Annual Review of United Nations Affairs

2006/2007

VOLUME IV

Edited by
Joachim Müller
and
Karl P. Sauvant

Oceana®
NEW YORK

OXFORD
UNIVERSITY PRESS

Oxford University Press, Inc., publishes works that further Oxford University's objective of excellence in research, scholarship, and education.

Published by Oxford University Press, Inc.
198 Madison Avenue, New York, New York 10016

ISSN: 0066-4340

ISBN: 978-0-19-533731-0 (2006/2007, Volume IV)

Note to Readers:

This publication is designed to provide accurate and authoritative information in regard to the subject matter covered. It is based upon sources believed to be accurate and reliable and is intended to be current as of the time it was written. It is sold with the understanding that the publisher is not engaged in rendering legal, accounting, or other professional services. If legal advice or other expert assistance is required, the services of a competent professional person should be sought. Also, to confirm that the information has not been affected or changed by recent developments, traditional legal research techniques should be used, including checking primary sources where appropriate.

(*Based on the Declaration of Principles jointly adopted by a Committee of the American Bar Association and a Committee of Publishers and Associations.*)

SUMMARY TABLE OF CONTENTS

VOLUME I

VOLUME II

VOLUME III

VOLUME IV

VOLUME V

TABLE OF CONTENTS VOLUME IV

CHAPTER 7

Selected Reports of Intergovernmental Bodies, Expert Groups and the United Nations Secretariat

CHAPTER 7

Selected Reports of Intergovernmental Bodies, Expert Groups and the United Nations Secretariat

I. United Nations System and Secretariat matters

1. Annual Overview Report of the United Nations System Chief Executive Board for Coordination for 2006/2007 (E/2007/69)

Summary

The present report provides an overview of major developments in inter-agency cooperation within the framework of the United Nations System Chief Executives Board for Coordination (CEB), during the period covering its fall 2006 and spring 2007 sessions, during which CEB initiated a dialogue encompassing the main global policy issues facing the international community, initiated a process of harmonization of United Nations management practices and addressed the integration of policy, management and operational activities within its framework.

During the reporting period, CEB, supported by its High-level Committee on Programmes, addressed a number of programme issues with system-wide implications. Those included issues that required the development of a coordinated response from the United Nations system, such as employment and decent work and the midterm review of the Brussels Programme of Action for the Least Developed Countries. Other topics were addressed from the perspective of developing common understanding and coherent responses to emerging issues on the international agenda, and ranged from system-wide coherence and the "One United Nations" system at the country level to aid-for-trade.

CEB continued its integrated and concrete consideration of management issues with the support of its High-level Committee on Management. The Committee and its networks devoted considerable time and attention to the subject of management harmonization and reform, with the aim of sharing information, avoiding duplication and setting common directions for future work. A number of important and emerging issues were on the Committee's agenda, including: the harmonization of United Nations system business practices, the confidentiality of internal audit reports, and the United Nations security management system.

The High-level Committee on Programmes and the High-level Committee on Management continued the innovative practice of holding joint meetings, which they had begun in 2006, in order to address cross-cutting issues from both a programme and a management perspective. Those meetings were intended to address major issues relevant to the work of both committees that were of importance across the work of the United Nations system. Issues addressed included gender equality and gender mainstreaming, results-based management, the United Nations System Staff College, and the establishment of a United Nations system-wide evaluation mechanism.

Renewed attention was given to enhancing the effectiveness of CEB itself in addressing the major strategic challenges facing the United Nations system, in order to respond more effectively to major global issues and to ensure that all the analytical and operational capacities available in the system were brought to bear on meeting those challenges, and to maximize the system's responsiveness to the requirements of Member States and the international community. The Secretary-General had requested the directors-general of the International

Labour Organization and the World Trade Organization to lead a review of the functioning of CEB to that end. The review was an important step forward in the evolution of CEB to more fully assume a strengthened role in the management of system-wide coordination under the leadership of the Secretary-General, and to develop a more integrated CEB framework that addressed policy, management and operational issues coherently.

I. Introduction

1. A consistent focus of the work of the United Nations System Chief Executives Board for Coordination (CEB) over the years has been to capitalize on the unique legitimacy and combined strengths of the organizations of the United Nations system, in order to maximize the system's responsiveness to the requirements of Member States and the international community. During 2006/07, renewed attention was given to enhancing the effectiveness of CEB itself, in addressing the major strategic challenges facing the United Nations system and in helping to ensure that all the analytical and operational capacities available in the system were brought to bear in a coherent way in meeting those challenges.

2. A number of factors were converging in creating, within the system, a new sense of urgency as well as of opportunity: a sense that the international community needed a strong, effective and united United Nations system; and a recognition that there were currently new, stronger foundations for advancing in that direction. A combination of circumstances currently existed that both compelled and facilitated a renewed effort on the part of CEB to maximize its contribution to that end.

3. The changing patterns of globalization and the opportunities for progress they offered and the risks they presented, including global challenges from climate change to international migration, all called for concerted, cross-sectoral responses. At the institutional level, the emergence on the international scene of new actors, including new issue-based organizations and global funds, was adding to the diversity of, and capacity for, responses by the international community, but was, at the same time, increasing the risk of duplication and fragmentation.

4. The breadth and scope of the policy foundations on which the system could currently rely to mount a renewed effort at enhancing coherence and impact were unprecedented. The Millennium Declaration, the internationally agreed development goals that had emerged from the United Nations conferences and summits, with the Millennium Development Goals prominent among them, and the outcome document of the 2005 World Summit, provided a solid keystone that supported and bound together the strategies and policies of the organizations of the system. They had played a crucial role in shaping the sense of common purpose that currently guided the system. The organizations of the system, acting together, had a key role to play in helping bridge the gap between commitment and action and in translating those international agreements into practical outcomes that had real impact in the lives of communities and peoples.

5. The priorities outlined by the new Secretary-General, Ban Ki-moon, Chair of CEB, in assuming office, the release of the report of the High-level Panel on System-wide Coherence and the initiation of intergovernmental deliberations on its recommendations, and the renewed momentum for reform that prevailed within and outside the system, had all strengthened a conviction on the part of the membership of CEB to seize the opportunity for a renewed effort at fully exploring the potential CEB carried as a driving force for enhanced coherence and effectiveness system-wide.

6. As part of the review of its own functioning, CEB was endeavouring to instil in interagency work a new level of ambition that fully recognized and respected the individual mandates and different governance structures and constituencies of its member organizations and sought to maximize the value of that diversity as an asset in terms of the breadth and scope of the services provided to the membership.

7. The strong sense of common purpose that increasingly characterized the work of CEB enabled the Board to address more decisively the problems of overlap and duplication that the system was encountering. The new level of ambition that CEB was endeavouring to introduce in its work was being targeted equally at policy development and implementation; at enhancing the strategic contribution of CEB to addressing the global challenges that the international community was facing; and at bringing the collective authority of the executive heads to bear on the effectiveness and coherence of the system's actions at the country level in response to country-defined strategies and priorities.

II. Programme issues

8. Over the 2006/07 period, CEB addressed a number of emerging and important programme issues with system-wide implications. Those included issues that required the development of a coordinated response from the United Nations, such as international migration and development, the midterm review of the Brussels Programme of Action for the Least Developed Countries, and the cross-cutting issue of employment and decent work. Other topics were addressed from the perspective of developing common understanding and coherent responses to emerging issues on the international agenda, ranging from aid-for-trade to system-wide coherence and "One United Nations" at the country level.

9. The Board considered the new mandates entrusted to the Economic and Social Council by the 2005 World Summit and further elaborated by the General Assembly in its resolution 61/16 in the context of the need to improve policy and programme coordination in the United Nations system. The Annual Ministerial Review of progress on the internationally agreed development goals, including the Millennium Development Goals, held the potential for establishing the Council as a central forum for intergovernmental oversight and assessment of the implementation of the United Nations development agenda. The biannual Development Cooperation Forum would be launched at the Council's forthcoming July meeting and would provide a global platform where all stakeholders would be able to engage in high-level dialogue on new trends and key policy issues affecting development cooperation.

10. In its deliberations, CEB reiterated the potential that the new functions entrusted to the Economic and Social Council carried to enhance the relevance and impact of its work. The new mandates entrusted to the Council provided new opportunities for a meaningful policy dialogue between the Council and the United Nations system on system-wide coordination and policy coherence.

A. "One United Nations" at the country level

11. CEB considered that a principal determinant of the United Nations system's image in donor as well as recipient countries was its work at the country level. The system could not, therefore, afford to be perceived as a disparate group of competing organizations. CEB members should instead strive to work as a coherent system devoted to bringing its diverse

capacities to bear, in a concerted way, on the priorities defined by developing countries. How best to harness the limited resources available to United Nations organizations to maximize their impact remained a major challenge.

12. While intergovernmental discussions on the whole package of reforms put forward in the Secretary-General's report on the recommendations of the High-level Panel on System-wide Coherence were under way, work on the eight "One United Nations" projects at the country level was serving to bring the United Nations family closer together. The necessity of showing real results from the pilots by the end of the year was underscored. The main challenge in that regard was setting strategic priorities that corresponded to national requirements and the country's own priorities. The pooling of resources in response to national priorities was an important next step in order to eliminate unnecessary competition in resource mobilization. CEB agreed that "Delivering as one" was a more accurate slogan than "One United Nations" as the intent was not to merge mandates, but rather to deliver together.

13. The Board expressed appreciation to the Administrator of the United Nations Development Programme (UNDP)/Chair of the United Nations Development Group (UNDG) for the work that had been accomplished so far on "One United Nations" at the country level through the eight pilot projects. Attempts to make the models for those pilot projects flexible to respond to different country requirements and to reflect the diversity of the system should be clarified and strengthened, and the Board generally concurred that the success of the pilot projects would be important in demonstrating the ability of the system to deliver as one. As the pilot projects were still in their early stages, a number of issues remained to be addressed. The Board stressed the experimental nature of the pilot projects and emphasized that progress on the projects should not prejudge the outcome of the intergovernmental deliberations on that issue in the General Assembly.

14. It was suggested that the eight pilot projects were not necessarily representative of the totality of the system's work at the country level. The development assistance programme in the United Nations Development Assistance Framework (UNDAF) often did not reflect the totality of the contribution that the United Nations system was making in response to country requirements and priorities. There was, thus, greater need for sensitizing resident coordinators with regard to the fuller services and expertise that non-resident agencies offered. Technical assistance and capacity-building of such agencies was highly specialized and targeted and should be taken into account in pursuing the objectives of "One United Nations" at the country level.

15. CEB recognized the crucial role of resident coordinators in realizing the "One United Nations" approach and stressed the need to ensure that clear and coherent direction was provided to them and that an appropriate framework was developed for managing their work. Resident coordinators should have clear reporting lines and be accountable to the system as a whole. As part of the overall effort to deliver as one, the Board gave broad support for the establishment under CEB of thematic clusters of interested organizations as a means to ensure that the system's country-level actions were guided by coherent policy frameworks and that the comparative advantages of the agencies directly engaged were fully drawn on. The Board further agreed that national ownership, comparative advantage, accountability and maximum effectiveness should be the principles guiding the system's efforts to deliver as one.

16. The Board fully endorsed the establishment of an evaluation process of the pilot projects, noting at the same time that lessons to be drawn might not be applicable to all the system's country-level work. In that regard, CEB called upon the United Nations Evaluation Group (UNEG) to urgently establish the substantive parameters and process for the evaluation of the pilot projects and requested to be kept fully and regularly informed of progress. As a first step, UNEG was mandated to begin work urgently on the development of evaluability criteria and baselines for the evaluation.

B. Employment and decent work

17. CEB addressed the issue of employment and decent work both in an initial preparatory discussion at its fall 2006 session and on the basis of further preparation by the High-level Committee on Programmes at its spring 2007 session in the light of increasingly strong political support for addressing full employment and decent work for all. That support had been manifested at high-level international gatherings in various regions, such as the African Union Extraordinary Summit on Employment and Poverty Alleviation and the Fourth Summit of the Americas.

18. At the 2005 World Summit, heads of State had supported fair globalization and the goals of full and productive employment and decent work for all, and subsequently, the Economic and Social Council 2006 Ministerial Declaration had underscored the significance of full and productive employment and decent work for all as an end in itself and as a means to achieve the Millennium Development Goals, including poverty eradication. In addition, the Secretary-General, in his annual report to the General Assembly at its sixty-first session, proposed that full employment and decent work for all be formally included as a new target under Millennium Development Goal 1.

19. CEB addressed several aspects of the employment and decent work agenda during the reporting period, including the potential for small-and medium-sized enterprises, especially in rural areas, to generate employment; advancing entrepreneurship and supporting development of small-and medium-sized businesses; and technologies that enhance the productivity of youth. A coherent United Nations system working together on the issue was seen by CEB as contributing to operationalizing the concept of "One United Nations" around an objective that was increasingly emerging as a priority at both the national and the international levels.

20. The High-level Committee on Programmes undertook the development of a toolkit to mainstream employment and decent work objectives in United Nations system organizations. The intent was to generate reflection throughout the system on how policies and programmes of the United Nations could contribute to maximizing job creation in the most effective way possible.

21. The methodology used in constructing the toolkit was a collective process led by the International Labour Organization (ILO) under the guidance of the High-level Committee on Programmes. The toolkit had the practical purpose of providing a means to facilitate policy coherence around shared common objectives. It was conceived along the structure of the decent work agenda, which consisted of the following four pillars: employment creation and enterprise development; social protection; standards and rights at work; and governance and social dialogue.

22. The objective of the toolkit was to assist the system support countries in achieving their objectives for full and productive employment and decent work through: mainstreaming the issue in policies and programmes; identifying areas of common interest, as well as linkages and synergies; deepening, sharing and expanding knowledge and tools in areas of common interest, and improving and pooling capacity to respond to country priorities.

23. In the next phase, CEB members will carry out initial self-assessments, as proposed in the toolkit, to establish a baseline to mark progress in 2010 and 2015. Initial assessments would be reported back in September 2007 so that CEB could provide an input to the Commission for Social Development on the theme of employment and decent work in February 2008.

24. CEB strongly supported the initiative and considered that the methodology that had been developed for the toolkit could be replicated in other areas as an integral part of the effort to advance policy coherence within the system. Practical responses were needed for the system to support countries in order to derive concrete benefit from such initiatives. The recent joint ILO-World Trade Organization study on trade and employment was cited as an example in that regard. It was clear that Millennium Development Goal 1 could not be achieved without employment generation and that for every 10 children being born, only one job was being created. In 2007 for the first time, 50 per cent of the global population would be living in urban areas, and by 2030 two thirds of the world's population would be living in urban areas with a majority in slums and squatter settlements.

25. In order to design appropriate interventions, it was important for all parts of the United Nations system to be well versed in the policy issues that were at the core of development. In that regard, ILO had provided training to resident coordinators on the decent work agenda in order to assist them in mainstreaming those objectives at the country level.

26. CEB gave its full endorsement to the toolkit and agreed to review progress in its operationalization at the forthcoming session of CEB, with a view to contributing to the work of the Commission for Social Development on employment and decent work.

C. Aid-for-trade

27. The Hong Kong Ministerial Declaration created a new WTO aid-for-trade work programme to complement the conclusion of the Doha Development Round. WTO had, in that regard, been mandated to monitor and evaluate aid-for-trade so as to create more incentives through greater transparency in honouring commitments, meeting needs, improving effectiveness and reinforcing mutual accountability. With the onset of the implementation phase of that initiative, the full involvement of the United Nations system was required.

28. CEB supported the need to further the objectives of the aid-for-trade initiative and noted that the reduction of trade barriers alone was not sufficient to put developing countries on the path to sustainable growth. The need to increase resources for trade capacity-building in developing countries in order to help them benefit from improved market access was an essential aspect of a successful trade regime.

29. Monitoring of the aid-for-trade work programme would take place on three levels: global monitoring, donor monitoring and self-evaluation, and recipient country monitoring based on in-country assessments. The World Bank and the regional development banks

would take the lead on regional reviews through preparatory meetings intended to enable all stakeholders to focus on real needs and challenges on the ground, prioritize needs and deliver business plans. Those would culminate in an annual aid-for-trade event, the first of which was scheduled for 2007. The initiative was not about creating new mechanisms, but rather about enabling WTO to work with others on implementing a work programme.

30. The central role of CEB members would be to help developing countries identify priorities, mainstream trade and national strategies and work on developing regional approaches, which were key factors to ensuring success. The challenge to the system was to maximize the positive aspects, while at the same time dealing with the negative impacts of trade liberalization. Aid-for-trade was seen as an essential complement to a successful Doha Round, i.e., helping countries deal with supply-side constraints while fully exploiting their trade potential. Raising awareness of trade issues among resident coordinators at the country level was seen as a very important issue to ensure that measures supporting countries in the development of capacity for trade featured appropriately in country programmes.

31. CEB noted that while there was no legal link between the aid-for-trade initiative and multilateral trade negotiations, there was an obvious political link. Aid-for-trade would take place irrespective of the status of negotiations; however, it could only complement and not substitute for progress on tariffs and subsidies. There was a need for policy coordination within the system in respect of industry, agriculture and services, and given the wide expression of support for the process, the Board decided that consideration should be given to the establishment of a cluster dealing with trade and productive capacity to help CEB make a useful and coherent contribution to the process.

D. Brussels Programme of Action for the Least Developed Countries

32. CEB also addressed the outcome of the midterm review by the General Assembly of the Brussels Programme of Action for the Least Developed Countries for the Decade 2001–2010. CEB highlighted the need to make every effort to accelerate the implementation of the Brussels Programme of Action as a major integral part of the drive towards meeting the internationally agreed development goals, including the Millennium Development Goals.

33. Despite some significant progress by some least developed countries, their gains as a group had been insufficient to meet the goals agreed upon in Brussels. Available data on recent poverty trends were not encouraging, with life expectancy declining in several least developed countries affected by HIV/AIDS and civil strife.

34. Further action was required under national leadership with international support in terms of market access, debt relief and more and better development assistance, with the United Nations supporting those objectives by working in concert at both the policy and operational levels.

35. In response to the General Assembly's call for action, CEB decided to respond with a three-prong approach to the outcome of the review: (a) United Nations system organizations would redouble their efforts to accelerate the implementation of the Brussels Programme of Action in their respective fields of competence; (b) twenty United Nations system entities and agencies had already adopted decisions in their respective governing bodies to mainstream the implementation of the Brussels Programme of Action in their work programmes, and other relevant entities would take similar action; and (c) on the

basis of the experience gained from the inter-agency consultation in the preparation of the review, further work would be undertaken on information sharing and building synergies around concrete objectives. It was agreed that the inter-agency consultations should be transformed into an inter-agency consultative group for the accelerated implementation of the Brussels Programme of Action.

E. Other programme matters

1. International migration and development

36. CEB took up the issue of international migration and development on the basis of an initial assessment of the implications for the system, as discussed by the General Assembly at the High-level Dialogue on International Migration and Development; CEB would seek to identify the steps needed to work towards greater policy coherence and programmatic and operational coordination in that area. In that regard, an effort by the Global Migration Group to improve the knowledge base through an inventory of available data sources in each of its member organizations was supported. The Group was also urged to take into account the issue of environmental degradation as a major push factor for migration.

37. CEB noted the initiative for convening a global forum on migration and development that would enable an ongoing dialogue among Governments on policies and practices that best contributed to progress. The importance of effective cooperation between the global forum, as an intergovernmental body, and the Global Migration Group, as an inter-agency mechanism well placed to support the forum, particularly in the areas of policy development and capacity-building was stressed. The Global Migration Group would be adopting new and more effective methods of work in the coming period and would address migration both as an economic issue linked to development and as a human rights issue.

2. Food security theme groups at the country level

38. Recognizing the importance of substantive thematic coordination in responding to the needs and priorities of partner countries, the Food and Agriculture Organization of the United Nations (FAO), the International Fund for Agricultural Development (IFAD) and the World Food Programme (WFP) informed CEB that the three organizations had decided to combine their complementary capacities and comparative advantages within food security theme groups at the country level. The groups are based on a jointly agreed twin-track approach whereby food assistance and rural agricultural development were required in many country contexts for achieving Millennium Development Goal 1. When relevant to national situations, the three organizations worked together to jointly identify thematic coordination opportunities drawing on poverty reduction strategies. They also sought to work with national Governments and civil society, through national alliances against hunger where they existed, and to explore opportunities for thematic groups based on knowledge-sharing.

F. Emerging issues on the agenda of the Chief Executives Board

1. Support to African development

39. CEB reviewed current economic and social trends in African development and the serious problems that many African countries continued to face in their efforts to achieve the Millennium Development Goals and recalled its earlier decision to place African development as a regular item on its agenda.

40. With the midpoint target date to meet the Millennium Development Goals approaching fast, it was incumbent on the United Nations system to make a strong renewed effort to revitalize its common endeavours in support of Africa. CEB concurred with the need to adopt innovative approaches to addressing African development in the future. The Board called for an inclusive preparatory process to the CEB discussions engaging, as necessary, outside experts to develop clear analyses and specific action-oriented recommendations to strengthen the system support to African development for further consideration by CEB. The Secretary-General observed that the gap between developing countries, particularly in Africa, and the developed world, rather than narrowing, appeared to be widening. At the same time, some countries, including some African countries, were registering very encouraging progress in the path towards the Millennium Development Goals. CEB agreed that Africa should be on the agenda of the next CEB session and the consideration of the issue should proceed on the basis of a thorough preparation for that discussion. CEB also decided that the specific implications for Africa of the Board's discussion on thematic issues should be highlighted.

2. Climate change

41. CEB was informed of the initiative of the Secretary-General to address the issue of climate change both through high-level envoys and through the possibility of convening a high-level meeting at the forthcoming session of the General Assembly. A wide-ranging discussion was undertaken by CEB on the scientific evidence emerging from the Intergovernmental Panel on Climate Change and the need for the Board to develop a clear system-wide approach and strategy to address the multifaceted challenges of climate change. The importance of a full preparation for the next session of CEB to be undertaken by the High Level Committee on Programmes was highlighted, as well as the cluster of executive heads most involved in that issue. CEB agreed to put climate change on the agenda of its regular session in fall 2007.

III. Management issues

42. CEB continued its consideration of management issues in a more integrated and concrete fashion over the 2006/07 period with the support of its High-level Committee on Management. The Committee and its networks had recently given considerable time and attention to the subject of management harmonization and reform within the competence of United Nations system executive heads, with the aim of sharing information, avoiding duplication of efforts, identifying successful experiences as benchmarks and setting common directions for future work. In a new environment which called for a focus on delivery and results, there was an increased need for adjusting the management of United Nations system organizations to the new environment. A strong internal commitment to deliver was creating a very positive momentum for harmonized management reform throughout the system. The system-wide adoption of international public sector accounting standards offered further impetus for the United Nations system organizations to work together.

43. In the area of information and communication technology (ICT), the High-level Committee on Management had established an ICT strategic framework which included a range of initiatives intended to strengthen cooperation on ICT-related activities among the organizations of the United Nations system. Two areas addressed in particular were

enterprise resource planning and ICT training. The overall objective in the Committee on the concept of common shared ICT services was to find ways for providing enhanced services at lower cost instead of each organization investing heavily and separately in its own ICT infrastructure.

44. Concerning the safety and security of staff, at its fall 2006 session the Board took note of progress made by the Department for Safety and Security since its establishment and the consultative approach adopted by the Department within the framework of the inter-agency security management network. The network had made specific recommendations concerning the production and launch of an inter-agency learning course on advanced security in the field and the development of a training package for inclusion in the forthcoming workshops for field security officers on how to cope with mass casualties, the improvement of security measures for women and cooperation of non-governmental organizations. The High-level Committee on Management had established a technical working group for reprioritizing the activities of the Department and corresponding funding mechanisms to meet the objectives set for 2008-2009 within the 2006-2007 cost-shared budget ceiling and to develop an effective surge capacity should resources become available.

45. CEB expressed satisfaction that the focus of the Committee's work had increasingly shifted from administrative matters to management policy, and called for further efforts to coordinate more closely with the work of the United Nations Development Group concerning management issues at the country level.

46. A number of important and emerging issues were on the Committee's agenda at its spring 2007 session, as outlined below.

A. Harmonization of United Nations system business practices

47. Extensive discussions had taken place within the High-level Committee on Management on harmonization and reform of business practices. The approach taken to the reform of business practices in the United Nations system was to be driven by programme priorities rather than by bureaucratic considerations and would be based on clear business logic and demonstrated system-wide benefits, concentrating on areas of harmonization and reform within the purview of executive heads.

48. A comprehensive proposal for the reform and harmonization of United Nations system business practices was being developed within the High-level Committee on Management. The proposal addressed six major categories: cross-cutting areas of general management; accountability and oversight; data warehouses; human resources management; financial management and knowledge-sharing.

49. A coherent approach focusing on the six areas identified would eventually constitute a draft action plan on United Nations business practices geared to provide a comprehensive approach to enhancing system-wide coherence. The Board was informed that the High-level Committee on Management had heard the views of staff representatives who had urged that the initiative should lead to an improvement of system-wide conditions on the basis of best practices rather than the lowest common denominator and who had asked for a regular consultation process. The Board considered that the success of the initiative would ultimately depend on the leadership and will of executive heads who should provide a strong mandate in that regard to their heads of management attending the High-level Committee on Management.

The Committee had set up an intersessional task force to take the matter further in order to develop a full-fledged action plan for CEB endorsement at the fall 2007 session.

50. The Board expressed strong support for that initiative as an important element of the drive towards greater system-wide coherence and recalled that the harmonization of business practices had emerged as a central recommendation of the High-level Panel on System-wide Coherence. The Board endorsed the initiative of the High-level Committee on Management on the development of the proposed Action Plan and decided to revert to it at its fall 2007 session. The Board also endorsed a proposal of High-level Committee on Management for the preparation of a study by the CEB secretariat on the functioning of the International Civil Service Commission for the Board's subsequent consideration.

B. Confidentiality of internal audit reports

51. The High-level Committee on Management reviewed current practices within the system for sharing information contained in internal audit reports through its finance and budget network. In that regard, initial criteria that could serve to guide the exercise were under consideration with a view to establishing a common approach to disclosure of information contained in internal audit reports. Further consultations would be held within the community of internal auditors and the Finance and Budget Network and the eventual criteria would take into account consultations with the Board of External Auditors and the Institute of Internal Auditors, as well as the need to respect the legislative decisions of governing bodies of United Nations system organizations.

52. CEB underlined the importance of internal audit reports as a vital management tool for executive heads as well as the need to distinguish between internal and external audits and their separate functions. The need to preserve the integrity of the internal audit as a management tool was acknowledged and, at the same time, the Board also acknowledged that the system was faced with growing demand for transparency and accountability to which it had to respond. CEB would revert to that matter at its forthcoming session on the basis of further consultations by the High-level Committee on Management.

C. United Nations security management system

53. The Board reviewed the financing of the United Nations security management system and the pending agreement on the cost-sharing formula for the system. The Board noted that the only outstanding matter in that regard was the concurrence of the World Bank on the formula on the basis of further information to be provided by the United Nations. CEB expected a full agreement would be forthcoming on that important issue shortly.

D. Senior Management Network

54. In line with the earlier discussion of CEB, the Senior Management Network and its Leadership Development Programme had been launched. The key objective of those initiatives was to inculcate among senior officials a new corporate culture to further system-wide coherence. Senior Management Network membership would initially consist of approximately 600 to 1,000 senior staff. The Board highlighted the need to strengthen the competencies and training of staff. The Board also noted in that regard, that further efforts to promote staff mobility were required and highlighted the need to strengthen staff training and its potential contribution to supporting staff mobility.

E. United Nations Convention against Corruption

55. CEB agreed to study further the applicability of the principles and standards of the United Nations Convention against Corruption in order to combat corruption and strengthen institutional integrity and respond to demands for accountability system-wide. The Board requested the High Level Committee on Programmes and the High-level Committee on Management and its relevant networks to be actively engaged in pursuing the matter further with the United Nations Office on Drugs and Crime, with a view to establishing a concrete proposal for CEB.

IV. Cross-cutting issues

56. During the reporting period, the High Level Committee on Programmes and the High-level Committee on Management continued the innovative practice of joint meetings that they had begun in 2006 in order to address cross-cutting issues from both a programme and a management perspective. Those meetings were intended to address major emerging issues relevant to the work of both committees that were of importance across the work of the United Nations system. Issues addressed included gender equality and gender mainstreaming, results-based management, the United Nations System Staff College, and the establishment of a United Nations system-wide evaluation mechanism.

A. Gender equality and gender mainstreaming

57. The issue of gender equality and gender mainstreaming was considered by all executive heads as an area in which insufficient progress had been made and further change was required. To that end, the Special Adviser on Gender Issues and Advancement of Women presented the Board at its fall 2006 session with a proposed system-wide policy on gender equality and a strategy on gender mainstreaming.

58. CEB noted that commitment at the highest level and overall leadership and accountability were required to address gender equality and gender mainstreaming in the United Nations system. The evaluation of the system-wide action plan for the implementation of Security Council resolution 1325 (2000) on women, peace and security had validated the various analyses carried out among inter-agency bodies and had identified deficiencies that existed in those areas as a main obstacle to progress. CEB endorsed the policy on gender equality and the strategy on gender mainstreaming as a first step in a new effort to meet the challenges facing the system in that area.[1]

B. Results-based management

59. CEB agreed that results-based management was a key part of the effort to reform the business practices of institutions throughout the United Nations system. It decided to expand its analysis of the subject to include the related issue of performance management, in order to review the incentives that existed within the system to enhance performance.

C. United Nations System Staff College

60. The Board addressed the establishment of a new curriculum and business plan for the United Nations System Staff College (UNSSC) on the basis of preparations by the High Level Committee on Programmes and the High-level Committee on Management. It was noted that a strong Staff College designed to nurture a common staff culture rooted in common values was essential in sustaining the effort towards system-wide coherence.

61. Three main areas of concentration for the work of the College had been identified:

(a) Senior Management Network: training tailored to meet requirements of senior United Nations managers;

(b) Peace and security: the College had been working on a special agreement with the Department of Safety and Security and other entities for training mission leaders. Actual training of trainers had already been initiated;

(c) Training programme for resident coordinators: the programme was ongoing and would be expanded to include country teams together with national teams.

62. CEB members expressed appreciation for the new directions being taken by the Staff College and committed the system to making full and effective use of its facilities as an integral part of the renewed effort to advance a learning culture system-wide.

D. Establishment of a United Nations system-wide evaluation mechanism

63. The United Nations Evaluation Group had prepared a proposal for the joint High Level Committee on Programmes-High-level Committee on Management spring session 2007 concerning the establishment of a United Nations system-wide evaluation mechanism linked to CEB to fill the current gap concerning evaluation of system-wide processes. It was stressed that such a mechanism must be independent in order to be credible and must at the same time meet the priority needs of its stakeholders. In order to advance transparency, accountability and learning, such a mechanism would promote the quality and independence of all United Nations evaluation work, foster harmonization of evaluation systems across the United Nations, undertake evaluations of system-wide strategic issues, and promote the development of evaluation capacity in member countries, including the promotion of a culture of independent evaluation to enable them to take the lead in the evaluation of programmes at the country level.

64. The High Level Committee on Programmes and High-level Committee on Management jointly endorsed the approach suggested by the United Nations Evaluation Group and emphasized that on the basis of the subsidiarity principle, work should be undertaken within the evaluation system at the most appropriate level.

V. Review of the functioning of the United Nations system Chief Executives Board for Coordination

65. At its October 2006 retreat and in the framework of broader discussions on the reform of the United Nations, CEB began a reflection on the future challenges facing the multilateral system, as well as the need to improve system-wide coherence. In the course of a wide-ranging discussion, the central importance and potential of CEB as an instrument for improving coherence across the system was underlined. Executive heads agreed that a new opportunity existed to undertake a more ambitious approach to strengthening the relevance and functioning of CEB. On behalf of CEB, the Secretary-General requested the directors-general of ILO and WTO to lead a review of the functioning of CEB and to report back the preliminary recommendations for consideration at the CEB meeting in April 2007.

66. An extensive consultative process involving all executive heads was undertaken by the directors-general of ILO and WTO, including comprehensive written inputs from executive heads. The overall exercise was carried out by executive heads themselves, marking a

difference with previous reviews of CEB. The central conclusion of the exercise was that if CEB was to become a stronger and more effective instrument for inter-agency coordination it would require the investment of more time and the direct involvement of executive heads supported by an integrated CEB structure incorporating policy, management and operational issues. The review was an important step forward in the evolution of CEB in the ownership and management of system-wide coordination under the leadership of the Secretary-General.

67. Consultations undertaken in the course of the review resulted in a common view that a major overhaul of CEB was not necessary, but that the review should envisage an incremental process of tightening the work of CEB and its machinery over the next two to three years on the basis of a pragmatic approach. CEB members acknowledged the critical role of CEB as a unique body of the multilateral system bringing together under the aegis and leadership of the Secretary-General, the executive heads of the specialized agencies, the World Bank, the International Monetary Fund, WTO and relevant United Nations entities, funds and programmes. As the apex inter-agency mechanism, CEB should provide inter-secretariat policy guidance by the chief executive officers of the secretariats of the organizations of the system. In that regard, individual mandates, respective strengths, capacities and areas of action, as well as different governance structures and constituencies of member organizations, needed to be recognized and respected.

68. A number of key issues were identified as central to the functioning of CEB. The first was the harmonization of business practices, systems and procedures across the system which was seen as being of primary importance. A second broad area identified was that of global policy issues. CEB would define and select a limited number of cross-cutting policy issues of concern to the whole system, to which it could make a specific contribution over the next two to three years. There was strong support for action to be taken immediately on climate change, fair and equitable globalization, gender equality and support to African development.

69. With respect to the third area of country operations, it was noted that with reform efforts for increased system-wide coherence and the focus on country-level results, operational activities should become an integral part of the major responsibilities of CEB, connecting with that policy, programme and management functions and seeking mutual support and reinforcement across them. While CEB should develop an overall monitoring capacity, it would not involve itself in specific country activities. A fundamental principle underlying that approach would be to bring the normative work of the United Nations and its country work closer together with the ownership of all relevant organizations. That was seen as critical given the new responsibilities expected of the resident coordinator system as lead representative of the United Nations system at the country level. In that regard, CEB endorsed the proposal for the integration of the United Nations Development Group within the CEB framework.

70. It was agreed that an integrated high-level committee structure would underpin the role of CEB as the pinnacle of inter-agency coordination and bring together vertical and horizontal coordination at the global, regional and country levels across the wide spectrum of mandates and expertise of CEB members.

71. A number of steps in the CEB review process were identified for the next stage of the review, including the mapping of all inter-agency coordination mechanisms, and further analysis of coherence and the different dimensions of policy coherence. CEB would also look at the financing of CEB, including the level of funding required for the appropriate functioning of CEB and its machinery. Finally, the review would also examine ways to strengthen Secretariat arrangements to appropriately service and provide substantive and logistical support to CEB, its clusters and committees and their interlinkages; improve reporting and transparency to intergovernmental bodies; and monitor the implementation of decisions.

72. CEB had endorsed the general principles contained in the proposal for its review and outlined specific measures to continue the review process. The High-level Committee on Management was required to proceed with the finalization of a plan of action for harmonization and reform of business practices and to develop proposals on dealing with additional functions proposed for it in managing country-level operations and monitoring resource flows to the system. The High Level Committee on Programmes was tasked to proceed with its work on global policy issues and make proposals for the consideration of CEB on the sequencing of issues for future CEB sessions. The High Level Committee on Programmes would also propose a methodology for the analysis of mandates and duplication and the study of different dimensions of policy coherence. With regard to the work of the three committees and the integration of the United Nations Development Group into CEB, the chairs of the three committees were asked to develop a set of proposed arrangements for the further consideration of CEB.

73. The review was seen as the first step in developing a far-sighted strategic vision for CEB based on a pragmatic approach with the intention of seeking concrete improvements within a two to three year period. Executive heads, in proceeding with the review, showed their commitment to assume fully their responsibilities in the ownership and management of CEB. The review took a holistic approach to the task of CEB which encompassed the main global policy issues faced by the multilateral system, its common managerial challenges, and the provision of guidance and oversight for country operations.

---

* E/2007/100.

[1] For further information, see CEB/2006/2, annex.

2. Climate Change 2007: A Report of Working Group I of the Intergovernmental Panel on Climate Change

Summary for Policymakers*

Drafting Authors:

Richard B. Alley, Terje Berntsen, Nathaniel L. Bindoff, Zhenlin Chen, Amnat Chidthaisong, Pierre Friedlingstein, Jonathan M. Gregory, Gabriele C. Hegerl, Martin Heimann, Bruce Hewitson, Brian J. Hoskins, Fortunat Joos, Jean Jouzel, Vladimir Kattsov, Ulrike Lohmann, Martin Manning, Taroh Matsuno, Mario Molina, Neville Nicholls, Jonathan Overpeck, Dahe Qin, Graciela Raga, Venkatachalam Ramaswamy, Jiawen Ren, Matilde Rusticucci, Susan Solomon, Richard Somerville, Thomas F. Stocker, Peter A. Stott, Ronald J. Stouffer, Penny Whetton, Richard A. Wood, David Wratt

Draft Contributing Authors:

J. Arblaster, G. Brasseur, J.H. Christensen, K.L. Denman, D.W. Fahey, P. Forster, E. Jansen, P.D. Jones, R. Knutti, H. Le Treut, P. Lemke, G. Meehl, P. Mote, D.A. Randall, D.A. Stone, K.E. Trenberth, J. Willebrand, F. Zwiers

Introduction

The Working Group I contribution to the IPCC Fourth Assessment Report describes progress in understanding of the human and natural drivers of climate change,[1] observed climate change, climate processes and attribution, and estimates of projected future climate change. It builds upon past IPCC assessments and incorporates new findings from the past six years of research. Scientific progress since the Third Assessment Report (TAR) is based upon large amounts of new and more comprehensive data, more sophisticated analyses of data, improvements in understanding of processes and their simulation in models and more extensive exploration of uncertainty ranges.

The basis for substantive paragraphs in this Summary for Policymakers can be found in the chapter sections specified in curly brackets.

---

* **This Summary for Policymakers should be cited as:**

IPCC, 2007: Summary for Policymakers. In: *Climate Change 2007: The Physical Science Basis. Contribution of Working Group I to the Fourth Assessment Report of the Intergovernmental Panel on Climate Change* [Solomon, S., D. Qin, M. Manning, Z. Chen, M. Marquis, K.B. Averyt, M.Tignor and H.L. Miller (eds.)]. Cambridge University Press, Cambridge, United Kingdom and New York, NY, USA.

Human and Natural Drivers of Climate Change

Changes in the atmospheric abundance of greenhouse gases and aerosols, in solar radiation and in land surface properties alter the energy balance of the climate system. These changes are expressed in terms of radiative forcing,[2] which is used to compare how a range of human and natural factors drive warming or cooling influences on global climate. Since the TAR, new observations and related modelling of greenhouse gases, solar activity, land surface properties and some aspects of aerosols have led to improvements in the quantitative estimates of radiative forcing.

Global atmospheric concentrations of carbon dioxide, methane and nitrous oxide have increased markedly as a result of human activities since 1750 and now far exceed pre-industrial values determined from ice cores spanning many thousands of years (see Figure SPM.1). The global increases in carbon dioxide concentration are due primarily to fossil fuel use and land use change, while those of methane and nitrous oxide are primarily due to agriculture. {Book Reference Omitted}

- Carbon dioxide is the most important anthropogenic greenhouse gas (see Figure SPM.2). The global atmospheric concentration of carbon dioxide has increased from a pre-industrial value of about 280 ppm to 379 ppm[3] in 2005. The atmospheric concentration of carbon dioxide in 2005 exceeds by far the natural range over the last 650,000 years (180 to 300 ppm) as determined from ice cores. The annual carbon dioxide concentration growth rate was larger during the last 10 years (1995–2005 average: 1.9 ppm per year), than it has been since the beginning of continuous direct atmospheric measurements (1960–2005 average: 1.4 ppm per year) although there is year-to-year variability in growth rates. {Book Reference Omitted}
- The primary source of the increased atmospheric concentration of carbon dioxide since the pre-industrial period results from fossil fuel use, with land-use change providing another significant but smaller contribution. Annual fossil carbon dioxide emissions[4] increased from an average of 6.4 [6.0 to 6.8][5] GtC (23.5 [22.0 to 25.0] $GtCO_2$) per year in the 1990s to 7.2 [6.9 to 7.5] GtC (26.4 [25.3 to 27.5] $GtCO_2$) per year in 2000–2005 (2004 and 2005 data are interim estimates). Carbon dioxide emissions associated with land-use change are estimated to be 1.6 [0.5 to 2.7] GtC (5.9 [1.8 to 9.9] $GtCO_2$) per year over the 1990s, although these estimates have a large uncertainty. {Book Reference Omitted}
- The global atmospheric concentration of methane has increased from a pre-industrial value of about 715 ppb to 1732 ppb in the early 1990s, and was 1774 ppb in 2005. The atmospheric concentration of methane in 2005 exceeds by far the natural range of the last 650,000 years (320 to 790 ppb) as determined from ice cores. Growth rates have declined since the early 1990s, consistent with total emissions (sum of anthropogenic and natural sources) being nearly constant during this period. It is *very likely*[6] that the observed increase in methane concentration is due to anthropogenic activities, predominantly agriculture and fossil fuel use, but relative contributions from different source types are not well determined. {Book Reference Omitted}
- The global atmospheric nitrous oxide concentration increased from a pre-industrial value of about 270 ppb to 319 ppb in 2005. The growth rate has been approximately constant since 1980. More than a third of all nitrous oxide emissions are anthropogenic and are primarily due to agriculture. {Book Reference Omitted}

CHANGES IN GREENHOUSE GASES FROM ICE CORE AND MODERN DATA

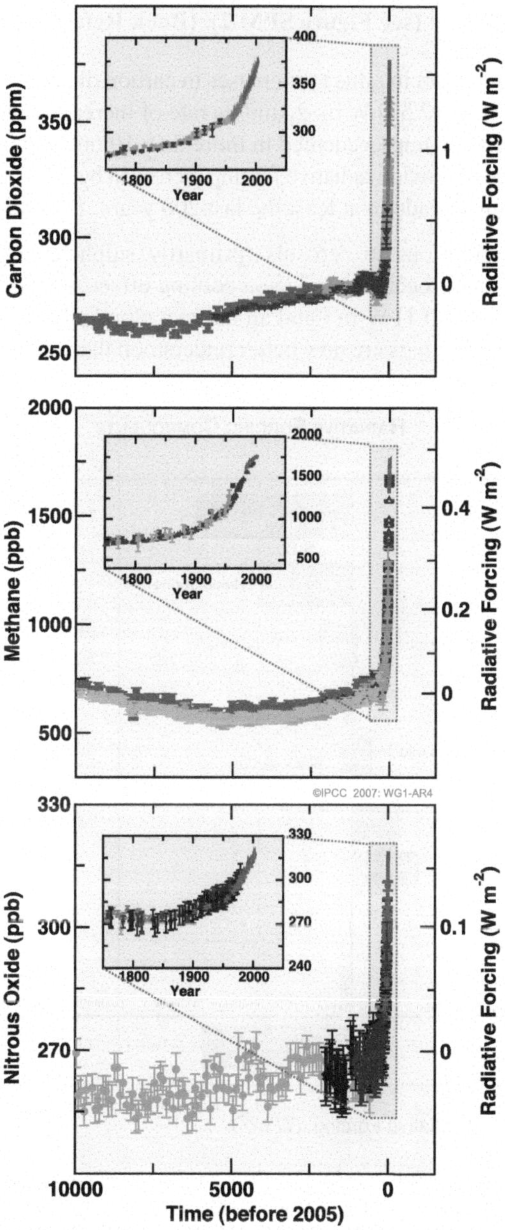

Figure SPM.1. Atmospheric concentrations of carbon dioxide, methane and nitrous oxide over the last 10,000 years (large panels) and since 1750 (inset panels). Measurements are shown from ice cores (symbols with different colours for different studies) and atmospheric samples (red lines). The corresponding radiative forcings are shown on the right hand axes of the large panels. {Book Reference Omitted}

The understanding of anthropogenic warming and cooling influences on climate has improved since the TAR, leading to *very high confidence*' that the global average net effect of human activities since 1750 has been one of warming, with a radiative forcing of +1.6 [+0.6 to +2.4] W m^{-2} (see Figure SPM.2). {Book Reference Omitted}

- The combined radiative forcing due to increases in carbon dioxide, methane, and nitrous oxide is +2.30 [+2.07 to +2.53] W m–2, and its rate of increase during the industrial era is *very likely* to have been unprecedented in more than 10,000 years (see Figures SPM.1 and SPM.2). The carbon dioxide radiative forcing increased by 20% from 1995 to 2005, the largest change for any decade in at least the last 200 years. {Book Reference Omitted}
- Anthropogenic contributions to aerosols (primarily sulphate, organic carbon, black carbon, nitrate and dust) together produce a cooling effect, with a total direct radiative forcing of –0.5 [–0.9 to –0.1] W m^{-2} and an indirect cloud albedo forcing of –0.7 [–1.8 to –0.3] W m^{-2}. These forcings are now better understood than at the time of the TAR due

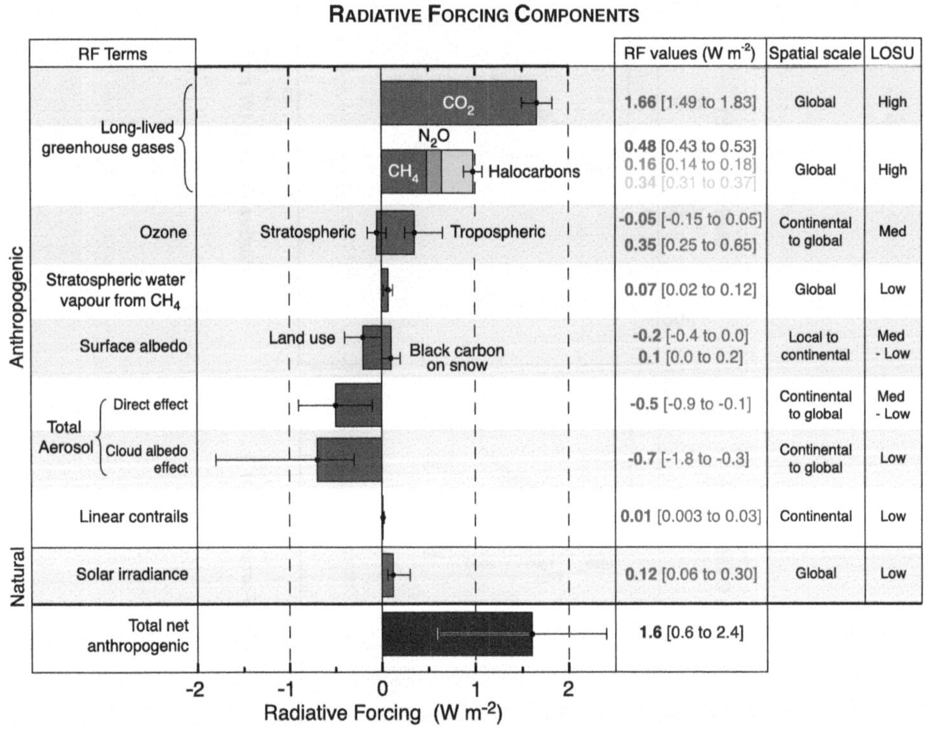

Figure SPM.2. Global average radiative forcing (RF) estimates and ranges in 2005 for anthropogenic carbon dioxide (CO_2), methane (CH^4), nitrous oxide (N2O) and other important agents and mechanisms, together with the typical geographical extent (spatial scale) of the forcing and the assessed level of scientific understanding (LOSU). The net anthropogenic radiative forcing and its range are also shown. These require summing asymmetric uncertainty estimates from the component terms, and cannot be obtained by simple addition. Additional forcing factors not included here are considered to have a very low LOSU. Volcanic aerosols contribute an additional natural forcing but are not included in this figure due to their episodic nature. The range for linear contrails does not include other possible effects of aviation on cloudiness. {Book Reference Omitted}

to improved *in situ*, satellite and ground-based measurements and more comprehensive modelling, but remain the dominant uncertainty in radiative forcing. Aerosols also influence cloud lifetime and precipitation. {Book Reference Omitted}

- Significant anthropogenic contributions to radiative forcing come from several other sources. Tropospheric ozone changes due to emissions of ozone-forming chemicals (nitrogen oxides, carbon monoxide, and hydrocarbons) contribute +0.35 [+0.25 to +0.65] W m^{-2}. The direct radiative forcing due to changes in halocarbons[8] is +0.34 [+0.31 to +0.37] W m^{-2}. Changes in surface albedo, due to land cover changes and deposition of black carbon aerosols on snow, exert respective forcings of –0.2 [–0.4 to 0.0] and +0.1 [0.0 to +0.2] W m^{-2}. Additional terms smaller than ±0.1 W m^{-2} are shown in Figure SPM.2. {Book Reference Omitted}
- Changes in solar irradiance since 1750 are estimated to cause a radiative forcing of +0.12 [+0.06 to +0.30] W m^{-2}, which is less than half the estimate given in the TAR. {Book Reference Omitted}

Direct Observations of Recent Climate Change

Since the TAR, progress in understanding how climate is changing in space and in time has been gained through improvements and extensions of numerous datasets and data analyses, broader geographical coverage, better understanding of uncertainties, and a wider variety of measurements. Increasingly comprehensive observations are available for glaciers and snow cover since the 1960s, and for sea level and ice sheets since about the past decade. However, data coverage remains limited in some regions.

Warming of the climate system is unequivocal, as is now evident from observations of increases in global average air and ocean temperatures, widespread melting of snow and ice, and rising global average sea level (see Figure SPM.3). {Book Reference Omitted}

- Eleven of the last twelve years (1995–2006) rank among the 12 warmest years in the instrumental record of global surface temperature[9] (since 1850). The updated 100-year linear trend (1906 to 2005) of 0.74°C [0.56°C to 0.92°C] is therefore larger than the corresponding trend for 1901 to 2000 given in the TAR of 0.6°C [0.4°C to 0.8°C]. The linear warming trend over the last 50 years (0.13°C [0.10°C to 0.16°C] per decade) is nearly twice that for the last 100 years. The total temperature increase from 1850–1899 to 2001–2005 is 0.76°C [0.57°C to 0.95°C]. Urban heat island effects are real but local, and have a negligible influence (less than 0.006°C per decade over land and zero over the oceans) on these values. {Book Reference Omitted}
- New analyses of balloon-borne and satellite measurements of lower- and mid-tropospheric temperature show warming rates that are similar to those of the surface temperature record and are consistent within their respective uncertainties, largely reconciling a discrepancy noted in the TAR. {Book Reference Omitted}
- The average atmospheric water vapour content has increased since at least the 1980s over land and ocean as well as in the upper troposphere. The increase is broadly consistent with the extra water vapour that warmer air can hold. {Book Reference Omitted}
- Observations since 1961 show that the average temperature of the global ocean has increased to depths of at least 3000 m and that the ocean has been absorbing more than 80% of the heat added to the climate system. Such warming causes seawater to expand, contributing to sea level rise (see Table SPM.1). {Book Reference Omitted}

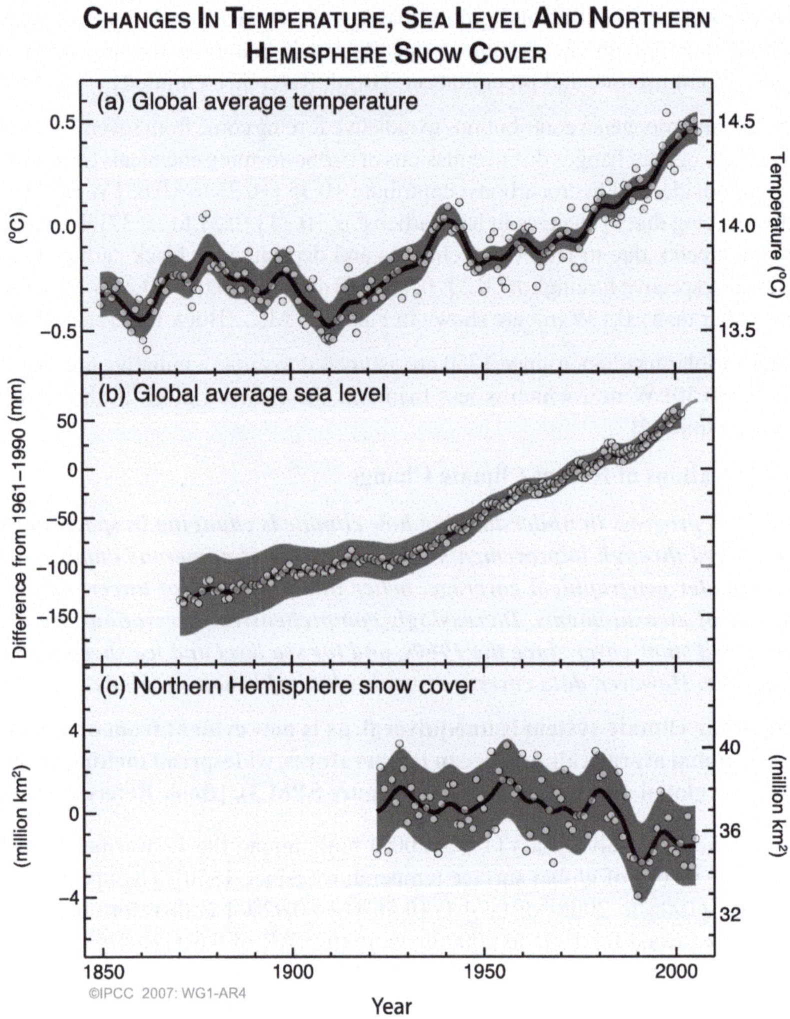

Figure SPM.3. Observed changes in (a) global average surface temperature, (b) global average sea level from tide gauge (blue) and satellite (red) data and (c) Northern Hemisphere snow cover for March-April. All changes are relative to corresponding averages for the period 1961–1990. Smoothed curves represent decadal average values while circles show yearly values. The shaded areas are the uncertainty intervals estimated from a comprehensive analysis of known uncertainties (a and b) and from the time series (c). {Book Reference Omitted}

- Mountain glaciers and snow cover have declined on average in both hemispheres. Widespread decreases in glaciers and ice caps have contributed to sea level rise (ice caps do not include contributions from the Greenland and Antarctic Ice Sheets). (See Table SPM.1.) {Book Reference Omitted}
- New data since the TAR now show that losses from the ice sheets of Greenland and Antarctica have *very likely* contributed to sea level rise over 1993 to 2003 (see Table SPM.1). Flow speed has increased for some Greenland and Antarctic outlet glaciers, which drain ice from the interior of the ice sheets. The corresponding increased

Table SPM.1. Observed Rate of Sea Level Rise and Estimated Contributions From Different Sources. {5.5, Table 5.3}

	Rate of sea level rise (mm per year)	
Source of sea level rise	*1961–2003*	*1993–2003*
Thermal expansion	0.42 ± 0.12	1.6 ± 0.5
Glaciers and ice caps	0.50 ± 0.18	0.77 ± 0.22
Greenland Ice Sheet	0.05 ± 0.12	0.21 ± 0.07
Antarctic Ice Sheet	0.14 ± 0.41	0.21 ± 0.35
Sum of individual climate contributions to sea level rise	1.1 ± 0.5	2.8 ± 0.7
Observed total sea level rise	1.8 ± 0.5[a]	3.1 ± 0.7[a]
Difference(Observed minus sum of estimated climate contributions)	0.7 ± 0.7	0.3 ± 1.0

[a] Data prior to 1993 are from tide gauges and after 1993 are from satellite altimetry

ice sheet mass loss has often followed thinning, reduction or loss of ice shelves or loss of floating glacier tongues. Such dynamical ice loss is sufficient to explain most of the Antarctic net mass loss and approximately half of the Greenland net mass loss. The remainder of the ice loss from Greenland has occurred because losses due to melting have exceeded accumulation due to snowfall. {Book Reference Omitted}

- Global average sea level rose at an average rate of 1.8 [1.3 to 2.3] mm per year over 1961 to 2003. The rate was faster over 1993 to 2003: about 3.1 [2.4 to 3.8] mm per year. Whether the faster rate for 1993 to 2003 reflects decadal variability or an increase in the longer-term trend is unclear. There is *high confidence* that the rate of observed sea level rise increased from the 19th to the 20th century. The total 20th-century rise is estimated to be 0.17 [0.12 to 0.22] m. {Book Reference Omitted}
- For 1993 to 2003, the sum of the climate contributions is consistent within uncertainties with the total sea level rise that is directly observed (see Table SPM.1). These estimates are based on improved satellite and *in situ* data now available. For the period 1961 to 2003, the sum of climate contributions is estimated to be smaller than the observed sea level rise. The TAR reported a similar discrepancy for 1910 to 1990. {Book Reference Omitted}

At continental, regional and ocean basin scales, numerous long-term changes in climate have been observed. These include changes in arctic temperatures and ice, widespread changes in precipitation amounts, ocean salinity, wind patterns and aspects of extreme weather including droughts, heavy precipitation, heat waves and the intensity of tropical cyclones.[10] {Book Reference Omitted}

- Average arctic temperatures increased at almost twice the global average rate in the past 100 years. Arctic temperatures have high decadal variability, and a warm period was also observed from 1925 to 1945. {Book Reference Omitted}
- Satellite data since 1978 show that annual average arctic sea ice extent has shrunk by 2.7 [2.1 to 3.3]% per decade, with larger decreases in summer of 7.4 [5.0 to 9.8]% per decade. These values are consistent with those reported in the TAR. {Book Reference Omitted}
- Temperatures at the top of the permafrost layer have generally increased since the 1980s in the Arctic (by up to 3°C). The maximum area covered by seasonally frozen ground has

decreased by about 7% in the Northern Hemisphere since 1900, with a decrease in spring of up to 15%. {Book Reference Omitted}

- Long-term trends from 1900 to 2005 have been observed in precipitation amount over many large regions.11 Significantly increased precipitation has been observed in eastern parts of North and South America, northern Europe and northern and central Asia. Drying has been observed in the Sahel, the Mediterranean, southern Africa and parts of southern Asia. Precipitation is highly variable spatially and temporally, and data are limited in some regions. Long-term trends have not been observed for the other large regions assessed.[11] {Book Reference Omitted}
- Changes in precipitation and evaporation over the oceans are suggested by freshening of mid-and high-latitude waters together with increased salinity in low-latitude waters. {Book Reference Omitted}
- Mid-latitude westerly winds have strengthened in both hemispheres since the 1960s. {Book Reference Omitted}
- More intense and longer droughts have been observed over wider areas since the 1970s, particularly in the tropics and subtropics. Increased drying linked with higher temperatures and decreased precipitation has contributed to changes in drought. Changes in sea surface temperatures, wind patterns and decreased snowpack and snow cover have also been linked to droughts. {Book Reference Omitted}
- The frequency of heavy precipitation events has increased over most land areas, consistent with warming and observed increases of atmospheric water vapour. {Book Reference Omitted}
- Widespread changes in extreme temperatures have been observed over the last 50 years. Cold days, cold nights and frost have become less frequent, while hot days, hot nights and heat waves have become more frequent (see Table SPM.2). {Book Reference Omitted}
- There is observational evidence for an increase in intense tropical cyclone activity in the North Atlantic since about 1970, correlated with increases of tropical sea surface temperatures. There are also suggestions of increased intense tropical cyclone activity in some other regions where concerns over data quality are greater. Multi-decadal variability and the quality of the tropical cyclone records prior to routine satellite observations in about 1970 complicate the detection of long-term trends in tropical cyclone activity. There is no clear trend in the annual numbers of tropical cyclones. {Book Reference Omitted}

Some aspects of climate have not been observed to change. {Book Reference Omitted}

- A decrease in diurnal temperature range (DTR) was reported in the TAR, but the data available then extended only from 1950 to 1993. Updated observations reveal that DTR has not changed from 1979 to 2004 as both day-and night-time temperature have risen at about the same rate. The trends are highly variable from one region to another. {Book Reference Omitted}
- Antarctic sea ice extent continues to show interannual variability and localised changes but no statistically significant average trends, consistent with the lack of warming reflected in atmospheric temperatures averaged across the region. {Book Reference Omitted}
- There is insufficient evidence to determine whether trends exist in the meridional overturning circulation (MOC) of the global ocean or in small-scale phenomena such as tornadoes, hail, lightning and dust-storms. {Book Reference Omitted}

Table SPM.2. Recent trends, assessment of human influence on the trend and projections for extreme weather events for which there is an observed late-20th century trend. {Tables 3.7, 3.8, 9.4; Sections 3.8, 5.5, 9.7, 11.2–11.9}

Phenomenon[a] and direction of trend	*Likelihood that trend occurred in late 20th century (typically post 1960)*	*Likelihood of a human contribution to observed trend[b]*	*Likelihood of future trends based on projections for 21st century using SRES scenarios*
Warmer and fewer cold days and nights over most land areas	*Very likely*[c]	*Likely*[d]	*Virtually certain*[d]
Warmer and more frequent hot days and nights over most land areas	*Very likely*[e]	*Likely (nights)*[d]	*Virtually certain*[d]
Warm spells/heat waves. Frequency increases over most land areas	*Likely*	*More likely than not*[f]	*Very likely*
Heavy precipitation events. Frequency (or proportion of total rainfall from heavy falls) increases over most areas	*Likely*	*More likely than not*[f]	*Very likely*
Area affected by droughts increases	*Likely in many* regions since 1970s	*More likely than not*	*Likely*
Intense tropical cyclone activity increases	*Likely in some* regions since 1970	*More likely than not*[f]	*Likely*
Increased incidence of extreme high sea level (excludes tsunamis)[g]	*Likely*	*More likely than not*[f,h]	*Likely*[i]

[a] See Table 3.7 for further details regarding definitions.
[b] See Table TS.4, Box TS.5 and Table 9.4.
[c] Decreased frequency of cold days and nights (coldest 10%).
[d] Warming of the most extreme days and nights each year.
[e] Increased frequency of hot days and nights (hottest 10%).
[f] Magnitude of anthropogenic contributions not assessed. Attribution for these phenomena based on expert judgement rather than formal attribution studies.
[g] Extreme high sea level depends on average sea level and on regional weather systems. It is defined here as the highest 1% of hourly values of observed sea level at a station for a given reference period.
[h] Changes in observed extreme high sea level closely follow the changes in average sea level. {Book Reference Omitted} It is *very likely* that anthropogenic activity contributed to a rise in average sea level. {Book Reference Omitted}
[i] In all scenarios, the projected global average sea level at 2100 is higher than in the reference period. {Book Reference Omitted} The effect of changes in regional weather systems on sea level extremes has not been assessed.

A Palaeoclimatic Perspective

Palaeoclimatic studies use changes in climatically sensitive indicators to infer past changes in global climate on time scales ranging from decades to millions of years. Such proxy data (e.g., tree ring width) may be influenced by both local temperature and other factors such as precipitation, and are often representative of particular seasons rather than full years. Studies since the TAR draw increased confidence from additional data showing coherent behaviour across multiple indicators in different parts of the world. However, uncertainties generally increase with time into the past due to increasingly limited spatial coverage.

Palaeoclimatic information supports the interpretation that the warmth of the last half century is unusual in at least the previous 1,300 years. The last time the polar regions were significantly warmer than present for an extended period (about 125,000 years ago), reductions in polar ice volume led to 4 to 6 m of sea level rise. {Book Reference Omitted}

- Average Northern Hemisphere temperatures during the second half of the 20th century were *very likely* higher than during any other 50-year period in the last 500 years and *likely* the highest in at least the past 1,300 years. Some recent studies indicate greater variability in Northern Hemisphere temperatures than suggested in the TAR, particularly finding that cooler periods existed in the 12th to 14th, 17th and 19th centuries. Warmer periods prior to the 20th century are within the uncertainty range given in the TAR. {Book Reference Omitted}
- Global average sea level in the last interglacial period (about 125,000 years ago) was *likely* 4 to 6 m higher than during the 20th century, mainly due to the retreat of polar ice. Ice core data indicate that average polar temperatures at that time were 3°C to 5°C higher than present, because of differences in the Earth's orbit. The Greenland Ice Sheet and other arctic ice fields *likely* contributed no more than 4 m of the observed sea level rise. There may also have been a contribution from Antarctica. {Book Reference Omitted}

Understanding and Attributing Climate Change

This assessment considers longer and improved records, an expanded range of observations and improvements in the simulation of many aspects of climate and its variability based on studies since the TAR. It also considers the results of new attribution studies that have evaluated whether observed changes are quantitatively consistent with the expected response to external forcings and inconsistent with alternative physically plausible explanations.

Most of the observed increase in global average temperatures since the mid-20th century is *very likely* due to the observed increase in anthropogenic greenhouse gas concentrations.[12] This is an advance since the TAR's conclusion that "most of the observed warming over the last 50 years is *likely* to have been due to the increase in greenhouse gas concentrations". Discernible human influences now extend to other aspects of climate, including ocean warming, continental-average temperatures, temperature extremes and wind patterns (see Figure SPM.4 and Table SPM.2). {Book Reference Omitted}

- It is *likely* that increases in greenhouse gas concentrations alone would have caused more warming than observed because volcanic and anthropogenic aerosols have offset some warming that would otherwise have taken place. {Book Reference Omitted}
- The observed widespread warming of the atmosphere and ocean, together with ice mass loss, support the conclusion that it is *extremely unlikely* that global climate change of the past 50 years can be explained without external forcing, and *very likely* that it is not due to known natural causes alone. {Book Reference Omitted}
- Warming of the climate system has been detected in changes of surface and atmospheric temperatures in the upper several hundred metres of the ocean, and in contributions to sea level rise. Attribution studies have established anthropogenic contributions to all of these changes. The observed pattern of tropospheric warming and stratospheric cooling is *very likely* due to the combined influences of greenhouse gas increases and stratospheric ozone depletion. {Book Reference Omitted}

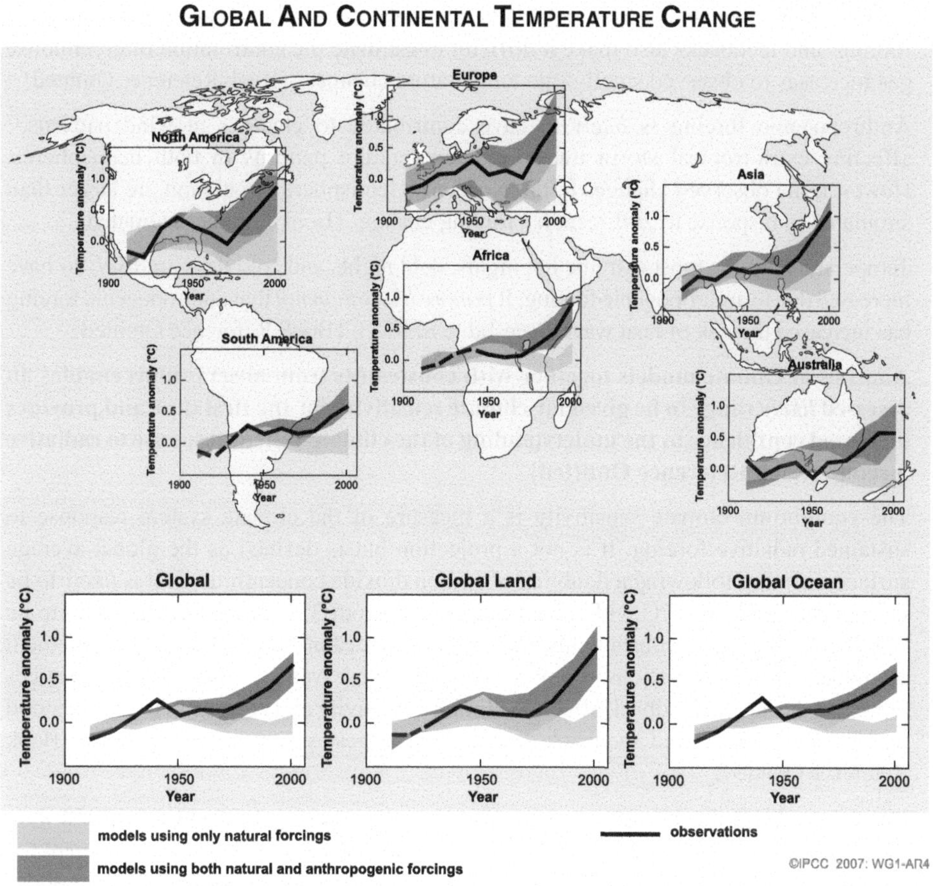

Figure SPM.4. Comparison of observed continental- and global-scale changes in surface temperature with results simulated by climate models using natural and anthropogenic forcings. Decadal averages of observations are shown for the period 1906 to 2005 (black line) plotted against the centre of the decade and relative to the corresponding average for 1901–1950. Lines are dashed where spatial coverage is less than 50%. Blue shaded bands show the 5–95% range for 19 simulations from five climate models using only the natural forcings due to solar activity and volcanoes. Red shaded bands show the 5–95% range for 58 simulations from 14 climate models using both natural and anthropogenic forcings. {Book Reference Omitted}

- It is *likely* that there has been significant anthropogenic warming over the past 50 years averaged over each continent except Antarctica (see Figure SPM.4). The observed patterns of warming, including greater warming over land than over the ocean, and their changes over time, are only simulated by models that include anthropogenic forcing. The ability of coupled climate models to simulate the observed temperature evolution on each of six continents provides stronger evidence of human influence on climate than was available in the TAR. {Book Reference Omitted}
- Difficulties remain in reliably simulating and attributing observed temperature changes at smaller scales. On these scales, natural climate variability is relatively larger, making

it harder to distinguish changes expected due to external forcings. Uncertainties in local forcings and feedbacks also make it difficult to estimate the contribution of greenhouse gas increases to observed small-scale temperature changes. {Book Reference Omitted}

- Anthropogenic forcing is *likely* to have contributed to changes in wind patterns,[13] affecting extra-tropical storm tracks and temperature patterns in both hemispheres. However, the observed changes in the Northern Hemisphere circulation are larger than simulated in response to 20th-century forcing change. {Book Reference Omitted}
- Temperatures of the most extreme hot nights, cold nights and cold days are *likely* to have increased due to anthropogenic forcing. It is *more likely than not* that anthropogenic forcing has increased the risk of heat waves (see Table SPM.2). {Book Reference Omitted}

Analysis of climate models together with constraints from observations enables an assessed *likely* range to be given for climate sensitivity for the first time and provides increased confidence in the understanding of the climate system response to radiative forcing. {Book Reference Omitted}

- The equilibrium climate sensitivity is a measure of the climate system response to sustained radiative forcing. It is not a projection but is defined as the global average surface warming following a doubling of carbon dioxide concentrations. It is *likely* to be in the range 2°C to 4.5°C with a best estimate of about 3°C, and is *very unlikely* to be less than 1.5°C. Values substantially higher than 4.5°C cannot be excluded, but agreement of models with observations is not as good for those values. Water vapour changes represent the largest feedback affecting climate sensitivity and are now better understood than in the TAR. Cloud feedbacks remain the largest source of uncertainty. {Book Reference Omitted}
- It is *very unlikely* that climate changes of at least the seven centuries prior to 1950 were due to variability generated within the climate system alone. A significant fraction of the reconstructed Northern Hemisphere inter-decadal temperature variability over those centuries is *very likely* attributable to volcanic eruptions and changes in solar irradiance, and it is *likely* that anthropogenic forcing contributed to the early 20th-century warming evident in these records. {Book Reference Omitted}

Projections of Future Changes in Climate

A major advance of this assessment of climate change projections compared with the TAR is the large number of simulations available from a broader range of models. Taken together with additional information from observations, these provide a quantitative basis for estimating likelihoods for many aspects of future climate change. Model simulations cover a range of possible futures including idealised emission or concentration assumptions. These include SRES[14] illustrative marker scenarios for the 2000 to 2100 period and model experiments with greenhouse gases and aerosol concentrations held constant after year 2000 or 2100.

For the next two decades, a warming of about 0.2°C per decade is projected for a range of SRES emission scenarios. Even if the concentrations of all greenhouse gases and aerosols had been kept constant at year 2000 levels, a further warming of about 0.1°C per decade would be expected. {Book Reference Omitted}

- Since IPCC's first report in 1990, assessed projections have suggested global average temperature increases between about 0.15°C and 0.3°C per decade for 1990 to 2005. This can now be compared with observed values of about 0.2°C per decade, strengthening confidence in near-term projections. {Book Reference Omitted}
- Model experiments show that even if all radiative forcing agents were held constant at year 2000 levels, a further warming trend would occur in the next two decades at a rate of about 0.1°C per decade, due mainly to the slow response of the oceans. About twice as much warming (0.2°C per decade) would be expected if emissions are within the range of the SRES scenarios. Best-estimate projections from models indicate that decadal average warming over each inhabited continent by 2030 is insensitive to the choice among SRES scenarios and is *very likely* to be at least twice as large as the corresponding model-estimated natural variability during the 20th century. {Book Reference Omitted}

Continued greenhouse gas emissions at or above current rates would cause further warming and induce many changes in the global climate system during the 21st century that would *very likely* be larger than those observed during the 20th century. {Book Reference Omitted}

- Advances in climate change modelling now enable best estimates and *likely* assessed uncertainty ranges to be given for projected warming for different emission scenarios. Results for different emission scenarios are provided explicitly in this report to avoid loss of this policy-relevant information. Projected global average surface warmings for the end of the 21st century (2090–2099) relative to 1980–1999 are shown in Table SPM.3. These illustrate the differences between lower and higher SRES emission scenarios, and the projected warming uncertainty associated with these scenarios. {Book Reference Omitted}
- Best estimates and *likely* ranges for global average surface air warming for six SRES emissions marker scenarios are given in this assessment and are shown in Table SPM.3. For example, the best estimate for the low scenario (B1) is 1.8°C (*likely* range is 1.1°C to 2.9°C), and the best estimate for the high scenario (A1FI) is 4.0°C (*likely* range is 2.4°C to 6.4°C). Although these projections are broadly consistent with the span quoted in the TAR (1.4°C to 5.8°C), they are not directly comparable (see Figure SPM.5). The Fourth Assessment Report is more advanced as it provides best estimates and an assessed likelihood range for each of the marker scenarios. The new assessment of the *likely* ranges now relies on a larger number of climate models of increasing complexity and realism, as well as new information regarding the nature of feedbacks from the carbon cycle and constraints on climate response from observations. {Book Reference Omitted}
- Warming tends to reduce land and ocean uptake of atmospheric carbon dioxide, increasing the fraction of anthropogenic emissions that remains in the atmosphere. For the A2 scenario, for example, the climate-carbon cycle feedback increases the corresponding global average warming at 2100 by more than 1°C. Assessed upper ranges for temperature projections are larger than in the TAR (see Table SPM.3) mainly because the broader range of models now available suggests stronger climate-carbon cycle feedbacks. {Book Reference Omitted}
- Model-based projections of global average sea level rise at the end of the 21st century (2090–2099) are shown in Table SPM.3. For each scenario, the midpoint of the range in Table SPM.3 is within 10% of the TAR model average for 2090–2099. The ranges are

narrower than in the TAR mainly because of improved information about some uncertainties in the projected contributions.[15] {Book Reference Omitted}

- Models used to date do not include uncertainties in climate-carbon cycle feedback nor do they include the full effects of changes in ice sheet flow, because a basis in published literature is lacking. The projections include a contribution due to increased ice flow from Greenland and Antarctica at the rates observed for 1993 to 2003, but these flow rates could increase or decrease in the future. For example, if this contribution were to grow linearly with global average temperature change, the upper ranges of sea level rise for SRES scenarios shown in Table SPM.3 would increase by 0.1 to 0.2 m. Larger values cannot be excluded, but understanding of these effects is too limited to assess their likelihood or provide a best estimate or an upper bound for sea level rise. {Book Reference Omitted}
- Increasing atmospheric carbon dioxide concentrations lead to increasing acidification of the ocean. Projections based on SRES scenarios give reductions in average global surface ocean pH[16] of between 0.14 and 0.35 units over the 21st century, adding to the present decrease of 0.1 units since pre-industrial times. {Book Reference Omitted}

There is now higher confidence in projected patterns of warming and other regional-scale features, including changes in wind patterns, precipitation and some aspects of extremes and of ice. {Book Reference Omitted}

- Projected warming in the 21st century shows scenario-independent geographical patterns similar to those observed over the past several decades. Warming is expected to be greatest over land and at most high northern latitudes, and least over the Southern Ocean and parts of the North Atlantic Ocean (see Figure SPM.6). {Book Reference Omitted}
- Snow cover is projected to contract. Widespread increases in thaw depth are projected over most permafrost regions. {Book Reference Omitted}

Table SPM.3. Projected global average surface warming and sea level rise at the end of the 21st century. {Book Reference Omitted}

	Temperature Change (°C at 2090-2099 relative to 1980-1999)[a]		*Sea Level Rise (m at 2090-2099 relative to 1980-1999)*
Case	*Best estimate*	*Likely range*	*Model-based range excluding future rapid dynamical changes in ice flow*
Constant Year 2000 concentrations[b]	0.6	0.3 – 0.9	NA
B1 scenario	1.8	1.1 – 2.9	0.18 – 0.38
A1T scenario	2.4	1.4 – 3.8	0.20 – 0.45
B2 scenario	2.4	1.4 – 3.8	0.20 – 0.43
A1B scenario	2.8	1.7 – 4.4	0.21 – 0.48
A2 scenario	3.4	2.0 – 5.4	0.23 – 0.51
A1FI scenario	4.0	2.4 – 6.4	0.26 – 0.59

[a] These estimates are assessed from a hierarchy of models that encompass a simple climate model, several Earth System Models of Intermediate Complexity and a large number of Atmosphere-Ocean General Circulation Models (AOGCMs).

[b] Year 2000 constant composition is derived from AOGCMs only.

MULTI-MODEL AVERAGES AND ASSESSED RANGES FOR SURFACE WARMING

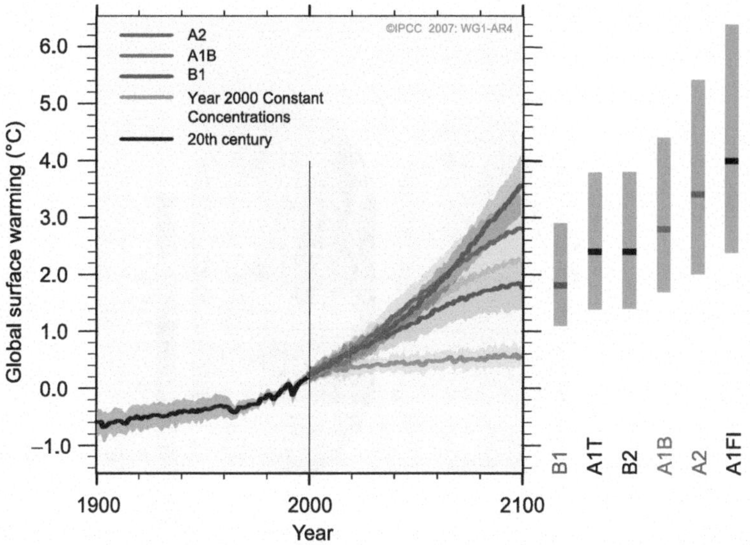

Figure SPM.5. Solid lines are multi-model global averages of surface warming (relative to 1980–1999) for the scenarios A2, A1B and B1, shown as continuations of the 20th century simulations. Shading denotes the ±1 standard deviation range of individual model annual averages. The orange line is for the experiment where concentrations were held constant at year 2000 values. The grey bars at right indicate the best estimate (solid line within each bar) and the ***likely*** range assessed for the six SRES marker scenarios. The assessment of the best estimate and ***likely*** ranges in the grey bars includes the AOGCMs in the left part of the figure, as well as results from a hierarchy of independent models and observational constraints. {Book Reference Omitted}

- Sea ice is projected to shrink in both the Arctic and Antarctic under all SRES scenarios. In some projections, arctic late-summer sea ice disappears almost entirely by the latter part of the 21st century. {Book Reference Omitted}
- It is *very likely* that hot extremes, heat waves and heavy precipitation events will continue to become more frequent. {Book Reference Omitted}
- Based on a range of models, it is *likely* that future tropical cyclones (typhoons and hurricanes) will become more intense, with larger peak wind speeds and more heavy precipitation associated with ongoing increases of tropical sea surface temperatures. There is less confidence in projections of a global decrease in numbers of tropical cyclones. The apparent increase in the proportion of very intense storms since 1970 in some regions is much larger than simulated by current models for that period. {Book Reference Omitted}
- Extratropical storm tracks are projected to move poleward, with consequent changes in wind, precipitation and temperature patterns, continuing the broad pattern of observed trends over the last half-century. {Book Reference Omitted}
- Since the TAR, there is an improving understanding of projected patterns of precipitation. Increases in the amount of precipitation are *very likely* in high latitudes, while decreases are *likely* in most subtropical land regions (by as much as about 20% in the A1B scenario in 2100, see Figure SPM.7), continuing observed patterns in recent trends. {Book Reference Omitted}

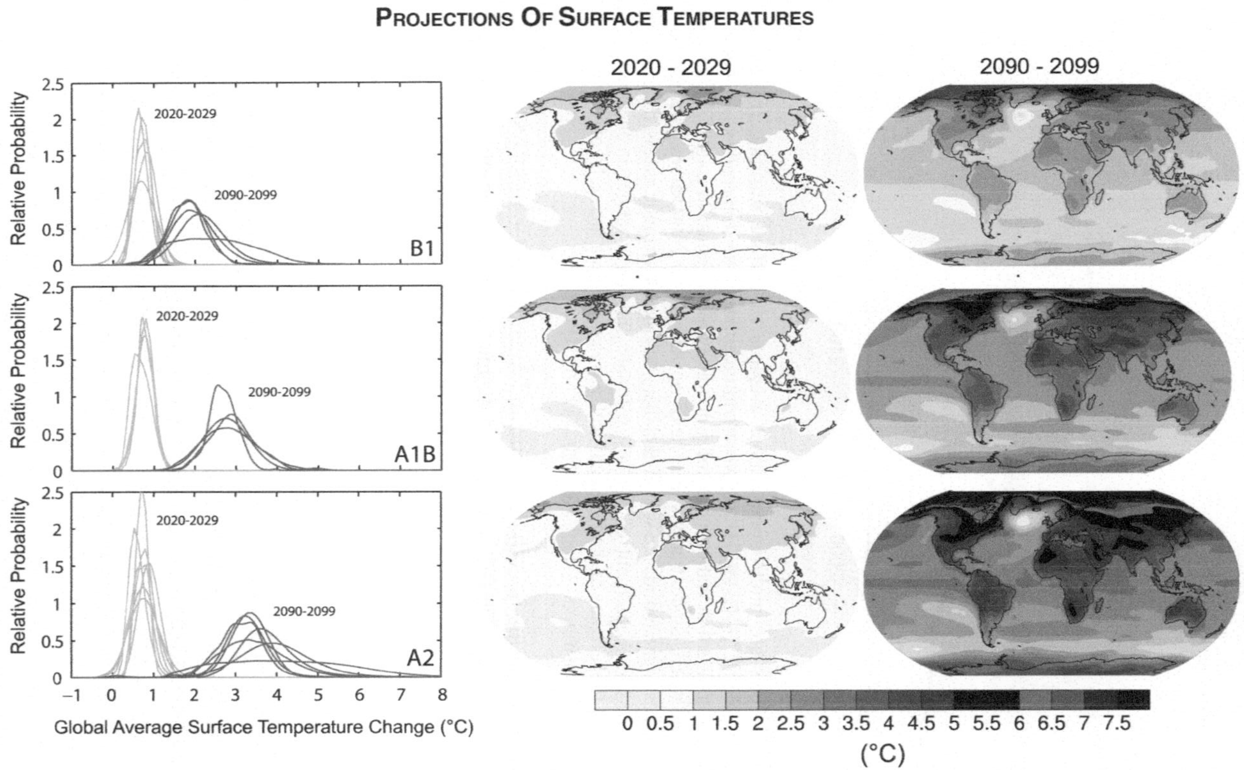

Figure SPM.6. Projected surface temperature changes for the early and late 21st century relative to the period 1980–1999. The central and right panels show the AOGCM multi-model average projections for the B1 (top), A1B (middle) and A2 (bottom) SRES scenarios averaged over the decades 2020– 2029 (centre) and 2090–2099 (right). The left panels show corresponding uncertainties as the relative probabilities of estimated global average warming from several different AOGCM and Earth System Model of Intermediate Complexity studies for the same periods. Some studies present results only for a subset of the SRES scenarios, or for various model versions. Therefore the difference in the number of curves shown in the left-hand panels is due only to differences in the availability of results. {Book Reference Omitted}

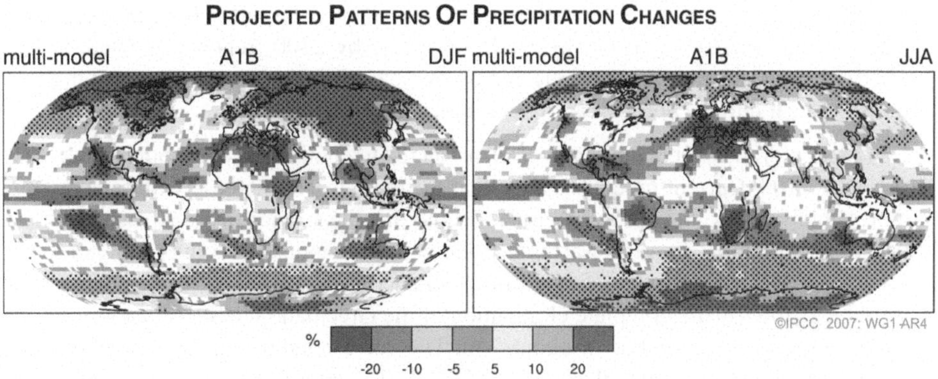

Figure SPM.7. Relative changes in precipitation (in percent) for the period 2090–2099, relative to 1980–1999. Values are multi-model averages based on the SRES A1B scenario for December to February (left) and June to August (right). White areas are where less than 66% of the models agree in the sign of the change and stippled areas are where more than 90% of the models agree in the sign of the change. {Book Reference Omitted}.

- Based on current model simulations, it is *very likely* that the meridional overturning circulation (MOC) of the Atlantic Ocean will slow down during the 21st century. The multi-model average reduction by 2100 is 25% (range from zero to about 50%) for SRES emission scenario A1B. Temperatures in the Atlantic region are projected to increase despite such changes due to the much larger warming associated with projected increases in greenhouse gases. It is *very unlikely* that the MOC will undergo a large abrupt transition during the 21st century. Longer-term changes in the MOC cannot be assessed with confidence. {Book Reference Omitted}

Anthropogenic warming and sea level rise would continue for centuries due to the time scales associated with climate processes and feedbacks, even if greenhouse gas concentrations were to be stabilised. {Book Reference Omitted}

- Climate-carbon cycle coupling is expected to add carbon dioxide to the atmosphere as the climate system warms, but the magnitude of this feedback is uncertain. This increases the uncertainty in the trajectory of carbon dioxide emissions required to achieve a particular stabilisation level of atmospheric carbon dioxide concentration. Based on current understanding of climate-carbon cycle feedback, model studies suggest that to stabilise at 450 ppm carbon dioxide could require that cumulative emissions over the 21st century be reduced from an average of approximately 670 [630 to 710] GtC (2460 [2310 to 2600] $GtCO_2$) to approximately 490 [375 to 600] GtC (1800 [1370 to 2200] $GtCO_2$). Similarly, to stabilise at 1000 ppm, this feedback could require that cumulative emissions be reduced from a model average of approximately 1415 [1340 to 1490] GtC (5190 [4910 to 5460] $GtCO_2$) to approximately 1100 [980 to 1250] GtC (4030 [3590 to 4580] $GtCO_2$). {Book Reference Omitted}
- If radiative forcing were to be stabilised in 2100 at B1 or A1B levels[14] a further increase in global average temperature of about 0.5°C would still be expected, mostly by 2200. {Book Reference Omitted}

- If radiative forcing were to be stabilised in 2100 at A1B levels14, thermal expansion alone would lead to 0.3 to 0.8 m of sea level rise by 2300 (relative to 1980–1999). Thermal expansion would continue for many centuries, due to the time required to transport heat into the deep ocean. {Book Reference Omitted}
- Contraction of the Greenland Ice Sheet is projected to continue to contribute to sea level rise after 2100. Current models suggest that ice mass losses increase with temperature more rapidly than gains due to precipitation and that the surface mass balance becomes negative at a global average warming (relative to pre-industrial values) in excess of 1.9°C to 4.6°C. If a negative surface mass balance were sustained for millennia, that would lead to virtually complete elimination of the Greenland Ice Sheet and a resulting contribution to sea level rise of about 7 m. The corresponding future temperatures in Greenland are comparable to those inferred for the last interglacial period 125,000 years ago, when palaeoclimatic information suggests reductions of polar land ice extent and 4 to 6 m of sea level rise. {Book Reference Omitted}
- Dynamical processes related to ice flow not included in current models but suggested by recent observations could increase the vulnerability of the ice sheets to warming, increasing future sea level rise. Understanding of these processes is limited and there is no consensus on their magnitude. {Book Reference Omitted}
- Current global model studies project that the Antarctic Ice Sheet will remain too cold for widespread surface melting and is expected to gain in mass due to increased snowfall. However, net loss of ice mass could occur if dynamical ice discharge dominates the ice sheet mass balance. {Book Reference Omitted}
- Both past and future anthropogenic carbon dioxide emissions will continue to contribute to warming and sea level rise for more than a millennium, due to the time scales required for removal of this gas from the atmosphere. {Book Reference Omitted}

The Emission Scenarios of the IPCC Special Report on Emission Scenarios (SRES)[17]

A1. The A1 storyline and scenario family describes a future world of very rapid economic growth, global population that peaks in mid-century and declines thereafter, and the rapid introduction of new and more efficient technologies. Major underlying themes are convergence among regions, capacity building and increased cultural and social interactions, with a substantial reduction in regional differences in per capita income. The A1 scenario family develops into three groups that describe alternative directions of technological change in the energy system. The three A1 groups are distinguished by their technological emphasis: fossil-intensive (A1FI), non-fossil energy sources (A1T) or a balance across all sources (A1B) (where balanced is defined as not relying too heavily on one particular energy source, on the assumption that similar improvement rates apply to all energy supply and end use technologies).

A2. The A2 storyline and scenario family describes a very heterogeneous world. The underlying theme is self-reliance and preservation of local identities. Fertility patterns across regions converge very slowly, which results in continuously increasing population. Economic development is primarily regionally oriented and per capita economic growth and technological change more fragmented and slower than other storylines.

B1. The B1 storyline and scenario family describes a convergent world with the same global population, that peaks in mid-century and declines thereafter, as in the A1 storyline, but with rapid change in economic structures toward a service and information economy, with reductions in material intensity and the introduction of clean and resource-efficient technologies. The emphasis is on global solutions to economic, social and environmental sustainability, including improved equity, but without additional climate initiatives.

B2. The B2 storyline and scenario family describes a world in which the emphasis is on local solutions to economic, social and environmental sustainability. It is a world with continuously increasing global population, at a rate lower than A2, intermediate levels of economic development, and less rapid and more diverse technological change than in the B1 and A1 storylines. While the scenario is also oriented towards environmental protection and social equity, it focuses on local and regional levels.

An illustrative scenario was chosen for each of the six scenario groups A1B, A1FI, A1T, A2, B1 and B2. All should be considered equally sound.

The SRES scenarios do not include additional climate initiatives, which means that no scenarios are included that explicitly assume implementation of the United Nations Framework Convention on Climate Change or the emissions targets of the Kyoto Protocol.

---

[1] *Climate change* in IPCC usage refers to any change in climate over time, whether due to natural variability or as a result of human activity. This usage differs from that in the United Nations Framework Convention on Climate Change, where climate change refers to a change of climate that is attributed directly or indirectly to human activity that alters the composition of the global atmosphere and that is in addition to natural climate variability observed over comparable time periods.

[2] *Radiative forcing* is a measure of the influence that a factor has in altering the balance of incoming and outgoing energy in the Earth-atmosphere system and is an index of the importance of the factor as a potential climate change mechanism. Positive forcing tends to warm the surface while negative forcing tends to cool it. In this report, radiative forcing values are for 2005 relative to pre-industrial conditions defined at 1750 and are expressed in watts per square metre ($W m^{-2}$). See Glossary and Section 2.2 for further details.

[3] ppm (parts per million) or ppb (parts per billion, 1 billion = 1,000 million) is the ratio of the number of greenhouse gas molecules to the total number of molecules of dry air. For example, 300 ppm means 300 molecules of a greenhouse gas per million molecules of dry air.

[4] Fossil carbon dioxide emissions include those from the production, distribution and consumption of fossil fuels and as a by-product from cement production. An emission of 1 GtC corresponds to 3.67 $GtCO_2$.

[5] In general, uncertainty ranges for results given in this Summary for Policymakers are 90% uncertainty intervals unless stated otherwise, that is, there is an estimated 5% likelihood that the value could be above the range given in square brackets and 5% likelihood that the value could be below that range. Best estimates are given where available. Assessed uncertainty intervals are not always symmetric about the corresponding best estimate. Note that a number of uncertainty ranges in the Working Group I TAR corresponded to 2 standard deviations (95%), often using expert judgement.

[6] In this Summary for Policymakers, the following terms have been used to indicate the assessed likelihood, using expert judgement, of an outcome or a result: *Virtually certain* > 99% probability of occurrence, *Extremely likely* > 95%, *Very likely* > 90%, *Likely* > 66%, *More likely than not* > 50%, *Unlikely* < 33%, *Very unlikely* < 10%, *Extremely unlikely* < 5% (see Box TS.1 for more details).

[7] In this Summary for Policymakers the following levels of confidence have been used to express expert judgements on the correctness of the underlying science: *very high confidence* represents at least a 9 out of 10 chance of being correct; *high confidence* represents about an 8 out of 10 chance of being correct (see Box TS.1)

[8] Halocarbon radiative forcing has been recently assessed in detail in *IPCC's Special Report on Safeguarding the Ozone Layer and the Global Climate System (2005).*

[9] The average of near-surface air temperature over land and sea surface temperature.

[10] Tropical cyclones include hurricanes and typhoons.

[11] The assessed regions are those considered in the regional projections chapter of the TAR and in Chapter 11 of this report.

[12] Consideration of remaining uncertainty is based on current methodologies.

[13] In particular, the Southern and Northern Annular Modes and related changes in the North Atlantic Oscillation. {3.6, 9.5, Box TS.2}

[14] SRES refers to the *IPCC Special Report on Emission Scenarios* (2000). The SRES scenario families and illustrative cases, which did not include additional climate initiatives, are summarised in a box at the end of this Summary for Policymakers. Approximate carbon dioxide equivalent concentrations corresponding to the computed radiative forcing due to anthropogenic greenhouse gases and aerosols in 2100 (see p. 823 of the TAR) for the SRES B1, A1T, B2, A1B, A2 and A1FI illustrative marker scenarios are about 600, 700, 800, 850, 1250 and 1,550 ppm respectively. Scenarios B1, A1B and A2 have been the focus of model intercomparison studies and many of those results are assessed in this report.

[15] TAR projections were made for 2100, whereas projections in this report are for 2090–2099. The TAR would have had similar ranges to those in Table SPM.3 if it had treated the uncertainties in the same way.

[16] Decreases in pH correspond to increases in acidity of a solution. See Glossary for further details.

[17] Emission scenarios are not assessed in this Working Group I Report of the IPCC. This box summarising the SRES scenarios is taken from the TAR and has been subject to prior line-by-line approval by the Panel.

3. Delivering as One: Report of the High-level Panel on United Nations System-wide Coherence in the areas of development, humanitarian assistance and the environment, 20 November 2006 (A/61/583)

Note by the Secretary-General

1. In the Outcome document of the 2005 World Summit (resolution 60/1), the Heads of State and Government recognized the importance of the unique expertise and resources that the United Nations system brings to global issues. The global leaders commended the extensive experience and expertise of the various development-related United Nations organizations and their important contributions to the achievement of the Millennium Development Goals and other broader development objectives.

2. However, the leaders recognized the need to build on ongoing reforms aiming at a more effective, coherent and better performing United Nations country presence. They specifically invited me to "launch work to further strengthen the management and coordination of United Nations operational activities so that they can make an even more effective contribution to the achievement of the internationally agreed development goals, including the Millennium Development Goals". The principal challenge for this work was identified as being in the fields of development, humanitarian assistance and the environment, while taking into account the cross-cutting areas of gender equality, sustainable development and human rights.

3. In putting in place arrangements for the study to be carried out in an expeditious and focused manner, it was my view that the United Nations system needed to further accelerate its efforts to support countries in meeting the Millennium Development Goals. Without a substantial renewed effort, the international community would not be able to live up to the ambition of the Millennium Development Goals. I considered that we required advice that brought together high-calibre political insight and managerial and operational know-how.

4. I asked three serving Prime Ministers, Prime Minister Shaukat Aziz of Pakistan, Prime Minister Luísa Dias Diogo of Mozambique and Prime Minister Jens Stoltenberg of Norway, to co-chair a High-level Panel on United Nations System-wide Coherence in the areas of development, humanitarian assistance and the environment. The Panel was composed of former Presidents Ricardo Lagos of Chile and Benjamin W. Mkapa of the United Republic of Tanzania and the following eminent international figures, Chancellor of the Exchequer Gordon Brown (United Kingdom of Great Britain and Northern Ireland), former Chief Executive Officer and Chairman of the Global Environment Facility Mohamed T. El-Ashry (Egypt), President of the Canadian International Development Agency Robert Greenhill (Canada), Former Director-General for Development Cooperation Ruth Jacoby (Sweden), European Union Commissioner for Development and Humanitarian Aid Louis Michel (Belgium), Director General of the French Development Agency Jean-Michel Severino (France), Under Secretary for Economic, Business and Agricultural Affairs of the United States Department of State Josette S. Sheeran (United States of America) and Former State Secretary for Foreign Affairs Keizo Takemi (Japan). Representing the United Nations system, Kemal Derviþ (Turkey) and Lennart Båge (Sweden) served as ex officio members of the Panel.

5. The Panel presented me with its report on 9 November 2006 and two co-chairs, Prime Minister Shaukat Aziz and Prime Minister Stoltenberg, joined me to launch the report at the informal briefing to the General Assembly, under the auspices of the President of the General Assembly.

6. The Panel report, entitled "Delivering as one", provides a clear and balanced analysis and series of ambitious but practical recommendations that can have a significant and long-lasting impact on the effectiveness and relevance of the United Nations system. In the area of development, the report recommends a "One United Nations" at the country level that has full country ownership, and is supported by a strengthened and more consolidated funding structure to substantially increase the effectiveness of United Nations interventions. Practical measures related to humanitarian assistance, environmental protection and gender equality and women's advancement will also strengthen the coherence, sustainability and impact of the United Nations delivery. The Panel has also proposed measures to strengthen coherence at the centre in the areas of governance, funding and management that are critical for a revamped United Nations development system. Moreover, many of the proposals are meant to ensure a much more effective integration and strengthening of the policy and normative role of the United Nations and better alignment with operational roles and structures.

7. I am very pleased to transmit the report of the Panel herewith to Member States for their consideration with my strong support for its recommendations. I urge the General Assembly to support their implementation as well.

Consultation process

8. I am also transmitting the Panel's report to my successor, Ban Ki-moon, to enable him to formulate specific proposals on how the Panel's recommendations should be taken forward. The new Secretary-General may wish to present a more detailed report on the Panel's recommendations once he has taken office. In this regard, I will be proposing to the new Secretary-General that he ensure that his office remain engaged in the oversight, coordination and tracking of the implementation of the report.

9. The Panel's report is very rich in terms of analysis and recommendations, and covers a great deal of ground. Therefore, it will be essential for there to be a process of informal dialogue on the Panel's report to build broad-based common understanding of its objectives, contents and proposals. These consultations should involve all delegations, senior officials from across the United Nations system and, if possible, Government officials, country-level practitioners and other experts. This would allow for different perspectives to be heard and stakeholders to become equally informed and aware of the recommendations and their implications.

10. Although the General Assembly will play a critical role in the consultation and decision-making process related to the critical recommendations of the report, other policymakers and actors need to be brought into the discussion to build deeper understanding and ownership of the proposals. This would include consultations within the Economic and Social Council and its commissions, and the governing bodies of United Nations system organizations. In this regard, I have already requested the executive heads of the United Nations specialized agencies, funds and programmes to transmit the report to their individual governing bodies for consideration.

11. Existing conferences and meetings of regional and other groupings could also afford opportunities for informal discussions on the Panel's report. These dialogues could be organized on the report as a whole, or on the various thematic areas contained in the report. Participants should be drawn from all relevant stakeholders.

12. This process of informal consultations/dialogue could culminate in a formal meeting of the plenary of the General Assembly some time in 2007. Once this process is complete, the President of the General Assembly could initiate consultations in "a working group" mode, in order for the General Assembly to consider a resolution on the Panel's report.

13. There will also be extensive United Nations inter-agency discussions on the Panel's recommendations, guided by and respectful of the intergovernmental consideration of the Panel's report. This dialogue will be essential as implementation of the Panel's recommendations will demand not only strong and sustained support from Member States, but also collective leadership and ownership within the United Nations system. Many of the changes proposed will require that individual United Nations agencies, funds and programmes take a broader view in the overall interest of a more coherent United Nations.

14. In this regard, I was very encouraged by the positive preliminary reaction to the Panel's work that was expressed during the Fall session of the United Nations System Chief Executives Board for Coordination (CEB). I have taken this reaction to be a positive signal in terms of our prospects for enacting the necessary system-wide reforms. The United Nations system is clearly united in its desire to improve its coherence and coordination.

Moving forward

15. I have decided to move forward on some of these recommendations, especially since many build on reforms and initiatives that are already being carried out by the executive heads of the United Nations agencies, funds and programmes.

16. The first such recommendation is the establishment of the five pilot One Country Programmes by 2007. A number of countries have already expressed an interest in being among the pilot countries, and we are in the process of determining appropriate criteria to carefully select them. In order to maximize results, we will need to ensure that the One Country Programme is piloted in countries at different stages of development, where United Nations agencies, funds and programmes and their counterparts are eager to work together to carry forward this pilot exercise. Some of the countries that are expressing an interest in being a pilot country would be building on the considerable progress already made in enhancing the coherence, effectiveness and efficiency of the United Nations at the country level. Well-designed and executed pilot programmes based on the principal of country ownership will provide the basis for further developing and expanding the One United Nations approach, as well as providing input to forthcoming deliberations on the triennial comprehensive policy review of operational activities for development of the United Nations system.

17. The second area that I will be moving forward is in the area of business practices. Great strides in improving performance and delivering results can be realized by implementing this set of recommendations, which clearly build on, and provide impetus to, many of the advances that the United Nations system has already made in this field. It will be essential that we swiftly modernize and achieve full compatibility on processes for resource

planning, human resources, common services and evaluation, as these are important drivers of coherence in the United Nations system. In this regard, it is significant to note that the CEB High-Level Committee on Management is making real progress, including on human resource practices, results-based budgeting and the approval of the adoption of International Public Sector Accounting Standards by 1 January 2010. The Panel's recommendations will provide further impetus to this United Nations system-wide effort.

18. The third recommendation that I am taking forward concerns CEB, which I chair. CEB has been asked to undertake a review of its functioning, in the light of experience gained since its establishment in 2001, with a view to improving its performance and accountability for system-wide coherence. Such a review was discussed at the fall session of CEB, and was unanimously welcomed. The Director-General of the International Labour Organization (ILO), Juan Somavia, and the Director-General of the World Trade Organization (WTO), Pascal Lamy, have agreed to lead such a review.

19. I urge the executive heads of the United Nations agencies, funds and programmes to do everything possible to move these recommendations forward.

20. Finally, I have started the process to take forward the recommendation on strengthening the United Nations gender architecture in order to provide one strong and coherent voice on women's issues in the United Nations system, which can better contribute to the overall efforts to achieve the goals of gender equality and empowerment of women. In this regard, I have initiated the necessary steps to request the establishment of the Under-Secretary-General for Gender Equality and Empowerment of Women who would lead a consolidated and strengthened United Nations gender architecture once it is approved by the relevant intergovernmental process. The detailed proposal will be presented to the General Assembly in November 2006. I urge Member States to support it.

Letter dated 9 November 2006 from the Co-Chairs of the High-level Panel on United Nations System-wide Coherence in the areas of development, humanitarian assistance and the environment addressed to the Secretary-General

We have the privilege to transmit to you the report of the High-level Panel on United Nations System-wide Coherence in the areas of development, humanitarian assistance and the environment, entitled "Delivering as one".

The report puts forward a series of recommendations to overcome the fragmentation of the United Nations so that the system can deliver as one, in true partnership with and serving the needs of all countries in their efforts to achieve the Millennium Development Goals and other internationally agreed development goals.

Our research and consultations revealed that the United Nations system has both strengths and weaknesses. It is an indispensable instrument in an age of growing interconnection between peace and security, sustainable development and human rights. However, bold reforms are needed to improve the effectiveness of the United Nations in delivering its mandate and responding to new and growing challenges. A more united system would be a stronger, more responsive and effective United Nations. A system reconfigured to optimally use its assets and expertise in support of country needs and demands would strengthen the voice and action of the United Nations in development, humanitarian assistance and the environment. A repositioned United Nations—delivering as one—would be much more than the sum of its parts.

Our proposals encompass a framework for a unified and coherent United Nations structure at the country level. These are matched by more coherent governance, funding and management arrangements at the centre. We have sought to consolidate existing entities wherever necessary, and to eliminate unnecessary duplication and competition. In all areas, our proposals identify the comparative advantage of organizations and delineate functions, roles and responsibilities. We have formulated mechanisms that would enable policy consistency and strategies to modernize business practices for better performance and accountability. We have renewed our commitment to put into practice the principles of good multilateral donorship, and to ensure adequate, sustained and secure funding for organizations that upgrade their efficiency and deliver results.

The members of the Panel, while having different perspectives on some issues, all endorse the report and generally agree with its findings. From our extensive consultation process, we can assure you that there are important constituencies of support for each of the Panel's proposals. We believe that, if taken together and implemented, our recommendations will result in a stronger United Nations system, one that is fit to play the central role envisaged for it in the 2005 World Summit Outcome document.

Our report is addressed to you, but many of our recommendations will require commitment from and action by heads of Government and organizations of the wider United Nations system. Only through their leadership—and the commitment of the incoming Secretary-General—can we realistically forge the consensus and action required for a more cohesive United Nations system.

It has been an honour to take part in this work, and we thank you for the trust you have placed in us to lead this study. We also want to express our deep respect and thanks to all Panel members, who injected total commitment, enthusiasm and creativity into this important task.

We were supported in our work by a secretariat under the leadership of Executive Director Adnan Amin. Mr. Amin and his devoted staff allowed us to benefit from their great experience, invaluable knowledge and astute judgement during and between our deliberations. We are thankful for their dedication and hard work which allowed us to complete our work on time.

(*Signed*) Shaukat **Aziz**
Co-Chair
Prime Minister of the Islamic Republic of Pakistan

(*Signed*) Luísa Dias **Diogo**
Co-Chair
Prime Minister of Mozambique

(*Signed*) Jens **Stoltenberg**
Co-Chair
Prime Minister of Norway

Summary

In facing up to the challenges of their times, the world leaders of 60 years ago created new multilateral institutions—the United Nations, the International Monetary Fund and the World Bank—in the conviction that international cooperation was the best way to solve the challenges of the post-war world.

Today we too face significant challenges: ours is an era of global change that is unprecedented in its speed, scope and scale. As the world becomes more interdependent, we are increasingly exposed to acute and growing social and economic inequalities. Poverty, environmental degradation, and lagging development exacerbate vulnerability and instability to the detriment of us all. Achieving the Millennium Development Goals and wider internationally agreed development goals is central to our global economic stability and prosperity.

The United Nations played a crucial role in articulating the Millennium Development Goals. Now it needs to take action to achieve these and the other development goals and to support Governments in implementing their national plans. However, without ambitious and far-reaching reforms the United Nations will be unable to deliver on its promises and maintain its legitimate position at the heart of the multilateral system. Despite its unique legitimacy, including the universality of its membership, the status of the United Nations as a central actor in the multilateral system is undermined by a lack of focus on results, thereby failing, more than anyone else, the poorest and most vulnerable.

The 2005 World Summit in New York gave new impetus to the need for United Nations reform. At the initiative of the Secretary-General, the High-level Panel on System-wide Coherence in the areas of development, humanitarian assistance and the environment has worked for over six months to consider how the United Nations system can most effectively respond to the global development, environmental and humanitarian challenges of the twenty-first century.

We have undertaken a thorough assessment of the strengths and weaknesses of the United Nations system, holding consultations with stakeholders around the world. We commend the United Nations as the indispensable force that drives forward the discourse on human development by defining and creating a global consensus in support of the Millennium Development Goals and the other internationally agreed development goals; playing a leading role in developing the concept of sustainable development; responding rapidly to humanitarian disasters; and mobilizing international action for the protection of the environment. The United Nations system also continues to play an essential role as a convener, setting norms and standards and advising countries on their implementation at the global, regional, national and local levels.

However, we have also seen how the work of the United Nations in the areas of development and the environment is often fragmented and weak. Inefficient and ineffective governance and unpredictable funding have contributed to policy incoherence, duplication and operational ineffectiveness across the system. Cooperation between organizations has been hindered by competition for funding, mission creep and outdated business practices.

Delivering as one and overcoming systemic fragmentation is a central theme of our report. Taken as a whole, our recommendations could result in a step change in the way the United Nations operates at Headquarters, in each region and in each country. If implemented, the recommendations could deliver a better focus on performance, efficiency, accountability and results within the United Nations system, and could also enhance the role and voice of developing countries. These changes would secure and strengthen the role of the United Nations at the heart of the multilateral system.

We have developed a set of clear recommendations that are based on the following five strategic directions:

- Ensure coherence and consolidation of United Nations activities, in line with the principle of country ownership, at all levels (country, regional, Headquarters).
- Establish appropriate governance, managerial and funding mechanisms to empower and support consolidation, and link the performance and results of United Nations organizations to their funding.
- Overhaul business practices of the United Nations system to ensure a focus on outcomes, responsiveness to needs and the delivery of results by the United Nations system, as measured in advancing the Millennium Development Goals.
- Ensure significant further opportunities for consolidation and effective delivery of "One United Nations" through an in-depth review.
- Undertake implementation urgently but not in an ill-planned and hasty manner that could compromise permanent and effective change.

"One" is a central concept in the present report: the United Nations needs to overcome its fragmentation and deliver as one through a stronger commitment to working together on the implementation of one strategy, in the pursuit of one set of goals. We have come up with ambitious but realistic recommendations with the potential to radically change the way the organizations operate at Headquarters, in each region and in each country so as to enable the United Nations to achieve more than the sum of its parts.

The essence of our vision is for the United Nations to deliver as one in the areas of development, humanitarian assistance and the environment. The normative and analytic expertise of the United Nations, its operational and coordination capabilities and its advocacy role would be more effectively brought together at the country, regional and global levels. Member States should shape the governance structures, the funding framework and the business practices to make it so.

One United Nations for development—at the country level

> **We recommend the establishment of One United Nations at the country level, with one leader, one programme, one budget and, where appropriate, one office.**

One third of United Nations country programmes include more than 10 United Nations agencies and in almost one third of them, less than US$ 2 million is spent by each United Nations agency. One United Nations should be based on a consolidation of all United Nations programme activities at the country level, where the country wishes it. The programme must be developed and owned by the country, in line with its own national priorities. Effective delivery requires a single budgetary framework.

To manage the One United Nations country programme there needs to be one leader—an empowered resident coordinator. The resident coordinator shall be selected on the basis of merit and competition demonstrably open to candidates outside the United Nations

Development Programme (UNDP) and the United Nations system. To ensure system-wide ownership of the resident coordinator system, the role of UNDP must change. It should focus and strengthen its operational work on policy coherence and positioning of the United Nations country team, and should withdraw from sector-focused policy and capacity work being carried out by other United Nations entities.

We recommend that 5 One United Nations country pilots be established by 2007 and, subject to satisfactory review, 20 One United Nations country programmes by 2009, 40 by 2010 and all other appropriate programmes by 2012.

One United Nations for development—at the headquarters level

We recommend the establishment of a Sustainable Development Board to oversee the One United Nations country programmes.

A coordinating board is necessary to provide oversight for the One United Nations country programme, in particular to provide system-wide coherence, ensure coordination and monitor the performance of global activities. We propose that the existing joint meetings of the boards of UNDP/the United Nations Population Fund (UNFPA), the United Nations Children's Fund (UNICEF) and the World Food Programme (WFP) be merged into this strategic oversight body—the Sustainable Development Board—which would report to the Economic and Social Council.

The Board should comprise a representative subset of Member States on the basis of equitable geographic representation, and should enhance the participation and voice of developing countries. The Board would be responsible for endorsing the One United Nations country programme, allocating funding and evaluating its performance in advancing the objectives agreed with the programme country. The Board should also maintain a strategic overview of the system to drive coordination and joint planning among all funds, programmes and agencies, and to monitor overlaps and gaps.

We recommend that the Secretary-General appoint a Development Coordinator, with responsibility for the performance and accountability of United Nations development activities.

The UNDP Administrator should serve as the Development Coordinator. The Development Coordinator should report to the Board and be supported by a high-level coordination group, comprising the heads of principal development agencies and an expert secretariat drawn from across the United Nations system. The evolution of the role of UNDP as manager of the resident coordinator system requires the establishment of a code of conduct and a firewall between its streamlined operational activities and other functions.

We recommend that the Secretary-General establish an independent task force to further eliminate duplication within the United Nations system and consolidate United Nations entities, where necessary.

We do not advocate a single United Nations entity because many individual agencies can best achieve their vital role in providing global public goods, advocacy, research, promoting best practices and establishing global norms and standards by operating individually in their specific sectors.

However, it is clear that the United Nations system suffers from a large number of overlapping functions, coordination failures and policy inconsistencies. An independent task force should clearly delineate the roles performed by United Nations funds, programmes, specialized agencies and regional entities, including the United Nations Secretariat. It should make concrete recommendations for merging or consolidating duplicative functions and ensure the complementarity of mandates. The task force should report by the end of 2007 to the Secretary-General, with clear recommendations for early implementation. This exercise has the potential to release significant annual savings, possibly in the range of 20 per cent per annum; the exact amount should be assessed by analysis of the task force review. Efficiency savings should be recycled to the One United Nations country programmes.

Results-based funding, performance and accountability

> **We recommend the establishment of a Millennium Development Goals funding mechanism to provide multi-year funding for the One United Nations country programmes as well as for agencies that are performing well.**

If the United Nations is to work more coherently and effectively, both at the country level and globally, significant changes are needed to the way donor funding is managed. Current United Nations funding patterns are highly fragmented, unpredictable and constrained by too much earmarking, which has encouraged duplication and inefficiency. This limits the United Nations and programme countries from making strategic decisions, and undermines the principles of multilateralism and country ownership.

A new Millennium Development Goals funding mechanism for voluntary donor funding (public, private and United Nations organizations) would provide multi-year funding for the One United Nations country programmes as well as for agencies that are performing well. The Sustainable Development Board would govern this mechanism. Donor contributions would be voluntary and could be specified. There should also be additional funding available at the discretion of the Board to reward headquarters of funds, programmes and specialized agencies that are performing well and to fund programmatic gaps and priorities in the system. To deliver maximum impact in advancing country priorities, we urge donors to contribute multi-year funding and substantially to reduce earmarking.

> **We recommend that United Nations organizations committed to and demonstrating reform receive full, multi-year core funding.**

Donors should support consolidated multi-year funding for the One United Nations country programme and core budgets of United Nations entities committed to reform. Donors would demonstrate by their actions that funding and performance are linked to results and reform.

Multi-year funding frameworks can be managed to increase focus on strategic priorities. Funding cycles of United Nations funds and programmes should be aligned to facilitate overall strategic coordination of United Nations programmatic work. The assessed budgets of the specialized agencies should be reviewed to ensure that they have sufficient core resources to deliver against strategic mandates.

The performance, funding and accountability of United Nations organizations are integrally linked. Funding must follow performance and reward results both for the One United Nations country programmes and Headquarters funding. The purpose of linking funding to performance is not to reduce funding but to improve outcomes. In fact, a more effective

United Nations could be an important partner in effectively using additional official development assistance. The price of poor performance should not be paid by reduced United Nations funding into countries but by the management and institutions. A reformed United Nations system demonstrating improved outcomes would be better placed to capture increased aid.

The Sustainable Development Board, assisted by a special Development Finance and Performance Unit in its secretariat, should publish internal evaluations of United Nations system spending and performance, as well as evaluations of the plans of individual funds, programmes and agencies, to which the Board would have access. The performance of United Nations organizations in advancing internationally agreed development goals should be measured. These assessments would inform funding decisions, both by donors making direct contributions and through the discretionary funding mechanism for the Millennium Development Goals to be made available to the Board as discussed above.

The modernization and reform of business practices, to be led by the Secretary-General, should be implemented urgently. Processes for resource planning, human resources, common services and evaluation must achieve full compatibility as major drivers of coherence in the United Nations system. There should be greater opportunities for staff mobility and a system-wide agreement on results-based management, as well as independent United Nations system-wide evaluation and common evaluation methodologies and benchmarking. The United Nations must systematically grasp opportunities for expanding joint services.

Programme countries and donors should be able to see and compare the true overhead costs of delivery through the introduction and publication of consistent administration and back office costs.

To promote transparency and accountability, we recommend that a United Nations common evaluation system be established by 2008, on the basis of a common evaluation methodology.

Humanitarian assistance

The United Nations has a unique and leading role to play in humanitarian disasters and emergencies. We recommend that this role be further enhanced by:

- Stronger coordination between the United Nations, national Governments and non-governmental organizations, including the International Federation of Red Cross and Red Crescent Societies, through a "cluster" approach to establish lead roles in the delivery of specific assistance, such as shelter, water, food, etc.
- Fully funding the Central Emergency Response Fund to facilitate quicker, more effective flows of funds in response to disasters.
- Clarifying United Nations mandates with regard to responsibility for internally displaced persons.
- More investment in risk reduction, early-warning and innovative disaster assistance strategies and mechanisms.
- Stronger leadership, quicker funding and better cooperation in post-conflict and post-disaster transition, with a clear lead role for UNDP once humanitarian coordination winds down.

- Periodic assessment and review of the performance of United Nations agencies and non-governmental organizations involved in humanitarian assistance.

Environment

There is an increasingly compelling case for taking urgent action on the environment. Environmental priorities have too often been compartmentalized in isolation from economic development priorities. However, global environmental degradation—including climate change—will have far-reaching economic and social implications that affect the world's ability to meet the Millennium Development Goals. Because the impacts are global and felt disproportionately by the poor, coordinated multilateral action to promote environmental sustainability is urgently required.

> **We recommend that international environmental governance be strengthened and made more coherent in order to improve the effectiveness and targeted action of environmental activities in the United Nations system.**
>
> **We recommend that, as a basis for reforms to improve system-wide coherence, the Secretary-General commission an independent assessment of international environmental governance within the United Nations system and related reform.**
>
> **We recommend that the United Nations Environment Programme be upgraded and given real authority as the environmental policy pillar of the United Nations system.**
>
> **We further recommend that United Nations entities cooperate more effectively on a thematic basis and through partnerships, with a dedicated agency at the centre.**

As the major financial mechanism for the global environment, the Global Environment Facility should be strengthened to help developing countries build their capacity. It should have a significant increase in resources to address the challenge posed by climate change and other environmental issues.

We have also made a number of recommendations to make sure that the United Nations helps countries mainstream environment in their strategies and actions, to elevate the status of sustainable development in the United Nations institutional architecture and in country activities, and to achieve the needed balance among the three pillars (economic, social and environmental) of sustainable development.

Gender: a key to effective development

> **We recommend the establishment of one dynamic United Nations entity focused on gender equality and women's empowerment.**

We consider gender equality to be central to the delivery of effective development outcomes, and the Secretary-General tasked us with a specific mandate to suggest radical changes for improving performance. We therefore propose a step change in the United Nations delivery of gender equality and women's empowerment, as follows:

- The three existing United Nations entities should be consolidated into an enhanced and independent gender entity, headed by an Executive Director with the rank of Under-Secretary-General, appointed through a meritocratic competition demonstrably open to those outside the United Nations.

- The gender entity would have a strengthened normative and advocacy role combined with a targeted programming role.
- The gender entity must be fully and ambitiously funded.
- Gender equality would be a component of all One United Nations country programmes.
- The commitment to gender equality is and should remain the mandate of the entire United Nations system.

Coordination with other multilateral agencies

The United Nations and the Bretton Woods institutions were established with the intention that they would work together in a complementary way. Over time both the World Bank and United Nations institutions have gradually expanded their roles, so that there is increasing overlap and duplication in their work. A balance needs to be struck between healthy competition and inefficient overlap and unfilled gaps. The Bretton Woods institutions and the United Nations need to work more closely together to remove unnecessary duplication and build on their respective strengths.

> **We therefore recommend, as a matter of urgency, that the Secretary-General, the President of the World Bank and the Executive Director of the International Monetary Fund set up a process to review, update and conclude formal agreements on their respective roles and relations at the global and country levels. These reviews must be periodically updated as well as assessed. This process should be undertaken on the basis of the enhanced performance, strengthened delivery and more influential role that the United Nations will have if our reforms are implemented.**

Implementation

We have proposed a comprehensive set of recommendations that taken together could make the United Nations much more responsive to the needs of its Member States, in particular developing countries. The United Nations would become more effective, more focused and better able to deliver results. If United Nations system organizations, Member States and all stakeholders act on our recommendations, the United Nations could become a driver in development to eradicate poverty, in partnership with civil society and the private sector. A reformed United Nations would be able to capture the increases in development resources that were committed in 2005, strengthening its enabling role in development and delivering more effective global public goods for the benefit of all.

The present recommendations are not a menu of options but an integrated whole. Each is individually vital to make the system greater than the sum of its parts, not smaller as has sometimes been the case. The recommendations should each be implemented with vigour and urgency and without diluting their purpose.

We recognize that implementing these reforms will involve significant challenges and sometimes the sacrifice of individual interests for United Nations agencies, funds and programmes. They will need to work more closely and effectively with the rest of the United Nations system in the interests of a greater common good. Donors will also be challenged by these recommendations, which propose changing the way they fund the United Nations in line with the principles of multilateralism and national ownership at different levels.

Our most important constituency are the billions who do not enjoy the prosperity and well-being that many of us take for granted and whose deprivation inspired a global call to action—the Millennium Development Goals. It is for the sake of the poor and the destitute that we need an efficient United Nations, one that is well governed and well funded and will remain a global repository of hope.

We have it within our grasp to make a real and lasting difference through the essential reforms set out in these proposals. All stakeholders in the United Nations system have a responsibility to seize this opportunity. Our actions and decision on reforms will for millions around the world make the difference between hope and despair, and for some the difference between life and death.

I. The case for reform

> The world needs a coherent and strong multilateral framework with the United Nations at its centre to meet the challenges of development, humanitarian assistance and the environment in a globalizing world. The United Nations needs to overcome its current fragmentation and to deliver as one. It should help the world accomplish the ambitious agenda endorsed by the 2005 World Summit, the Millennium Development Goals and other internationally agreed development goals. It should enable and support countries to lead their development processes and help address global challenges such as poverty, environmental degradation, disease and conflict.

1. In facing up to the challenges of their times, the world leaders of 60 years ago created new international institutions—the United Nations, the World Bank and the International Monetary Fund (IMF)—and demonstrated by their actions that international cooperation was the only way to solve the economic and political challenges of the post-war world. The architects of these institutions built for their time and their generation not only a whole set of new rules for the international system—they gave expression to a new public purpose based on high ideals.

2. Just as they did 60 years ago, we face a changing world today. Ours is the era of globalization, of global change unprecedented in its speed, scope and scale. As the world becomes ever more interdependent, sharp social and economic inequalities persist. Some of the poorest countries and communities remain isolated from economic integration and the benefits of globalization, and are disproportionately vulnerable to crisis and social upheaval. There is greater awareness of the acceleration of environmental degradation and climate change, and its effects on agricultural productivity and food security. More conflicts are within States than between them, and the risk of terrorism and infectious disease illustrate that security threats travel across borders.

3. Poverty, environmental degradation and lagging development heighten vulnerability and instability to the detriment of all. Now, more than ever, dealing with inequality—by achieving the Millennium Development Goals and wider development objectives—is central to economic stability and global security. In the face of unacceptable poverty we have a clear moral imperative to act when we have the knowledge, ability and resources to do so.

4. We know that when the flows of goods, services, capital and people are global, the challenges that arise can be solved only through globally concerted action. Globalization makes multilateralism indispensable, and the United Nations is the heart of multilateralism. Promoting development, eradicating poverty, protecting the environment for future

generations and preventing and assisting in humanitarian crises cannot be undertaken without the United Nations. Its universal values and representativeness create the political legitimacy and authority essential to the actions needed globally, regionally, nationally and locally.

5. Despite deep divides in the international community in the past, in particular during the cold war, the United Nations has been able to build a set of norms and internationally agreed development goals that frame the efforts of most nations and institutions. The United Nations has demonstrated intellectual leadership across a range of issues. For example, the annual Human Development Report, launched in the early 1990s, played a leading role in developing the concept of sustainable development and placed the well-being and dignity of people at the heart of the development agenda. At the 2000 Millennium Summit, 191 Member States, with 147 represented at the level of Head of State and Government, endorsed the United Nations Millennium Declaration. The United Nations can bring parties together, based on the unique legitimacy of its universal membership and on its diverse roles as a standard-setter, capacity-builder and advocate. Many of today's globally accepted norms and standards have originated from United Nations forums.

6. The United Nations has an opportunity in the unprecedented consensus reached on a common framework for the future, most recently reaffirmed by the 2005 World Summit. The framework is contained in the internationally agreed development goals of recent global conferences, ranging from social development to the empowerment of women, but is most compellingly outlined in the Millennium Development Goals. Never before have rich and poor countries alike formally embraced such concrete commitments. Never before have the United Nations, the World Bank, IMF and all parts of the international system come together behind the same set of development commitments and stood ready to be held accountable for them.

7. The United Nations has a key role in ensuring progress towards the Millennium Development Goals and other internationally agreed development goals. But it must reform to do so. Through the Secretary-General's High-level Panel on System-wide Coherence in the areas of development, humanitarian assistance and the environment, the international community has a unique opportunity to ensure that the United Nations can respond to the global challenges of the twenty-first century and play a full and effective role in the multilateral system.

8. The Monterrey Consensus of 2002 established a partnership for development, with donors making more official development assistance (ODA) and debt relief available within a context of continuing reform in developing countries, which was further elaborated in the Paris Declaration on Aid Effectiveness. In 2005 donors made further commitments to increase ODA by US$ 50 billion by 2010 and to provide US$ 55 billion in debt relief. A more effective and efficient United Nations should be an important partner in ensuring that those resources deliver results and accelerate progress towards the Millennium Development Goals.

9. These commitments go hand in hand with the Panel's recognition that the primary responsibility for action lies with each Member State. Country ownership of development plans and donor commitment to principles of aid effectiveness and good donorship have to underpin the work of the United Nations. Decades of piecemeal and failed development

efforts demonstrate that assistance policies cannot be imposed—they must be owned not only by Governments but by their people and communities. While this concept is broadly accepted, it must now be put into practice.

10. We know that the United Nations has been seen by some to fail in delivering some of the vision and mission we expect from it. There are many reasons why the United Nations has become fragmented and weak: from a lack of buy-in and mixed messages from Member States between capitals and representatives in various bodies, to a proliferation of agencies, mandates and offices, creating duplication and dulling the focus on outcomes, with moribund entities never discontinued. Even when mandates intersect, United Nations entities tend to operate alone with little synergy and coordination between them. The United Nations system now encompasses 17 specialized agencies and related organizations, 14 funds and programmes, 17 departments and offices of the United Nations Secretariat, 5 regional commissions, 5 research and training institutes and a plethora of regional and country-level structures. The loss of cohesion prevents the United Nations from being more than the sum of its parts.

- At the country level, operational incoherence between United Nations funds, programmes and agencies is most evident. More than one third of United Nations country teams include 10 or more United Nations agencies on the ground at any one time. Several teams include 20 or more. This has led to incoherent programme interventions and excessive administrative costs. It also burdens the capacity of developing countries to deal with multiple agencies. Of 60 countries analysed by the Panel, 17 country teams had an annual budget of less than US$ 2 million per agency. Nor does the normative and analytical expertise of non-resident agencies sufficiently support United Nations country team efforts. Without authoritative leadership by the United Nations resident coordinator, and system-wide ownership of the resident coordinator system, incentives for better coordination remain limited.
- Signs of fragmentation are also apparent at the regional level. Regional offices of different United Nations agencies are scattered in different locations, and definitions of regions can differ from one agency to another. In some regions strong regional and subregional institutions either exist or are rapidly evolving while others have strayed from their original mandates. This calls for a review of the United Nations regional roles and settings, including the regional commissions, to address regional needs, avoid duplication and overlapping functions and seek a coherent regional institutional landscape.
- More synergy is also needed at the global level. In some sectors, such as water and energy, more than 20 United Nations agencies are active and compete for limited resources without a clear collaborative framework. More than 30 United Nations agencies and programmes have a stake in environmental management. On specific issues, such as internally displaced people, several agencies have a legitimate interest, but none has a clear lead. Merging United Nations agencies does not always lead to better outcomes. But we believe there must be a significant streamlining of United Nations agencies so that the United Nations can "deliver as one", reduce duplication and significantly reduce the burdens it currently places on recipient and donor Governments, without diluting the performance and expertise of individual organizations.

- Inadequate and unpredictable funding of the system also contributes to fragmentation, undermining the multilateral character of the United Nations. The exponential growth of extrabudgetary (non-core) versus core resources has encouraged supply-driven rather than demand-driven approaches to assistance, undermining the principle of country ownership. Lack of donor coordination and competition for non-core resources among United Nations agencies squander significant time and effort on fund-raising, undermining the ability of the United Nations to make long-term strategic decisions that would deliver more effective results. Nor does the United Nations have a common system for its overall development funding or for measuring results transparently and systematically.

11. The international community has a duty to ensure that the United Nations is fit for purpose, reinvigorated and strengthened to meet the global challenges and diverse needs of an ever more interdependent world. To do this, the United Nations must be coherent and flexible enough to respond to demands for a variety of policy and operational services. A one-size-fits-all approach would be inappropriate.

12. As stakeholders in the United Nations system, we have a responsibility to agree on and present ambitious recommendations to improve the coherence of the United Nations so that it delivers as one in the areas of development, humanitarian assistance and the environment. The most radical decision we could take is to maintain the status quo. It would represent a victory for inertia and parochial, short-term institutional and national interests to maintain a system that has grown over time, and which no one facing the challenges we do today would design as it is. The Panel believes that reform to improve the coherence of the United Nations system must be underpinned by clear principles:

- *National ownership and people-centred approaches.* National sovereignty and national ownership of development plans must remain the bedrock of effective development. The system must be realigned to a demand-driven approach and to programmes delivered as close to beneficiaries as possible.
- *Core comparative advantage.* The United Nations needs to be flexible enough to respond to the operational and policy needs of all countries and to advocate global standards and norms. In each country it should focus on where it is best able to provide leadership—and withdraw from areas where it does not—to deliver results in response to country programme needs. The added value of the system lies in harnessing the full array of capabilities under its umbrella in an integrated way, not in seeking out narrow niches.
- *Maximum effectiveness and accountability.* Change must prepare the United Nations to address new challenges and to improve its performance measured by outcomes. Responsibility and authority must be clarified, and staff given the means to deliver on their mandates and be held accountable for them. Efficiency gains must be pursued through better business practices.

13. We must ensure that the United Nations is reformed and strengthened to deliver more effectively on its mandate to empower the vulnerable and the excluded. A United Nations able to respond flexibly can help to provide prosperity and justice for all. Our report is the starting point of a process to develop a commonly owned vision among all stakeholders for a coherent and effective United Nations system. It will require leadership by the Secretary-General, as well as sustained commitment and effort on the part of Member States and

United Nations agencies. We are convinced that the implementation of this bold but realistic programme of recommendations will help to ensure that the United Nations development system remains fit to rise to the challenges of the twenty-first century.

II. Development, Humanitarian assistance and the Environment

A. Development: delivering as one at the country level

To bring about real progress towards the Millennium Development Goals and other internationally agreed development goals, we believe that the United Nations system needs to deliver as one at the country level. To focus on outcomes and improve its effectiveness, the United Nations should accelerate and deepen reforms to establish unified United Nations country teams—with one leader, one programme, one budgetary framework and, where appropriate, one office (see box 1). To deliver as one, United Nations country teams should also have an integrated capacity to provide a coherent approach to cross-cutting issues, including sustainable development, gender equality and human rights.

Recommendation: The United Nations should deliver as one by establishing, by 2007, five One Country Programmes as pilots. Subject to continuous positive assessment, demonstrated effectiveness and proven results, these should be expanded to 20 One Country Programmes by 2009, 40 by 2010 and all other appropriate country programmes by 2012.

14. The Panel has been guided in its work by assessing whether the current structure and functioning of the United Nations system are fit for the development challenges of today and tomorrow. We have focused on the United Nations development activities at the country level, but we recognize that the role of the United Nations in development goes beyond its direct support to countries. The United Nations has a central role in promoting global policies that improve the development prospects of countries, and countries are increasingly turning to the United Nations for advice to address the challenges of globalization and other cross-border issues. Most important, the United Nations has provided Member States with a forum to reach consensus on internationally agreed development goals. These goals respond to the needs and aspirations of people, communities and countries everywhere and provide a framework for a comprehensive approach to development.

15. The success of these global commitments—from fighting hunger and poverty, to upholding core labour standards, to containing the global HIV/AIDS pandemic—can be measured only by their translation into concrete results for countries and communities. Development objectives can be achieved only if countries define, own and drive their development processes at all levels. Country-led development frameworks, such as poverty reduction strategies, are seen as the main vehicle to achieve the internationally agreed development goals. They serve as a platform for aligning all partners' contributions to national development priorities and provide an inclusive forum for policy dialogue. We believe that the United Nations needs to be a more active player in this context—as an adviser to Governments, as a convener of stakeholders, as an advocate for international norms and standards and as a source of technical assistance and advice on how to build and strengthen institutions.

16. At the country level, the United Nations often struggles to fulfil such strategic roles, working with systems and approaches (from programming to funding to reporting) that are fragmented, piecemeal and not designed for this purpose. More than a third of the United

Nations country teams include more than 10 United Nations entities, some more than 20. The cost of doing business with the United Nations is thus too high for both recipient countries and donors. Today there are many other actors active in development, such as NGOs, foundations and the private sector, and the country presence of bilateral donors is growing. In this new development landscape—with many players providing multifaceted contributions to development—the United Nations needs to reposition itself to deploy its normative and policy capacity more effectively.

17. The current design of the United Nations system risks perpetuating a myriad of niche players, which individually will not have the influence and authority to secure a strong voice in national and global debates. We have heard in our consultations that unifying the United Nations at country level would compromise the characteristics and dynamism of individual agencies. But failing to strategically position the United Nations in its entirety risks marginalizing the whole system in the long term.

Box 1 One United Nations at the country level—key features

One programme

- Country owned and signed off by Government, responsive to the national development framework, strategy and vision, including the internationally agreed development goals.
- Building on the United Nations country team's common country assessment or national analysis and reflecting the United Nations added value in the specific country context.
- Strategic, focused and results-based, with clear outcomes and priorities, while leaving flexibility to reallocate resources to changes in priorities.
- Drawing on all United Nations services and expertise, including those of non-resident agencies, in order to effectively deliver a multisectoral approach to development (with due attention to cross-cutting issues).

One leader

- Resident coordinator authority to negotiate the One Country Programme with the Government on behalf of the entire United Nations system and to shape the One Country Programme (including the authority to allocate resources from pooled and central funding mechanisms).
- Clear accountability framework for resident coordinators and an effective oversight mechanism for the resident coordinator system.
- Resident coordinator authority to hold members of the team accountable to agreed outcomes and for compliance with the strategic plan. The resident coordinator should also be accountable to the members of the United Nations country team.
- Strengthened resident coordinator capacity with adequate staff support to manage United Nations country team processes and ensure effective dialogue and communication with partners.

- Competitive selection of resident coordinator candidates, drawn from the best talent within and outside the United Nations system.

One budgetary framework

- Transparency, management, and the effective implementation of the One Country Programme through one budgetary framework.
- Funding should be linked to the performance of the United Nations country team preparing and implementing a strategic One Country Programme.
- The budget should be completely transparent, showing clearly the overheads and transaction costs of the United Nations and all of its funds, programmes and specialized agencies in the country.

One office

- One integrated results-based management system, with integrated support services.
- Joint premises (where appropriate).
- A common security infrastructure and clear lines of accountability.

18. Recent changes to the resident coordinator system have somewhat improved the way the United Nations operates in countries, but resident coordinators are not equipped with the authority to provide effective leadership to all the United Nations entities operating in the country. Too often, "reform" has meant adding extra layers of bureaucracy, outweighing potential benefits. And successful reform has depended too heavily on the commitment of individuals rather than on institutional capacity, needed to ensure that a good practice becomes the best global practice. Greater ownership and accountability of the resident coordinator system to all organizations of the United Nations needs to be secured.

Recommendation: United Nations resident coordinators should have the authority to lead the One Country Programme. To perform this function, resident coordinators should have appropriate competencies, capabilities and support capacities. Their enhanced authority should be matched by a clear accountability framework and an effective oversight mechanism to ensure system-wide ownership of the resident coordinator system.

19. To effectively implement the "One United Nations" at the country level, significant changes would be needed in the governance and funding of the United Nations development activities (recommendations in this regard are made in chap. III below). The role of the United Nations Development Programme (UNDP) in managing the resident coordinator system would also have to evolve significantly to engender ownership among other United Nations agencies, and eliminate duplication of programmatic activities.

Recommendation: UNDP will consolidate and focus its operational work on strengthening the coherence and positioning of the United Nations country team delivering the One Country Programme. As manager of the resident coordinator system, UNDP should set a clear target by 2008 to withdraw from sector-focused policy and capacity work for which other United Nations entities have competencies. UNDP programmatic work should be limited to interventions that strengthen the coherence and overall positioning of the United Nations country team:

- Promoting and supporting the United Nations work to help countries achieve the Millennium Development Goals and other internationally agreed development goals and poverty reduction through supporting governments in integrating the Millennium Development Goals into their national development strategies, assessing needs and monitoring results.
- Leading the United Nations support to governance.
- Leading and coordinating the United Nations work in crisis prevention, post-conflict, post-disaster and early recovery (see chap. II.B).

In addition, UNDP would continue its support to mainstreaming environmental issues into national development strategies at the country level, in cooperation with the United Nations Environment Programme (UNEP) and other relevant United Nations organizations (see chap. II.D).

Recommendation: To ensure that there is no potential for, or perception of, a conflict of interest, UNDP should establish an institutional firewall between the management of its programmatic role and management of the resident coordinator system (including system-wide strategic and policy support). This separation of functions will also ensure that all parts of the United Nations system have a greater stake in the ownership of the resident coordinator system. UNDP will develop a code of conduct, including a transparent mechanism to evaluate the performance of its country operations. This should be done in consultation with all relevant United Nations organizations and the agreed code of conduct should be formally approved by the Sustainable Development Board (see chap. III). The redesign of the UNDP organizational structure should include a clear separation of responsibilities, senior managers and budgets between UNDP management of the resident coordinator system and its programmatic activities.

Milestone: By the end of 2007 UNDP will have finalized a code of conduct and by the end of 2008 it will have implemented the firewall and restructuring.

B. Humanitarian assistance and the transition from relief to development: strengthening the capacity to respond

Humanitarian response should be improved through a closer partnership between the United Nations, Governments and NGOs, making full use of the coordination role of the United Nations. The Central Emergency Response Fund must be fully funded from additional resources. There should be clear responsibilities within the United Nations system for addressing the needs of internally displaced persons. Development should be an integral part of any peace process. There should be clear leadership by UNDP on early recovery from conflict and natural disasters, as well as flexible United Nations funding. National development strategies and donors should invest more in risk reduction and early warning, building on existing international initiatives. The private sector and communities should be included in formulating strategies.

Humanitarian assistance

20. Since the appointment of the Emergency Relief Coordinator in 1991 and the establishment of the Office for the Coordination of Humanitarian Affairs in 1997, the United Nations emergency response capacity has become stronger. Operational agencies—such as the World Food Programme (WFP), the Office of the United Nations High Commissioner for Refugees (UNHCR) and the United Nations Children's Fund (UNICEF)—continue to respond well in humanitarian relief, based on established principles of humanity, impartiality and neutrality. Mechanisms for inter-agency coordination, such as the Inter-Agency Standing Committee and the Executive Committee for Humanitarian Affairs, have enhanced coordination between the humanitarian organizations of the United Nations and with non-United Nations partners. For 2006 United Nations humanitarian appeals amount to US$ 4.7 billion, for some 31 million beneficiaries in 26 countries. Significant challenges remain, however, in both coordination and funding.

21. To build strong United Nations leadership at the field level and support country ownership and cooperation, efforts to strengthen the humanitarian coordinator need to be intensified. The cluster lead agency system, adopted by the United Nations system in 2005, helped identify organizational leaders in different areas of humanitarian response, but the experience of its first year of implementation indicates that it should need to broaden to include national partners, NGOs and the Red Cross movement.

22. As a result of the increase in intrastate conflict, there are more than 25 million internally displaced persons, compared with 10 million refugees. The humanitarian system must evolve further to address this growing problem. A clear allocation of responsibility within the United Nations system is needed. UNHCR must reposition itself to provide protection and assistance for displaced people in need, regardless of whether they have crossed an international border.

23. Humanitarian funding remains crucial in influencing the United Nations response capacity, and there has been progress in developing a more coherent approach. But the consolidated appeals process, with all United Nations agencies and some non-United Nations agencies participating, still suffers from unpredictability and under-funding. And three years after the adoption of the good humanitarian donorship principles, the predictability of assistance has not yet improved substantially. The recently established Central Emergency Response Fund has facilitated faster, more effective responses, but current funding (US$ 262 million) is only halfway to the funding target.

24. Steps towards greater coherence must include efforts to increase United Nations accountability through more effective communication with affected populations and donors. Better information flows are crucial for the United Nations to be even more effective in emergency situations. Transparent, periodic and independent assessments of the global response to humanitarian emergencies can help identify gaps in coherence and failures of coordination. The Panel therefore recommends that the United Nations take the lead in preparing a regular and independent assessment of the performance of the United Nations and the wider humanitarian system in responding to humanitarian emergencies.

Recommendation: To avoid a fragmented approach to humanitarian assistance, there should be stronger partnership arrangements between the United Nations, national

Governments, the International Federation of Red Cross and Red Crescent Societies and NGOs, based on the coordination and leadership roles of the Emergency Relief Coordinator at the global level and the humanitarian coordinator at the country level. These arrangements should support and ensure effective and inclusive participation in the cluster lead agency approach. Procedures, including the definition of "provider of last resort" and how this relates to the position of cluster leader, need to be clarified.

Recommendation: The Central Emergency Response Fund should be fully funded to its three-year target of US$ 500 million from additional resources. A substantial increase should be considered over the coming five years, following a review of its performance. Donors must implement the agreed principles of good humanitarian donorship and provide adequate resources based on needs assessments, particularly to crisis situations now under-funded. They should ensure that their pledges are honoured promptly. The Consolidated Appeals Process should set clearer priorities, based on joint assessments, coordination and action.

Recommendation: The humanitarian agencies should clarify their mandates and enhance their cooperation on internally displaced persons. In particular, the role of UNHCR should be reviewed, to establish a clear mandate and to further strengthen the effectiveness of the United Nations approach to addressing the needs of internally displaced persons.

Transition from relief to development

25. For countries emerging from conflict, the immediate international response is dominated by political mediation and reconciliation. The current United Nations approach tacitly emphasizes immediate stability over sustainable peace. Symptoms of conflict are often addressed, while root causes are often not addressed. For countries recovering from natural disaster, and in supporting nationally owned strategies, it is imperative to integrate vulnerability and risk reduction into all phases of recovery and development planning. In July 2006, the Tsunami Evaluation Coalition stated that successful post-disaster reconstruction required an understanding of ongoing political, economic and social processes that enable and constrain affected populations as they rebuild their lives. A clear lead capacity on the development aspects of the post-disaster recovery process, charged with early coordination and planning, should be established at United Nations Headquarters within UNDP.

26. Since the 2000 Brahimi report on peacekeeping operations, integrated United Nations peacekeeping and peacebuilding missions have improved coordination by bringing the development arm of the United Nations under the direct leadership of the Special Representative of the Secretary-General. Better development strategies for post-conflict peacebuilding are needed to guide such missions. The Peacebuilding Commission should be the forum that encourages the development of peacebuilding strategies on the ground.

27. Unlike peacekeeping operations, which are funded by assessed contributions, humanitarian and development activities depend on unpredictable voluntary pledging conferences. The management of funds in support of development in conflict countries has increasingly been placed in the hands of the World Bank, often disbursed only when Government structures are firmly in place. In many countries the donors have sought flexibility and directly transferred funds to UNDP trust funds, especially when Government capacity is not strong. Cooperation between the United Nations and the World Bank requires a clearer division of

labour based on realities on the ground. Efforts should be made to strengthen response with more flexible United Nations interim funding mechanisms that could address transition issues faster and more effectively.

Recommendation: The repositioned UNDP should become the United Nations leader and coordinator for early recovery. While building standing and surge capacity to take the lead role when humanitarian coordination winds down, UNDP should work closely with the World Bank and other development and humanitarian agencies, using the sectoral programming capacity of other relevant United Nations agencies. All early recovery activities should conform to national priorities, with national authorities managing the recovery process as soon as they have the capacity to do so.

Recommendation: Adequate funding for the United Nations role in early recovery should be ensured, even before a donor conference is held or a United Nations/World Bank Multi-Donor Trust Fund is operational. If the Peacebuilding Fund or the UNDP Thematic Trust Fund for Crisis Prevention and Recovery is not able to provide resources immediately, a country-specific fund for early recovery can be set up, linked to these overall funding mechanisms. The initial funding target of the Peacebuilding Fund of US$ 250 million should be met by 2007.

Recommendation: To build long-term food security and break the cycle of recurring famines, especially in sub-Saharan Africa, WFP, the Food and Agriculture Organization of the United Nations (FAO) and the International Fund for Agricultural Development should review their respective approaches and enhance inter-agency coordination. Complementary strategies should be further developed to strengthen local capacity and resilience to mitigate and cope with consequences of famines.

Reducing risk

28. In the first eight months of 2006, 91 million people had their lives devastated by natural disasters. Reducing the risk of disaster must be linked to humanitarian, development and environmental approaches. With more than 75 per cent of the world's people living in disaster-prone areas, risk reduction has been recognized as a cost-effective strategy to protecting livelihoods and achieving the internationally agreed development goals. The Hyogo Framework for Action (2005-2015), agreed to by Governments in 2005 as the international framework for disaster reduction, has created an agenda, taking into account the need for a strong sense of ownership, including collaboration with civil society and the private sector, and ensuring the awareness and capacity of local governments and communities. The International Strategy for Disaster Reduction and the new World Bank-hosted Global Facility for Disaster Reduction and Recovery are making progress on this, but more coherent action is required.

29. There is insufficient "disaster-proofing of the Millennium Development Goals", through mainstreaming risk reduction in development strategies. The Tsunami Evaluation Coalition revealed that, despite advances in early warning systems, the Tsunami response had failed to enhance local preparedness or reduce long-term vulnerability. Further investment at country and community levels is required, and the responsibilities and capacities of the United Nations system have to be further specified and enhanced.

Recommendation: The United Nations efforts on risk reduction should be urgently enhanced, through full implementation and funding of international agreements and

other recent initiatives and the involvement of communities. National development strategies should address risk reduction explicitly and should be the basis on which donors plan their contributions to risk reduction and how they report these contributions as part of international and national risk reduction targets. UNDP should take the lead on this issue in the United Nations, particularly at the country level. In addition, the Office for the Coordination of Humanitarian Affairs, UNDP, UNEP, the World Meteorological Organization (WMO), and WFP with the International Strategy for Disaster Reduction secretariat should build a joint programme for early warning, drawing on existing capacities of funds, programmes and specialized agencies.

Recommendation: The United Nations should continue to build innovative disaster assistance mechanisms, such as private risk insurance markets, as means to provide contingency funding for natural disasters and other emergencies. Consideration should be given to efforts such as the WFP pilot humanitarian insurance policy in Ethiopia to provide coverage in the case of an extreme drought during the country's 2006 agricultural season. The Emergency Relief Coordinator should work with United Nations country teams and agencies on designing such event-specific contingency funding to reduce the reliance on the Central Emergency Response Fund.

C. Environment: building a global consensus and capacity for action

Deteriorating environmental trends have far-reaching economic, social and health implications and affect the world's ability to meet the Millennium Development Goals. Substantial gains in efficiency and effective responses can be made through enhanced coordination and improved normative and operational capacity, in particular through the integration of environment into national development strategies and United Nations system country operations. To improve effectiveness and targeted action of environmental activities, the system of international environmental governance should be strengthened and more coherent, featuring an upgraded UNEP with real authority as the United Nations environment policy pillar. Synergy needs to be pursued between the United Nations organizations that address environment, and multilateral environmental agreements should continue to pursue efficiencies and coordination among themselves. An independent assessment of the current United Nations system of international environmental governance is required to support ongoing efforts at reform.

30. There can be no long-term development without environmental care. In a global and interdependent world economic objectives and environmental objectives increasingly reinforce each other. Environmental priorities—including climate change—have too often been compartmentalized and separated from economic development priorities. However, because the impacts are global and felt disproportionately by the poor, environmental sustainability is not an option—it is an imperative. The Panel is united in its conviction that addressing worsening trends of environmental degradation is one of the greatest collective challenges for economic development and human welfare.

31. We possess fairly comprehensive knowledge and understanding of what we individually and collectively need to do to reverse these trends—all spelled out in reports, declarations, treaties and summits since the early 1970s. While we have made significant advances within the United Nations framework, what is needed now is a substantially strengthened and streamlined international environmental governance structure, to support the incentives for change required at all levels.

32. The Panel recognizes that relatively little headway has been made in integrating the environment in development strategies at the country level, or in implementing internationally agreed goals. Environmental issues and goals must now be better integrated within United Nations system country operations, as critical components of national poverty reduction strategies and sustainable development plans. Bearing in mind that environmental sustainability is the foundation for achieving all the other Millennium Development Goals, there must be a strengthening of human, technical and financial capacities in developing countries to mainstream environmental issues in national decision-making, particularly through the resident coordinator.

33. The increase in the incidence and severity of natural disasters with environmental causes demonstrates the need to strengthen the links between environmental and humanitarian activities and between environmental and development activities. The United Nations system needs to incorporate more knowledge in its work on preparedness and risk reduction for natural disasters and for post-disaster recovery and reconstruction.

34. The United Nations institutions for the environment must be optimally organized and tooled, drawing on expertise in different parts of the United Nations system. Unless the United Nations adopts more comprehensive approaches, it will continue to fall short of its goals. The Panel is cognizant of the ongoing General Assembly informal consultative process on international environmental governance and has interacted with the process. Our recommendations should give it greater impetus.

35. Fragmented institutional structures do not offer an operational framework to address global issues, including water and energy. Water is an essential element in the lives of people and societies, and the lack of access to water for basic needs inflicts hardship on more than 1 billion people. Similarly, energy is a main driver of development, but current systems of energy supply and use are not sustainable (more than 2 billion people in developing countries do not have access to modern energy services). More than 20 United Nations organizations are engaged at some level in water and energy work, but there is little evidence of overall impact.

36. The inadequacy of the current system is the result of having outgrown its original design. Developing countries are unable to cope with the extensive reporting and participation requirements of the current multilateral environmental structure, which has depleted expertise and resources for implementation. A survey by the Panel revealed that the three Rio Conventions (biodiversity, climate and desertification) have up to 230 meeting days annually. Add the figures for seven other major global environmental agreements (not including regional agreements) and that number rises to almost 400 days.

37. As environmental issues have become more clearly defined and interlinked, they have come to influence the work of practically every United Nations organization, all competing for the same limited resources. The institutional complexity is further complicated by the substantial environment portfolios of the World Bank and regional development banks, which are not well coordinated with the rest of the United Nations system. In addition, UNEP, the principal environment organization of the United Nations—with its normative, scientific, analytical and coordinating mandate—is considered weak, under-funded and ineffective in its core functions.

38. Climate change, desertification, ecosystem decline, and dispersion of hazardous chemical substances have the potential to affect every part of the globe and require clear and forceful responses by the United Nations system. Cooperation should be close among UNEP, UNDP, WMO, the Global Environment Facility (GEF) and the World Bank for building scientific and technical capacity, managing investment and infrastructure components, supporting adaptation measures and facilitating an effective integration of global environmental concerns into the development policy frameworks at the country level. GEF, the specialized funding instrument to help developing countries undertake projects and programmes that protect the global environment, has been replenished in 2006—but will require a significant increase in resources to address future challenges. Its policy requirements and operational procedures need to be made much more simple and compatible with the development framework at the country level.

39. It is the judgement of the Panel that the international community must transcend differences and move forward. Economic growth, social justice and environmental care, advance best when they advance together. It is in our shared interest to have institutions that enable us to respond collectively to the threats of environmental degradation that challenge us all. To deliver on the internationally agreed goals and commitments, the United Nations will require stronger leadership and greater capacity for environmental activities. In this regard, cooperation and partnerships with civil society organizations, including the private sector, are essential.

Recommendation: International environmental governance should be strengthened and more coherent in order to improve effectiveness and targeted action of environmental activities in the United Nations system. It should be strengthened by upgrading UNEP with a renewed mandate and improved funding.

Recommendation: An upgraded UNEP should have real authority as the environment policy pillar of the United Nations system, backed by normative and analytical capacity and with broad responsibility to review progress towards improving the global environment. UNEP should provide substantive leadership and guidance on environmental issues.

- The technical and scientific capacity of UNEP should be strengthened as the environmental early-warning mechanism of the international community and for monitoring, assessing and reporting on the state of the global environment. This can be achieved through a system of networking and drawing on the work of existing bodies, including academic institutions and centres of excellence and the scientific competence of relevant specialized agencies and scientific subsidiary bodies of multilateral environmental agreements.
- Capacity should be built to promote the implementation of international commitments. The Bali Strategic Plan for Technology Support and Capacity-building should be strategically implemented to provide cutting-edge expertise and knowledge resources for the sustained expansion of capacity at the country level. Where necessary, UNEP should participate in United Nations country teams through the resident coordinator system, as part of One United Nations at the country level.
- UNEP should take the lead in assisting countries in the two-step process of quantifying environmental costs and benefits and incorporating them into mainstream policymaking,

in cooperation with UNDP and the Department of Economic and Social Affairs of the Secretariat.

Recommendation: United Nations agencies, programmes and funds with responsibilities in the area of the environment should cooperate more effectively on a thematic basis and through partnerships with a dedicated agency at the centre (such as air and water pollution, forests, water scarcity, access to energy and renewable energy). This would be based on a combined effort towards agreed common activities and policy objectives to eliminate duplication and focus on results.

- Greater coordination at Headquarters should promote coherence at the country level, and greater coordination efforts at the country level should promote coherence at the international level. There is a need to strengthen UNEP coordination of system-wide environmental policies in order to improve cohesion and consistency. In this regard, the Environmental Management Group should be given a clearer mandate and be better utilized. It should be linked with the broader framework of sustainable development coordination.

Recommendation: Efficiencies and substantive coordination should be pursued by diverse treaty bodies to support effective implementation of major multilateral environmental agreements. Such coordination is being pursued by the Basel, Rotterdam and Stockholm convention secretariats (pending decisions of their respective conferences of the parties).

- Stronger efforts should be made to reduce costs and reporting burdens and to streamline implementation. National reporting requirements for related multilateral environmental agreements should be consolidated into one comprehensive annual report, to ease the burden on countries and improve coherence.
- Countries should consider integrating implementation needs of multilateral environmental agreements into their national sustainable development strategies, as part of the One Country Programme.
- Governing bodies of multilateral environmental agreements should promote administrative efficiencies, reducing the frequency and duration of meetings, moving to joint administrative functions, convening back-to-back or joint meetings of bureaux of related conventions, rationalizing knowledge management and developing a consistent methodological approach to enable measurement of enforcement and compliance.

Recommendation: GEF should be strengthened as the major financial mechanism for the global environment. Its contribution in assisting developing countries in implementing the conventions and in building their capacities should be clarified, in conjunction with its implementing and executing agencies. A significant increase in resources will be required to address future challenges effectively.

Recommendation: The Secretary-General should commission an independent and authoritative assessment of the current United Nations system of international environmental governance. To be completed as soon as possible and taking previous work into account, the assessment would review global needs as well as the specific roles and mandates of UNEP and other United Nations agencies and multilateral environmental agreements. It would provide the basis for further reforms towards improving system-wide coherence, effectiveness and targeted action. It should be complementary to the General Assembly informal consultative process on the institutional framework for the United Nations environmental activities, which should continue its work and provide guidance on the subject. The assessment should include an analysis of proposals to upgrade UNEP from among a range of organizational models.

D. Cross-cutting issues: sustainable development, gender equality and human rights

40. In promoting sustainable development, gender equality and human rights, the United Nations has strong mandates and Member States have committed themselves to achieving ambitious goals. The Panel recommends that cross-cutting issues must be an integral part of United Nations activities, particularly when delivering as One United Nations at the country level.

Sustainable development

> *The status of sustainable development should be elevated within the United Nations institutional architecture and in country activities. The United Nations system must strive for greater integration, efficiency and coordination of the economic, social and environmental dimensions of sustainable development. At the operational level, the Panel supports a strong partnership between UNEP (normative) and UNDP (operational) and a sharper focus on environment by the resident coordinator system as part of the One United Nations at the country level. The Panel calls for the Economic and Social Council to establish a sustainable development segment—and for continuing reform of the Commission on Sustainable Development that truly leads to integrated decision-making on economic, social and environmental issues.*

41. The visionary blueprint for sustainable development, outlined in Agenda 21 and adopted at the 1992 United Nations Conference on Environment and Development, is under way but has yet to be realized. Even though the General Assembly adopted sustainable development as part of the overarching framework of United Nations activities, the international community is still falling short in implementation and needs to improve the institutional framework for sustainable development.

42. This was clearly acknowledged by world leaders in 2002 at the World Summit on Sustainable Development. They stressed the need for greater integration, efficiency and coordination of the economic, social and environmental dimensions of sustainable development. Governments also agreed that strengthening the international institutional framework for sustainable development is evolutionary. The international community needs to keep relevant arrangements under constant review, identifying gaps and eliminating duplication.

43. Member States and international institutions continue to treat poverty, human health and environmental degradation as standalone threats. The United Nations system should assist countries in their integration, tackling the challenges of sustainable development across different sectors and issues.

44. The Commission on Sustainable Development was envisaged as a high-level forum that would bring economic and environmental decision makers together and provide an opportunity for frank dialogue, deliberation and problem-solving. The Panel believes that the Commission has proved successful as a model for incorporating stakeholders and as a forum to interact and exchange ideas. It has been far less effective in ensuring that the promise of integrating environment and development is fulfilled. The Commission's

mandate has been broadened considerably to include sectoral assessments of natural resources. Focusing on environmental issues alone, the Commission has contributed to overlaps and often unclear divisions of labour.

45. The Panel's recommendations for development, humanitarian assistance, environment and gender equality and human rights should be viewed in the context of sustainable development. The recommendations here deal more with elevating the status of sustainable development in the United Nations institutional architecture and in country activities—and with achieving the needed balance among the three pillars (economic, social and environmental) of sustainable development.

Recommendation: A stronger partnership between UNEP (normative) and UNDP (operational) should build on their complementarities. They should:

- Integrate environment in country-owned development strategies through the resident coordinator system.
- Strengthen the analytical and technical capacities of national institutions.
- Work with countries in implementing multilateral environmental agreements.
- Contribute the environmental perspective in disaster preparedness and post-disaster recovery and reconstruction.
- Implement the strategic approach agreed to in the Bali Strategic Plan for Technology Support and Capacity-building. This requires environmental expertise from UNEP in United Nations country teams.

Recommendation: Sustainable development should be mainstreamed into the work of the Economic and Social Council. This would be done through substantive consideration of reports emanating from subsidiary bodies, the Governing Council/Global Ministerial Environment Forum of UNEP and other relevant intergovernmental bodies, including the Sustainable Development Board (see chap. III.A).

- A "sustainable development" segment should be instituted in the Economic and Social Council. It would: (a) help promote a balance between the three pillars of sustainable development; (b) focus on sustainability issues arising from the Council's functional commissions and feed conclusions back to those commissions; and (c) coordinate recommendations to United Nations system organizations and their governing bodies.
- The reform of the Commission on Sustainable Development following the 2002 World Summit on Sustainable Development should be pursued further by focusing on implementation, including approaches for integrating environmental and social concerns into economic planning, and for identifying and sharing best practices.

Gender equality and women's empowerment

Gender equality is central to sustainable development that responds to the needs, rights, aspirations and talents of half the world's people. The Panel believes that the United Nations needs to replace several current weak structures with a dynamic United Nations entity focused on gender equality and women's empowerment. This entity should mobilize forces of change at the global level and inspire enhanced results at the country level. The promotion of gender equality must remain the mandate of all United Nations entities.

46. Within the United Nations framework the international community has made strong commitments over the past six decades to gender equality and women's empowerment. It has entrusted the United Nations with an enormously important mandate in this area. The Secretary-General called upon us to include in our work an assessment of how gender equality could be better and more fully addressed by the United Nations, in particular—where it matters most—in the Organization's operational activities on the ground.

47. We have listened carefully to Governments in programme and donor countries, to civil society representatives and to United Nations staff at Headquarters and at regional and country offices. The message is clear: while the United Nations remains a key actor in supporting countries to achieve gender equality and women's empowerment, there is a strong sense that the United Nations system's contribution has been incoherent, under-resourced and fragmented.

48. We believe that the importance of achieving gender equality cannot be overstated. For both reasons of human rights and development effectiveness, the United Nations needs to pursue these objectives far more vigorously. While there are inspiring examples of United Nations initiatives that have helped to change women's lives, these have unfortunately remained isolated "best practices".

49. We propose a new way forward based on fundamentals that we believe need to constitute the guiding principles of any efforts to strengthen United Nations performance on gender equality and women's empowerment:

- The United Nations needs a much stronger voice on women's issues to ensure that gender equality and women's empowerment are taken seriously throughout the United Nations system and to ensure that the United Nations works more effectively with Governments and civil society in this mission. We believe that a gender entity—based on the principles of coherence and consolidation—is required to advance this key United Nations agenda.
- But it is also our strong belief that the commitment to gender equality is and should remain the mandate of the entire United Nations system. Responsibility and accountability for the integration of gender equality concerns cannot be held by one United Nations agency or entity alone, regardless of its size and influence.
- And finally, in our recommendations, we seek to combine greater visibility for gender issues at the centre with enhanced results on the ground, where the United Nations performance will be assessed.

Recommendation: The Panel recommends strengthening the coherence and impact of the United Nations institutional gender architecture by streamlining and consolidating three of the United Nations existing gender institutions as a consolidated United Nations gender equality and women's empowerment programme.

Box 2 Mandate and structure of the consolidated gender entity

Governance

The gender entity would consolidate three of the United Nations existing entities under two organizational divisions. The "normative, analytical and monitoring" division would subsume the Office of the Special Adviser on Gender Issues and the Advancement of Women and the Division for the Advancement of Women. The "policy advisory and programming" division would subsume the current activities of the United Nations Development Fund for Women (UNIFEM). The Office of Human Resources Management of the Secretariat would take over the human resource functions, currently performed by the Office of the Special Adviser, aimed at improving the status of women in the Secretariat and the United Nations system.

The Executive Director of the consolidated entity should have the rank of Under-Secretary-General, consistent with that of other heads of agency, to guarantee organizational stature and influence in United Nations system-wide decision-making. The position should be recruited

through a meritocratic competition demonstrably open to those outside the United Nations and an open and transparent global search process.

The Executive Director would act as the chief adviser to the Secretary-General on gender equality and women's empowerment issues. The Executive Director would report to the Economic and Social Council and the General Assembly (through the Secretary-General), and to the UNDP/UNFPA Executive Board (which would be renamed to reflect the entity's name). To reduce costs and increase effectiveness, the entity would share common services at United Nations Headquarters and at the field level, in particular with UNDP, where available.

The gender entity would be a full member of the United Nations System Chief Executives Board for Coordination (CEB) and the proposed Development Policy and Operations Group (see chap. III.A).

Mandate

The gender entity would be entrusted with a dual mandate combining normative, analytical and monitoring functions with policy advisory and targeted programming functions. Where necessary, United Nations country teams would include senior gender expertise provided by the gender entity.

The entity's mandate under the normative, analytical and monitoring division would include:

- Facilitating and advising on system-wide policies for gender equality and women's empowerment.
- Undertaking global advocacy efforts on issues critical to women's empowerment and gender equality, including the publication of flagship reports.
- Monitoring and evaluating, on behalf of the Secretary-General, the integration of gender equality objectives across the United Nations system, including the funds, programmes, Secretariat departments and specialized agencies.
- Supporting the integration of gender equality and women's empowerment concerns in intergovernmental bodies for development, humanitarian assistance, environment, human rights, peacekeeping and peacebuilding.

- Providing substantive and technical servicing to the Commission on the Status of Women.

The Panel believes that the gender entity should have sharply focused operations on gender equality and women's empowerment issues, equipped with high-quality technical and substantive expertise, to provide leadership in regions and countries. Under the policy advisory and programming division, the entity's mandate would include:

- Providing policy advice and guidance to United Nations country and regional teams to ensure that gender equality concerns are mainstreamed in the support provided to nationally led poverty reduction and development plans.
- Undertaking regional and national advocacy to put issues critical to women's empowerment on the policy agenda.
- Facilitating innovation, sharing lessons and enabling institutional learning throughout the system.
- Supporting targeted and innovative activities, benefiting women in line with national and regional priorities and the objectives set out in the Beijing Platform for Action and Security Council resolution 1325 (2000) on women and peace and security.
- Strengthening and monitoring accountability across the resident coordinator system and assisting resident coordinators and United Nations country teams to meet their responsibilities for gender mainstreaming.

The gender entity would continue to work closely with Governments and civil society organizations, strengthening networks already established at the global, national and local levels. The operations of the United Nations gender entity would be undertaken as part of One United Nations in each country.

Funding

To be effective in this role, the gender entity needs adequate, stable and predictable funding. The work of the normative and analytical division should continue to be funded as it is now from the United Nations regular budget, supplemented by voluntary contributions. The policy advisory and programming division should be fully and ambitiously funded.

The Panel strongly believes that substantially increased funding for the gender entity should constitute only part of the overall commitment of the United Nations to gender equality. Other United Nations entities need to dedicate significantly more resources to gender mainstreaming in all their work and decisions, in particular at the country level, and to monitor and report regularly on progress.

Human rights

The necessary international human rights agreements and institutions are now in place, but responsibilities need to be clarified within the United Nations system. The Office of the United Nations High Commissioner for Human Rights (OHCHR) should lead the effort on protection and work with and through the resident coordinator and the United Nations country team to promote human rights, and strengthen the capacities of Governments, relevant institutions, civil society and individuals.

50. We support the Secretary-General's contention that "we will not enjoy development without security, we will not enjoy security without development, and we will not enjoy either without respect for human rights" (A/59/2005, para. 17). The responsibility to make this happen lies with countries, and the necessary human rights instruments and agreements are now in place. At the 2005 World Summit Member States reaffirmed their commitment to address human rights through a new Human Rights Council, and gave unprecedented political backing for the further mainstreaming of human rights in the work of the United Nations. We remain deeply concerned, however, that the global implementation of human rights lags far behind its articulation.

51. The legitimacy of the United Nations to address human rights has been reaffirmed in our consultations, including support to national counterparts in their pursuit of international human rights commitments. Yet an assessment of the decade's worth of effort to mainstream human rights in all areas of United Nations work shows limited progress, in part because of widespread misunderstanding about where responsibility lies for human rights promotion and protection.

Recommendation: Resident coordinators and United Nations country teams should be held accountable and be better equipped to support countries in their efforts to protect and promote human rights. They should assist countries in implementing their human rights obligations and commitments as part of their national development strategies.

Recommendation: OHCHR, the centre of excellence on human rights, should provide dedicated support to the resident coordinator system. It should ensure appropriate linkages with and coordination between the resident coordinator system and the United Nations human rights special procedures and mechanisms. It should take the lead on human rights protection, including the provision of technical assistance at the request of countries to assist Member States in fulfilling their existing human rights obligations and commitments.

Recommendation: All United Nations agencies and programmes must further support the development of policies, directives and guidelines to integrate human rights in all aspects of United Nations work. The United Nations common understanding on a human rights-based approach to programming and the United Nations-wide Action 2 Programme—developed and adopted by 21 heads of United Nations agencies, programmes and departments—should provide useful guidance in this.

III. Governance, funding and management

52. We have already recommended changes to the way the United Nations is managed at the country level. A more coherent and better functioning United Nations would benefit developing countries. For these changes to be effective, they need to be supported by similar coherence of functions at the centre.

53. Substantial change is required in governance, management and funding arrangements to realize the vision of a more effective and coherent United Nations. Having examined the intergovernmental and organizational structures from this perspective, the Panel believes that achieving a more effective and coherent United Nations calls for consolidating some functions and strengthening others, as well as devising new modalities. This process should be designed to enhance the flexibility, responsiveness and coherence of the United Nations

system. The principles underlying these proposals for reform of governance, funding and management are ownership, effectiveness, transparency and coherence.

54. The Panel believes that stronger and more effective mechanisms must be developed for governance and funding. These mechanisms must incorporate clear lines of accountability and robust oversight of performance and results. To deliver lasting change, they must be transparent, inclusive and decisive. We have therefore proposed the creation of bodies that have the power to take decisions. This process will involve significant changes for United Nations agencies, developing countries and donors alike. United Nations agencies need to work more closely and effectively with the rest of the United Nations system in the interests of a greater common good. Donors, too, will need to change the way they fund the United Nations so that it is in line with the principles of multilateralism. These changes are essential if we are to be successful in the management and delivery of One United Nations.

A. Governance: consolidating some functions, strengthening others

Effective governance is at the core of coherence. To enable the United Nations to "deliver as one" on global development challenges, and in particular to make the "One United Nations" at the country level a reality for developing countries, the Panel proposes the following series of measures.

Intergovernmental level

- *To provide a high-level forum for strategic guidance on sustainable development policy and global public goods, a Global Leaders Forum should be established.*
- *A Sustainable Development Board should be established to provide operational oversight and supervision of the "One United Nations" at the country level. The Board would also take decisions on pooled voluntary funding for country programmes.*

Regional level

- *The important regional work of the United Nations must be streamlined by establishing regional hubs to support United Nations country teams and clarifying the roles of regional commissions.*

Organizational level

- *The United Nations System Chief Executives Board for Coordination should improve its decision-making role on overall reform and effectively drive managerial reform.*
- *The Development Policy and Operations Group should be the central coordinating mechanism for United Nations work on development at the country level. It will bring policy and operational roles together and will be chaired by a Development Coordinator. The Group would comprise the major development organizations in the United Nations.*
- *A clear firewall and accountability framework should be established between a repositioned UNDP support to the resident coordinator system and its*

reduced operations role. This will allow the full ownership of the United Nations system in the resident coordinator system (see chap. II.A).

- *A Development Finance and Performance Unit should support the Development Policy and Operations Group in providing information and analysis on United Nations system funding, expenditures and results.*

Streamlining and consolidation

55. The Panel has benefited from extensive consultations on the functioning of the United Nations system at the country, regional and global levels. It has also concentrated on the key drivers and incentives required for coherence from a bottom-up approach. More detailed and specific proposals for further streamlining and consolidation to improve system-wide coherence require a more in-depth analysis than was feasible within the context of our work. The Panel believes that it is important to build on its work by further considering the removal of unnecessary duplication in the United Nations system and by ensuring the clear delineation of roles and mandates.

56. We do not however advocate a single United Nations entity because some individual agencies can best achieve their vital role in the provision of global public goods, advocacy, research, promoting best practice and global norms and standards by operating individually in their specific sectors.

Recommendation: The Panel recommends that the Secretary-General establish an independent task force to build on the foundation of its work. It would:

- Clearly delineate the roles of the United Nations and its funds, programmes and specialized agencies to ensure complementarity of mandates and to eliminate duplicated functions, making concrete recommendations for consolidating or merging United Nations entities where necessary. Such a process has the potential to lead to significant annual savings, possibly up to 20 per cent, which should be redirected to supporting the One United Nations at the country level.
- Review the assessed funding required by United Nations specialized agencies—to address the current imbalance between assessed and voluntary resources dedicated to the implementation of normative mandates. The review should determine whether the current policy of zero real growth can allow United Nations agencies to deliver on global mandates.
- Review the functioning and continuing relevance of existing regional structures in addressing regional needs, taking into account the different needs of regions and the emergence of strong regional and subregional institutions. The review should also consider options for streamlining and consolidation.

Intergovernmental structures

Economic and Social Council

57. The General Assembly is the highest intergovernmental body for formulating policy on economic, social and related matters. The Economic and Social Council is the main body for coordination, policy review, policy dialogue and recommendations on economic and social development and for the review and follow-up of the internationally agreed development goals.

58. The Council's mandate has been far greater than its exercise of it. Despite many attempts to strengthen its role, the Council continues to lack effectiveness and influence. Its oversight of the funds and programmes remains perfunctory and is almost non-existent for the specialized agencies. The Council needs to improve its operational and coordination functions with regard to the entire system.

59. Much can be done to improve the Council within its current mandate, but it will require new forms of functioning. Leaders at the 2005 World Summit took steps to enable the Council to play an effective policy coordination role as envisaged in the Charter of the United Nations. The Panel believes that the vision for the Council in the 2005 Summit should be faithfully implemented, and that the Council should be further empowered through the involvement in its work of Member States at the highest possible political level.

Recommendation: A Global Leaders Forum of the Economic and Social Council should be established. The Forum would comprise the leaders of half its members, rotating on the basis of equitable geographic representation, with the participation of the executive heads of the major international economic and financial institutions. Its meetings could be preceded by a preparatory meeting of ministers for foreign affairs and economic, social and related ministries.

Box 3 Role of the Global Leaders Forum

- Provide leadership and guidance to the international community on development and global public goods related issues.
- Develop a long-term strategic policy framework to secure consistency in the policy goals of the major international organizations.
- Promote consensus-building among Governments on integrated solutions for global economic, social and environmental issues.

Sustainable Development Board

60. The Panel believes that a new governance mechanism is required to provide oversight for the One United Nations at the country level. Current board structures of the United Nations system provide only for individual funds, programmes and agencies to report separately to their respective boards for their country, regional and global work. There is a need to provide operational guidance and direction to the separate organizations for the coherence and effectiveness of the United Nations system at the country level. The Panel recommends the establishment of a Sustainable Development Board, reporting to the Economic and Social Council. It will be responsible for operational coherence and coordination, and system-wide implementation of policies, for allocations of voluntary funding and for performance of the One United Nations at the country level.

61. Individual boards should continue to consider issues that require particular agency focus, including those relating to multi-year funding frameworks that reflect the approved strategic focus of each agency. The Sustainable Development Board will review the consolidated One Country Programme, which will include components developed by individual organizations, reflecting the policies and directives of their respective boards.

Recommendation: A Sustainable Development Board should be established. Reporting to the Economic and Social Council, the Board would provide the decision-making and monitoring framework for implementation of One United Nations at the country level. The Board would be responsible for oversight of the implementation of the pilot programme to create unified United Nations country programmes.

Recommendation: Meetings of the Sustainable Development Board should supersede the joint meeting of the boards of UNDP/UNFPA/gender entity, WFP and UNICEF. After three years the effectiveness of the Board should be assessed. This assessment should include consideration of the scope for integrating the boards of UNDP/UNFPA and UNICEF as segments of the Sustainable Development Board, rather than maintaining them as stand-alone boards.

Milestone: Member States should agree on the composition and mandate of the Sustainable Development Board by September 2007, and the Board should convene its first session by June 2008. The new bodies necessary to support the Board (Development Policy and Operations Group, including the Development Finance and Performance Unit and the Independent Evaluation Unit) should have been established by June 2007. By 2010 an independent assessment of the Board's effectiveness should be commissioned.

Box-4 Role and mandate of the Sustainable Development Board

- **Endorse One Country Programmes and approve related allocations** of voluntary donor finance from the Millennium Development Goal funding mechanism (see box 6). Following an inclusive planning process by the United Nations country team, in line with the principle of country ownership, and approval of the programme by the country, the Sustainable Development Board will endorse unified country programmes and approve the allocation of voluntary funds. It would ensure agency alignment with jointly agreed United Nations priorities.
- **Maintain a strategic overview of the system** to drive coordination and joint planning between all funds, programmes and agencies to monitor overlaps and gaps.
- **Review the implementation of global analytical and normative work of the United Nations in relation to the One United Nations at the country level,** to progress towards the internationally agreed development goals and to provide strategic guidance on the policy and analytical work of United Nations sustainable development activities.
- **Oversee the management of the funding mechanism for the Millennium Development Goals**, which will coordinate donor resources and consolidate allocations. The Board's decisions, particularly on allocations, will be informed by strategic policy and operational advice provided by the Development Policy and Operations Group, under the leadership of the Development Coordinator. To fulfil this role the Group requires an internal Development Finance and Performance Unit to manage voluntary donor finance and monitor system-wide performance (see chap. III.B).

- **Review the performance of the resident coordinator system**, taking all necessary steps to strengthen coherence and delivery. This will include monitoring the implementation and delivery of efficiencies, results-based management and the harmonization of business practices. It will also cover the provision of common services to all funds, programmes and specialized agencies in the field.
- **Consider and comment on the implementation of the strategic plans of funds, programmes and specialized agencies** with a role in delivering the Millennium Development Goals, the other internationally agreed goals and normative activities relating to sustainable development, particularly in the context of the One Country Programme. The Board would assess and strengthen system-wide operational and normative coherence, performance and effectiveness of United Nations system-wide sustainable development activities. There should be additional discretionary funding available to the Board to provide incentives for good performance of Headquarters of funds, programmes and specialized agencies and to fund programmatic gaps and priorities.
- **Commission periodic strategic reviews of One Country Programmes**. The Board will ensure that the One Country Programmes are aligned with national development plans, have full country ownership established through inclusive consultative processes and are focused on internationally agreed development goals. Strategic reviews will be prepared for the Board's consideration under the direction of the Development Coordinator. The Board should provide clear guidance and directions to relevant stakeholders to implement the recommendations of such reviews.
- **Consider and act on independent evaluation, risk management and audit findings**, submitted by the new Independent Evaluation Unit, established by the Secretary-General and reporting to the Board. This Unit will strengthen evaluation across the development system and provide timely, independent performance information to improve the system and its processes (see chap. III.B).

Membership and reporting

The Economic and Social Council should establish the Board and determine its membership in line with experience gained from the composition of the executive boards of the funds, programmes and specialized agencies. The Board will comprise a subset of Member States on the basis of equitable geographic representation. Senior staff from development, planning, finance and foreign ministries, with the appropriate skills and competencies, should represent Member States. The Board should convene at the ministerial level when required. It should enable major non-United Nations intergovernmental organizations with a key role in the international development architecture to fully participate in its meetings. The Board's decisions should be communicated to all relevant United Nations intergovernmental bodies. Executive heads of United Nations agencies, or their deputies, with significant operational and normative programmes, should take part as ex officio members. When allocating funding for a One Country Programme, a high-level representative from that country should be invited. The Board should invite independent experts, senior officials of the Bretton Woods institutions and NGOs to participate in discussions and to inform the Board's decision-making, when necessary.

Organizational structures

62. A more coherent development system would unify and integrate the global analytical and normative work of the United Nations, with regional perspectives and country level interventions, and maximize synergies between them. It would create a mechanism to deploy the multidimensional perspectives of the United Nations in support of policy advice and technical services to all countries. This would help the United Nations to secure its place as a unique, credible and complementary partner in the international development architecture. Through consolidation, priority-setting and the elimination of duplication, a reconfigured development system will improve performance and increase cost-effectiveness. It will significantly increase managerial accountability and effectiveness without creating a large centralized bureaucracy. And at the country level, it would provide the framework for One United Nations.

United Nations System Chief Executives Board for Coordination

63. CEB, established in 2000, has led to some improvement in inter-agency coordination. The High-level Committees on Programmes and Management have developed more coherent approaches to system-wide themes and coordinated approaches to reform business processes. But the Board's potential has been underexploited and its decision-making role has been underused. An effective results-oriented CEB as a counterpart to a better functioning Economic and Social Council would enhance coherence throughout the system.

Recommendation: CEB should review its functions, in the light of experience gained since its establishment five years ago, with a view to improving its performance and accountability for system-wide coherence.

Development Policy and Operations Group

64. The Panel believes that a Development Policy and Operations Group should be established for organizational coherence, within the CEB framework, to unify and integrate the United Nations global analytical and normative work with regional perspectives and country operations. The Group would provide vision to bring together economic, social and environmental policies and activities into an integrated whole. It would subsume the current United Nations Development Group and the Executive Committee on Economic and Social Affairs. It would be served by a secretariat comprising talented officials from all parts of the United Nations system.

65. The Panel proposes that the Secretary-General appoint the UNDP Administrator as the Development Coordinator to chair the Development Policy and Operations Group. The Panel also proposes that the Group comprise the executive heads of United Nations funds, programmes, regional commissions, specialized agencies and the United Nations Secretariat. The Panel proposes that the Chair of the Group be supported by the head of the Department of Economic and Social Affairs, acting in the capacity of United Nations chief economist, and an executive head of a United Nations specialized agency with a significant operational portfolio, serving on a rotating basis. An Executive Committee consisting of the heads of United Nations funds, programmes and specialized agencies with significant portfolios and those with major cross-cutting mandates would be formed, including the Head of the Department of Economic and Social Affairs. The Development Coordinator would report and be accountable to the Sustainable Development Board.

Recommendation: The Secretary-General should appoint the UNDP Administrator as the Development Coordinator to chair the Development Policy and Operations Group that would support One United Nations at the country level. The Development Coordinator would report and be accountable to the Sustainable Development Board on the implementation of the One United Nations. A Development Finance and Performance Review Unit should be established to support the Development Policy and Operations Group.

Box 5

The role of the Development Policy and Operations Group

- Provide an inclusive forum for strategic decision-making, improve the effectiveness of the United Nations operational activities at the country level, build system-wide ownership of the resident coordinator system and enable member agencies to work collectively and deliver as One United Nations at the country level.
- Provide a framework to link normative, analytical and technical expertise to support nationally owned and led development programmes.
- Provide knowledge networking, sharing best practices and technical expertise to support regional and subregional programming.
- Create an incentive system for coherence, efficiency, cost-effectiveness and networking in deploying United Nations resources.
- Support the Development Coordinator in reporting to the Sustainable Development Board.

The Development Finance and Performance Unit, under the Development Policy and Operations Group, would

- Act as a coordinating clearing house and database of all United Nations funding sources and spending to assist the Sustainable Development Board with strategic financial planning and allocations.
- Provide advice to the Board on country and regional financial allocations and allocations for global policy work.
- Provide advice to the Board on setting and delivering efficiency measures to maximize investment in programming, based on internal country and regional performance reports and audits.
- Provide a common internal audit system for all United Nations sustainable development activities.
- Provide an annual performance and financial report on all United Nations sustainable development activities.

Regional structures and coordination

66. The regional economic commissions were established to promote economic and social development in their regions. And United Nations funds, programmes and agencies have developed regional mechanisms to provide technical and management support to their country offices. The result is a broad regional presence for the United Nations, providing a vast potential of assets and expertise, but increasing duplication, fragmentation and incoherence.

67. Over time, certain regional commissions have continued to meet regional needs while others have lost focus in applying their comparative strength in conducting regional analysis, developing policy frameworks and norms and supporting regional integration efforts and activities—instead devoting attention to operational activities at the country level. Strong institutional arrangements are now needed to ensure complementarities and build a genuine culture of cooperation among all United Nations organizations active in each region, as well as between the United Nations and non-United Nations regional entities.

Recommendation: United Nations entities at the regional level should be reconfigured and the United Nations regional setting should be reorganized around two interrelated sets of functions:

- Focusing on analytical and normative work, as well as activities of a transboundary nature. The regional commissions would act as a catalyst for these functions, using, inter alia, their convening power at both the intergovernmental and Secretariat levels.
- Focusing on coordinating the servicing of the United Nations country teams. Being responsible for managing the resident coordinator system, UNDP would act as the catalyst for these functions.

Recommendation: Regional offices of United Nations entities should be co-located and the definition of regions among all United Nations entities should be standardized to ensure consistency and coherence in the work of the United Nations at the regional level.

Coherence at the national level

68. Global development issues are interconnected, but in national Governments, responsibilities usually fall within separate line ministries (for trade, aid, debt, agriculture, environment, labour employment, health and education). As the global economy becomes more integrated, so will the linkages among these issues. Without coherent policy and leadership within national governments, disparate policies and fragmented implementation will undermine the effectiveness of multilateral organizations. Greater coherence within governmental structures, particularly for donors, can ensure coherence of policy development and implementation, both bilaterally and through multilateral institutions.

69. National Governments must also do more to ensure coherence and exercise good donorship in accordance with the mutual obligations of donors and recipients as set out in the Monterrey Consensus and the Paris Declaration on Aid Effectiveness. A candid international examination should be made of the developed countries' policy choices and the fulfilment of their commitments, including that by the Development Assistance Committee of the Organization for Economic Cooperation and Development.

Recommendation: At the national level, Governments should establish an "all-of-government" approach to international development to ensure coordination in the positions taken by their representatives in the decision-making structures of all relevant organizations, including the Bretton Woods institutions and the World Trade Organization. Pursuing consistent policies in the different settings can ensure that all relevant governing bodies effectively promote system-wide coherence to achieve internationally agreed goals.

Recommendation: The United Nations should establish benchmarks by 2008 to ensure the implementation of principles of good multilateral donorship, so that the funding provided at headquarters and at the country level do not undermine the coherence of development efforts and funding of the United Nations development system.

Relations with the World Bank and the International Monetary Fund

70. System-wide coherence at the United Nations cannot be discussed in a vacuum. It needs to be placed in a broader contextual framework of a dynamic international setting in which there are a large number of other relevant international actors and efforts. Today's consensus on the international development agenda is a result of the internationally agreed development goals and of platforms for their implementation through nationally owned development strategies and support by the donor community. This adds to the need for credible engagement of the United Nations with other development actors, since the success of this common agenda can be realized only through coherence in implementation.

71. Given the universality of the United Nations and the complementary role of the Organization and the Bretton Woods institutions in economic, social and related fields, there is an urgent need for a more credible and meaningful engagement between the United Nations system and the international financial institutions. This is needed to secure policy consistency and enable countries to achieve their development objectives. The United Nations and the Bretton Woods institutions were established with the intention that they would work together in a complementary way. Over time both the World Bank and the United Nations institutions have gradually expanded their roles so that there is increasing overlap and duplication in their work. There is a balance to be struck between healthy competition and inefficient overlap and unfilled gaps. The Bretton Woods institutions and the United Nations need to work more closely together to remove unnecessary duplication, and to build on their respective strengths.

Recommendation: As a matter of urgency the Secretary-General, the President of the World Bank and the Executive Director of IMF should set up a process to review, update and conclude formal agreements on their respective roles and relations at the global and country level. These reviews must be periodically updated as well as assessed. This process should be undertaken on the basis of the enhanced performance, strengthened delivery and more influential role that the United Nations will have if our reforms are implemented.

- *Global level.* The participation of the Bretton Woods institutions in the annual spring meetings of the Economic and Social Council and the biennial high-level dialogue of the General Assembly should be more substantive. The focus should be on areas of common interest and on concrete measures to promote policy consistency to achieve the internationally agreed development goals. The United Nations status and participation in the Development Committee should be enhanced. Joint research and staff exchanges and peer reviews should become regular. The sharing of information and opinions on draft reports and strategic documents should be improved.

- *Country level.* The United Nations, the World Bank and IMF should cooperate closely in supporting countries on their national development strategies, including poverty reduction strategies and Millennium Development Goal strategies. Common frameworks to collect data and measure results should be developed. The World Bank and the United Nations should work jointly on needs assessments, with full national ownership. The skills and legitimacy of the United Nations in capacity-building should be fully used.
- *Post-conflict transition.* The United Nations and the World Bank should clarify the terms of collaboration in post-conflict situations and institutionalize a dialogue with clear counterparts on both sides. The United Nations should take the lead in the political and governance aspects of post-conflict issues, including deteriorating governance, and on electoral issues, as well as in supporting and funding early recovery when the capacity and processes are not in place yet to have a regular development process. The World Bank should be involved early in these processes and can assist in setting up multi-donor trust funds and more regular funding based on nationally owned recovery and development strategies.

Recommendation: To review cooperation within the international development structure, and to ensure policy consistency and coordination, an annual meeting should be chaired by the Secretary-General, with the participation of the President of the World Bank, the Managing Director of IMF, the Development Coordinator and relevant heads of agencies, funds and programmes, including the Directors-General of the World Health Organization (WHO), the Food and Agriculture Organization of the United Nations (FAO), the International Labour Organization (ILO), the United Nations Educational, Scientific and Cultural Organization (UNESCO) and others, depending on the issue under discussion.

Engaging civil society organizations and the private sector

72. Progress towards the internationally agreed development goals has improved through the active engagement of the United Nations with different actors at various levels, including partnerships with Governments, civil society and the private sector.

73. Civil society organizations can drive the United Nations development agenda forward. They are indispensable partners in delivering services to the poor, and they can catalyse action within countries, mobilize broad-based movements and hold leaders accountable for their commitments. In crisis, post-conflict and post-disaster countries, national and international NGOs are vital implementing partners—without them, United Nations humanitarian assistance could not be delivered.

74. The private sector has a vital role in generating new investments, creating full and productive employment, contributing to financing for development and managing natural resources and the environment. Coalitions of private foundations and public-private alliances have emerged as some of the more dynamic means of transferring financial and technical resources to realize sustainable development goals. They are also important platforms to promote corporate social responsibility and accountability.

75. While Governments remain the primary interlocutors for country-level engagement with the United Nations, civil society and private sector inputs into the preparation of the

One Country Programme are important to ensure full national ownership and relevance. United Nations country teams should work with Governments to support an enabling environment for productive employment and enterprise development, and to encourage knowledge development, partnerships, corporate social responsibility, skills transfer and public-private networking across regions.

76. While the relationship between the United Nations and civil society is as old as the Charter, United Nations cooperation with civil society organizations and the private sector needs to be systematized and upgraded to enable these partnerships to contribute more effectively to the implementation of internationally agreed development goals.

Recommendation: The capacity of the resident coordinator's office to advocate, promote and broker partnerships between Government and relevant civil society organizations and the private sector should be enhanced to build stakeholder consensus and realize country-specific goals as embodied in the national development plans.

B. Funding the United Nations system for results

For coherent action to help achieve the Millennium Development Goals and other internationally agreed development goals, the United Nations needs sustained funding for the One Country Programme, as well as secure core funding for United Nations entities that have a demonstrable commitment to reform. Donors should increasingly pool their contributions at country or headquarters level, based on the performance of the United Nations in pilot cases.

77. For development at the country level, the role of the United Nations is not that of a major financial resource provider, but that of convener, policy adviser, commodity provider and capacity-builder. Exceptions are post-conflict situations, where the United Nations plays a major role, often with trust fund resources. The total ODA channelled through the United Nations annually is approximately US$ 10 billion.

78. To make the One Country Programme a success and to tackle global challenges, United Nations funding practices and mechanisms need urgent review. Current practices for funding the United Nations are fragmented and unpredictable. They constrain the United Nations and recipient countries from making strategic choices for the use of funds and in contributing to the Millennium Development Goals and other internationally agreed goals. The Development Coordinator should convene a meeting of the Development Policy and Operations Group with major donors to discuss and elaborate the practical changes required in donor practices to fund the One Country Programmes.

79. There is too much earmarked funding and too little funding for the core budget of United Nations organizations. Moreover, funding is unpredictable, and burden-sharing procedures are unclear. So United Nations organizations are only to some extent masters of their own budgets, with donor priorities rather than multilateral mandates determining some of their actions. Even in specialized agencies, assessed contributions have not increased for years, leaving them to rely on voluntary funding for core activities.

80. Current funding practices also lead to competition and fragmentation, often with relatively small budgets per agency at the country level, while the common programme is left with insufficient resources. A review of 10 United Nations country teams found on average that only 40 per cent of their resources are mobilized through core resources. United Nations

organizations have to put considerable effort into fund-raising. Some argue that the resident coordinator system should be funded through assessed contributions, in line with an agreed contributions scale, which is how the United Nations Secretariat, peacekeeping operations and core specialized agency budgets are funded.

81. Sustained and consolidated funding is the key to reversing the fragmentation of the United Nations system. More secure funding has to go hand in hand with better performance, oversight, accountability, efficiency and results. That is why the Panel devoted considerable attention to governance and management and recommends steps to resolve them, based on the following principles:

- United Nations organizations that have a demonstrable commitment to reform, effectiveness and working together need sufficient sustained core funding—or, where applicable, assessed funding—to fulfil their missions. There should also be sufficient funding for supporting and strengthening the resident coordinator system.
- There should be one budgetary framework for the One Country Programme, reflecting all contributions. Donors should increasingly pool their contributions at the country or headquarters level, based on United Nations performance in pilot cases. They should increasingly refrain from funding country-level interventions by the United Nations system outside the One Country Programme.
- While pursuing greater coherence, diversity has brought the United Nations system many resource mobilization opportunities and successful brands, allowing both donors and recipient countries a degree of choice. Some diversity in the system is thus to be welcomed.

Recommendation: Funding for the One Country Programmes should be predictable and multi-year. The five One Country Programme pilots should be funded by pooled country-level funding. Subject to continuous positive assessment, demonstrated effectiveness and proven results, they should be expanded to 20 One Country Programmes by 2009, 40 by 2010 and all other appropriate country programmes by 2012. Following the five pilots, the One Country Programmes will also be funded by voluntary contributions to a consolidated funding mechanism, the Millennium Development Goal funding mechanism (see box 6).

Recommendation: There should be full core funding for individual United Nations organizations committed to reform.

- There should be full core funding for individual funds and programmes demonstrably committed to reform, effectiveness and working together, through strengthened and improved multi-year funding frameworks, with strategic priorities, related funding priorities and robust indicators. By 2008 funds and programmes should align their multi-year funding cycles to facilitate strategic coordination.
- There should also be a review of assessed funding of the specialized agencies, to enable them to continue their essential work on global norms and standards and assess whether the current policies of zero real growth is adequate.
- The strengthened resident coordinator system should be fully funded. Resources earmarked for supporting the system should continue to be managed separately from UNDP programme resources.

Box 6 Funding the United Nations system for results

Full funding for the One Country Programme

At the country-level, contributions to the One Country Programme should be consolidated within a single budgetary framework, which would not constitute a legal constraint on the spending authority of funds, programmes and specialized agencies. The one budgetary framework brings together all contributions to the One Country Programme. To fund the One Country Programme through this single budgetary framework, the Panel recommends the following funding sources:

- The five pilots of the One Country Programme should be funded by pooling funding in the country. For donor contributions to each pilot, a country-level Millennium Development Goal strategy support fund should be established, to be administered by the resident coordinator, in line with national priorities. In principle, funding from all sources for the One Country Programme should flow through these country funds. Donors would be strongly encouraged to contribute through these funds.
- A Millennium Development Goal funding mechanism should be established following the five pilots. This voluntary mechanism would coordinate overall resource flows enabling global oversight of funding available for contributions to the One Country Programme. The mechanism should be governed by the Sustainable Development Board under the supervision of the development coordinator. Donors are strongly encouraged to make funds available to this mechanism at the central or country level. United Nations organizations could also contribute core funding for the One Country Programme within the framework of this mechanism.

Recommendation: The United Nations should drive reform by channelling reform savings back into the system through mechanisms, such as an empowerment fund. This fund would demonstrate to the world's poorest citizens, communities and local entrepreneurs that United Nations savings will be invested directly in their empowerment. It would be financed with minimal overhead through efficiency cost savings resulting from reforming, consolidating and streamlining United Nations functions and organizations, as recommended by the task force to be established by the Secretary-General (see chap. III.A). This fund could redirect savings from efficiency reforms back to country-level strategies (One Country Programme) with a special emphasis on helping countries achieve the Millennium Development Goals.

C. Reforming United Nations system business practices: building institutions of public trust

Business practices for resource planning, human resources, common services and evaluation must achieve full compatibility as major drivers of coherence in the United Nations system. There should be greater opportunities for staff mobility and a system-wide agreement on results-based management as well as an independent United Nations system-wide evaluation mechanism and common evaluation methodologies and benchmarking. The United Nations must systematically examine opportunities and possibilities for joint services.

82. The business practices, processes and culture of the United Nations system have evolved in an incremental and ad hoc manner over 60 years, in response to specific situations and agency needs. This has widened the disconnection between organizations of the system, contributed to inefficiency and hindered the development of a common management culture that is accountable and results-oriented. To boost public trust, the United Nations needs to demonstrate more transparency and accountability.

83. There is no central management authority in the United Nations to implement common rules and practices. So individual organizations pursue various initiatives, without incentives to harmonize for the benefit of the United Nations system as a whole. Without explicit commitment from organizational leaders, common services cannot work. We believe the time has come to establish a process leading to a common framework for business practices in the United Nations. This will transform the way the United Nations works, build a culture of collaboration, improve the system's effectiveness in achieving organization-wide programmatic results and lead to significant savings. Harmonized business practices will enhance the United Nations system's capacity to deliver the One Country Programmes. Savings from efficiency gains will be redirected to these programmes.

84. Harmonizing systems in itself does not achieve coherence. Needed first is an agreement on standards, to ensure that value is added in pursuing change. Using internationally recognized standards would facilitate the simplification and harmonization of business practices within the United Nations system.

85. Public trust will be reinforced through measurable results. Evaluations throughout the system use different measurement criteria, which are often too narrowly defined by quantifiable terms, rather than by measurements of longer term impact.

86. Attracting and retaining the most qualified staff for an effective and independent civil service is not possible with a human resource system based on different performance evaluation systems, entitlements and contracts. To encourage mobility and cross-fertilization and to prepare staff for positions of greater responsibility, the system's appraisals must be based on performance, not seniority. A competitive and incentive-based system is required. The International Civil Service Commission has become a politicized body that represents the interests of Member States, rather than operational priorities. It is too slow and needs substantial change.

87. Current governance mechanisms need to be modernized. Without an overarching management system to drive change, there can be no management control and little progress towards coherence. For CEB to work more effectively, the United Nations agencies must first commit to the need for its revised terms of reference.

Recommendation: CEB, chaired by the Secretary-General, should lead efforts to improve management efficiency, transparency and accountability of the United Nations system. It should be used more effectively in its principal role as a high-level decision-making forum in the United Nations system on substantive and management issues. CEB reporting and transparency to intergovernmental structures should be improved.

Recommendation: The business practices of the United Nations system should be harmonized:

- International Public Sector Accounting Standards, which will be implemented across the entire United Nations system by 2010, must provide an important basis for simplifying and harmonizing business practices.
- To break down barriers to programmatic and administrative collaboration, enterprise resource planning standards, and data warehouses for reporting, should be harmonized across the system by 2010. Entities currently selecting enterprise resource planning systems (including the United Nations Secretariat) should base their selection on data-sharing compatibility and interconnectivity.
- Improvements in results-based management, results-based budgeting, evaluation and other measures to increase transparency and accountability should be in place by 2008. This should include harmonizing the principles, terms and methods of results-based management and the audit procedures across the United Nations system.
- A system-wide security management system based on common policies, standards and operating procedures should be established at the country level, particularly for humanitarian affairs.

Recommendation: Evaluation mechanisms should be established for transparency and accountability. A United Nations system-wide independent evaluation mechanism should be established by 2008, and taking into account the evolving role of the Office of Internal Oversight Services, to monitor how system-wide goals are being delivered. A separate system to enable peer reviews across organizations should also be developed. A common evaluation methodology should be applied across the United Nations system by 2010 to permit benchmarking and inter-agency comparisons and facilitate exchanges of best practices. Standardized information and data related to United Nations activities, programme delivery, budgets, staffing and cost-effectiveness should be transparent and publicly available. Harmonizing systems and methodologies will provide Member States with a more transparent overview of United Nations system results and financial figures by area of interest and type of activity.

Recommendation: Human resource policies and practices should be updated and harmonized. An authoritative and independent external evaluation to reform the International Civil Service Commission should be carried out in 2007. Human resource management policies and contractual arrangements should be simplified, harmonized and updated in line with an emphasis on results, performance management systems and accountability frameworks. Recruitment and promotion policies should be underpinned by the principle of "meritocracy with equity and representation" and developed to improve staff capabilities and ensure a culture of management for results.

Human resource policies must enable mobility of the staff across the system and the transferability of pensions. Host countries should be encouraged to enable the employment of spouses of United Nations staff. A fundamental overhaul of staff training and career development programmes should be carried out by 2010 to ensure that, at all levels of the system, staff serving the United Nations are motivated and have appropriate professional skills. The United Nations System Staff College should have the capacity to provide executive leadership training to senior United Nations managers. This would enable more effective management of change processes and contribute to a common management culture in the United Nations system.

Recommendation: Executives should be selected according to clear criteria, and for limited terms. All appointments or elections to executive positions in United Nations organizations should be in line with clear and effective criteria, limited to two terms of four or five years.

Recommendation: Change should be managed at the highest levels. The overall management of reform of business practices should be invested in the Secretary-General, in his capacity as chairman of CEB, assisted by a bureau of staff specialists as part of the CEB machinery. All chief executives in the United Nations system should develop plans to reform the business practices in their organizations together with resource requirements for investing in change processes.

88. The Panel is of the view that implementing the reforms necessary to enable the United Nations to deliver as one will require time and energy. A dedicated team will be needed at a senior level within in the United Nations system to ensure that progress is being made on the changes being recommended.

Recommendation: The Panel recommends that the Secretary-General appoint a senior member of his staff and provide the necessary resources to form a senior change management team. The team would be responsible for tracking and supporting implementation, and reporting regularly to the Secretary-General and Member States on progress to implement the recommendations of the High-level Panel on United Nations System-wide Coherence, in the areas of development, humanitarian assistance and the environment.

Annex I
Terms of reference of the Panel, issued on 15 February 2006

Background

1. In the Outcome document adopted at the 2005 World Summit in New York global leaders called for much stronger system-wide coherence across the various development-related agencies, funds and programmes of the United Nations. In addition to supporting current, ongoing reforms at building a more effective, coherent and better-performing United Nations country presence, it specifically invited the Secretary-General to "launch work to further strengthen the management and coordination of United Nations operational activities". They also called for such work to be focused on ensuring that the United Nations maximized its contribution to achieving internationally agreed development goals, including the Millennium Development Goals, including proposals for "more tightly managed entities" in the field of development, humanitarian assistance and the environment.

2. The Secretary-General intends to commission a small panel, supported by Adnan Amin, United Nations Environment Programme (UNEP), as Executive Director, and appropriate research and analytical capacity from inside and outside the United Nations system, to develop concrete and comprehensive analysis and recommendations in this regard. The Secretary-General is determined to ensure that while this work is under way, existing reform initiatives endorsed in the Outcome document, including those for a strengthened role for special representatives of the Secretary-General and resident coordinators, and the strengthening of the United Nations country team through a common management programming and monitoring framework should continue. The Secretary-General considers that the outcome of this exercise would provide an important complement to the ongoing reform deliberations in the General Assembly.

Timeline

3. The Panel will seek to consult on an interim basis with the United Nations System Chief Executives Board for Coordination (CEB) at its meeting in April 2006. This would allow for further consultation with member states at the Economic and Social Council in July 2006 and for the full study to be completed by the next session of the General Assembly to allow for embarking on possible implementation in 2007.

Scope

4. As set out in the Outcome document, the three elements of the study will need to have slightly different scope:

(a) In the field of humanitarian assistance significant progress has been made in recent years in providing more coordinated response to emergencies at the country level. The Outcome document also commits the General Assembly to strengthening the coordination of humanitarian and disaster relief assistance of the United Nations and separate follow-up work is already under way in this regard. However, the growing scale and scope of disasters, particularly natural disasters, underlines the importance of improving the timeliness and predictability of humanitarian funding, mainly by improving the Central Emergency Response Fund, in part through a thorough evaluation of lessons learned from recent experience. This part of the study will also need to focus on ways of developing and improving mechanisms for the use of emergency standby capacities for a timely response to humanitarian emergencies;

(b) In the field of environmental activities, two separate issues need to be addressed. First, in the normative area, a full assessment should be made of how the United Nations can best provide more comprehensive and coherent management and monitoring of the growing range of multilateral environmental agreements. This should include the development of stronger scientific and analytic capacity in monitoring, assessing and reporting on critical environmental trends. Second is the need for better integration of the environmental perspective within the broad principle of sustainable development in United Nations country-level activities and in particular capacity-building and technology support undertaken by the entire United Nations system. The General Assembly may launch its own deliberations on the issue of international environmental governance issues in early 2006 and it would be important to ensure that these efforts are complementary;

(c) In development, despite wide-ranging reforms over the past five years strengthening the role of the resident coordinator and the United Nations country team, developing and donor countries alike remain concerned that, overall, United Nations development at the country level remains overly fragmented and supply-driven. The Outcome document commits all countries to map out their own national strategies to meet international conference goals, including the Millennium Development Goals. In this context, the study will need to analyse how the United Nations system as a whole can be better reoriented to provide more efficient, coherent demand-driven support to national partners by building on its core normative, technical assistance and capacity-building strengths to partner with the longer-term financing and other support brought by the World Bank and other international partners. In this regard, it will be particularly important to consider how to strengthen linkages between the normative work and the operational activities of the system. It will also need to examine how this work can support and complement the wider role the Outcome document envisages for the Economic and Social Council in ensuring follow-up and assessing progress of the outcomes of the major United Nations conferences and summits, including the internationally agreed development goals; and playing a major role in the overall coordination of funds, programmes and agencies, ensuring coherence among them and avoiding duplication of mandates and activities.

5. In all three areas, the study will need to encompass both organizational and funding issues, ranging from the duplication and overlap of work products across United Nations agencies, funds and programmes to prospects for joint, multi-year funding and programming arrangements. The broad issue of more predictable financing of the United Nations system—from the consolidated appeals process to the growth in non-core funding of funds and programmes to the appropriate role of assessed contributions—and its impact on existing systems and proposed reform will need to be a central element.

6. The overarching aim of the study is to seek recommendations on a process of rationalization that will maximize the available resources for relief and development programmes in the United Nations system while minimizing overhead and administrative costs. As such,

the study will need to explore ways of fully exploiting synergies between the normative and analytical institutions and departments of the United Nations, such as the Department of Economic and Social Affairs and the United Nations Conference on Trade and Development (UNCTAD), and operational agencies. It will also need to address how the United Nations system works and can best exercise its comparative advantages with international partners, including the Bretton Woods institutions, the European Commission and other regional actors, donors, civil society and the private sector. While the primary focus will be on increasing impact at the country level, in making concrete proposals for improved management, coordination and effectiveness, it will need to make findings with regard to work both at United Nations headquarters, regional and country level.

7. In terms of recommendations, the study should seek to identify a short, medium and longer-term vision and benchmarks, thus laying a platform for an actionable plan of implementation rather than open-ended proposals. Change may need to occur in phases, with first initial proposals for rationalization of the current system without major structural changes; then proposals for preliminary restructuring of the current system to minimize duplication and overlap; and finally recommendations for comprehensive revitalization and restructuring of the United Nations operational role in environment, humanitarian and development work.

Consultation

8. The Outcome document calls for greater coordination between the governing boards of various operational agencies so as to ensure a more coherent policy in assigning mandates and allocating resources throughout the system. In this spirit—and to ensure wide acceptance and subsequent implementation of the findings—it will be essential for the Panel to consult widely with all stakeholders, including the management and governing boards of relevant agencies, funds and programmes, prior to submission of their final report to the Secretary-General.

Additional request from the Secretary-General: gender equality

9. In addition, the Secretary-General called upon the High-level Panel on United Nations System-wide Coherence in the areas of development, humanitarian assistance and the environment to review contribution of the United Nations system to achieving gender equality and to make recommendations on how gender equality perspectives can be better integrated into the work of the United Nations. In his recent report on the mandate review, the Secretary-General states that there is a need to move towards "improved clarity on institutional responsibilities and more concerted action in relation to gender equality. There is a need to assess the progress made across the system, the gaps and challenges remaining, and ways to improve outcomes". He requested the Panel "to include in its work an assessment of how gender equality, including through gender mainstreaming, can be better and more fully addressed in the work of the United Nations, particularly in its operational activities on the ground" (A/60/733, para. 131).

Excerpt from General Assembly resolution 60/1

10. General Assembly resolution 60/1 states, in part:

> 168. We recognize that the United Nations brings together a unique wealth of expertise and resources on global issues. We commend the extensive experience

and expertise of the various development-related organizations, agencies, funds and programmes of the United Nations system in their diverse and complementary fields of activity and their important contributions to the achievement of the Millennium Development Goals and the other development objectives established by various United Nations conferences.

169. We support stronger system-wide coherence by implementing the following measures:

Policy

- Strengthening linkages between the normative work of the United Nations system and its operational activities
- Coordinating our representation on the governing boards of the various development and humanitarian agencies so as to ensure that they pursue a coherent policy in assigning mandates and allocating resources throughout the system
- Ensuring that the main horizontal policy themes, such as sustainable development, human rights and gender, are taken into account in decision-making throughout the United Nations

Operational activities

- Implementing current reforms aimed at a more effective, efficient, coherent, coordinated and better-performing United Nations country presence with a strengthened role for the senior resident official, whether special representative, resident coordinator or humanitarian coordinator, including appropriate authority, resources and accountability, and a common management, programming and monitoring framework
- Inviting the Secretary-General to launch work to further strengthen the management and coordination of United Nations operational activities so that they can make an even more effective contribution to the achievement of the internationally agreed development goals, including the Millennium Development Goals, including proposals for consideration by Member States for more tightly managed entities in the fields of development, humanitarian assistance and the environment

Humanitarian assistance

- Upholding and respecting the humanitarian principles of humanity, neutrality, impartiality and independence and ensuring that humanitarian actors have safe and unhindered access to populations in need in conformity with the relevant provisions of international law and national laws
- Supporting the efforts of countries, in particular developing countries, to strengthen their capacities at all levels in order to prepare for and respond rapidly to natural disasters and mitigate their impact
- Strengthening the effectiveness of the United Nations humanitarian response, inter alia, by improving the timeliness and predictability of humanitarian funding, in part by improving the Central Emergency Revolving Fund

- Further developing and improving, as required, mechanisms for the use of emergency standby capacities, under the auspices of the United Nations, for a timely response to humanitarian emergencies
- *Environmental activities*
- Recognizing the need for more efficient environmental activities in the United Nations system, with enhanced coordination, improved policy advice and guidance, strengthened scientific knowledge, assessment and cooperation, better treaty compliance, while respecting the legal autonomy of the treaties, and better integration of environmental activities in the broader sustainable development framework at the operational level, including through capacity-building, we agree to explore the possibility of a more coherent institutional framework to address this need, including a more integrated structure, building on existing institutions and internationally agreed instruments, as well as the treaty bodies and the specialized agencies

Annex II
Panel members

Shaukat Aziz, Pakistan (Co-Chair)
Prime Minister, Pakistan

Luísa Dias Diogo, Mozambique (Co-Chair)
Prime Minister, Mozambique

Jens Stoltenberg, Norway (Co-Chair)
Prime Minister, Norway

Gordon Brown, MP, United Kingdom of Great Britain and Northern Ireland
Chancellor of the Exchequer

Mohamed T. El-Ashry, Egypt
Senior Fellow, United Nations Foundation and Former Chairman and Chief Executive Officer, Global Environment Facility

Robert Greenhill, Canada
President, Canadian International Development Agency

Ruth Jacoby, Sweden
Ambassador of Sweden to Germany
Ministry of Foreign Affairs, Sweden
Former Director-General for Development Cooperation

Ricardo Lagos, Chile
Former President, Republic of Chile

Louis Michel, Belgium
European Commissioner for Development and Humanitarian Aid

Benjamin W. Mkapa, United Republic of Tanzania
Former President, United Republic of Tanzania

Jean-Michel Severino, France
Director General, French Development Agency

Josette S. Sheeran, United States of America
Under Secretary for Economic, Business and Agricultural Affairs, United States Department of State

Keizo Takemi, Japan
Senior Vice-Minister of Health, Labour and Welfare
Former State Secretary for Foreign Affairs of Japan

Ex officio

Lennart Båge
President, International Fund for Agricultural Development

Kemal Derviş
Administrator, United Nations Development Programme

Annex III
Panel secretariat

Adnan Z. Amin (Executive Director)

Koen Davidse (Research Director)

Moustapha Soumaré (Research Director)

Kai Buchholz

Mohamed El-Farnawany

Fabienne Fon Sing

Treena Huang

Maaike Jansen

Ruth McCoy

Zazie Schafer

Annex IV
Consultative process

1. To ensure that its deliberations were informed by a broad range of perspectives from all key stakeholders, the Panel agreed that it was essential to undertake a wide-ranging, but focused consultative process, in accordance with the scope of the study outlined in the Panel's terms of reference. Members considered that an inclusive consultative process was important not only to enrich the work of the Panel, but also to ensure the engagement and commitment of concerned stakeholders, a fundamental step to developing relevant and realistic recommendations and making sure that the Panel's work would lead to genuine reform.

2. The consultative process resulted in the development of an analytical base and options for consideration by the Panel. Consultations drew on research and analytical capacity from inside and outside the United Nations system, and enabled contacts with Member States, the United Nations system, intergovernmental forums, international financial institutions, academia and civil society organizations.

3. Several Panel members participated in a series of consultations at the regional and country level, in Africa, Asia, Arab States and Latin America and the Caribbean. Each consultation

undertook a broad assessment of experience from six countries within that region, bringing together United Nations country teams, Government representatives, regional organizations, donors and civil society. The objectives of these consultations included enhancing understanding among Panel members of the expected role of the United Nations at country level, canvassing information on good practices as well as major challenges to the United Nations country level coherence and allowing for the integration of the views of practitioners from each region into the overall deliberations of the Panel. In addition, one Panel member undertook country visits to Indonesia, Cambodia and Thailand to analyse challenges to a coherent and effective United Nations at the country level, identify good practices and assess the country level aspects of the issues to be addressed by the Panel.

4. Similarly, a number of thematic consultations were held on the environment, the resident coordinator system, the transition from relief to development, international financial institutions, business practices and funding. These consultations allowed for interaction between Panel members and key stakeholders, including experts, the United Nations system and civil society organizations—and for building an understanding of key challenges and the type of recommendations that could be put forward. A rich consultation was also held with civil society organizations, particularly focusing on sustainable development, gender equality, gender mainstreaming and human rights.

5. Panel members held consultative meetings with intergovernmental forums (the General Assembly and the Economic and Social Council), as well as smaller briefings for regional groupings (the Group of 77 and China, the European Union, the African Group and the Latin America and Caribbean Group). Panel members were also sensitive to their responsibility to build on the United Nations system's own experience and aspirations, meeting with United Nations system organizations, through the United Nations System Chief Executives Board for Coordination (CEB), as well as smaller groupings of organizations (in Rome, Vienna and Geneva), and the regional commissions.

6. The consultative process also benefited from meetings that aimed to provide input to the Panel's work, including consultations hosted by permanent missions to the United Nations (Egypt and France) and United Nations inter-agency bodies (the CEB High-Level Committees on Programmes and Management). In addition, members of the Secretariat held a large number of bilateral meetings with Government representatives (from various ministries and/or permanent missions to the United Nations), United Nations system organizations and civil society organizations.

7. Furthermore, papers were commissioned that fed into the consultative process, including those on gender, business practices, funding, humanitarian assistance, the transition from relief to development and the United Nations institutional architecture.

Panel meetings and consultations, 2006

Meeting	*Date*	*Venue*
First Panel meeting	4 and 5 April	New York
Meeting with the General Assembly	6 April	New York
Meeting with the United Nations System Chief Executives Board for Coordination	7 and 8 April	Segovia

Meeting	*Date*	*Venue*
Consultation on the environment	4 and 5 May	Nairobi
Regional consultation for Africa	8 and 9 May	Maputo
Consultation on the resident coordinator system	15 May	Vienna
Consultation on transition from relief to development	19 May	Rome
Meeting with executive heads of Rome-based agencies	20 May	Rome
Regional consultation for Asia	24 and 25 May	Islamabad
Second Panel meeting	1 and 2 June	Geneva
Meeting with executive heads of Geneva-based agencies	3 June	Geneva
Regional consultation for Arab States	20 and 21 June	Cairo
Consultation with international financial institutions	26 June	Washington, D.C.
Consultation on business practices	26 June	Washington, D.C.
Consultation on funding	29 June	London
Meeting of Sherpas in preparation for the third Panel meeting	30 June	London
Consultation with civil society organizations	2 July	Geneva
Third Panel meeting	3 and 4 July	Geneva
Dialogue with the Economic and Social Council	4 July	Geneva
Meeting with the regional commissions	4 July	Geneva
Regional consultation for Latin America and the Caribbean	28 and 29 July	Bridgetown
Meeting of Sherpas in preparation for the fourth Panel meeting	17 and 18 August	New York
Fourth Panel meeting	31 August and 1 September	Oslo

Annex V
The United Nations system

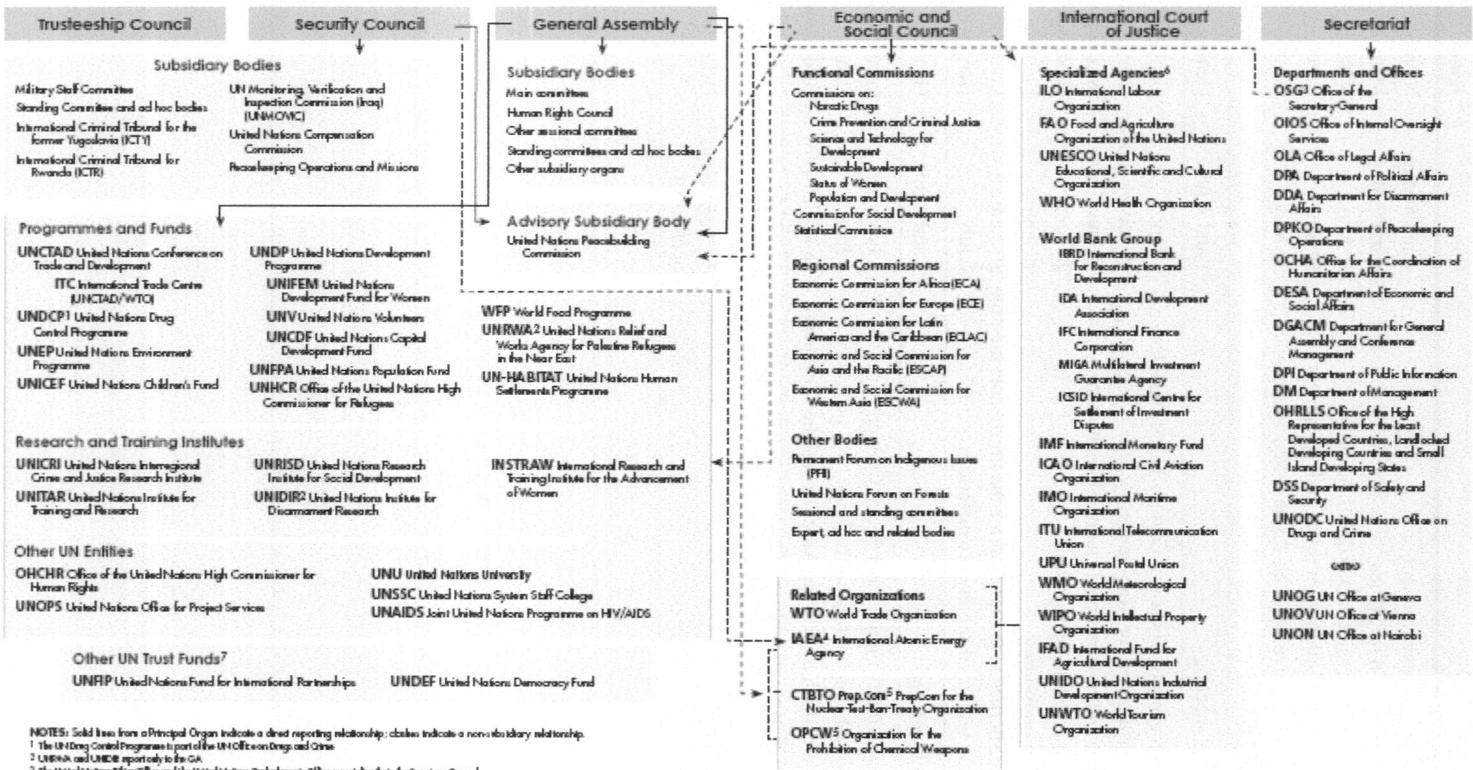

NOTES: Solid lines from a Principal Organ indicate a direct reporting relationship; dashes indicate a non-subsidiary relationship.
[1] The UN Drug Control Programme is part of the UN Office on Drugs and Crime
[2] UNRWA and UNIDIR report only to the GA
[3] The United Nations Ethics Office and the United Nations Ombudsman's Office report directly to the Secretary-General
[4] IAEA reports to the Security Council and the General Assembly (GA)
[5] The CTBTO Prep.Com and OPCW report to the GA
[6] Specialized agencies are autonomous organizations working with the UN and each other through the coordinating machinery of the ECOSOC at the intergovernmental level, and through the Chief Executives Board for coordination (CEB) at the inter-secretariat level
[7] UNFIP is an autonomous trust fund operating under the leadership of the United Nations Deputy Secretary-General. UNDEF's advisory board recommends funding proposals for approval by the Secretary-General.

Annex V
The United Nations system

Acknowledgements

The members of the High-Level Panel on United Nations System-Wide Coherence in the areas of development, humanitarian assistance and the environment would like to express sincere appreciation to their respective aides and advisers for their substantive contributions and dedication.

The Panel's work was made possible by generous financial contributions to a dedicated trust fund. In this regard, the Panel expresses its deep gratitude to the Governments of Belgium, Canada, Denmark, Finland, France, Germany, Ireland, Japan, Luxembourg, the Netherlands, Norway, Sweden, the United Kingdom of Great Britain and Northern Ireland and the United States of America.

Contributions in-kind supporting the work of the Panel secretariat were gratefully received from the International Labour Organization (ILO), the Netherlands Ministry of Foreign Affairs, the United Nations System Chief Executives Board for Coordination (CEB) secretariat, the United Nations Development Group office, the United Nations Development Programme, the United Nations Environment Programme (UNEP), the United Nations Population Fund (UNFPA) and the World Food Programme (WFP). Particularly appreciation is extended to UNEP for its generous gesture in providing office space for the Panel secretariat.

The Panel would also like to extend its gratitude to the Governments and United Nations organizations that hosted consultations and meetings, including: the Governments of Austria, Barbados, Egypt, Italy, Kenya, Mozambique, Norway, Pakistan, Spain and the United Kingdom; the Permanent Missions to the United Nations of Egypt, France and Norway in New York; UNEP, ILO, the United Nations Industrial Development Organization, the United Nations Foundation, the United Nations Office at Geneva, the World Bank, WFP, the World Health Organization, the World Tourism Organization and relevant resident coordinators and United Nations country teams, in particular those in Barbados, Egypt, Mozambique and Pakistan.

The Panel's work also benefited greatly from the views of a large number of Government, United Nations organization and civil society representatives and individual experts who provided valuable perspectives to the Panel in the course of its consultative process, in particular Donald Skerrett, who donated his time and expertise in the area of business practices. UNFPA kindly made available the services of Brendan O'Brien to support country-level consultations. The Panel's work was further enriched by the many insightful written contributions that it received.

The Panel would like to express its deep appreciation to the Secretary-General for having entrusted the members of the Panel with such an important task, and having brought together a remarkable mixture of perspectives and experience in order to formulate recommendations that we hope will effect a major and lasting change on the enhanced functioning of the United Nations system. We would also like to thank the Deputy Secretary-General for his valuable support throughout this process.

Finally, the Panel expresses its sincere appreciation to members of the Panel secretariat for their extensive substantive and administrative support and commitment.

All of these contributions are much appreciated and gratefully acknowledged.

4. Delivering as One: Report of the High-level Panel on United Nations System-wide Coherence in the Areas of Development, Humanitarian Assistance and the Environment, Report of the Secretary-General, 20 November 2006 (A/61/586)

I.Introduction

1. In an ever more interdependent world, a coherent and strong United Nations is needed to meet an immense set of global challenges and a wide diversity of needs. The United Nations has a key role in ensuring progress towards the Millennium Development Goals and the other internationally agreed development goals, enabling countries to lead their development processes and helping to address such global challenges as disease, conflict and the environment, as well as to promote the realization of all rights. The United Nations must be flexible and coherent enough to respond to the operational and policy needs of developing countries, States experiencing conflict, stable low-income countries, emerging economies and developed countries. It should advocate global standards and norms and, in each country, should be focused on delivering results in line with country needs.

2. However, in the face of the preceding challenges, the United Nations is not optimally configured. The Organization urgently needs more coherence and synergy so it can perform as one and be more than the sum of its parts. It should utilize its unique universality, neutrality and capacity to operate in the security, development and humanitarian spheres. It should more successfully perform its roles of convener, standard-setter, advocate, expert, monitor, coordinator and manager of programmes. It should respond to the diverse needs of countries and perform as one at the country level, and have the governance, management and funding practices in place to support those efforts.

3. The recommendations contained in the report of the Secretary-General's High-level Panel on System-wide Coherence in the areas of development, humanitarian assistance and the environment (A/61/583), "Delivering as one", present an important opportunity to address those issues in a comprehensive and consistent manner, to ensure that the Organization can respond to the global challenges of the twenty-first century and play a full and effective role at the heart of the multilateral system.

4. Having reviewed and assessed the recommendations put forward by the High-Level Panel, and in the light of the counsel provided by my predecessor, who commissioned the Panel's work, and with the benefit of having engaged in a range of informal consultations on different aspects of the Panel's report, I am pleased to signal my broad support for the principle of a stronger, more coherent United Nations and for the recommendations contained in the report.

5. The Panel's report puts forward a vision of significantly enhanced United Nations system-wide coherence, which I perceive to be very much in line with the demands and objectives of Member States and the concerns they have and continue to voice. That vision is predicated on overcoming fragmentation and bringing together the system's many assets in order to "deliver as one" at all levels, but particularly at the country level, in line with the principle of country ownership. I believe that this is vital, and as I was quoted as saying in

the report of the Panel, "the true measure of the success for the United Nations is not how much we promise but how much we deliver for those who need us most".

6. The Panel's vision also gives due prominence to the need for the United Nations system to be results based and focused on performance and accountability. This imperative of efficiency, transparency and accountability is also very much at the heart of the demands from Member States for United Nations reform, and forms a cornerstone of my own priorities for the Organization.

7. The present report provides an overview of how I view the Panel's recommendations in the context of the wider United Nations reform agenda and suggests elements of a process for consideration of ways to take forward intergovernmental consideration of the Panel's report.

II. Consideration of the Panel's recommendations

8. As noted by my predecessor, the Panel's report is very rich in terms of analysis and recommendations and covers a great deal of ground. As he suggested in his transmittal note, the report merits a process of review and dialogue to build broad-based common understanding of its objectives, contents and proposals. Although the main consideration of and decision-making regarding the report's recommendations should be done by the General Assembly, other policymakers and actors need to be brought into the discussion to build deeper understanding and ownership of the proposals. Those steps include consultations within the Economic and Social Council and with the governing bodies of organizations of the United Nations system.

9. I believe that the proposals in the report should be pursued as an integrated and coherent whole, as the report was crafted as such with many of the recommendations connected to one another. Arrangements for its review should ensure that the different proposals in the report are addressed on their own merits, with outcomes that reinforce each other and advance, together, the overall objectives set by the Panel.

10. The report should be considered within the context of a number of ongoing reform processes. Clearly, the Panel, in formulating its recommendations, was mindful of the other processes and the progress and obstacles they have encountered. In that regard, many of its recommendations are consistent with existing mandates for reform. In those cases, the United Nations system should move ahead to improve coherence without unnecessary delays so as to avoid duplication of effort. Other areas will require fuller discussions and deliberations.

11. One such process, which is highly relevant in terms of the Panel's recommendations related to enhancing the coherence, effectiveness and efficiency of the United Nations at the country level, is the forthcoming triennial comprehensive policy review of operational activities for development of the United Nations system. A number of the Panel's recommendations reaffirm and give renewed impetus to ongoing reform initiatives mandated by the 2001 and 2004 triennial comprehensive policy reviews, which constitute the policy framework agreed at the intergovernmental level for the operational activities of the United Nations system. The 2007 triennial comprehensive policy review provides an important opportunity to consider and take forward relevant recommendations of the Panel, including assessing progress with regard to the pilot "One Country Programmes" recommended by the Panel.

12. Following consultations and at the request of interested Member States, the United Nations Development Group has initiated eight pilots in which the "One United Nations" approach will be tested. The pilots are being undertaken on a voluntary basis under government leadership and will consist of a subset of about 20 joint offices that the Organization has committed to initiate under the triennial comprehensive policy review implementation plan approved by the Economic and Social Council. This exercise will provide an essential test of the application of the principles advocated by the Panel in different countries, and an analysis of the results and experiences will be presented to the relevant governing bodies at the end of the year. I have endorsed the present exercise and encouraged the Chair of the United Nations Development Group to proceed. A number of issues related to the development of the One United Nations approach will need to be considered, including the following: the central concept of national ownership; the authority and accountability of the United Nations Resident Coordinator; and the role of the United Nations Development Programme (UNDP), as manager of the resident coordinator system on the one hand and in its programmatic role on the other. There should be clear delineations of responsibilities in the form of an internal "firewall" in UNDP. At the same time, the United Nations Development Programme's programmatic role should be supportive of the overall cohesion effort and be strategic and cross-cutting rather than sector or project focused. There also needs to be more clarity with regard to what would constitute an effective unified budgetary framework at the country level.

13. Similarly, there is an existing process dealing with United Nations reform issues in the area of the environment, namely the General Assembly informal consultative process on the institutional framework for the United Nations environmental activities. The Panel was cognizant of this process and interacted with it, emphasizing that its recommendations were complementary and intended to provide an impetus to deliberations in that forum. Consultations on the environment-related recommendations put forward by the Panel could thus be taken up by the Assembly's informal consultative process, as appropriate, taking into consideration relevant discussions and decisions in other intergovernmental forums, including the Global Ministerial Environmental Forum of the United Nations Environment Programme Governing Council, the Council of the Global Environment Facility and the conferences of the parties to relevant multilateral environmental agreements. I will be giving due attention, in the light of the intergovernmental process, to the Panel's recommendation that I commission an independent and authoritative assessment of the current United Nations system of international environmental governance.

14. Progress is already being made with regard to the Panel's recommendation that the United Nations System Chief Executives Board for Coordination (CEB) undertake a review of its functioning, in the light of experience gained since its establishment five years ago, with a view to improving its performance and accountability for system-wide coherence. At the session of the CEB held during the fourth quarter of 2006, executive heads unanimously welcomed the broad thrust of the Panel's recommendations and were united in their desire to improve coherence and coordination and enact the necessary system-wide reforms. The Director-General of the International Labour Organization, Juan Somavia, and the Director-General of the World Trade Organization, Pascal Lamy, have been entrusted with the task of leading the CEB review, seeking the full engagement of all executive heads. The intention is for the first session of the CEB, which I will chair, in April 2007, to consider a preliminary set of proposals for action to strengthen the effectiveness and relevance of that

body as a responsive and transparent high-level mechanism under the chairmanship of the Secretary-General, geared to advancing the overall coherence and impact of the United Nations system.

15. The Panel's recommendations are providing further impetus to reform measures on United Nations business practices, which are aimed at significantly enhancing performance and delivery of results. The recommendations are clearly very much in line with my priorities in such areas as transparency, accountability, efficiency and human resources development, including the promotion of staff mobility, and should be actively pursued in all relevant forums. Modernizing and achieving full compatibility on processes for resource planning, human resources, common services and evaluation are essential to turning the concepts of a more unified and coherent United Nations into reality. As much of the work falls within the purview of the CEB High Level Committee on Management, which encompasses representatives of all the agencies, funds and programmes of the United Nations system, a comprehensive progress report from CEB on its work in harmonizing business practices may be helpful to the General Assembly in facilitating its consideration of these matters.

16. Another area in which progress is already being made is with regard to certain recommendations in the humanitarian assistance section of the Panel's report. With respect to food security, advanced discussions among the Rome-based agencies of the United Nations system have already taken place, with a view to developing proposals for the consideration of relevant intergovernmental bodies. However, more needs to be done to further strengthen the Organization's role as a coordinator in terms of enhancing partnerships and its capacities to deal with the transition phase from relief to development. Moreover, more investment is urgently required in risk reduction and early warning, building on existing international initiatives to help mitigate or prevent natural disasters. The Panel makes good recommendations in those and other areas that should be further considered.

17. With regard to the Panel's recommendations to strengthen the Organization's gender architecture, I am in full agreement with the Panel's assessment of the need to consolidate and strengthen several current structures in a dynamic United Nations entity focused on gender equality and women's empowerment, which should mobilize forces of change at the global level and inspire enhanced results at the country level. It is also essential to stress that gender equality will remain the mandate of all United Nations entities. I will also continue to recruit competent women to become part of my senior team.

18. With regard to the proposal on gender equality and women's empowerment, including the establishment of an Under-Secretary-General for Gender Equality and Empowerment of Women, who would lead a consolidated and strengthened United Nations gender architecture subject to approval by the relevant intergovernmental process, the United Nations system and many Member States are united in their conviction that the recommendations would contribute to overall efforts to achieve the goals of gender equality and empowerment of women. However, I will await the outcome of the substantive discussions and consultations by Member States on the proposal in order to be guided further by the intergovernmental process. I hope that Member States will be able to reach a positive early agreement on this proposal so that we can take it forward.

19. With regard to the Panel's recommendations in the area of human rights, I am in full agreement with the Panel that human rights and other cross-cutting issues should be an

integral part of United Nations activities. The United Nations High Commissioner for Human Rights, as the highest official of the United Nations responsible for human rights, should ensure the linkages between the normative work of the United Nations human rights mechanisms and operational activities. It is of utmost importance to support the Human Rights Council to make it into a truly effective body that has the credibility and authority to take forward the Human Rights agenda of the United Nations.

20. One area of the Panel's report which merits in-depth intergovernmental consideration is that of governance. I urge Member States to give due consideration to the recommendations of the Panel in that regard. In the view of the Panel, their recommendations taken together would encompass a framework for a unified and coherent United Nations structure at the country level, matched by more coherent governance, funding and management arrangements at the centre as well as by consistency and coherence at the regional level. The report's recommendations in this area constitute an important starting point for a process that requires further deliberation and discussion to develop a commonly owned vision that should enhance the coherence and efficiency of the intergovernmental structure and reflect the principle of country ownership. The preceding set of issues includes consideration of the proposals made by the Panel relating to the strengthening of the Economic and Social Council as the authoritative forum to ensure more efficient implementation of our common development agenda; the establishment of a Sustainable Development Board as an inclusive strategic overview and governance framework for the implementation of the "One United Nations" approach at the country level; and ensuring support to the Sustainable Development Board, once it is created, through an inter-agency Development Policy and Operations Group, within the CEB framework. This Group could either replace the United Nations Development Group or be a subgroup of the United Nations Development Group explicitly given the task of supporting the new Board. I believe that the aim should be greater coherence at the Headquarters level to support coherence in the field.

21. With that in mind, I concur with the Panel's conclusion that more detailed and specific proposals for further streamlining and consolidation would require a more in-depth technical analysis than was feasible in the time frame available to the Panel. I will thus be giving due consideration to the Panel's proposal that I establish an independent task force to further eliminate duplication within the United Nations system, and consolidate United Nations entities, where necessary, building on the foundations of the Panel's work.

22. I intend to work and consult closely with Member States, the President of the General Assembly and the relevant intergovernmental bodies, which will play a critical role in moving the report forward. In that regard, I have asked the Deputy Secretary-General to oversee and support implementation of the system-wide coherence reform agenda. The Deputy Secretary-General will work closely with relevant senior United Nations officials who will be at the disposal of Member States to facilitate discussion in their respective areas of responsibility. The United Nations system is conscious of the need to urgently take steps to enhance overall coherence and effectiveness, but is equally aware of the need to ensure that efforts to act on the Panel's recommendations are guided by and respectful of the intergovernmental consideration of the Panel's report.

5. Secretariat Reform: Peace Operations and Disarmament, Letter dated 15 February 2007 from the Secretary-General Addressed to the President of the General Assembly, 23 February 2007 (A/61/749)

I am writing to request that you bring to the attention of the General Assembly the present letter and its annexes outlining my intentions with regard to strengthening the capacity of the Organization to manage and sustain peace and security operations and to advance the disarmament agenda.

The annexes provide clarification and additional detail sought by Member States in response to proposals I described in informal consultations with members of the General Assembly on 5 February 2007. Since that time, I have carried out extensive consultations with regional groups and Member States and have continued to refine the proposals in the light of suggestions, views and concerns expressed by Member States. I am grateful for the consultations you have undertaken in this regard and hope you will continue to facilitate the consultation process further. I am also hopeful that the Assembly will be in a position to expeditiously express its approval, in principle, of the attached proposals.

Annex I pertains to measures for strengthening the capacity of the Organization to manage and sustain peace operations. I will present, within a matter of weeks, a report further elaborating the proposals contained in that annex and providing further details, including their full financial implications, for the consideration of the General Assembly during its sixty-first session, in accordance with established procedures. It should be noted at the outset that I intend for these proposals to be resource-neutral with respect to the programme budget for the biennium 2006-2007. Any additional resources required to strengthen the Secretariat, notably the new Department of Peace Operations and Department of Field Support, will be reflected in the forthcoming submission on the support account for peacekeeping operations, together with such requirements as may arise with the latest wave of growth in peacekeeping activity in the field mandated by the Security Council.

Annex II, on advancing the disarmament agenda: a new approach, underscores that general and complete disarmament under strict and effective international control remains a central issue on the global agenda. Current challenges point to the need to revitalize the disarmament and non-proliferation agenda through a more focused effort. I am personally committed to taking action on that agenda. I therefore intend to strengthen the work of the Organization in the area of arms control, disarmament, non-proliferation and related security matters and propose that the Department for Disarmament Affairs be constituted as a separate office in the Secretariat, with a separate budget section, headed by a High Representative.

I should be grateful if you would circulate the present letter and its annexes as a document of the General Assembly under agenda item 112.

(*Signed*) **Ban** Ki-moon

Annex I
Strengthening the capacity of the Organization to manage and sustain peace operations

I. Introduction

1. I intend to undertake a series of measures, outlined below, to strengthen the Secretariat's capacity to manage and sustain United Nations peace operations. I propose a reconfiguration of the current Department of Peacekeeping Operations to create two departments—the Department of Peace Operations and the Department of Field Support. In conjunction with this realignment, I also propose measures to better align authority, responsibilities and resources presently assigned to various Secretariat departments engaged in providing support to peace operations with a view to facilitating clearer performance accountability.

2. The full implementation of these proposals, in my view, would lead to better planning, faster deployment and a more responsive system of support for tens of thousands of United Nations peacekeepers in the field, many of whom are deployed in austere and insecure environments. It would also lead to the more effective, efficient and transparent use of resources placed by Member States at the Secretariat's disposal to implement legislative mandates.

II. The urgency for reform

3. Since the moment I was honoured to be elected by the General Assembly as Secretary-General, I have been consulting widely with Member States, United Nations staff and outside experts to identify areas of the Secretariat in the most pressing need of reform. During these past months, no issue has been mentioned more frequently to me than the need to strengthen the Secretariat's capacity at Headquarters to plan, rapidly deploy, manage and sustain United Nations peace operations.

4. It is widely acknowledged that the Department of Peacekeeping Operations has undergone more intensive reform and strengthening than any other part of the Secretariat, especially since the issuance of the report of the Panel on United Nations Peace Operations (the "Brahimi report") in 2000 (A/55/305-S/2000/809). Such reforms have enabled the Department to confront the enormous challenges of the past six years. It is important to recall that the objective of the 2000 reform agenda was to equip the Department with sufficient capability to launch one new multidisciplinary mission per year. Yet, the past 36 months alone have seen the start-up or expansion of nine field missions, with three additional missions currently in active start-up. Over the course of the next year, the number of personnel in United Nations peace operations could increase by as much as 40 per cent.

5. The unique nature of United Nations peace operations, and a proven record on the ground, has led the Member States to place ever-increasing demands on United Nations peacekeeping. The number of peace operations is at an all-time high, with almost 100,000 personnel in the field. It appears that the figure will rise still further in 2007. Last year alone, the United Nations started negotiations for memorandums of understanding with more than 100 troop-contributing countries, transported more than 800,000 passengers and 160,000 tons of cargo by air and operated more than 200 hospitals and clinics in the field. Furthermore, more than half of the staff of the Secretariat serve in field operations. No other multinational actor deploys the same number of military and civilian personnel. No bilateral partner engages in multiple field operations of such scope and complexity.

6. Because of the surge in demand, and despite the diligent efforts of our colleagues in peacekeeping, our system is dramatically strained and overstretched. This comes at a time when we can least afford it, as we plan and prepare for new peace operations in Darfur and elsewhere around the world. I have provided a more detailed account of the nature and implications of the surge in peacekeeping activity in my recently issued report on the implementation of the recommendations of the Special Committee on Peacekeeping Operations (A/61/668 and Add.1). There are many non-structurally-related initiatives proposed in that report that seek to strengthen the Secretariat's ability to address the surge in demand. These include measures to strengthen the operational capacity of Headquarters military and police components, the reinforcement of an integrated approach to support for the enforcement and reform of the rule of law and a greater focus on core business so as to enable the timely and sustainable drawdown of United Nations peace operations. I look forward to the Secretariat's dialogue with the Special Committee on Peacekeeping Operations on those initiatives, as well as on the relevant details regarding the implementation of the proposals outlined herein.

7. Without wishing to prejudge the outcome of Member States' deliberations in the Special Committee and other appropriate bodies, including the Fifth Committee and the Advisory Committee on Administrative and Budgetary Questions, my consultations to date with Member States appear to indicate near consensus on one stark reality: the United Nations faces a real problem; the current approach to mounting and sustaining peacekeeping operations in the field will not sustain the explosive growth in the demand for and complexity of those operations without significant change.

8. The ability of the Department of Peacekeeping Operations to keep up with the growing demand is challenged in nearly every dimension: the leadership—dedicated and hard-working—is impossibly overstretched. The Department's Senior Management Team, comprising a single Under-Secretary-General, two Assistant Secretaries-General, Director-level Military and Police Advisers, a Director of Change Management and a Director for Mine Action, oversee the vast stretch of operations in the field. This small group must manage and attend to every aspect of peace operations, large and small. Everything from the timely planning of missions to sensitive political negotiations and ensuring the timely delivery of critical spare parts can and do require their personal attention. They are, of course, supported by committed and expert staff at various levels, whose numbers also require strengthening, but the requirement for greater leadership and senior-level management is ever present. In addition, the growing complexity of field operations in every dimension—from the intricacies of multi-layered political processes to the highly technical nature of support services to the specialized requirements necessitated by United Nations rules and regulations—place an added premium on senior personnel who are experts not only on substance but also on management.

9. Moreover, current systems in place to support operations in the field simply cannot keep up with the continuous, often simultaneous, demand for resources, services and staff that has grown several times over in the past three years alone. Many examples exist in multiple areas. Routine procurement transactions are now stalled under the sheer weight of their volume. The budget process for field missions is now nearly year-round, as new missions continue to evolve and significant adjustments are made to existing missions. Annual mission staff turnover averages 30 per cent, with it being extremely difficult to keep some of our most difficult missions reliably staffed—especially in critical technical functions.

10. Compounding these difficulties, the diffusion of authority and responsibility among field offices and multiple departments at Headquarters make it impossible to fix responsibility for fully delivering timely and reliable supplies and services to the field. Simply put, there is no single place in the United Nations system right now with the full responsibility, authority and resources necessary to ensure that peacekeeping missions have what they need, when they need it, to succeed in their mandates. Having said this, I am mindful that appropriate controls to mitigate risk and ensure competent oversight must be maintained. But these measures are an incomplete guarantee for successful, efficient operations when the foregoing alignment of conditions is absent.

11. In essence, a variety of problems need to be addressed urgently. The foregoing discussion demonstrates that there is a clear case for consolidating all responsibility, authority and resources currently assigned to different departments in the Secretariat within a single department dedicated to planning, deploying, managing and sustaining all peacekeeping and related field operations. On the other hand, such a consolidation under a single Under-Secretary-General for Peace Operations would fail to address the problem of managerial overstretching. It would not address the fact that other parts of the Secretariat manage field-based activities as well, albeit at a fraction of the scale. It could undermine the important independent role that must be played by such critical actors as the Legal Counsel or the Controller on behalf of the Secretariat as a whole, and it could challenge efforts to preserve Organization-wide standards and coherence.

12. I have thus concluded that the best way to reconcile these competing demands is through a substantial consolidation of authority, responsibility and resources under one Under-Secretary-General for Field Support heading a department that specializes in that function. I believe this move would dramatically reduce duplication of effort and provide focused attention to this vital area of expertise. In general, I firmly believe in the necessity to promote clearer lines of accountability and a sharper differentiation of roles and responsibilities among my most senior staff. At the same time, I recognize that the creation of two Under-Secretaries-General—where one presently exists—creates a new set of challenges, given the interrelated nature of operations and support in virtually all aspects of peacekeeping. The challenge is therefore to enable the two departments to fulfil their specialized responsibilities while concurrently ensuring that where the operational need exists they act as one, in an integrated manner at all levels. In reacting to my evolving thinking on the matter during informal consultations, Member States urged that I examine these challenges and propose means of addressing them while ensuring adherence to certain key principles. The key principles include:

- Clarity of departmental roles and responsibilities
- Unity of command and integration of effort
- Alignment of responsibilities and consolidation of resources
- Preserving Organization-wide standards and coherence

13. I am confident that the proposals outlined below will respond to the urgent challenges facing the Organization while adhering to these principles and making the Secretariat more responsive to the needs of our women and men in the field.

III. Proposed roles and responsibilities of the Department of Peace Operations and the Department of Field Support

14. As I have discussed with Member States, I propose to establish a new Department of Field Support. The entirety of the current Office of Mission Support of the Department of Peacekeeping Operations would be transferred to the Department of Field Support, as would some additional resources from the Department of Management. The Department of Field Support would also require additional new resources funded through the support account for peacekeeping operations that would in any event have been requested for the Office of Mission Support and the Department of Management in direct response to the ongoing surge in peacekeeping demands.

15. Within the overall policy and oversight framework established by the Department of Management on my behalf, I intend to empower and hold accountable the Department of Field Support in undertaking the administration and management of field personnel, procurement, information and communication technology and finances for United Nations peace operations. Responsibilities and resources will continue to be centralized where services are provided Organization- or system-wide and where significant economies of scale are achieved.

16. This consolidation of support functions would lead to:

- More effective, coherent and responsive support to field operations
- More efficient management of Member States' resources
- Clearer lines of responsibility and accountability through the establishment of a single entry point for the full range of field support needs

It would also allow a separate, concentrated Department of Peace Operations to focus on the work it needs to do: strategic as well as day-to-day direction and management of peace-keeping operations; new mission planning; implementation of policies and standards; and fostering partnerships with a broad range of United Nations and non-United Nations actors, including regional organizations.

17. The creation of two departments would not only improve structural capacity, it would also give peace operations desperately needed additional senior posts. It would help to strengthen the heavily overburdened senior management team of today's Department of Peacekeeping Operations, which performs its tasks with outstanding commitment but under relentless and unsustainable pressure.

18. Taken together, these measures would bolster and improve the assistance that Headquarters provides to field missions and to field personnel contributed by the Member States. It would mean more and better policy guidance from a dedicated Department of Peace Operations; enhanced responsiveness from a Department of Field Support properly equipped and specialized to address mission support needs; and, by equipping the departments expeditiously with the human, material and financial resources they need to do their jobs, a better way to ensure the safety and security of personnel and the prospects for successful mandate implementation.

19. By increasing capacity and designating clear responsibilities, we can also strengthen training and maximize oversight—both of which are essential in ensuring the highest

standards of conduct and discipline among United Nations peacekeeping personnel. I am determined to ensure that we protect and uphold the sacred trust that needs to exist between the United Nations and the populations we serve and to implement our zero-tolerance policy on sexual abuse and exploitation.

20. The proposed organization charts for the Department of Peace Operations and the Department of Field Support are attached (see appendix, sects. A and B). Detailed information outlining the roles and responsibilities of each of the components indicated in the charts has been prepared and can readily be made available.

IV. Unity of command and integration of effort

21. Clearly, these proposals can succeed only if the envisaged realignment preserves the principles of unity of command and integration of effort. There are very few operational issues and decisions that do not have significant support implications and vice versa. Success cannot be achieved if the two departments do not work in an integrated manner, at all levels, in the field and at Headquarters.

22. I intend to maintain unity of command and integration of effort at the field level by preserving the existing overall authority of my special representatives and heads of mission over all mission components, including the military, police and administrative components. Directors and Chiefs of Administration will report directly and exclusively to the Special Representative of the Secretary-General or Head of Mission. (This is a change in current arrangements, whereby Directors and Chiefs of Administration have a second reporting line to the Assistant Secretary-General for Mission Support on matters pertaining to the staff and financial regulations and rules.) It must be understood that the Special Representative of the Secretary-General or Head of Mission will be the ultimate authority at the mission level for all aspects of United Nations operations and support. In strengthening the authority of the heads of mission, I also intend to hold them accountable for proper resource management in accordance with established policies and procedures.

23. The Special Representative of the Secretary-General or Head of Mission will have a single, clear reporting line to the Secretary-General through the Under-Secretary-General for Peace Operations. Existing command and control arrangements applicable to force commanders in the field will not change.

24. To ensure unity of command and integration of effort at the Headquarters level, the Under-Secretary-General for Field Support will report to and receive direction from the Under-Secretary-General for Peace Operations on all issues that fall under the purview of United Nations peacekeeping. This arrangement will be an improvement over the current situation because the Department of Peace Operations will have directive authority over a department—the Department of Field Support—which will be more empowered and equipped than the current Office of Mission Support to address field support needs.

25. To facilitate the integration of effort between the joint decision-making bodies of the two departments, information-sharing mechanisms and shared resources will be set up. Joint senior decision-making bodies will be established to address cross-cutting and strategic issues on policy formulation, resources, information management, public information and engagement with United Nations and non-United Nations partners. Senior officials of the two departments will jointly address strategic and emergency issues in specific

missions through regular meetings chaired by the Department of Peace Operations. Joint morning meetings at the Director level, weekly staff town hall meetings and shared Intranet resource platforms will be key information-sharing mechanisms to support unity of command and effort.

26. Certain resource capacities (which will include a mix of political, support, military and police personnel, as appropriate) will be shared by the two departments, encouraging unity of approach and policy coherence but also enabling efficiency gains. The two departments will share policy development as well as a common doctrine, best practices (in which the gender and HIV/AIDS advisers will remain) and evaluation and training capacities, all to be located in the Department of Peace Operations. They will also both draw upon a capacity intended to identify and develop strategic peacekeeping partnerships with a wide range of United Nations and non-United Nations actors as well as a public information and external relations support capacity located in the Office of the Under-Secretary-General for Peace Operations. A crisis management response capacity will also be shared through the Situation Centre, located in the Department of Peace Operations. This will facilitate an integrated response to crises and emergencies in the field. The Department of Field Support, meanwhile, will be responsible for the management and administration of information management capacity for peacekeeping, as well as for conduct and discipline, and for providing secretariat support to the senior field leadership selection process. To facilitate close working relationships at all levels, the two departments will be co-located. A shared Executive Office will support the administration of both departments.

27. Arguably the most essential vehicle to unity and coherence is the establishment and reinforcement of integrated structures and processes. The central vehicle for the integrated planning and conduct of United Nations peace operations is the integrated operational team concept introduced in 2006 as part of the peacekeeping reform agenda entitled "Peace operations 2010". The Department of Peace Operations will be responsible for leading the establishment and management of integrated operational teams, bringing together expertise from both departments to provide integrated policy and operational backstopping for field missions as well as integrated advice for senior management. Integrated operational teams will also provide a single entry point for troop- and police-contributing countries and United Nations and non-United Nations partners to engage in the planning and conduct of integrated peacekeeping operations. Military and police personnel from the Department of Peace Operations and support specialists from the Department of Field Support will be outposted to integrated operational teams. The structure of the teams is depicted in section C of the appendix. Details of the envisaged roles and responsibilities of the teams can readily be made available.

28. The successful functioning of integrated operational teams will depend on the extent to which coherent guidance and processes are in place to enable integrated planning and operational support. The integrated mission planning process is essential in this regard. Significant progress has already been made in developing the integrated mission planning process as a system-wide model for integrated United Nations operations. In order to ensure the continued development and implementation of the planning process throughout Headquarters and in the field, a dedicated integrated mission planning process support capacity will be established in the Department of Peace Operations to support integrated operational teams in providing coherent, responsive planning and support for United

Nations peacekeeping operations. Integrated mission planning process guidance will be delivered at Headquarters and in the field to all relevant personnel of the two departments.

V. Interrelationships with other departments: alignment of responsibilities and resources

29. The measures set out above will help to clarify the roles and responsibilities of the Department of Peace Operations and the Department of Field Support as well as the expectations of how they will work together as one. Likewise, it is essential to clarify the division of labour between the Department of Field Support and the Department of Management. The latter will continue to play its role on my behalf in providing the policy direction and oversight needed to ensure the appropriate as well as consistent implementation of General Assembly resolutions. Authority, responsibility, accountability and resources will be aligned to preserve Organization-wide coherence and economies of scale while ensuring operational effectiveness in the areas of human resources management, finance, information technology and procurement. Measures to satisfy these imperatives in support of United Nations peace operations are set out below. On broader management issues, the Department of Field Support will work together with the Department of Management, under the guidance of the Deputy Secretary-General, to ensure the system-wide coherence of management practices.

Field personnel

30. The responsibility for delivering mandates entrusted to peacekeeping operations rests on the shoulders of our personnel serving in the field. In many respects, we are only as good as the quality and timeliness of our deployments and our ability to get the right people to the right place at the right time. The dramatic expansion of peacekeeping activities in the post-cold-war period has demonstrated that the human resources management processes and systems designed over the course of nearly 50 years to meet the traditional and stable needs of our Organization were ill suited to respond to the current and projected operational tempo. Just as the failure to put boots on the ground can damage the preservation of a fragile peace, so too can the failure to deploy civilian personnel as rapidly as required damage significantly our ability to support those troops and carry out the full range of duties entrusted to this Organization in a post-conflict environment. Those we serve deserve to be sent our best and brightest, with urgency and diligence.

31. To address those needs, in 1994 the Office of Human Resources Management of the Department of Management delegated a broad range of authority to the Department of Peacekeeping Operations. While the exercise of such authority has led to the development of rapid-deployment mechanisms and administrative procedures that respond more adequately to operational needs, the dynamic evolution of the mandates of United Nations field operations demands that we improve still further our responsiveness and effectiveness. To this end, expanded delegated authority will be vested in the Department of Field Support to empower and hold it accountable for the recruitment, management and administration of field personnel. Decision-making authority will be given, in particular, in areas where the casework related to the recruitment or placement of staff is already being reviewed at both the mission and Headquarters levels or where, as certified by the Office of Human Resources Management, resident Department of Field Support expertise exists,

for example, to design and classify jobs for United Nations peace operations against International Civil Service Commission and organizational standards. Processes will be further streamlined to eliminate review stages where little or no value is added.

32. The structures and systems needed to carry out this additional authority and fulfil the new roles and responsibilities already reside in great part in the current field personnel function in the Department of Peacekeeping Operations. The direction and management structure, field personnel support capacities and quality assurance mechanisms will, however, need to be strengthened to address the breadth and depth of the delegated authority and the size and scope of field mission human resources requirements and related responsibilities exercised at Headquarters and in the field.

33. Central authority for the establishment of Organization-wide policies and standards governing all human resources management matters will be retained by the Office of Human Resources Management, in line with its mandate as the central authority within the Secretariat to interpret and enforce the Staff Regulations and Rules and ensure consistency of standards Organization-wide. This includes the determination of contractual arrangements and conditions of service Organization- and/or system-wide and the establishment of salary scales for locally recruited staff, mission subsistence allowance rates and other benefits and entitlements. The Office of Human Resources Management will continue to represent the Secretariat before the General Assembly, the International Civil Service Commission, the High Level Committee on Management of the United Nations Chief Executives Board for Coordination and other bodies on Organization-wide human resources management and compensation issues, with support from the Department of Field Support on matters related to field personnel. The Office of Human Resources Management will also maintain its responsibility to monitor and evaluate the exercise of its delegated human resources management authority.

34. Finally, the Office of Human Resources Management will retain overall authority to establish, review and monitor overall health policy for the United Nations, including staff counselling, health and fitness standards, standards of health care and service delivery and clinical standards and qualifications for United Nations health-care professionals. The authority to plan and assess medical support for field operations and to approve and conduct medical evacuation and clearance procedures will be exercised by the Department of Field Support, in consultation with the Office of Human Resources Management.

35. The resources allocated to the Office of Human Resources Management related to the exercise of its responsibilities with respect to policies and standards governing all human resources management matters, Organization- and/or system-wide conditions of service and oversight and monitoring of authority delegated to the Department of Field Support will remain intact. The allocation of responsibilities and resources related to internal justice will be dealt with separately in the context of the implementation of internal justice system reform.

Field budget and finance

36. The current budgetary process for peacekeeping operations does not fully meet requirements. Budget personnel from missions currently engage with two departments at Headquarters (the Department of Peacekeeping Operations and the Department of Management) to prepare their budgets in a timely manner. Lines of communication need to be rationalized. Deadlines are often not met and budgets do not serve their appropriate role

as strategic policy and management documents required to put resources to their fullest and most effective use.

37. To correct these shortcomings and to streamline the budgetary process, I intend to strengthen the capabilities of the Finance Management and Support Service so as to ensure that the Department of Field Support has the analytical and information-processing capacity required to prepare budget proposals and performance reports at a standard appropriate for submission to the General Assembly. Such strengthening would include greater attention to the application of consistent and coherent costing standards. In line with the best public practice principles, the Department of Management will retain the final authority to submit budgets to the Assembly on my behalf. In addition, the Department of Management will reorient its focus on and strengthen its strategic analysis of peacekeeping budgeting.

Field communications and information technology

38. The rationalization of processes also applies to the area of information and communication technology. The Information Technology Services Division of the Department of Management and the Communications and Information Technology Service of the Department of Peacekeeping Operations currently share responsibility for some aspects of the provision of information and communication technology services to field missions. For example, while the Communications and Information Technology Service is responsible for the management of over 350 satellite Earth stations located in the field, it does not manage the one at United Nations Headquarters, which provides a vital link from New York to the field. I intend to propose the streamlining and consolidation of this service under the new Department of Field Support to reduce the duplication of responsibilities and enhance the provision of reliable and uninterrupted service to the field. In addition, at present, the secure voice and data network, which provides secure services for the exchange of confidential information, is managed within the Information Technology Services Division. This capability is essential for the management of field missions and so should be consolidated, again, in the Department of Field Support. Finally, as the new office of the Chief Information Technology Officer takes shape, I will ensure that the Department of Field Support discharges its responsibilities in the area of field information management and systems consistently within the overall system-wide policy direction set by that office.

Field procurement

39. To address the multitude of time-critical field support functions in a responsive manner, procurement management must be streamlined and strengthened. I believe that integrating the procurement function with operational delivery will work best to support field operations.

40. I draw this conclusion in part because of the very different circumstances that drive Headquarters procurement as compared with procurement for field operations. Headquarters procurement is embedded in and relies on established and well-functioning markets operating under strong regulatory regimes where multiple vendors of high-quality products and services exist. Redundant and reliable lines of communication for product and service delivery readily support the procurement process, and contract failure can often be quickly mitigated with substitute vendors (while redress against non-performance is pursued). In this kind of commercial and physical environment, a premium can and is placed on the need to secure the best value.

41. In contrast, many—indeed most—of our peacekeeping and other missions in the field simply do not enjoy the same advantages. Markets are often weak, with some sectors completely non-viable. Regulatory frameworks suffer from a general absence of the rule of law, and lines of communication are long, subject to easy interdiction and increasingly dangerous. In this kind of commercial and physical environment, a balance must be struck among the equally important factors of value, quality and timeliness of delivery. In addition, contract failure can present a major impediment to mandate implementation, as many weeks and months are lost in the search for a replacement vendor. In my view, these factors argue strongly for a dedicated and separate capacity to deal with the specialized needs of field procurement.

42. I therefore intend to vest authority for field support procurement with the Department of Field Support by delegating procurement authority to that department as well as the authority to appoint procurement officers at Headquarters and in the field. This change in authority will entail a transfer of resources from the present Procurement Division in the Department of Management to the Department of Field Support. I do not, however, intend to promote or have duplicative structures. Therefore, a common vendor database, a joint vendor review committee, a common procurement manual that takes fully into account the needs of field procurement and common information technology systems for both field and Headquarters procurement will be maintained. A considerably strengthened and nearly full-time Headquarters Committee on Contracts, including representation from the Department of Field Support, will facilitate the handling of the growing volume of field procurement actions and will report to the Department of Field Support for peacekeeping procurement and to the Department of Management for other requirements. Procedures will be put in place to ensure that threshold levels for review by the Headquarters Committee on Contracts are established jointly by the Department of Management and the Department of Field Support and that appropriate priority is given to immediate review in cases of urgent operational requirements.

43. In addition, I intend to examine the possibility of establishing regional procurement offices to significantly enhance the procurement opportunities for developing countries and countries with economies in transition. More details regarding this and the other responsibilities I am proposing for the Department of Field Support will be forthcoming in subsequent reports. I welcome the opportunity to discuss this and other aspects of this initiative during the current session of the General Assembly.

Support for public information components in field operations

44. I believe that the measures noted in the preceding sections substantially clarify the roles and responsibilities of the Department of Peace Operations, the Department of Field Support and the Department of Management and the interrelationships between them. I believe that it is warranted to do so as well with respect to the roles and responsibilities of the Department of Peace Operations and the Department of Public Information, in particular with respect to the backstopping of public information needs in peace operations.

45. An effective public information component is widely acknowledged to be a political and operational necessity for the success of any peace operation. It serves an invaluable function in explaining the mandate of the mission, establishing direct communication with host communities and promoting an atmosphere of constructive dialogue and reconciliation.

The ongoing growth in peace operations also highlights the need for troop, police and financial contributors to be able to demonstrate to domestic constituencies the tangible improvements resulting from their participation in and support for United Nations peacekeeping, as well as explaining the measures in place to prevent and respond to misconduct that undermines confidence in the United Nations as a whole. The Brahimi report placed considerable emphasis on this subject in 2000, and since then Member States have increased the percentage of mission budgets dedicated to public information, which is often the largest substantive civilian component of peacekeeping operations. However, during this period of increase in the scope and complexity of public information work, the capacity at Headquarters to support field components and to ensure the best staff and most effective use of resources has remained static. In the light of these coming challenges, the current public information configuration at Headquarters is no longer tenable.

46. The responsibility for supporting the wide range of public information activities relating to peace operations is currently divided between the Department of Public Information and the Department of Peacekeeping Operations. While the Department of Public Information has a limited number of posts dedicated to such activities, the Department of Peacekeeping Operations has never had a dedicated public information capacity and has compensated for this by shifting internal resources in a limited and ad hoc manner to meet the demand. The unprecedented surge in United Nations peacekeeping has clearly overstretched the relevant capabilities of both departments. The consolidation of support resources that I propose will provide a much-needed opportunity to reclarify roles and maximize existing resources, leveraging the comparative advantages of each department and protecting the significant investment of the international community in public information in the field. To this end, I intend to establish a public affairs unit within the Department of Peace Operations that will assume responsibility for media relations, departmental publicity, external relations and corporate messaging/internal communications. The new unit will also provide advice on budgetary, administrative, staffing and technical matters to public information components in the field and integrated operations teams at Headquarters. The Departments of Public Information, Peace Operations and Field Support will work jointly on planning, policy, training and evaluation. In line with its overall mandate for United Nations public information and in accordance with General Assembly resolution 61/121 B, the Department of Public Information will also continue to play an important role by providing strategic communications support to United Nations peace operations. The new unit in the Department of Peace Operations will allow for better use of the comparative advantages of all three departments and will promote greater efficiency, increase accountability and ensure more effective use of existing resources.

Preservation of existing arrangements with respect to other departments' allocated resources and responsibilities for support to peacekeeping

47. There are three other departments with resources allocated from the support account that have distinct responsibilities for Headquarters support to peacekeeping: the Office of Legal Affairs, the Department of Safety and Security and the Office of Internal Oversight Services.

48. In order to maintain the independence of the Legal Counsel and the role of the Office of Legal Affairs as the central legal service of the Organization, and thereby the consistency of legal advice provided throughout the Organization, I do not propose to transfer to the

Department of Field Support or the Department of Peace Operations existing authority, responsibilities or resources presently allocated to the Office of Legal Affairs for support to peacekeeping. The provision of a small legal capacity in the Office of the Under-Secretary-General for Field Support is required, however, to facilitate timely and effective interactions between the Office of Legal Affairs and the Department of Field Support on what will be an even greater volume of support issues requiring legal review and expert legal advice.

49. With regard to the safety and security of field personnel, I am mindful that a significant investment has been made only recently to upgrade the capacity of the United Nations to promote the security and safety of civilian personnel in the field, including through the establishment of the Department of Safety and Security. Therefore, I do not intend to change the roles and responsibilities of that department with respect to peacekeeping. However, the Departments of Safety and Security, Peace Operations and Field Support will need to review and revise certain existing standard operating procedures to take into account the proposed realignment of the Department of Peacekeeping Operations.

50. With regard to oversight and in accordance with its existing mandate, the Office of Internal Oversight Services will continue to provide internal oversight over the activities of the Department of Peace Operations and the Department of Field Support through independent auditing, monitoring, inspection, evaluation and investigation of Headquarters activities and peace operations in the field. To that end, the Office will continue to review internal controls and management practices and, where necessary, make recommendations to promote the responsible administration of resources, assign accountability, improve transparency and enhance efficiency and effectiveness in the management of peace operations.

VI. Conclusion

51. The proposals I have set out above may appear, at first glance, to be a radical overhaul of the way the Secretariat is structured and organized to support peace operations. Together, however, they represent the continuation and culmination of the collective efforts of Member States to address the fundamental issue of how we can best equip this Organization to carry out the responsibilities and tasks mandated in support of international peace and security. The Brahimi report of 2000, the report of the High-level Panel on Threats, Challenges and Change (A/59/565, annex), the 2005 World Summit Outcome (resolution 60/1) and the peacekeeping reform agenda outlined in "Peace operations 2010" have been distinct stages during the process to establish responsive, effective and accountable United Nations peace operations.

52. I am mindful of my responsibility to contribute to the collective effort to enable United Nations peace operations to meet the challenges of the future. The success of United Nations peacekeeping depends on the ability of the Organization to evolve at the same rate as the new challenges and demands confronting it. We owe it to the millions of people around the world who put their faith in United Nations peace operations on a daily basis. I look forward to working with the Member States to build on this confidence and to ensure that peacekeeping remains a flagship of activity not only for the United Nations, but for the global community.

Appendix
Organization chart

A. Department of Peace Operations

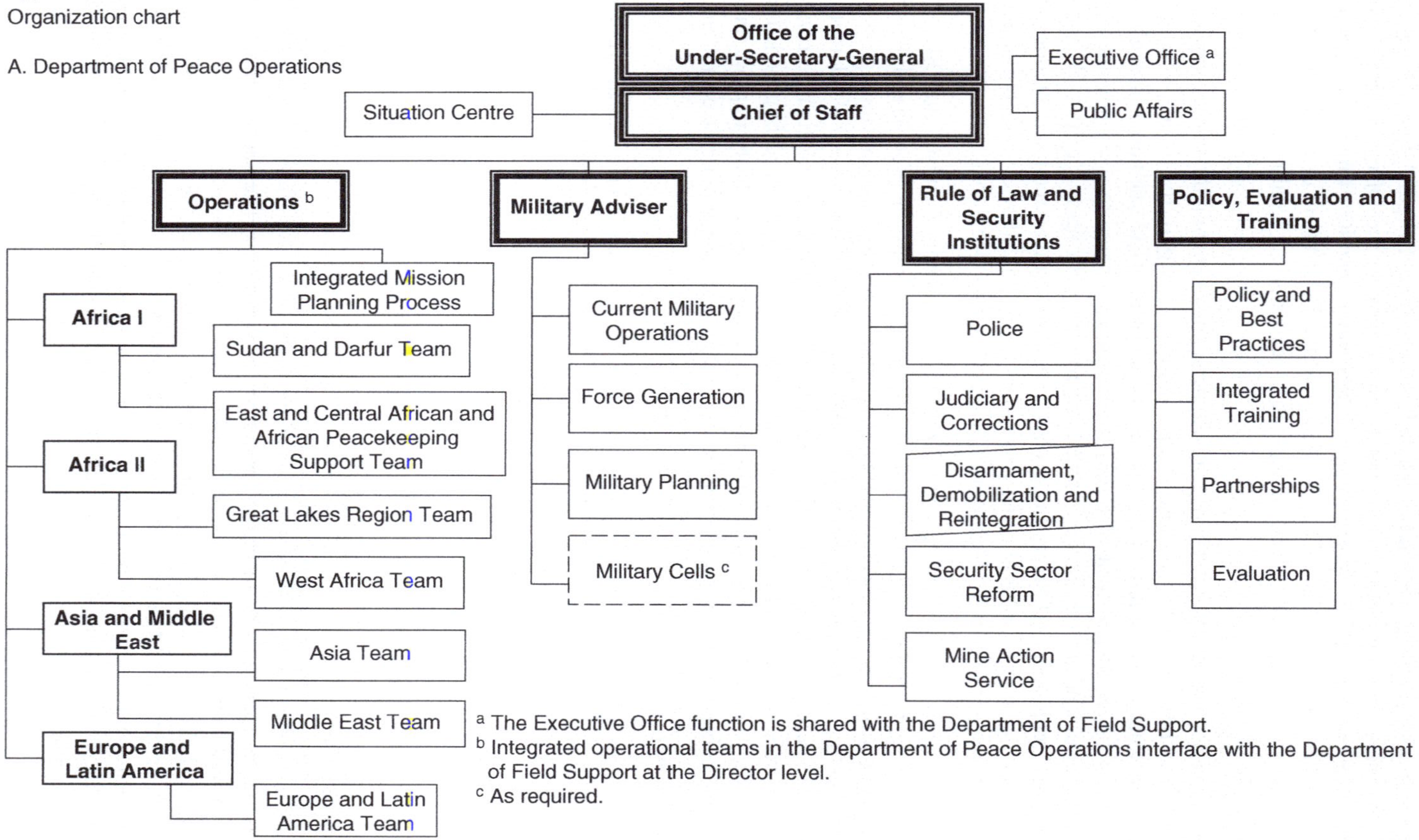

[a] The Executive Office function is shared with the Department of Field Support.
[b] Integrated operational teams in the Department of Peace Operations interface with the Department of Field Support at the Director level.
[c] As required.

B. Department of Field Support[a]

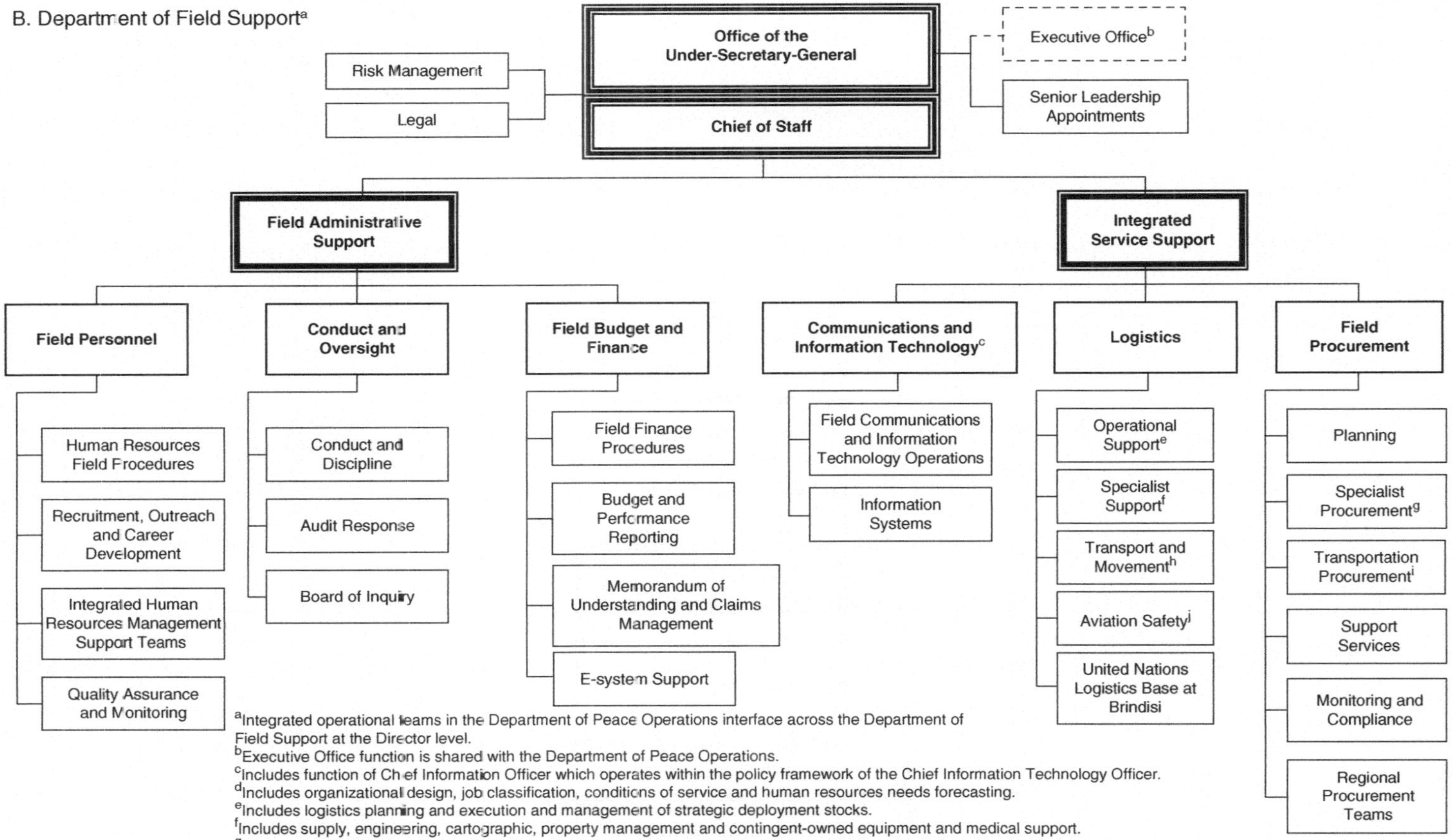

[a]Integrated operational teams in the Department of Peace Operations interface across the Department of Field Support at the Director level.
[b]Executive Office function is shared with the Department of Peace Operations.
[c]Includes function of Chief Information Officer which operates within the policy framework of the Chief Information Technology Officer.
[d]Includes organizational design, job classification, conditions of service and human resources needs forecasting.
[e]Includes logistics planning and execution and management of strategic deployment stocks.
[f]Includes supply, engineering, cartographic, property management and contingent-owned equipment and medical support.
[g]Procurement activity in support of supply, engineering, cartography, medical, communications and information technology.
[h]Includes air and surface transport and movement control functions.
[i]Procurement activity in support of air and surface transport functions.
[j]Aviation safety function could be transferred to the Department of Safety and Security.

C. Integrated operational teams

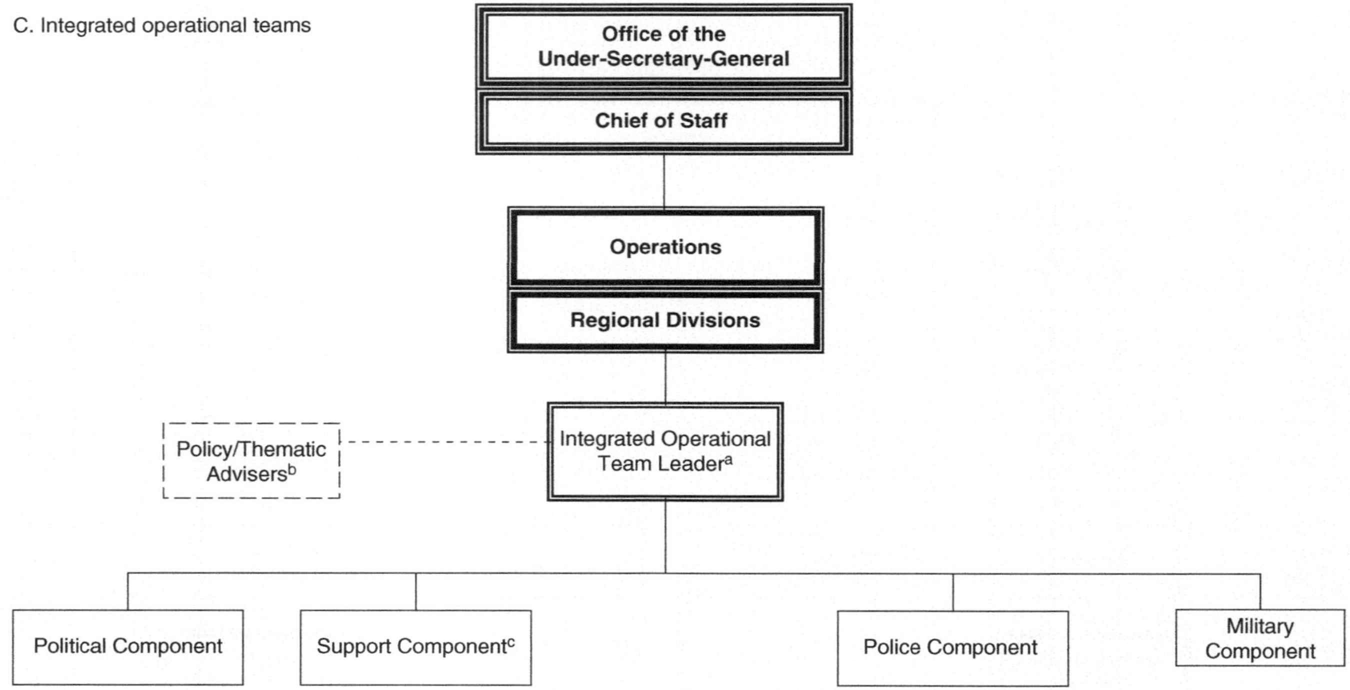

Composition
Team leader
Political Affairs Officers
Two military officers — Military advice to integrated operational team and liaison to Military Division
Two police officers — police advice to integrated operational team and liaison to Military Division
One Administrative Department of Field Support mission support specialist
One logistics Department of Field Support mission support specialist

[a]Each of the seven operational teams is headed by a team leader reporting to the Director of one of the four regional divisions in Operations.
[b]Integrated operational teams will draw on the expertise of the policy and thematic advisers.
[c]Support includes administration and logistics personnel and other Department of Field Support specialists as required.

Annex II
Advancing the disarmament agenda: a new approach

I. The urgency of reform

1. At the 2005 World Summit, Heads of State and Government underscored a difficult and challenging moment for disarmament and non-proliferation and the need for more decisive international efforts in those fields. The absence of meaningful outcomes in certain areas (for example, the failure of the 2005 Review Conference of the Parties to the Treaty on the Non-Proliferation of Nuclear Weapons, the deadlock in the Conference on Disarmament on its priorities, the need for new impetus for the entry into force of the Comprehensive Nuclear Test Ban Treaty and the outcome of the United Nations Conference to Review Progress made in the Implementation of the Programme of Action to Prevent, Combat and Eradicate the Illicit Trade in Small Arms and Light Weapons in All Its Aspects) underscores the need for determined leadership at the highest level to revitalize the disarmament agenda.

2. This deeply alarming situation makes clear the need to revitalize the disarmament and non-proliferation agenda through a more focused effort. I believe in the need for a greater role and personal involvement of the Secretary-General in this regard.

3. I strongly believe, therefore, that a new emphasis needs to be imparted on the essential functions of the existing Department for Disarmament Affairs through a combination of high-level commitment and appropriate institutional support. This must ensure that the United Nations has a strengthened institutional foundation and management mechanism to succeed in its central role and primary responsibility in supporting Member States in their disarmament and non-proliferation efforts.

4. I have thus concluded that what is needed is an office headed by a High Representative so as to maximize the flexibility, agility and proximity to the Secretary-General required to facilitate ongoing and new disarmament and non-proliferation efforts. It would also allow for more systematic interaction between the Secretary-General and the High Representative.

II. Proposed role and responsibilities of the Office for Disarmament Affairs

5. For the reasons articulated above, a managerial reorganization of the Department for Disarmament Affairs will be effected so that the new office, with a direct line to me, will ensure effective interaction with my office and relevant United Nations departments. The new office will be in place to respond effectively to the priorities of Member States in the disarmament and non-proliferation area and will ensure effective interaction with the General Assembly, the Security Council and other legislative bodies.

6. The establishment of the Office takes fully into account current trends and developments, as well as Member States' expressed interest in finding ways to address new challenges in the area of disarmament and non-proliferation. Its mandate will continue to derive from the priorities established in relevant General Assembly resolutions and decisions in the field of disarmament, including the Final Document of the Tenth Special Session of the General Assembly, adopted by consensus at the first special session devoted to disarmament (resolution S-10/2). The programme of the Office will also be guided by

the United Nations Millennium Declaration (resolution 55/2) and will take into account other relevant United Nations resolutions.

7. In this connection, it is recalled that the fifth preambular paragraph of General Assembly resolution 61/60 indicated that the convening of a fourth special session of the Assembly devoted to disarmament "would offer an opportunity to review, from a perspective more in tune with the current international situation, the most critical aspects of the process of disarmament and to mobilize the international community and public opinion in favour of the elimination of nuclear and other weapons of mass destruction and of the control and reduction of conventional weapons". In the seventh preambular paragraph of the resolution, Member States reiterated their "conviction that a special session of the General Assembly devoted to disarmament can set the future course of action in the fields of disarmament, arms control, non-proliferation and related international security matters".

8. The Office will retain the current five branches of the Department for Disarmament Affairs (see appendix) and functions and will continue to implement existing mandates. It will continue to provide substantive and organizational support for norm-setting in the area of disarmament through the work of the General Assembly and its First Committee, the Disarmament Commission, the Conference on Disarmament and other bodies. The Director-General of the United Nations Office at Geneva will continue to act as the Secretary-General of the Conference on Disarmament and the Personal Representative of the Secretary-General to the Conference, reporting directly to the Secretary-General on matters pertaining to the Conference.

9. Under a High Representative, the work would be re-energized for simultaneous action on both disarmament and non-proliferation in all its aspects. The two objectives are inextricably linked, and neither can advance without the other. The Office will continue its work in support of universal adherence to international disarmament and non-proliferation treaties and agreements and their full and effective implementation.

10. Weapons of mass destruction, in particular nuclear weapons, continue to be of primary concern to the Organization. The Office will continue to assist Member States in promoting, strengthening and consolidating multilaterally negotiated principles and norms in all areas of disarmament and non-proliferation in all its aspects in order to help maintain international peace and security and to contribute to global efforts against terrorism. It will also support efforts aimed at further advancement in nuclear disarmament, which will contribute to consolidating the international regime for nuclear non-proliferation and thereby to ensuring international peace and security.

11. Conventional weapons, especially small arms and light weapons and landmines, continue to receive increased attention from the international community in view of the havoc that these weapons are inflicting on peoples' daily lives, particularly in conflict-ridden regions. The Office will continue to support efforts for the further implementation of the Programme of Action adopted at the United Nations Conference on the Illicit Trade in Small Arms and Light Weapons in All Its Aspects, as well as Member States' efforts to establish common international standards for the import, export and transfer of conventional arms. It will promote transparency, based on the principle of undiminished security for all, and confidence-building measures in the field of disarmament. Through its regional centres for peace and disarmament, the Office will assist Member States in promoting

regional approaches to disarmament, non-proliferation in all its aspects and regional and international peace and security.

12. The Office will continue to contribute to efforts to enhance disarmament expertise in Member States, particularly in developing countries. New emphasis will be put on tailored dialogue, cooperation and assistance to Member States in order to help States build capacity to counter the proliferation of weapons of mass destruction, as well as to tackle the proliferation of small arms and light weapons.

13. The Office will also carry out such emerging mandates as Member States may entrust to the Organization. Any programmatic adjustments would result only from the successful conclusion of negotiations in the appropriate multilateral forums.

III. Functions and responsibilities of the High Representative for Disarmament Affairs

14. The functions of the High Representative will be focused on four core areas:

(a) Policy development and coordination functions in the area of disarmament and non-proliferation in all its aspects in support of the Secretary-General;

(b) Advocacy of disarmament and non-proliferation issues with Member States and civil society;

(c) Promotion and support of multilateral efforts on disarmament and the non-proliferation of weapons of mass destruction, in particular nuclear weapons;

(d) Promotion and support of disarmament efforts in the field of conventional disarmament, especially with regard to major weapons systems, small arms and light weapons and landmines.

15. The High Representative will be able to operate with more flexibility and have more systematic interaction with Member States. He or she will also have more flexibility in establishing cooperation and conducting dialogue with Governments and other interested actors, and would act as a facilitator in finding solutions to issues of concern.

16. As a diplomat and manager, the High Representative will actively seek to engage the international community, bringing together key actors within and outside the United Nations to promote more concerted and effective responses to challenges in the area of disarmament and non-proliferation in all its aspects.

17. Proximity to the Secretary-General will allow for a strengthened advocacy role in mobilizing political will to overcome the stalemate in disarmament and non-proliferation. The High Representative will also act as a catalyst with civil society organizations, which play a vital role in building and activating public opinion for disarmament and non-proliferation. He or she will undertake appropriate advocacy work/initiatives in partnership with the relevant parts of the United Nations as well as with civil society, the media, academia and foundations.

18. At the same time, the High Representative will encourage and facilitate the development of networking and foster international cooperation to support efforts on all arms control, disarmament, non-proliferation and related security matters.

19. The High Representative will also actively encourage and support Member States in their efforts to improve the United Nations disarmament machinery and to make it more responsive to the needs of the Member States.

20. The High Representative will report directly to the Secretary-General and will:

(a) Be responsible for all the activities of the Office as well as its administration;

(b) Provide the Secretary-General with advice and support on all arms control, disarmament and related security matters and, in that respect, represent the Secretary-General, as required;

(c) Undertake appropriate advocacy work to advance the disarmament agenda, in partnership with the relevant parts of the United Nations as well as with civil society, the media, academia and foundations;

(d) Provide authoritative analysis and assessment of developments in the field of disarmament and international security for policy guidance and decision-making purposes;

(e) Represent the Office in the meetings of the Senior Management Group, senior advisers' meetings, the Executive Committee on Peace and Security and the Policy Committee;

(f) Act as the focal point between the Secretariat and Member States for information on all arms control, disarmament and related security matters;

(g) Act as a focal point between the Secretariat and global and regional intergovernmental organizations on all arms control, disarmament, non-proliferation and related security matters.

IV. Administrative and financial matters

21. The proposal will be implemented within existing resources. The allocation of responsibilities will be as currently contained in the programme budget for the biennium 2006–2007 in order to allow the Office for Disarmament Affairs to fulfil its responsibilities with respect to the mandates entrusted to it by the General Assembly and to preserve its ability to undertake the necessary activities in that regard. The reorganization into the new office will not affect its objectives for the next biennium, as approved in the strategic framework for the period 2008-2009 (see A/61/6 (Prog. 3) and resolution 61/235).

V. Conclusion

22. The proposal I have set out above may appear, at first glance, to weaken the way in which the Secretariat is structured and organized to support disarmament and non-proliferation efforts. I believe, however, that the new approach will lead to greater visibility of disarmament and non-proliferation issues and that the new office will have a stronger impact in support of Member States' efforts to address the threats and challenges that are before the international community.

23. I also believe that the elements set out above help to clarify the roles and responsibilities of the High Representative for Disarmament Affairs as well as the expectations of how

he or she will play a leadership role in providing the policy direction and guidance needed to ensure the implementation of General Assembly resolutions in the area of disarmament and non-proliferation.

24. I am mindful of my responsibility to contribute to our collective effort in this important area. The full implementation of this proposal, in my view, would strengthen existing synergies across the field of peace and security and, at the same time, would help to build more functional and effective cooperation with Member States, as well as with global and regional intergovernmental organizations. I intend to undertake a thorough review of the implementation of mandates under this reorganization proposal and to report on the outcome at the sixty-third session of the General Assembly.

Appendix
Office for Disarmament Affairs: organizational structure for the biennium 2008-2009

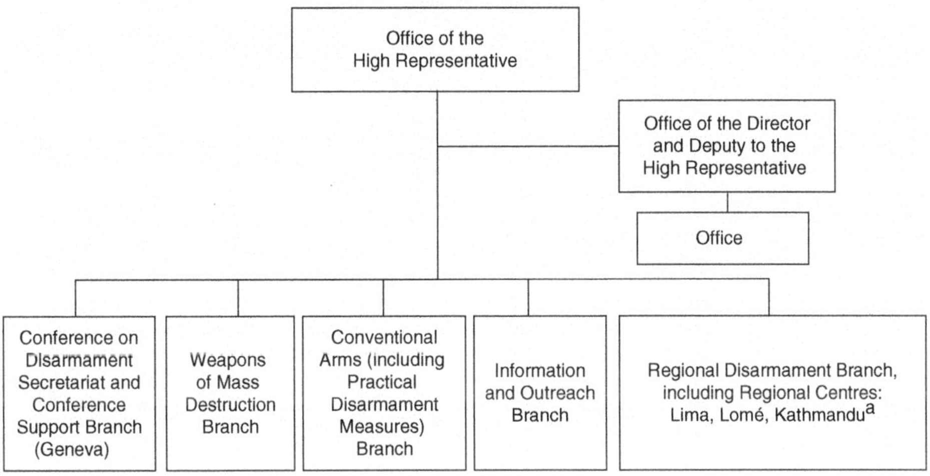

[a]Operating from New York.

6. Security Council Reform: Report of the Facilitators to the President of the General Assembly on the Consultations, 19 April 2007

I. Introduction

The question of equitable representation on and increase in the membership of the Security Council was first introduced in our agenda in 1979, during the thirty-fourth session of the General Assembly. At its forty-eighth session the General Assembly adopted resolution 48/26, of 3 December 1993, by which it decided to establish the *Open-ended Working Group on the Question of Equitable Representation on and Increase in the Membership of the Security Council and Other Matters Related to the Security Council.*

After more than a decade of intensive discussions on this important matter, both in the General Assembly and within the *Open-ended Working Group*, no concrete result has been achieved thus far.

At the 2005 World Summit, stressing the need to complete Security Council reform—as an essential element of our overall effort to reform the United Nations—Heads of State and government expressed support for early reform of the Security Council, in order to make it more representative, efficient and transparent, and to further enhance its effectiveness and the legitimacy of its decisions.

On 11 December 2006, when opening the plenary debate on Security Council reform, the President stated that after many years of inconclusive debate the time had come to make a realistic assessment of the whole issue; and to be prepared to look at this matter with a fresh and open mind if the General Assembly were to make substantial progress.

Against this backdrop, in her letter dated 24 January 2007, the President of the General Assembly invited the membership to start consultations around five key issues, namely: *categories of membership; the question of the veto; the question of regional representation; the size of an enlarged Security Council; and, the working methods of the Security Council and the relationship between the Security Council and the General Assembly.* Subsequently, on 8 February 2007, the President of the General Assembly appointed five facilitators in their individual capacity to assist her during the consultation process on the five preceding issues respectively: H. E. Mr. Ali Hachani, the Permanent Representative of Tunisia; H. E. Mr. Andreas D. Mavroyiannis, the Permanent Representative Cyprus; H.E. Mrs. Mirjana Mladineo, the Permanent Representative of Croatia; H. E. Mr. Heraldo Muñoz, the Permanent Representative of Chile; and, H. E. Mr. Frank Majoor, the Permanent Representative of Netherlands.

The President of the General Assembly mandated the five facilitators to conduct open, transparent and inclusive consultations with a view to making the most accurate possible assessment on the state of play on Security Council reform, for the purpose of establishing the appropriate process which would enable the General Assembly to fulfill the challenging task of reforming the Council.

Furthermore, the President requested the five facilitators to prepare a consolidated report on the result of their work, in order to allow the membership to have an informed follow up discussion on the way forward.

From 20 to 23 February 2007, the facilitators held a series of six informal meetings. The facilitators also convened an informal interactive panel discussion on 13 March 2007. These informal meetings, which took place in the framework of the Open-ended Working Group on the Question of Equitable Representation on and Increase in the Membership of the Security Council and Other Matters related to the Security Council, provided the Member States with opportunities to comprehensively discuss all related aspects of the reform of the Council while focussing on each of the five aforementioned main issues identified by the President of the General Assembly.

In addition, the five facilitators conducted, separately or jointly, wide-ranging consultations and met with individual States and various groups of States. These contacts also allowed them to interact with delegations which did not participate in the open-ended informal meetings so as to take the fullest possible account of the views of all Member States.

The purpose of this report is to provide the President of the General Assembly with the outcome of the consultations the facilitators carried out over the past three months. The report includes a descriptive annex that gives an account and assessment of the views expressed by Member States on the different issues under consideration, and a more analytical part providing a number of notions on the way to move the process forward. The annex contains largely the evaluations of each facilitator responsible for his/her respective theme. The section "Notions on the Way Forward" reflects the common views of the facilitators. The facilitators hope that Member States would, in the next stage of the process, give special attention to the Notions on the Way Forward presented in this report.

II. Notions on the Way Forward

As stated in the introduction, the facilitators, guided by the President of the General Assembly, undertook an inclusive process of consultations to elicit an accurate reflection of the positions and suggestions of the membership on the main questions regarding Security Council reform. Based on those consultations, as well as on the assessments contained in the annex, below are a set of notions of reform that may serve as a framework for result-oriented negotiations, a process over which Member States should have collective ownership.

The objective of the facilitators was to map out what seems most feasible at this stage, so that Member States themselves might proceed to work out all possible configurations guided by the notions identified below as prospective ways of moving forward.

1. Security Council enlargement is an integral part of the United Nations reform process. Member States consider that the United Nations reform would be incomplete without meaningful Security Council reform. Maintaining the Status quo is not acceptable to an overwhelming majority of Member States that feel that the current situation should be improved.

2. Flexibility is key in order to move forward on Security Council reform; but flexibility must be effectively shown and shared by all concerned. A significant number of Member States tend to agree that their ideal solution may not be possible at this stage, and believe that it may be more reasonable to consider the best possible substantial solution for now.

3. The positions of the major interest groups, well-known to the membership for some time, are not likely to be fully realized at this stage. It was encouraging that, in order to move

forward with the process and despite the reiteration of initial positions, flexibility was displayed in the form of willingness to explore a viable compromise solution.

4. The General Assembly should opt for a Security Council reform formula that can garner the widest possible political acceptance by the membership, and in any case, well above the required majority in the General Assembly, including the acquiescence by the current permanent members of the Council, bearing in mind the ratification process of any amendment to the Charter as stipulated in its article 108.

5. Any achievable solution must address the concerns of the wide majority of United Nations Member States aimed at enhancing their access, both in terms of increasing their chances to serve as members of the Council and by being more intensively involved with its work while not a member. Especially the second element was a source of concern for small States and for those who have an item inscribed on the Council's agenda.

6. Enlargement and working methods need to be dealt with in a comprehensive manner. They are closely linked and reform will be incomplete without either one. However, in any scenario, continued efforts should be made to improve the working methods.

7. Expansion needs to be based both on Member States' contribution to the maintenance of international peace and security and to the other purposes of the Organization as well as equitable geographical distribution, as stipulated in the Charter. Maintaining the current regional groups, any enlargement should address the under-representation of developing countries as well as small States. The wide diversity in the membership of the Organization might be taken into account.

8. Under the present state of affairs, Member States, while retaining their initial positions, may wish to explore new and emerging ideas concerning a transitional approach to Security Council reform. A transitional approach assumes an intermediary arrangement and should have as an integral component a mandatory review to take place at a predetermined date. Within the transitional approach there are different options and variations that Member States may wish to further explore. The negotiables include the content and duration of the intermediary arrangement and the nature of the review. Issues on which Member States will not agree in the negotiations would have to be deferred to the review. Consequently, at this stage none of the stakeholders has to give up its original position.

9. As regards categories, the transitional approach, without prejudice to the prospect of creating new permanent seats, could explore the creation of new non-permanent seats as well as an intermediate category. Member States may wish to consider, among others, the following variations of an intermediate category;

- Extended seats that could be allocated for the full duration of the intermediary arrangement, including the possibility of recall.
- Extended seats, which would be for a longer period than the regular two-year term, but with the possibility of re-election. The length of the terms as well as the re-election modalities should be decided in negotiations.
- Extended seats, which would be for a longer period than the regular two-year term, but without the possibility of re-election. The length of the term should be decided in the negotiations.
- Non-permanent two-year seats with the possibility of immediate re-election.

10. Regarding the veto, some Member States favour and some oppose its elimination; some demand and some oppose its extension. Therefore, as a definitive solution might not be feasible at this stage, Member States may wish to address this question within the framework of the review.

In the meantime, Member States may wish to consider forms of limitation in the use of the veto. These might include, among others:

- Ways of enhancing accountability for the use of the veto.
- Limitations of the scope of application of the veto.
- Individual or collective pledges to refrain from its use in certain instances.

11. Regarding regional representation, in the sense of Member States representing regional views, the notion of accountability, both in the election process and while serving in the Council, might be explored. To take into account this aspect, the following ideas could be considered:

- Future candidatures to the Security Council could be proposed directly by Member States or through regional consensus, it being understood that the final decision is to be taken by the General Assembly through the election process as set out in the Charter.
- Elected Members of the Council should be deemed, if they so wish, to also represent, through internal arrangements, the views of the groups to which they belong while continuing to act in accordance with the purposes and principles of the United Nations.

12. As regards the question of the expansion of the size of the Security Council, Member States may decide to consider the following options:

- A limited expansion, believed to be supported by those Member States particularly concerned about the efficiency of the Council.
- A large expansion, believed to be supported by those Member States particularly concerned about the Security Council's representativity
- A medium-size expansion that could reconcile the concerns of those who argue for an efficient Council with the views of those who underscore its representativity.
- A limited expansion in a first stage and a further expansion in the framework of the review.

13. Any reform scenario should enhance access for non-Council members by improving the working methods of the Security Council. Since any enlargement will only modestly improve the chances of individual Member States to become a member of the Council, better access for non-Council members is deemed an essential and integral part of a reform package. At the same time, improvement of the working methods can be seen as a continuous, dynamic process. At this stage, Member States may wish to consider the following options:

- Establishment of a mechanism ensuring that Member States whose interests are specially affected will be heard upon request in private meetings of the Council (more vigorous implementation of articles 31 and 32 of the Charter), and expansion of consultation and cooperation with regional organizations and countries in the region, not only in thematic, public meetings, but also in private meetings.

- Creation of additional opportunities for non-Council members whose interests are specially affected to be heard in the work of the subsidiary bodies; in case of resolutions that call into being far-reaching obligations of Member States, an extended consultation process could be established.
- Implementation of consistent consultations with potential Troop Contributing Countries in the early phase of a new operation, and regular substantive meetings during ongoing operations; Troop Contributing Countries and, as appropriate host countries, to be invited to private meetings of the Security Council in which the mandate of a Peacekeeping Operation is discussed.
- Increase in the transparency of the Council's work by: encouraging formal adoption of rules of procedure, stimulating thematic reports by the Security Council for discussion in the General Assembly and ensuring regular consultations between the Presidents of the principal organs on the implementation of the respective mandates, in accordance with the Charter.

III. Conclusions

The present report represents the facilitators' honest evaluation of the state of affairs on Security Council reform. It reflects months of extensive and inclusive consultations, where the facilitators carefully listened to the views and concerns of Member States. The facilitators have tried to make a fair assessment, as contained in the annex, of the different aspects related to the reform.

On the basis of the consultations and the assessment, the facilitators have prepared the above notions that Member States might want to further discuss in order to explore feasible solutions for the way forward, aimed at facilitating tangible progress on a key and integral component of United Nations reform. As such, an attempt has been made to identify new and emerging ideas that might be worth exploring. At the same time, as stressed before, the facilitators underline that Member States may wish to pursue other options. Those identified here are not necessarily exhaustive.

The facilitators trust that the report will contribute to productive further discussions in which Security Council reform can be brought to a next stage. This could include an agreement on a negotiating process that is conducive to timely decision-making. The facilitators believe that there is a path forward that Members States could build on towards meaningful negotiations, taking advantage of the current momentum. The reform process ahead needs to continue to be all-inclusive and transparent.

Annex
Assessments on Clusters

Categories of Membership

The issue of categories of membership proved to be one of the key issues of the entire process. One of the main purposes of the facilitation was to explore whether innovative ideas heard during consultations could help to reconcile existing positions with a view of advancing the process. The following views were expressed during consultations:

- A large group of States continued to call for the enlargement of the Security Council in both categories of membership (permanent and non-permanent seats).
- A group of States, while defending an enlargement of the Security Council in both categories, is proposing that any new permanent seats holders enjoy all prerogatives of permanent members including veto right in case it is maintained.
- Another group of States reiterated its position seeking the creation of a category of membership which is of a permanent character but, at least initially, without exercising the veto. Addition of new non-permanent seats is also proposed by this group.
- A group of States reiterated its position of accepting enlargement only in the category of non-permanent seats, while considering that no initial positions should be pre-empted for any future discussions of the issue. The creation of only non-permanent seats is also considered by a group of States as a possible fall back position in case no other satisfactory solution is found.
- Some Member States encouraged the exploration of a sort of an "interim" or "transitional solution" based on a longer term renewability of seats. Likewise, other Member States expressed their readiness to explore a solution that would move the process ahead while enjoying broad acceptance.
- Some delegations, especially from small States, expressed the view that any solution should enhance their aspiration to serve in the Security Council.
- A large number of delegations expressed the view that there is a need for ensuring, in any expansion, a strengthened representation of developing countries and small states. A number of delegations stressed the need to take into account the wide cultural diversity within the international community.
- Some delegations expressed their wish to have the question of categories, as well the other issue-areas ascertained through a "questionnaire" addressed to Member States.
- The notion of accountability, both at the time of election (art 23.2 of the Charter) and while serving in the Council (art 24.2 of the Charter) has been addressed by delegations in relation with categories of membership:

  – A group belonging to a specific region is of the view that this region would be responsible for the selection of its representative States in an enlarged Security Council, which would be accountable to it.

  – Other Member States expressed the view that accountability could be ensured through a process of "challenge" in a review mechanism.

Signals of flexibility were shown during the consultations: Despite the reiteration of initial positions, readiness for some flexibility was expressed by the main groups especially on the question of permanency:

- Delegations defending permanency would accept to submit the status of any new permanent seats to challenge.
- Delegations contesting the permanency would admit the possibility for a number of States to be in the Council for a longer period of time than that initially envisaged by the Charter.
- Members of a group of States, although remaining firm in their initial positions, expressed readiness to refer any new proposed elements regarding Security Council reform to their highest political authorities at the earliest possible opportunity.

The question of the veto

Given the sui generis character of the veto, the extent of member states' flexibility and the scope of possible veto reform were explored through extensive bilateral consultations with a cross-regional sample incorporating small, medium-sized and large states, states having items on the Council's agenda and the states currently holding the veto. Member states addressed the issue on two levels: ideal and attainable reform. The veto was criticised on various grounds by the significant majority of member states, many of whom relayed a perception at the same time that elimination is not realistic at this stage. Trends regarding the veto included the restriction of its use, prevention of its extension, resignation from its reform at this stage and extension of it to all permanent members so long as it exists.

In terms of restricting the veto, suggestions included limiting the instances where it can be used (e.g. to exclude instances such as genocide, war crimes, crimes against humanity), establishing criteria for when and in which situations the veto can be used, formalising explanations for the use of veto, limiting the scope of application of the veto (either restricting it to Chapter VII decisions or disallowing its use in Chapter VI decisions), restricting its use to only vital issues, barring the veto where a permanent member is a party to a conflict, changing its weight (e.g. requiring two negative votes to reject a draft resolution), overruling it, and placing a cap on the total number of negative votes that can be cast by a permanent member.

Member states considered that extension of the veto pre-supposes agreement on the addition of new permanent members. Permanent members themselves did not rule out extending the veto, depending on the number of prospective new permanent members and which those would be. Their position ranged from offering qualified support to the G4 draft resolution, to being ready to add one or two new members to the P5 group and to extending the veto to a representative from a region currently without it.

Among states in support of expansion in permanent and non-permanent members, three tendencies were identifiable; a) the veto is a tool for inaction that does not contribute to the effectiveness of the Council and should not be extended to new permanent members, b) in principle extension of the veto, accompanied by a commitment not to use it until a future review, and c) automatic extension of the veto to new permanent members. The second option gathered the most support, also because it was expressed as a fallback position by many states supporting options one and three. For those supporting extension of the veto at this stage, the second option would provide future prospect to this end while for those supporting non-extension of the veto, the second option would satisfy their position now without pre-empting the eventual settlement of the issue.

The general perception of the permanent members regarding the veto, despite nuances on certain aspects of this issue, is that the veto is at the core and is the sustaining force of the system of collective security. It is considered inherently different from other elements discussed in the reform process, as it is the result of a political understanding that preexisted the Charter and thus could not be reformed by the wider membership. Its reform could only be governed by the same historical rationale that initially brought it into being as a tool of restricting the scope of the collective security system according to their major policy considerations.

Permanent members recognized that the wider membership had concerns regarding the veto but did not consider it was misused; rather, they insisted that the veto is exercised with restraint. However, they did not exclude the prospect of finding ways amongst themselves to appease those concerns, including for most of them through a) a voluntary commitment in this respect or b) an oral understanding that permanent members would agree to a non-legally binding statement once the reform process has been agreed.

Despite nuances, permanent members alluded to the limits of what could be agreed vis-à-vis the veto. The latter's abolition or modification would not be ratifiable through Charter amendment. This includes legally-binding regulation of the veto or General Assembly guidelines on how to exercise it. General Assembly involvement in matters falling within what permanent members consider to be exclusive competence of the Security Council is not amenable, nor is explanation of the use of veto before the General Assembly (the P5 consider the two organs to stand on equal footing). Most permanent members based their acceptance of enlargement and other reform of the Council on preserving the essence of their veto power.

The limited span between what the current holders of the veto could accept and what the wider membership is seeking prompted member states to contemplate the option of bypassing, at this stage, substantial veto reform while maintaining strong preference for the veto to be explicitly included on the agenda of a possible future review. The latter requires further exploration, as there does not seem to be across the board agreement on it. The assessment of the facilitator is that, although desirable for the majority of member states, veto reform alone might not be the single factor that will seal or break the reform deal at this stage, provided that the rest of the reform package will be substantial.

States that have thus far insisted on new permanent members obtaining the same rights and privileges as the incumbents, including the veto, were frequently mentioned as key to the process of Security Council reform. Such states, when consulted, reiterated their collective official position but appeared to be willing to consider alternatives on condition that those would be concrete and sufficiently attractive. While these states did not rule out the prospect of a provisional solution, it was quite clear that no definitive views could be provided by them on this level of consultation and at this stage.

Member states who addressed the use of the veto as a source of non-action on the part of the United Nations expressed varying views on whether and how this could be remedied. The mechanism created through General Assembly resolution 377 (V) was accepted as an alternative by some but deemed either ineffective and/or undesirable by others. No concrete suggestions were suggested on how the General Assembly might exercise a subsidiary role in those instances where the primary responsibility of the Council for the maintenance of international peace and security is not exercised because of a veto. Member states did however stress that the General Assembly should do more to fully exercise its competencies under articles 10-12 of the Charter, including by examining matters of peace and security, and calling on the Security Council to take relevant action. This could exhort the Security Council to take action on a situation, provide the viewpoint of the wider membership to the Security Council on a particular issue, and contain the veto through input that would deter its use. The awareness by the Security Council of the pronouncement of the General Assembly on a certain issue would make it difficult for the Council to subsequently ignore the collective will of the international community and be silent on account of a veto.

Through the above consultations it transpired that a pragmatic option concerning veto reform at this stage is the possibility of a pledge by the permanent members to exercise the veto with restraint. While this would not amount to a legally binding measure, some member states have indicated that this would have an impact in practical terms. It was reasoned that indirect limitation/regulation of the veto and the influence of permanent members could be achieved to some degree through the cumulative impact of reform. It was also suggested that enlargement itself amounts to a de facto limitation of the power of the veto because permanent members will constitute less than 25% of the Council and the responsibility to block action through veto will be substantially heavier. As the veto is viewed as synonymous with P5 influence, it is particularly pertinent to note that the enhanced presence and voting might of members other than the P5 is believed by many to limit the influence of permanent members on decision making as well as decision-making that is exclusively power balance-driven. Lastly, it was suggested that the power stemming from possession of the veto (implicit veto) would diminish if the Council operated in a manner that allowed for less pressure to be exerted on non-permanent members.

The question of regional representation

There seemed to be a common understanding that the Security Council in its current composition does not reflect the geopolitical realities and thus needs to be adequately rebalanced.

- The majority of delegations were of the view that the rebalancing of the Security Council needs to be based on "the contribution to the maintenance of international peace and security and to the other purposes of the Organization", as well as on equitable geographical representation, as stipulated in article 23 of the Charter.
- Nevertheless, some delegations pointed out that additional objectives and measurable criteria had yet to be worked out to define the necessary capabilities of States relevant to the maintenance of international peace and security. Proposals included, *inter-alia*, the level of financial contribution to the United Nations, population, regional role and standing, size of military forces, as well as contributions to peacekeeping operations.

In the course of the discussion there seemed to be a two-fold understanding of the term "regional representation".

- Some delegations identified the term "regional representation" as identical to the "equitable geographical distribution" as contained in article 23.1 of the Charter.

- Other delegations expressed the view that the term "regional representation" should be understood as the regional seat leading to regional accountability. They argued that the notion of regional representation, in the sense of Member States representing regional views, could be explored further. Different options were suggested, such as candidatures to be proposed directly by Member States or through regional consensus, it being understood that the final decision is to be taken by the General Assembly through the election process as set out in the Charter. Another suggestion was that Members of the Council should be deemed, if they so wish, to also represent the views of regional groups to which they belong while continuing to act in accordance with the purposes and principles of the United Nations.
- However, a wide number of delegations felt that, at this stage, the non-permanent members of the Council, although proposed on a regional basis, could not represent their respective regions. Rather, as members of the Security Council, they should have a global accountability as well as an obligation to the international community as a whole.
- In addition, many delegations were of the view that the concept of the regional seat, given the different character of each regional group as well as the existing differences in their internal working procedures, was not feasible at this stage.

Although the composition of the existing regional groups was challenged in terms of not accurately reflecting geopolitical realities, there seems to be a wide understanding that the restructuring of the current system is not realistic. The majority is thus still of the view that the principle of the equitable geographic distribution should be exercised through the existing structures. Nevertheless, opinions varied on how to amend the situation, in particular with respect to defining the underrepresented.

The discussion brought out several interpretations within the category of the underrepresented. Accordingly, the underrepresented were classified in the following manner:

- Within the existing group arrangements, there was a general feeling that Africa, Asia and GRULAC were underrepresented. Some opined that the EEG was underrepresented as well.
- There was also a broad understanding that small and developing countries are underrepresented as a general rule. In addition, some delegations pointed out that small and developing countries from Africa, Asia and GRULAC were underrepresented in particular.
- Some delegations were of the opinion that there was a need for an enlarged Security Council to represent all cultures, religions and civilizations. In that respect, although various political organizations were mentioned as candidates for the Security Council seat, the majority of delegations argued it would contradict the intergovernmental nature of the United Nations and therefore proposed that their legitimate concerns should be accommodated through other means.

Bearing in mind the inseparable links between the *Regional Representation* cluster and those of *Size* and *Categories of Membership*, it might prove to be very difficult to devise any workable solution prior to the agreement on the number of seats to be distributed. However, since it can be argued that the notions of contribution to the maintenance of international peace and security and equitable geographical distribution constitute the fundamental elements of any future fair and just solution, they should be taken into account as a general principle during deliberations as well as at the early stages of the eventual future negotiations on size and categories.

The size of an enlarged Security Council

During consultations Member States agreed with an enlargement in the size of the Security Council. No Member State opposed expansion. Below, are some of the main opinions expressed by Member States in the consultations:

- The size of an enlarged Security Council cannot be judged in isolation from other conditioning issues, such as equitable regional representation and the categories of membership. Determining the size of an enlarged Council was guided, for example, by the aspirations of regions to be satisfied with their representation, rather than a theoretical number decided a priori.
- Opinions as to the size of an enlarged Security Council vary. Many Member States gave specific preferred numbers, while others expressed that they are open to suggestions, some of them provided that additional considerations are taken into account.
- Some Member States expressed that among the main criteria that ought to be considered in determining the size of an expanded Security Council are equitable geographical distribution, enhanced credibility, efficiency and effectiveness of the Council. A number of delegations added criteria such as the financial and diplomatic contributions to the United Nations, as well as respect for democracy and human rights. Others prefer to adhere solely to the criteria enunciated in Article 23 (1) of the Charter, *i.e.* "due regard being specially paid, in the first instance to the contribution of Members of the United Nations to the maintenance of international peace and security and to the other purposes of the Organization, and also to equitable geographical distribution."
- The "efficiency" and "effectiveness" of an enlarged Security Council were considered by some delegations, particularly but not only permanent members of the Security Council, as paramount elements for a Council that is supposed to act swiftly in the face of crises. Other delegations argued that efficiency does not necessarily result from a reduced size, and that efficiency (or efficacy) could ultimately improve by enlargement in more representative higher numbers.
- Some Member States lamented the current configuration of regional groups, as not representative of like-minded States, but agreed, as most members did, that it would not be advisable to revisit existing regional groups, notwithstanding the wish expressed by some that an expanded Council should consider seats for small States or States of particular cultures and civilizations.
- A significant number of Member States, both developed and developing, from different regions, believe that the size of an expanded Security Council should remedy the under-representation of developing countries, particularly from Africa, Asia, Latin America and the Caribbean.
- A number of delegations, while stressing that the Security Council should properly represent current world reality, expressed their desire to see an adequate correlation between the number of members in the Council and the membership of the General

Assembly. They pointed out that the ratio between Security Council and the general membership of the U.N. was 21% in 1945 (a ratio of 1:5), 13% in 1965 (a ratio of 1:8) and less than 8% (a ratio of 1:13) at present.

- A limited expansion of seats has been advocated by Member States on grounds of efficiency and agility of the Council to confront crises. Other member States favor a larger expansion of seats based on representativity of the Council.
- In the view of some Member States, an increase in the number of seats, even if solely in the non-permanent category, would entail a re-balancing of the power structure within the Security Council. More members would require new higher proportions of votes to approve resolutions, as the weight percentage of permanent members would decline.
- While some Member States addressed the question of size from the perspective of a one-time expansion, some Member States felt that a Review Conference should revisit the issue of size in the context of a transitional approach.
- Despite the fact that views on the exact size of an expanded Security Council differ among Member States, they do not seem irreconcilable.

The working methods of the Security Council and the relationship between the Security Council and the General Assembly

A wide majority of Member States felt that the working methods are an essential and integral part of Security Council reform. Some Member States opined that expansion and working methods should not be seen as inseparable. They argued that reform of the working methods, which would not require a Charter amendment, should be seen as a continuous process. Ultimately, a widely shared conclusion was that the working methods should be part of any reform package. If agreement on a package would not be attainable, efforts to reform the working methods could, and in the eyes of many, should still be continued.

- Some Member States offered another perspective on the relationship between the working methods and expansion of the Council. Many (smaller) Member States serve relatively sporadically on the Council, even in case of an expansion. For those Member States, improved working methods, and thus better access as non-Council member to the work of the Council, is of essential importance.
- Member States alluded to the relationship of the Security Council with the General Assembly. Most Member States put this issue in the context of the so-called encroachment of the Security Council on the General Assembly. It was argued that this had much to do with the broadening definition of "security". Working with this broad definition, the Security Council was increasingly discussing subjects that would, arguably, fall under the competence of the General Assembly. Most however felt that it was difficult to address this issue in the context of Security Council reform.
- As to the substance of the working methods, many Member States welcomed several initiatives that have recently been taken, such as the draft resolution by Costa Rica, Jordan, Liechtenstein, Singapore and Switzerland (S5) and the recent Note by the President of the Security Council on working methods (S/2006/507). Many Member States saw as the central aim of improved working methods to ensure better access for non-Council members to the work of the Security Council. The access seemed to have distinct components: information, consultation and cooperation.

- With regard to access through information, Member States felt that timely and substantive information on the work of the Council would lead to more transparency. This would not only enable them to better follow the proceedings, but would also allow Member States to informally exert influence on the decision making process. Concrete suggestions that were made by Member States:
  - Better notification to all Member States of all Council meetings, including unscheduled meetings and early distribution of draft resolutions.
  - More frequent briefings by the President of the Security Council, as well as by the Chairmen of the subsidiary bodies. Distribution to all Member States of reports of the meetings of the subsidiary bodies.
  - Institutionalized periodic review of the implementation of Council mandates and decisions.
- On better access through consultations, Member States indicated an interest to have direct, real access to the Council in cases where their interests were specially affected, and in particular when they have an item on the agenda (both in open and private meetings). It was widely felt that this would increase the legitimacy of the Council's decisions, without necessarily infringing on the prerogatives of the Council. Suggestions that were made:
  - A mechanism should be established to ensure that Member States whose interests are specially affected will be heard upon request in private meetings of the Council, as well as in the work of the subsidiary bodies.
  - Consistent consultations with potential TCC's in the early phase of a new operation, with the participation of the host country, where appropriate, and regular substantive meetings during ongoing operations.
- As already stated, it was also argued that better access could be achieved by means of expanding on the mechanisms for interaction between UN bodies, most notably between the Security Council and General Assembly. Suggestions that were made:
  - The Security Council should issue special subject-oriented reports (article 24.3 Charter) for discussion in the General Assembly. This could include reports on the understanding of the mandate of the Security Council, e.g. what is the definition of "international peace and security".
  - In addition to increased cooperation between the SC and GA, also a regularized, substantive dialogue should be established with ECOSOC, the Human Rights Council and the PBC (also on the implementation of the respective mandates).

As stated before, most Member States felt that measures as described above should be part of a reform package, that would eventually be voted on in the General Assembly. By and large, the permanent members indicated that they supported some level of reform of the working methods. Some of them stated that these measures should be adopted by the Security Council itself, and could not be 'imposed' by the General Assembly. This is a matter that would require further consultation.

7. Security Council Reform: Report to the President of the General Assembly on the Consultations, 26 June 2007

I. Introduction

1. On 22 May 2007, the President of the General Assembly appointed H.E. Mr. Heraldo Muñoz, the Permanent Representative of Chile and H.E. Mr. Christian Wenaweser, the Permanent Representative of Liechtenstein, (hereafter referred to as "the authors of this report"), to conduct consultations with the membership on how to move the process forward, in formats they should deem useful. The President asked the two Permanent Representatives to use the five Facilitators' report of 9 April 2007 as the basis for those consultations, and to report back on the outcome before the end of June 2007.

2. Moreover, in view of their significant contribution to the deliberations on Security Council reform, the President of the General Assembly asked the facilitators appointed on 8 February 2007, to continue to advise her on this important matter.

II. Background

3. This report is submitted in accordance with the mandate contained in the abovementioned letter of 22 May. In keeping with this mandate and building upon the momentum created by the Facilitators' report, the authors of this report have conducted inclusive and extensive consultations. In this context, they approached existing groups—those that have taken a position on Security Council reform in the past as well as others—and thus reached out to the membership in the course of their consultations. In addition, they also held numerous bilateral talks.

4. The authors of this report also benefited from the views offered during the informal plenary meetings held on 3 and 4 May 2007, as well as from the insight provided by the Facilitators advising the President of the General Assembly.

5. Throughout this latest stage of consultations, many Member States have reiterated that Security Council reform is an integral part of the ongoing United Nations reform process, and that United Nations reform would be incomplete without a meaningful reform of the Council. In this regard, the status quo is not acceptable to an overwhelming majority of Member States. There is thus a continued strong commitment to Security Council reform in accordance with paragraphs 152 to 154 of the Outcome Document of September 2005.

6. Furthermore, Member States underscored that to move forward on Security Council reform, flexibility had to be effectively shown and shared by all concerned. Such flexibility would imply a concrete commitment to find the widest possible political agreement.

7. Both the Facilitators' report and the informal plenary meetings made it clear that those who have taken a distinct position on Security Council reform in the past still maintain those positions. This report is thus without prejudice to positions expressed by Member States in the past and in particular to the proposals on Security Council reform submitted in the past by the G-4 (A/59/L.64), the Uniting for Consensus Group (A/59/L.68) and the African Group (A/59/L.67). The same applies to the proposal submitted by the S-5, which dealt exclusively with the working methods of the Security Council (A/60/L.49).

8. The consultations have reaffirmed that at this stage of the process, the positions of the major interest groups from the past are unlikely to be fully realized. Therefore, as stated in the five facilitators' report, under the present state of affairs, Member States, including those supporting the above-cited draft resolutions, while retaining their initial positions, may be open to explore further a transitional approach to Security Council reform. At present, there is considerable interest in and openness to the transitional or intermediary approach; yet, a deeper understanding is needed to advance the process. This report is intended to assist in such a possible exploration.

III. The Intermediary Approach

9. The positions taken in the past have revealed stark differences of opinion on a number of issues such as size of an enlarged Council, the veto and on whether new permanent seats should be created. The intermediary approach, as outlined in the Facilitators' report, is intended to reconcile these positions to the extent possible and is therefore by definition a compromise. At the same time, it is not meant to reflect a lowest common denominator, but rather a possible solution that is at the same time politically sustainable and framed in a manner that is flexible enough to allow the membership to take further reform steps in the future. It is clear that the goal of any proposal on Security Council reform should be finding the formula that garners the strongest possible agreement of the membership - preferably expressed through support exceeding the legally required two-thirds majority, thus facilitating an early entry into force of the necessary Charter amendments.

10. Such a solid political majority will have to take into account the interests and concerns of all major interest groups and States, including of those who do not fully subscribe to any of the proposals submitted in the past. This includes small States who emphasize their particular interest in the issue of working methods, in particular the aspect of access to information and decision-making within the Council - to which those who have an item inscribed on the Council's agenda also attach particular importance - as well as enhancing their possibility to serve in the Council.

11. A transitional approach assumes an interim arrangement and should have as an integral component a mandatory review to take place at a predetermined date to review and assess the adequacy of this arrangement. Issues on which Member States will not agree in the negotiations would have to be deferred to the review.

IV. Notions for Discussion

12. Paragraph 8 of the five Facilitators' report states that "States may wish to explore new and emerging ideas concerning a transitional approach to Security Council reform." It goes on to say that "within the transitional approach there are different options and variations that Member States may wish to further explore." The following notions are intended to assist Member States in such a further exploration of a transitional approach, if they so wish.

Size and categories of membership

13. The size of an expanded Security Council depends on striking an adequate balance between the general satisfaction about the geographical representation of the Council, in particular in terms of the representation of developing countries and of small States, and the desire to maintain its efficient functioning. In their consideration of the size of the Council, States may want to examine the linkages between the size and the scope of the

review clause, and address the issue of access of States that are not members of the Council to its decision-making process in the context of the discussions concerning the improvement of the working methods.

14. The intermediary approach entails the creation of a category of membership not currently provided for under the Charter. Within the intermediary or transitional approach, Member States may wish to consider, inter alia, creating extended seats that could be allocated for the full duration of the intermediary arrangement, up to the review; extended seats for a longer period than the existing non permanent seats with the possibility of re-election; or extended seats for a longer term than the existing non permanent seats but without the possibility of re-election.

15. Any of these options can be combined with enlargement in the regular non-permanent category, in accordance with article 23.2 of the Charter.

16. The options in size range from a limited to a large expansion, a decision which could be adopted either in one step or in stages—i.e., a given number at first and a further expansion in the review.

17. The length of the extended seats would have to be considered together with their re-election modalities, as appropriate, and the geographic distribution of the new seats. This constitutes an essential negotiable and is also tied to the review.

Elections of New Members

18. Member States may wish to consider the modalities for electing members in the new category of seats. While such elections would have to be held in accordance with the relevant provisions of the Charter, States may want to consider whether the elections for additional seats and the regular two-year seats take place simultaneously. Furthermore, Member States may wish to add a provision which would prevent countries from presenting candidatures for both the new category and the traditional non-permanent category at the same time or in short intervals.

Veto

19. Within the intermediary approach, States may want to examine the question of rules concerning the exercise of the veto, including forms of limitations of its use, possibly in the framework of a decision on working methods. Given that none of the options under the intermediary approach entail the creation of new vetoes, this possibility would under any of the options be left for consideration in the course of a review. The use of the veto is linked to the issue of working methods as well as to categories of membership and the review.

Regional representation

20. As far as regional representation, States may wish to reflect on the notions presented in the Facilitators' report in their possible further consideration of an intermediary approach. This issue is linked in particular to the question of size and composition.

Review

21. A review clause may open the way to take further reform steps in the future. Within an intermediary approach, special weight must be given to a review clause. Such a review must be mandatory and take place after a specified number of years following the entry

into force of Charter amendments related to Security Council reform. It is further indispensable to clearly define the scope of the review.

22. While the review plays a central role in the consideration of an intermediary approach, further changes to any aspect of the composition of the Security Council will require a separate decision by the General Assembly on a further amendment of the UN Charter and a separate ratification process.

23. The central role of a review clause is linked to all other aspects of Security Council reform and in particular to those aspects on which Member States will not agree in negotiations. These might include the question of the creation of permanent seats including the question of the veto, the creation of additional non-permanent seats in accordance with Article 23, paragraph 2 of the Charter of the United Nations and the further consideration of arrangements regarding the use of non-concurring votes by Permanent members of the Security Council in accordance with Article 27, paragraph 3 of the Charter. The review should also entail undertaking a comprehensive reassessment of the Security Council, including its composition and working methods.

Working methods

24. There is general agreement on the high importance of working methods. Enlargement and working methods need to be dealt with in a comprehensive manner, and reform would be incomplete without either one. The complementary nature of the two areas of Security Council reform is generally recognized, within which the possibility of advancing independently on the two aspects is also put forward. The different nature of the two aspects of reform, with only enlargement requiring a Charter amendment, has to be taken into account in this regard. The issue of working methods is linked to the review, the veto and the size of an enlarged Council, in particular through enhancing the access of non-members to the decision-making process of the Council.

V. Future Steps

25. A large number of Member States expressed the view that the President of the General Assembly has established favourable conditions to advance toward a process of negotiations among Member States. Delegations expressed the view that instead of further consultations, the next stage should consist of negotiations.

26. While the continued leadership of the President of the General Assembly will be essential, substantive input from Member States will be indispensable in order to take the discussions to the next stage, i.e. intergovernmental negotiations, with a view to continuing moving forward, so as to achieve further concrete steps within the sixty-second session of the General Assembly.

27. Future negotiations would need to be conducted on the basis of a text containing concrete elements on all the negotiables identified in this report. Member States should have primary ownership of such a process.

28. This report is intended to enable tangible progress through which Security Council reform can be brought to a next stage that could include—in concrete terms—an agreement on an intergovernmental negotiating process, as the only way to move forward.

29. Flexibility must be effectively shown and shared by all concerned in a process that would need to continue to be all-inclusive and transparent. There have been years of discussions, without substantial results. The time has come to bring the process closer to decision-making. It is therefore important that the current momentum be maintained in order to develop a common understanding conducive to the attainment of the Security Council reform.

30. This report represents a genuine effort of the two Permanent Representatives to fulfil the mandate given to them by the President of the General Assembly in her letter of 22 May. It thus brings to an end their work under this mandate.

II. UN Focus Issues During 2006/2007

A. Congo

1. Twenty-second report of the Secretary-General on the United Nations Organization Mission in the Democratic Republic of the Congo, 21 September 2006 (S/2006/759)

I. Introduction

1. The present report is submitted pursuant to Security Council resolution 1635 (2005) of 28 October 2005, by which the Council extended the mandate of the United Nations Organization Mission in the Democratic Republic of the Congo (MONUC) until 30 September 2006, and resolution 1565 (2004) of 1 October 2004, by which the Council requested me to keep it regularly informed of developments in the Mission area. This report covers major developments since my last report to the Council, dated 13 June 2006 (S/2006/390), and provides recommendations on the mandate of MONUC.

II. Political developments

Developments towards the holding of national elections

2. The first democratic elections in more than 40 years in the Democratic Republic of the Congo were held on 30 July 2006. During the preceding weeks, a number of political and civil society leaders, including the Conférence episcopale nationale du Congo (CENCO), raised concerns about the conduct and organization of the elections and called for the holding of national consultations to address them. On 27 June, the President of Gabon, Omar Bongo Ondimba, convened a meeting in Libreville of Congolese leaders, including the Chairperson of CENCO and several presidential candidates, to discuss issues related to the conduct of the campaign. On 30 June, the main political parties—except the People's Party for Reconstruction and Democracy (PPRD), the Union for Democracy and Social Progress (UDPS) and the Unified Lumumbist Party (PALU)—expressed concern about an alleged lack of impartiality and transparency in the electoral process, particularly regarding the number of supplementary ballot papers and the publication of the voters list. UDPS called for demonstrations in Kinshasa against the holding of the elections, and in Kasaï Oriental and Kasaï Occidental, UDPS supporters participated in a number of demonstrations including a "ville morte", and called for a boycott of the elections.

3. On 29 July, at an inter-institutional meeting, the espace présidentiel, the institutions in support of democracy and the Presidents of the two houses of the Transitional Parliament discussed the timetable for the Provincial Assembly elections and a possible second round of the presidential election. It was agreed that for logistical and financial reasons the polls could not be held before the end of October. The Independent Electoral Commission subsequently published, together with the final list of the 13,500 candidates for the Provincial Assembly elections, the electoral calendar, which scheduled these elections for 29 October.

4. To lend moral authority to the five institutions in support of democracy and assist them in strengthening confidence in the electoral process, MONUC facilitated the establishment of the International Committee of Eminent Persons, which held its first meeting on 28 July

under the chairmanship of the former President of Mozambique, Joachim Chissano. Currently the other committee members are the former Prime Minister of Senegal, Madior Boye, Judge Lewis Makame, Chairman of the National Electoral Commission of Tanzania and Kai Eide (Norway), who has served as my Special Representative in Bosnia and Herzegovina, and most recently as Permanent Representative of Norway to the North Atlantic Treaty Organization. The full composition of the Committee is being finalized.

The electoral campaign

5. On 29 June, the Independent Electoral Commission officially launched the month-long electoral campaign for the presidential and National Assembly elections, which took place in a generally peaceful atmosphere. While some candidates campaigned throughout the country, others did not have the financial means of doing so. This and other discrepancies, including the lack of legislation on the financing of political parties, led some candidates to question the fairness of the campaign. On 5 July, a group of 19 presidential candidates requested the suspension of the electoral campaign until alleged irregularities in the electoral process had been rectified.

6. Despite its generally peaceful and democratic character, the campaign was marked by a number of isolated violent incidents, including clashes between supporters of candidates in Kinshasa, Kindu and Mbandaka, and the destruction of candidates' posters and signs throughout the country. International observers also reported some cases of misconduct by national and local authorities, in particular through the misuse of security personnel to obstruct candidates they did not support, and by imposing bureaucratic and practical obstacles on their constitutionally guaranteed freedoms of movement and assembly. Despite efforts by the High Media Authority, there was a problem of inequitable access to media by candidates and politically biased coverage throughout the campaign, as well as intimidation of journalists in some areas.

7. On 27 July, presidential candidate Vice-President Jean-Pierre Bemba was met by a crowd of enthusiastic supporters on his return to Kinshasa following the completion of his campaign in other parts of the country. Many supporters followed him from the airport to downtown Kinshasa where he addressed a large rally. Clashes between the Vice-President's supporters and police were reported and shots were fired during a confrontation between the Vice-President's security guards and the Congolese National Police (PNC). Four people were reportedly killed and 17 injured. Several police stations were attacked and looted, and the properties of two individuals, reportedly supporters of President Kabila, were set on fire. The offices of the High Media Authority and the Human Rights Monitoring Commission were looted and destroyed. A warehouse at the official residence of Vice-President Bemba in Kinshasa was also burnt down. PNC is investigating but has not yet determined whether the incident was accidental or related to the events of the day. Reports have been received of the deaths of a number of children of Bemba's guards at the compound. On 28 July, President Kabila addressed some 15,000 supporters in Kinshasa and no incidents were reported.

Election day and announcement of the provisional results

8. On 30 July, the presidential and National Assembly elections took place in a generally peaceful and orderly manner, amidst wide popular enthusiasm. Some 70.54 per cent of the more than 25 million registered voters participated, with a high turnout of women. The polls

were observed by some 47,500 national observers, 466,000 political party witnesses and 1,773 international observers. The African Union, the Association of European Parliamentarians for Africa, the Carter Center, the Electoral Institute of Southern Africa, the European Union, the International Organization of la Francophonie, the Electoral Commissions Forum of the Southern African Development Community (SADC), and the SADC Parliamentary Forum, were among the organizations fielding observer missions. Several diplomatic missions in Kinshasa also fielded a number of observers.

9. Problems were experienced in approximately 239 of the 50,000 polling stations, all located in the Kasaïs: 172 polling stations in Kasaï Oriental, most of them in Mbuji-Mayi, experienced delivery delays following the burning of trucks delivering electoral material. Nine stations were set on fire. In Kasaï Occidental, violence between supporters of rival political candidates resulted in the destruction of 58 polling stations. As a result, polling in those stations took place on 31 July and 1 August, after the Independent Electoral Commission, with MONUC support, dispatched replacement material and PNC and MONUC reinforced security.

10. Counting began immediately after the closing of the polling stations and in most sites continued into the early hours of 31 July. After having posted the results at each polling station, results sheets and other important materials were transported to the local results compilation centres. This process was slowed by the transportation difficulties in the country. In Kinshasa, during the first few days after the vote, the centres were overwhelmed by the deliveries of huge quantities of ballot papers, which resulted in their careless handling in some cases. However, the Independent Electoral Commission addressed the situation and ensured order promptly, and the deadline for completing the compilation of presidential results within 14 days was met, allowing for the declaration of the provisional results on 20 August. The Independent Electoral Commission Media Centre was an important resource for the Commission communication strategy.

11. In a joint statement issued on 1 August, international electoral observer missions, while acknowledging some shortcomings, noted that they had been impressed by the strong voter turnout and high level of participation of political party witnesses and national observers. Electoral observers also raised a number of concerns about the results compilation process, including the burning of a number of used and unused ballots—after they had been counted—and other electoral material outside an election office in Kinshasa. While the incident did not affect the compilation of results, it could cast doubt on the validity of any recount, should it become necessary. In subsequent separate statements, observer missions noted areas requiring improvement, including the collection of results, education of the public and candidates about the electoral process and the training of electoral workers.

12. The period between the elections on 30 July and the announcement of the provisional results on 20 August was rife with speculation about the electoral process, notably by candidate-owned or controlled media outlets. Several candidates expressed concern regarding alleged serious irregularities, emphasizing their intention not to accept the results unless they were investigated. The international community, including the International Committee in Support of the Transition (CIAT) and the International Committee of Eminent Persons, called for restraint, reaffirmed the role of the Independent Electoral Commission as the only institution authorized to release the official results, and reminded candidates of the mechanisms established for dealing with electoral claims and complaints. The Commission,

in conjunction with the High Media Authority, also recalled its exclusive prerogative to compile and release the provisional results, and on 1 August, issued a joint statement condemning media outlets that had published unofficial results.

13. In the late afternoon, on 20 August, a few hours before the scheduled announcement of the provisional results, PNC and Vice-President Bemba's security guards exchanged fire in downtown Kinshasa. Intermittent fighting ensued into the evening also reportedly involving the Republican Guard, which is mandated to protect the President and presidential premises. Armed elements also fired at MONUC vehicles, including that of my Special Representative and his convoy. Following interventions by the international community, calm was restored late in the evening and the Independent Electoral Commission announced the provisional results of the presidential elections. In the days prior to the outbreak of violence, media outlets owned by Vice-President Bemba had aired programmes, which included personal attacks against President Kabila, who complained to MONUC, which urged Vice-President Bemba to stop such broadcasts. On 21 August, the media outlets of the Vice-President were shut down by supporters of President Kabila.

14. President Kabila won 44.81 per cent of the votes, followed by Vice-President Bemba (20.03 per cent), Antoine Gizenga (13.06 per cent) and Nzanga Mobutu (4.77 per cent). No single candidate won an absolute majority of the votes. Therefore, in accordance with the electoral law, President Kabila and Vice-President Bemba, being the two candidates with the highest percentage of the votes, would contest a run-off presidential election.

15. In the days leading up to the announcement of provisional results President Kabila and his Alliance pour la majorité présidentielle (AMP) increasingly advocated for the upholding of the provisions of article 71 of the Constitution, which they interpreted to stipulate that the second round of presidential elections must be held 15 days after the announcement of the first round. They also argued that the second presidential round should be separated from the Provincial Assembly elections, which they claimed would reduce overall costs and allow for an advancement of the date for holding the second round.

16. My Special Representative and CIAT underlined that article 71 of the Constitution states that if one candidate does not win an absolute majority of the votes in the first round, the Independent Electoral Commission would "proceed" to the second round within 15 days, i.e., first steps must be taken to organize the elections. Moreover, separating the two rounds would duplicate logistical requirements and thus double the cost of holding them concurrently, and would not shorten the preparation time needed for each election.

17. On the morning of 21 August, at the request of my Special Representative, CIAT held a meeting, attended by the International Committee of Eminent Persons, to discuss concerns over the high level of tension between the supporters of President Kabila and Vice-President Bemba, and the call for the holding of the second presidential round 15 days after the announcement of the final results of the first.

18. Earlier in the day, the MONUC Force Commander was informed by the Chief of Defence Staff of the Armed Forces of the Democratic Republic of the Congo (FARDC) that troops would be deployed in Kinshasa to maintain law and order, and, in that regard, to forcibly disarm the security elements of the four Vice-Presidents. The Chief of Defence Staff was strongly advised that PNC should be allowed to maintain law and order and that discussions should be held with the Vice-Presidents in regard to any proposed disarmament

of their security personnel. Vice-President Bemba also expressed deep concern to my Special Representative that the Republican Guard intended to attack his residence.

19. Shortly after the CIAT meeting had begun at the residence of Vice-President Bemba, small automatic and heavy arms fire was heard around the house, making it impossible for CIAT members to leave. MONUC troops, troops of the European Union force (Eufor R. D. Congo) and the MONUC Chief of Security were immediately alerted and moved to the area. My Special Representative established contact with President Kabila and his advisers, while the Force Commander established contact with the FARDC Chief of Staff. After discussions, two MONUC companies and one Eufor R. D. Congo company undertook a closely coordinated operation to extract CIAT members and stabilize the situation. Eufor R. D. Congo took action within its mandate in Kinshasa, as authorized by the Security Council in its resolution 1671 (2006) of 25 April, and deployed along a key section of the main boulevard in central Kinshasa.

20. MONUC and Eufor R. D. Congo troops dispatched in the vicinity reported that a company of the Republican Guard, with three armoured personnel carriers, one with a 90 mm mounted gun, and two howitzer guns, were assembled at a strategic junction on the 30 June Boulevard, apparently ready to advance towards the residence of the Vice-President. Meanwhile, small groups of the Republican Guard were seen in the area exchanging fire with a group of some 200 of Vice-President Bemba's guards, who were positioned among the houses around his residence. During the fighting, Vice-President Bemba's personal helicopter, located in the courtyard in front of his office building, approximately 300 metres from his residence, was destroyed.

21. From the outset, my Special Representative worked actively to arrange a cessation of hostilities and restore calm, including through arranging a direct telephone conversation between President Kabila and Vice-President Bemba. Meanwhile, the Secretary-General spoke with both Vice-President Bemba and President Kabila to warn them that the fighting was jeopardizing the achievements of the transitional process, and called for an immediate cessation of hostilities. Senior officials from several CIAT member States made similar calls.

22. My Special Representative emphasized to Vice-President Bemba and President Kabila that: (a) hostilities should immediately cease; (b) the forces of both camps should disengage and withdraw to their earlier positions; and (c) President Kabila and Vice-President Bemba should meet as soon as possible, with international mediation or not, and commit to some basic rules of conduct to be adhered to during the electoral process.

23. Calm was restored by early evening, as the Republican Guard withdrew most of its personnel together with the armoured vehicles and armaments. MONUC and Eufor R. D. Congo units deployed at key road junctions in the city centre. Furthermore, MONUC deployed troops with 20 armoured personnel carriers around the residence of the Vice-President to stabilize the situation and provide security. Soon thereafter, MONUC safely extracted my Special Representative and the CIAT Ambassadors from the residence.

24. Following further interventions by my Special Representative and other members of the international community, MONUC facilitated the establishment of a working group comprising the Ministers of Defence and the Interior, the FARDC Chief of Staff, the PNC Inspector General, representatives of the Vice-President's guards, the commander of the Republican Guard, as well as the Eufor R. D. Congo and MONUC Force Commanders to

identify and establish confidence-building measures, to encourage dialogue and resolve immediate security disputes between both parties. The group reviews, inter alia, the reports of daily joint verification missions comprising the above parties.

25. Meanwhile, President Kabila and Vice-President Bemba also agreed to my Special Representative's proposal to establish a joint commission, facilitated by MONUC, with two subcommissions tasked to conduct an impartial, preliminary inquiry into the events of 20 to 22 August, and to foster agreement between the two candidates concerning rules of conduct for themselves and their supporters during the electoral campaign and the second presidential election round, as well as a memorandum of understanding on the post-electoral period. The two candidates have agreed, in principle, to a weapons-free zone in Kinshasa, the details of which are under discussion. Further progress was made on 13 September, when President Kabila met Vice-President Bemba for the first time since the events in August, together with Vice-Presidents Azerias Ruberwa and Arthur Zahidi N'Goma, to discuss the recent violence.

26. On 26 August, at the request of the High Media Authority, representatives of seven media outlets (Radio Libérté, Radio Télévision Nationale Congolaise, Digital Congo, Canal Congo Télévision, Canal Kin TV, Molière TV and Radio Lisanga Télévision) signed an agreement in the presence of CIAT and a group of Congolese media representatives committing themselves to respect the rules of journalistic ethics during the electoral period. A media monitoring mechanism was established to analyse key print and broadcast media during the electoral campaign for incidents of incitement to hatred or violence, based on data provided to MONUC by the European Union Electoral Observation Mission in the Democratic Republic of the Congo.

27. In accordance with the electoral timetable, the Supreme Court was to receive and review the provisional results of the presidential elections and any electoral complaints from 21 to 23 August. However, that was not possible until after MONUC secured the Court's premises on 25 August, when the Independent Electoral Commission transmitted the provisional results to the Court. On 14 September, after it had reviewed the electoral complaints, the Supreme Court validated the provisional results of the first round and confirmed that President Kabila and Vice-President Bemba would contest a second presidential round.

28. On 7 September, the Independent Electoral Commission announced the provisional results for the National Assembly elections, which indicated that the platform of parties supporting President Kabila, AMP, had won 224 of the 500 seats, followed by the Regroupement des nationalistes congolais (RENACO), the parties supporting Vice-President Bemba, with 116 seats. The Coalition des démocrates congolais (CODECO), the coalition supporting Pierre Pay-Pay, won 25 seats and Vice-President Ruberwa's Rassemblement congolais pour la démocratie (RCD) won 15 seats, while President Kabila's party, PPRD, won 111 seats and Vice-President Bemba's party Mouvement de libération du Congo (MLC) won 64 seats.

29. The installation of the National Assembly is scheduled to take place on 22 September, and the inauguration of the President on 10 December. The Provincial Assemblies will elect the members of the Senate in a vote scheduled for 29 December. With the endorsement of the new National Assembly, the elected President is to appoint a Prime Minister, who will be entrusted with the formation of a government. The completion of this process may take

until the end of the year, and possibly longer. The calendar for the local elections, which can be held only after the National Assembly has adopted the decentralization law, has yet to be discussed.

Electoral operations

30. The Independent Electoral Commission was generally successful in carrying out the timely organization of such large and complex elections. Some 80 per cent of the 50,000 polling centres opened as scheduled, while most of the remaining centres opened with minor delays. The Commission trained some 260,000 election workers for deployment to the 49,746 polling stations, clustered in 9,104 polling centres. 170 different ballots were printed and delivered to 14 logistical hubs, from which MONUC transported the material to the 210 sites from which the Commission had the responsibility of ensuring its transportation to some 9,104 polling centres, under PNC escort.

31. To assist the Commission in safely deploying electoral materials, implement civic education programmes and collect and deliver the electoral results, MONUC deployed electoral, police, military observer and security officers to 78 locations across the country, including to all 64 Commission Liaison Offices. The South African Government also provided staff, through the United Nations Development Programme (UNDP), to work alongside the Commission at the local results compilation centres. On polling day, United Nations teams visited polling centres to help the Commission staff identify and quickly resolve problems. A national network, led by the Association of Female Lawyers and comprising several non-governmental organization partners, monitored the security of women during the elections.

32. Civic education efforts were enhanced to inform the Congolese population about basic electoral principles and to urge them to vote. The Independent Electoral Commission, MONUC and international partners met regularly to coordinate their civic education and public information activities for the elections. Radio Okapi broadcast voter education programmes and a daily debate giving equal air time to political parties and presidential candidates, and produced video clips on the rights and responsibilities of voters. MONUC particularly targeted women and youth in its programming.

33. A major challenge during the electoral process was the payment of electoral workers throughout the country. With the support of UNDP and MONUC, the Independent Electoral Commission paid some 260,000 polling station workers and 73,000 police officers who participated in the 30 July polls at 210 sites.

34. The extension of the electoral calendar beyond the original timeline, according to which the transitional process would have ended in June, raised the costs of the first round of the presidential and National Assembly elections. On 24 July, the Steering Committee of the UNDP-managed project in support of the elections approved a revised 2006 budget of $144 million. I would like to thank donors, which have provided funding for the elections, and in particular note the support of the Government of South Africa, which provided substantial in-kind contributions for the production and transportation of ballot papers. I would also like to acknowledge the response to my recent requests to address a critical funding gap from Belgium, France, Norway, Spain, Sweden, Switzerland, the United Kingdom of Great Britain and Northern Ireland and the European Commission, which has reduced the shortfall for the electoral budget to $9 million.

National security plans for the elections

35. The national police are responsible for the security of the electoral process, including the maintenance of law and order and the protection of the electoral staff, facilities and equipment. In accordance with the national security plan for the elections, 72,258 Congolese security officers provided security for the electoral process, including 53,274 territorial police officers, 2,588 intelligence officers and 14,000 crowd control officers. They were supported, where necessary, by 2,396 FARDC personnel. MONUC police and military liaised closely with their national counterparts throughout the process.

36. During the reporting period, MONUC trained 4,793 Congolese police officers, including 26 instructors, and 1,370 territorial police officers, during one-week essential skills programmes on security for the polling centres. The six formed police units from Bangladesh, India and Senegal deployed at five strategic locations (Kananga, Kinshasa, Kisangani, Lubumbashi and Mbuji-Mayi) provided training in crowd control techniques to 1,703 police officers, and conducted joint patrols with PNC units.

Preparations for the second presidential round and ProvincialAssembly elections

37. In two rulings issued on 13 and 15 September, the Supreme Court of Justice reaffirmed the requirements under article 71 of the Constitution with respect to the time of holding a second round for the presidential election, but also acknowledged the logistical challenges, and concluded that it was not possible for the Independent Electoral Commission to complete all preparations within the 15-day period. It therefore granted an extension of the constitutional deadline and allowed the Commission to conduct the second round up to 50 days after the announcement of the final results of the first round. The 50-day period became effective on 16 September.

38. Preparations for the second round of the presidential elections and the provincial assembly elections are ongoing. The ballot papers are being printed in South Africa. MONUC, UNDP and the Government of South Africa are undertaking the transportation of 60,000 electoral kits and 1,260 metric tons of ballots to the 14 hubs in the Democratic Republic of the Congo. MONUC will transport the kits and ballots to 166 territorial centres and cities, and the Commission will be responsible for their movement to the polling centres.

Regional relations

39. During the reporting period, no meetings of the Tripartite Plus Joint Commission and the joint verification mechanisms took place. There have been signs of a further gradual improvement of relations between the Democratic Republic of the Congo and Rwanda. On 1 August, the Government of Rwanda reiterated its intention to open a diplomatic mission in Kinshasa after the elections. The formal exchange of Ambassadors would be a major step towards the restoration of peace, security and development in the region.

40. Meanwhile, the Democratic Republic of the Congo and Uganda have continued to seek solutions to issues of mutual concern, including regarding elements of Lord's Resistance Army (LRA) which may be present on Congolese territory.

III. Implementation of the Mission mandate

Ituri

41. There were a number of positive developments in the Ituri district of Oriental Province during the reporting period; however, the security situation remained volatile. Armed groups continue to operate in Djugu and Irumu territories, regularly harassing the local population, as well as MONUC and FARDC troops. During the reporting period, MONUC and FARDC continued joint operations to protect the civilian population and compel recalcitrant militia groups to disarm.

42. In Djugu territory, a joint MONUC and FARDC operation was launched on 20 May to dislodge and capture elements of the Front des nationalistes et integrationistes (FNI), led by Peter Karim. On 28 May, a MONUC Nepalese unit was attacked by FNI during a cordon and search operation. One MONUC soldier was killed, three were injured and seven were captured and held by FNI. Two of the soldiers were safely released to MONUC on 27 June and the remaining five on 28 July.

43. During the negotiations leading to the release of the seven soldiers, Peter Karim indicated that FNI wanted to join FARDC. On 10 July, Karim and the Government signed an agreement on the terms of the FNI integration in FARDC. Since then, the Government has not taken action to formally incorporate Karim into FARDC, and the demobilization and brassage of the FNI elements has been delayed. In the meantime, Karim is reportedly recruiting new militia elements.

44. On 5 June, the Government reopened the disarmament and demobilization process in Ituri. As of 8 September, 4,758 militia elements had surrendered with 2,332 weapons. However, operational, managerial and financial difficulties of the national disarmament, demobilization and reintegration agency, the National Commission for Disarmament, Demobilization and Reintegration (CONADER), have significantly hampered the demobilization process.

45. MONUC has also continued to focus on the two remaining militia groups in Ituri, the Mouvement révolutionnaire congolais (MRC) of Mathieu N'Gudjolo and the Forces de résistance patriotique de l'Ituri (FRPI) of Cobra Matata. On 26 July, MONUC facilitated discussions between MRC and the Government, pursuant to which MRC would discontinue hostilities and integrate into FARDC. Sensitization of MRC elements began immediately, but the Government and MRC have yet to reach agreement on a timetable for integration or on a mutually-acceptable venue for talks. MONUC is assisting in overcoming these problems.

North and South Kivu

46. The overall situation in North Kivu remains stable but fragile. During the reporting period, the presence of non-*brassaged* former brigades of the Armée nationale congolaise (ANC) and their resistance to the deployment of integrated brigades remained a serious concern. Upon receiving reports that renegade General Laurent Nkunda and ex-ANC hardliners intended to cause instability, and given the persistent threat of Rwandan and Ugandan foreign armed groups, MONUC increased patrols and monitored the situation closely to prevent any escalation of violence. The arrival of additional integrated brigades in North Kivu helped further restrict the activities of militias in the province and ease the burden on

the overstretched Eighth Military Region. However, standoffs and tensions between the integrated brigades and the pro-Nkunda brigades over their areas of responsibility continue to be problematic, and MONUC is monitoring the situation closely.

47. MONUC continued to take proactive measures to ensure a stable security situation in South Kivu. The activities of the Forces démocratiques de libération du Rwanda (FDLR) and uncontrolled armed groups have decreased considerably, and only a few incidents of looting and killings were reported. MONUC patrols have enhanced security for the local population and deterred militia activities. It is expected that the security situation will continue to improve with the arrival of additional integrated FARDC brigades in the post-election period.

Katanga

48. Katanga remained relatively calm, with the exception of the northern and central area of the province where Mayi-Mayi groups remained reluctant to demobilize. On 12 May, the Mayi-Mayi leader known as "Gédéon" surrendered along with several commanders and approximately 750 followers. However, splinter factions continue to commit atrocities, especially in the Pweto, Mitwaba and Manono triangle. On 28 August, Fidele N'tumbi surrendered and, as of 8 September, 171 of his followers had disarmed. The unpaid and non-*brassaged* FARDC brigades in the area are a security risk, as they continue to prey on the local population causing displacements.

49. During the reporting period, MONUC deployed an additional battalion of four companies (India), a level 2 hospital (Jordan) and an aviation unit (South Africa) in Kamina. These forces joined the present battalion (Benin) stationed in Kalemie, Nyunzu and Manono. MONUC, the Sixth Military Region Commander, and the humanitarian community are working together to identify operational requirements to provide security and confidence for internally displaced persons to return to their villages.

Western Democratic Republic of the Congo

50. The security situation in Kinshasa remained tense following serious clashes between the guards of Vice-President Bemba and the Republican Guard from 20 to 22 August. The commitment of both camps to disarm or significantly reduce their forces ahead of the second presidential round campaign will have a significant impact on the security situation in the coming weeks.

51. The development of Kinshasa as a flash point has required the redeployment of Western Brigade troops to the capital. On 23 August, the Western Brigade was reinforced by a special forces company (South Africa) stationed in Lumubashi.

52. On 29 July 2006, Eufor R. D. Congo, authorized under Security Council resolution 1671 (2006) of 25 April to support MONUC, reached its full operational capacity, with 1,100 troops stationed in the country and 1,307 troops stationed in Gabon. Eufor R. D. Congo is now capable of responding within capability and agreed tasking to a MONUC request for assistance. MONUC and Eufor R. D. Congo have engaged in a programme of planning and coordination to ensure maximization of operational efficiency.

53. The robust presence of the Western Brigade in Kinshasa supported by Eufor R. D. Congo, as well as several military and political confidence-building measures aimed to

restore security in the capital, will help ensure that the campaign for the second round can be held in a relatively secure environment.

Arms embargo

54. Pursuant to Security Council resolution 1596 (2005) of 18 April, MONUC inspected a shipment of military equipment and related materials, including tanks, armoured personnel vehicles and ammunition, at the Matadi port on 29 July. The Government had neither informed the Security Council Committee established pursuant to resolution 1533 (2004) prior to the arrival of the cargo, nor invited the Mission to verify the type and quantity of military material, in violation of the resolution.

55. On 24 and 25 August, without notice, FARDC moved seven truckloads of ammunition from Matadi to Kinshasa. FARDC acknowledged the movements, but declined to provide further details. MONUC conducted a number of verification missions, and was informed on 12 September that nine T-55 tanks had been delivered during the night, bringing the equipment now stored at a FARDC logistics base in Kinshasa to 12 T-55 tanks, 20 infantry combat vehicles and one recovery tank. In view of the fighting in Kinshasa between 20 and 22 August, these developments are of considerable concern.

56. During the reporting period, representatives of the Agence nationale de renseignement (ANR) in Beni expressed concern to MONUC about the alleged continued smuggling of arms from Uganda to Butembo. MONUC intends to submit a comprehensive report of its verification inspections to assist the work of the Security Council Committee established pursuant to resolution 1533 (2004) and the Group of Experts established pursuant to resolution 1698 (2006).

Disarmament, demobilization, repatriation, resettlement and reintegration

57. On 24 August, Major Ninja, an FDLR leader active in North and South Kivu, and 84 of his followers were disarmed. Of those, 26 FDLR elements were repatriated to Rwanda, while 58 Congolese elements entered the national disarmament and demobilization programme. Major Ninja was a well-known source of destabilization in the Kivus, and his repatriation is likely to further weaken FDLR command and control in the Democratic Republic of the Congo, and encourage remaining rank and file FDLR combatants to also undergo disarmament, demobilization, repatriation, resettlement and reintegration. During the reporting period, some 600 additional FDLR elements voluntarily repatriated to Rwanda, bringing the total of voluntary repatriation of foreign armed groups under the facilitation of MONUC to 13,000 combatants and dependents.

Security sector reform

Army integration

58. The Joint Commission on Security Sector Reform and its technical military subcommission continued to meet regularly under the chairmanship of Vice-President Ruberwa and my Special Representative. The Joint Commission decided to undertake a more coherent and cost-effective deployment of the remaining integrated brigades. The Joint Commission has also requested my Special Representative to chair a meeting in early September of the Government and key donors on the transparency of the defence budget.

59. As of 13 September, the Government had established 13 out of the 18 integrated brigades it had planned to create before the elections. Owing to financial problems, the formation of the remaining five integrated brigades is several weeks behind schedule.

60. While there is broad agreement among international actors that security sector reform is a key issue, donors need to harmonize their support to the Government in developing a security sector reform strategy. MONUC is currently discussing this issue with its security sector reform partners with the view to presenting an agreed approach to the new Government.

61. Meanwhile, the lack of operational support for the integrated brigades conducting joint operations with MONUC continues to impede FARDC's capacity to maintain stability following such operations. In this connection, the Government and MONUC have jointly prepared a project document with the view to seeking donor funds necessary to address the immediate operational needs of integrated brigades conducting joint operations with MONUC. At the same time, the European Union Mission of Assistance for Security Sector Reform (EUSEC) is assisting the Government in taking immediate measures to address urgent financial and administrative issues in this regard.

Disarmament, demobilization and reintegration

62. As of 8 September, CONADER had demobilized more than 76,614 ex-combatants, including 19,000 children. Meanwhile, some 85,000 elements have yet to undergo the disarmament, demobilization and reintegration process. However, the budget of some $200 million of CONADER, provided by donors through the Multi-Country Demobilization and Reintegration Programme (MDRP), has been exhausted. The World Bank has indicated that additional funding from MDRP would be contingent on its assessment of CONADER operations, which would be reviewed at an MDRP meeting in mid-November.

63. The financial crisis facing the Government structures related to disarmament, demobilization and reintegration has had a significant impact on the *brassage* process. As *brassage* follows demobilization, delays in demobilization have a direct impact on army integration, inter alia, creating difficulties for the stabilization of the Kivus, Katanga and Ituri. Delays in the payment of safety net and demobilization allowances, as well as the implementation of reinsertion projects, has caused discontent among ex-combatants.

64. The Joint Commission for Security Sector Reform has decided that priority for disarmament, demobilization and reintegration of the outstanding caseload would be accorded to the more than 44,000 troops from the Sixth, Eighth and Tenth Military Regions (North Kivu, South Kivu, Katanga), while discussions would start on the *brassage* of the Republican Guard and the Kinshasa Garrison (30,000 troops total).

Police and penal reform

65. The joint working group on the reform and reorganization of PNC has completed its recommendations on the reform and restructuring of the force, for discussion with the new Government. These include conducting a census of the police, including the vetting and certification of police officers, to allow, among other things, for the proper budgeting of salaries and the establishment of an effective payment system. Following the holding of the census, the design and delivery of a comprehensive training programme for the national police needs to be undertaken.

66. The dilapidated state of the country's penitentiary facilities has resulted in frequent detention centre breakouts. During the reporting period, 258 convicts, including FARDC soldiers and PNC officers responsible for serious human rights violations, escaped from prison. On 4 June, 193 detainees escaped from Bukavu prison, including Colonel Biyoyo, the first army officer sentenced for child soldier recruitment. Serving prisoners, confined alongside pre-trial detainees, continue to endure appalling conditions of detention. MONUC has deployed 12 detention experts throughout the country to advise the authorities on improving prison conditions.

Human rights

67. In addition to the human rights concerns mentioned under the review of the electoral process above, a number of other issues of concern arose during the reporting period. On 30 June, heavily armed FARDC soldiers, not trained for crowd control, were deployed to prevent a political demonstration in Matadi (Bas-Congo Province). They fired indiscriminately at protesters after a soldier was killed by the enraged crowd. Thirteen people were killed and 20 injured.

68. On the night of 27 June, 12 UDPS supporters were arbitrarily arrested by ANR and detained in Mbuji-Mayi in a military camp, while ANR in Kalemie, Lubumbashi and Uvira made a number of arrests for political reasons and mistreated detainees, some of whom were tortured. MONUC was denied access to the victims in some of these cases, and in Kinshasa, is systematically denied access to ANR holding cells. The Chief of ANR has thus far refused to meet with MONUC to discuss these concerns.

69. The Republican Guard committed a number of politically-motivated human rights violations during the electoral campaign, including the arbitrary arrest of journalists, the intimidation of presidential candidates and their families and ill-treatment of detainees arrested for political reasons.

70. MONUC has learned with concern that the Mai-Mai leader Kyungu Kasongo Mutanga, known as "Gédéon", may be given a command position and an officer's rank upon being integrated into the army. MONUC has written to the Auditeur militaire, asking him to expedite the judicial investigation into the crimes of which Gédéon is suspected. In the letter, MONUC also refers to the case of the Mayi-Mayi leaders "Tshinja-Tshinja", the Kilwa massacre in October 2004, the December 2004 massacres in North Kivu and the situation of several Ituri militia leaders who have been in custody for up to 16 months without trial. All these investigations are effectively blocked, in most cases by political and military interference in the judicial process.

71. On 20 June, 42 soldiers were sentenced by a military court in Mbandaka for murder and rape, as crimes against humanity, committed during a mutiny on 3 to 4 July 2005. With respect to past unpunished crimes, preparations for the deployment of a team to map the most serious human rights violations committed between 1993 and 2003 and to recommend appropriate measures to deal with such violations are under way, in close cooperation with the Office of the High Commissioner for Human Rights.

Child protection

72. Of serious concern are the recent abductions and attempts to re-recruit children formerly associated with armed forces and groups in North Kivu, primarily by elements of the former

ANC brigades loyal to Laurent Nkunda. On 22 June, 13 children were abducted near Kitchanga in Masisi territory by elements of the 835th Battalion. They reported that they had been severely beaten by their abductors. On 30 July, two of these children were traced to their home by members of the 835th Battalion, who tried again to lure them back to the military.

73. Given the number of children who, after being reunified with families, have begun returning to transit centres in Goma seeking protection from intimidation or re-recruitment, child protection partners have temporarily suspended all family reunification of children formerly associated with armed forces and groups in Masisi. The area is also becoming increasingly insecure for child protection organizations.

Humanitarian situation

74. The number of newly displaced persons increased dramatically in the first eight months of 2006. The majority of the 45,000 IDPs at the Geti camp in southern Irumu territory (Ituri) have refused to return home because of insecurity. FARDC imposed a security perimeter to prevent militia from mixing with the camp population. Human rights monitors continue to report rapes and the killing of individuals who have risked venturing out of the camp. A World Food Programme food distribution to the camp has been delayed owing to a lack of stocks, leading to increasing malnutrition and an average of six deaths per day, twice the humanitarian alert level. MONUC is facilitating the temporary return of some internally displaced persons to their home communities in order to harvest their crops.

75. The demobilization of 500 Mayi-Mayi elements in Mitwaba and the deployment of the FARDC 63rd Brigade have provided the opportunity for the 160,000 IDPs, who had fled the hostilities between the FARDC and the Mayi-Mayi, to return. During the reporting period, MONUC facilitated the transportation of 62 metric tons of non-humanitarian cargo, including food and medicines, medical equipment and other non-food items for IDPs in Bukiringi (60 km south of Bunia), as well as for 20,000 internally displaced persons in Mitwaba, Katanga, and for various groups of returnees in the Kivus.

Conduct and discipline

76. The MONUC Conduct and Discipline Team further clarified its role and mandate and strengthened its monitoring functions while it continued to receive and follow up on allegations of misconduct and to train mission personnel. To that end, a number of directives and procedures were issued to all mission personnel on reporting allegations of misconduct, and on the investigation process. The concerns expressed in my previous report regarding the investigating capacity of the Office of Internal Oversight Services continued to present a challenge, as very few final investigation reports were received during the period.

77. To improve coordination with other United Nations agencies, the sexual exploitation and abuse inter-agency focal points network has been reactivated. Its priorities include the adoption of a common code of conduct, the sharing of training materials and the coordination of a referral system for the assistance to victims of sexual exploitation and abuse by United Nations personnel.

IV. Administration

78. During the reporting period, MONUC restructured the support component on the basis of a comprehensive review, carried out pursuant to recommendations of the General

Assembly. The logistics hub in Entebbe, Uganda, is being strengthened to better support operations in eastern Democratic Republic of the Congo. Coordination regarding support is also being further strengthened with other missions in the region.

79. The Mission vacancy rate has been significantly reduced. However, personnel retention remains a challenge. The increasing demands placed on staff members, combined with security problems and associated restrictions in the execution of tasks, are contributing to a high rate of attrition.

80. The Mission continued to provide limited logistical support to FARDC units conducting joint operations with MONUC in eastern Democratic Republic of the Congo. Limited progress has been achieved in efforts to mobilize voluntary contributions for this.

81. MONUC effectively met the formidable challenge of providing logistical support to elections of an unprecedented scope in United Nations operations. The Mission has also supported the requirements of United Nations funds, programmes and agencies as well as other partners, particularly with respect to the elections, including logistical support to Eufor R. D. Congo, on a cost-recovery basis. This has placed a significant strain on the Mission's support component, and MONUC will be continuing these activities through the next phase of the electoral process. It is important that, as roles are agreed upon between members of the United Nations country team in implementing a post-electoral strategy, close attention is paid to sharing costs.

V. Financial aspects

82. The General Assembly, by its resolution 60/121 B of 30 June 2006, appropriated the total amount of $1,091,242,800, equivalent to $90,936,900 per month, for MONUC for the period from 1 July 2006 to 30 June 2007. Should the Security Council decide to extend the mandate of MONUC beyond 30 September 2006, the cost of maintaining the Mission until 30 June 2007 would be limited to the amounts approved by the General Assembly.

83. As at 30 June 2006, unpaid assessed contributions to the Special Account for MONUC amounted to $160.4 million. The total outstanding assessed contributions for all peacekeeping operations as at that date amounted to $1,265 million.

84. As at 31 July 2006, amounts owed to troop and formed-police contributors totalled $55.9 million. Reimbursement of troop and contingent-owned equipment costs have been made for the period up to 30 April 2006 and 31 March 2006 respectively, in accordance with the quarterly payment schedule.

VI. Observations and recommendations

85. I would like to commend the Congolese people and the political parties for their commitment to the democratic process, as demonstrated by the high voter turnout at the first round of the presidential elections and the National Assembly elections on 30 July, and the generally peaceful atmosphere in which the polls were conducted. While there were some concerns over irregularities, and isolated incidents of violence, the successful holding of the polls was a landmark step in the peace process in the Democratic Republic of the Congo. The Independent Electoral Commission and its national and international partners effectively met the enormous organizational challenges involved in ensuring that the elections were held under the best possible conditions. The support provided by MONUC,

UNDP, the European Commission and the Government of South Africa deserves a particular note of appreciation.

86. In the light of the ruling of the Supreme Court of Justice on 15 September, in which it acknowledged that it would not be possible to meet the constitutional deadline for holding the second round of the presidential election, I encourage President Kabila and Vice-President Bemba to reaffirm their commitment to the electoral calendar, which established 29 October as the date for the second round. The United Nations is committed to providing all possible support in ensuring the timely and successful holding of these elections

87. It is vital that the parties and candidates take all possible steps to ensure that the electoral campaign is freely contested across the country and that the elections are held under secure conditions and are credible and transparent. It should be emphasized that any resort to incitement to hatred or violence during the electoral process is unacceptable, and that perpetrators must be held accountable. Meanwhile, the transitional institutions need to continue to operate effectively until the legislative and executive institutions have been duly installed. At this critical juncture, I would urge the Congolese parties to continue to work assiduously to build on the significant gains made so far in the transitional process and ensure its successful conclusion in the coming months. The recent generous support of several donors has reduced significantly the outstanding shortfall in the electoral budget to some $9 million. I would urge donors to give due consideration to meeting the remaining gap as soon as possible, so the electoral preparations can proceed unhindered.

88. The violent incidents of 20 to 22 August in Kinshasa were of deep concern. President Kabila and Vice-President Bemba should be encouraged to work in good faith with the facilitation mechanisms established by my Special Representative, and to reach early agreement on rules of conduct for the campaign for the second round of the presidential elections and also on mutual assurances of security and political engagement following the elections. They should also continue to work with the joint monitoring mechanisms established by MONUC with the assistance of Eufor R. D. Congo, and institute measures to prevent a recurrence of violence in Kinshasa or elsewhere in the country during the electoral process. The robust deployment of the Western Brigade in Kinshasa, supported by Eufor R. D. Congo, will help in ensuring stability in the capital during the electoral period. It is also important that the electoral campaign focus on the key issues facing the country. Furthermore, the establishment of as inclusive a Government as possible would lay the foundation for national reconciliation and broad-based efforts towards the consolidation of peace.

89. The use of the media to incite hatred and violence during the electoral process is a worrisome development. The establishment of a mechanism to monitor the situation is a welcome step and the agreements reached recently by several major media outlets on respect for journalistic ethics during the campaign period need to be strictly adhered to. It is important that the relevant Government institutions ensure that such misuse of the media is prevented, and that no unilateral action is taken by others in this regard.

90. The reports on the importation of arms into the country, without prior notification being given to the Security Council Committee established pursuant to resolution 1533 (2004), are of concern. I call on the parties to fully cooperate with MONUC and allow the Mission to properly monitor and inspect any shipments of arms into the country.

91. The national police and the armed forces continue to face a range of problems, including poor discipline, insufficient training and equipment, and inadequate systems for the delivery of salaries. A comprehensive plan for security sector reform is urgently required to address these and other challenges to enhance the capacity of the security services to effectively maintain security nationwide. International partners should urgently strengthen their support to the Government in the development and implementation of an effective security sector reform plan, which will be vital in ensuring long-term stability in the country. The assessment of CONADER operations should be conducted as soon as possible and an agreement reached on the urgent provision of additional financial support for disarmament, demobilization and reintegration.

92. In the post-elections period, addressing the many challenges facing the Democratic Republic of the Congo will require the continuing support of a United Nations peacekeeping operation. It is envisaged that post-electoral tasks of MONUC, in cooperation with the United Nations country team and the international community, would include: providing support to the new Government and civil society in strengthening democratic institutions; promoting the rule of law and basic human rights; building an adequate security environment and architecture; strengthening economic management; and establishing and consolidating State authority nationwide. In the context of long-term institution-building, including governance and security sector reform, natural resource management and decentralization, MONUC would work to advocate, facilitate and support national planning and reform processes that will enable donors to coherently assist the implementation of such programmes.

93. I have asked my Special Representative to consult the new Government as soon as possible on the proposed role of MONUC, including its strategy, objectives and benchmarks for achievement in areas of support.

94. In the post-elections period, international assistance for the Democratic Republic of the Congo should be strengthened and sustained in support of the peace consolidation efforts of the Government. Further progress in the implementation of political and governance reforms will be vital in laying the foundations for durable peace and stability and, in this context, I would encourage the finalization of the proposed "Governance Compact", being developed under the lead of the United Nations, the World Bank and the European Commission, and its early consideration by the Government.

95. International stakeholders should also give urgent consideration to the establishment of a coordination and support mechanism, to replace the International Committee in Support of the Transition. It is envisaged that, in agreement with the Government, such a mechanism could play an important role in ensuring effective donor coordination, promoting good governance and serving as a forum for policy dialogue with the elected Government. I have asked my Special Representative to undertake consultations with relevant stakeholders in this regard.

96. In the meantime, I would recommend an extension of the current mandate of MONUC for a period of four and a half months, from 1 October 2006 to 15 February 2007, to allow sufficient time for consultations with the new Government on the Mission's future role.

97. In its resolution 1692 (2006) of 30 June, the Security Council decided to extend until 30 September 2006 the authorization contained in resolution 1669 for the Secretary-General to redeploy temporarily troops from the United Nations Operation in Burundi

(ONUB) to MONUC. Moreover, in its resolution 1693 (2006) of 30 June, the Security Council decided to extend until 30 September the increase in the military and civilian police strength of MONUC authorized by resolutions 1621 (2006) and 1635 (2006). I am extremely grateful for the action taken by the Security Council to strengthen the capacity of MONUC in this period. In the light of recent developments and the vital importance of maintaining MONUC's current authorized strength to ensure a peaceful and successful completion of the electoral process, I would like to recommend for the Security Council's consideration that it extend, until 15 February 2007, the authorization to redeploy the troops from ONUB to MONUC in accordance with resolution 1669 (2006). I intend to submit further recommendations with respect to these redeployed troops before the end of January 2007. I would also like to recommend for the Security Council's consideration a further extension, until 15 February 2007, of the increase in the military and civilian police strength of MONUC authorized by resolutions 1621 (2006) and 1635 (2006).

98. Finally, I would like to thank my Special Representative, the Force Commander and all the civilian and military women and men of the United Nations family in the Democratic Republic of the Congo for their untiring efforts and commitment to bringing peace and security to the Democratic Republic of the Congo, particularly in regard to the assistance they have provided to the electoral process. I would also like to pay tribute to the military and civilian members of the United Nations, including its security personnel, for their work in stabilizing the situation in Kinshasa and ensuring the safety and security of all United Nations personnel. A note of appreciation also goes to the men and women of Eufor R. D. Congo, for the support provided to MONUC.

Annex
United Nations Organization Mission in the Democratic Republic of the Congo: military and civilian police strength (as at 31 August 2006)

	Military component				
Country	*Military observers*	*Staff officers*	*Troops*	*Total deployed*	*Police officers*
Algeria	6	0	0	6	
Argentina					2
Bangladesh	17	10	1 351	1 378	250
Belgium	0	9	0	9	
Benin	20	0	751	771	8
Bolivia	7	3	200	210	
Bosnia and Herzegovina	5	0	0	5	
Burkina Faso	12	0	0	12	76
Cameroon	1	1	0	2	49
Canada	0	9	0	9	
Central African Republic					7
Chad					6
China	14	0	218	232	
Côte d'Ivoire					1
Czech Republic	1	0	0	1	
Denmark	1	1	0	2	
Egypt	18	5	0	23	13
France	0	6	0	6	10
Ghana	21	2	462	485	
Guatemala	8	1	105	114	
Guinea	2	0	0	2	53
India	36	13	4 349	4 398	250
Indonesia	9	4	175	188	
Ireland	2	1	0	3	
Jordan	22	6	66	94	3
Kenya	28	7	0	35	4
Madagascar					7
Malawi	26	0	109	135	
Malaysia	5	12	0	17	
Mali	32	0	0	32	24
Mozambique	4	0	0	4	
Mongolia	2	0	0	2	
Morocco	1	3	807	811	
Nepal	18	2	1 052	1 072	
Netherlands	0	1	0	1	
Niger	19	1	0	20	37
Nigeria	30	1	0	31	

Continued

Country	Military component				Police officers
	Military observers	Staff officers	Troops	Total deployed	
Pakistan	30	17	3 560	3 607	
Paraguay	19	0	0	19	
Peru	7	0	0	7	
Poland	3	0	0	3	
Romania	20	0	0	20	1
Russian Federation	21	2	0	23	5
Senegal	11	14	459	484	290
South Africa	5	25	1 183	1 213	
Serbia	0	0	6	6	
Spain	2	0	0	2	
Sri Lanka	2	0	0	2	
Sweden	5	0	0	5	3
Switzerland	1	1	0	2	
Togo	1	0	0	1	
Tunisia	30	3	464	497	
Turkey					14
Ukraine	11	0	0	11	3
United Kingdom	0	6	0	6	
Uruguay	34	12	1 324	1 370	
Vanuatu					2
Yemen					1
Zambia	22	5	0	27	
Total	**592**	**183**	**16 641**	**17 416**	**1 119**

Includes military personnel deployed under MONUC and ONUB authorized troop strengths.

2. Twenty-third report of the Secretary-General on the United Nations Organization Mission in the Democratic Republic of the Congo, 20 March 2007 (S/2007/156)

I. Introduction

1. The present report is submitted pursuant to Security Council resolution 1711 (2006) of 29 September 2006, by which the Council extended the mandate of the United Nations Organization Mission in the Democratic Republic of the Congo (MONUC) until 15 February 2007; welcomed my intention to consult closely with the new Congolese authorities on an adjustment of the mandate and capacities of MONUC after the completion of the national elections; and requested me to submit recommendations in this regard by the end of January 2007. In its resolution 1736 (2006) of 22 December 2006, the Security Council authorized, from 1 January 2007 until the expiry of the current MONUC mandate, an increase in the military strength of up to 916 personnel, to allow for the continued deployment of the infantry battalion and the military hospital previously authorized under the mandate of the United Nations Operation in Burundi. In its resolution 1742 (2007) the Council provided a further extension of the MONUC mandate until 15 April 2007. The present report covers major developments since my last report to the Council, dated 21 September 2006 (S/2006/759), and provides recommendations on the future mandate of MONUC.

II. Situational update

A. Political developments

2. Following the successful presidential, National Assembly and Provincial Assembly elections in the Democratic Republic of the Congo, the National Assembly was installed on 22 September 2006 and President Joseph Kabila was inaugurated on 6 December 2006, bringing the transition process envisaged by the Global and All-Inclusive Agreement of 2002 to a formal conclusion. On 30 December 2006, President Kabila appointed as Prime Minister Antoine Gizenga, who announced the formation of his cabinet on 5 February. The Provincial Assemblies elected members of the Senate and Governors in January. However, those indirect elections were marred by widespread allegations of corrupt practices in the conduct of the vote. In this regard, it is notable that gubernatorial candidates affiliated with the Alliance pour la majorité presidentielle (AMP) were elected in Kinshasa and Bas-Congo province, despite the fact that the majorities in both of the relevant Provincial Assemblies are affiliated with the Union pour la nation (UPN).

3. On 29 October 2006, the second round of the presidential and Provincial Assembly elections took place in a generally peaceful environment. The Independent Electoral Commission improved its performance in the conduct of the polls, the vote count and the compilation of results. Voter turnout was lower than in the first presidential round, held on 30 July 2006, with 65 per cent of the electorate casting votes. Isolated incidents were reported in 3 of the 189 constituencies in Equateur and Ituri, where polling was rescheduled for 31 October and 2 November 2006. National and international observer missions, including those of the African Union, the European Union, South Africa and the Carter Center, widely regarded the elections as technically sound, transparent and credible.

4. Despite tensions and mutual accusations in advance of the second round of presidential elections, representatives of President Joseph Kabila and Vice-President Jean Pierre Bemba met regularly in confidence-building forums. The President of the Independent Electoral Commission, Abbé Malu Malu, regularly briefed both parties on electoral developments and technical issues. The Comité international des sages, chaired by Joaquim Chissano, former President of Mozambique, also met frequently with the parties to discuss, inter alia, the conduct of the campaign. The parties signed several agreements reaffirming their commitment to a peaceful electoral process, agreeing to accept the outcome of the polls without recourse to violence, and to demilitarize the capital and major urban centres.

5. On 15 November 2006, the President of the Independent Electoral Commission announced the provisional results of the second presidential round, declaring President Kabila the winner with 58.05 per cent of the vote. On 18 November, Vice-President Bemba submitted an appeal to the Supreme Court, alleging electoral irregularities. On 21 November, violent demonstrations outside the Supreme Court building caused a temporary suspension of the Court's review of the provisional results. Order was quickly restored with MONUC assistance, and on 27 November the Supreme Court ruled that the complaints of irregularities were unfounded and officially declared Joseph Kabila President-elect. On 28 November, Vice-President Bemba stated that, in the interest of maintaining peace, he accepted the results and would lead a strong and republican opposition.

6. President Kabila's inaugural speech on 6 December outlined a broad and ambitious agenda of reform to end the cycle of crises in the Democratic Republic of the Congo and to improve living conditions. He cited as priorities improvements in infrastructure, education, employment, water and electricity supplies, health care and good governance. He emphasized that the security and development challenges facing the country transcended partisan interests, and that there was "room for everybody" in a democracy.

7. Meanwhile, two broad alliances emerged in the 500-seat National Assembly: AMP, the Parti lumumbiste unifié and the Union des démocrates mobutistes, having more than 300 seats, formed a bloc supporting President Kabila, while parties supporting former Vice-President Bemba in his presidential bid, including the Mouvement de libération du Congo (MLC) and a number of former presidential candidates formed a political opposition, UPN, with some 116 seats. Vital Kamerhe was elected Assembly President and presides over the Assembly Bureau, elected on 28 December, whose seven members are all affiliated with AMP.

8. On 19 January, the 11 Provincial Assemblies elected members of the Senate. Among those elected were some who had been prominent figures during the transition, including former Vice-Presidents Bemba and Abdoulaye Yerodia. Nine Provincial Assemblies elected Governors and Vice-Governors on 27 January. Gubernatorial polls in Kasai Occidental and Kasai Oriental were delayed until 15 February. AMP-affiliated candidates won 10 governorships, with a UPN candidate winning the governorship of Equateur province. Following widespread allegations of corruption in forms such as vote-buying, appeals were filed in appeals courts in nine provinces. Candidates from Bas-Congo, Kinshasa, Bandundu, Kasai Oriental and Maniema contested the provisional results in the Supreme Court, which upheld the results in all but Maniema, for which a decision is still pending.

9. On 24 February, the parliament adopted the Government programme for 2007-2011, marking the formal establishment of the new Government. The programme reflects the

priorities identified in the country's poverty reduction strategy paper adopted in 2006. The proposed budget for the 2007-2011 programme is some $14 billion, half of which the Government hopes will be funded by donors. In a welcome development, the Government annexed to its programme a "governance contract", which is closely modelled on and reflects the priorities of the governance compact developed during the transition.

10. The representation of women in the Government is, regrettably, very low: 9 of 60 Ministers, 42 of 500 members of the National Assembly, 5 of 108 Senators; and 43 of 690 Provincial Assembly members are women. Only one woman was elected Vice-Governor, out of 22 gubernatorial posts.

11. I visited the Democratic Republic of the Congo from 26 to 28 January. I congratulated President Kabila and the National Assembly and urged leaders of the Democratic Republic of the Congo to work together towards the consolidation of peace and reconstruction. I came away deeply impressed by the magnitude of the tasks facing the Government and the people of the country, and the scope of MONUC operations.

B. Security

12. While Kinshasa and most other urban areas are generally calm and peaceful, frequent outbreaks of fighting continue in the east, resulting in civilian casualties and displacement. The serious violence that erupted in Bas-Congo province after the gubernatorial elections demonstrated the dangerous fragility of the situation and serious deficiencies in the security forces. Incidents of unrest, often caused by disgruntled former combatants, continue throughout the country, and in some areas armed robbery and criminal activities have increased.

13. In North Kivu, fighting broke out in Sake on 25 November between non-integrated brigades loyal to Laurent Nkunda and the Armed Forces of the Democratic Republic of the Congo (FARDC). This conflict reflects deep underlying local tensions, in particular concerns among the minority Tutsi population regarding their security and lack of representation in Government. On 4 January, an agreement was reached, with important facilitation by the Government of Rwanda, between representatives of both sides to merge Nkunda-led elements with FARDC brigades from South Kivu. This mixing process helped bring an end to fighting. However, effective brassage of the former combatants, the professionalization of FARDC and a comprehensive strategy for reconciliation and economic development are preconditions for long-term stability in the eastern Democratic Republic of the Congo.

14. In Bas-Congo, serious incidents of civil unrest on 31 January and 1 February between a politico-religious movement, Bundu Dia Kongo (BDK), and the Congolese security forces resulted in more than 100 deaths, mainly of civilians. The violent disturbances were reportedly precipitated by a BDK call for a *ville morte* following the announcement of the provisional gubernatorial results by the Independent Electoral Commission, declaring the election of AMP-affiliated candidates as Governor and Vice-Governor. UPN, and some members of BDK, contested the results at the Bas-Congo Court of Appeals, alleging serious corrupt practices, given that the majority of seats in the Provincial Assembly had been won by UPN-affiliated candidates.

15. A MONUC investigation into the disturbances noted the Government's limited law enforcement capacity and the poor discipline of some Congolese national police and

FARDC personnel, who responded to the unrest with a disproportionate use of force and, in some cases, with summary executions. Violent action taken by some BDK elements and other demonstrators exacerbated the situation. In addition to deploying a formed police unit, troops and humanitarian and human rights teams of MONUC, my Special Representative continues to work with the Government, the national police and opposition supporters to prevent further violence in Bas-Congo, impressing on the authorities the need to scrupulously keep their pledge to ensure democracy and create political space for the opposition.

16. On 3 March, an incident of cross-border fire from the Democratic Republic of the Congo territory near Kibumba (30 km north of Goma) directed at Rwandan troops on the other side of the border was reportedly followed by a further exchange of fire on 4 March. The Rwandan Defence Forces subsequently addressed a letter to MONUC expressing concern about recent cross-border incidents allegedly involving combatants of the Democratic Forces for the Liberation of Rwanda (FDLR) present in the Democratic Republic of the Congo. MONUC has encouraged the Governments of the Democratic Republic of the Congo and Rwanda to discuss this incident and to seek a solution to the broader question of the remaining FDLR elements on the territory of the Democratic Republic of the Congo.

17. On 6 March, FARDC issued a communiqué ordering all personal guards of the Vice-Presidents and other senior transitional government officials to report with their weapons to FARDC sites by 15 March. It also indicated that their duties would be assumed by the national police and private security companies. The communiqué resulted in tensions in Kinshasa between the close-protection force of former Vice-President Bemba and FARDC. MONUC has increased patrols to defuse the situation and is actively engaged in facilitating contacts between the parties to find a peaceful solution.

18. The Lord's Resistance Army (LRA), which maintains a small presence in the remote Garamba Park border region in the north-eastern Democratic Republic of the Congo, poses a major security challenge and a continuing source of tension for the Democratic Republic of the Congo and neighbouring States. MONUC is supporting efforts to facilitate dialogue aimed at a lasting solution to the LRA problem, and it promotes active deterrence of the group's activities by supporting FARDC operations.

C. Disarmament, demobilization and reintegration

19. In 2006, the Government reached provisional disarmament, demobilization and reintegration agreements with the three remaining Ituri armed groups, comprising 4,500 combatants. Despite those agreements, on 24 December sporadic fighting broke out between FARDC and one group, the Front nationaliste intégrationniste (FNI) militia led by Peter Karim. By 9 March, following joint FARDC and MONUC operations to contain FNI elements, some 600 fighters had presented themselves for disarmament, demobilization and reintegration. Continued pressure is still required to induce remaining elements of the armed groups to undergo disarmament, demobilization and reintegration and *brassage*. In Katanga, local armed groups, including some 3,000 Mayi-Mayi elements, are to participate in community stabilization programmes following their disarmament.

D. Elections

20. In a letter addressed to me dated 1 March, Prime Minister Gizenga indicated that the local elections should be held as soon as possible. He requested United Nations technical

and logistical assistance, along with support in mobilizing resources for the preparation and conduct of both direct and indirect local elections. He also requested that the United Nations coordinate all international electoral assistance. The United Nations is prepared to support that request and is consulting with the Government regarding the election plan.

E. Regional developments

21. The signing on 15 December of the Pact on Security, Stability and Development in the Great Lakes Region was a historic development. Upon ratifying the Pact, participating States will commit themselves to adhering to the principle of non-aggression, the promotion of democracy and good governance, regional integration and mutual assistance on key human rights and humanitarian issues. The Pact and its protocols provide for the mandatory disarmament and extradition of foreign armed groups, the prevention of illicit flows of small arms, close collaboration with the United Nations and the establishment of joint security management mechanisms along common borders.

22. Military representatives from the Democratic Republic of the Congo, the Sudan and Uganda met on 7 February in Arua, north-western Uganda, to address issues of joint border security. Furthermore, from 26 to 28 February, the Democratic Republic of the Congo Government hosted the first meeting of parliamentarians of the Great Lakes region in Kinshasa. The parliamentarians agreed to the establishment of a regional parliamentary forum and declared their commitment to promoting the Pact's ratification and implementation.

III. The post-transitional period

23. The Transitional Government, with massive support from the United Nations and the international community, made considerable progress towards the objectives of the 2002 Global and All-Inclusive Agreement, particularly regarding the reunification of the country; the initial integration of FARDC; the adoption, through a national referendum, of the new Constitution; and the holding of national elections. However, significant aspects of the transition agenda remain to be completed, particularly with respect to armed groups, local elections, transitional justice and the promotion of reconciliation relating to ethnic tension and serious human rights violations.

24. The Global and All-Inclusive Agreement envisaged the establishment of a new political order based on constitutional and democratic government. The objectives for achieving this were outlined in President Kabila's inaugural speech and further elaborated in the Government programme for 2007-2011. The programme and the "governance contract" annexed to it place particular emphasis on good governance and rule of law, security sector reform, transparency and the fight against corruption, improved management of public funds and natural resources, civil service reform, local governance and an enhanced investment climate, including reform of publicly owned enterprises. Those documents set out widely agreed immediate steps for setting the country on a sustainable path towards meeting the Millennium Development Goals. The coupling of the Government programme and the "governance contract" is a welcome sign that the new Government recognizes the link between economic and social progress and democratic norms of transparency and accountability.

25. In carrying out its programme, the Government will face a number of immediate challenges complicated by severe security and fiscal constraints, lack of infrastructure and inadequate institutional capacity. It will need to extend State authority throughout the

country and develop and implement strategic plans to stabilize the eastern provinces and to reform the security sector. Early and effective measures will also be needed to provide basic social services and improve living conditions for the people of the Democratic Republic of the Congo.

A. Democratic institutions and processes

26. The Government will need to continue, in a transparent and determined manner, the establishment of the new institutions and mechanisms of the State at the national and provincial levels, in accordance with the Constitution. Legislation will be needed to establish the new High Courts and related institutions. Immediate steps will need to be taken towards empowering the new provincial governments and Assemblies through, inter alia, determining the most effective means for realizing the constitutional provision for decentralization. A key measure of the Government's commitment to consolidating democracy will be concrete steps to eliminate corruption and to ensure the systematic promotion of and respect for human rights throughout its institutions, particularly by the army and the police.

27. The Government will also need to ensure that there is an open, transparent political process that ensures popular participation in decision-making. Inclusiveness and consultation with opposition parties and broader civil society will be key indicators of the Government's commitment to democracy, as will its willingness to ensure the effective functioning of a multiparty political system as it approaches local elections and decentralization.

28. The dilapidated state of the civil administration will require urgent Government attention. Civil administration is weak, non-existent, or unduly influenced by local power brokers, particularly in areas affected by conflict. Strengthening the civil service at the central and provincial levels will be critical for improving security, the rule of law and living standards.

B. Security environment and security sector reform

29. The security situation remains precarious in many areas; Equateur, Ituri, the Kivus, Katanga, the Kasais, Bas-Congo and Kinshasa are particular areas of concern. FARDC remains fragile because of weak command and control; high levels of corruption; poor operational planning and tactical skills; poor administrative and logistical capacity to oversee the deployment, payment, sustenance and equipping of troops; very limited training capacity; and questionable loyalty on the part of some troops. While 14 of an intended 18 integrated brigades have been established, none can be considered effective without MONUC logistical support and, on occasion, operational training. The capacity of the national police has improved with the help of the United Nations and bilateral donors. However, it is still severely limited by deficiencies in training, a lack of unified and accountable command structures and systems for registering and vetting personnel and a lack of equipment.

30. Security and respect for the rule of law are key preconditions for progress. The Government, with international support, needs to urgently develop a comprehensive national security strategy and plan for security sector reform aimed at building the capacity of the defence sector, the police and the administration of justice so as to ensure the existence of professional, well-managed security institutions functioning within a framework of rule of law and respect for human rights. MONUC facilitation and co-chairmanship of the Joint Commission on Security Sector Reform played an important role, while donors such

as Angola, Belgium, South Africa and the United States of America have provided critical bilateral training support to FARDC. The European Union security sector reform mission has also provided valuable support for security sector reform. Other international partners, including Japan, the Netherlands, South Africa, the United Kingdom of Great Britain and Northern Ireland, the European Union—including through its police mission in Kinshasa—and the European Commission have also provided valuable support to the National Police, and Canada and the United Kingdom to the civilian and military judiciary. The European Union has indicated a willingness to coordinate international support for security sector reform.

Military

31. During the transition period, a primary focus of security sector reform, in tandem with the disarmament, demobilization and reintegration programme, was to build the capacity of the national army through restructuring, limited training projects and the integration of former belligerent forces. Through this Government-led process, some 96,478 combatants have been demobilized, with 50,541 integrated into the armed forces. The disarmament of another 44,046 former combatants has been completed. The Government will need to develop mechanisms to integrate an additional 34,786 elements, including the Kinshasa garrison and the Republican Guard.

32. Accelerated disarmament, demobilization and reintegration efforts are needed to disband the remaining armed groups, and to consolidate gains through improved law enforcement and reintegration processes. However, the disarmament, demobilization and reintegration of an estimated remaining 70,000 former combatants risks being jeopardized by a lack of funding. The Multi-Country Demobilization and Reintegration Programme is currently mobilizing resources through the World Bank and its partners for a follow-up project to support the national disarmament, demobilization and reintegration programme. The funding will be conditional on changes in the arrangements for implementing that programme and improved governance. Working with its international partners, the Government of the Democratic Republic of the Congo should provide the political support for the demobilization of remaining troops and militia.

33. The record of FARDC personnel as major perpetrators of human rights abuses is aggravated by a lack of accountability for those and other crimes, which is due to an inadequately resourced military justice system and interference in the judicial process. Continued appointments of alleged human rights violators to high ranking positions within FARDC are a source of concern. MONUC documents reports of human rights violations by FARDC and regularly submits its reports to the authorities. Reform of FARDC and effective measures to combat impunity would significantly reduce the level of human rights violations in much of the Democratic Republic of the Congo.

Police

34. During the transition period, 53,000 Congolese police received basic training, largely for election security. MONUC also oversaw the provision of basic equipment for some 32,000 national police personnel through a $52 million trust fund administered by the United Nations Development Programme (UNDP). A police reform commission, comprising Government and international members, prepared a comprehensive set of recommendations for a legal framework and the restructuring and rebuilding of the national police,

including on the development of basic operational, technical, and administrative capacities. The recommendations include those on the early implementation of a police census featuring the vetting and certification of officers and the adoption of legislation on longer-term modernization.

Justice

35. The justice sector severely lacks operational capacity. It has historically lacked independence and an ability to prosecute crimes and enforce judgements. Low salaries have compounded corruption, and few citizens have access to legal representation. Fewer than 60 of the required 180 first-instance courts exist, laws are obsolete and judicial facilities and prisons are extremely dilapidated.

36. Despite a few recent convictions by military courts relating to violations of human rights, the Democratic Republic of the Congo faces a pervasive climate of impunity. Of the few convictions for serious offences in the reporting period was a verdict issued by the Military Tribunal of Ituri district, on 19 February, convicting six of seven suspects for the murder of two United Nations military observers in May 2003.

37. The United Nations has contributed to capacity-building through technical advice and training, transport of judges and the MONUC prison support programme. Significant support from international partners is urgently needed for building the capacity of the justice system.

C. Economic management

38. Most of the population has failed to benefit from the natural resource wealth of the Democratic Republic of the Congo because of protracted war, civil disturbances, mismanagement and corruption. Social indicators are dismal. Life expectancy stands at 43 years, and mortality of children under 5 years of age is above 220 per thousand. An estimated 16 million people suffer critical food needs. Gross domestic product per capita stood at about $120 in 2005, and 75 per cent of the population lives on less than one dollar a day. The Democratic Republic of the Congo ranked 167th out of the 177 countries in the UNDP *Human Development Report 2006*. Uncontrolled and insufficient State revenues, budget leakages, serious irregularities in the allocation of concessions for the exploitation of natural resources, patronage in public enterprises and lack of transparency in budget execution and procurement undermine the country's sovereignty and the effective functioning of the State. The "governance contract", described in paragraph 24 above, commits the new Government to new approaches to the management of State finances, including opening the budgetary process to public scrutiny and parliamentary oversight.

39. In March, the International Monetary Fund suspended its regular stabilization programme and cash support after the Transitional Government failed to meet its targets. Uncontrolled public spending, financed partially by the issuance of currency, has contributed to a significant accumulated national debt and a worsening inflation rate. In 2007, the new Government is likely to face a considerable budget gap, which is expected to hamper its ability to pay public-sector salaries.

40. World Bank President Paul Wolfowitz and the European Commissioner for Development and Humanitarian Aid, Louis Michel, visited the Democratic Republic of the Congo on 8 and 9 March. During their visit, they called on the international community to provide

support for the new Government's peacebuilding and reconstruction efforts. Mr. Wolfowitz announced that the World Bank would provide $1.5 billion in reconstruction assistance over the next three years, and Mr. Michel announced that the European Union was providing €161 million in 2007 for that purpose.

D. Human Rights

41. The human rights situation remains critical throughout the Democratic Republic of the Congo. Although the number of gross human rights violations reported to and investigated by MONUC decreased considerably in 2006 relative to 2005, violence against civilians continues. Summary executions, politically motivated mass arbitrary arrests, ill-treatment and torture of civilians, beatings and rape continue to be committed, mainly by security service personnel. Despite the adoption in July 2006 of laws on sexual violence, rape is widespread, including incidents of mass rape.

42. In a landmark step towards fighting impunity, on 29 January the International Criminal Court confirmed the charges against former militia leader Thomas Lubanga for war crimes committed in Ituri during 2002 and 2003.

IV. Post-transition mandate of the Mission

43. The Democratic Republic of the Congo has entered a new political era. However, significant core stabilization tasks in the current MONUC mandate remain to be completed, including the creation of a stable security environment: disarmament, demobilization, repatriation, resettlement and reintegration of foreign armed groups; disarmament, demobilization and reintegration of Congolese combatants; and support for the large and complex local election process. Having consulted the Government, I believe that during the next phase MONUC will also need to play a strong role in supporting the consolidation of democracy, maximize its contribution to security sector reform, contribute to the normalization of regional relations and help to ensure that significant benchmarks are achieved in key areas identified in consultation with the Government.

44. I therefore propose that the principal elements of the MONUC mandate, as an integrated Mission working in close collaboration with the United Nations country team and donors, would be to assist the Government of the Democratic Republic of the Congo in (a) building a stable security environment, (b) consolidating democracy, (c) planning security sector reform and participating in its early stages, (d) protecting human rights and strengthening the rule of law, (e) the protection of civilians and (f) the conduct of local elections. The United Nations would also contribute actively, if requested to do so by the Government, to the coordination of international assistance.

45. In all areas of its work, MONUC will emphasize the role of civil society in political dialogue and decision-making, ensuring a rights-based approach, as defined by the General Assembly, and the implementation of Security Council resolutions 1325 (2000) on women and peace and security and 1612 (2005) regarding the protection of children. As the focus of United Nations efforts shifts increasingly towards longer-term goals, the United Nations country team is expected to play an increasingly important role in the post-transition period.

A. Building a stable security environment

Protection of civilians and security operations

46. Under a mandate based on Chapter VII of the Charter of the United Nations, MONUC would continue to support the Government of the Democratic Republic of the Congo in creating a stable security environment in the country, within its capabilities and where it is deployed, by protecting civilians under imminent threat of violence, securing national borders and monitoring illegal arms flows, protecting humanitarian personnel and securing United Nations personnel and activities. Through support for FARDC operations, MONUC would compel recalcitrant local armed groups to join the disarmament, demobilization and reintegration process, maintain pressure on foreign armed groups (including FDLR and LRA) and interdict illegal economic activities and support for illegal armed groups.

47. The security responsibilities of MONUC would be gradually turned over to the Congolese authorities in line with clear, agreed benchmarks to be achieved through an enhanced security sector reform programme in which MONUC would participate in line with its mandate, resources and expertise. If requested to do so by the Government and in coordination with international partners, MONUC would assist in security sector reform at the policy level as the Government takes the lead in establishing a comprehensive security sector reform process. That process would include strengthening command and control of the military and police forces and building an effective military justice system.

Security sector reform

48. It will be essential to ensure that as MONUC disengages, significant progress is being made in security sector reform. Long-term and comprehensive capacity-building of FARDC can be carried out only in cooperation with bilateral donors. However, its capacity to conduct joint operations needs to be urgently improved. In this regard, in areas where MONUC is present it would provide short-term, basic, individual and unit-level training to integrated FARDC brigades deployed in the eastern Democratic Republic of the Congo in order to improve their capability to hold ground and secure the gains made, and so that they could earn the confidence and support of the population. Human rights would be an important component of all training activities. MONUC would also continue to mentor FARDC at all levels to promote a single, effective and accountable line of command.

49. Since 2005, MONUC has provided FARDC with limited material support to enable it to conduct joint operations. Without such assistance, which includes sustenance, medical support, fuel for transportation, communications equipment and occasional airlifts, FARDC units would lack sufficient operational mobility and face shortages in rations and other combat supplies. When essential for joint operations, MONUC would need to continue providing such support, pending enhanced bilateral assistance programmes and progress in the Government's own efforts to enhance the capabilities of FARDC.

Police

50. MONUC would continue to develop the capacity of the national police and related law enforcement agencies, in accordance with internationally recognized human rights and criminal justice norms and standards. MONUC would provide policy advice, technical assistance and training, in coordination with other international partners, as well as mentoring and on-the-job training through co-location of MONUC police advisers at the command and

field levels. It would also conduct on-the-job training at the national and provincial levels in operational and resource planning, the creation of coordination mechanisms and the establishment of professional standards and disciplinary units to ensure prompt follow-up on human rights violations and unprofessional conduct by police and law enforcement officials. Significant efforts by international partners, including technical training and resources, will be required during the MONUC mandate and beyond.

51. The formed police units of MONUC would, in areas of deployment, continue to train Congolese counterparts at the local level, provide perimeter security for United Nations installations and, together with national police crowd-control units, conduct joint patrols to increase security in the event of civil disturbances. MONUC would continue to advise and train the national police to ensure that the use of force is proportionate to the threat and in accordance with internationally accepted crowd-control methods.

Justice

52. MONUC would continue to work with its national and international partners to provide strategic and operational policy advice in this vital area, especially with regard to means for coordinating between police, justice and prison systems and for facilitating coordination between justice officials and the promotion of professional standards. MONUC would provide on-the-job training and co-locate experts with officials of the Democratic Republic of the Congo, provide technical assistance and train instructors.

53. Together with bilateral and multilateral partners, MONUC would support the Government in strengthening the capacity of the justice and prison system by assisting in the development of a long-term justice and prison reform strategy; mobilizing donor assistance; enhancing capacity to investigate and prosecute serious criminal cases and for court and prison management; improving national academic capacity for professional training; and bringing State-provided justice to all communities in the Democratic Republic of the Congo. MONUC would also enhance military justice, by initiating a military justice needs assessment and follow-up; by evaluating the role of military justice with a view to restricting its jurisdiction to military offences and personnel; by mobilizing assistance to improve a minimum number of military prisons; and by deploying military justice personnel.

Authorized strength of the Mission

54. In projecting the mandated strength that MONUC requires, it should be taken into consideration that the security situation in the Democratic Republic of the Congo remains fragile, with the potential for violence to erupt simultaneously in several locations. MONUC military and police remain a unique and indispensable pillar for helping ensure stability.

55. An immediate reduction in the MONUC troop level would weaken the ability of FARDC and the Mission to maintain military pressure on the remaining armed groups in Ituri, the Kivus and Katanga, thus delaying the pacification of those areas. Any quick reduction would also leave the Democratic Republic of the Congo without a capacity to respond to multiple incidents in different regions. The reduction or removal of MONUC formed police units would seriously disrupt ongoing programmes to build the capacity of the national police to deal with civil disorder, while depriving MONUC of a non-lethal option to protect its own personnel and facilities in the event of violence. Furthermore, it is likely that political tensions will rise in the run-up to the local elections. MONUC will require a significant

military, police and logistical presence to support countrywide local elections effectively. In order for the Mission to carry out the tasks envisaged in the next phase, it would require its current authorized military strength of 17,030 (all ranks, not inclusive of military observers), its 391 police trainers and its six formed police units (750, all ranks) until at least 31 December 2007.

56. In accordance with established practice, the Secretariat will conduct a technical assessment mission to the Democratic Republic of the Congo before September to assist MONUC in its strategic planning for the next phase of the Mission. That technical mission will focus in particular on the establishment of benchmarks in key sectors to guide the eventual drawdown and withdrawal of MONUC. Accordingly, I propose to present further recommendations regarding the force strength, deployment and operations of MONUC to the Security Council in a report to be issued in November 2007.

B. Consolidating democracy

Strengthening democratic institutions and processes

57. In the next phase, MONUC and the United Nations country team would work very closely with the Government to help the Democratic Republic of the Congo acquire capacity at the national, provincial, regional and local levels. The efforts of MONUC would focus on strengthening democratic institutions and processes; promoting justice, human rights and child protection; gender issues; and supporting humanitarian operations. MONUC would play an essential role countrywide in supporting the Government's efforts for decentralization and the extension of State authority.

58. MONUC would play a role in promoting good governance and accountability, advancing national reconciliation and engaging with and coordinating partners and international support. It would also support the strengthening of civil society using a variety of means, including Radio Okapi. Working closely with the Government and the United Nations country team, MONUC would also support the implementation of the Government programme for 2007-2011 and facilitate the implementation of the Country Assistance Framework.

Promoting human rights

59. The integrated United Nations Human Rights Office, which includes MONUC human rights officers, would continue its human rights monitoring role, assist the Government in putting an end to impunity, strengthen national capacity in the area of human rights and assist in building civil society's capacity to monitor and advocate for human rights. The integrated Office would also support the Government and civil society in establishing an independent and credible national human rights institution in accordance with the Paris Principles. It would also help develop and implement a transitional justice strategy, including through assistance to the Office of the United Nations High Commissioner for Human Rights in implementing a mapping exercise of the most serious violations of human rights and international humanitarian law committed between March 1993 and June 2003. That mapping exercise, which is important for long-term national reconciliation and justice in the country, would require donor funding. MONUC would also continue to cooperate with efforts to ensure that those responsible for serious violations of human rights and international humanitarian law are brought to justice.

Promoting child protection

60. MONUC would continue to assist the Government and civil society actors to strengthen their capacity in the area of child protection in close cooperation with national and international partners, and continue monitoring and reporting on violations of children's rights, in accordance with Security Council resolution 1612 (2005). It would support the Government in developing and adopting the necessary legal, judicial, security and other measures to enhance the protection of children.

Gender

61. Together with national and non-governmental organizations, MONUC and the United Nations country team would assist the Government and civil society in integrating and reinforcing the gender perspective in national programmes. MONUC would support the parliament's adoption of a law on gender equality, as stipulated in the Constitution, and its review of existing legislation pertaining to women's rights to ensure that it reflects international standards. In collaboration with the Ministry of Women's and Family Affairs and women's groups, MONUC would also help develop a national plan of action on Security Council resolution 1325 (2000) and assist the national authorities, the security forces and civil society in developing programmes on peace and security and women's issues.

C. Support for local elections

62. The local elections form an integral part of the electoral process envisaged under the Global and All-Inclusive Agreement. They are essential for implementing the constitutional decentralization process and for the participation of communities in governance and reconstruction. The process will entail the election, by universal suffrage, of 98 municipal and 5,400 local community councils, followed by indirect elections of 98 burgomasters, 21 mayors and over 700 sector chiefs and their deputies. With 6,037 local (as opposed to 385 national and provincial) constituencies, the local elections will be a challenge equal to, if not surpassing, that of organizing and supporting the national elections. The local elections will take place across the country in several phases and are expected to require at least 12 months to complete.

63. In response to the Government's request, the assistance of MONUC would include advising on a legal framework for the National Independent Electoral Commission as a successor to the Independent Electoral Commission; helping to establish the National Independent Electoral Commission and consolidate its institutional capacity; and providing logistical and security support. MONUC and UNDP would also assist the Government in mobilizing sufficient international assistance for the holding of the local elections. The Mission and other partners would help the National Independent Electoral Commission develop operational plans and promote a high degree of participation by women candidates.

64. MONUC would also continue to assist the Government in completing outstanding work related to the elections, including updating voters' lists. MONUC and UNDP will work through integrated structures in supporting the local elections, as they did for the national elections. The Government, MONUC, UNDP and other donors are working to confirm the overall plan, budget and financing and support arrangements.

D. Humanitarian issues

65. Persistent violence against civilians and localized conflicts have dire consequences for the population. Between December 2006 and January 2007 an estimated 115,000 people were forced to flee their homes in North Kivu following the confrontation between FARDC and elements loyal to Laurent Nkunda. In Ituri district, renewed fighting between FNI and FARDC led to the displacement of some 35,000 persons towards the end of January 2007. Just over 1 million persons remain displaced, and there are 413,000 Congolese refugees in neighbouring countries. While the humanitarian needs in the country remain immense, the increased capacity of the humanitarian community to respond, coupled with better security conditions in some areas of the country, allowed for the provision in 2006 of assistance to more than 600,000 displaced persons and facilitated the return of 550,000 internally displaced persons, as well as the repatriation of 35,000 Congolese refugees.

66. Over the past year, the Office for the Coordination of Humanitarian Affairs has reinforced its operations in the east of the country and improved the coordination of humanitarian response. The donor community has increased its support by contributing some $351 million to the 2006 humanitarian action plan. The 2007 humanitarian action plan, launched on 30 November 2006, totals $687 million and focuses on rapid responses to emergencies and the recovery of affected populations. Almost 70 per cent of the 2007 requirements are targeted for the eastern Democratic Republic of the Congo.

67. In the western provinces, UNDP and MONUC would continue to support the Humanitarian Coordinator and the Office for the Coordination of Humanitarian Affairs by facilitating inter-agency coordination for life-saving, emergency protection and recovery projects until the United Nations country team can deploy additional resources for that purpose. The Mission would also continue to assist the Government in building capacity for mine action, including the development of medium- and long-term responses and mechanisms for the coordination of mine action activities.

E. Conduct and discipline

68. My Special Representative and the MONUC senior management team continue to give high priority to the prevention of sexual exploitation and sexual abuse and other types of misconduct, including through a policy of strong preventive measures and an ambitious training strategy. In 2006, thousands of United Nations personnel were briefed and trained on the code of conduct through numerous briefing sessions, including train-the-trainer workshops for military personnel. A database monitoring system and strengthened procedures for monitoring, reporting and processing allegations have been put in place, enabling the Mission to report more systematically on allegations of misconduct by all categories of personnel.

69. During 2006, 176 allegations of sexual exploitation and abuse were reported to the Office of Internal Oversight Services. Investigations were completed against 49 personnel; as a result, three military contingent members were repatriated on disciplinary grounds. The remaining allegations are under active investigation. In cooperation with the MONUC Conduct and Discipline Team, the Office of Internal Oversight Services has made considerable progress in addressing the concerns expressed in my previous reports with regard to the length of, and delays in, investigations. However, those aspects, as well as the limited investigative capacity of the Office of Internal Oversight Services, need to be urgently addressed.

70. I intend to monitor closely the progress made towards eliminating sexual exploitation and abuse by United Nations personnel wherever deployed, and ensuring that whenever it occurs, those responsible are held accountable. During my visit to the Democratic Republic of the Congo in January, I stressed to MONUC personnel that the policy of zero tolerance for sexual exploitation and abuse will be vigorously applied.

F. Coordination of international support

71. The Government of the Democratic Republic of the Congo requires the sustained support of international partners in addressing the priorities set out in its programme for 2007–2011. This will necessitate an effective platform for regular consultation between the Government and the international community in order to ensure that key partners clearly understand the Government's goals and initiatives, to help maintain international engagement, and to ensure concerted action by international partners of the Democratic Republic of the Congo in averting or responding to potential crises. Such a platform would also provide active support for the Government in its efforts to move the democratic process forward. A partnership arrangement, chaired by the Prime Minister or another senior Government official, with my Special Representative as Vice-Chair, might provide such a forum. If requested to do so by the Government, MONUC would be prepared to facilitate and provide the secretariat for such a forum. It is expected that development assistance will also be coordinated under the strong leadership of the Government through mechanisms supported by the World Bank and the United Nations Resident Coordinator.

V. Financial aspects

72. The General Assembly, by its resolution 60/121 B, appropriated the total amount of $1,091,242,800, equivalent to $90,936,900 per month, for MONUC for the period from 1 July 2006 to 30 June 2007. Should the Security Council decide to extend the mandate of MONUC beyond 15 April 2007, the cost of maintaining the Mission until 30 June 2007 would be limited to the amounts approved by the General Assembly.

73. As at 31 December 2006, unpaid assessed contributions to the special account for MONUC amounted to $349.3 million. The total outstanding assessed contributions for all peacekeeping operations as at that date amounted to $1,760 million.

74. As at 31 January, amounts owed to troop and formed-police contributors totalled $56.9 million. Reimbursements of troop and contingent-owned equipment costs have been made for the period up 31 October 2006 and 31 March 2006, respectively.

VI. Observations and recommendations

75. With the successful conduct of the 2006 elections and the installation of the new Government, the Democratic Republic of the Congo has reached a historic turning point. In his inaugural speech, President Kabila captured the significance of this moment. He called for respect for democratic principles, tolerance and inclusiveness, and for setting visionary goals for reducing poverty and raising living standards. His words articulated the long-held aspirations of the Congolese people to break with the past and establish a new culture of democracy, reconciliation, human rights and development.

76. The Government now faces the daunting task of realizing its ambitious programme for 2007-2011. By including in its programme the "governance contract", the Government

expressed its commitment to governance principles endorsed by the Congolese people and by the international community. Faithful implementation of the contract would bring major benefits for the people of the Democratic Republic of the Congo. I therefore urge the international community to support the Government in its efforts to put its historic programme into effect.

77. The Government has requested the assistance of MONUC to support the holding of local elections as soon as possible, and has begun preparing the necessary legislation. Those elections will be another important step in the democratization of the country. The United Nations is prepared to provide technical advice and to facilitate that crucial exercise, as well as to extend logistical and security support to the National Independent Electoral Commission that is to be established.

78. The largely peaceful and orderly passage from the transition period to the new dispensation has not been without cause for concern. Some of the most recent political developments in the Democratic Republic of the Congo have been worrying. I am concerned at the alleged widespread electoral corruption believed to have influenced the results in several gubernatorial contests. Furthermore, the narrowing of the political space for an effective political opposition, including the exclusion of opposition members from the Bureau of the National Assembly, as well as the incitement to violence by some members of opposition parties, represent troubling tendencies that, if not reversed, threaten the nascent democracy of the Democratic Republic of the Congo.

79. I strongly urge the political leaders in the Democratic Republic of the Congo to respect the principles of transparency, inclusiveness and tolerance of dissent. At the same time, opposition parties should adhere to those same democratic norms, voicing their views responsibly and without resort to violence. Failure to adhere to these democratic principles would seriously undermine the credibility and ultimate legitimacy of the country's political leaders and institutions.

80. Inadequate participation by women in political structures at the national and provincial levels is also a cause for concern. A concerted effort should be made by all political parties and the Government to promote the participation of women candidates and to engage women in civic and voter education.

81. Assisting the Democratic Republic of the Congo in addressing the security challenges posed by armed groups in the east will remain a core element of the MONUC mandate. In Ituri, strong Government efforts to ensure the entry of all remaining militia elements into disarmament, demobilization and reintegration remain vital, including through continued military pressure by FARDC, supported by MONUC. In North and South Kivu, developments show prospects for improvement. In this regard, I commend the efforts of the Governments of the Democratic Republic of the Congo and Rwanda to resolve the problems posed by the forces of renegade commander Laurent Nkunda and other armed elements.

82. The Government should urgently develop a coherent plan for achieving security in the East, including through the completion of disarmament, demobilization and reintegration, which should be accompanied by efforts to promote national reconciliation, recovery and development in the region. MONUC will continue to work closely with FARDC to bring an end to the threats posed by FDLR and non-integrated militias, including Mayi-Mayi and

other groups. The FDLR problem should be addressed through a combination of political engagement, military dissuasion and possible relocation.

83. The presence of LRA in the north-eastern Democratic Republic of the Congo remains a destabilizing element in the region that must be addressed with determination. The United Nations continues to support Uganda's efforts to address this problem through dialogue and the efforts of my Special Envoy for the LRA-affected areas, Joaquim Chissano.

84. Progress in security sector reform is key to the restoration and consolidation of peace in the Democratic Republic of the Congo and the exit strategy for MONUC. International stakeholders should reach agreement with the Congolese authorities on the way forward on security sector reform as soon as possible. A comprehensive security sector reform plan should take into account immediate and long-term needs and identify the key priorities in the areas of defence sector reform, police and justice. The achievement of specific benchmarks of operational performance by the security forces of the Democratic Republic of the Congo will be critical for the eventual disengagement of MONUC. Much useful preliminary work has been done by the international partners of the Democratic Republic of the Congo, in particular the European Union, to assess needs and outline possible approaches to security sector reform. I would encourage the Government and those partners to reach early agreement on effective coordination arrangements for security sector reform and to proceed with that vital process in earnest, building on earlier efforts. Assisting the Government in identifying resources for long- and short-term funding and encouraging the support of a wide range of international partners will be essential elements for success.

85. The establishment of the new Government offers an opportunity for the Democratic Republic of the Congo to normalize its relations with neighbouring States. I would urge the Democratic Republic of the Congo to establish full diplomatic relations with its neighbours as soon as possible and to address mutual concerns over security and border issues constructively. The recently signed Pact on Security, Stability and Development in the Great Lakes Region offers a promising mechanism for regional cooperation, and I would urge the parliaments of the signatory States to ensure its early ratification.

86. My Special Representative has consulted with President Kabila and Prime Minister Gizenga, as well as with National Assembly President Kamerhe, regarding the future mandate of MONUC. He has also discussed it with representatives of the Governments of Angola, Belgium, France, Germany, South Africa, the United Kingdom of Great Britain and Northern Ireland and the United States of America. He has also met with Javier Solana, High Representative for Common Foreign and Security Policy of the European Union, and senior European Commission officials, as well as with Paul Wolfowitz, President of the World Bank.

87. In the light of these consultations, and taking into consideration the factors discussed above, I recommend that the Security Council approve the post-transition mandate for MONUC as outlined in section IV above, including a military strength of 17,030 personnel and 760 military observers and a civilian police strength of 391 police advisers and six formed police units of 125 members each (all ranks) until 31 December 2007. MONUC would continue to operate as a fully integrated Mission in which its work and that of the United Nations country team reinforce and complement each other.

88. An operational plan for the gradual downsizing and eventual withdrawal of MONUC and a responsible exit strategy will require clear linkages between the achievement of benchmarks in key areas—including in the political sphere—and the handover of responsibility to other actors, including the Government, the United Nations agencies, funds and programmes, the World Bank and other bilateral and multilateral stakeholders. Following the multidisciplinary technical assessment mission to the Democratic Republic of the Congo described in paragraph 56 above, I intend to report to the Security Council in November on benchmarks in key sectors and tentative timetables for achieving them, which would guide a gradual and phased withdrawal of MONUC.

89. I would like to thank my Special Representative, William Lacy Swing, and all the women and men of MONUC and the United Nations country team for their determination and dedication, particularly over the past difficult months. Their service, often under difficult conditions, has been instrumental in the realization of the aspirations of the people of the Democratic Republic of the Congo for the holding of national elections. My appreciation also goes to the countries contributing police and troops to MONUC and to donor countries and the multilateral and non-governmental organizations that continue to provide invaluable support to the Democratic Republic of the Congo.

Annex
United Nations Organization Mission in the Democratic Republic of the Congo: military and civilian police strength as at 28 February 2007

	Military component				
Country	*Military observers*	*Staff officers*	*Troops*	*Total deployed*	*Civilian police*
Algeria	5	0	0	5	3
Argentina	0	0	0	0	0
Bangladesh	15	9	1 331	1 355	250
Belgium	0	9	0	9	0
Benin	13	0	750	763	10
Bolivia	8	0	200	208	0
Bosnia and Herzegovina	5	0	0	5	0
Burkina Faso	11	0	0	11	55
Cameroon	0	0	0	0	55
Canada	0	9	0	9	0
Central African Republic	0	0	0	0	7
Chad	0	0	0	0	2
China	10	2	218	230	0
Côte d'Ivoire	0	0	0	0	7
Czech Republic	3	0	0	3	0
Denmark	1	1	0	2	0
Egypt	19	4	0	23	1
France	0	6	0	6	9
Ghana	22	3	462	487	30
Guatemala	5	1	105	111	0
Guinea	0	0	0	0	0
India	36	13	4 372	4 421	250
Indonesia	9	4	175	188	0
Ireland	0	23	0	23	0
Jordan	21	5	66	92	4
Kenya	29	7	0	36	4
Madagascar	0	0	0	0	4
Malawi	26	0	109	135	0
Malaysia	4	5	0	16	0
Mali	20	0	0	20	19
Mozambique	0	0	0	0	0
Mongolia	2	0	0	2	0
Morocco	1	3	809	813	0
Nepal	19	1	1 030	1 050	0
Netherlands	0	0	0	0	0
Niger	17	1	0	18	48
Nigeria	30	1	0	31	0
Pakistan	36	15	3 556	3 607	0

	Military component				
Country	*Military observers*	*Staff officers*	*Troops*	*Total deployed*	*Civilian police*
Paraguay	17	0	0	17	0
Peru	4	0	0	4	0
Poland	3	0	0	3	0
Romania	24	0	0	24	1
Russian Federation	22	1	0	23	4
Senegal	12	14	459	485	275
South Africa	2	14	1 184	1 200	0
Serbia	0	0	6	6	0
Spain	2	0	0	2	0
Sri Lanka	2	0	0	2	0
Sweden	5	0	0	5	3
Switzerland	1	1	0	2	0
Tunisia	26	5	464	495	0
Turkey	0	0	0	0	5
Ukraine	11	0	0	11	3
United Kingdom	0	6	0	6	0
Uruguay	33	12	1 324	1 369	0
Vanuatu	0	0	0	0	2
Yemen	4	0	0	4	1
Zambia	20	4	0	24	
Total	**555**	**167**	**16 620**	**17 342**	**1 024**

B. Haiti

1. Report of the Secretary-General on the United Nations Stabilization Mission in Haiti, 19 December 2006 (S/2006/1003)

I. Introduction

1. By its resolution 1702 (2006), the Security Council extended the mandate of the United Nations Stabilization Mission in Haiti (MINUSTAH) until 15 February 2007 and requested me to report on its implementation not later than 31 December 2006. The present report covers major developments since my report of 28 July 2006 (S/2006/592), and progress made and problems encountered in the implementation of the mandate of the Mission as contained in Security Council resolutions 1542 (2004), 1608 (2005) and 1702 (2006).

II. Political developments

2. During the reporting period, the largely successful completion of the electoral process marked a further significant step in the reinforcement of Haiti's democratic process. On 3 December, approximately 29,000 candidates competed for some 8,000 municipal and local positions in the first such elections in 10 years, and a second round was held for 3 senatorial and 11 deputy seats postponed from the earlier legislative elections as a result of interruptions in voting. As compared with previous elections, the Provisional Electoral Council assumed increased responsibility for technical and administrative aspects of the process, including full responsibility for training and payment of some 40,000 poll workers.

3. The Mission provided logistical and security assistance for the electoral process. Among the tasks undertaken by the Mission were the distribution of voter lists to 140 Communal Electoral Offices and of 2,000 kits for the training of poll workers, and assistance with the logistics for the collection and storage of sensitive and non-sensitive material from some 9,231 polling stations throughout the country. MINUSTAH worked closely with the Haitian National Police to implement a joint security plan. The military component provided static security for voting centres in areas identified as high-risk, and the Haitian National Police and MINUSTAH police patrolled assigned areas. MINUSTAH police also recruited and trained approximately 4,000 electoral guards.

4. While some security incidents occurred, voter turnout, which was estimated at approximately 30 per cent, was higher than expected. Overall, the Haitian electoral authorities declared themselves satisfied with the process. However, a number of appeals are anticipated, which the Provisional Electoral Council will address in the coming weeks. In addition, given the destruction of some voting centres and the related loss of electoral data, reruns are likely to be held in several affected constituencies.

5. Members of the forty-eighth legislature were convoked to extraordinary sessions on a number of occasions, including for the adoption of the State budget in September. To date, eight draft bills submitted to Parliament have been studied by the Senate and five by the Chamber of Deputies. The various parliamentary committees have been meeting regularly, including for consultation with experts and with national and international partners. In October and November, groups of parliamentarians undertook a series of visits to each of the 10 regions where MINUSTAH provides logistical and security support. The Government

opted to maintain all departmental delegates, vice-delegates and municipal authorities for the remainder of 2006. The measure was taken in order to avoid a precipitous change among local government officials prior to the 3 December elections, and to allow time for parliamentary debate and scrutiny of the decentralization and deconcentration bills.

6. The implementation of the proposal by the Prime Minister for a *Programme d'apaisement* social (social pacification programme) has not advanced significantly. Bilateral support will be crucial to permit the tangible improvements envisaged in the programme, which are crucial in order to promote stability and encourage further political progress. During the International Conference for Haiti's Economic and Social Development held in Port-au-Prince on 25 July 2006, international participants pledged 750 million dollars for much-needed programmes to finance the budget deficit and the Government's public investment programme for the coming fiscal year. They expressed their readiness to work towards greater transparency in international aid through firm commitments to budget cycles, as proposed by the Government. The international participants reiterated their long-term support for the Government's reform efforts in the areas of economic governance, fighting corruption, smuggling and tax evasion, and reaffirmed their willingness to work with the Government in support of the reform of the Haitian National Police and the judicial system, as well as of efforts for social development and the disarmament, demobilization and reintegration process. The follow-up conference in Madrid on 30 November further helped to maintain international focus on Haiti and resulted in a number of sizeable pledges, although it was not formally a pledging event.

7. The demonstrations that took place in October suggest the potential for violent expressions of frustration, which could have implications for Haitian and international efforts to promote progress. On 24 October, a group of some 30 students gathered near a United Nations Day ceremony in Port-au-Prince, holding anti-MINUSTAH placards and calling for the withdrawal of the peacekeepers. The next day, some 600 students held a similar protest near the Presidential Palace, and roadblocks with burning tyres were erected. In response, the Minister for Foreign Affairs urged students not to resort to violence, but noted that the demonstrations illustrated the public's impatience at the lack of socio-economic progress.

8. Following the reintegration of Haiti into the Caribbean Community (CARICOM), on 18 October, a high-level delegation from CARICOM, headed by the Prime Minister of Saint Kitts and Nevis, who is the current Chairman of the organization, visited Haiti. The delegation discussed with the Haitian authorities the prospects for the full integration of Haiti into the organization, including the common market. The visit coincided with a CARICOM assessment mission, during which the participants discussed the possibilities of opening an office in Port-au-Prince. The preceding initiatives were conducted within the framework of the organization's response to a request from President René Préval for support for Haiti's development.

9. The continued repatriation of Haitian nationals continued to present a potential problem along the border area with the Dominican Republic. On 21 November, MINUSTAH facilitated a meeting that brought together representatives of the authorities of Haiti and the Dominican Republic and non-governmental organizations to discuss the application of the Protocol of Understanding on the mechanisms of repatriation and other key areas of concern.

III. Security situation

Security operations

10. During the reporting period, the overall security environment continued to be relatively stable in most of the country and there were signs of improvement in some critical areas. However, the overall situation remained fragile and volatile. Much of the violence continued to take place in the capital; other regions of the country enjoyed a greater level of stability, with the exception of isolated incidents reported in Fort Liberté, Cap Haïtien and Gonaïves. Although kidnappings continued to take place at a high rate throughout Port-au-Prince, they occurred less frequently than last year, and murder rates also showed some decline. However, armed attacks against MINUSTAH and violent demonstrations increased. The development of Haitian National Police capacity remained at a very early stage, and the Mission's military and police components continued to play a key role in promoting its capacity in the face of substantial challenges, working in close cooperation with the Haitian political and police leadership.

11. On 19 July, armed groups gathered in Port-au-Prince, firing weapons and creating panic in the vicinity of Cité Soleil and the airport, expressing their frustration for the perceived inaction on the part of the Government to meet their demands for amnesty in return for participation in a disarmament programme. On the following day, the armed groups opened fire on the Jordanian Battalion camp and a nearby Haitian National Police station, injuring one police officer, while five of the gang members were killed and another five injured. Over the following two days, 6 civilians were killed, approximately 80 injured and an unknown number were abducted.

12. In response to the outbreak of violence, my Special Representative intensified his discussions with President Préval and Government officials to develop a coordinated response. To highlight the partnership between the Mission and the Government, President Préval visited Cité Militaire on 9 August, together with other officials from the Government and the Mission. After talking to local residents, the President issued a statement stressing that, while his Government had initiated dialogue with some armed groups in an effort to launch a disarmament, demobilization and reintegration programme, he would not hesitate to use force to neutralize armed groups that refused to disarm voluntarily.

13. On 25 August, Haitian and MINUSTAH officials agreed to an enhanced security plan, which established 12 additional Haitian National Police/MINUSTAH checkpoints and 23 additional Haitian National Police checkpoints around Port-au-Prince. Three MINUSTAH platoons were redeployed from the outlying regions to Cité Soleil to support the increased tempo of operations in that area. The configuration of formed police units was also adjusted.

14. By mid-September, the security situation began to improve owing to the measures taken by the Haitian National Police and MINUSTAH, and relative calm was observed in Cité Soleil and Cité Militaire, following the reinforcement of the Mission's presence there. Furthermore, on 2 October, MINUSTAH and the Government agreed to establish a communication mechanism at the highest level to plan future joint operations in Cité Soleil and set up a coordination, monitoring and verification mechanism for such operations. On the following day, Haitian National Police officers accompanied by MINUSTAH visited Cité Soleil to meet local residents and community leaders and to look into the possibility of resuming patrols and re-establishing a Haitian National Police presence in the area.

This first visit of the Haitian police to Cité Soleil in almost three years was welcomed by local residents, who expressed their readiness to work alongside the Haitian National Police to restore peace to the area. The Haitian National Police have subsequently carried out patrols in Cité Soleil during daylight hours.

15. Tensions remained high in the Martissant area of Port-au-Prince throughout the reporting period. On a number of occasions MINUSTAH troops have found bodies in the area, with the deaths attributed to suspicious causes. As part of the joint Government/MINUSTAH plan to restore security, the Mission organized a series of meetings between local authorities and residents. On 27 September, MINUSTAH troops apprehended a significant armed group leader who had been linked to the large-scale killings in Martissant in both 2005 and 2006. On 3 November, a group of armed criminals in Martissant were confronted by the Haitian National Police and a MINUSTAH formed police unit, resulting in the death of one civilian and the wounding of one formed police unit member. Eight individuals were arrested by the Haitian National Police, but were subsequently released.

16. MINUSTAH troops and police were shot at on a number of occasions during the reporting period, and on 10 November, two MINUSTAH soldiers were killed as they returned to their base. The ongoing violence has also taken a toll on the Haitian National Police, with seven police officers murdered in the capital since August.

17. The advances that have been made in the area of security remain fragile and should be consolidated. In order to do this, it will be essential to reinforce the close collaboration that has developed between MINUSTAH and the Haitian political and security authorities and to continue to increase the tempo of operations in the rural and urban areas. In addition to continued activities in Port-au-Prince, the Mission plans to enhance its presence and undertake deterrent actions along the border, in ports and on outlying islands in order to buttress the Government's minimal capacity to deal with trafficking activities (see S/2006/592, para. 54). To mitigate such illicit activities, MINUSTAH and the Haitian Coast Guard will perform joint operations, bearing in mind the Coast Guard's limited capability.

18. In the above context, it will be vital to avoid premature changes in the Mission's force configuration. As noted below, a long-term process will be required to develop a full security capability for Haiti, including an ability to assume tasks that go beyond essential policing. Therefore, barring a dramatic improvement in the security situation, the continued contribution of the military and police components, at their currently authorized ceilings of 7,200 troops and 1,951 police officers (including eight formed police units), will remain indispensable for the coming months. Future reductions in international troops and police should take place within a measured and carefully prepared process, drawing on consultations with the Haitian authorities, as proportionate improvement in Haitian capacity permits the handover of specific tasks.

19. At the same time, supplementary bilateral assistance will be crucial to address problems presented by the smuggling of narcotics and weapons. Those illicit activities far surpass the ability of national authorities and of MINUSTAH to control them and pose a grave problem to the country's long-term stability. It will also be essential to make further efforts to promote small-scale humanitarian and development activities that can follow up on and reinforce the impact of security operations.

Disarmament, demobilization and reintegration and violence reduction

20. MINUSTAH has continued to work with the relevant national authorities to develop a process of disarmament and reintegration that is appropriate to the country's security needs. The process requires a particular focus on community violence reduction through social and economic investment and the return of local government to volatile neighbourhoods, in accordance with the vision outlined in Security Council resolution 1702 (2006).

21. As reflected in his public remarks on the issue, President René Préval has favoured a dual-track strategy according to which increased pressure by security forces in Cité Militaire and Cité Soleil would be accompanied by ongoing discussions between his Government and armed group leaders. On 29 August, the Government appointed a seven-member National Commission for Disarmament, Dismantlement and Reintegration, which has taken the lead in implementing the Government's disarmament programme.

22. While the above-mentioned process is still at an early stage, progress to date has remained limited. Only two groups totalling 104 individuals have formally entered the disarmament and reintegration programme. Furthermore, while their participation may have contributed to a decline in violence and kidnappings in the short term, it is clear that it has not resulted in a meaningful step towards the dismantlement of the gangs. Several participants are suspected of continuing their engagement in criminal activities. Meanwhile, MINUSTAH and the United Nations Development Programme (UNDP) are working in close coordination with the Government to support the strengthening of the legislative framework for small arms control; to build community capacity for violence reduction in collaboration with the new local government structures; and to maintain a focus on women affected by the violence and (in collaboration with the United Nations Children's Fund (UNICEF)) on children associated with armed groups.

23. The task of adapting disarmament processes to the circumstances in Haiti and effectively dismantling gangs remains a complex and significant challenge. However, it will be important to continue to pursue this objective, in view of the importance attached to the programme by the Government as a necessary complement to security operations, security sector reform and the return of local government to volatile zones. The Mission will continue to work closely with the Government to find an appropriate solution, while also pursuing related community-based measures.

IV. Reform of rule-of-law structures

Strengthening Haitian security capacity

24. A significant step towards reforming and strengthening Haiti's security structure was taken by the Government when Prime Minister Jacques-Edouard Alexis signed the Haitian National Police reform plan on 8 August (see S/2006/726, annex). The reform plan was the product of an extended review and consultation between relevant Haitian police and political officials, with support from the United Nations. This blueprint lays out a clear and comprehensive outline for the development of a basic policing capacity within Haiti, drawing on experience in the country and internationally. The plan also provides a practical road map for collaboration between Haitians and international partners. Its adoption could mark a starting point for a truly effective process of reform of the Haitian National Police.

25. According to the benchmarks established in the reform plan, it is envisaged that the Haitian National Police would increase from its current strength by a rate of approximately 1,500 officers a year, to 14,000 by 2011. The plan notes that the latter figure should be sufficient to undertake essential policing functions. At the same time, it indicates that further security capacity, up to a total staffing of 20,000, would be required to undertake the full range of security tasks, and that an appropriate plan would need to be devised for its development. To date, some 8,070 Haitian National Police officers and 1,580 civilian employees have been registered within a United Nations police database which will also serve the Haitian National Police. A further 600 candidates for the Haitian National Police, including 30 women, will begin training courses in January 2007. With regard to gender representation, some 6.5 per cent of Haitian National Police officers and 12 per cent of Haitian National Police employees are women. In an effort to combat discrimination against women within the institution and ensure that gender is mainstreamed in all their activities, the Haitian National Police have recently established gender focal points throughout the country. They are currently undergoing training in collaboration with MINUSTAH. The Mission, the Joint United Nations Programme on HIV/AIDS (UNAIDS) and the United Nations Population Fund (UNFPA) supported the Haitian National Police HIV-awareness and prevention programme through training at the Haitian National Police Training Centre and throughout the country.

26. As noted previously (see S/2006/592), the Haitian National Police reform plan foresees the implementation of three main processes: vetting, training and the strengthening of institutional capacities. On 9 November, the Haitian National Police announced the beginning of the vetting process, which assesses professional skills and disciplinary background and draws on the efforts of combined teams of MINUSTAH and Haitian police. The 25 most senior officers of the Haitian National Police, including the Director General and Inspector General, are currently undergoing this process, as are 10 Haitian National Police investigators who will themselves be involved in future vetting. Officers who do not meet the requisite disciplinary standards will be dismissed, while deficiencies in terms of skills will be remedied through additional training.

27. In addition to its contribution to the vetting process, the Mission plays a crucial role in supporting the training and institutional development of the police envisaged by the Haitian National Police reform plan. The Mission's 951 police advisers will continue to monitor and advise Haitian National Police counterparts in Port-au-Prince and in the provinces, while supporting development of Haitian National Police policies and institutions. MINUSTAH will also need to provide further specialized advice, drawing on civilian skills, in order to ensure the effective development of the Haitian National Police administration.

28. Generous bilateral assistance will be indispensable to build on and sustain the basic level of support provided through MINUSTAH. This will include in particular assistance for the required capital investments, which the United Nations Development Programme and MINUSTAH can help to coordinate.

Justice and prison systems

29. As previously reported, the criminal justice system in Haiti remains largely dysfunctional and the lack of cooperation between the police and justice systems presents a significant problem. Prison overcrowding and prolonged pre-trial detention continue to be a source of grave concern. Juvenile justice also remains problematic. The juvenile court of

Port-au-Prince has been paralysed for several months because of the refusal of judges assigned to the court to work in the shanty town of Bel-Air, where it is located.

30. In response, MINUSTAH is providing assistance and advice to the Ministry of Justice and Public Security, especially on the drafting of new or urgent legislation, the restructuring of key institutions, the reopening of the *Ecole de la magistrature* (school for magistrates), and the professionalization of the Ministry. The Minister has prepared an action plan looking at short- and mid-term activities that could help address structural problems such as the judiciary's lack of independence and prolonged pre-trial detention. In addition, with the support of MINUSTAH, he adopted an overall strategic plan for the reform of the justice system that he intends to use as the basis for the Ministry's five-year institutional development plan. He also held a first meeting with all donors involved in the justice sector, which has led to the establishment of a new coordination mechanism for assistance.

31. The Ministry has prepared three bills (on the *Statut de la magistrature* (status of the magistrates), the *Ecole de la magistrature* and the *Conseil supérieur du pouvoir judiciaire* (Supreme Council of the Judiciary)) which are intended to strengthen the independence of the judiciary. The bills are now awaiting approval by the Council of Ministers before being presented to the Parliament. MINUSTAH and UNICEF continue to provide technical expertise and training to the judicial authorities to improve the juvenile justice system, in particular the situation of children in conflict with the law.

32. The Mission also provides professional resources to support the judicial actors themselves, combining direct technical assistance and advice, with the main objective of improving the criminal process, and addressing the aforementioned problem of pre-trial detention. MINUSTAH has also worked with bilateral partners providing training to over 250 justices of the peace and registry clerks and to nearly 70 public prosecutors and coordinating donor support.

33. Overcrowding in the prisons, exacerbated by weak infrastructure and low corrections staffing, remains worrying in terms of security and human rights. The risks inherent in this situation were highlighted by a prison break on 4 December, although it was limited in scale. The Mission is working with the Ministry on the establishment of commissions on detention throughout the country to address the crucial issues of prison overcrowding and prolonged pre-trial detentions. MINUSTAH has sought to strengthen prison management through support for reform of budget control and expenditure procedures, as well as a monitoring system for stock and personnel. MINUSTAII, the National Prison Administration and the International Committee of the Red Cross are developing a comprehensive approach towards addressing health and nutritional problems in prisons.

34. While the engagement of the newly elected authorities in outlining plans for reform of long-needed problems in the justice sector has provided a vital basis for future activity, the continued involvement of MINUSTAH will be crucial to realizing their potential. Through continued advice on policy and practical issues, experts within the Mission's Justice Section will continue to serve as a vital resource for the personnel in the Ministry of Justice and Public Security and in the judicial and corrections system as they seek to transform the plans into reality. Likewise, the 16 correction officers seconded from Member States, as authorized by resolution 1702 (2006), will follow up on reforms in detention centres throughout the country through direct assistance and advice to prison management.

V. Human rights

35. The installation of the new Government and subsequent high-level appointments in the area of rule of law have improved the prospects for a more efficient response to serious shortcomings in respecting human rights. The commitment of the new authorities will be crucial in addressing the human rights situation in Haiti, which remained a concern during the reporting period. Many Haitians continued to be affected by daily violence, particularly in the shanty towns of Port-au-Prince. At least a dozen people, including a local human rights activist, were reported killed in September 2006 by armed groups operating in the Port-au-Prince neighbourhoods of Martissant and Fontamara. On 12 October, also in Port-au-Prince, at least five individuals were executed and a dozen injured by shooting in the Bel-Air area of the capital. The perpetrators were allegedly armed group members chased from the area by the population in September 2006. Progress in the judicial investigation into the 7 July killings in Martissant (see S/2006/592, para. 13) has not been significant and has been hindered by serious technical shortcomings, including a lack of proper forensic evidence and flawed collaboration between police and judicial authorities.

36. Some progress was made regarding the case of former Prime Minister Yvon Neptune (see S/2006/592, para. 29), who was granted provisional release on 27 July after more than two years on pre-trial detention. Four high-profile Lavalas activists were released on 8 August after almost two and a half years in pre-trial detention.

37. In the course of an official visit to Haiti in October 2006, the United Nations High Commissioner for Human Rights expressed concern regarding shortcomings in respect of civil and political rights, including the overcrowding of prisons and the issue of pre-trial detention, as well as in respect of social and economic rights. At the same time, she welcomed the willingness of the Government to take concrete steps to address the situation.

38. With the support of the Office of the United Nations High Commissioner for Human Rights (OHCHR), the Mission has augmented its training, civic education and advisory activities. The Mission's regional offices continued to conduct monitoring activities and periodic refresher courses on human rights standards and Haitian legal provisions organized in targeted police stations, prosecutors' offices, courts and prisons across the country. In collaboration with the Haitian National Police, MINUSTAH is developing training materials aimed at mainstreaming human rights standards into all aspects of basic police training.

39. The Mission continues to be a member of the *Table de concertation nationale pour la prévention des violences spécifiques faites aux femmes et leur prise en charge* (National Round Table on the Prevention of Violence against Women and on their Protection) led by the Ministry of Women's Affairs and Rights. MINUSTAH is specifically involved in programmes relating to the establishment of a database to harmonize data collection relating to violence, the creation of reception units within Haitian National Police stations for women exposed to violence and the capacity-building of a national non-governmental organization created by men for men to combat violence against women.

40. Further efforts will be required to address human rights problems and strengthen the human rights institutions of Haiti. MINUSTAH will continue to pursue its capacity-building activities in Port-au-Prince and throughout the country and its assistance to relevant State institutions in developing skills and expertise. At the same time, the continued commitment

of the Haitian leadership will be crucial for progress, including through the approval of legislation aimed at redefining the status and role of the Office of the Ombudsman.

Child protection

41. Grave violations against children, especially in the areas of Port-au-Prince affected by armed violence, continued to be a serious concern, as well as widespread rape and other grave sexual abuse of girls. The strengthening of the *Brigade de protection des mineurs* (Brigade for the Protection of Minors) of the Haitian National Police as well as the institution of a programme of training for the police on children's rights and protection are priorities, as is the resumed functioning of the juvenile court. MINUSTAH and UNICEF have also initiated a process of training and capacity-building for the parliamentary commission on children's rights.

VI. Democratic governance and State institutions

42. Over the reporting period, MINUSTAH played a key role in support of the completion of elections at the local, municipal and national levels, which has paved the way for consolidation of the democratic structures of governance in Haiti. Furthermore, drawing on the new momentum provided by the installation of democratically elected authorities, the Mission has begun to strengthen State institutions. However, much more remains to be done to ensure a basic level of capacity, requiring continued assistance from the Mission and from donors. At the same time, political decisions will be required to clarify the ways in which the various institutions will function and how they will relate to one another.

43. The Mission has provided advice to the Executive Branch at the central level, in particular through contacts with the Ministry of Interior and Territorial Collectivities, the Ministry of Planning and External Cooperation and the Ministry of Economy and Finance, in order to support the extension of State authority throughout the country. Further specialized assistance will be essential to support national authorities in developing skills and policies in other areas that are crucial for stability, including security and customs. The Mission participated in and contributed to, through funds for quick-impact projects, an eight-week training programme for local financial comptrollers working jointly with the Ministry of Economy and Finance. With regard to the legislature, the Mission has established a parliamentary liaison office and is working closely with the presidents of the two chambers and the leaders of parliamentary groups to assess parliamentarians' needs and promote coordination of international assistance.

44. In addition, in close cooperation with national authorities, the Mission has designed training programmes for a number of appointed and elected officials, particularly at the local level, to help the majority of the 140 communes to reach a basic level of functioning governance. Implementation will begin upon clarification of who will be assuming these responsibilities in the coming year. One of the initiatives was the preparation of a training programme for departmental delegates and vice-delegates, which was jointly designed with the Ministry of the Interior and Territorial Collectivities. The training programme will cover such topics as local finances, budgetary principles and management; an evaluation, together with the Ministry of Economy and Finance and a local non-governmental organization, of gaps in the knowledge of 1,800 local candidates for office in order to develop training methods for future elected officials; and the elaboration of modules to be used to train newly elected officials between mid-December and February 2007.

45. The Mission, in cooperation with central and local authorities, has also continued to identify the most urgent needs in terms of infrastructure. It has also drawn on the quick-impact project mechanism for small infrastructure projects, such as the rehabilitation or construction of town halls, tribunals, police stations and offices of delegates, providing State institutions with the minimal means to deliver services, while longer-term projects are planned with the assistance of donors.

46. Overall, while activities over the reporting period have helped to lay a foundation for progress, much of the work of professionalizing and training staff in State institutions has yet to be done. The Mission is making a substantial contribution to meeting the most urgent requirements through continued support for development of training materials and provision of guidance, including by making available specialized expertise to key ministries. However, that effort needs to be complemented by bilateral initiatives to fulfil the requirements that may be less closely linked to stability but nonetheless must be met to enable the State to function at an adequate level to meet the needs of its citizens. In addition, substantial and sustained donor support will be essential for an effective response to the country's infrastructure needs beyond the basic contributions that can be made through the Mission. Such projects include road rehabilitation and building projects in the North and other locations and rehabilitation of the main electricity grid throughout the country, funded by the Inter-American Development Bank. Likewise, while the comparatively smooth functioning of the present electoral cycle demonstrated the enhanced capability of the provisional electoral authorities, further international assistance will be essential in order to advance towards the creation of permanent electoral bodies and enable them to manage future electoral processes. Efforts by MINUSTAH in this regard could be complemented by other actors.

47. Progress will also depend on a number of key decisions facing the leadership and people of Haiti. They include the determination of the most appropriate balance for the distribution of responsibilities between central and local authorities, and of which tasks should be assumed respectively by elected authorities (decentralization) and by the delegates appointed by the executive branch (deconcentration). It will also be necessary to consider how best to respond to the considerable financial and practical implications of maintaining an extended network of authorities at the local level. Another issue that will require attention in the coming year concerns the provisions within the Constitution according to which one third of Senate seats would be subject to election in November 2007. It will be important to find a way to continue to promote respect for constitutionally mandated processes while bearing in mind the limited availability of financial and logistical resources within the country to support further electoral exercises.

VII. Humanitarian, recovery and development activities

48. Living in the poorest nation in the Western Hemisphere, Haitians continue to suffer from lack of access to basic social services. Haiti's recently approved budget for 2006–2007 amounts to 1.6 billion dollars, of which international loans and donors will constitute up to 65 per cent. Increasing Government revenues and revitalizing the economy are paramount goals.

49. As stated above, the Mission is seeking to enhance the Government's ability to generate income through expert advice in related areas. At the same time, MINUSTAH has worked closely with local officials in all regions to plan and coordinate the delivery of basic social services and developmental activities. With the objective of tackling the most immediate

problems related to the delivery of basic services, MINUSTAH has supported the Government in establishing coordination roundtables throughout the country, involving departmental delegates, the Ministry of Planning and External Cooperation, the organizations and agencies of the United Nations system, and non-governmental and civil society organizations.

50. Haiti's vulnerability to natural disasters continues to be of great concern. During the reporting period, Hurricane Ernesto, which struck the island on 27 August, affected over 4,000 people and resulted in 4 deaths, 3 people missing, 515 people in temporary shelters, 83 houses destroyed and 759 houses damaged. Heavy rains also caused a succession of floods and landslides during September and October in the north of Haiti. Two municipalities in the north-west were also affected by a tornado and a tidal surge on 8 October. Floods in Grande-Saline affected 300 families on 30 September. On 23 and 24 November, heavy rains caused extensive damage in the departments of Grande-Anse, Nippes and Nord-Ouest, resulting in six deaths and five people injured, with social infrastructure damage to two hospitals, eight water supply systems and 10 schools, and damage to or destruction of 792 houses. Extensive agricultural damage, including destroyed crops, was also reported.

51. The Mission has continued to assist the Haitian authorities in responding to disasters, with personnel in the regions undertaking emergency evaluation missions and supporting the coordination of humanitarian response with local authorities and non-governmental organizations. The United Nations contingency plan for natural disasters, in support of Haiti's efforts, was activated in response to Hurricane Ernesto. Following landslides in Cap Haïtien on 27 October, MINUSTAH engineers immediately began working with local authorities to remove large quantities of earth blocking a major drainage channel in the city centre to avoid future flooding. The World Health Organization (WHO), UNDP and the International Organization for Migration (IOM) also continued their assistance to victims of previous floods while strengthening national capacity for natural disaster preparedness and response through the provision of equipment to local institutions, the building of water-resistant structures and the training of personnel and transfer of appropriate technology to communities at risk. The projects, which employ national workers, benefit approximately one million people living in natural disaster-prone areas. In addition, the United Nations Educational, Scientific and Cultural Organization (UNESCO) intensified its efforts, through research and studies, to increase national capacity for sustainable water resource management.

52. The reporting period was marked by increased delivery of programmes managed by the United Nations that focused on increased access to basic services and rapid job creation. Various United Nations organizations and agencies of the United Nations system estimate their projects to have collectively generated over 650,840 additional person days of work during the third quarter of 2006.

53. Throughout the reporting period, the Food and Agriculture Organization of the United Nations (FAO) and the World Food Programme (WFP) intensified their support in both building the necessary structures for domestic food production and in providing immediate food assistance to the most vulnerable segments of the population, including children, pregnant women and people living with HIV/AIDS and tuberculosis. Altogether, 6,722 tons of food aid were distributed to more than 245,500 recipients, 65 per cent of whom reside outside the capital. School canteens benefited more than 50,000 pupils within Port-au-Prince and more than 240,000 outside the capital. Nearly 84 tons of emergency food aid have also been distributed in the shanty towns of the capital.

54. A number of agencies initiated a series of labour-intensive projects to clean up, repair or build Haiti's basic infrastructure, including canals, bridges, roads, schools and common areas. Many efforts, such as the rehabilitation by the United Nations Office for Project Services' (UNOPS) of four small hydropower plants, focused on locations in the provinces as well as in shanty towns such as Cité Soleil, where IOM, UNOPS, UNICEF and the Pan American Health Organization (PAHO)/WHO assisted in the clean-up of canals and roads, the improvement of sanitary and hygienic conditions in over 40 schools and the provision of water to over 200,000 residents. The current and expected impact of those initiatives on job creation is estimated at 200,000 persons per day, including 5,400 persons per day for youth at risk.

55. In cooperation with the Government and international partners, UNESCO launched a programme to promote the elimination of illiteracy. UNICEF provided assistance to 271 schools and their teachers, covering violence-affected areas in Port-au-Prince. Jointly with the Ministry of Education and Professional Training, UNESCO and the World Bank, UNICEF is supporting the national strategy of reform in education, in particular through the promotion of the zero-fees initiative to include as many children as possible in the school system nationwide.

56. The United Nations Population Fund continued its support to reproductive health services, with particular attention to emergency obstetric care to prevent maternal mortality and morbidity, assistance to women and girls that are victims of sexual violence and HIV/AIDS prevention and treatment. Through a joint UNFPA/UNICEF programme, and in cooperation with the Ministry of Public Health and Population, 50,000 pregnant women are currently receiving prenatal, childbirth and post-natal care services throughout the country. UNICEF has increased its support for the Ministry's national programme of immunization in cooperation with PAHO/WHO through the provision of equipment, supplies and related training. More than 1,250,000 children under five years of age and 600,000 women have been immunized, double the number immunized in 2004.

57. The Mission will continue to play an important role in promoting development and supporting humanitarian assistance, including through the efforts of the Deputy Special Representative of the Secretary-General in coordinating the work of the United Nations country team. However, the provision of adequate bilateral support will be crucial in enabling real progress. In this context, in order to promote the swift provision of tangible benefits, a transitional appeal will be launched on 18 December. The appeal constitutes a broad package in support of the Government's *Programme d'apaisement social* and priorities in 2007, with a focus on institutional strengthening, economic growth and recovery and a more balanced delivery of basic services countrywide. Further steps have also been taken to ensure enhanced coordination between the United Nations country team and MINUSTAH and with the various development actors in Haiti, as well as improved monitoring and reporting on the overall impact of humanitarian and development efforts.

VIII. Conduct and discipline of United Nations personnel

58. During the reporting period, MINUSTAH strove to maintain the highest standards of integrity and discipline. In that regard, MINUSTAH is training all categories of Mission personnel in the prevention of sexual exploitation and abuse, conducting outreach activities with the local community, including women's groups and non-governmental organizations, and enforcing off-limit locations. The Mission's national staff have received special training

to enhance their understanding of their rights and duties and also to foster better understanding between the Mission and the Haitian population.

IX. Financial implications

59. In its resolution 60/18 B of 30 June 2006, the General Assembly appropriated the amount of $489,207,100, equivalent to $40,767,258 per month, for the maintenance of MINUSTAH for the period from 1 July 2006 to 30 June 2007. Should the Security Council decide to extend the mandate of MINUSTAH beyond 15 February 2007, the cost of maintaining the Mission until 30 June 2007 would be limited to the amounts approved by the General Assembly.

60. As at 31 October 2006, unpaid assessed contributions to the Special Account for the United Nations Stabilization Mission in Haiti amounted to $195.5 million. The total outstanding assessed contributions for all peacekeeping operations as at that date amounted to $2,541.8 million.

61. As at 30 November 2006, amounts owed to troop and formed police contributors to MINUSTAH totalled $17.2 million for the period from 1 September 2006 to 31 October 2006. Reimbursement of troop costs has been made for the period up to 31 August 2006 and, for costs of contingent-owned equipment, up to 30 June 2006, in accordance with the quarterly payment schedule.

X. Observations

62. Following the election of the new President and Parliament, I travelled to Haiti in August 2006. The visit made it possible for me to witness how, in spite of the fragility of the country's foundation for democracy and stability, a renewed political dialogue has created a unique opportunity to tackle key underlying problems in the areas of security, institution-building and socio-economic development. The completion of the electoral process and the installation of elected representatives at all levels of Government can bring further progress. However, the realization of those possibilities will require sustained and close collaboration between the Haitian authorities, the United Nations Stabilization Mission in Haiti and the wider international community.

63. Primary responsibility for taking advantage of this opportunity and for ensuring progress remains with the Haitian leadership and people. As pointed out by my Haitian interlocutors during my visit, all parties—the Government, the private sector, civil society and the international community alike—will need to continue to work in partnership to consolidate strong State institutions and national capacities. The Government will continue to face significant challenges in the coming months, including such issues as the distribution of responsibilities between central and local authorities; how best to meet the full security requirements of the country, beyond essential policing tasks; determination of the appropriate response to armed groups and development of relevant disarmament, demobilization and reintegration programmes; finalization of plans for reform of the justice system and prompt adoption of key related bills; development of a means to resolve the problem of pre-trial detentions; and adoption of an appropriate legislative framework for the Office of the Ombudsman. As exemplified by the adoption of the Haitian National Police reform plan, clear decisions in such areas, drawing on input from all relevant stakeholders, could provide

an indispensable framework for efforts to promote progress. However, unless swift results are achieved in those key areas, the situation might deteriorate.

64. The Mission's continued deployment will be essential, since destabilizing forces continue to use violence to attain their objectives. The continued engagement of the Mission's military and police will remain crucial in responding to significant threats at a time when Haiti's own security capacity is still at an early stage of development. Any reductions in the international security presence from its current force levels should be linked to proportionate increases in the ability of Haitian institutions to assume relevant tasks, taking into account any changes in the security environment.

65. With the completion of the electoral cycle, MINUSTAH has been supporting the new Government in establishing strong and sustainable State institutions for governance and the rule of law. MINUSTAH is also supporting the enhancement of human rights capacity and coordinating development and humanitarian activities. The priorities have been shaped in consideration of Haitian needs and focus on those areas most closely linked to stability, where the Mission can make a key contribution in the initial phases of a longer-term process. However, the work has only begun, and continued involvement by the Mission will be required.

66. Accordingly, I recommend that the Mission be extended for a further 12-month period, with the mandate provided in resolutions 1542 (2004), 1608 (2005) and 1702 (2006), and with its present authorized troop and police ceilings. At the same time, the ability of the Mission to succeed will depend on the closest collaboration with the Haitian authorities in all its areas of activity. I urge the Haitian leadership to continue to work with MINUSTAH in reinforcing the close partnership that has made a key contribution to enabling progress to date.

67. It should be borne in mind that MINUSTAH can respond only to Haiti's most immediate needs. Sustained bilateral assistance will be indispensable to further reinforce and strengthen democratic structures of governance and rule of law, including through meeting key infrastructural requirements. This will also be crucial to bringing tangible improvements to the daily lives of Haitians. While the statements issued during the international donor conferences which took place in Port-au-Prince in July and Madrid in November provided encouraging indications of continuing commitment, the rate of disbursement of international aid appears to fall far short of what is required. Delays in programmatic funding for capacity-building and institutional support might pose a serious challenge to stability. The transitional appeal for Haiti that will be issued at the end of December will identify a number of key areas where swift response to needs is particularly important. Tangible improvements in the socio-economic conditions of the general population, including through job creation, is essential to forestall an increase in popular discontent that could unravel all that has been accomplished thus far.

68. I would like to reiterate my gratitude to the Member States contributing troops and police personnel to MINUSTAH, as well as the Core Group, for their support in the implementation of the Mission's mandate. I would like to pay special tribute to the two Jordanian peacekeepers who made the ultimate sacrifice in November while seeking to promote stability in Haiti. Finally, I should like to express my deep appreciation to my Special Representative, Edmond Mulet, and to all MINUSTAH staff for their dedication and work in advancing the democratic process in Haiti.

Annex I
United Nations Stabilization Mission in Haiti: countries providing military staff and contingents (as at 10 December 2006)

Country	*Staff officers*	*Troops*	*Total*
Argentina	9	548	557
Bolivia	2	215	217
Brazil*	13	1 198	1 211
Canada	6	—	6
Chile	6	497	503
Croatia	1	—	1
Ecuador	1	73	74
France	2	—	2
Guatemala	5	100	105
Jordan	11	750	761
Morocco	1	—	1
Nepal	7	749	756
Pakistan	1	—	1
Paraguay	3	—	3
Peru	5	205	210
Philippines	2	154	156
Sri Lanka	9	950	959
United States of America	3	—	3
Uruguay	14	1 122	1 136
Total	**101**	**6 561**	**6 662**

* Including the Force Commander

Annex II
United Nations Stabilization Mission in Haiti: countries providing police officers and formed police units (as at 10 December 2006)

Country	*Police officers*	*Formed police units*	*Total*
Australia	1	—	1
Argentina	4	—	4
Benin	30	—	30
Burkina Faso	73	—	73
Cameroon	43	—	43
Canada	79	—	79
Chad	8	—	8
Chile	10	—	10
China	5	125	130
Colombia	2	—	2
Egypt	7	—	7
El Salvador	2	—	2
France	73	—	73
Grenada	1	—	1
Guinea	59	—	59
Jordan	4	288	292
Madagascar	1	—	1
Mali	24	—	24
Mauritius	2	—	2
Nepal	7	124	131
Niger	59	—	59
Nigeria	—	125	125
Pakistan	—	249	249
Philippines	41	—	41
Romania	10	—	10
Russian Federation	8	—	8
Rwanda	11	—	11
Senegal	40	84	124
Sierra Leone	2	—	2
Spain	46	—	46
Togo	9	—	9
Turkey	28	—	28
United States of America	48	—	48
Uruguay	4	—	4
Vanuatu	3	—	3
Yemen	3	—	3
Total	**747**	**995**	**1 742**

2. Report of the Secretary-General on the United Nations Stabilization Mission in Haiti, 22 August 2007 (S/2007/503)

I. Introduction

1. By its resolution 1743 (2007), the Security Council extended the mandate of the United Nations Stabilization Mission in Haiti (MINUSTAH) until 15 October 2007, and requested me to report on its implementation no later than 31 August 2007. The present report covers major developments since my report of 19 December 2006 (S/2006/1003) and progress made in the implementation of the mandate of the Mission as contained in Security Council resolutions 1542 (2004), 1608 (2005), 1658 (2006), 1702 (2006) and 1743 (2007), and also presents recommendations for the future.

II. Political developments

2. The multiparty Government of Haiti established by President Préval in May 2006 continued to benefit from broad public support, based in particular on improvements in security. The Government's economic achievements included the stabilization of the local currency and a noteworthy reduction in inflation. President Préval sought to anchor the rule of law through initiatives to promote judicial reform and curb corruption and drug trafficking. During my visit to Haiti on 1 and 2 August, the President urged continued United Nations support and requested that MINUSTAH reorient itself with a greater focus on judicial reform, institutional support and the provision of basic services and that it assume additional tasks, such as border management. President Préval also pursued efforts to reinforce regional cooperation, in particular with the Caribbean Community, including through visits to a number of key partners in and beyond the region.

3. On 18 May, President Préval called on Haitians to participate in a war against corruption and to root out bribe-taking officials. He demonstrated his commitment to that policy with prompt and decisive action after tackling the security situation in the urban shanty towns. In June, the second largest seizure of illegal drugs in the history of Haiti led to the arrest of a dozen individuals, half of whom were police officers. Some weeks later, four businessmen were arrested in connection with a high-profile banking corruption scandal. Efforts to fight organized crime continued with the arrests of several key figures connected with drug trafficking and of two prominent businessmen charged with fraud.

4. The President maintained his multiparty Government through continued dialogue with political parties, legislators and civil-society representatives. However, the relationship between the Government and the parliament remained strained as a result of, inter alia, the lower House's summoning of several ministers and some legislators to replace the Prime Minister. Late in July, the Minister for Culture and Communication was the subject of a vote of no confidence, on the basis of allegations of misuse of public funds, and he resigned early in August. There have also been a number of allegations of corruption against legislators.

5. Political blocs in the parliament have remained fluid, and the rate of absenteeism has frequently caused sessions to be postponed. During the first ordinary session, in January 2007, the legislature adopted the State budget, passed five bills on State loans and one related to development programmes and ratified four international conventions. The pace of work intensified during the extraordinary session held in June. Various committees met

with ministers to review budgetary and administrative issues and to inquire into high-profile controversies. In a welcome development, the Senate recently passed two of three bills on the independence of the judiciary (see para. 41).

6. Some of the main political parties struggled with internal conflicts and a lack of unity with their representatives in the parliament and local government. In June, some parties initiated a national review of draft legislation on political party reform, which will be presented to civil society through regional meetings. Also in June, Lespwa, the electoral coalition that brought President Préval to power, began organizing regional meetings to promote its transformation into a political party.

7. There has been significant political interest in devising a process to review provisions in the 1987 Constitution that have been criticized as contradictory or impractical. Additional focus on this issue has been generated by the forthcoming senatorial elections. No agreement has emerged concerning the best method of undertaking such reforms. Several political parties insist that constitutional reform should take place through the mechanisms stipulated in the Constitution. Others have advocated for the drafting of a new Constitution. There are also divergent positions on such key related issues as the electoral system, dual nationality and the status of the army.

8. President Préval has extended his outreach efforts beyond the capital to the municipalities and has demonstrated interest in decentralization and the empowerment of local governance. On four occasions he invited all mayors and deputy mayors to meet with Government officials. President Préval has encouraged the mayors to be proactive in increasing local revenue and fighting corruption. However, the newly elected local authorities are constrained by inadequate resources and an incomplete legal framework. Municipal administrations, which derive the bulk of their revenue from transfers from the central Government, often lack the means to deliver services to the population. Some communal authorities lack the necessary physical facilities to operate effectively. Relations with State representatives in the departments are complicated because of the fact that they were appointed by the Transitional Government and have not been confirmed or replaced by the current Government.

Elections

9. On 29 April, partial reruns for the local and municipal elections were held without serious incident. Some 300,000 citizens were eligible to cast votes. Voter turnout was relatively uneven, ranging from less than 10 per cent to over 40 per cent. MINUSTAH facilitated the conduct of the elections by providing logistical and administrative assistance to the Provisional Electoral Council and, together with electoral guards and the Haitian National Police, ensured security. Based on the results of those and previous elections, the members of the multiparty Government (Lespwa, Fusion, Organisation du Peuple en Lutte, Union, Alyans and Fanmi Lavalas) govern in 93 of the 140 municipalities. Lespwa took 27 municipalities, more than any other party. The participation rate of women as voters and candidates was higher than in previous elections. Twenty-five women were elected as mayors, a sharp increase from the six elected in 2000.

10. The sub-communal assembly results were published on 7 August. The Constitution now calls for indirect elections to be held to establish councils and assemblies at the municipal, departmental and interdepartmental levels and to designate members of a permanent

electoral council, as well as judges up to the appeals level. Draft legislation defining the modalities for such indirect elections has yet to be submitted to the parliament. Once the legislation has been passed, the process of organizing the indirect elections is expected to take at least three months. Funding for the elections (estimated at $500,000) has been secured. In addition, the mandates of one third of the members of the Senate will expire on 14 January 2008, and senatorial elections should be held by the end of 2007. Funding for the senatorial elections (estimated at $16 million) has not yet been secured. MINUSTAH is ready to provide logistical and security support for both elections.

11. A voter registration process to be launched by the Haitian National Office of Identification and the Provisional Electoral Council in collaboration with the Organization of American States will seek to update voter rolls before the senatorial elections are held. It will address mainly those who have turned 18 since the 2005 registration and those who did not register at that time.

Institutional support and the strengthening of the State

12. The effectiveness of the institutions of governance of Haiti will depend above all on the commitment of the political leadership and civil society to ongoing dialogue and constructive collaboration, although the provision of expertise and material support will also be crucial. Elected officials inherited weak institutions that suffer from shortages of qualified personnel, inadequate infrastructure and limited budgetary and material resources. In response, MINUSTAH is continuing to enhance skills and to promote coordination among international assistance efforts, while providing urgent technical assistance and expert advice for the development of key institutions, including the Office of the President, major ministries, the parliament and relevant local bodies.

13. MINUSTAH has cooperated closely with the Government and legislators, including through advice aimed at strengthening the internal organization of the parliament. It has facilitated contacts between the parliament, civil society and local government and supported thematic meetings between parliamentarians and the international community. Further assistance to the parliament will be provided through the sharing of best practices of other national legislatures and the promotion of efforts to coordinate international support. MINUSTAH will continue to support parliamentary outreach through multimedia centres in the 10 departments.

14. In order to enhance the impact and sustainability of international cooperation, MINUSTAH and the wider United Nations system have promoted regular coordination meetings between donors and national authorities at the technical and political levels, including discussions between the Government and the international community task force regarding those areas that have been particularly affected by gang violence (see para. 60). The Mission also facilitated monthly consultations between the President, the Prime Minister and the Core Group.

15. MINUSTAH has assisted the Ministry of Interior and Local Government in establishing municipal councils by providing technical expertise on topics such as budgetary principles and management. The Mission also supported training programmes for 58 comptrollers. In order to respond to urgent needs and to help local authorities to deliver a minimum level of functioning local governance, MINUSTAH supported 166 quick-impact projects ($2.02 million), including 92 to rehabilitate public buildings essential for the functioning of local

government. An additional quick-impact project ($200,000) is being implemented with the Ministry of Interior and Local Government to provide all mayors and departmental delegates and vice-delegates with municipal start-up kits. Those projects not only provided support for local government at a time when other assistance was not forthcoming, but also paved the way for enhanced support for MINUSTAH by the newly elected officials.

16. In keeping with Government priorities, the Mission, together with the United Nations country team, will continue to focus on extending State authority and building local capacity, particularly with regard to public service delivery, the development of local taxation and the promotion of good governance. In doing so, it will be essential to foster links between institutions at the local level, support State reform and decentralization and promote transparency and the fight against corruption. Complementary bilateral support is crucial to meet infrastructure requirements and to supplement the Mission's expertise, particularly in areas such as the property register, capacity-building, including of the civil service, and the generation of local revenue.

Integrated border management

17. Lack of control by Haiti of its land and sea borders is a factor of instability affecting the sustainability of the political and economic governance, security and institutional development of the country. Given its 1,600 miles of unprotected coastline, its unguarded seaports and its numerous clandestine airstrips, the country is subject to penetration by those engaged in illicit trafficking, including in arms and drugs, whose activities could create renewed instability if they are not stopped. There have been widespread reports of trafficking activities across the land border and via the ports and coastline, as well as the many small airstrips, of Haiti. The Mission's threat assessment (see para. 26) identified illicit trafficking and the consequent corruption of institutions as significant threats to stability. The loss of State revenue resulting from the dysfunctional customs service and port administration is also significant.

18. The lack of effective basic border management directly affects the joint efforts of the Haitian authorities and MINUSTAH to enhance security, the rule of law and institutional support. The Government has approved a three-year strategic plan for strengthening the Haitian customs system, which was prepared by the customs service with support from the International Monetary Fund (IMF). However, an integrated approach will be required if the State is to extend its authority to the borders in a comprehensive manner and thereby play a central role in solidifying stability. In this regard, the Government has recently indicated its interest in establishing an appropriate comprehensive border management mechanism.

19. The Mission has identified four crucial objectives in this area: supporting the establishment of an integrated border management strategy and strengthening the related State institutions; improving border security, which should reduce illicit trafficking; increasing revenue and tax collection; and supporting cross-border arrangements.

20. MINUSTAH could make a key contribution by supporting the extension of State authority to the land and maritime borders pending the formulation and implementation of a comprehensive border management strategy endorsed by the Government. With regard to improving border security, it will be necessary for MINUSTAH to redeploy and reorient certain elements of its military and police personnel to assist the Government in controlling the land and maritime borders (see paras. 28 and 29 below). International expertise is

essential to assist the Government in the formulation and implementation of such a strategy, as well as to guide the Mission's overall efforts to assist the Government of Haiti in border management.

III. Security situation

Security operations

21. There have been significant improvements in the security situation, particularly in the urban areas that had previously been under gang control. The restoration of those areas to State authority represents an important stride forward. In the regions, the security situation remains relatively calm. However, the situation is still fragile (see para. 26 below), and the gains achieved need to be consolidated in order to prevent backsliding and promote long-term stability.

22. The dialogue with members of armed groups initiated by the Government in July 2006 aimed at achieving voluntary disarmament proved unfruitful, prompting the Government and MINUSTAH to increase pressure on the gangs. A series of intensive and intelligence-driven security operations in urban areas, particularly in Port-au-Prince and Gonaïves, restored them to State authority. From 22 December 2006 to 28 February 2007, MINUSTAH and the Haitian National Police conducted a total of 19 security operations in Cité Soleil and Martissant. Those operations dislodged the main gang leaders and, together with other joint operations throughout the country, led to the arrest of some 850 suspected gang members by the end of July. Initially, members of armed groups launched sustained counter-attacks, injuring six peacekeepers. However, armed resistance decreased markedly after two main gang leaders fled the area. Those operations paved the way for the Haitian National Police, supported by MINUSTAH, to return to those areas and, in March, to begin joint patrols in Cité Soleil.

23. In Martissant, gang rivalry was a source of violence. In January alone, 29 bodies were discovered. MINUSTAH and the Haitian National Police conducted a series of targeted arrests that led to a sharp decrease in the level of violence. On 22 January, an office was established co-locating MINUSTAH military, police and civilian components with the Haitian National Police. The Haitian National Police and MINUSTAH now carry out joint patrols, which have been welcomed by the population. However, while gang violence has declined, there has been a corresponding increase in public lynching.

24. Recent security operations also brought significant improvement in Gonaïves, where gangs had become entrenched. Following a number of violent incidents, including the brutal murders of a Fanmi Lavalas spokesman and of the Director of Radio Gonaïves, MINUSTAH and the Haitian National Police stepped up security operations in early May. During two months of intensified activity focusing largely on the volatile shanty towns, some 90 individuals were arrested.

25. Initial progress has also been made against drug trafficking. The counter-drug unit of the Haitian National Police has conducted limited operations, facilitated by support from the United States of America, including an operation that took place in Léogâne on 31 May that resulted in the seizure of 420 kilograms of cocaine and the arrests of five Haitian National Police officers and of foreign nationals. That seizure gives some indication of the use of Haiti as a significant transit point for the shipment of drugs to the United States and Europe.

26. In July, the Mission conducted a detailed threat assessment, which identified three security threats facing Haiti. First, there is the likelihood of civil unrest, which is increased by an environment marked by the persistence of a deep socio-economic divide and compounded by high unemployment and high expectations on the part of the people. Secondly, the potential for renewed armed violence within the country remains considerable. Despite the fact that many suspected criminals have been apprehended in 2007, relatively few weapons have been confiscated, and many former gang members, who could be persuaded to resume their gang activities by spoilers with political or criminal motives, remain at large. Thirdly, the illicit traffic in drugs, arms and contraband remains a critical factor. If not addressed, illicit trafficking will continue to corrupt State institutions. Corruption, and its acceptance throughout society, will continue to foster impunity. It should be noted that, while incidents of kidnapping have significantly decreased in 2007, the phenomenon still represents a threat.

27. Despite marginal improvements in Haitian National Police capability, it remains unable to undertake crucial security tasks unaided (see para. 38), and MINUSTAH security forces will need to undertake key mandated activities so as to ensure a safe and secure environment and to shore up the gains made thus far. A significant security presence in Port-au-Prince will continue to be required to solidify the security situation there. In the regions, the absence of effective and visible State institutions necessitates a basic security presence on the part of MINUSTAH to monitor developments, promote a sense of stability and prevent incidents. It will also be crucial for MINUSTAH to establish a minimum security presence along the land and maritime borders of the country—a mandated task not yet addressed because of other priorities.

28. Accordingly, MINUSTAH should retain its military and police components at this time, with some adjustments in composition being made to reflect the changing circumstances and priorities, which call for the military to enhance its capabilities in border control, engineering and mobility, while decreasing its infantry capabilities. It is recommended that the Mission's military force level be reduced by one company (some 140 troops) and that certain heavy equipment be repatriated. The remaining 7,060 troops would be reconfigured in line with the threat assessment. The Mission would reduce its military presence in calmer rural and urban areas, where increased Haitian and international policing capacity would facilitate the transfer of some basic patrolling duties, and would redeploy military personnel to establish patrols within maritime and land border areas, in cooperation with the Haitian National Police and MINUSTAH police. Pending the development of the Haitian National Police maritime policing capacity, coastal patrolling would be undertaken by means of small craft based at key sites around the country. Up to 16 small craft would be required. Some additional engineering capability would also be necessary, as would the retention of a mobile force reserve to address specific incidents.

29. Given the military redeployment and the continuing limitations in Haitian National Police operational capacity, the MINUSTAH police component will need to increase its support for maintaining law and order. It is therefore recommended that the police component be increased, with one additional formed police unit of up to 140 officers. That additional capability would enhance the Mission's ability to support the Haitian National Police in undertaking key basic policing functions, consolidating the progress that has been made in securing and stabilizing urban areas over the past six months and limiting the risk of

reversal that might result from a somewhat smaller military component assuming additional border-related tasks. Individual MINUSTAH police officers would support the development of the maritime police within the Haitian National Police and would mentor and monitor Haitian National Police personnel engaged in border responsibilities. Those activities would be aligned with the Mission's overall strategy to progressively transfer geographical and functional responsibilities to Haitian counterparts and to facilitate Haitian National Police engagement in conventional law and order duties, in accordance with the Haitian National Police reform plan. Alongside the Mission's efforts, bilateral support for the Haitian Coast Guard will remain essential if the transitional process is to advance.

30. The combined MINUSTAH and Haitian National Police security assets in Haiti will remain below 20,000 personnel, which has been conservatively identified in the Haitian National Police reform plan as the minimum required to maintain the country's security. The relatively high degree of mobility of the Mission's military and police components should help avoid any major setback. Those arrangements will be kept under review as the security environment continues to evolve and Haitian National Police capacity develops.

Community violence reduction

31. Although violence in Haiti diminished during the reporting period, it remains a serious concern, in particular because of the prevalence of small arms held by private citizens and the fact that non-traditional actors are involved in fomenting instability. Traditional approaches to disarmament, however, do not address the unique circumstances in Haiti. Recognizing the need for a fresh approach, the Mission worked closely with national counterparts, the United Nations country team and donors to develop a community violence reduction programme. That process was informed by a United Nations assessment mission, as well as by a conference of leading national and international experts dealing with gang violence, which was held in Port-au-Prince.

32. The Mission's reoriented programme focuses on institutional support for and the capacity-building of the National Commission for Disarmament, Dismantlement and Reintegration. The programme will also concentrate on labour-intensive projects to provide an alternative to criminality for those in the violence-affected communities, pending larger-scale economic recovery efforts to be undertaken by the Government and its development partners. It will also support the development of a weapons registry, the revision of current laws on the importation and possession of arms and the reform of the weapons permit system. The programme will include Haitian National Police officers found by the vetting process to be unsuitable for service for reasons other than criminality. Efforts by the national authorities and MINUSTAH to reduce violence can succeed only with strong complementary bilateral assistance, including for promoting employment in gang-affected areas. MINUSTAH will coordinate activities with humanitarian and development partners, including through a steering group.

33. MINUSTAH continued to provide operational support to the National Commission for Disarmament, Dismantlement and Reintegration. In the period since 19 December 2006, 27 reinsertion and community-based projects (valued at $2.1 million) have reached various stages of implementation. Those projects are facilitating the return of former gang members to their communities, reinforcing the capacity of local communities to resolve conflicts peacefully, promoting a culture of peace, assisting victims of violence and supporting the

creation of temporary employment. Several of the projects specifically target women, both as victims and as perpetrators of armed violence. So far, 381 individuals have entered the reinsertion programme. Approximately 200 weapons have been handed over.

IV. Reform of rule-of-law structures

Strengthening Haitian security capacity

34. Further progress was made to strengthen the Haitian National Police. Some 7,728 Haitian National Police officers are now undertaking policing duties. A further 633 officers from the nineteenth class at the Police Academy are scheduled to begin patrolling in late September 2007. This is in line with the Haitian National Police reform plan, which envisaged that some 1,500 officers would graduate per year. The police have adopted a new seven-month curriculum for basic training, which is followed by three months of field training. The Mission is supporting both the Academy and the curriculum. For officers who are already serving, the monitoring and mentoring role of MINUSTAH police, including in field training, has helped reinforce core values and raise skill levels as high as those of Academy graduates.

35. MINUSTAH, together with the United Nations Development Programme (UNDP), continues to work closely with the leadership of Haiti in developing the institutional capacity of the Haitian National Police, including through close coordination with donors. Pledges and contributions by donors now total some $46 million in support of the reform plan and are supporting the establishment of a new General Inspectorate headquarters, the refurbishment of some police stations, the provision of equipment for regular operations and the construction of a new national Police Academy. MINUSTAH and the Haitian National Police are working together on the preparation of a maritime police development plan aimed at developing a local capacity capable of gradually assuming the coastal patrolling responsibilities that MINUSTAH will undertake in the meantime. Bilateral support to develop the country's coast-guard capacity remains essential.

36. On 18 January 2007, 220 Haitian National Police officers officially entered the vetting programme in Jérémie. Their files are being reviewed and investigated by the joint Haitian National Police-MINUSTAH teams. The teams have now begun their work in Les Cayes, where they have opened 280 case files. In parallel, 30 additional case files were opened in Port-au-Prince for senior managers of the Haitian National Police. Background checks on officers undergoing training in the Police Academy were completed for the eighteenth and nineteenth classes. Twenty-six recruits have been dismissed to date as a result of background checks. The Inspector General is conducting a separate internal affairs investigation, and about 540 cases have been finalized by the Minister for Justice and Public Security, leading to termination of employment.

37. MINUSTAH continued to mainstream gender issues in the Haitian National Police through the development of educational material for instructors at the Police Academy and training in connection with Haitian National Police gender focal points. The participation of women in the Haitian National Police is gradually increasing. Women currently constitute 6 per cent of police officers, and approximately 12 per cent of cadets in the current class are female. In August, the Haitian National Police, with MINUSTAH support, carried out a registration exercise to encourage women to join the police service, and thousands of women applied for some 150 places in the Academy's next class. MINUSTAH has also

supported the establishment of reception units within police stations for female victims of violence.

38. While progress in police reform is encouraging, Haitian National Police capacity remains below the level required to ensure law and order in Haiti. Skill levels are basic, and institutional development is incomplete and fragile. The lack of key resources continues to limit the capacity of the Haitian National Police to operate outside Port-au-Prince. The number of police officers remains far below that required, and the ongoing vetting of police officers will limit staffing in the immediate future. Attaining a viable security structure is a long-term process. In accordance with the reform plan timelines, and assuming that there are no unforeseen obstacles, it will take four more years before the Haitian National Police can reach 14,000—the minimum figure for basic policing duties.

Judicial system

39. On 27 March, President Préval convened a special public meeting on the reform of the rule-of-law institutions—a priority issue for his presidency. As a result, an ad hoc committee on judicial reform was established. This so-called follow-up committee is chaired by the Minister for Justice and Public Security and includes representatives from civil society, the Bar Association, human rights organizations, political parties, the parliament and MINUSTAH. On 13 June, the committee presented a report with 18 short-term recommendations to initiate the reform process, which was strongly supported by the Independent Expert of the Secretary-General on the situation of human rights in Haiti. The committee subsequently produced a road map, with timelines, for the implementation of the 18 recommendations.

40. Meanwhile, the Government has continued to work to promote judicial reform, particularly in connection with a legislative framework and strategic planning. In June, the Minister for Justice and Public Security established a small working group to prepare an overall strategic plan for judicial reform, to be finalized and adopted by the Government in liaison with national and international partners in the framework of the poverty reduction strategic plan. The Ministry has also prepared a circular instructing all judges and prosecutors about new procedures for criminal forensic investigations and is developing legal assistance initiatives, in particular to provide basic judicial assistance and legal advice to residents in areas torn by violence.

41. On 31 July and 2 August 2007, the Senate unanimously adopted two bills prepared by the Minister for Justice and Public Security on, respectively, the status of magistrates and the Superior Council, which oversees their functions. The bills are currently before the Chamber of Deputies, while a third bill, on a school for magistrates, remains before the Senate. The progress on those bills constitutes a crucial step towards judicial reform, since they would provide a framework, tools and mechanisms to fight corruption, impunity and ethical and disciplinary problems within the judiciary, as well as establish arrangements for the certification of judges and prosecutors.

42. MINUSTAH, in coordination with its partners, will continue to provide technical advice both to institutions and to individual actors within the judicial system. Particular areas of activity will include assistance to the Ministry of Justice and Public Security, collaboration with Haitian efforts to professionalize judicial actors, including through *accompagnement* (mentoring) and certification programmes, and support for the Government's efforts to ensure effective legal follow-up to major criminal activities. The Mission will continue to

assist the Government in promoting the coordination of bilateral assistance, particularly in such areas as restructuring the Ministry, certifying magistrates, legal aid for the most vulnerable and modernizing key legislation.

Prison system

43. The security and human rights situations in Haitian prisons remain unacceptable. As of August 2007, more than 6,000 detainees were being held within 17 prisons in an area that, in accordance with international standards, should not accommodate more than 1,088 inmates. The National Penitentiary in Port-au-Prince currently houses 2,700 inmates in accommodation adequate for 800. As of July 2007, 82.5 per cent of prisoners are pretrial detainees (90.4 per cent male, 5.3 per cent female; 3.6 per cent male minors, 0.7 per cent female minors).

44. The early work of the Consultative Commission on Prolonged Pretrial Detention, which was established in February 2007, is encouraging. On 2 July, the Commission submitted its first report, leading to the release of 150 persons, including pregnant women and minors. Given the high rate of illegal pretrial detention, that initiative is of key importance. On 6 August, the Commission presented its second report, on juvenile detention and justice. The Commission has also supported measures by the Minister for Justice and Public Security and the Chief Prosecutor to improve due process and safeguard the penal chain.

45. The National Prison Administration, with assistance from MINUSTAH and UNDP, developed a comprehensive strategic plan, including cost estimates, for prison reform for the next five years, which was approved by the Prime Minister on 7 August. The plan has six elements: (a) the reinforcement of security in corrections facilities; (b) the improvement of prison conditions; (c) the improvement of working conditions for staff; (d) the professionalization of staff; (e) the restructuring of the prison system; and (f) the rehabilitation and social reintegration of inmates.

46. MINUSTAH and UNDP will now support the National Prison Administration in facilitating donor coordination. MINUSTAH and UNDP have also provided technical advice regarding the building of new facilities consistent with international standards. As an urgent measure, MINUSTAH has implemented six quick-impact projects to improve the sanitary conditions in six prisons. International corrections officers will continue to work in the regions, implementing mentoring and training programmes. Continued United Nations and bilateral donor engagement will be essential for the successful implementation of the strategic plan for penal management.

V. Human rights

47. Crime and urban violence remain of concern, although more Haitians have enjoyed increased security and freedom of movement as a result of the security operations. At the same time, the improvements in the security situation have brought the weakness of the judicial system to the fore, as law enforcement, court and prison systems remain unable to manage the influx of persons arrested and detained.

48. Particular concern continued to be generated by reports of arbitrary arrests, unlawful police custody, ill-treatment and excessive use of force. The Haitian National Police still needs to make improvements in the areas of respect for judicial oversight, legal procedures,

professional and scientific investigation techniques and the maintenance of operational and legal records. Meanwhile, lack of technical expertise, poor communications, negligence and apparent corruption on the part of judicial authorities have resulted in numerous unlawful arrests, prolonged pretrial detention and a low number of court decisions.

49. MINUSTAH continued its regular monitoring of police commissariats, prosecutors' offices, justices of the peace, courts and prisons. It has also provided local authorities and the public with information on developments in the human rights situation and on the institutional functioning of key rule-of-law institutions. In February 2007, MINUSTAH organized two national seminars during which judicial and police authorities dealt with complex challenges pertaining to the protection of judicial guarantees. The Mission has also supported the institutional development of the Haitian National Police General Inspectorate in human rights through training and the exchange of information on individual cases. MINUSTAH also conducted a wide array of advocacy efforts, working closely with civil society, including human rights organizations, women's associations, professional interest groups and the media.

50. As a reflection of public distrust of the judicial system, many Haitians appear to avoid the formal court system and rely on other methods to arbitrate or handle disputes, including lynching. Over the past six months, MINUSTAH has received reports of 60 people having been killed by lynching and of 28 people having been seriously injured or maimed as a result of attempted lynchings. While many of those attacks were spontaneous, others were premeditated acts carried out in response to robberies, family disputes, gang activity or accusations of witchcraft. Unfortunately, the lynching phenomenon has, historically, garnered little public scrutiny from the State or from civil society. However, during the reporting period some 20 individuals were arrested for their participation in lynchings.

51. From 15 to 20 April, in collaboration with the Ministry of Women's Affairs and Rights, MINUSTAH hosted a high-level delegation from the United Nations Division for the Advancement of Women. The delegation initiated the provision of technical support to the Government on the implementation of the Convention on the Elimination of All Forms of Discrimination against Women.

52. MINUSTAH will continue its monitoring and training activities aimed at strengthening capacities and facilitating institutional reform, while producing periodic and thematic reports to inform key public institutions, including the police, the judicial system, local administrative authorities and the parliament, about the protection of human rights, the fight against impunity and institutional reform. MINUSTAH will ensure that human rights standards are integrated into the vetting of the Haitian National Police, which it will also monitor. In its training activities for law enforcement, judicial and administrative authorities, MINUSTAH will seek to address the key human rights violations and procedural irregularities observed in the field. Support will also be provided to the Government in developing a human rights action plan and in reporting to international treaty bodies on human rights, as well as to the parliament and civil society. Particular emphasis will be placed on strengthening programmatic capacities within the Office of the Ombudsman. MINUSTAH will also augment its civic education efforts to raise awareness among the broader public of human rights and rule-of-law issues, including those related to law enforcement, justice, the fight against impunity and economic, social and cultural rights.

Child protection

53. Despite the recent improvements, a large number of children continue to be affected by armed violence. MINUSTAH continues to receive reports of the widespread rape and other grave sexual abuse of girls. The holding of minors in prolonged pretrial detention remains a source of concern. On a positive note, the Juvenile Court of Port-au-Prince resumed functioning in January 2007, with support from MINUSTAH and the United Nations Children's Fund (UNICEF), and the Consultative Commission on Prolonged Pretrial Detention is prioritizing juvenile justice. MINUSTAH and UNICEF continued to provide training on child protection and juvenile justice to judicial actors and Haitian National Police officers.

54. The situation of children in institutional care centres and of children who are victims of trafficking is of great concern. MINUSTAH provided technical assistance to the Brigade for the Protection of Minors, the Institute of Social Well-being and Research and the Office of the Ombudsman to facilitate investigation and family reunification, and it is prioritizing support for the Ministry of Social Affairs to reinforce monitoring of institutional care centres. Lastly, the situation of restavek children (children who are forced into domestic labour) remains worrying. UNICEF estimates that there are approximately 173,000 restavek children working in Haiti, of whom 60 per cent are girls. They live in appalling conditions and are often beaten and abused.

VI. Humanitarian recovery and development

Socio-economic situation

55. Haiti has made progress in stabilizing the economy over the past three years. In May 2007 the annual inflation rate declined to 8.3 per cent, the currency stabilized, international reserves reached close to $250 million and growth, although modest, resumed. On 23 July, the IMF Executive Board completed the first review of the country's economic programme under the Poverty Reduction and Growth Facility arrangement, making some $11.7 million immediately available for disbursement. Haiti can also now benefit from the multilateral debt relief initiatives of the World Bank and the Inter-American Development Bank. Prospects for private sector growth were also enhanced by the adoption by the United States Congress of the Hemispheric Opportunity through Partnership Encouragement Act, which provides preferential tariffs for textiles, the largest export sector in Haiti.

56. If Haiti maintains its current path, real growth is expected in its gross domestic product, which should increase from 2.5 per cent in fiscal year 2005/06 to 3.5 per cent in the current fiscal year and to about 4 per cent over the medium term. Such progress will require continued improvement in terms of security, as well as efforts to foster economic stability and create a more predictable business environment. The spending and implementation capacity of the Government remains limited. Various structural and institutional factors, such as supply bottlenecks in the construction sector, dilapidated infrastructure and the inadequate supply and high cost of basic utility services, need to be addressed. Similarly, education and health services and regulatory frameworks for property rights need to be improved.

57. Despite the macroeconomic improvements, the majority of the population remains in dire poverty. The lack of employment opportunities and public services, exacerbated by rapid population growth, are a source of growing frustration, as are ongoing socio-economic disparities. Further pressure is created by environmental degradation. It remains

urgent to address the humanitarian needs and socio-economic realities of daily life, the extreme hardship of which poses an implicit threat to all efforts to stabilize the country.

58. MINUSTAH and the United Nations country team strive to maximize the impact of their assistance through closer integration and joint programmes. However, their effectiveness will depend on cooperation and strong support from bilateral donors and the re-engagement of the private sector. The international community should give priority to developing innovative approaches for delivering a peace dividend, including through the generation of short-term employment opportunities.

59. While addressing short-term needs, it is also important to prepare for the longer term. The poverty reduction strategy paper, which is expected to be finalized by September 2007, will provide the framework for international assistance by defining concrete programmes and projects in the context of a midterm development framework endorsed by the Government and aimed at fulfilling the Millennium Development Goals. Under the leadership of the Government, and with support from UNDP, the United Nations Population Fund and MINUSTAH, the poverty reduction strategy paper is being prepared through a broad country-wide consultative process. The United Nations system will also develop a new United Nations Development Assistance Framework for 2009 to 2011.

Humanitarian and socio-economic needs

60. An international task force, comprising MINUSTAH, the United Nations country team, key partners and donors, was launched in January to help ameliorate the dismal situation in the shanty towns of Port-au-Prince. Its aim is to identify a broad strategy as well as short- and medium-term activities for those areas. The Government launched its own task force for Cité Soleil to reinforce coordination and implement a coherent development strategy. Together, the two task forces developed a comprehensive plan, with projects worth some $42 million that are benefiting approximately 300,000 people—implemented or planned by MINUSTAH, the United Nations country team and non-governmental organizations—to address, inter alia, nutrition, water and sanitation and emergency food aid. UNDP and MINUSTAH also began implementing a pilot project funded by the Government of Norway for supporting the most disadvantaged areas of Haiti, while the International Organization for Migration (IOM) undertook complementary confidence-building and reconciliation activities.

61. Haiti has been affected by inclement weather in 2007, including heavy rains in May, affecting over 12,000 families. MINUSTAH, the Office for the Coordination of Humanitarian Affairs, UNDP, UNICEF, the World Food Programme (WFP) and the Food and Agriculture Organization of the United Nations (FAO) provided assistance. Contingency plans for a potentially severe hurricane season were updated by the Office for the Coordination of Humanitarian Affairs in cooperation with the Government. MINUSTAH strengthened its joint operations centre to augment the country's disaster-response capacity through improved logistics, communication and coordination. The Office for the Coordination of Humanitarian Affairs organized a humanitarian and development forum every two weeks to share information and discuss humanitarian issues.

62. An appeal covering the period from January 2007 to June 2008 was launched by the United Nations system for a total of $97.9 million to support the Government's priorities, pending the implementation of the United Nations Development Assistance Framework. Donor response has so far been limited (10 per cent of overall estimated needs). Funding from

Canada, Norway and Spain was used for activities in the areas of disaster prevention, agriculture, maternal health and the protection of vulnerable segments of the population, as well as for initiatives at the land border.

63. The United Nations Educational, Scientific and Cultural Organization, UNICEF, the World Bank and bilateral donors supported the Government in developing a national strategy for education. As part of its health programmes targeting pregnant women and malnourished children, WFP distributed more than 6,310 tons of direct food assistance to some 193,000 beneficiaries. School canteens received 3,048 tons of food assistance, providing a daily food supplement for some 312,000 schoolchildren. The WFP food-for-work programme provided 412,000 people with some 829 tons of food assistance and, together with IOM, FAO and UNDP, generated over 1 million person days of employment. The Pan American Health Organization working in collaboration with the World Health Organization, as well as UNICEF and MINUSTAH assisted the Government in organizing a mass immunization campaign that will have an impact on some 7 million people. The United Nations Office for Project Services provided management and support services to the Mission's communications centres as well as to multimedia centres in Haiti that promote dialogue with civil society, local media and the local authorities. It also renovated two hydropower stations.

VII. Mission support

64. In addition to routine tasks, key mission support activities included logistical assistance for elections in April, the handover of the University of Tabarre to local authorities and the relocation of the Brazilian contingent. Logistical support was also provided for security operations and the establishment of a MINUSTAH office in Martissant. A new joint operations centre was constructed in the Mission's headquarters.

65. Promoting adherence to standards of conduct for personnel and enforcing a zero-tolerance policy for sexual exploitation and abuse remained priorities. MINUSTAH undertook an awareness campaign on the prevention of sexual exploitation, targeting both the public and MINUSTAH personnel. The number of international and national staff who underwent relevant training increased, and two integrated training modules were created for military and police personnel. Additional training on conduct and discipline issues is being provided for all personnel with supervisory, managerial and command responsibilities.

66. Since January 2007, 7 MINUSTAH personnel have died in the course of duty (not from hostile fire), 35 have been medically evacuated to locations outside Haiti and 40 have been medically evacuated to higher-level care within Haiti. Diseases that can have serious health consequences remain a major concern for personnel. Mission personnel also continue to confront serious security hazards. Since January, 8 national staff members have been kidnapped, and approximately 30 staff members, both national and international, have been assaulted.

VIII. Financial aspects

67. By its resolution 61/284, the General Assembly appropriated the amount of $535,372,800, equivalent to $44,614,400 per month, for the maintenance of MINUSTAH for the period from 1 July 2007 to 30 June 2008. Should the Security Council decide to extend the mandate of MINUSTAH beyond 15 October 2007, the cost of maintaining the Mission until 30 June 2008 would be limited to the amounts approved by the General Assembly.

68. As at 30 April 2007, unpaid assessed contributions to the Special Account for MINUSTAH amounted to $164.8 million. The total outstanding assessed contributions for all peacekeeping operations as at that date amounted to $2,074.6 million.

69. As at 31 July 2007, amounts owed to troop and formed police contributors to MINUSTAH totalled $15.1 million. Reimbursement of troop costs has been made for the period up to 31 May 2007 and, for contingent-owned equipment, up to 31 March 2007, in accordance with the quarterly payment schedule.

IX. Observations

70. On 1 and 2 August, I travelled to Haiti to assess the stabilization process and to reaffirm the United Nations commitment to Haiti. I held extensive discussions with members of the Haitian Government and parliament, as well as other influential members of Haitian society, and reviewed the work of the Mission. My visit gave me a first-hand awareness of the degree to which Haiti now stands at a moment of hope unlike anything that has been possible for decades. My optimism is based upon the considerable achievements thus far, and the determination of the Haitian leadership and people to address root causes of Haiti's crisis, with the support of the international community. However, the length of the journey ahead and the fragility of recent gains were also starkly apparent, as was the real possibility that this moment of hope could dissipate unless it is supported through long-term commitment and vision. Haitian and international engagement is essential to consolidate these initial achievements and ensure that they become a firm basis for further progress towards stability and sustainable development.

71. The responsibility for Haiti's continued stabilization continues to rest first and foremost with its leadership and people. All actors must set aside divisive approaches and embrace the dialogue and collaboration promoted by President Préval. Recent progress towards the adoption of key legislation related to judicial reform is an encouraging development in this regard. Equally important are decisions to strengthen institutions of governance, such as local authorities, and to establish a permanent electoral council. Respect for the rule of law and State institutions can be further buttressed by support for President Préval's initiatives to end impunity and to curb corruption. These values must be reinforced, including by members of civil society and the private sector.

72. Consolidation of the recent achievements will require sustained and substantial international support, including through the continued deployment of MINUSTAH, as called for by President Préval during my visit. The assistance of MINUSTAH remains essential to support Haiti's efforts to achieve key objectives in such areas as governance, security, rule of law, the reinforcement of State institutions and respect for human rights, so as to create an enabling environment for socio-economic development.

73. I therefore recommend that the Security Council extend the mandate of the Mission for 12 months, while retaining the responsibilities established in its prior resolutions. After carefully listening to President Préval's priorities and assessing the situation on the ground, I do not see the need for a change in the current mandate, but I believe that MINUSTAH should progressively reorient and reconfigure itself to reflect changing circumstances on the ground.

74. While the democratic legitimacy of the Haitian leadership has laid the foundations for a new beginning, stability will depend on the capacity of the authorities at all levels to formulate policy and deliver public services. New areas where MINUSTAH may need to provide technical expertise at the national level would include border management, security strategies and anti-corruption. Appropriate MINUSTAH staff, experienced in border management issues, will be essential to support the efforts of the Government of Haiti in this area. The Mission will also need to help local authorities to attain a minimum level of capacity to serve their constituents. The provision of quick-impact projects continues to make a crucial difference, including by fostering public support for MINUSTAH and the implementation of its mandate and by promoting the safety and security of its personnel.

75. Substantial gains have been made in restoring gang-controlled urban areas to State authority. A review of security threats, challenges and risks has shown, however, that the situation remains fragile, and the root causes of instability are still present. Renewed political or criminal violence could re-emerge, as could civil disturbance. In addition, the absence of security forces along the border severely undermines efforts to stabilize the country. International peacekeepers will continue to assume the bulk of security-related responsibilities, pending the gradual development of the Haitian National Police. However, the current force of MINUSTAH needs to be adjusted to address effectively the present situation and possible threats, as well as to support the priorities outlined by President Préval. Accordingly, I recommend that the Mission's security components be reconfigured in line with the concepts outlined in paragraphs 28 and 29 of the present report, and that its troop strength be reduced by one company, to a total of 7,060, while its police component would be increased by an additional formed police unit, making a total of 2,091 police (out of which 1,140 would consist of officers in nine formed police units).

76. These arrangements would fall within the overall framework of a gradual transition towards reliance on Haitian structures to maintain stability, with a progressive transfer of functional or geographical responsibilities as corresponding capacity of the Haitian National Police develops. To this end, MINUSTAH will continue to strengthen the Haitian National Police. The Mission will also cooperate closely with the Haitian authorities in support of a comprehensive programme for judicial reform. These processes must be complemented by renewed efforts to shore up the prison system, where conditions remain unacceptable. MINUSTAH support for institutional strengthening and the promotion of good governance remain essential.

77. During the coming mandate period, MINUSTAH would develop a consolidation plan, with clear benchmarks for progress. Further details and elaboration on the Mission's transition strategy will be provided in my next report to the Security Council. However, the efforts of the Mission can be successful only if they are complemented by robust bilateral assistance in priority areas, including elections. Above all, bilateral actors and the private sector must assist with the economic recovery of the country and promote the generation of employment.

78. In conclusion, I would like to express my appreciation for the courage and dedication of the military, police and civilian personnel of MINUSTAH, and to those Governments that have provided troops and police to the operation. I would also like to place on record my sincere gratitude to my outgoing Special Representative, Edmond Mulet, whose leadership, determination and political skills have made a key contribution to ensuring substantial progress towards the stabilization of the country.

Annex I
United Nations Stabilization Mission in Haiti: countries providing military staff and contingents (as at 15 August 2007)

Country	*Staff officers*	*Troops*	*Total*
Argentina	10	552	562
Bolivia	3	215	218
Brazil[a]	15	1 196	1 211
Canada	4	—	4
Chile	5	497	502
Croatia	3	—	3
Ecuador	1	66	67
France	2	—	2
Guatemala	5	114	119
Jordan	10	746	756
Nepal	10	1 098	1 108
Pakistan	1	—	1
Paraguay	Nil	31	31
Peru	5	205	210
Philippines	1	155	156
Sri Lanka	10	950	960
United States of America	3	—	3
Uruguay	13	1 134	1 147
Total	**101**	**6 979**	**7 080**

[a] Including the Force Commander.

Annex II
United Nations Stabilization Mission in Haiti: countries providing police officers and formed police units (as at 15 August 2007)

Country	*Police officers*	*Formed police units*	*Total*
Australia	1	—	1
Argentina	4	—	4
Benin	52	—	52
Brazil	4	—	4
Burkina Faso	57	—	57
Cameroon	42	—	42
Canada	57	—	57
Central African Republic	1	—	1
Chad	1	—	1
Chile	13	—	13
China	11	125	136
Colombia	2	—	2
Egypt	11	—	11
El Salvador	3	—	3
France	71	—	71
Guinea	48	—	48
Jordan	4	290	294
Madagascar	1	—	1
Mali	61	—	61
Mauritius	1	—	1
Nepal	21	125	146
Niger	73	—	73
Nigeria	4	125	129
Pakistan	—	249	249
Philippines	11	—	11
Romania	10	—	10
Russian Federation	6	—	6
Rwanda	11	—	11
Senegal	66	85	151
Spain	41	—	41
Togo	11	—	11
Turkey	22	—	22
United States of America	49	—	49
Uruguay	2	—	2
Total	**760**	**999**	**1 770**

C. Iraq

1. Report of the Secretary-General pursuant to paragraph 30 of Resolution 1546 (2004), 1 September 2006 (S/2006/706)

I. Introduction

1. In paragraph 30 of its resolution 1546 (2004), the Security Council requested the Secretary-General to report to the Council on a quarterly basis on the fulfilment of the responsibilities of the United Nations Assistance Mission for Iraq (UNAMI). The present report is the ninth submitted pursuant to that resolution.

2. The report provides an update on United Nations activities in Iraq since the previous report (S/2006/360 of 2 June 2006). It presents a summary of key political developments in the period under review, particularly concerning the efforts of the Government of Iraq to promote national reconciliation and to improve the security situation throughout the country, as well as regional and international developments pertaining to Iraq. The report also provides an update on the activities of my Special Representative for Iraq, Ashraf Jehangir Qazi, the activities of UNAMI, an assessment of the security situation and an update on operational and security matters.

3. On 11 August 2006, the Security Council adopted resolution 1700 (2006), by which the Council extended the mandate of UNAMI for an additional period of 12 months, as requested by the Government of Iraq on 3 August 2006. In the resolution, the Council recognized that there continues to be a vital role for UNAMI in assisting Iraqi efforts to build a productive and prosperous nation at peace with itself and its neighbours. The Council also expressed its intention to review the mandate of UNAMI in 12 months or sooner, if requested by the Government of Iraq.

II. Summary of Key Developments in Iraq

A. Political developments

4. During the period under review, Iraq was faced with growing violence and insecurity, particularly in Baghdad and the southern and western regions. In response to those challenges, the first constitutionally elected Government of Iraq following its appointment on 20 May 2006, focused its political efforts on promoting national reconciliation and dialogue.

5. On 8 June 2006, the Council of Representatives completed the Government formation process by approving the appointment of Mohammed Abdulqadir al-Obaidi as Minister for Defence, Jawad Bolani from the Al-Fadila party of the United Iraqi Alliance as Minister of the Interior, and Sherwan al-Waili from Al-Daawa of the United Iraqi Alliance as Minister of State for National Security.

6. On 14 June 2006, the Government launched a security plan for Baghdad aimed at addressing the increased level of violence and growing criminality, which are undermining its efforts of reconciliation and dialogue. The second phase of the Baghdad security plan was initiated at the beginning of August 2006 with the redeployment of additional troops of the Multinational Force to the capital.

7. On 25 June 2006, the Prime Minister, Nouri al-Maliki, unveiled the National Reconciliation Plan. The 24-point Plan called for a qualified amnesty, the release of detainees, the reform of the legal and judicial systems, the provision of assistance to areas that are prone to violence, the facilitation of dialogue on constitutional and related matters, and the resolution of the problem of militias. The Plan also acknowledged the idea of an Iraqi-led Baghdad peace initiative, emphasized the need for regional support to achieve peace and stability in Iraq, and recognized the efforts of the League of Arab States to convene a conference on Iraqi national accord. The Plan also provided for the establishment of the High Committee for National Reconciliation, which held its first session on 22 July 2006. The composition of the Committee has not yet been finalized owing to a difference in views concerning membership criteria.

8. In his statement to mark the launch of the National Reconciliation Plan, my Special Representative welcomed the Plan and commended the efforts of the Government of Iraq in promoting dialogue and peace. He called upon all concerned, including regional and international actors, to support the initiative. He also reiterated that the United Nations remained fully committed to facilitate and assist in the implementation of the issues outlined in the reconciliation project of the Prime Minister, in accordance with its mandate.

9. Prior to the August recess of Parliament, the Council of Representatives established 19 of its 24 parliamentary committees. Extensive debate on the internal rules of procedure and the powers of the Speaker of the Council delayed parliamentary deliberations and the work of the committees. The kidnapping on 1 July 2006 of Tayseer Mashhadani, member of parliament from the Tawafoq coalition, resulted in further delay when the Tawafoq bloc temporarily suspended its participation in the Council of Representatives. Tawafoq resumed its participation after receiving assurances of Ms. Mashhadani's release, which occurred on 26 August 2006.

10. On 16 and 25 July, the Council of Representatives conducted its first and second readings of the draft law on the establishment of the Independent High Electoral Commission. The Council decided that it would resume its discussions on that subject in September. It also decided to extend the caretaker mandate of the Independent Electoral Commission of Iraq for an additional two months, until 10 October 2006. In addition, the Council continued its consultations on the draft law for the establishment of a national human rights commission in Iraq.

B. Regional developments

11. At the invitation of the Government of the Islamic Republic of Iran, the Foreign Ministers of the countries neighbouring Iraq held their ninth meeting in Tehran on 8 and 9 July 2006. The meeting was attended by the Foreign Ministers of Bahrain, Egypt, Iran (Islamic Republic of), Iraq, Jordan, Kuwait, Saudi Arabia, the Syrian Arab Republic and Turkey, as well as the Secretaries-General of the League of Arab States and the Organization of the Islamic Conference. My Special Representative for Iraq also attended the meeting. In the final communiqué of the meeting, the Ministers welcomed the establishment of a broad-based Government with the participation of all segments of the Iraqi population.

12. The League of Arab States continued preparations for the convening of the conference on Iraqi national accord. At the invitation of the League of Arab States, UNAMI sent a team to participate in the preparatory meeting for the conference, which was held in Cairo from

25 to 27 July 2006. It was decided that the next preparatory meeting would be held in November 2006. My Special Representative has remained in close contact with the Secretary-General of the League, Amre Moussa, and its Envoy to Iraq, Mukhtar Lamani, in support of this initiative.

C. International developments

13. On 16 June 2006, I accepted the request by the Government of Iraq for the United Nations to provide support in developing the International Compact with Iraq. The Compact is an initiative of the Government for a new partnership with the international community. Its purpose is to achieve a national vision for Iraq with the aim of consolidating peace and pursuing political, economic and social development over the next five years. The primary focus will be to build a framework for the economic transformation of Iraq and its integration into the regional and global economy. The Compact will also reflect the interconnectedness of political and security developments with Iraq's recovery, which is a prerequisite for sustainable regional investments. The Compact is co-chaired by the Deputy Prime Minister of Iraq, Barham Salih, and my Deputy Secretary-General, Mark Malloch Brown. My Special Representative for Iraq has been designated as my focal point for the Compact in Iraq.

14. On 5 and 6 July, my Deputy Secretary-General visited Baghdad to consult with the Government of Iraq, the United Nations Development Group, United Nations agencies, the World Bank, and the international donor community on the process of developing the Compact. The co-chairs are assisted by a preparatory group of countries and organizations to develop the Compact via a consultative process. The group provides support, advice and guidance on the Compact. The co-chairs have appointed an executive committee that will manage the process towards the adoption of the Compact and beyond. The committee includes representatives of the Government of Iraq, the United Nations, the World Bank, the International Monetary Fund, the Arab Fund for Economic and Social Development and the Islamic Development Bank.

15. On 27 July, the co-chairs issued a joint statement formally launching the Compact, in which they invited the international community to commit their support to the process and to join as valued partners in the International Compact with Iraq. It is envisaged that the finalized Compact, including key priorities, benchmarks and commitments, will be presented by the Government of Iraq by the end of 2006.

16. In order to engage in a strategy dialogue on the future of Iraq, on 18 September, I will convene a meeting of Foreign Ministers at Headquarters in New York. The purpose of the meeting will be to review progress in the implementation of Security Council resolution 1546 (2004) and the commitment of the United Nations to provide the necessary assistance to the Government of Iraq. Participants will include Iraq and its neighbouring countries, the permanent members of the Security Council, key donors and representatives of concerned regional and international organizations. The meeting will provide an opportunity to review the progress being made by the Government in the political, security and economic fields, and to seek broader international support and engagement with the Government. The meeting will also provide a unique opportunity for the Government to present an outline of its programme for the reconstruction of Iraq over the next five years inside the framework of the International Compact.

III. Update on activities of the Mission

A. Political activities of the Special Representative of theSecretary-General

17. During the period under review, my Special Representative remained in close contact with all key Iraqi political, community and religious leaders to promote the National Reconciliation Plan of the Government. He also encouraged all concerned to exert their influence to protect civilian lives and dedicate their efforts to ensure mutual respect and dialogue and to discuss tangible steps to reduce violence and build trust in State institutions. He also continued his consultations with political, tribal and religious leaders to discuss mechanisms for exploring the Iraqi-led Baghdad peace initiative.

18. In the context of his regular contacts with the League of Arab States on the continuing efforts to convene the conference on Iraqi national accord, my Special Representative, on 12 June 2006, met the delegation of the League led by Assistant Secretary-General Ahmad Bin Hilli to discuss preparations for the conference.

19. On 8 and 9 July, my Special Representative visited Tehran to participate in the ninth meeting of the Foreign Ministers of the countries neighbouring Iraq. At the meeting, my Special Representative stressed the need for regional support to achieve peace and stability in Iraq and that all of Iraq's neighbours have a stake in the success of the Compact. He held separate meetings with the Foreign Minister of the Islamic Republic of Iran, Manouchehr Mottaki, and the Foreign Minister of Iraq, Hoshyar Zebari, to discuss matters of regional interest, including preparations for the International Compact. He also met the Secretary-General of the League of Arab States, Amre Moussa, and the Secretary-General of the Organization of the Islamic Conference, Ekmeleddin Ihsanoglu.

20. My Special Representative received the Governor of Karbala and members of the Karbala Provincial Council. He also met with senior commanders of the Multinational Force, as well as with the Ambassadors of Denmark, France, Turkey, the United Kingdom of Great Britain and Northern Ireland and the United States of America, and the representative of the European Union in Iraq. In addition, within the framework of the ongoing preparations for the International Compact, my Special Representative held consultations with members of the Government of Iraq as well as with representatives of the diplomatic and the donor community in Baghdad.

B. Constitutional support activities

21. During the period under review, the UNAMI Office of Constitutional Support continued to play a leading role in promoting dialogue and consensus-building on the Constitution of Iraq. The Office met with a broad spectrum of political and community leaders, academic institutions and non-governmental organizations to discuss issues pertaining to the review, amendment and implementation of the Constitution.

22. In July 2006, the Office completed its seminar programme, which was launched in February 2006, to promote multiparty dialogue. The programme engaged senior political leaders, technocrats and members of civil society in focused discussions on critical constitutional issues. The programme concentrated on the constitutional themes of decentralization and federalism, the rule of law and human rights, and issues relating to accountable governance. Specific topics included multilateral dialogue on the subjects of the rule of law and the judiciary system, human rights, oil and gas, federalism, fiscal federalism, and governance.

23. The Office continued to provide advice and assistance to the Government and the Council of Representatives on issues relating to the establishment of the constitutional review committee. It also continued to contribute to UNAMI reconciliation activities, in particular those targeted at the resolution of potentially divisive constitutional issues.

C. Electoral assistance activities

24. On 2 July 2006, the Council of Representatives requested the assistance of the United Nations in the drafting of the legal framework for the establishment of a permanent electoral commission along with other related issues, such as the conduct of upcoming electoral events. In response to the request of the Council of Representatives, the UNAMI Electoral Assistance Team provided technical assistance to the Legal Committee of the Council in the drafting of the law establishing the Independent High Electoral Commission, as well as on the formulation of the new electoral law.

25. On 16 and 25 July, the Council of Representatives conducted its first and second readings of the draft law on the establishment of the Commission. The Council decided that it would resume its discussions on the matter in September. In the meantime, the Council decided to extend the caretaker mandate of the Independent Electoral Commission of Iraq for an additional two months, until 10 October 2006.

26. In addition, the Electoral Assistance Team continued its efforts aimed at strengthening the capacity of the Independent Electoral Commission and the skills of its staff. The Team stands ready to provide required technical assistance to support the transition of the Commission to the new Independent High Electoral Commission.

D. Reconstruction, development and humanitarian assistance

27. Concern continues to grow over the displacement of civilians, primarily as a result of intercommunal violence, but also due to military operations. According to United Nations and Iraqi Government sources, the number of displaced families since the Samarra attack on 22 February 2006 exceeded 30,000 (approximately 200,000 individuals). National non-governmental organizations and the Iraqi Red Crescent Society have reported that their personnel are facing increased harassment and threats as a result of their efforts to assist internally displaced persons. As a consequence, volunteers have left the agencies, further diminishing the human resources available to assist those in need.

28. The rapidly increasing number of internally displaced persons underlines the need for additional resources to address the deteriorating humanitarian situation. United Nations agencies, funds and programmes have nearly exhausted their resources earmarked for emergency humanitarian activities, as most were funded from donations received following the last United Nations consolidated appeal for Iraq in 2003, as well as from their respective core resources. Similarly, the Government of Iraq is constrained in its ability to adequately respond to the situation. There is now an urgent need for substantial new funding to meet the needs of those who have been displaced by the conflict.

29. The Mission has also provided the Government with guidance on addressing the needs of internally displaced persons in regard to shelter and assistance, in an effort to avoid the establishment of tented camps that would pose long-term problems and potentially jeopardize the security and dignity of the displaced. Other advocacy issues include respect for humanitarian access and space, and other principles of international humanitarian law.

30. The United Nations country team continues to work according to its plans, with a new focus on area-based development as a result of its internal consultations. Numerous missions and regular dialogue have allowed UNAMI to help address the specific needs of communities in various regions. As a part of that process, UNAMI continued to support the initiative of the Ministry of Planning and Development Cooperation to enhance coordination and interaction between the provincial and central authorities on reconstruction and development challenges. The assignment of an international adviser to the Ministry has been completed. Discussions are under way to determine whether the need exists to continue the arrangement.

31. A revised concept for the establishment of an emergency coordination and response cell was submitted to the Office of the Prime Minister during the reporting period. The UNAMI Humanitarian Adviser assigned to the Office will be returning to Baghdad soon to work on the cell. Frequent visits to Iraq by my Deputy Special Representative for Humanitarian, Reconstruction and Development Affairs have helped to raise awareness within the Government of the concept for the cell.

32. Support to civil society remains high on the United Nations agenda in Iraq. Capacity-building, grants for the provision of services to communities and the convening of regional coordination meetings for non-governmental organizations are ongoing activities. A United Nations International Adviser recently arrived in Baghdad to work with the State Ministry for Civil Society Affairs, focusing on the drafting of the law on non-governmental organizations, and providing support for institution-building and training.

33. In my previous report, it was anticipated that there would be a meeting of the Donor Committee of the International Reconstruction Fund Facility for Iraq during the current reporting period. However, the preparations for the International Compact provide for a recalibration of the Facility mechanism to accelerate the gradual channelling of bilateral and multilateral support directly to the Government of Iraq.

E. Human rights activities

34. Iraq is experiencing an acute human rights and humanitarian crisis, with indiscriminate killings, targeted attacks, crime and corruption contributing to the lack of law and order. Despite efforts by the new Government to address the situation, State institutions have been unable to protect individuals from gross human rights violations or grant redress or compensation to the rapidly growing number of victims. I remain concerned by reports that militia elements have infiltrated governmental and law enforcement institutions, thus undermining the confidence of the Iraqi people in State institutions. The existence of death squads, some of which are linked to the existing armed militias, and even to sectors of Government security forces, is highlighted by the daily appearance, in various parts of the country, of dozens of bodies of murdered persons bearing signs of torture and execution.

35. Violence in Iraq continues to disproportionately affect civilians. According to figures provided by the Ministry of Health, 3,149 civilians were killed in June while at least 3,438 were reportedly killed in July. Numerous attacks and mass kidnappings of civilians revealed a pattern of targeting based on sectarian affiliation, with a clear intent to provoke fear and take vengeance. The impact on women, children and ethnic and religious minorities has been particularly alarming. Women continue to see their rights and freedom curtailed. A significant number of "honour crimes" have been reported, although precise figures

remain difficult to obtain. Children also continue to suffer not only from indiscriminate violence, including kidnapping, but also from acts of abuse. The violence has led to an increase in the number of internally displaced children, who require basic services and psychosocial support. Ethnic and religious minorities also continue to be targeted by violence, often resulting in forced migration and internal displacement.

36. The number of detainees held in the country also remains a source of concern. The Ministry of Human Rights reported that approximately 26,398 detainees were being held in detention centres countrywide at the end of July 2006, including some 13,000 detainees in the custody of the Multinational Force. The figures include a number of detainees in the region of Kurdistan, amounting to 2,147 at the end of June. The Mission continues to work with the Iraqi authorities and the Multinational Force to ensure that the release and transfer of detainees is carried out promptly and in accordance with international human rights standards. However, thousands of detainees continue to be held in violation of the existing legal framework and still lack the right of due process, in part because of the lack of required capacity in Iraqi courts. I welcome the release of some 3,300 individuals in June and July as an attempt to bolster the National Reconciliation Plan of the Government.

37. I remain very concerned that arbitrary detention and torture of detainees in Iraqi prisons continue to be widespread. On 1 June 2006, a joint inspection of a prison site by representatives of the Iraqi Government and the Multinational Force found 1,431 detainees with signs of physical and psychological abuse. A total of 52 arrest warrants have been issued against officials of the Ministry of the Interior, but they have yet to be served. On 1 and 2 July 2006, the Special Rapporteur on the question of torture, Manfred Nowak, met with Iraqi non-governmental organizations and representatives of the Ministry of Human Rights in Amman to survey the situation in Iraq. On 19 July, the United Nations High Commissioner for Human Rights wrote to the Iraqi Prime Minister, commending him for his efforts to promote national reconciliation, in particular the release of detainees. She also reiterated her previous call for the immediate release of the report on the investigation into allegations of detainee abuse at the Al-Jadiriya detention centre in November 2005.

38. On 21 June 2006, following the assassination of Khamis al-Obeidi, a lawyer representing Saddam Hussein, the defence counsel boycotted several court sessions. On 27 July 2006, the court recessed until 16 October 2006, when it is scheduled to announce the verdict of the Dujail case. The current trial, which will consider the Anfal campaign in northern Iraq against Kurdish populations during the late 1980s, began on 21 August 2006. Mr. Hussein and six other co-defendants are charged with war crimes related to an internal armed conflict and crimes against humanity. Saddam Hussein and Ali-Hassan al-Majid are also charged with genocide.

39. The Mission continues to work with Iraqi ministries, judicial institutions and civil society organizations in the development of a strong human rights system. Progress was made in the drafting of a law for the establishment of a national human rights commission. The Human Rights Office also continued to support the Rule of Law Sector Working Group, a group composed of representatives of Iraqi ministries and donor countries to develop a comprehensive strategy on the rule of law.

40. On 22 and 23 July, the Human Rights Office, the Office of the United Nations High Commissioner for Human Rights and the International Centre for Transitional Justice, in

partnership with the Ministry of Human Rights, organized a meeting on transitional justice in Iraq. Numerous calls were made for greater United Nations involvement and expertise. It was agreed that further mechanisms would be established within UNAMI to support the implementation of the National Reconciliation Plan, which includes transitional justice as a key component.

IV. International Reconstruction Fund Facility for Iraq

41. As at 31 July 2006, the total contributions to the United Nations Development Group Iraq Trust Fund, one of the two funds of the International Reconstruction Fund Facility for Iraq, equalled $934 million. A total of 101 projects valued at $831 million were approved as at the end of July 2006 for funding under the Iraq Trust Fund. Continuing the significant progress in implementation, contracts worth cumulatively $637 million (77 per cent of approved funding) have been initiated and $522 million (63 per cent of approved funding) have been disbursed.

42. On 24 May 2006, the United Nations and the World Bank hosted an informal meeting on the progress of Fund Facility activities in Amman. The meeting was attended by the officials of the Government of Iraq and 38 officials from 16 countries. The briefing focused on the third six-month progress reports from the World Bank and the United nations, as well as on the findings of external reviews of United Nations and World Bank operations. The participants recognized the many positive features of the Fund Facility, particularly the success achieved in a very difficult environment, the quality of the reports and the transparency of the information provided on the dedicated web site (www.irffi.org). The meeting strongly supported the need to retain the Fund Facility as an important instrument to support Iraq in the next stages of its reconstruction process.

43. Participants commended the United Nations on its work in Iraq, especially in the areas of electoral assistance, constitutional support and the provision of basic services. The European Commission in particular welcomed the convening of the informal meeting and the opportunity to discuss the progress reports, the reviews and the prospects for both trust funds. Subsequently, the European Commission announced that it would grant an additional €120 million to the Iraq Trust Fund to support the ongoing work on basic services and governance. The United Nations is highly appreciative of this major new contribution to the Iraq Trust Fund.

44. In follow-up to the Amman meeting, the Chair of the Fund Facility visited Baghdad from 16 to 19 July 2006 to convey the views of the Donor Committee to the new Government of Iraq. The Deputy Prime Minister and the new Minister for Planning and Development Cooperation confirmed their support for a new revitalized and refocused Facility. There was general agreement on the concept of continuing to use the Facility as a funding mechanism for rapid response to basic services and needs, but also with a greater focus on support to Iraqi institutions that would elaborate and operationalize the strategic policy and economic reforms that may result from the Compact.

V. International Advisory and Monitoring Board

45. On 17 and 18 July 2006, the International Advisory and Monitoring Board, which oversees the use of resources of the Development Fund for Iraq, met in New York and reviewed draft audit reports by Ernst & Young covering the audits of Iraqi oil export sales and Fund

operations for the period from 1 July to 31 December 2005. In its statement issued on 10 August 2006, the Board noted that audit reports continued to be critical of the financial and accounting control systems in place in the spending ministries, the United States agencies in respect of the outstanding commitments using Fund resources, and the Iraqi administration of Fund resources. The Board urged the Government of Iraq to take concrete steps to address the audit findings and recommendations to ensure that oil resources were better protected.

VI. Security and operational issues

A. Assessment of the security situation

46. The level of violence in Iraq continues to rise in many areas of the country, and United Nations staff members remain at risk. The sectarian nature of most of the violence, together with resistance groups, extremist-led armed groups and organized criminal groups, combine to create a very complex and dangerous operating environment. The current level of violence and disorder is likely to continue for some time.

47. Daily civilian casualties remain high. Large-scale kidnappings are now common, as are false checkpoints and summary executions by various Shiite and Sunni armed groups. Despite the Government's introduction of the Baghdad security plan in June 2006, the levels of violence in the city have actually risen, indicating the worrisome capability of insurgents, armed opposition groups and criminal gangs. Early in August 2006, the Government of Iraq announced a second phase of the Baghdad security plan in which more than 3,700 Multinational Force troops and their armoured fighting vehicles were deployed in the city in another attempt to contain the intensifying violence.

48. However, the security situation in Iraq varies widely. Next to Baghdad, the western province of Al-Anbar is considered the most dangerous area in the country. As a result, the United Nations is unable to conduct operations there. In Baghdad, many districts have been effectively out of bounds for United Nations operations for extended periods. Large numbers of civilians, as well as personnel of Iraqi security forces and troops of the Multinational Force, are killed every week. On 12 July 2006, security responsibilities in the province of Al-Muthana in the south were handed over by the Multinational Force to Iraqi security forces. No significant acts of violence against the Government or other entities in the province have been reported.

49. The security of United Nations staff and operations in the international zone are under constant review by UNAMI and the Department for Safety and Security. Although indirect fire attacks occur, they are mostly ineffective. However, United Nations staff continue to wear personal body armour whenever moving inside the international zone and must use armoured vehicles. Although incidents are often reported from the many pedestrian and vehicular checkpoints into the international zone, and explosions and gunfire can be heard on most days, the perimeter of the international zone and its heavily controlled entrance checkpoints remain robust and safe. A roadside explosion on 7 August 2006, apparently aimed at the convoy of the Deputy Special Representative, underlined the dangers of moving inside the red zone, regardless of the fact that the incident resulted in no injuries. The incident is under investigation to determine the facts and to identify any lessons learned so that a maximum level of protection can be ensured during such movements.

50. The situation in Basra remains tense and the Multinational Force has made arrests of high-profile militia leaders in the province. In response, the levels of violence increased during the quarter, including indirect fire attacks in the Basra Palace area, which houses United Nations offices. As a result, the United Nations temporarily relocated some members of the United Nations liaison detachment staff from Basra in July. Erbil continues to be stable and calm. Nevertheless, recent reports of potential threats kept UNAMI staff on moderate alert for numerous weeks during the reporting period. Several demonstrations over the rising prices and poor services were held in the Kurdish region, some of which led to a violent response by the police, resulting in one death and several injuries.

51. United Nations national staff members have been directly and indirectly affected by the violence, particularly in Baghdad and Basra. One national staff member of the World Health Organization has been missing since early May 2006 and several others have been threatened. The immediate relatives of several other staff members have been kidnapped, and subsequently released in return for ransom, or murdered. United Nations national staff members in Basra have been directly threatened and, in a few cases, their family members or close relatives have been killed. United Nations staff members are exposed to the effects of violence on a regular basis. Therefore, exceptional measures have been adopted, including flexible working hours, biweekly security briefings, the establishment of a national staff security working group, limited temporary accommodation in the international zone, and subsequent interaction with the Multinational Force, the Government of Iraq and other entities, when appropriate. Assisting its national staff members remains one of the Mission's foremost concerns.

52. In conclusion, the Organization's presence and its ability to operate effectively in Iraq remain severely constrained by the security environment. The United Nations is highly dependent on the Multinational Force for movement security and threat information. However, UNAMI is gradually developing methodologies and capabilities within its safety and security unit to ensure it is able to operate safely and effectively in this environment should it need to function with more self-reliance.

B. Facilities, logistics and support

53. UNAMI has commenced the planned transition from the facilities managed by the Multinational Force to the new premises managed by the Mission. On 22 August, the Mission moved its Baghdad staff from the Al-Rasheed Hotel to a temporary United Nations compound inside the international zone. The compound will serve as an interim accommodation site until a long-term and integrated facility is completed. A permanent site for that purpose has been allocated by the Government of Iraq and plans for its development, including a technical survey and site clearance, are under way. In Erbil, staff members are accommodated in the new Area Office. Improvements to the compound continue in keeping with the surrounding environment. In Basra, the new Area Office is ready for occupation by staff currently accommodated in the facilities of the Multinational Force. However, owing to recent security concerns in Basra, the planned move of staff to the United Nations compound was put on hold until further notice. Development plans are also under way for a logistics base and air terminal at Baghdad International Airport to support a dedicated aircraft when it becomes available, as well as to improve the handling of staff and cargo at the airport.

54. While the acquisition of air assets for the United Nations presence in Iraq has been a major challenge, some progress has recently been made. The Government of Japan and the United Nations have recently finalized arrangements for the provision of a dedicated weekly flight for UNAMI. The Government of Denmark has also offered to provide a dedicated aircraft to UNAMI. I look forward to the finalization of the modalities of this offer as soon as possible. I am grateful to the Government of Japan and the Government of Denmark for their offer of air support, which will significantly improve the mobility of the Mission.

C. Agreements

55. The status-of-mission agreement between the United Nations and the Government of Iraq was signed on 3 June 2005, but its entry into force remains pending. While the United Nations sent a note to the Government of Iraq on 6 June 2005 confirming the acceptance of the agreement, the confirmation of the Government remains pending, despite repeated reminders. I call upon the Government to take action on the approval of the agreement by way of a corresponding note.

56. The Mission continues to pursue the negotiation of a series of supplementary arrangements with the Multinational Force to implement the agreement concerning the establishment of security for UNAMI, concluded between the United Nations and the Government of the United States on 8 December 2005. I look forward to the early finalization of these arrangements, which will form a core aspect of continued security support for the presence of the United Nations in Iraq.

VII. Observations

57. Over the past three years, the people of Iraq have made many sacrifices to support the political transition of their country. Through their active participation in two elections, the constitutional process and the constitutional referendum, they have demonstrated their commitment to a peaceful, democratic and prosperous Iraq, despite the very tight transitional timetable and challenging security environment. The Iraqi people now have every right to expect their elected leaders, and first and foremost their constitutionally-elected Government, to do everything possible to deliver tangible improvements in their day-to-day lives.

58. Despite the significant achievements in the political transition process, meeting the benchmarks endorsed by the Security Council in resolution 1546 (2004) has not translated into an improved security and human rights situation. This remains a major challenge. Insurgent, militia and terrorist attacks, as well as gross violations of human rights, including killings, kidnappings and torture, continued unabated in many parts of the country. Many of the victims are women, children and minorities. Iraq today has become one of the most violent conflict areas in the world. According to the latest Government figures, the number of civilians killed has increased considerably and stands at an average of 100 people per day, while more than 14,000 were reportedly wounded per month. Since the Samarra attack on 22 February 2006, approximately 200,000 individuals have been displaced. These are worrisome trends, and if they continue, the social and political fabric of the country could be endangered.

59. While I note the efforts of the Government of Iraq to take concrete measures to improve security, such as the Baghdad security plan, and the efforts by the Multinational Force to

train Iraqi security forces, there can ultimately be no military solutions to the many challenges facing Iraq. As a case in point, growing militia activities are both a cause of and a response to the rising level of insecurity and human rights violations. As long as the people of Iraq do not have full confidence in the impartiality and accountability of the new Government and its security forces, there is the danger of a vicious cycle in which rising levels of militia activities breed more fear and insecurity, which in turn will lead to a further increase in militia activities. This cycle must be broken.

60. In such a difficult environment, the burden of leadership is a heavy one. Those who are in a position to bring their influence to bear must not only take robust measures to protect the lives of innocent civilians, but also hold those responsible for violent acts accountable and bring them to justice, address legitimate grievances, and ensure that their own actions are in full accordance with international humanitarian and human rights law. The Government of Iraq has a special responsibility to ensure that all those who speak and act on its behalf do so in the interest of all Iraqi citizens, and refrain from responding to particular constituencies or interests. It must do everything possible to progressively foster an environment conducive to the demobilization, disarming and reintegration of militias.

61. A vital element in the quest for addressing the security and human rights situation is the improvement of living conditions for all Iraqis. The people of Iraq have witnessed three decades of war, internal conflict, political instability and sanctions. Most Iraqis today live without reliable access to proper health care, social services, education, employment and other economic opportunities. These needs must be addressed without delay.

62. One important economic initiative of the Government of Iraq is the International Compact, co-chaired by the Government and the United Nations, for a new partnership with the international community. Considerable preparatory work has been initiated to create an effective framework for the Compact in which the Government can develop its economic programme according to clearly defined priorities, benchmarks and commitments. While the focus of the Compact will be economic, due account needs to be taken of the interlinkages with the political and security challenges facing Iraq and the policies the Government has adopted to effectively address them. The Compact will also need to be as inclusive as possible to ensure a constructive and interactive regional and international engagement. The Government of Iraq and the international community must work together closely to develop and implement the Compact with a view to building a strong Iraqi economy, reintegrating it into the regional and global economy, and ensuring that its benefits are made available to all Iraqis. The United Nations looks forward to working with all concerned towards the successful outcome of the Compact.

63. Any strategy for the reconstruction of the country requires an enabling framework for peace and reconciliation, that addresses the causes of violence, insecurity and human rights violations. Such a framework requires political solutions based on genuine dialogue and consensus-building among the many diverse communities in Iraq, which should be seen as a source of strength rather than of division and conflict. The Government and the Council of Representatives must therefore lead in the development of a national agenda that is responsive to the needs and aspirations of all Iraqi constituencies. The Iraqi people expect and deserve no less. I welcome Prime Minister Al-Maliki's National Reconciliation Plan, in which key issues requiring effective action are identified. The Iraqi-led Baghdad peace

initiative can make an important contribution to realizing the goals of the Plan, and the United Nations stands ready to assist.

64. Regional countries have an important role in supporting national reconciliation in Iraq, given the symbiotic relationship between Iraq and the region as a whole in terms of their security and prosperity. While Iraq needs to recognize the legitimate concerns of regional countries about the situation inside its own country, regional countries must be responsive to Iraqi needs. The United Nations therefore continues to support the planned League of Arab States conference on Iraqi national accord, and my Special Representative is working closely with the League on the necessary preparations. I also welcome the periodic meetings of the Foreign and Interior Ministers of the States neighbouring Iraq. These meetings have helped to promote dialogue and interaction between Iraq and its neighbours. However, much more needs to be done through such forums to promote concrete confidence-building measures, since the situation on both sides of the Iraqi border remains difficult. In the coming months, I therefore intend to explore this issue further with Member States.

65. While regional support for national reconciliation is important, the primary responsibility clearly rests with the people of Iraq. The constitutional review could become an important vehicle to establish a firm foundation for the reconciliation process. The series of multiparty seminars held by UNAMI on key outstanding constitutional issues has shown that apparently divisive issues can be resolved if approached in constructive and imaginative ways. An effective review process thus has the potential to generate buy-in from all Iraqi constituencies. It could also create important benefits for the International Compact, establishing a solid basis for the economic reconstruction of Iraq and increasing donor and investor confidence. The United Nations therefore hopes that the Council of Representatives will initiate the constitutional review as soon as possible, and remains fully committed to providing the necessary support.

66. The United Nations also stands ready to provide assistance in drafting the legal framework for the establishment of the new Independent High Electoral Commission, as requested by the Council of Representatives. I urge those concerned to respect international experience in preserving the integrity and independence of the officials both in the commission and its governorate offices. Only a genuinely independent electoral commission can ensure successful and credible elections, which are central to the maturing democracy of Iraq.

67. The United Nations remains fully committed to continuing to fulfil its mandate pursuant to Security Council resolution 1546 (2004), as circumstances permit. I therefore welcome the 12-month extension of the UNAMI mandate by the Security Council, as requested by the Government of Iraq. While the United Nations remains responsive to the current challenges facing Iraq, it is keen to engage in a strategic dialogue on plans for the future of the country. To this end, I will convene a meeting in New York on 18 September 2006 with the representatives of Iraq and its neighbours, the permanent members of the Security Council, key donors and regional and international organizations. I hope that the participants will seize that opportunity to engage in a frank and forward-looking dialogue.

68. While the Organization's presence and ability to operate effectively remains severely constrained by the security environment, UNAMI is exploring how it can maximize its impact and which tasks can be prioritized. I would like to reiterate my appreciation to Member States, from both within and outside the Multinational Force, who support the

United Nations in Iraq, by providing military advisers, guard forces and movement and aviation support.

69. Following the formal completion of the political transition of Iraq, the time has come for its constitutionally elected Government and the international community to place the safety and welfare of the Iraqi people at the front and centre of all their collective efforts. The Iraqi people and their leaders have arrived at an important crossroads: if they are able to build firm foundations for the common interest of all Iraqis, the promise of peace and prosperity will be within reach. However, if current patterns of discord and violence prevail for much longer, there is a grave danger of a breakdown of the Iraqi State, and potentially of civil war, which would be detrimental not only to the Iraqi people, but also to countries in the region and the international community in general. I therefore hope that, at this critical time, the Iraqi people will resolve to unite with a view to building a better future for all, living up to the country's significant human and natural potential. They will need the active support from the region and the international community in general, which must recognize that overcoming the many challenges facing Iraq will require long-term solutions that can only be achieved through a sustained commitment of cooperation and support.

70. Based on the extended mandate of UNAMI, the United Nations will continue to stand by the people of Iraq and their political, religious and community leaders, and will make every effort to play its part to help generate tangible progress for a democratic and prosperous Iraq, at peace with itself, its neighbours and the international community in general. I wish to thank my Special Representative, Ashraf Jehangir Qazi, for his leadership and the Mission's national and international staff, as well as the personnel of the United Nations agencies, programmes and funds, for their dedication in fulfilling their duties in implementing the UNAMI mandate under extremely difficult conditions.

2. Report of the Secretary-General pursuant to paragraph 30 of Resolution 1546 (2004), 5 December 2006 (S/2006/945)

I. Introduction

1. In paragraph 30 of resolution 1546 (2004), the Security Council requested the Secretary-General to report to the Council on a quarterly basis on the fulfilment of the responsibilities of the United Nations Assistance Mission for Iraq (UNAMI). The present report is the tenth submitted pursuant to that resolution.

2. The report provides an update on United Nations activities in Iraq since the last report (S/2006/706) of 1 September 2006. It presents a summary of key political developments in the period under review, particularly concerning the efforts of the Government of Iraq to promote national reconciliation and to improve the security situation, as well as regional and international developments pertaining to Iraq. The report also provides an update on the activities of my Special Representative for Iraq, Ashraf Jehangir Qazi, and UNAMI, an assessment of the security situation and an update on operational and security matters.

II. Summary of key developments in Iraq

A. Political developments

3. The period under review was marked by a significant increase in sectarian violence, insurgent and terrorist attacks, and criminal activities, with civilian casualties reaching an all-time high. Across many parts of the country an increasing number of Iraqis have been affected by growing violence and insecurity.

4. A joint effort by the Government of Iraq and the multinational force to stem the rising level of violence under the Baghdad security plan appears to have had very limited success. Control of access to and from Baghdad, curfew extensions and house-to-house cordon and search operations were some of the additional security measures employed to stabilize the capital. Despite those efforts, in large areas of Baghdad and other parts of the country, insurgent and militia activities remain uncontrolled. The most serious recent incidents, such as the mass abduction of some 100 employees of and visitors at the Ministry of Higher Education in Baghdad and the heinous terrorist attacks in Sadr City on 23 November, which left over 200 people dead and scores injured, have deepened public concerns over the ability of the Government to control the security environment.

5. The succession of various initiatives to promote national reconciliation both inside and outside Iraq does not appear to have had a significant impact on the scale and nature of the violence in the country. The proliferation of initiatives has led to widespread scepticism about their viability both inside and outside Iraq. The Government has also been unable to supplement its security initiatives with the implementation of projects to improve the delivery of essential services, provide jobs and rebuild socio-economic infrastructure. Institutional capacity limitations have also impeded the ability of the Government to implement the 2006 budget.

6. During the period under review, the Council of Representatives, which reconvened on 5 September 2006 after the summer recess, finalized the establishment of its 24 parliamentary

committees and considered several pieces of legislation, including some key bills related to the implementation of the Constitution. Through these committees, the Council adopted a number of pieces of legislation, including a law on the import and retailing of oil products; amendments to the criminal code; amendments to the general prosecution law of 1979; and a law on national investment. Discussions at the political and technical levels on a draft national hydrocarbon law are ongoing.

7. On 12 September 2006, a group of parliamentarians from the Sadrist block of the Shia coalition, the United Iraqi Alliance, and from Sunni political parties called for a timetable for the withdrawal of the multinational force. As a result, the Defence Committee of the Council of Representatives held discussions on the status of the multinational force.

8. On 25 September 2006, the Council of Representatives established the Constitutional Review Committee, which is composed of 27 members in proportional representation to the distribution of seats in the Council. On 15 November 2006, following a prolonged debate over its chairmanship, the Committee held its first formal session and elected Sheikh Humam Hamoudi (United Iraqi Alliance) as its Chair, and Ayad Sammaraie (Tawafoq) and Fouad Massoum (Kurdistan Alliance) as the Deputy Chairs. The Committee agreed that the Committee leadership should take decisions by consensus.

9. On 8 October 2006, the Council of Representatives renewed for another 30 days the state of emergency that has been in place across the country since November 2004, with the exception of the Kurdistan region.

10. On 11 October 2006, the Council of Representatives adopted the law on the formation of regions. The drafting of the law was contentious. Several Sunni political parties, spear-headed by Tawafoq and joined by Fadhila, the Sadrists and some independents, argued that the law should be enacted only after the completion of the constitutional review process. The United Iraqi Alliance and the Kurdistan Alliance called for its enactment prior to a six-month deadline set forth in the Constitution. The draft law was finally put to a vote as a result of a compromise "package deal" reached on 24 September, according to which the enacted law would not be implemented for 18 months and the Constitutional Review Committee would be given one year to complete its work. Notwithstanding that compromise, the law was passed by a very narrow margin, as a number of parliamentarians boycotted the vote in the Council of Representatives.

11. On 25 October 2006, as result of differences over security operations in Sadr City, the Government of Iraq and the multinational force announced the formation of a joint coordination committee. The committee, which is composed of the Iraqi National Security Adviser, the Iraqi Ministers of Defence and Interior, the multinational force Commander and the United States Ambassador to Iraq, was charged with accelerating the training of the Iraqi security forces and the transfer of responsibility for security to the Government of Iraq, including assumption of command and control over Iraqi forces.

12. In a letter dated 11 November 2006 addressed to the President of the Security Council (S/2006/888), Prime Minister Al-Maliki, on behalf of the Government of Iraq, requested that the mandate of the multinational force be extended for an additional 12 months. On 28 November 2006, the Security Council unanimously adopted resolution 1723 (2006) extending the mandate of the multinational force until 31 December 2007. The Council also decided that this mandate could be reviewed at the request of the Government of Iraq

or no later than 15 June 2007, and that it would terminate the mandate earlier if requested by the Government of Iraq.

13. During the period under review, Prime Minister Al-Maliki pushed forward the implementation of his National Reconciliation Plan. Following a conference of tribal leaders in August 2006, he held a meeting with a spectrum of civil society figures and institutions on 16 September. The conference with political leaders, originally scheduled for October, has been postponed several times.

14. On 2 October, Prime Minister Al-Maliki announced a four-point Ramadan accord, which was supported by major political parties. A key element of the agreement included the establishment of local security committees composed of political, religious, police and army figures. The Prime Minister also initiated direct contacts through his personal representatives with Iraqi opposition groups within Iraq and in Jordan, Egypt and other neighbouring countries.

15. Reconciliation initiatives in Iraq have been complemented by the efforts of regional actors. On 20 October 2006, Iraqi Shiite and Sunni religious leaders, in a meeting sponsored by the Organization of the Islamic Conference, issued in Mecca a declaration calling for an end to sectarian bloodshed in Iraq. The agreement was welcomed by political and religious leaders both inside and outside of Iraq.

16. On 1 September 2006, Masoud Barzani, President of the Iraqi Kurdistan region, banned the Iraqi national flag within the Kurdistan region and replaced it with the flag of that region. In response, Prime Minister Al-Maliki ordered that the Iraqi national flag be used throughout the country. At the same time, he called upon the Parliament to consider adopting a new national flag. Meanwhile, Mr. Barzani, while continuing to refuse to fly the current national flag, agreed to fly the 1958 Iraqi flag within the Region. On 24 September, a draft constitution for the Kurdistan region of Iraq was read in the Kurdistan National Assembly on 24 September and was submitted for a period of public comment that will run through April 2007.

17. During the period under review, the Government-appointed committee established under article 140 of the Constitution for the normalization of the situation in Kirkuk held five sessions and established a number of sub-offices in the area. On 11 October 2006, the Council of Representatives established a parliamentary committee to oversee the work of the Government article 140 committee.

B. Regional developments

18. During the period under review, Prime Minister Al-Maliki and members of his cabinet made several visits to Iraq's neighbouring States as part of the efforts of the Government to foster their cooperation in stabilizing Iraq. In that context, on 12 and 13 September 2006, Prime Minister Al-Maliki visited Iran for meetings with Ayatollah Ali Khamenei and President Mahmoud Ahmadinejad.

19. On 18 September 2006, the Interior Ministers of the countries neighbouring Iraq held their third meeting in Jeddah, Saudi Arabia. The participants adopted a protocol on combating terrorism, illegal border infiltration and organized crime. On 21 September 2006, the tenth meeting of the foreign ministers of the neighbouring countries of Iraq was held in New York.

C. International developments

20. The United Nations, as a co-chair of the International Compact with Iraq, continued to provide support to the Government of Iraq in the development of the Compact document. The United Nations also assisted in organizing the high-level and technical meetings of the Preparatory Group. In addition, the United Nations hosted two meetings at Headquarters to broaden international support for the Compact beyond the Preparatory Group. In that context, on 18 September 2006, I convened a high-level meeting at United Nations Headquarters to review progress in the implementation of Security Council resolution 1546 (2004) and in developing the Compact. The meeting, which included the permanent members of the Security Council, Iraq's neighbouring countries, key donors and representatives of concerned regional and international organizations, provided an opportunity to review the progress being made by the Government of Iraq in the political, security and economic fields. The meeting also permitted the mobilization of greater and broader international support and engagement with the Government of Iraq on the Compact.

21. On 10 September 2006, the Deputy Secretary-General, Mark Malloch Brown and the Iraqi Deputy Prime Minister, Barham Salih, co-chaired the first high-level meeting of the International Compact with Iraq Preparatory Group in Abu Dhabi. At the meeting participants adopted the Abu Dhabi Declaration, in which the members of the Preparatory Group recognized the need to expeditiously complete the development of the Compact through a broad consultative process at the national, regional and international levels. On 31 October 2006, my Special Representative for Iraq co-chaired the second high-level meeting of the Preparatory Group of the Compact in Kuwait City. The meeting focused on substantive issues related to the Compact document and its implementation. During the meeting, participants recognized the progress in drafting the Compact document, in particular the inclusion of the political and security sections, as well as a presentation of specific benchmarks and the Joint Monitoring Matrix. I would like to thank the Governments of Kuwait and the United Arab Emirates for hosting the two high-level meetings of the Preparatory Group. I look forward to the formal launch of the International Compact with Iraq. The date and venue for the final event are under consideration.

22. On 13 November 2006, the Deputy Secretary-General convened a meeting at United Nations Headquarters to brief all Member States on the progress being made to develop the Compact, following the high-level Preparatory Group meeting held in Kuwait City. The meeting also provided the opportunity to discuss external support to the Government of Iraq, particularly in the areas of debt relief and new financial contributions.

III. Update on activities of the Mission

A. Political activities of the Special Representative of the Secretary-General

23. During the period under review, my Special Representative continued his consultations with a broad spectrum of key political, civil society, tribal and religious leaders in the effort to promote genuine dialogue and address the volatile security situation. He met frequently with leading members of the Iraqi Government, the Speaker of the Iraq Council of Representatives and parliamentary committee chairs, as well as other political and religious leaders, to discuss the Government's legislative agenda, the constitutional review process and other matters relating to UNAMI priorities. In his meetings he encouraged the strengthening of the legal and institutional foundation of the country, while supporting efforts aimed at

stemming the prevailing violence in the country. He also worked to promote the implementation of the Government's National Reconciliation Plan.

24. On 7 September 2006, my Special Representative visited Amman, where he held discussions with the Foreign Minister of Jordan and senior officials of the Government of Jordan. He also interacted with a cross-section of representatives of Iraqi political and tribal groups currently based in Jordan to discuss national reconciliation in Iraq.

25. As my focal point for the International Compact in Iraq, my Special Representative coordinated preparatory activities for the elaboration of the Compact document with key Iraqi and international counterparts in Baghdad. On 10 September and 31 October 2006, he participated in the high-level Preparatory Group meetings in Abu Dhabi and Kuwait City. He also presided over a series of technical and executive meetings related to the International Compact in Baghdad.

26. During his trip to New York and Washington, D.C., from 12 to 22 September 2006, my Special Representative attended the high-level meeting on Iraq and the tenth meeting of the foreign ministers of the neighbouring countries of Iraq, chaired by Turkey in New York. In Washington, D.C., my Special Representative held discussions with the United States National Security Adviser and senior officials of the United States Department of State.

B. Constitutional support activities

27. During the period under review, the UNAMI Office of Constitutional Support continued its support to the Council of Representatives in developing the required legislation for advancing the implementation of the Constitution. UNAMI/Office of Constitutional Support also engaged key members of Parliament concerning the establishment of the Constitutional Review Committee and relevant legislative issues.

28. Following the establishment of the Constitutional Review Committee, at the request of the Speaker of the Council of Representatives, UNAMI/Office of Constitutional Support initiated discussion with the leadership of the Committee on how best it could support the process, particularly through technical assistance, as well as substantive and procedural advice. The United Nations intends to provide strong support to the constitutional review process, drawing on best practice from around the world. If approached with the necessary political will for dialogue and compromise by Iraq's leaders, this process could provide a key vehicle for national reconciliation by resolving fundamental issues (e.g. federalism; allocation of power and resources).

C. Electoral assistance activities

29. The draft law for the establishment of the Independent High Electoral Commission of Iraq remains outstanding, as discussions continue with regard to the rights and responsibilities of the provincial election commissions. Pending the establishment of the Commission, the Independent Electoral Commission of Iraq has operated under a series of one-month extensions, the last of which expired on 10 November 2006 without further extension.

30. Throughout the period under review, the UNAMI Office of Electoral Assistance continued its engagement with the Council of Representatives on the legal framework for the establishment of the Independent High Electoral Commission of Iraq. It also provided advice on the electoral aspects of the law on the formation of regions.

31. The UNAMI Office of Electoral Assistance is also providing support for the process of the transition from the Independent Electoral Commission to the future Independent High Electoral Commission of Iraq. This process involves the identification and planning of the required infrastructure, staffing and financial resources, as well as logistical and security needs for the establishment of the Independent High Electoral Commission of Iraq. UNAMI is also providing support for the planning and updating of the voter rolls in preparation for future electoral events.

D. Reconstruction, development and humanitarian assistance

32. UNAMI and United Nations agencies, programmes and funds continued to support the Government of Iraq by working to strengthen ministerial capacities, to provide and coordinate access to basic services and to restore public infrastructure. During the period under review, the primary focus was on providing substantive support to the Government in preparation for the International Compact with Iraq.

33. The implications of the content and direction of the Compact have influenced the strategic planning of the United Nations role in Iraq. The United Nations country team has recalibrated its focus and programming to complement the Compact. In this regard, a two-pronged assistance strategy is being employed whereby the United Nations will continue to focus on providing assistance for the delivery of essential social services, while providing targeted institutional and operational capacity-building support to the Government of Iraq.

34. UNAMI continued to emphasize the need for Iraqi leadership of humanitarian development initiatives as an essential means to promote national stability. To this end, the consultancy services of a contingency planning adviser from the Office for the Coordination of Humanitarian Affairs, as well as a civil society legal adviser provided through the United Nations Office for Project Services, have been secured and made available to the relevant government institutions, including the Office of the Prime Minister and the Ministry of Civil Society Affairs.

35. Sectarian violence and ongoing military operations continue to adversely affect large numbers of Iraqi civilians in many areas of the country. The number of displaced Iraqis continues to increase, either because of threats or acts of aggression by various elements. According to the Office of the United Nations High Commissioner for Refugees (UNHCR), the International Organization for Migration and Government sources at the time of the publication of the present report, the number of displaced persons since the Samarra attack on 22 February 2006 exceeds 450,000, including approximately 27,000 individuals displaced in Al-Anbar Governorate alone, as a result of recent military operations. That total added to displacements previous to the Samarra events brings the total number of displaced persons in Iraq to over 1.6 million people. With the approaching winter, there are increasing concerns about the well-being and basic rights of the displaced, especially women, children, the disabled and the elderly.

36. UNHCR estimates that an additional 1.6 million people have become refugees outside the country since 2003, of which between 500,000 and 700,000 are currently in Jordan; approximately 600,000 are in Syria, and about 100,000 are in Saudi Arabia and Kuwait. A total of 436,000 Iraqis have moved to Europe, the Americas, Africa and Asia. Every day approximately 2,000 Iraqis flee the country to the Syrian Arab Republic and 1,000 to Jordan. The United Nations agencies and their partners continue to provide food, shelter

and non-food items to as many displaced Iraqis as resources permit. However, the resources available are not sufficient to adequately address the growing humanitarian crisis faced by Iraqis displaced within and outside of the country.

37. In order to address the overall human security situation in Iraq, my Emergency Relief Coordinator convened a series of meetings with donors to raise awareness and promote an integrated approach that would address the immediate and long-term needs of Iraqi civilians. In this regard, I encourage the international community to identify additional means for supporting United Nations agencies in their work with displaced Iraqis. In all instances, the United Nations will continue to actively assist all displaced persons and affected host communities and prepare for all likely scenarios by developing contingency plans.

E. Human rights activities

38. Although the Government of Iraq has resolved to promote the protection of human rights and the rule of law, human rights violations continue to rise. Abuses continue to be committed by terrorists, insurgents, militias and criminal armed groups. The excessive use of force by the multinational force and the Iraqi security forces in responding to these elements is also a matter of concern. Ongoing military operations also continue to challenge the principles of international humanitarian law as civilian casualties mount and access to public services by the affected populations is limited or obstructed. The sectarian carnage has resulted in a vicious cycle of violence fuelled by revenge killings. The end result is an environment of lawlessness and insecurity.

39. I remain particularly concerned by the abhorrent bombings and other attacks inflicting death and injury on civilians, as well as the kidnappings and murder of scores of people by death squads, allegedly operating in collusion with law enforcement agencies. According to the Ministry of Health, the number of civilians violently killed in the country was 3,345 in September and 3,709 in October, compared to 3,590 in July and 3,009 in August. The number of wounded reached 3,481 in September and 3,944 in October. In Baghdad alone the total number of civilians violently killed in September and October was 4,984.

40. Estimates by apparently reputable sources of the number of Iraqis killed over the past three and a half years are truly shocking and indicate the possibility of a humanitarian and human rights catastrophe in Iraq. Previous reporting by the Iraqi Body Count estimated that approximately 50,000 civilians have been killed since March 2003. However, recent estimates put the human toll of the conflict much higher than previously thought. On 9 November 2006, the Minister of Health of Iraq estimated that 150,000 civilians had been killed, while a study by the Johns Hopkins University Bloomberg School of Public Health published in the October 2006 issue of *The Lancet* estimated that 601,027 excess violent deaths have occurred in Iraq since March 2003. While questions on the methodology contained in the Johns Hopkins study have been raised by, inter alia, the Iraq Body Count, it nonetheless represents a serious attempt to quantify the loss of life in Iraq during this period.

41. The UNAMI Human Rights Office continues to work closely with Iraqi institutions, including the Higher Judicial Council, the Ministry of Human Rights and the Ministry of Justice, among others, to strengthen the rule of law and create a strong and effective national human rights protection system. A draft law on the establishment of a national human rights commission, prepared by the Human Rights Committee of the Council of Representatives during the previous period, has yet to be approved. Thirty leading

parliamentarians who participated in a workshop, jointly organized by the Office of the High Commissioner for Human Rights and UNAMI in Amman on 17 and 18 October 2006, stressed the urgency for the Council of Representatives to enact this law to establish this important independent commission.

42. On 5 November 2006, the Iraqi Higher Criminal Tribunal sentenced former President Saddam Hussein and two other co-defendants to death for their role in the 1984 execution of 148 people convicted of involvement in the attempted assassination of the former President in Dujail. On the same day, the United Nations High Commissioner for Human Rights, Louise Arbour, issued a statement urging the Iraqi authorities to ensure that the right of appeal of persons convicted and sentenced by the Tribunal would be fully respected. The High Commissioner also expressed the hope that the Government would observe a moratorium on executions.

43. I am also concerned about the targeting of various professional and minority groups inside Iraq. An increasing number of journalists and media workers are apparently targeted specifically because of their work, putting the right to freedom of expression under threat. Minorities continue to be targeted, and attacks against Christians have intensified since September. Members of the Sabean-Mandean community and other minority groups report continuous suffering at the hands of extremists. In addition, the situation of women has deteriorated further and an increasing number were recorded to be either victims of religious extremists or of "honour killings". The targeting of academics, including teachers and professors, as well as students, is seriously disrupting the education system, and has forced some to leave the country.

44. Significant progress in defending human rights will be difficult unless the professionalism and discipline of the country's law enforcement agencies are enhanced. The lack of proper training, standing orders and internal accountability systems continue to undermine respect for human rights and have consequentially eroded public confidence in Iraqi security forces. Perpetrators of criminal activities remain unpunished due to the shortage and intimidation of judges, prosecutors and court officials. Additionally, living conditions in prisons do not meet minimum international standards, and, although there have been some reports of improvement regarding the treatment of prisoners, the UNAMI Human Rights Office continues to receive reports of torture and other inhuman and degrading treatment of detainees, especially among juveniles. I am also concerned about reports of police and militias colluding to abduct people to extract bribes from their families. I welcome the decision of the Ministry of Interior to intensify the screening of police officers and commence more stringent vetting measures, including the suspension of police officers involved in abductions, the mistreatment of detainees and assassinations.

45. According to the Ministry of Human Rights, the total number of detainees for the entire country was 29,256 (13,571 of whom are in multinational force detention facilities) at the end of October, a slight decrease from the 30,104 detainees reported in September. In spite of ongoing efforts to release detainees and bring them under the jurisdiction of the Ministry of Justice, I remain troubled by the continued detention of thousands of Iraqis, which, in the absence of speedy judicial oversight, amounts to de facto arbitrary detention.

46. More than one year after the discovery of a secret detention facility in Al-Jadiriya, I would like to reiterate the call made by the United Nations High Commissioner for Human

Rights and my Special Representative for the immediate release of the report on the Government investigation of this case. That issue notwithstanding, I take note of the action recently announced by the Minister of Interior with respect to human rights violations committed by officials of the Ministry at the detention centre known as Site 4. Prosecution of those responsible is necessary in order to combat the prevailing impunity and will act as a deterrent against further violations.

47. Vibrant and independent non-governmental organizations are critical components of a democracy based on the rule of law and respect for human rights. However, the activities and freedoms of civil society organizations operating in Iraq could be curtailed if a law recently drafted by the Iraq Ministry of Civil Society Affairs is passed by the Council of Representatives. Therefore, I am hopeful that the legislation being considered will ultimately conform to international standards and best practices.

48. On 6 September 2006, 27 individuals, including one woman, were executed in Baghdad for murder, kidnapping and terrorism-related charges. Officially, since the reinstatement of the death penalty in 2004, more than 150 individuals have received death sentences, 51 of whom have already been executed. My Special Representative expressed his concern over these death sentences to the Iraqi presidency and called for moratorium. I urge the Government of Iraq to abolish capital punishment and implement a moratorium on death sentences.

49. Discussions on the future of the de-Baathification process in Iraq continued during the reporting period. It is important that this process embrace the principle of individual responsibility as opposed to collective punishment. At the same time, a comprehensive general amnesty currently being considered as part of the Prime Minister's National Reconciliation Plan is a possible means to promote peace and reconciliation. Draft legislation has yet to be circulated, although it is expected that amnesty in Iraq will primarily benefit individuals currently in detention, mostly those who have neither been charged nor convicted, as well as individual members of the insurgency, militias and other armed groups who renounce violence and, consistent with international standards, have not been responsible for war crimes, crimes against humanity or genocide. While recognizing the need for amnesty, I firmly believe this should not prejudice the victims' rights to truth and reparations.

IV. International Reconstruction Fund Facility for Iraq

50. As of 31 October 2006, the total contributions to the United Nations Development Group (UNDG) Iraq Trust Fund, one of the two funds of the International Reconstruction Fund Facility for Iraq, equalled $1.11 billion. A total of 104 projects valued at $869 million were approved as at the end of October 2006 for funding under the UNDG Iraq Trust Fund. Continuing the significant progress in implementation, contracts worth cumulatively $664 million (76 per cent of approved funding) have been initiated and $558 million (64 per cent of approved funding) have been disbursed.

51. On 10 November 2006, the Fourth Consolidated Six Monthly report of the Administrative Agent on UNDG Iraq Trust Fund progress was submitted to donors. The report, which covers the period from 1 January to 30 June 2006 (with an informal update to end of September 2006) highlights UNDG Iraq Trust Fund progress as a whole, focusing on programme implementation in the areas of governance and basic services. The report builds on the three official reports issued to date in May 2005, November 2005 and May 2006.

Although overall progress on governance was less than expected, reflecting, inter alia, delays in the establishment of the Constitutional Review Committee, further strong progress was made in delivering basic services. That included 10 quick-impact projects in basic services, namely education, health, water and sanitation, which were discussed at the July 2005 International Reconstruction Fund Facility for Iraq donor meeting, which have virtually been completed. They have led to the rehabilitation of 262 schools, 192 primary health centres, and 160 water and sanitation systems. Thanks to these projects, polio and cholera have been kept under control. Expenditures under the UNDG Iraq Trust Fund rose during the reporting period by $90.5 million, to a total of almost $600 million.

52. The International Reconstruction Fund Facility for Iraq will continue to be a valuable tool under the International Compact with Iraq and will continue to provide rapid response to basic services and needs. The details of the alignment of the International Reconstruction Fund Facility for Iraq to the Compact are being negotiated between the Government of Iraq, the Chair of the International Reconstruction Fund Facility for Iraq Donor Committee, the World Bank and the United Nations.

V. Security and operational issues

A. Assessment of the security situation

53. The level of violence in Iraq remains elevated, with casualty levels among civilians at their highest since March 2006. The violence is characterized by a conflict that is increasingly sectarian in nature, a continuing insurgency, and violence by extremist groups, some affiliated with Al-Qaida in Iraq. Intracommunal violence is also on the rise, with clashes reported between some Sunni tribes and among Shia groups in the south of Iraq.

54. Baghdad remains the focus of armed activity and of efforts by the Government of Iraq and the multinational force to reduce the violence. By the end of October, violent incidents in the city had increased 22 per cent over the previous month. That trend was consistent with the spike in violence experienced during the holy month of Ramadan in the previous two years.

55. In areas near Baghdad, the insurgency remains potent, and since September there has been a marked increase in a number of significant attacks against Iraqi security forces, as well as the multinational forces. In particular, the international zone remains a target for armed groups from across the spectrum. The primary means of attack is indirect fire from the surrounding areas. During October there was a direct rocket strike on a concrete car shelter in the UNAMI compound. The incident occurred in the late evening and there were no casualties. Checkpoints leading into the international zone also remain subject to sporadic attacks.

56. During the period under review, the situation in north-western and north-central parts of Iraq, such as the Governorates of Ta'mim, Mosul and Diyala, was increasingly volatile. In the west, Al-Anbar Governorate continues to witness heavy fighting involving tribal, Al-Qaida and armed groups. The situation in southern governorates remained tense. From 19 to 21 October 2006, the predominantly Shiite town of Ammara was witness to violent clashes between rival militias seeking to establish control over the city. Incident rates are rising in the Governorates of Qadissiya, Maysan, Wassit, Karbala and Babil. In northern Iraq, the security situation varies in intensity and character. In the far north, violence is mostly concentrated in Mosul, with Erbil remaining relatively peaceful.

57. Basra has witnessed a high number of incidents since August and appears to be in turmoil. The fragile political balance in the Governorate Council is challenged on the street by a nexus of informal groups associated with smuggling and criminal activities. The Basra Palace compound and other multinational force centres are the primary targets. Indirect fire is a constant threat and a frequent occurrence. United Nations staff presence in Basra continues to be maintained at an absolute minimum, with accommodation in hardened facilities.

58. United Nations international staff in the international zone continue to be exposed to a medium level of risk. Staff numbers are continuously reviewed and monitored to ensure that they are kept at acceptable levels. Nevertheless, the risk to national staff remains very high due to the rampant violence afflicting Baghdad. They are at risk of abduction, serious physical injury and death, particularly as they enter and exit the international zone.

59. The deteriorating security situation in Iraq has put severe constraints on the ability of the Organization to carry out its activities. UNAMI continues to work to adjust its operating procedures to respond to these changing conditions and to promote effective Mission operations that are compatible with the security environment. Although there appears to be greater Iraqi and international support for a more active United Nations role, should there be a further deterioration of the security situation, the viability of maintaining a significant United Nations presence in Iraq might be called into question. There can be no tolerance for exposing United Nations personnel to unacceptable risk.

B. Facilities, logistics and support

60. Following the relocation of UNAMI from Al-Rasheed Hotel to a new compound in the international zone on 22 August 2006, preparations have begun to construct overhead protection for the two thirds of the compound that lacks such protection. The compound will serve as an interim accommodation facility until the long-term and integrated UNAMI site is completed. This site, allocated for United Nations use by the Government of Iraq, has undergone site clearance and technical surveys, and development plans are complete.

61. In Erbil, staff members are accommodated in the new Area Office. Improvements to the compound continue, in keeping with the surrounding environment. In Basra, the work on the new premises of the United Nations Liaison Detachment has been completed and United Nations staff still in Basra are currently accommodated in these facilities. A UNAMI administrative team recently visited Basra to finalize the improvement of hardened accommodation, should the full complement of the United Nations Liaison Detachment return to Basra.

62. The Government of Japan and the United Nations have finalized arrangements for the provision of a dedicated weekly flight for UNAMI, and a once-weekly flight is now successfully operational. The Government of Denmark has also offered to provide a dedicated aircraft to UNAMI, and a specialized fact-finding team continues to meet with UNAMI to finalize the requirements for its deployment. I remain grateful to the Governments of Japan and Denmark for their air support to the Mission, which greatly enhances the ability of the Mission to conduct its work.

63. In this regard, I am very grateful to a number of Member States for their continued support in providing protection and logistical support to UNAMI. In particular, I would like to thank the Government of Fiji for providing UNAMI with personal security details and guard units, and the Governments of Georgia, the Republic of Korea and Romania for

providing "middle-ring" protection. In 2004, in accordance with Security Council resolution 1546 (2004), a trust fund was established to support a distinct entity under the unified command of the multinational force with a dedicated mission to provide security for the United Nations presence in Iraq. Since its establishment, the fund has received over $20 million in contributions from 16 Member States. However, after three years of payments, the funds will likely be exhausted by March 2007. I therefore call upon Member States to continue to support this trust fund with a new financial commitment.

C. Agreements

64. The status of mission agreement between the United Nations and the Government of Iraq was signed on 3 June 2005, but will enter into force only following formal ratification by the Council of Representatives. However, despite several approaches made by the United Nations, confirmation from the Government of Iraq remains pending. The United Nations has been advised by the Office of the Prime Minister that the matter has been presented to the Council of Representatives for action. I urge the Government of Iraq to expedite the ratification of the status of mission agreement and issue the required official confirmation note. Once entered into force, the status of mission agreement will accord to UNAMI the required legal status under customary international law to fulfil its mandated tasks.

65. Negotiations have continued between UNAMI and the multinational force regarding the supplemental arrangements under the agreement between the United Nations and the Government of the United States concluded on 8 December 2005 governing UNAMI security. At present, two of three components of the subordinate arrangements are near completion. While I note the constructive spirit with which these discussions have been held, I call for the process to be expedited and for the early finalization of these arrangements, which will form a core aspect of continued security support for the presence of the United Nations in Iraq.

Observations

66. In my last report, I stated that Iraq was at an important crossroads and that the Iraqi people and their leaders faced a fundamental choice between taking the high road to negotiation and compromise or descending further into fratricidal sectarian conflict. Three months onwards, the situation in Iraq has further deteriorated in many parts of the country with a significant rise in sectarian violence, insurgent and terrorist attacks, and criminal activities. The growing militia activities have led to further destabilization. Across many parts of the country, an increasing number of Iraqis have been affected by growing violence and insecurity. High levels of civilian casualties and displacement on a daily basis are breeding an increasing sense of insecurity and deep pessimism among Iraqis. The prospects of all-out civil war and even a regional conflict have become much more real. Therefore, the challenge is not only to contain and defuse the current violence, but also to prevent its escalation.

67. Although the figures on civilian casualties since March 2003 vary between 50,000 and more than 600,000, depending on the sources, the real issue is the predicament of the Iraqi people. The deteriorating security situation has continued to adversely impact on the human rights, humanitarian situations and overall living standards. The large number of casualties is having a much wider social impact than immediate death or injury. Fatal incidents invariably produce widows, orphans and female-headed households who must bear the burden of lost breadwinners and broken families. This is becoming a permanent disabling factor for human development and greatly adds to the burden of reliable access to proper health care,

social services, education, employment and economic opportunities, which remain largely absent in Iraq today.

68. While I note the efforts of the Government of Iraq to improve security and promote national reconciliation, it must undertake an urgent review of strategies, policies and measures, with the aim of implementing a consensus-based action plan to halt and reverse current political and security trends in the country, which needs to be supported by a much broader and inclusive regional and international effort. In this effort, the Government faces three overarching challenges.

69. First, it needs to develop a fully inclusive political process that is focused on bringing all disenfranchised and marginalized communities into the political mainstream. While this will require hard political choices, the Government must ensure equitable access to political power, the institutions of the State and its natural resources by all Iraqi communities. This will require, inter alia, an approach to resource-sharing that is guided by the broader national interest rather than the interests of particular constituencies. Only when all Iraqi constituencies have a real stake in the future of the country will Iraq be on a path towards greater stability and prosperity.

70. Secondly, the Government must establish a monopoly over the use of force through the instruments of security and law enforcement within the framework of the rule of law. This will require addressing the terrorist, insurgency, sectarian and criminal violence, and will have to include dealing with the problem of militias inside the communities of Iraq, as well as the removal of militia elements from all ministries and the Iraqi security forces.

71. Thirdly, there is a need to cultivate a regional environment that is supportive of Iraq's transition. The Government has a special responsibility to normalize its relations with its neighbours, which in turn requires the neighbours to work towards fostering greater stability and security in Iraq.

72. To meet these challenges, the Government must now be fully empowered to deliver concrete results on all fronts—security, political, economic and human rights. The limited impact of existing policies has demonstrated that there is an urgent need for new approaches at the national, regional and international levels.

73. At the national level, the constitutional review process that has just begun and is supported by the United Nations offers a real opportunity for all Iraqi communities to reach a broad consensus on the fundamental issues that continue to divide them. I therefore once again urge Iraqi leaders and key international actors to demonstrate their commitment and make this review a top priority. Other important initiatives, such as key pieces of new legislation, including the law on the formation of regions and the hydrocarbon law, should satisfy the legitimate interests of all Iraqi communities, and thereby provide a firm basis for national reconciliation. In addition, there is a particular need to promote confidence-building measures between communities in potential flashpoint areas, such as Kirkuk. The United Nations stands ready to assist in this effort. Increased efforts are also needed to review the de-Baathification process and to pass an amnesty law without prejudice to the victims' rights to truth and reparation.

74. At the regional level, there is an increasing realization that a worsening conflict in Iraq would have implications not only for cross-border security, but that it could also aggravate

a range of underlying tensions in neighbouring countries. I have for some time now been urging Iraq's neighbours to contribute in a tangible manner to the stabilization of Iraq, which would also be beneficial to their own security. I welcome the ongoing dialogue between Iraq and its neighbours through periodic meetings of regional Foreign Ministers and Interior Ministers, in which my Special Representative regularly participates. However, in the light of the deteriorating situation in Iraq and its potentially grave regional implications, it may be necessary to consider more creative ways for fostering regional dialogue and understanding, which could result in concrete confidence-building measures between Iraq and its neighbours. This process could be broadened to include the permanent members of the Security Council. The United Nations is prepared to explore the possibilities of such a process in consultation with all concerned.

75. At the international level, the International Compact with Iraq, supported by the United Nations and the international community, provides an important framework for mobilizing national, regional and international actors in support of Iraq's transition. However, the Compact can only become a genuine partnership if it is based on a consensus on the way forward shared by all the major stakeholders inside Iraq. Its success will ultimately depend on the ability of the Government of Iraq and the international community to deliver on their mutual commitments. Achieving tangible progress during the first six months of its implementation will therefore be critical.

76. There is an urgent need to promote convergence at the national, regional and international levels to stabilize the situation in Iraq. In this regard, as I have publicly stated recently, beyond the measures mentioned above, it may be worthwhile to consider a larger framework for fostering dialogue and understanding at all three levels. Drawing on the positive experiences of the United Nations in other parts of the world, such as the Bonn peace accords for Afghanistan, it may be worthwhile to consider an arrangement that could bring Iraqi political parties together, possibly outside Iraq, with the United Nations playing a facilitating role. This would also require the active engagement of regional countries and the international community. The recent positive experience of the International Compact with Iraq in which national, regional and international actors have been engaged, demonstrates that the political will for such a process can be effectively mobilized.

77. During the 10 years of my tenure as Secretary-General, Iraq has been one of the biggest challenges for the Organization. Certainly one of the darkest moments in my career was the bombing of the United Nations compound on 19 August 2003, in which the United Nations lost 22 friends and colleagues, including the head of the mission, Sergio Vieira de Mello. This tragedy serves as a constant reminder of both the importance of remaining vigilant with respect to staff security, and the need for the United Nations to continue its work in Iraq. Despite the loss of United Nations staff, and bearing in mind the limits of what the United Nations can do under the prevailing circumstances, the Organization has remained steadfast in its support for the people of Iraq who have suffered so much.

78. Based on its mandate under resolution 1546 (2004), the United Nations has been implementing its tasks "as circumstances permit", while continuously assessing the extent to which the Organization is able to implement these tasks in the light of the very challenging security environment and its limited capacity. This assessment has enabled the United Nations to maximize its impact and prioritize its tasks with a focus on its core political, electoral and constitutional activities under paragraph 7 (a) of its mandate under resolution

1546 (2004). Due to the security situation, activities in the areas of reconstruction, development, human rights and the rule of law under paragraph 7 (b) of its mandate have remained limited and have continued to be carried out mainly from outside Iraq. However, I am pleased that over the past six months, the United Nations has been able to play a lead role in the development of the International Compact, which provides a tangible long-term framework for the reconstruction and development of the country.

79. I would like to reiterate my appreciation to Member States, from both within and outside the multinational force, that have supported the United Nations in Iraq by providing military advisers and guard forces, as well as movement and aviation support. Despite efforts to increase our own security and logistical support, the United Nations will remain dependent on the support of the multinational force for the foreseeable future, owing to the complex security situation. In addition, if there is a further deterioration of the security situation, maintaining a United Nations presence in Iraq might be called into question.

80. I also wish to take this opportunity to thank my Special Representative for Iraq, Ashraf Jehangir Qazi, for his outstanding leadership and the Mission's national and international staff, as well as the personnel of United Nations agencies, programmes and funds, for their dedicated work in fulfilling their mandated tasks under extremely difficult conditions.

3. Report of the Secretary-General pursuant to paragraph 30 of Resolution 1546 (2004), 7 March 2007 (S/2007/126)

I. Introduction

1. In paragraph 30 of resolution 1546 (2004), the Security Council requested the Secretary-General to report to the Council on a quarterly basis on the fulfilment of the responsibilities of the United Nations Assistance Mission for Iraq (UNAMI). The present report is the eleventh submitted pursuant to that resolution.

2. The report provides an update on United Nations activities in Iraq since the last report (S/2006/945) of 5 December 2006. It presents a summary of key political developments during the period under review, particularly concerning the efforts of the Government of Iraq to promote national reconciliation and improve the security situation, as well as regional and international developments pertaining to Iraq. The report also provides an update on the activities of my Special Representative for Iraq, Ashraf Jehangir Qazi, and UNAMI, an assessment of the security situation and an update on operational and security matters.

II. Summary of key developments in Iraq

A. Political developments

3. During the period under review, high levels of violence in Iraq continued to overshadow political and reconstruction efforts by the Government of Iraq and the international community. It has also had an adverse impact on the humanitarian and human rights situation. The deteriorating situation has further undermined the social and political fabric of the country, with the number of internally displaced persons and refugees reaching new highs.

4. The worsening security situation, particularly in Baghdad and in the southern and western regions, continues to undermine the ability of the Government of Iraq to deliver essential services, create jobs, and reconstruct socio-economic infrastructure. In particular, as a result of curfews and general insecurity, access to health services continues to be very difficult, and treatment is not always guaranteed, owing to the severe shortage of medical equipment and drugs. According to the Iraqi Ministry of Education, school attendance has drastically fallen to approximately 50 per cent in 2006. Given the worsening situation, many Iraqis are turning to local groups or militias for protection or the provision of basic services. In response, the Government of Iraq has focused its efforts on countering the prevailing violence through the launch of the new Baghdad security plan, code named Operation Fardh al-Qanoon (Operation Imposing Law).

5. On 10 January 2007, President Bush outlined the details of the new United States strategy for Iraq in a televised policy speech. In addition to security operations, the approach includes military, social and economic milestones intended to bolster progress on the ground. The intention is for the Government of Iraq to take responsibility for security in all provinces by November 2007; hold provincial elections no later than the end of 2007; ensure the fair allocation of $10 billion of Iraqi funds for reconstruction and infrastructure projects to create new jobs; finalize legislation on the equitable sharing of oil revenues;

revise the de-Baathification law; and establish a fair process for the review of the Iraqi Constitution. In the same policy speech, President Bush asserted the intention of the United States of America to interrupt activities emanating from the Islamic Republic of Iran and the Syrian Arab Republic, in particular those that are allegedly supporting attacks on American troops. Subsequent interventions by the multinational force in Iraq against Iranian nationals, including arrests in Erbil and Baghdad, have heightened diplomatic tensions. The Islamic Republic of Iran denied the allegations, and the Foreign Minister of the Islamic Republic of Iran stated that the arrested officials were in Iraq at the invitation of the Government of Iraq.

6. On 16 and 17 December 2006, Prime Minister Al-Maliki hosted a conference of political parties and entities as part of the Government's national reconciliation plan. The event was largely attended by political parties within the national unity government, while those with ties to the Ba'ath Party, the Sadrist bloc, the Iraqiya list of Ayad Allawi, and the Iraqi Front for National Dialogue led by Saleh al-Mutlak did not officially attend. However, numerous members of each group participated in their own personal capacity. The conference concluded with a statement recommending, among other items, the dissolution of militias, the expedited withdrawal of the multinational force, and the re-incorporation of veteran army personnel.

7. The Council of Representatives was unable to establish a quorum throughout much of December 2006 and January 2007, partly owing to a boycott by the 30 Sadrist bloc members, thereby delaying the adoption of numerous important laws. The Sadrist bloc resumed participation in the Government and the Council of Representatives on 21 January 2007, after suspending involvement on 30 November 2006. When the full Parliament reconvened on 23 January 2007, the law on the formation of the Independent High Electoral Commission was passed, as well as the state of emergency law, which had lapsed on 31 December 2006. The Council of Representatives also approved the 2007 budget on 8 February 2007, which, at $41 billion, is the largest budget in the history of Iraq. The budget indicates a $7 billion deficit, and it will reportedly draw from the surplus from the 2006 fiscal year.

8. Additional legislation considered to be central to the national reconciliation strategy, as envisaged by the Baghdad security plan, remains pending. In particular, the hydrocarbon law, which is essential for both national unity and the economic development of Iraq, is still under consideration. The draft law, along with complementary legislation, aims to establish investment and management procedures for the oil industry and to make progress towards reaching an agreement on the sharing of the nation's oil revenues and federal oversight of regionally negotiated oil contracts. Following extensive negotiations, the draft law was endorsed by the Council of Ministers on 27 February 2007, and will be submitted to Parliament, which will reconvene in March. Other key pieces of legislation are pending, including those on de-Baathification, provincial elections and a possible amnesty law.

9. The Baghdad security plan was formally launched on 13 February 2007 in a live televised address by General Qanbar, Commander of Baghdad security plan operations. General Qanbar announced that the launch of the Baghdad security plans would be accompanied by closure of the borders with the Syrian Arab Republic and the Islamic Republic of Iran for a period of 72 hours and the extension of curfew hours in Baghdad. Illegal occupants of real estate property belonging to displaced persons were given 15 days to vacate and return such properties with their assets to their legal owners. Prime Minister Al-Maliki

distinguished the new plan from past efforts by highlighting Iraqi control of security operations with United States troop support, the decision to confront all armed groups regardless of religious or political affiliation, and the combination of reconciliation and economic measures.

10. Following the start of the Baghdad security plan there was a decrease in civilian casualties in Baghdad, particularly in the number of unidentified bodies found in the city, and in the frequency of car bomb attacks. Car bombings resumed shortly after the implementation of the plan, apparently in an attempt to discredit the plan, cause large numbers of civilian casualties and provoke retaliatory actions. The initial reduction of violence in Baghdad has been attributed by some commentators to the decision of militias to keep a low profile during the security operations, thus prompting concern that they will quickly re-emerge once the security plan is completed. The plan also enjoyed initial political support, as indicated by the parliamentary vote on 25 January, when all 160 members of Parliament present at the session voted in favour of the plan. However, leaders on all sides started voicing scepticism weeks after the security operations commenced.

11. On 6 February 2007, the High Commission on the Implementation of Article 140, regarding the status of Kirkuk, announced Orders Nos. 3 and 4, which were intended to commence the process of relocating Arab families that moved to Kirkuk during the "Arabization" campaign of Saddam Hussein. The Orders, which require approval by the executive branch, offer compensation to relocated families. The announcement by the Commission was followed by demonstrations in Kirkuk by opponents of the measure, who claimed it was tantamount to forced displacement. In response, Commissioners clarified that the relocation and compensation mechanisms were strictly voluntary and that 7,000 families had reportedly registered for relocation. It is not clear how the cases handled by the High Commission will relate to those processed by the Commission for Resolution of Real Property Disputes, which is responsible for settling claims by people who lost property as a result of actions of the Ba'athist regime during the period from 1968 to April 2003. More than 50,000 Kirkuk-related claims have been filed with the Commission for Resolution of Real Property Disputes to date.

12. Kirkuk remains a highly sensitive issue, which should be approached cautiously, as it could worsen an already complex situation both inside Iraq and in the region. United Nations experts believe that before a successful referendum on Kirkuk and disputed territories can be conducted, as mandated under article 140 of the Iraqi Constitution, several outstanding technical issues must be resolved. These include clarification of the specific issues on which people would be voting; the definition of the boundaries of the territories subject to the referendum; the establishment of a credible voters' register; criteria for identifying the threshold for passage of the referendum; and the completion of a census prior to the referendum.

13. In the prevailing atmosphere of mistrust among Iraqi communities, recent attempts to reach across the ethnic and religious divide have been welcomed. On 7 February 2007, Grand Ayatollah Ali al-Sistani released a statement that listed commonalities between Shiite and Sunni Muslims, called for unity and coexistence based on mutual respect, and asserted the sanctity of Muslim blood. In addition to denouncing false fatwas made in his name, the Grand Ayatollah declared that it was the duty of all Muslims to reduce tensions caused by political disputes and focus on strengthening ties between the children of the

nation of Iraq. On 10 February 2007, dozens of Shia and Sunnis gathered for the re-opening of a Sunni mosque in Shiite-dominated Sadr City. A month earlier, on 10 January 2007, a senior Sadrist official concluded an agreement with the Sunni Iraqi Islamic Party to form joint committees in mixed neighbourhoods in Baghdad to cooperate on security and returns of internally displaced persons. In Basra, joint Sunni and Shiite committees were formed in February 2007 to reopen and protect Sunni mosques closed in the aftermath of the attack on the Samarra shrine in February 2006. More initiatives of these kinds are essential to help build confidence and encourage Iraqi communities to end their mistrust of each other.

B. Regional developments

14. During the period under review, several developments and events pertaining to Iraq took place in the region. A meeting of a contact group on Iraq of the League of Arab States, which took place in Cairo on 5 December 2006, expressed solidarity with Iraq and rejected all forms of violence in the country. On 10 December 2006, the Iraqi National Security Adviser attended a regional security summit in Bahrain and reiterated the centrality of national reconciliation in the strategy of the Iraqi Government to establish security in the country. Most notably, on 14 January 2007, President Talabani paid an official visit to the Syrian Arab Republic, the first by an Iraqi head of State in nearly 30 years. At the end of his visit, a joint communiqué between the Governments of Iraq and the Syrian Arab Republic called for greater political coordination, economic cooperation and improved water resource management between the two countries.

15. The increasing number of Iraqi refugees and internally displaced persons continues to be a serious concern for neighbouring countries. In response to the growing unease in the region, the United Nations High Commissioner for Refugees visited Saudi Arabia, Jordan and the Syrian Arab Republic during the month of February 2007, to highlight the plight of Iraqi refugees residing in these respective countries. That effort followed a $60-million appeal launched by the Office of the United Nations High Commissioner for Refugees (UNHCR) on 8 January 2007 to provide support for the hundreds of thousands of Iraqi refugees and internally displaced persons in the region. The High Commissioner praised the generosity of Jordan and the Syrian Arab Republic for hosting such large numbers of Iraqis.

16. In an effort to promote greater regional dialogue, the Government of Iraq has invited neighbouring States to participate in a preparatory meeting of the Foreign Ministers' meeting of Iraq's neighbours, to be held in Baghdad at the level of senior official on 10 March 2007. I welcome this new diplomatic initiative, as it is in keeping with the United Nations call for the convergence of national, regional and international efforts in support of the people and Government of Iraq.

C. International developments

17. Preparatory activities for the International Compact with Iraq continued and resulted in the finalization of documentation. At the request of Prime Minister Al-Maliki, I have decided to host a meeting in New York on 16 March 2007, in an effort to brief Member States on the status of the International Compact with Iraq and to provide the Iraqi Government with an opportunity to inform potential donors on the progress made in the implementation of its commitments made under the Compact. I hope that the date and venue of the launch of the Compact will be identified as soon as possible. I also strongly

believe that positive political progress and a reduction of violence are essential preconditions for the success of this initiative.

18. On 23 February 2007, the High Commissioner for Refugees announced that UNHCR will convene an international conference in Geneva on 17 and 18 April 2007, to discuss the humanitarian needs of refugees and displaced people inside Iraq and neighbouring countries. The ministerial-level conference will bring together Iraqi authorities, neighbouring countries, major donor countries, resettlement countries, and concerned regional governmental and non-governmental organizations (NGOs). It will focus on a broad range of issues and objectives, including raising awareness on the dimensions of the displacement crisis and the protection and assistance needs of those affected. The conference will also consider ways to encourage the international community to work collectively to ease the suffering of millions of refugees and displaced persons in the region.

III. Update on activities of the Mission

A. Political activities of the Special Representative of the Secretary-General

19. During the period covered by the present report, my Special Representative, Ashraf Jehangir Qazi, maintained regular contacts with a wide spectrum of Iraqi political, religious and tribal actors. He met with officials at various levels of the Government of Iraq and the Council of Representatives in an effort to foster political dialogue and discuss legislative matters, as well as other priority concerns for UNAMI. In all of his meetings, he encouraged efforts to lessen the prevailing violence in Iraq and its impact on Iraqi citizens. My Special Representative also held regular meetings with diplomatic representatives in Baghdad and updated them on his contacts in Iraq and in the region.

20. In an effort to better understand regional perspectives on Iraq, my Special Representative undertook a tour of the region, meeting with senior government officials of the Islamic Republic of Iran, Jordan, Kuwait, Saudi Arabia, the Syrian Arab Republic and Turkey. The overall objective of the tour was to hear the views of key interlocutors and encourage their respective countries to adopt a more positive, proactive and shared approach to supporting the Government of Iraq in its efforts to reduce violence and promote national dialogue. They expressed deep concern about the deteriorating situation in Iraq and the prospects of the instability spreading to neighbouring countries. Some officials were also critical of the way in which the situation was being handled and the actions of some external actors inside Iraq. However, there was wide agreement that every effort should be made to find solutions and work towards preserving the unity and territorial integrity of Iraq. There also appeared to be broad support for a more active United Nations role to strengthen regional dialogue and promote confidence-building.

21. On 18 February 2007, my Special Representative attended the fifth United States-Islamic World Forum in Doha, hosted by the Brookings Institution, with the support of the Ministry of Foreign Affairs of the State of Qatar. In his address on Iraq, my Special Representative stressed the need for neighbouring States to come together and find common ground on the way forward in Iraq. Constructive policies by all the neighbouring States are essential to reduce violence and increase the prospects for a political settlement to take root in Iraq and pave the way for national reconciliation.

B. Constitutional support activities

22. The UNAMI Office of Constitutional Support continued to assist the Constitutional Review Committee of the Council of Representatives in its mandate to conduct a comprehensive review of the Iraqi Constitution. In addition to facilitating substantive dialogue among the members of the Committee and strengthening the Committee's outreach capacity to civil society during the constitutional review process, UNAMI, the Committee and the Council of Representatives agreed on a defined programme of support, including the staffing and equipment needs of the Committee that will be provided by the Mission. During the reporting period, the Office of Constitutional Support also provided technical assistance to the Iraqi judiciary on the issues of federalism, wealth and resource-sharing, the judicial architecture and human rights.

23. In December 2006, the Constitutional Review Committee began weekly plenary sessions to discuss priority issues in the constitutional text on the basis of an issues paper prepared by UNAMI. From 21 to 23 January a multi-party dialogue sponsored by the Office of Constitutional Support was held in Cairo on Iraqi judicial architecture under the theme "Mapping a new federal judicial system for Iraq". It was attended by representatives of the Constitutional Review Committee, the Council of Representatives, the Higher Judicial Council, the Prime Minister's Office, international experts, Iraqi academics, judges, and members of Iraqi civil society. Participants focused on constitutional amendments and implementation of legislation necessary to create a functional federal judiciary. In particular, the discussion focused on ways to strengthen and further define the Higher Judicial Council, the Federal Supreme Court and the Federal Court of Cassation, reinforce the independence of the judiciary, clarify the structure of the regional judiciary and adjudicate constitutional disputes.

24. In February 2007, the Office of Constitutional Support took members of the Constitutional Review Committee on study tours to three federal jurisdictions, in Spain, Germany and Malaysia, to gain from the experience of those countries with federal arrangements and to interact with parliamentarians, government officials and judges. From 25 to 28 February in Dubai, two inter-party dialogues relating to federalism and fiscal flows were facilitated by the Office of Constitutional Support and organized by the United Nations Office for Project Services (UNOPS) to allow Committee members to hold internal discussions on principal challenges and potential constitutional amendments required for the construction of a viable federal system. Leading international experts in these fields, including representatives from the World Bank, engaged the Iraqi delegation, which included members of the Committee, the Council of Representatives and the federal Government. Specifically, the topics included: collaboration, coordination and autonomy in the exercise of federal and regional powers; the modalities of intergovernmental collaboration and cooperation; constitutional provisions on fiscal flows and the current practice in Iraq; petroleum management, revenue management and taxation; criteria for fiscal equalization; federal Government roles in foreign affairs and federal interventions in the regions; modalities for transitioning from governorates to the regions; and the division of powers between the federal Government and the regions.

25. At the completion of each of the above events, the Office of Constitutional Support engaged with participants in Iraqi-only sessions to reflect on the issues presented and to discuss their application to the Iraqi Constitution. These sessions represented opportunities

for the Committee members representing all of Iraq's major political blocs to hold substantive discussions on specific topics potentially warranting amendments to the Constitution.

C. Electoral assistance activities

26. The law on the formation of the Independent High Electoral Commission was enacted by the Council of Representatives on 23 January 2007. The law is currently pending approval by the Presidency Council. Following ratification by the Presidency Council, the law provides for a period of 60 days for the selection of members of the new Commission. UNAMI will advise on the selection process and anticipates that a new Commission may be in office by April 2007. Pending the transition to the Independent High Electoral Commission, the Independent Electoral Commission of Iraq will continue to operate under a caretaker mandate.

27. UNAMI continues its engagement with the Independent Electoral Commission of Iraq and has undertaken a comprehensive capacity-building assessment of the institution. In close consultation with Iraqi counterparts, the assessment will form the framework for the planning and activities of the UNAMI Electoral Assistance Office for the first part of the year. It will include the induction of the new Commission and continued development of electoral infrastructure and the technical capacity of the administration.

28. Significant challenges remain in preparing for any future electoral events in Iraq. First and foremost, there is currently no fully empowered electoral commission. In addition, the core legal framework for electoral activities is not yet in place; it must include enabling legislation for referendums on disputed territories, including Kirkuk; governorate elections; and a referendum on constitutional amendments. Furthermore, no progress has been made on the voters' register or boundary delimitation issues, and the electoral budget has been significantly cut, thereby requiring additional funds if electoral activities are to be held. Assuming these conditions are met, the Independent Electoral Commission of Iraq believes that at least six months will be required to prepare and conduct an election event.

29. UNAMI will assist the Commission in meeting these challenges by supporting legislative drafting, developing a governorate-level electoral capacity, advising on electoral systems and developing a credible voters' list. Planning for the next electoral cycle will depend on the successful engagement of these processes under the deteriorating humanitarian and security conditions.

D. Reconstruction, development and humanitarian assistance

30. The humanitarian situation in Iraq has worsened steadily during the reporting period. Large-scale outflows are already taking place, with the number of people seeking refuge steadily rising. According to UNHCR, there are approximately 2 million Iraqi refugees in neighbouring countries, largely located in the Syrian Arab Republic and Jordan, placing a considerable strain on the resources of these States. Working closely with the relevant United Nations agencies and the Human Rights Office, UNAMI is monitoring the situation to ensure that needs are identified and addressed where possible within existing resources, while determining gaps that must be filled. According to UNHCR, International Organization for Migration and government sources, of the 1.9 million internally displaced persons in Iraq, approximately 712,000 have been displaced in the past 12 months as a result of sectarian violence and military operations. Nearly 80 per cent of these internally

displaced persons are from the central and southern governorates, indicating a massive movement of the population along ethnic and/or sectarian lines. Above all, Iraq is experiencing a protection and human rights crisis that has the potential of turning into a full-scale humanitarian emergency if the prevailing climate of fear, impunity and disorder is not addressed in conjunction with efforts to meet basic material needs.

31. Implications of this situation are far-reaching. An increasing number of children are unable to attend school, particularly in the Baghdad area. Brain drain continues, as professionals and skilled workers leave the country. Unemployment and inflation rates are escalating. The standard of living of all Iraqis has fallen, despite ongoing initiatives to reconstruct infrastructure and capacities to deliver basic services such as electricity, health, drinking water and sanitation. Food security is tenuous, with more than a third of the population dependent on a rapidly deteriorating food ration distribution system (public distribution system). The impact of this situation on children in particular is leading to increased chronic and acute malnutrition rates, school dropout rates and truancy rates. Access to health services is weakening, as insecurity jeopardizes efforts to maintain even the most basic services.

32. Advocacy efforts initiated by the Emergency Relief Coordinator have resulted in an initiative that is gathering momentum, and the Acting Emergency Relief Coordinator has worked to mobilize the United Nations system, donors and the Iraqi Government to assess the situation and determine possible courses of action. These include information-gathering and coordination mechanisms, with counterparts in neighbouring countries, in anticipation of worst case scenarios, namely, significant outflows of people from Iraq.

33. Relevant United Nations agencies, NGOs and the International Committee of the Red Cross (ICRC) also met in Geneva on 31 January 2007 to discuss the deteriorating humanitarian situation in Iraq. The meeting was co-chaired by the Acting Emergency Relief Coordinator and the Humanitarian Coordinator for Iraq. It reached an agreement to keep Iraq on the humanitarian agenda of the United Nations system while determining the scope and scale of the United Nations response to the situation. Consultations with donors and the Government of Iraq continued in February 2007 and will be followed by efforts to define the role of the United Nations system on the basis of gaps in assistance.

34. As the unfolding humanitarian crisis becomes more evident, the United Nations is increasingly called upon to provide leadership. UNAMI and the United Nations country team will continue their reconstruction and development programmes wherever possible in Iraq, including providing support for the International Compact with Iraq, while also maintaining a strong advocacy role in humanitarian and human rights issues. Addressing humanitarian issues could also create space for political and economic development initiatives.

E. Human rights activities

35. Civilians remain the primary victims of the prevailing security situation, which is characterized by terrorist acts, and action by armed groups, criminal gangs, religious extremists and militias, as well as operations by security and military forces. Daily acts of violence feed a cycle of retaliation involving mortar attacks, kidnappings and assassinations. The relentless violence has disrupted essential services, especially access to the most vulnerable groups, and has led to further displacement of civilian populations. In the absence of concrete measures by the Iraqi Government to address the prevailing climate of

impunity, the violence maintains a crippling effect on institutions that promote the rule of law, particularly the security forces and the judiciary.

36. According to the Iraq Ministry of Human Rights, there were 30,622 detainees in Iraq at the end of January 2007, including 13,989 detainees held by the multinational force. Following investigations into reported abuses at Ministry of Interior facilities, the Iraqi Government issued arrest warrants for 52 personnel from the Site 4 facility. Until now, those arrest warrants have not been enforced. In January 2007, joint prison inspections by the multinational force and Iraqi authorities resumed after a break of seven months. Holding law enforcement officials accountable is essential for removing a culture of impunity and strengthening the capacity of institutions to promote the rule of law. This is of particular importance now, as the implementation of the Baghdad security plan is expected to lead to additional detentions.

37. Armed groups continue to target professionals, such as academics, health workers and journalists. The Committee to Protect Journalists reported that 47 media workers died as a result of targeted assassinations, crossfire or other acts of war in 2006. Accurate casualty figures for medical professionals, who have been similarly targeted, are not currently available, as many have fled Iraq. Their departure has exacerbated the already depleted number of health workers across the country. The Iraqi Association of University Lecturers reported that some 300 academics and university administrators have been killed since March 2003. For example, Mustansiriyah University in Baghdad was the target of heinous terrorist attacks on 16 January and 25 February, resulting in the death of dozens of students and university workers.

38. The Palestinian community in Iraq, currently estimated at more than 15,000 persons, suffers from regular intimidation, kidnappings and assassinations. On 23 January 2007, unidentified men, some of whom were in police uniforms, abducted 60 Palestinians from their homes in three Baghdad neighbourhoods. When released, some victims showed signs of physical abuse. UNAMI records indicate that 186 Palestinians were killed between April 2004 and mid-January 2007. Approximately 700 Palestinians have sought refuge on the border between Iraq and the Syrian Arab Republic and at the Al-Waleed Camp on the Iraqi side of the border. UNHCR and its NGO partners are providing food, water, supplies and medicine, while ICRC is supplying tents and other essential relief items. On 8 February 2007, a senior representative of the Palestinian Authority visited Iraq, after several failed attempts. He sought assurances from President Talabani and Prime Minister Al-Maliki that Palestinians in Iraq will be protected.

39. On 26 December 2006, the Appeals Chamber of the Iraqi High Tribunal unanimously dismissed the appeals of Saddam Hussein and his two co-defendants, Barzan al-Tikriti and Awad al-Bandar, upholding all three death sentences. The Appeals Chamber returned the case of a fourth defendant, Taha Yassin Ramadan, to the Iraqi High Tribunal for re-sentencing, recommending a harsher sentence than the term of life imprisonment that he had received. The Special Rapporteur on the independence of judges and lawyers, in a statement made on 27 December 2006, expressed concern at the failure of the panel to address the grave shortcomings in the trial. He urged the Government not to carry out the death sentences following an allegedly procedurally flawed legal process. The United Nations High Commissioner for Human Rights, Louise Arbour, called for restraint by the Iraqi authorities and reiterated her concerns about the appeal process and fairness of the original trial.

Saddam Hussein, however, was executed on 30 December 2006. The other two co-defendants were executed on 15 January 2007.

40. On 8 February 2007, the United Nations High Commissioner for Human Rights filed a legal brief as amicus curiae with the Iraqi High Tribunal, arguing against the imposition of capital punishment in the case of Taha Yassin Ramadan. In her submission, the High Commissioner argued that

> "The egregious violations of human rights that took place in Iraq over decades have been well documented by the United Nations human rights system ... There is no doubt that the horrors of the past must be effectively addressed and their perpetrators must be brought to justice... At the same time, experience and history in very different contexts around the world have shown the absolute indispensability of the integrity of such proceedings, both in fact and perception, for true understanding of the past, for national reconciliation and for the construction of a just, durable, and sustainable society founded on the rule of law and respect for human rights of both victims and defendants."

On 12 February 2007, the Iraqi High Tribunal announced its decision to sentence Mr. Ramadan to death.

41. A series of meetings were organized in Baghdad in December 2006 to help the Ministry of Human Rights expand its programme, improve its cooperation with NGOs and the media, and strengthen its lobbying capacity. UNAMI also supported the High Judicial Council in its leadership of the sector working group on the rule of law, composed of the Iraqi Government, donors and the United Nations system. On 13 January 2007, the working group adopted a plan for justice sector reform.

IV. International Reconstruction Fund Facility for Iraq

42. As of 31 January 2007, the total contributions to the United Nations Development Group (UNDG) Iraq Trust Fund, one of the two funds of the International Reconstruction Fund Facility for Iraq, equalled $1.12 billion. A total of 113 projects, valued at $893 million, were approved as of the end of January 2007 for funding under the UNDG Iraq Trust Fund. Continuing the significant progress in implementation, contracts worth a cumulative $693 million (78 per cent of total approved funding) have been initiated and $591 million (66 per cent of total approved funding) have been disbursed.

43. At the invitation of the Government of Turkey, the fifth meeting of the International Reconstruction Fund Facility for Iraq Donor Committee will take place in Istanbul, Turkey, on 20 March 2007. At the Istanbul meeting, the United Nations and the World Bank will present reports on the activities undertaken through the two Funds and present an assessment of results achieved. The Donor Committee will also consider various strategic and policy issues related to the scope and future operations of the International Reconstruction Fund Facility for Iraq.

V. Security and operational issues

A. Assessment of the security situation

44. The security situation in Iraq remains complex and unpredictable, particularly as responsibility for security is transferred from the multinational force to the Iraqi security forces.

The ability of the Iraqi security forces to fulfil this requirement is yet to be fully tested. The security situation remained serious during the reporting period, with deepening conflict between various political parties, factions, militia groups and elements of the insurgency. This situation is graphically manifested in Baghdad, where the hostilities and violence have continued despite initial successes under the Baghdad security plan.

45. The United Nations presence and activities in Iraq continue to be severely limited by the prevailing security situation in the country. However, with significant mitigation measures and proper training of United Nations staff members, the risk level continues to be assessed at the medium level. The threat of indirect fire remains high and the use of false uniforms and identity cards by armed opposition groups pose a serious concern. Additionally, new tactics involving the use of chlorine gas in their weapons systems is worrisome. Of particular concern to the United Nations were the recent successful attacks on eight helicopters in Iraq. Six multinational force and two United States Department of State contractor helicopters have been attacked and destroyed since early January. Although all were involved in supporting combat operations, UNAMI continues to re-evaluate the level of risk posed to United Nations staff using this mode of transportation.

46. Serious security incidents continue at a high rate, with a daily average of 160. There has been a corresponding rise in the level of casualties among civilians, the multinational force and Iraqi security forces. The conflict continues to be characterized by attacks against the multinational force and sectarian violence by insurgents and militias. They use suicide bombings, assassinations, kidnappings and indiscriminate indirect fire attacks, using both rockets and mortars. Incidents against the multinational force are particularly intense in Ramadi and Falluja, with frequent roadside ambushes and sustained attacks against police and military bases. The alleged presence of Al-Qaeda in Iraq, in Diyala and al-Anbar provinces, has been a factor in sustaining and widening the conflict. Despite the focus on the security situation in Baghdad, it is not always apparent that violent incidents take place in almost all areas of Iraq.

47. While the Kurdish region remains relatively calm, a series of incidents have caused concern. Following the raid on the Iranian office in Erbil by the multinational force, there was a period of tension and friction between the multinational force and the local security forces. In February 2007, Kirkuk also suffered waves of car bombings. Also in the north, Mosul and Tal Afar witnessed multiple bomb attacks.

48. The multinational force continued intensive operations in the Diyala province, with extensive cordon-and-search operations in Balad Ruz and Baqubah. Numerous suspects were detained and weapons caches discovered. Despite these operations, the insurgency continues in Diyala and al-Anbar provinces. Major routes through Falluja and Ramadi are persistently ambushed by armed opposition groups employing increasingly effective explosive devices and improved tactics.

49. In Baghdad, Sunni and Shiite neighbourhoods are engaged in frequent reciprocal assaults, using improvised explosive devices, mortars and rocket attacks. Typically there can be as many as 15 bombs of varying sizes delivered to targets across the city in a given day, with retaliatory mortar attacks against residential communities. In the single deadliest attack, on 4 February 2007, a suicide bomber driving a truck loaded with one ton of explosives struck a market, killing 135 people and injuring 305. This situation is further compounded by high rates of kidnappings, drive-by shootings and the dumping of mutilated bodies.

50. Indirect fire attacks on the international zone in Baghdad increased from an average of one or two strikes per week in 2006 to over four per week at the beginning of 2007. Apart from the increased threat from indirect fire attacks, there were also a number of shooting incidents in the vicinity of the entry checkpoints to the international zone. On 14 January 2007, a car was stopped at an entry checkpoint carrying around 4 kilograms of explosives concealed within crates of vegetables in the trunk of the vehicle.

51. These security challenges to the integrity of the international zone, and the continuing threat of kidnapping, highlight the risks faced by the United Nations staff in Baghdad. However, extensive mitigation measures are in place within the international zone aimed at reducing the overall risk to United Nations staff. Movement of United Nations staff in the international zone is controlled with a curfew and limitations on travel. Visits to government buildings outside the international zone require armed escorts, and UNAMI has practised procedures for this requirement. National staff working at all locations in Iraq are exposed to high levels of risk, particularly when travelling to and from work. An Iraq-specific package of measures has been designed to reduce their risk.

52. Frequent revisions and adaptation of security precautions are required to meet emerging threats. The recent commando style raid by militants on the Provincial Joint Coordination Centre in Karbala is one such example. In that case, militants penetrated Iraqi army and police security checkpoints in Karbala on 20 January 2007 by disguising themselves in United States army uniforms and using look-alike vehicles. They succeeded in abducting and later killing five United States officers who were attending a meeting at the base.

53. During the observance of the Shiite holiday of Ashura (20-30 January 2007), a number of violent events took place across the country. On 12 February 2007, during a 15-minute pause to commemorate the first anniversary of the bombing of the Samarra shrine, a massive triple car bomb disrupted the silence and struck the Shorja market, killing 80 and injuring over 150 people. One extraordinary event involved a Shiite group, the Army of Heaven, which clashed with security forces outside Najaf. During the battle a United States attack helicopter was shot down and allegedly more than 200 militants were reportedly killed. Many new and modern weapons, including a truck-mounted anti-aircraft gun, were captured in the process.

54. The lower south region experienced a number of violent incidents. They involved the harassment, ambush and assassination of pilgrims returning from the hajj, particularly near Iskandariyaa. On 16 December 2006, a number of tribal leaders and provincial officials were killed on their return from the national reconciliation conference in Baghdad and, on 1 February 2007, 60 persons were killed by a car bomb in Hilla. In Basra and the surrounding areas, militias have continued to harass and attack the multinational force on a daily basis. Rocket and mortar attacks, particularly against the Basra Palace and the Old State Building, have increased in frequency and accuracy, with up to 10 rocket launchings against Basra Palace in a single day. The United Nations presence at Basra Palace is currently under review, in the light of the recent decision by the United Kingdom to consolidate its presence in the south.

B. Facilities, logistics and support

55. The incidence of indirect fire into the international zone in Baghdad has increased recently. However, only a part of the UNAMI interim accommodation facility has overhead

protection, which limits the number of staff who can be safely deployed to Baghdad. A contractor has been identified to construct overhead protection for the remaining area of the compound. It is anticipated that the construction will begin in the near future and be completed within three to four months following the signing of the contract. In the interim, emergency sleeping accommodations have been established in a barrack type facility that has overhead protection. For the future integrated United Nations headquarters in Baghdad, subject to availability of suitable contractor(s), UNAMI expects to start work within a few months on the site allocated by the Iraqi Government. Following site clearance and technical surveys, development plans, including a statement of work, are in the final stage of preparation. UNAMI will continue to use the LOGCAP and the 607 Agreement when there is no equivalent service provider available either because of the security situation or availability in the mission area.

56. Denmark has provided a dedicated fixed-wing aircraft for UNAMI use, and services commenced on 28 January 2007. Japan has continued to provide a dedicated flight on a weekly basis to UNAMI. These arrangements are time-limited and, in the absence of extensions, alternative options for fixed-wing support beyond 30 June 2007, including commercial options, will have to be explored. The feasibility of introducing commercial rotary-wing helicopter support is also currently under consideration. Helicopter support is critical for movements between Baghdad International Airport and the international zone, and for other movements within Iraq. The ability to maintain reduced risk levels for employing United Nations helicopters is however fundamental to the feasibility of this option.

57. I am very grateful to the Member States that continue to provide logistic and protection support to the United Nations presence in Iraq. UNAMI will face major challenges in 2007 in developing its own operational capacity to become gradually self-reliant. This will include the construction of a permanent office and accommodation facilities and development of independent transport capacities, to the extent possible. Under current security conditions, this will pose substantial logistic and financial challenges. Full support from Member States and the Iraqi Government will be required to achieve these goals. In this context, I remind Member States that the trust fund established in 2004 to support the distinct entity, in accordance with Security Council resolution 1546 (2004), will be exhausted by March 2007. The distinct entity, under multinational force command, has a dedicated mission to provide security for the United Nations presence in Iraq. Since its establishment, it has received over $20 million in contributions from 16 Member States.

C. Agreements

58. The status-of-mission agreement between the United Nations and the Government of Iraq was signed on 3 June 2005, but will enter into force only following formal ratification by the Council of Representatives. While the United Nations has been advised that the matter has been presented to the Council of Representatives for action, the decision is still pending. I strongly urge the Government of Iraq to expedite this process and issue the required official confirmation note as soon as possible.

D. Observations

59. The rising levels of violence, terrorist attacks and sectarian conflict that have gripped large parts of Iraq are increasingly acquiring a self-sustaining dynamic that could overwhelm the country's fragile political processes and institutions. The high level of civilian

casualties each day and the increasing number of displacements are deepening the sense of insecurity and pessimism among ordinary Iraqis. If the cycle of violence is not brought under control, efforts made over the past several years could be jeopardized.

60. I note the efforts of the Government of Iraq and the multinational force to improve the security situation, and I encourage all parties concerned to proceed in a manner that will improve the safety and security of the capital of the country for all Iraqis. Despite some initial success, it is too early to determine the effectiveness of the latest Baghdad security plan. While it will take time for this new security measure to show tangible results, its ultimate success will likely depend on the successful implementation of a wider set of measures aimed at promoting political dialogue, economic development and reconstruction.

61. It is of utmost importance that Iraqi leaders come together in a spirit of mutual respect and compromise. Attaining political objectives through violence will only breed further violence. Only the Iraqi people themselves can determine their common destiny and agree upon the structure of the Iraqi state. New institutions should be built on the principles of fair distribution of power and equitable sharing of national resources and wealth. This would allow all of Iraq's communities to attain greater security, peace and prosperity.

62. To give all Iraqi constituencies a real stake in the future of their country, I call on all parties concerned to support a genuine constitutional review process, which will offer an opportunity to achieve broad consensus on fundamental issues, including federalism and resource-sharing. I hope that the provisions of the new hydrocarbon law, currently before the Council of Representatives, will help safeguard Iraq's future economic prosperity and contribute to the process of national reconciliation. In the hopes of achieving consensus on other critical issues, it is also essential for Iraq's leaders to finalize key pieces of legislation that are still pending, including those on de-Baathification, provincial elections, and a possible amnesty law.

63. The worsening humanitarian and human rights situation has become a cause of serious concern. I note the alarming rate of displacement, which has reached an all-time high, with 2 million refugees in neighbouring countries and nearly 1.9 million displaced inside Iraq. While some of these refugees lived in neighbouring countries prior to March 2003, a substantial number fled following the bombing of the Al-Askari Mosque in Samarra on 22 February 2006. Displacement continues on a daily basis, owing to the ongoing level of violence and intimidation inside Iraq. There is an urgent need for greater international cooperation to address this growing humanitarian crisis. I welcome the generosity of a number of countries especially Jordan and the Syrian Arab Republic. I encourage the international community to support efforts by the United Nations to assist those in need. As civilians continue to bear the brunt of the violence in Iraq, I believe that the situation also calls for the establishment of a national protection system in Iraq based on respect for human rights and the rule of law. For its part, the United Nations will continue to monitor and report on the human rights situation in Iraq.

64. From a regional perspective, I strongly believe in the need to strengthen dialogue between Iraq and its neighbours. Regional actors could play a key role in assisting with the stabilization of Iraq, which could be beneficial to their own long-term security. I welcome the ongoing dialogue between Iraq and its neighbours, through regular bilateral contacts and periodic meetings of regional Foreign Ministers and Interior Ministers. However, given

the complexity of the situation inside Iraq, and its wider regional implications, there is a need for more creative thinking on how to improve dialogue between Iraq and all of its neighbours to promote concrete confidence-building measures.

65. In these difficult times, Iraqi politicians, religious leaders, tribal elders and influential members of civil society must not lose sight of the fundamental goal of preserving Iraq's national unity. They must work towards settling their differences peacefully and protecting the human dignity of all Iraqis, irrespective of their creed and ethnicity. Efforts to find political solutions will no doubt represent a daunting challenge, with major obstacles along the way to overcome. There will be no quick solutions; patience and perseverance will be required without artificially rigid timelines. Ultimately, the Iraqi people and their leaders face a fundamental choice, between seeking a negotiated political settlement or drawing further into the abyss of sectarian conflict. I believe that it is still not too late to turn the tide and prevent further escalation.

66. The United Nations is committed to its mandate under resolution 1546 (2004) to play a role in supporting Iraq's political and economic development. Under paragraph 7 (a) of the resolution, the United Nations will continue to engage in political facilitation and offer its good offices to all parties concerned. The United Nations is also committed to providing technical assistance for Iraq's electoral processes and in the building of new democratic and federal institutions. Under paragraph 7 (b) of the resolution, the United Nations will do all it can to support activities in the areas of human rights and the rule of law, as well as with respect to humanitarian assistance, reconstruction and economic development. At the regional and international levels, UNAMI will continue to support the International Compact for Iraq.

67. I would like to reiterate my appreciation to Member States that have supported the activities of the United Nations in Iraq, in particular by providing military advisers and security forces. The United Nations will continue to rely on such support, especially with regard to the distinct entity trust fund, which was established to fund a "middle-ring" force to protect the United Nations presence in Iraq. It is vital that fresh financial contributions are made to the trust fund to ensure that the "middle-ring" force is well resourced in the future. In addition, I am grateful to the Governments of Denmark and Japan for the provision of air support. These arrangements are crucial for the United Nations to operate in Iraq, and I hope that they will continue in the future.

68. I would also like to express my sincere appreciation for the continued efforts of my Special Representative for Iraq, Ashraf Jehangir Qazi. His unwavering commitment and leadership over the past several years is truly admirable. I would also like to extend my special thanks to all staff who have worked under very difficult and challenging circumstances to implement the United Nations mandate in Iraq.

4. Report of the Secretary-General pursuant to paragraph 30 of Resolution 1546 (2004), 5 June 2007 (S/2007/330)

I. Introduction

1. In paragraph 30 of resolution 1546 (2004), the Security Council requested the Secretary-General to report to the Council on a quarterly basis on the fulfilment of the responsibilities of the United Nations Assistance Mission for Iraq (UNAMI). The present report is the twelfth submitted pursuant to that resolution.

2. The report provides an update on United Nations activities in Iraq since the last report (S/2007/126), of 7 March 2007. It presents a summary of key political developments during the period under review, particularly efforts by the Government of Iraq to reduce the violence and promote national reconciliation, as well as regional and international developments pertaining to Iraq. The report provides an update on the activities of my Special Representative for Iraq, Ashraf Jehangir Qazi, an assessment of the security situation and an update on operational and security matters.

II. Summary of key developments in Iraq

A. Political developments

3. Despite the initial success of stepped-up security measures in recent months, the situation in Iraq remains precarious. Insurgent attacks persist and civilian casualties continue to mount. While there was a brief lull in the level of sectarian violence early in the reporting period, it now appears that militia forces are resuming their activities, including targeted killings and kidnappings. The threat that the violence poses to the political process was illustrated by the bombing in the Iraqi Parliament on 12 April that resulted in the death of one lawmaker and injured several others. The Council of Representatives met in an extraordinary session the following day to condemn the attack and show its defiance. South of Baghdad, rising political tension in Basra and Qadissiya provinces resulted in an escalation of violence in those governorates. The Government of Iraq continued to engage leaders from across the political and religious spectrum to promote its national reconciliation plan. The efforts of the Prime Minister, Nouri al-Maliki, to reconcile demands within his governing coalition were further challenged by the withdrawal of support by key allies in his Government.

4. On 7 March, the Fadhila Party, which holds 15 parliamentary seats, withdrew from the United Iraqi Alliance, the leading bloc in the National Unity Government. On 16 April 2007, the Sadrist bloc within the Alliance withdrew its six ministers from the Prime Minister's cabinet. Unlike in November 2006, the Sadrists this time did not suspend the participation of their 30 legislators in the Council of Representatives. On 24 May Prime Minister Al-Maliki presented his nominations for the six ministerial vacancies to the Council of Representatives.

5. Shortly thereafter, on 5 May, leaders of the Sunni parliamentarian bloc Tawafoq, including Vice-President Tareq al-Hashemi, threatened to withdraw from the governing coalition expressing their disenchantment with the ability and commitment of the Government to

address their concerns, particularly those related to the constitutional review process. On 7 May, following a meeting with Prime Minister Al-Maliki, the Office of Vice-President Al-Hashemi issued a statement saying that the meeting had helped move the political process forward. The Kurdish Alliance, which holds 53 seats in the Council of Representatives, also reportedly threatened to leave the Government at the end of March unless a referendum to decide the final status of Kirkuk was held by the end of 2007.

6. On 29 March 2007, the Minister of Justice, Hashim al-Shibli, announced that the Government had approved the recommendations made in February 2007 by the High Commission on the Implementation of Article 140 on determining the final status of Kirkuk and other disputed territories. Mr. Al-Shibli stressed that there would be no coercion or use of force in carrying out the decisions regarding the relocation and compensation of thousands of Arab families that had moved to Kirkuk under the "Arabization" campaign of the former regime. The Kurdistan Alliance praised the decision, while Turkomen and Sunni representatives, as well as Sadrists, denounced it for ignoring the rights of the concerned families and for failing to address the issue of property claims. Moqtada al-Sadr suspended two Sadrist ministers who had voted in favour of the recommendations.

7. Although the draft hydrocarbon law and its related annexes were endorsed by the Council of Ministers on 27 February, it has not been submitted to the Oil and Gas Committee of the Council of Representatives. There has been no decision on whether the hydrocarbon law will be voted on as part of a larger energy package with annexes and supporting laws or by itself. The four annexes currently under discussion address the allocation of oilfields, and related legislation is also being developed on revenue sharing, the structure of the Ministry of Oil, and the establishment of the Iraq national oil company. Under the proposed law, the national oil company would have jurisdiction over the country's oilfields and the authority to sign contracts. A federal oil and gas council would be established to set all policies related to contracts and other industry issues. A panel of oil experts from inside and outside Iraq would advise the federal council before it entered into any contracts.

8. Several parliamentarians and members of the Government, including Vice-President al-Hashemi, expressed the preference to consider these laws after the completion of the constitutional review, as it has direct implications for key provisions of the hydrocarbon law. Several political blocs expressed strong objections to certain provisions of the law. The Federation of Oil Unions articulated concern over potential production sharing arrangements and organized several demonstrations in Basra to voice its concerns.

9. On 26 March, the Presidency Council and the Office of the Prime Minister circulated a draft accountability and justice law that would amend the current de-Baathification process. According to the draft, there would be a three-month period to challenge former Baathists for their involvement in the repression instituted by the former regime, after which they would be immune from legal punishment for their past actions, would be eligible for employment in the public sector and receive their pension benefits. Former army officers and members of the security service above the rank of major would not be re-employed in the public sector, but they would receive their pension benefits. The draft law also weakens the powers of the De-Baathification Commission by vesting more powers in independent judges. It calls for the abolition of the Commission within six months after the law is ratified. The Chairman of the De-Baathification Commission, Ahmad Chalabi, produced his own draft law that is currently before the Legal Committee following a review

by the De-Baathification Committee of the Council of Representatives. The existence of competing drafts sparked intense political debate, and on 21 April the Sadrist bloc rejected the proposed amendments to the existing procedures of de-Baathification, declaring them unconstitutional.

10. On 11 May, Sadrist and Sunni parliamentarians collected the signatures of 144 parliamentarians calling for a timetable for the withdrawal of the multinational force from Iraq. The petition, which was signed by a majority of members of Parliament, was submitted to the Speaker of the Council of Representatives. Most members regarded the petition as non-binding, but it did call on the Government to set a deadline for the withdrawal of foreign troops and it requested the Ministers of Defence, the Interior and National Security to identify a date by which Iraqi forces would be ready to assume primary responsibility for security operations in the country.

11. On 11 May, the Supreme Council for Islamic Revolution in Iraq, the senior partner in the United Iraqi Alliance with 36 seats in Parliament, issued a 49-point communiqué declaring that it had changed its name to the Supreme Islamic Iraqi Council. The Prime Minister visited Ramadi on 13 March to meet with provincial officials, security chiefs and tribal leaders of Anbar governorate. This marked the Prime Minister's first visit to the majority Sunni province. On 6 April, the Office of the Prime Minister announced its decision adopted at the end of March on providing pension payments for senior officers of Saddam Hussein's armed forces. A conference of Anbar tribal sheikhs was convened on 15 April 2007 by the Anbar Salvation Front. The conference called for cooperation with the multinational and Iraqi forces. The Anbar Salvation Front, which includes 17 tribes, was established in September 2006 as a paramilitary wing to unite against the threat posed by Al-Qaida in Anbar province.

12. At the time of its formation in November 2006, the Constitutional Review Committee set a deadline of 15 May 2007 for the delivery to Parliament of its report on recommended constitutional amendments. The deadline was later extended to 22 May due to the recess schedule of Parliament. On 23 May, the Committee's presidency informed the Council of Representatives that the Committee had prepared a draft report based upon a consensus reached among its members, including proposals for the division of powers between the federal Government and the regions and the handling of oil revenues. The Committee requested a further one-month extension to attempt to resolve outstanding politically contentious issues including the treatment of article 140 (resolving the status of Kirkuk and other disputed territories) and the powers of the Presidency. To be adopted, the Committee's draft formulations will need to gain the backing of the full range of Iraq's political leaders and win popular support in a potential referendum. Iraq's political leadership is yet to endorse the Committee's draft recommendations.

B. Regional developments

13. During the period under review, several developments and events pertaining to Iraq took place in the region. On 10 March, a meeting of senior officials was convened in Baghdad to prepare for an expanded ministerial meeting of foreign ministers of neighbouring States. At the meeting, Prime Minister al-Maliki appealed to all participants to work together to help Iraq overcome its many challenges. It was agreed in principle to form three working groups to address the issues of border security, fuel and energy and refugees.

A number of the participants considered the meeting a good first step in promoting regional cooperation on Iraq.

14. On 4 May, the Government of Egypt hosted the expanded ministerial conference of neighbouring countries of Iraq in Sharm el-Sheikh. The meeting included representatives of the permanent members of the Security Council, the European Union, the G-8, Bahrain, Egypt, the League of Arab States, the Organization of the Islamic Conference and the United Nations. At the conclusion, the participants reaffirmed the sovereignty, territorial integrity, political independence and national unity of Iraq. They also committed themselves to the principle of non-interference in Iraq's internal affairs and good-neighbourly relations with all its neighbours. The participants endorsed the formation of the three working groups and pledged to support them with active participation and technical assistance. They recognized the role of the United Nations in supporting ongoing political processes in Iraq, as well as the positive contributions being made by the League of Arab States and the Organization of the Islamic Conference. It was agreed to hold the next ministerial conference in Istanbul.

15. On 28 May, the United States of America and the Islamic Republic of Iran held a meeting at the ambassadorial level in Baghdad, also attended by Prime Minister al-Maliki. It was the first such meeting between the two countries since diplomatic relations broke down in 1979. The parties limited their discussions to the security situation in Iraq. One principal concern for the Islamic Republic of Iran is the detention of five Iranian nationals on 10 January 2007 by coalition forces. Both the Government of Iraq and the President of the Kurdistan region have sought their release. Since their arrest, the multinational force has allowed the International Committee of the Red Cross (ICRC) to visit the detainees twice.

C. International developments

16. The Prime Minister of Iraq visited Japan and the Republic of Korea from 8 to 12 April. Japan announced that it would lend Iraq $862 million repayable over 40 years with a 10-year grace period. The money will be used to build an oil facility connecting pipelines in southern Iraq, fund fertilizer and oil refinery plants and improve the electricity supply. The loan is part of a $6 billion aid package that Japan pledged in 2003. On 5 April the Office of the Prime Minister of Iraq announced that it had negotiated a $500 million loan from the World Bank for reconstruction. On 12 April the Prime Minister signed a memorandum of understanding with the Republic of Korea on cooperation in the development of oilfields.

17. On 17 and 18 April, the Office of the United Nations High Commissioner for Refugees (UNHCR) convened an international conference in Geneva to address the humanitarian needs of displaced Iraqis, both inside Iraq and in neighbouring countries. The meeting brought together representatives of 60 nations, who agreed on the urgent need to stem the outflow of people, assist those in need and provide support to neighbouring countries which are hosting refugees. UNHCR welcomed the positive and constructive spirit of the meeting. The participants also recognized the importance of seeking a broader political solution and promoting national reconciliation to improve the conditions on the ground for the return of refugees and displaced persons.

18. On 3 May, the International Compact with Iraq was launched in Sharm el-Sheikh, Egypt. The event was preceded by a regional tour by Prime Minister Al-Maliki aimed at securing support for the International Compact. The Prime Minister and I co-chaired the

conference, which was attended by 75 delegations. The participants unanimously adopted a resolution reaffirming their shared commitment to work in partnership with the Government of Iraq to a secure and stable Iraq, while emphasizing the need for national dialogue, improved governance, anti-corruption measures, equal protection for all Iraqis and an institutional framework based on the rule of law. Participants agreed to meet regularly to coordinate their efforts and review progress on these reforms and assistance. Most notably, representatives made considerable pledges in the areas of debt relief and financial assistance. The meeting demonstrated broad international support for the people and Government of Iraq in rebuilding their country. I also pledged the full support of the United Nations for the implementation of the International Compact.

III. Update on the activities of the Mission

A. Political activities of the Special Representative of the Secretary-General

19. My Special Representative, Ashraf Jehangir Qazi, maintained contacts with Iraqi political, religious and tribal leaders. To ensure timely and effective assistance in electoral and constitutional areas, he met with officials from the Government of Iraq, the Council of Representatives and the diplomatic community. He repeatedly stressed the need for a more inclusive political approach in the implementation of the Baghdad security plan.

20. He supported the efforts of the Government of Iraq to engage with regional actors and the wider international community. On 10 March, he attended a meeting of senior-level officials which was convened in preparation for an expanded ministerial meeting on Iraq. On 16 March he was in New York to participate in a preparatory meeting on the International Compact with Iraq. On 3 and 4 May, my Special Representative attended the launch of the International Compact and the expanded ministerial conference of neighbouring countries of Iraq in Sharm el-Sheikh.

21. I visited Iraq on 22 March for the first time since becoming Secretary-General and met with a wide range of Iraqi leaders. The trip also allowed me to take stock of the important work of UNAMI in person. My Special Representative also hosted visits by the United Nations High Commissioner for Refugees, Antonio Guterres, on 30 and 31 March, and my Special Adviser, Ibrahim Gambari, from 6 to 9 April. Subsequently, my Special Representative attended the international conference on Iraqi refugees and displaced persons in Geneva on 17 and 18 April.

22. In Baghdad, my Special Representative and UNAMI worked closely with the Government of Iraq, the World Bank, the European Union and the co-chairs of the International Reconstruction Fund Facility in Iraq in the establishment of secretariats for both the Facility and the International Compact. He also received representations from Iraqis and others regarding human rights issues, including detainees. In wide-ranging discussions with Iraqi politicians and senior diplomats, the status of the implementation of article 140 of the Iraqi Constitution on Kirkuk emerged as a matter of increasing priority.

B. Constitutional support activities

23. The UNAMI Office of Constitutional Support, with significant funding from the European Union, has provided substantive and logistical assistance to the Constitutional Review Committee of the Council of Representatives. Following Parliament's return to session in March 2007, the Office provided advice to the Constitutional Review Committee in

the following specific areas: federalism, wealth sharing, the respective roles of the judiciary and independent institutions, the Iraqi Federation Council or upper house, the constitutional protection of human rights and procedural considerations relating to the constitutional review itself. The Office facilitated the constitutional review process by providing seven submissions in key areas of deliberation and responding to requests from the Committee for options for textual formulations. It maintained direct contact with the Committee throughout the review period.

24. To support its technical advice to the Constitutional Review Committee, UNAMI initiated a broad dialogue on the constitutional review and elements of Iraqi federalism with senior federal and provincial politicians and public servants. UNAMI organized two workshops in Erbil on 27 and 28 March 2007 on the constitutional review and Iraqi federalism, one for Iraqi governors and provincial council chairs, and one for members of the Kurdistan regional government. Participants discussed a range of issues including key challenges under the constitutional review process, principles of federalism and the distribution of powers, fiscal federalism and the sharing of wealth, legislation related to the formation of regions and the role of governorates, the importance of continuity in the provision of public goods and services during the transition from governorates to regions, mechanisms of intergovernmental coordination and the relationship between the Iraqi Constitution and future regional constitutions. In addition to these activities, the Office of Constitutional Support coordinated bilateral and international assistance through regular international coordination meetings.

25. In its interactions with the Constitutional Review Committee and Iraq's political leaders, the Office of Constitutional Support has focused on the core issues that will determine how Iraq's federal system will function. These include establishing a balanced division of powers between the federal Government and the regions and providing guarantees on the national sharing and automatic distribution of oil and gas revenues. These are also among the most politically contentious issues and achieving consensual agreement on them will be difficult. The Committee has seriously considered substantive amendments in these areas, although not necessarily exactly in line with the Office's recommendations or preferred formulations. However, if some of the amendments currently being discussed are ultimately agreed to, they could go some way towards establishing the basis for the national Government to play a necessary coordinating role within the decentralized federal system envisaged by Iraq's Constitution. The constructive nature of the Committee's deliberations indicates that its members are making an attempt to address the concerns held by each others' communities with respect to the Constitution.

26. Finally, the Office coordinated bilateral and international assistance through regular coordination meetings and developed commentaries on parallel legislative proposals with significant constitutional dimensions, such as the draft hydrocarbon law and the law on regional formation.

C. Electoral assistance activities

27. Following the adoption of the law to establish the permanent Independent High Electoral Commission in January 2007, the Council of Representatives voted on 28 April to accept the nomination of nine candidates for five-year terms as electoral commissioners. The selection process was observed by UNAMI electoral staff with full access to all applications and

deliberations of the nominating committee. UNAMI issued an observation report concluding that the selection process had been consistent with Iraqi legislation and the nominating committee's own procedures. The new Board of Commissioners selected officers for a one-year term, including the Chairman, Vice-Chairman, Chief Electoral Officer and Rapporteur. All major communities are represented on the Board, which has requested continued technical assistance from UNAMI.

28. The International Reconstruction Fund Facility in Iraq approved a $6 million capacity-building programme to train the staff and Board members of the Independent High Electoral Commission. UNAMI is doing all it can to support efforts to retain Iraqi electoral staff for the Electoral Commission, which has suffered a 30 per cent reduction since the last election in 2005. The offer by the Government of India to host orientation training and briefings in New Delhi in the first week of June is much appreciated. This will provide an opportunity for Indian electoral experts to share their extensive knowledge of international best practices with the new Board members.

29. Considerable challenges remain in preparing for future electoral events. Of great concern is the lack of progress in improving the Iraqi voter registry, which was last updated in 2005. Consultations in the Council of Representatives are ongoing to agree on legislation to enable a referendum on disputed territories including Kirkuk, governorate elections and a referendum on possible amendments to the Constitution. The capacity of the United Nations Assistance Mission for Iraq to facilitate such discussions and provide technical assistance is being hampered by increasing security restrictions at both the Iraqi Parliament and the premises of the Electoral Commission. Under these difficult conditions, UNAMI continues its efforts to strengthen the operational capacity of Electoral Commission staff and the new Board of Commissioners.

D. Human rights activities

30. UNAMI has continued to meet with Government and civil society representatives, as well as a wide range of Iraqi citizens, to assess the current state of the human rights situation in Iraq. I view favourably the recent decision by the Iraqi Ministry of the Interior to grant UNAMI access to all of its detention facilities. The Government's cooperation in this regard is most welcome. UNAMI intends to begin such visits in June.

31. There are a number of pressing human rights concerns in Iraq. These include the increase in the number of detainees and security internees during the past two months as a result of the intensified security operations; the need to do all possible to bring to justice law enforcement personnel suspected of serious human rights violations; intercommunal tensions and violence directed at ethnic and religious minorities; and the current conditions for freedom of expression, which worsen every time journalists and media workers are attacked. I continue to urge the Government of Iraq to do all possible to bring perpetrators of violence to justice and to strengthen the institutions that promote the rule of law, particularly the security forces and the judiciary.

32. On 25 April, UNAMI launched its tenth human rights report, covering the period from January to March 2007. The report reiterated that lasting stability and security can only be realized through the protection of fundamental rights and respect for basic human dignity. It highlighted a number of concerns relating to the accurate depiction of the current human rights situation in the country, particularly the systematic collection and processing of

information on casualties registered in hospitals and medico-legal institutes throughout the country. I have asked UNAMI and the Office of the United Nations High Commissioner for Human Rights to work closely with the Government on how best to address this and the other important issues referred to above with a view to realizing an early improvement in the human rights situation, which is a priority concern of the international community. I look forward to strengthening our cooperative relationship in this regard.

E. Reconstruction, development and humanitarian assistance

33. Despite growing awareness and concern regarding the humanitarian crisis in Iraq, the situation deteriorated steadily during the reporting period. The violence has resulted in a protection crisis which dominates discussions related to a humanitarian response. For every death reported in the news, six family members on average are left without a breadwinner. The rising number of displaced persons is also a cause for concern. UNHCR estimates that displacement has continued at an undiminished pace and over 800,000 Iraqis have been internally displaced since the Samarra mosque bombing in February 2006, while 30,000 to 50,000 flee to neighbouring countries each month.

34. The violence is also having a major impact on Iraqi children and their ability to attend school. The United Nations Children's Fund (UNICEF), the Central Organization for Statistics and Information Technology of the Ministry of Planning and Cooperation Development and the Kurdish Regional Statistics Office recently published a preliminary report of the Multiple Indicator Cluster Survey which estimated that 17 per cent of primary school-age children were not attending school in 2005 and 2006. This translates into approximately 765,000 children, of whom 61 per cent were girls, even before the recent escalation in the numbers of refugees and internally displaced persons. Dropout rates are also increasingly outstripping school participation. Only 34 per cent of girls and 43 per cent of boys of secondary school age were attending secondary school in 2005 and 2006.

35. On 17 and 18 April UNHCR convened an international conference in Geneva to discuss the humanitarian needs of persons displaced inside Iraq and in neighbouring countries. It called for urgent action by the Government and all relevant parties to find durable solutions based on national reconciliation and respect for fundamental human rights and humanitarian law. The conference recognized the heavy burden borne by neighbouring countries, which are generously hosting some 2 million Iraqis, and called for greater bilateral assistance to the affected countries. It welcomed the initial commitment by the Government of Iraq to provide $25 million to assist both internally and externally displaced Iraqis. The Government recognized the specific vulnerability of Palestinian refugees and undertook to enhance their protection. It also undertook to provide displaced Iraqis with appropriate documentation to ensure their access to essential services. Commitments in support of the $60 million appeal by UNHCR were made by the United States, the European Union, Turkey, Germany and France.

36. In order to address the basic needs of the civilian population of Iraq, United Nations agencies, funds and programmes continue lifesaving interventions as and where possible. Safe water is emerging as a primary concern for displaced families. United Nations support includes water tankering in six districts in Baghdad and two in Anbar, serving over 70,000 people per day. However, this might also have the long-term consequences of reducing water availability in surrounding areas. The only way to meet the needs of the broader

population, including the internally displaced, would be to renovate, extend and construct water supply systems.

37. Food has been identified as a priority need for many internally displaced persons, as preliminary figures indicate that 47 per cent of them do not have access to the public distribution system. The World Food Programme (WFP) is still providing food for tuberculosis patients, pregnant and lactating women, and malnourished children and their families across the country. At the same time, UNICEF has stated that about one child in 13 is underweight, and one in five is undersized for their age.

38. Consultations with donors and the Government of Iraq continued throughout the period in order to mobilize support for the Strategic Framework for Humanitarian Action in Iraq, devised by United Nations and humanitarian actors in the country. The Humanitarian Working Group in Iraq has been working on the operations plan, which is intended to operationalize the Strategic Framework by clearly articulating the agreed modalities for both implementation and coordination that need to be put into place for future humanitarian action in Iraq. Of primary importance was developing flexible yet effective coordination mechanisms that would recognize the operational challenges, as well as ensuring that credible information gathering was undertaken for accurate and appropriate response planning. Of equal importance was the development of an advocacy strategy, which comprises a significant portion of the Strategic Framework and will be responsible for ensuring continued support and awareness among all stakeholders, especially on protection issues.

39. There is also a need to consider ways for adequate resourcing to enable both national and international non-governmental organizations as well as United Nations agencies to undertake immediate humanitarian assistance. This should complement the response and support mobilized by the Government of Iraq to ensure the provision of basic social services and assistance to vulnerable populations in Iraq. As the strategy to address the humanitarian crisis gains operational momentum, the United Nations will have to identify modalities for increasing its capacity to meet the growing demands for its leadership in this area. An initial step is the re-establishment of the presence of the Office for the Coordination of Humanitarian Affairs in support of the Office of the Deputy Special Representative of the Secretary-General and United Nations Humanitarian Coordinator, with an office in Amman.

40. At the same time, UNAMI and the United Nations country team will continue reconstruction and development programmes, including providing support for the International Compact with Iraq. Maintaining the longer-term perspective through development activities designed to support the Iraqi population in terms of governance, capacity-building and provision of basic services remain the guiding strategy, as outlined in the joint priority action plan.

41. The United Nations will assist in the creation of a Compact secretariat to provide the necessary support to the Government of Iraq to monitor the progress made by the Government and implementing agencies alike in achieving the objectives of the International Compact. The secretariat will not only provide immediate capacity to the Government but will aim to transfer that capacity to the relevant governmental institutions for future initiatives.

42. Only through assistance from the international community in this difficult period can Iraq fulfil its enormous human and economic potential. These complementary efforts—of providing immediate assistance to displaced Iraqis, while setting in motion interventions

aimed at the medium and longer-term goals embodied in the International Compact—will be the strategic direction of the United Nations in Iraq for the coming period.

IV. International Reconstruction Fund Facility for Iraq

43. As of 30 April 2007, the total contributions to the United Nations Development Group Iraq Trust Fund, one of the two funds of the International Reconstruction Fund Facility for Iraq, equalled $1.167 billion. A total of 148 projects valued at $1.02 billion were approved as at the end of April 2007 for funding under the Trust Fund. Continuing the significant progress in implementation, contracts worth cumulatively $730 million (72 per cent of approved funding) have been initiated and $622 million (61 per cent of approved funding) have been disbursed.

44. The fifth meeting of the International Reconstruction Fund Facility for Iraq Donor Committee was held in Istanbul on 20 March 2007. It was preceded by a meeting of the Iraq Reconstruction Forum on 19 March 2007, which provided an opportunity for the Government of Iraq to present reconstruction priorities to donors. The meetings were graciously hosted by the Government of Turkey, which also pledged a contribution of $10 million to the Facility, enabling Turkey to become a full member of the Donor Committee.

45. During the Donor Committee meeting, progress reports were presented by the United Nations and the World Bank to update donors on trust fund programmes, achievements, challenges and lessons learned. The Donor Committee reaffirmed its support for the Facility and concluded that it should remain an important vehicle for donors to support the implementation of the International Compact with Iraq. A commitment to increased Iraqi leadership was made through the decision reached during the meeting to pass the chairmanship of the Donor Committee from Canada to the co-chairmanship of the Government of Iraq and the Government of Italy. I would like to express my thanks to Ambassador Michael Bell and the Government of Canada for their effective chairmanship of the Facility over the past two years.

V. Security and operational issues

A. Assessment of the security situation

46. The security situation in Iraq remains complex and unpredictable and is a major limiting factor for the United Nations presence and activities in Iraq. The major development in the reporting period was the increased threat of indirect fire into the International Zone. These attacks have become increasingly concentrated and accurate and often consist of multiple mortars and rockets landing within minutes of each other. The International Zone experienced 17 attacks in March, 30 in April and 39 by 22 May alone. Since 19 February, indirect fire attacks have reportedly resulted in the deaths of 26 people in the International Zone. The security situation has been further compounded by the increase in car bombs in the vicinity of entry checkpoints to the International Zone. Armed groups operating in Baghdad have demonstrated their ability to strike at well-protected, strategic targets, such as the suicide bombing inside the Parliament building on 12 April.

47. The overall security environment presents a major challenge for the United Nations, particularly for its staff in the International Zone in Baghdad. Extensive mitigation measures were put in place within the International Zone to reduce the overall risk to United Nations personnel. Movement of staff inside the International Zone is controlled with a

curfew and limitations on travel. Visits to government buildings outside the International Zone require armed escorts, and UNAMI has practiced procedures for this requirement. Due to the risks of indirect fire, the United Nations staff working in Baghdad have temporarily been relocated to more hardened accommodation facilities. With existing mitigation measures and training of United Nations staff, risk is still assessed at the medium level.

48. National staff working at all locations in Iraq are exposed to high levels of risk, particularly when travelling to and from work. During the reporting period one national staff member was kidnapped and, in a separate incident, a second was reported as missing. Both were returning from holidays abroad and were travelling through Anbar province. Their whereabouts are still unknown.

49. While there was a decline in civilian casualties in Baghdad, the multinational force and Iraqi security forces have suffered higher levels of casualties. Since the commencement of the Baghdad security plan, the multinational force and the Iraqi Security Force have attempted to open outposts inside neighbourhoods. Their location at small security outposts in high-risk areas has exposed them to frequent attacks by armed groups.

50. In Mosul and Kirkuk insurgents maintain a capability to use a wide range of methods to carry out attacks against security forces and civilians. In these two cities the use of car bombs against facilities of the two Kurdish parties is a frequent occurrence. In Tal Afar the frequent use of suicide bombs against civilians has led to increased tensions between the communities in the area. The recent use of high-explosive truck bombs in Erbil and Makhmour, some 70 km south-west of Erbil, resulting in hundreds of casualties, may indicate deterioration of the security situation in previously stable areas.

51. Baghdad security plan operations appear to have forced some insurgent activity out of Baghdad and into Diyala, Salah al Din and Tamim provinces. Although there have been reduced incident levels in Fallujah and Ramadi, the violence in Anbar has shifted to smaller towns and villages. This is partly a reflection of the growing conflict between Al-Qaida and the tribal leaders in Anbar province. In Basra the increase in indirect fire attacks on multinational force installations and Basra Palace led to a reduced United Nations presence. With redeployment of the multinational force from the Basra Palace to Basra Air Station, and consequent inability to provide adequate security at the site, all remaining United Nations staff and equipment were withdrawn from Basra Palace Island in April.

52. The addition of overhead protection to the UNAMI living accommodation in Baghdad is scheduled for completion soon. While this will significantly enhance the protection of United Nations staff, there is still concern that the level of overhead protection will not be sufficient to withstand direct impacts of larger-calibre ordnance, such as 107-mm and 122-mm rockets, which are increasingly used in attacks on the International Zone. The only long-term solution to this dilemma is the expeditious construction of a hardened integrated compound, with the necessary structural integrity to withstand impacts from high-calibre ordnance.

B. Facilities, logistics and support

53. Providing secure and adequate facilities for the United Nations staff in Iraq remains a priority support issue. Facilities currently available in Baghdad, on a lease or rental basis, fall far short of adequate long-term arrangements to provide secure working conditions for

United Nations staff. In light of this it would appear that the only way to sustain the mission in the coming months and years will be to construct purpose-built structures. These structures will need to meet the very challenging security environment in Baghdad. Their provision will make the difference between the United Nations mission being able to operate effectively in the future or having to wind down operations due to the unacceptable security risks currently faced by the Mission. Accordingly, it is my intention to make arrangements for the expeditious construction of a new United Nations building in Baghdad. Although the high level of specification for security features will inevitably lead to relatively high construction costs, it is felt that there is no realistic alternative if the Mission is to continue operations. With the support of the Security Council for this proposal, I intend to make arrangements for funding the new construction within the framework of the budgeting provisions for special political missions.

54. The redeployment of multinational forces from the Basra Palace compound has led to a reduction in perimeter security at the site. This in turn has led to the withdrawal of United Nations staff and assets from the UNAMI compound at the Basra Palace Island on 28 April 2007. Possibilities for establishing a United Nations presence at a new location in Basra are being explored. UNAMI and the United Nations country team are also considering the possibility of expanding the United Nations compound in Erbil and United Nations operations in the north of Iraq.

55. UNAMI continues to maintain offices in Kuwait city and Amman in support of operations in Iraq. However, there are plans to consolidate UNAMI offices outside Iraq in a single location in Amman by the end of 2008. This will result in the eventual closure of the UNAMI office in Kuwait.

56. As at 31 May, a total of \$2.6 million had been pledged in new contributions for the Distinct Entity Trust Fund. I am grateful to the Governments of Finland, Germany, Ireland, Luxembourg, the Netherlands, Poland and Sweden for their generous contributions. However, additional funding from other Member States is required to ensure that the force providing security for the United Nations presence under the distinct entity ("middle ring") is well-resourced for the remainder of the year.

57. In January 2007, the Government of Denmark provided the Mission with a dedicated fixed-wing aircraft which partially facilitated the independent movement of personnel and materials between Amman, Erbil, Kuwait and the Baghdad International Airport. Movement of personnel and staff between the airport and the International Zone is solely performed with multinational force support. Denmark is unable to extend the arrangement beyond June 2007. The deployment of alternative aircraft, including commercial rotary-wing helicopters, is being explored. I am grateful to the Government of Denmark for its support and I reiterate my request to Member States to be forthcoming in providing aviation support to UNAMI.

C. Agreements

58. The status-of-mission agreement between the United Nations and the Government of Iraq was signed in June 2005. It has been agreed between the two parties that the agreement is to go into effect on the basis of an exchange of diplomatic notes attesting to ratification. The United Nations submitted its note in 2005, but the corresponding note on the part of the Government of Iraq has not yet been delivered. Consequently, the agreement has not

been ratified, despite numerous follow-up requests. I hope that this ratification will be provided in short order, as this document provides a critical legal foundation for the ongoing work of the United Nations in Iraq.

59. The subordinate protocols mandated by the 8 December 2005 Agreement between the United Nations Organization and the Government of the United States of America Concerning the Establishment of Security for the United Nations Assistance Mission for Iraq, are virtually complete. However, as a result of the turnover of multinational force officials assigned to this file, the finalization and signature/receipt of these protocols has not yet been achieved. I hope that, as a result of the recent arrival of the replacement of the outgoing multinational force liaison officer to UNAMI, this process can be finalized by the end of July.

VI. Observations

60. Iraq's political and social fabric continued to come under considerable strain during the reporting period as a result of ongoing political, sectarian and criminal violence. Despite the efforts of the Iraqi and multinational security forces to stem violence, progress was slower than had been hoped when security initiatives were launched at the start of 2007. This has been demonstrated by continued attacks on the civilian population, physical infrastructure and political institutions such as the Council of Representatives.

61. From my discussions with Iraqi leaders, senior officials in the region and the wider international community, it is clear that there is a growing understanding that the complex problems facing Iraq are interconnected and their urgent resolution is in the interests of the region and, indeed, the world. Several initiatives displayed a new level of solidarity in tackling the impact of the crisis in Iraq. The April conference in Geneva on displaced Iraqis was an important first step in seeking collective solutions to a growing problem that is affecting the region as a whole. Similarly the discussions at the launch of the International Compact with Iraq in Sharm el-Sheikh on 3 May 2007 and at the meeting of the neighbouring States, the Permanent Five and G-8 the following day were notable for their sober appreciation of the need to shore up the Government of Iraq's reconciliation efforts by concerted international support. The decision to activate the neighbouring States' technical committees on security, displaced Iraqis and energy supplies was further evidence of a willingness to strengthen collaboration on issues important to Iraq and its neighbours. I encourage all concerned to maintain this momentum and seek further concrete ways to foster greater cooperation for addressing Iraqi and related regional problems.

62. The Sharm el-Sheikh meetings demonstrated that the international community, while recognizing the complexities of the situation, is willing to work together in solidarity with Iraq. It is now incumbent upon Iraqi leaders to implement the commitments for the benefit of the citizens of Iraq. Given the continued violence, which is testing the country's unity, additional efforts are needed for confidence-building through national dialogue. The United Nations stands ready to support the Government of Iraq in this regard.

63. The constitutional review process and the work of the Council of Representatives provided an opportunity for expanding political dialogue. The Constitutional Review Committee is to be commended for its constructive work. A package of its recommendations could address some of the perceived shortcomings of the Constitution. However, important constitutional issues remain unaddressed in the recommendations put forward to

the Council of Representatives. As a result, progress was delayed on other vital legislative requirements such as laws on hydrocarbons, provincial elections, de-Baathification and amnesty. The establishment of the Independent High Electoral Commission was a notable achievement during the reporting period.

64. The political process in Iraq is entering an exceptionally sensitive phase. It requires efforts at building bridges and calls for measures aimed at stabilizing the country. Therefore contentious issues, such as the referendum on Kirkuk and other disputed areas, must be approached carefully. Solutions must be found through sustained national dialogue, the patient search for compromise, and within the framework of the Constitution.

65. As was demonstrated through the preparations for the Sharm el-Sheikh meetings, the United Nations remains committed to assisting the Government of Iraq. There have been growing calls for a larger United Nations role in Iraq. Circumstance permitting, I would consider an expanded role and presence in Iraq where possible. For this, clear direction from the Security Council and the Government of Iraq would be essential and better coordination with our major international partners would also be welcomed. Of particular importance would be the creation of necessary infrastructure and operational conditions for the United Nations to play its role. This includes adequate protection and security arrangements, air support and, in particular, the construction of secure facilities. I am deeply appreciative of Member States that have contributed to the United Nations operations in Iraq by providing funds and technical assets or by deploying troops for protection. It is my hope that the Security Council and States Members of the United Nations will continue to provide strong political and logistical support for the Organization's presence in Iraq.

66. I wish to take this opportunity to thank my Special Representative for Iraq, Ashraf Jehangir Qazi, for his continued leadership and the Mission's national and international staff, as well as the personnel of United Nations agencies, programmes and funds, for their dedicated work in fulfilling their mandated tasks. Finally, I would like to thank my Deputy Special Representative for Iraq, Jean-Marie Fakhouri, who is leaving the Mission on 30 June, for his service and valuable work under extremely difficult conditions. He has made a lasting impact on the delivery of humanitarian assistance, development and reconstruction activities in Iraq, and I wish him all the best in his new endeavours.

D. Kosovo

1. Report of the Secretary-General on the United Nations Interim Administration Mission in Kosovo, 20 November 2006 (S/2006/906)

I. Introduction

1. The present report is submitted pursuant to Security Council resolution 1244 (1999) of 10 June 1999, by which the Council decided to establish the United Nations Interim Administration Mission in Kosovo (UNMIK) and requested the Secretary-General to report at regular intervals on the implementation of the mandate. It covers the activities of UNMIK and developments in Kosovo (Serbia), from 15 August to 31 October 2006.

II. Political Assessment

2. The future status process for Kosovo continued to advance during the reporting period. My Special Envoy for the future status process for Kosovo, Martti Ahtisaari, convened further rounds of direct talks between Belgrade and Pristina on decentralization, cultural and religious heritage and community rights on 7 and 8 September. The talks gave the sides an opportunity to engage in a substantial exchange of views on the issues at hand, without resulting, however, in any major shifts of position. Overall, the positions of the parties in each of the areas discussed remain far apart. Following the talks, my Special Envoy brought the sides together for another round of direct discussions on the delineation of new municipalities, including Mitrovica, in the context of the talks on decentralization which, however, did not result in any substantial progress. Expert-level consultations with the sides continued throughout the reporting period.

Political situation

3. The political situation in Kosovo during the reporting period was characterized by an intensified focus on the future status process, which continues to be the dominating factor in political life in Kosovo. High expectations on the part of Kosovo Albanians, coupled with recent speculations about a possible delay in the process, have led to a feeling of uncertainty as to the way ahead and are likely to be a source of instability if momentum slows. There is a widespread feeling among them that a tangible delay in the process would entail high political and economic costs. Fringe groups and extremists on all sides stand ready to exploit more widespread frustration. Uncertainty and frustration are also prevalent among the Serbs and other minority populations, raising the potential for instability pending a political solution.

4. Members of the Kosovo negotiating team have been confronted with increased pressures, both internally and externally. Many feel that the negotiation process is exhausted and that there is no more room for compromise. The issue of decentralization has led to protests in a number of Kosovo Albanian-majority municipalities affected by the decentralization plan proposed by the team. In the municipality of Gnjilane, demonstrations were organized by the local municipal leadership in concert with the War Veterans' Associations and the Self-Determination movement. Similar protests were held in Vitina, Novo Brdo and Kamenica.

5. The beginning of the Democratic League for Kosovo (LDK) party election process has been another source of pressure on the unity of the negotiating team and the Kosovo Government. On 5 September, the LDK Presidency proposed Kosovo President Sejdiu as its candidate for the party chief position, despite the stipulation in the constitutional framework that the President of Kosovo shall not hold any other office or employment. My Special Representative made it clear to President Sejdiu that, in the event of his election as party President, he would immediately have to decide either to resign as President of Kosovo or not to assume the office of party President. President Sejdiu nevertheless accepted the nomination and will run against the former Assembly President, Nexhat Daci.

6. The new Serbian Constitution, which describes Kosovo as an integral part of Serbia, was heavily criticized in a statement of the Kosovo Assembly. The referendum in Kosovo on the Serbian Constitution on 28 and 29 October was conducted without incident.

7. Security incidents involving Kosovo Serbs continued during the reporting period. On 26 August, a grenade attack on a café at the northern end of the main bridge over the river in Mitrovica injured 9 people, leading to protests by 300 Kosovo Serbs and the temporary closure of the main bridge. A Kosovo Albanian juvenile suspect was arrested in connection with the attack and remains under house detention. A grenade attack on a Kosovo Serb returnee family in the town of Klina on 19 September wounded a family of four and further raised tensions in the community. All leaders of the Kosovo Provisional Institutions of Self-Government and Kosovo Albanian political leaders condemned the attacks. Despite these incidents, the overall number of potentially ethnically motivated crimes has considerably decreased in the course of this year.

8. The Mission made strenuous and successful efforts to encourage members of the negotiating team and the Provisional Institutions more widely to reach out to majority and minority communities. Prime Minister Agim Çeku has been particularly active in reaching out to Kosovo's minority communities and in responding to security incidents, while the negotiating team has made efforts in explaining the political process and its role to citizens, particularly in areas that will be affected by the team's decentralization proposal in the negotiations.

9. There has still been virtually no Kosovo Serb participation in Kosovo's political institutions at the central level. Reserved positions in the Assembly and Government have not been taken up and the Minister of Communities and Returns remains the only Kosovo Serb member of the Government. While some participation of members of the Serbian List for Kosovo and Metohija in Assembly committee work has taken place and two more small, independent Kosovo Serb parties have been formed, the engagement of the Kosovo Serb community in and with the Provisional Institutions remains severely limited. This is particularly true in the northern municipalities dominated by the Serb National Council, which continue their boycott of contacts with the Provisional Institutions. While my Special Representative has worked to increase the level of communication with the leaders of the Serb National Council, they continue to operate a separate sphere of local governance, closely linked with the institutions of Serbia.

Security

10. Coordinated action by UNMIK police and the Kosovo Force (KFOR), supported by the international community, has for now stabilized the situation in the north of Kosovo, at least on the surface. Operations Stringent Security (focusing on preventing and investigating

crime against Kosovo Serbs) and Safety Chain (designed to prevent and resolve attacks with political motives) continued.

11. The Mission and the Provisional Institutions have moved forward in transferring aspects of security to greater local control. The establishment of the Kosovo Ministry of Justice is proceeding well, with good cooperation between the UNMIK Department of Justice and the Ministry, following the positive outcome of the interim review and the transfer of the second phase of competencies in April 2006 (see S/2006/707, para. 17). Attempts by the Ministry to exercise closer control over the Office of the Public Prosecutor of Kosovo is a cause for possible concern, but the drafting of a law on prosecutors is being closely monitored to ensure it meets European standards in safeguarding their independence. Also following the positive interim review and the transfer of additional competencies relating to oversight of the Kosovo Police Service (KPS), the consolidation of the Kosovo Ministry of Internal Affairs is progressing. The Kosovo Police Inspectorate has been established and its members are currently undergoing training by the Organization for Security and Cooperation in Europe (OSCE). With support from the European Agency for Reconstruction and the United Kingdom Department for International Development, the Ministry has developed its mission statement and strategic plan. UNMIK and the donor agencies are focusing on four priority areas: clarification of the role and authority of the Ministry vis-à-vis KPS; the creation of capacity for managing migration and repatriation; improved capability for emergency preparedness and response; and civil registration and documentation.

Standards

12. Sustained progress on standards has been an encouraging feature throughout 2006, and the Provisional Institutions deserve credit for continuing to give priority and emphasis to the programme. The standards programme in turn continues to strengthen the Kosovo institutions, which gain more experience in coordination and implementation, but its impact upon Kosovo Serb communities is limited by their own reluctance to cooperate with the Pristina authorities. The 13 priorities identified by the Contact Group in June continued to receive close attention. All were either achieved or show substantial progress. The Provisional Institutions are also now creating structures and workplans to implement the European Partnership Action Plan adopted in August (S/2006/707, para. 14). The standards programme now forms an integral part of that Plan. A detailed technical assessment of standards implementation for the period from 15 August to 31 October, prepared by my Special Representative, is contained in annex I to the present report.

Decentralization

13. Further progress has been made in the implementation of the three existing pilot municipal units in Kosovo. Each of the units now has the capability to issue civil status documents (birth, marriage and death certificates), certified by the Ministry of Public Services, and generate its own revenue, though this aspect remains limited at this stage. More importantly, the Kosovo Ministry of Local Government Administration, the Ministry of Finance and Economy, the three units and the host municipalities from which they are derived, signed a memorandum of understanding for the support for and gradual transfer of responsibilities from the host municipalities to the units. The 2007 budget cycle will treat the units as separate budget organizations, which is a necessary basis for their transformation into full-fledged municipalities in 2007. The units will also collect and distribute property taxes,

manage education and health grants and, in coordination with other signatories of the memorandum, jointly manage schools and primary health-care facilities. The Ministry will also conduct an assessment jointly with UNMIK on the current process of establishing other units and their performance. That assessment could serve as a valuable tool for implementation of the decentralization proposal led by the Office of the Special Envoy for the future status process for Kosovo.

Cultural and religious heritage

14. Weekly security meetings between UNMIK, UNMIK police, KPS and focal points on cultural heritage at the central and regional levels are now held to improve communication and raise the awareness of cultural heritage protection within KPS. There was a decrease in the incidents reported against Serbian Orthodox Church sites with a corresponding increase in the number of patrols by KPS to cultural heritage sites during the reporting period. In October, UNMIK also intervened through the Provisional Institutions to stop illegal constructions in the vicinity of the cultural heritage sites included by the Office of the Special Envoy in the list of sites for proposed protective zones. As September was Cultural Heritage Month, UNMIK organized a second round of its heritage-awareness campaign in 30 municipalities. On 9 October, the Assembly passed the Law on Cultural Heritage, including key passages insisted upon by the Special Envoy, the Council of Europe and UNMIK, with regard to additional legislation on religious communities and potential amendments to harmonize the law with future status agreements.

15. The reconstruction of Serbian Orthodox Churches damaged or destroyed during the violence of March 2004 has moved forward. Extensive interventions on seven sites under the direction of the Reconstruction Implementation Commission, chaired by the Council of Europe, have been under way since the end of August and will be completed by mid-December 2006. The United Nations Educational, Scientific and Cultural Organization (UNESCO) and UNMIK signed an umbrella memorandum of understanding on 11 September, which will provide a framework for the implementation of projects arising from the pledges made at the 2005 UNESCO donor conference. For implementation to begin, supplementary memorandums must be signed on a project-by-project basis. UNMIK and UNESCO are currently in the process of negotiating the first of these memorandums regarding a project funded by the United States of America.

Dialogue

16. The dialogue between Pristina and Belgrade on technical issues made moderate progress. The Working Group on Missing Persons met in closed session in Pristina on two occasions. On 1 September, the delegations agreed that work should focus on suspected burial sites where additional data should be sought and ensuring that no potential site has been omitted. The meeting on 19 October followed up on issues raised and commitments made at previous meetings. However, as at previous sessions, no new concrete information was offered by either delegation on the fate or location of missing persons. Discussions focused on objectives to be achieved in order for the Chair from the International Committee of the Red Cross, to be able to convene the next formal session of the Working Group.

17. Renewed commitment to the dialogue process was evident in relation to the work of the Working Group on Energy, which met in Belgrade on 26 October. Discussions covered energy transmission and supply, gas supply and possibilities for cooperation concerning

Belgrade's offers of unconditional supply of free electricity to Kosovo and bill collection in some areas. The Working Group on Returns has not met since 23 June owing to scheduling problems on all sides, and there have subsequently been delays in the establishment of a technical subgroup agreed upon at that meeting. The Working Group on Transport and Telecommunications remained dormant during the reporting period.

Returns

18. While remaining steady, the number of minority returns to Kosovo is unsatisfactory: UNHCR estimates that 1,173 minority community members returned from January to September 2006. The primary factors affecting returns continue to include lack of economic opportunities, uncertainty about the future status of Kosovo, and, to a much lesser degree than in the past, security. The attitude of receiving communities continues to improve. Municipalities are also demonstrating the capacity to directly implement components of returns projects, making them more sustainable and less expensive. The Office of the Prime Minister took corrective action to allocate remaining funds to support returns of internally displaced persons to Kosovo. However, a funding shortfall of €20 million affects 22 approved return projects, all of which have been recently re-evaluated with stakeholders to bring down projected costs. Cooperation on returns between the Provisional Institutions and the Government of Serbia continued at the local level, particularly on matters of humanitarian concern. From January to September 2006, the overall number of persons involuntarily repatriated from host countries reached 2,697. Repatriation functions are in the process of being transferred to the Provisional Institutions.

Economy

19. A number of significant economic developments took place during the reporting period. Following an agreement with the World Bank, other donors and UNMIK, the Kosovo Ministry of Energy and Mining issued, on 19 August, a request for expressions of interest for the development of a new lignite mining facility, its associated new electricity generating and transmission capacity, as well as the rehabilitation of some of Kosovo's existing electricity generating facilities. The issuance of the request was followed, on 10 and 11 October, by a Ministry-sponsored international investors' conference, promoting the project to potential investors and acquainting them with Kosovo's existing power generation capacities. On 24 August, the Special Representative signed a regulation that transformed the Banking and Payments Authority of Kosovo into the Central Banking Authority of Kosovo. One of its main objectives was to transfer to local control the Governing Board of that important institution, as well as to strengthen its powers in regulating and managing Kosovo's financial system. The newly established body has produced Kosovo's first balance of payments report in accordance with the guidelines of the International Monetary Fund.

Regional cooperation

20. During the reporting period, economic cooperation and trade with regional neighbours was the highlight in terms of regional cooperation. Two bilateral free trade agreements were signed on 28 September and 19 October, with Croatia and with Bosnia and Herzegovina, respectively. Negotiations on a single agreement for the region of South-East Europe were concluded in Brussels on 20 October. On 17 October, UNMIK and the Provisional Institutions signed two memorandums of understanding with Albania on cooperation in the field of energy and for the construction of a new 400 kV connection line between Kosovo and Albania.

Future international arrangements and transition

21. My Special Representative has intensified preparations for the end of the UNMIK mandate following an eventual political settlement, while recognizing that the Mission will retain all of its authority and existing responsibilities for as long as resolution 1244 (1999) remains in force. Planning has included an analysis of all tasks performed by UNMIK and of action necessary to achieve a successful transition. The Steering Group has continued to meet in Pristina under the chairmanship of my Special Representative, bringing together all interested parties from the international community, including representatives of the planned future International Civilian Office.

III. Observations

22. The future status process has enabled the parties to engage in focused negotiations, in which the representatives of Serbia and Kosovo have clearly delineated their respective positions. I remain disappointed that the process has resulted in only uneven progress and limited agreement on some specific elements, and that the two sides have not moved from their diametrically opposed views on the future status of Kosovo. At the same time, I call upon all sides to refrain from any unilateral actions and statements.

23. It is important to keep the momentum in the political process. Everyone needs clarity with regard to the future status of Kosovo. The sustained support of the Council and key Member States is essential, and I call upon them to keep Kosovo on their agenda as we move forward.

24. I welcome the commitment shown throughout 2006 by the Government of Kosovo to the implementation of the standards, and especially to the 13 priority points identified by the Contact Group. The progress made in the standards programme, and the experience and skills developed by implementing it, have strengthened the institutions of Kosovo and contributed to building a foundation for future development. As we look ahead, the leaders and people of Kosovo need to bear in mind that a political settlement will not be a panacea for all challenges ahead. It remains important for the Kosovo authorities to take the progress achieved still further, and not to lose sight of all the standards that are important to developing more stable and effective institutions and to improving the delivery of services to all people in Kosovo.

25. Progress will be achieved by demonstrating through actions, not words, that everyone has a future in Kosovo. It will be important that substantive actions take precedence over symbolism with the aim of promoting confidence and stability. I would urge the leaders of all communities not to yield to the temptation of divisive words and actions, but to embrace the opportunity to promote reconciliation and dialogue. It takes more courage and strength to do so, and the main burden rests with the leaders of the majority population.

26. I call on the members of the negotiating team to remain united and commend them for their efforts to reach out to all communities in Kosovo. I appeal to them to continue their efforts in order to keep the communities of Kosovo informed about the future status process and to prepare the population for the eventual settlement.

27. I note with dismay that violent attacks continue to be made by a few in an attempt to effect political change. I am resolute in condemning such violence and call upon the people of Kosovo to help their institutions defeat it. Political developments and timelines will not be dictated by the streets, and violence will not be tolerated. Leaders will be held responsible for managing expectations and controlling possible discontent.

28. I am disappointed that Kosovo Serb leaders continue to remain outside the political process in Kosovo. This is a disservice to their community. I once again call on the Belgrade authorities to remove all impediments to Kosovo Serb participation in Kosovo institutions, and on the Kosovo Serb leaders to engage with the Provisional Institutions.

29. I would like to extend my appreciation to my Special Representative, Joachim Rücker, for his dedication and work on behalf of the Organization. I also express my gratitude to the staff of UNMIK for their continued steadfastness in carrying out their challenging tasks, often in difficult circumstances. I would like to extend my appreciation to KFOR, our partners within UNMIK—the European Union and OSCE—and the United Nations agencies, funds and programmes as well as other organizations, contributors and donors for their commitment and valuable support. I welcome the close cooperation between all stakeholders in preparing the ground for a transition that will follow an eventual determination of the future status of Kosovo.

Annex I
Technical assessment of progress in implementation of the standards for Kosovo

Prepared by the Special Representative of the Secretary-General for Kosovo, 6 November 2006

1. The standards programme continued to benefit from the momentum built up during 2006, and from the continued attention and effort on the part of the Kosovo authorities. As a whole, the programme now presents a picture of institutions gradually gaining in strength and as a result improving their performance.

2. The 13 priority points presented to the Government of Kosovo by the Contact Group in June continued to be a focus of particular attention; the present report begins with an analysis of the progress made on them. The Provisional Institutions of Self-Government in Kosovo made a sustained effort to fulfil the tasks entailed and by the end of the reporting period, this subset of objectives had been either substantially or wholly achieved.

The 13 priorities for standards implementation

3. **Priority 1.** The Law on Freedom of Religion was adopted on 13 July by the Assembly and promulgated on 24 August. The Law on Cultural Heritage was approved by the Assembly on 9 October. On 27 July, the Assembly adopted the Law on Languages which provides for full equality of Albanian and Serbian as official languages of Kosovo, and requires other minority languages to be official in municipalities where the respective minority constitutes at least 5 per cent of the population. On 21 September, the Assembly adopted an amendment establishing Turkish as an official language in the municipality of Prizren, irrespective of the size of the Turkish community there. That law was promulgated on 20 October.

4. **Priority 2.** The Kosovo Protection Corps (KPC) was assigned a major role in completing operational aspects of the reconstruction work in Svinjarë/Svinjare. While the deadline of 31 October was not met, partly because of late availability of funding and partly because the original scope of the work was later extended, the bulk of the work is completed and the balance under way. A panel for resolving other claims, run by the Provisional Institutions, recommended to the Prime Minister on 30 October that 11 outstanding contractors' claims should be paid, but no recommendations were made on outstanding commercial claims.

5. **Priority 3.** The Kosovo Property Agency launched a rental scheme pilot project covering 200 of the 5,294 properties currently under its administration. To date, 195 property right holders have been contacted, of whom 111 have signed an agreement with the Agency. A total of 28 tenants have begun to pay rent. Following pressure from the Provisional Institutions, several banks have agreed to reduce their charges on transfers outside Kosovo. The Provisional Institutions have begun an advertising campaign on television to promote public awareness of the scheme. The pilot scheme now needs to be extended to all residential properties under administration.

6. **Priority 4.** A total of 1,150 Housing and Property Directorate decisions remain to be implemented, down from 2,804 in June. Standard operating procedures for the Kosovo Police Service (KPS) to deter and remedy reoccupation of houses after eviction were approved in August and are currently being amended in discussions between the police and the Kosovo Property Agency.

7. **Priority 5.** On 31 August, UNMIK and the Ministry of Transport and Communications signed a memorandum of understanding governing the transfer of the competency of UNMIK to provide humanitarian train and bus services for minority communities in Kosovo. There will be no change in the current service providers until 2008. Affected communities will be invited to participate in the selection of new bus routes in 2007.

8. **Priority 6.** The Government of Kosovo and UNMIK reached an agreement on 30 June on the allocation of the remaining €4,700,000 in returns project funds from the Ministry of Returns and Communities. Under the agreement, €1,100,000 was to be transferred to KPC in support of the Svinjarë/Svinjare reconstruction programme. However, it was found that the Ministry had spent the funds on other activities. The Government then identified €1,100,000 outside the Ministry's budget and allocated it to KPC as part of the mid-year review process.

9. **Priority 7.** Regarding March 2004 cases, of the 323 criminal charges originally made in local courts, excluding Minor Offences courts,1 198 have led to indictments which in turn have brought 134 convictions. A total of 28 cases remain under investigation. International courts have indicted 31 defendants, of whom 26 have been found guilty and 4 await trial. During the reporting period, police made a total of 12 arrests on charges of arson committed in the municipality of Fushë Kosovë/Kosovo Polje during the March 2004 disturbances. International prosecutors and UNMIK police are reviewing all reported incidents to compile an archive and database that will help to show how much remains to be done and facilitate future prosecutions.

10. **Priority 8.** On 1 September, the Ministry of Public Services issued administrative instruction No. MPS 2006/10 defining the rules and procedures of central-level monitoring of the use of official languages. The Government has also compiled the first CD-ROM containing all Government decisions and regulations in the official languages. Copies of the CD-ROM were distributed to ministries and municipalities. All ministries now have staffed translation units, but full implementation of the official language policy will require further training and even more staff, especially at the municipal level.

11. **Priority 9.** On 11 July, the Government distributed the first grants from its Minority Media Fund to 11 recipients.

12. **Priority 10.** All 11 planned Court Liaison Offices have been established and are now fully operational. On 6 September, the Police Commissioner and the Minister for Internal Affairs agreed to establish 17 new submunicipal police stations. To date, 10 are fully operational while the funding or logistical problems affecting the remainder are being addressed. Two proposed substations have not been accepted by their target communities.

13. **Priority 11.** A Director of the Anti-Corruption Agency was appointed on 17 July. The Agency currently employs 7 staff and the recruitment of another 15 is under way. Plans envisage a total of 35 staff members and a move to new premises in 2007. The Ministry of Justice and the Office of the Prime Minister have appointed officers responsible for maintaining a registry of gifts.

14. **Priority 12.** The Council of the Independent Media Commission was established on 28 August, thus finalizing the handover of regulating radio and television from UNMIK to the Provisional Institutions. The Commission replaces the institution of the temporary Media Commissioner, which was established in 2000. The Council, consisting of two international and five resident members, has selected a chairperson, a deputy chairperson and a chief executive officer.

15. **Priority 13.** The draft law to amend the Law on Public Procurement passed its first reading in the Assembly on 9 October.

Functioning democratic institutions

16. The Government continues to hold in trust the salaries of the Kosovo Serbs who have left the payroll of the Provisional Institutions.

17. An administrative instruction of 10 August of the Ministry of Finance and Economy on the implementation of fair share financing requires municipalities to submit by 15 December an annual plan for minority projects and expenditure for 2007 in consultation with the heads of the municipal community offices and the concerned minority communities.

18. Language units are established in 22 municipalities, while six have only one interpreter/translator and two (Zveçan/Zvečan and Zubin Potok) did not employ any interpreters or translators. All ministries and most municipalities now have simultaneous interpretation equipment, although some municipalities report that it is either underutilized or not properly installed. Most municipalities are fully or partially language-compliant in respect of road and streets signs and municipal buildings.

19. The Ministry of Public Services and the Ministry of Local Government Administration continued to monitor language compliance at the central and municipal levels, respectively, compiling statistics and producing reports, which they plan to issue on a monthly basis. To date, some 50 per cent of municipalities have reported to the Ministry of Local Government Administration.

20. Public grievance redressal offices have been established in all ministries and municipalities. Some of the offices have begun submitting reports on the number of complaints received and addressed.

21. Implementation of a long-term strategy to increase the number and improve the position of women in the Provisional Institutions, drafted by the Office of Gender Equality and approved by the Government on 3 May, has begun with training and the gathering of statistics.

22. Since the first edition of the Official Gazette of the Provisional Institutions in June, issues have been published on a monthly basis, including on the website of the Official Gazette.

23. Since its establishment at the end of August, the Independent Media Council has adopted its rules and procedures, a code of ethics and broadcast policy and sanctioning guidelines. The Council also established working groups regarding the future licensing process and related guidelines, cable regulation and advertising policies, as well as the protection of minors.

24. Little progress has been made in extending the reach of the signal of Kosovo Radio-Television (RTK) from the current 75 per cent of the population to 90 per cent, as required by law. In September, however, RTK started to broadcast its minority programmes via satellite, thus reaching minority community areas not covered terrestrially.

Functioning democratic institutions: challenges ahead

25. The unwillingness of many Kosovo Serbs to cooperate with the Provisional Institutions remains a challenge and an obstacle to the integration of Kosovo Serb communities into mainstream society.

26. While the monitoring of language compliance has improved, enforcement needs to develop further. An action plan is needed to implement the Law on Languages. Skills need to be developed to analyse collected data and derive policy recommendations.

27. The long-term strategy to increase the number and improve the position of women in the Provisional Institutions, drafted by the Office of Gender Equality and approved by the Government on 3 May, should be further implemented.

28. The Office of the Official Gazette needs additional capacity and resources to develop a systematic approach to the publication of laws and secondary legislation, as well as a database and index to make the extensive existing body of laws accessible.

Rule of law

29. The transfer of additional competencies to the Ministry of Justice and the Ministry of Internal Affairs continues within the parameters established in the relevant UNMIK legislation. Penal management and missing persons and forensics have been transferred to the Ministry of Justice. Minority representation stands at 10.97 per cent in the Ministry of Internal Affairs and 15.16 per cent in the Ministry of Justice. Both ministries are preparing their strategic action plans for the next five years and have adequate financial management systems in place.

30. On 31 August, following the transfer of border police stations and boundary crossings to KPS control, Gates 3 and 4 were handed over. Gates 5 and 6 followed on 13 September. Recently, the Regional Command West and Regional Command North also were transferred. The Directorate of Organized Crime has been partially transferred.

31. The Kosovo Police Service and the Kosovo Correctional Service continue to have a multi-ethnic composition, with 16.09 per cent of minority staff in the Police Service and 14.45 per cent in the Correctional Service.

32. As a result of a recruitment campaign for judges and prosecutors targeting members of underrepresented communities, 15 recommendations for judicial and prosecutorial appointments have been forwarded to the Special Representative of the Secretary-General for appointment, including 8 from underrepresented communities. Non-Albanian representation remained constant from the previous reporting period, accounting for 9 per cent of judges and 8 per cent of prosecutors. Women's representation also remained constant, at 26 and 18 per cent, respectively.

33. The civil court backlog increased 1.43 per cent in comparison to the previous reporting period, to 45,699 cases. A team of experts has been recruited by the European Agency for Reconstruction to assist with the implementation of the case management information system.

34. Inter-ethnic crime continues at a low level, though dramatic incidents, such as the hand grenade attack on the Dolce Vita bar in Mitrovicë/a on 26 August, continue to make headlines.

Rule of law: challenges ahead

35. More work is needed to develop and implement a comprehensive judicial and prosecutorial vetting procedure to ensure the integrity and competence of judges and prosecutors.

36. Further efforts are needed to protect witnesses from intimidation. Legislation on witness protection needs to be finalized.

37. To supplement the targeted recruitment drive, more work is needed to increase the number of underrepresented communities among judges and prosecutors. The Ministry of Justice needs to target non-Albanian communities and run an outreach programme to attract applications from recent law school graduates, especially Serbs.

38. Additional efforts are necessary to implement the case management information system to enable more efficient and transparent case management. Judges, prosecutors and court staff need to be encouraged to use the system.

Freedom of movement

39. The police continue to assess the security situation as stable but fragile. Regular surveys conducted by KPS show that over 94 per cent of minorities travel outside their area of residence and that their perception of freedom of movement remains good; between 91 and 96 per cent of those interviewed stated that the situation was satisfactory.

40. The main bridge across the Ibar in Mitrovicë/a was closed for several weeks following the incident reported in paragraph 34 above.

41. Political and institutional leaders continue to condemn incidents of violence and vandalism when they occur, such as the attack on Kosovo Serbs in Klinë/a on 20 September. The Prime Minister visited the victims shortly after the incidents.

42. On 8 September, the Prime Minister participated in a conference on inter-ethnic dialogue to show support for dialogue initiatives. The Confidence Building Task Force and the Communities Security Council established during the previous reporting period did not meet during the reporting period, though the latter initiative led to the approval of a number of quick-impact projects in vulnerable communities.

43. The number of vehicle technical control sites in non-Albanian communities continues to increase. There are currently seven inspection sites designated in such areas, of which four, including Leposaviq/ć, are operational, while the remaining three still need to fulfil the technical criteria for licensing.

44. Escorts and checkpoints continue to be reduced throughout Kosovo without affecting freedom of movement. Non-Albanian civil servants at the central and municipal levels travel to work without escorts.

45. The Kosovo Serb basketball team "Bambi" from Mitrovicë/a joined the Kosovo league and has played several games in various locations, despite intimidation of the trainer by members of the Kosovo Serb community.

Freedom of movement: challenges ahead

46. More direct contact between police and families is necessary in areas where juveniles still occasionally throw stones at vehicles thought to be carrying Serbs.

Sustainable returns and the rights of communities

47. An increasing number of municipalities have shown considerable progress in taking over the ownership of the returns process, while central-level involvement remains impeded by serious financial and administrative management problems in the Ministry of Returns and Communities.

48. All relevant municipalities have developed municipal returns strategies, though those in Zveçan/Zveçan and Leposaviq/č still need to be endorsed by the Municipal Assembly.

49. In all municipalities in which municipal working groups on returns are functioning, the chairmanship now lies with the municipality. Task forces are functioning in locations with ongoing organized returns as well as in Mitrovicë/a, where several task forces cover the gap left by the absence of a working group. In most cases, the displaced are represented in the working group and/or taskforce. With some exceptions (Leposaviq/ć, Malishevë/Mališevo, Gjakovë/Djakovica, Gjilan/Gnjilane, Lipjan/Lipljan and Kaçanik/Kačanik), municipalities are now giving support to the returns process.

50. While ever more returns projects are being developed by municipalities, lack of funding remains the single most important obstacle to returns. UNMIK and the Ministry of Returns and Communities jointly revised the budgets of all pending returns projects to cut costs and provide municipalities with a greater implementing role: as a result the funding gap was revised downwards by €6 million and now stands at €20 million for 22 approved organized returns projects. However, the budget submission for 2007 of the Ministry omitted those projects in favour of others that are not in conformity with the existing policies and have not been endorsed at the municipal level.

51. The Belgrade authorities have cooperated with the Kosovo institutions on humanitarian matters, particularly at the municipal level. A joint returns project is being implemented in Llugë/Lugovo and Gjurakovc/Djurakovac (Istog/k) and another project is being jointly developed in Badovc/Badovac (Prishtinë/Priština).

52. Terms of reference have been developed regarding the establishment of human rights units in ministries, which will be responsible for each ministry's compliance with the recommendations of the Ombudsperson Institution of Kosovo.

53. The President, the Prime Minister and ministers continued to visit communities. On 25 October, the Government approved a consolidated outreach plan for ministers among non-Albanian communities that will aim at encouraging participation of members of those communities in the Provisional Institutions.

Sustainable returns and the rights of communities: challenges ahead

54. The policy framework for voluntary returns is now in place. The success of its implementation depends on leadership and commitment from the central institutions. Valuable support for the returns process is being provided, in particular by the Ministry of Local Government Administration, but sustainable progress can only be achieved if the serious managerial issues facing the Ministry of Returns and Communities are addressed. Transfer of further competencies to that Ministry should depend on improvements in this field.

55. The repatriation of Kosovans returning from third countries after being denied legal status presents a huge potential problem of resources and organization. An estimated 90,000 are subject to deportation and return to Kosovo. UNMIK and the Provisional Institutions have developed a joint plan to address their needs and to manage the transfer of repatriation functions to the Provisional Institutions.

56. An administrative instruction on the Anti-Discrimination Law has been issued, but more efforts are needed for its implementation.

57. Displaced people, particularly women, need to be consulted more in the decision-making process, and a database of displaced persons is urgently needed.

58. The functioning of Communities Committees and Mediation Committees needs to be re-examined. There is generally poor participation and a lack of quorum.

Economy

59. The mid-year review of the 2006 budget, promulgated by the Special Representative of the Secretary-General on 19 September, was generally budget-neutral. The Ministry of Finance and Economy continues to enforce the authorized ceiling on the wage bill, and on 7 September the Government imposed a hiring freeze, with the exception of a few employment categories. There has been little progress, however, on public service reform and head-count reduction, and the wage bill is likely to remain higher than that recommended by the International Monetary Fund (IMF). The potential implementation of a number of laws on social benefits would have a significant upward effect on public expenditure. The 2007 budget is currently being prepared below the ceiling recommended by IMF. A final draft was submitted to the Government on 31 October.

60. The average revenue collection rate of the Kosovo electricity company (KEK) has increased from 32 per cent for the year 2005 to 36 per cent for the first half of 2006 (revenue collected against total energy supplied). The Company's ABC load-shedding scheme remains in place, and it has also introduced mobile cash collection offices. The courts have recently issued convictions against two criminal cases of debt to KEK. The Ministry of Energy and Mines has continued a public information campaign on the importance of paying bills and economical use of energy, with the support of the European Agency for Reconstruction.

61. The Statistical Office of Kosovo produces monthly trade and consumer price statistics; IMF has corrected certain errors in the compilation of the latter. Economic accounts for

2005 are overdue, and there is a lack of basic data (principally a business survey) for the compilation of future statistics. The Office faces difficulties in retaining experienced local staff.

62. At the end of September, the Office of the Auditor General conducted a preliminary review of follow-up on auditors' recommendations in 10 municipalities and two ministries. Preliminary findings indicate that little has been done. On 13 October, the Ministry of Finance and Economy addressed a letter to all budget organizations to undertake immediate measures to implement the Auditor General's recommendations.

63. The Mission has received a number of procedural complaints against the Tax Administration of Kosovo from various businesses. In addition, the Kosovo Trust Agency has complained to the Minister of Finance and Economy regarding the Administration's handling of tax-related issues of various socially owned enterprises. UNMIK Customs has noted that the Administration currently lacks a strategic planning component and work plans for 2006 and 2007, and also that it has failed to set up a working group in the context of the Fiscal Blueprints benchmarking exercise of the European Union, as requested by the European Commission at the Stabilization and Association Process Tracking Mechanism meeting held in July 2006.

64. The Board of Directors of the Kosovo Trust Agency has met regularly and agreed to launch the nineteenth and twentieth waves of privatization. The total proceeds of paid and pending contracts currently amounts to €236,152,396. The Deputy Special Representative of the Secretary-General for Pillar IV and the Minister for Local Government Administration have agreed on a list of criteria to be applied in processing municipal requests to use land owned by socially owned enterprises for the benefit of the public.

Economy: challenges ahead

65. Compliance with IMF recommendations remains a major medium/long-term challenge in the face of upward pressures on expenditure, including those potentially related to a status settlement.

66. The Tax Administration of Kosovo should investigate procedural complaints raised by the Kosovo Trust Agency and various businesses, develop annual working plans, and establish a working group for the purposes of the European Union Fiscal Blueprints benchmarking exercise.

67. Responsiveness to and implementation of auditors' recommendations needs to improve.

68. Despite some improvements in revenue collection, non-payment of bills remains a major problem for a number of public utilities and an obstacle to their attainment of economic viability.

69. The Ministry of Public Services and the Statistical Office of Kosovo need to develop a plan for the absorption of future technical assistance and the retention of experienced capacity in the Statistical Office.

Property rights

70. Legal reform relating to property rights is slowly moving forward. The law on housing is awaiting adoption by the Assembly. The draft law on the treatment of illegal constructions

is pending approval by the Prime Minister. Other bills are under review by the Assembly to ensure compliance with European standards.

71. A strategy is under discussion to reduce the backlog of disputes relating to property before the courts, which has reached 31,017 cases (two thirds of the overall civil case backlog; see para. 33), though these include 18,132 conflict claims lodged against UNMIK, KFOR and the Provisional Institutions by Kosovo Serbs, stayed at the request of the UNMIK Department of Justice. Another 2,939 claims of a similar nature were lodged by Kosovo Albanians against Serbia and individuals.

72. The Ministry of Environmental and Spatial Planning and the municipalities have allocated a budget to social housing programmes. The total budget allocated is €6,143,300.

73. Repossession is not usually the choice of the successful claimant (other options are administration of the property or withdrawal of the claim). The percentage of repossession thus remains low (15.74 per cent of 4,117 implemented category C cases). When repossession requests result in an eviction order, the number of cases in which the unlawful occupant voluntarily releases the property is low (562 cases, 13.6 per cent). In comparison, in 3,571 cases (86.4 per cent), a forced eviction has been necessary.

74. Illegal occupation of non-residential properties continues to be a widespread phenomenon. To date, the Kosovo Property Agency has received 4,022 claims related to agricultural and commercial property.

Property rights: challenges ahead

75. A strategy to address the backlog of property-related cases needs to be agreed upon and implemented.

76. Illegal construction remains rife. In addition to the legal reform now under way, there is an urgent need for a comprehensive policy at the central level to address the issue.

77. Municipalities, in cooperation with ministries, must remedy previous irregular expropriations and ensure that ongoing public works comply with the law.

78. The Kosovo Property Agency lacks funding for the duration of its mandate and still needs donor support, in addition to the €2.7 million provided through the Kosovo budget.

79. The Kosovo-wide medium- and long-term strategy and action plan on regularizing existing informal settlements and preventing new ones need to be developed and implemented.

Cultural heritage

80. Reconstruction and restoration of cultural heritage sites by the Reconstruction Implementation Commission continue. After an accelerated tender in early June, the replacement of the stolen roof of Ljeviska church was completed on 31 August, and work started on three other sites (St. George, St. Nicholas and Dević Monastery). A second round of tenders that included additional work to these sites as well as to three other sites (St. George Runović, Presentation of the Virgin and St. Elias) was evaluated early in September and works began on 2 October. A third round of additional work to a church (Holy Virgin Mary) was evaluated on 13 October and work should begin early in November.

81. Since the previous reporting period, there has been a decrease in the number of incidents relating to cultural heritage property and monuments. Between 7 August and 26 October, six incidents were reported, including one case of attempted theft at an Orthodox church. Two cases have been sent to the prosecutor.

82. Following the series of incidents during the previous reporting period, the Ministry of Culture, Youth and Sports initiated weekly security meetings with KPS. Additional protection measures now include increased local patrolling by KPS at cultural heritage and religious sites, especially Orthodox sites under reconstruction.

83. Progress has been made on the inventory of cultural heritage. The assessment of data already existing in the architectural, archaeological and movable inventories is ongoing. According to most recent updates, a total of 2,847 objects have been identified in the inventory process since 2003; of these, 426 objects have been listed under protection by law. The Ministry of Culture, Youth and Sports hopes to complete the inventory database by the end of 2006.

Cultural heritage: challenges ahead

84. Condemnation by political and community leaders of incidents affecting cultural heritage sites should continue, to encourage the public to respect cultural heritage and cooperate with law enforcement.

85. The Ministry of Culture, Youth and Sports needs a policy for the allocation of funding for cultural heritage protection. At present, funds are allocated on an ad hoc basis, which makes it hard for partner organizations to plan ahead.

86. Once the adopted Law on Cultural Heritage has been promulgated, subsidiary legislation needs to be drafted to implement the law.

Kosovo Protection Corps

87. Non-Albanian membership of the Kosovo Protection Corps has risen throughout 2006. From 180 at the start of the year, by 26 October there were 223 non-Albanian members, or 7.4 per cent of a total workforce of 3,030, including 58 Serbs (up from 52 in August). Intimidation from within the Kosovo Serb community itself is still an obstacle to the recruitment and retention of Kosovo Serbs. Throughout 2006, the focus has been on retention and support, which has included visits to non-Albanian communities.

88. Women are represented at all levels of KPC and continue to occupy relatively more senior ranks in comparison with men. The United Nations Development Fund for Women (UNIFEM) and KPS began gender-awareness training for KPC officer courses on 21 October, continuing a tradition of cooperation between UNIFEM and KPC in that area.

89. The continuing leadership of KPC in the reconstruction of properties damaged in March 2004 in Svinjarë/Svinjare village has remained a high-profile activity during the reporting period (see para. 4). The implementation of reconstruction and humanitarian projects, especially for non-Albanian and mixed communities, has been a consistent feature of KPC activity.

90. Disciplinary compliance continues to improve. On 29 August, the KPC Disciplinary Board convened for the second time under its new code. It reviewed 21 cases and recommended 12 KPC members for dismissal: 10 for absenteeism, including 8 Kosovo Serbs.

Absenteeism continues to be the most common disciplinary offence, but shows a declining trend.

91. In August, the Geneva International Centre for Humanitarian Demining conducted an independent assessment of the remaining mine and unexploded ordnance tasks in Kosovo, and judged that KPC would be ready to assume sole responsibility for all mine action in Kosovo as of late 2007. On 27 September, KPC began technical survey operations of all outstanding dangerous and suspicious areas, a new responsibility that further builds its capabilities. By 27 October, KPC, together with a number of non-governmental organizations, had cleared nearly 2.5 million square metres of land and located and destroyed 2,364 pieces of unexploded ordnance and other ordnance.

92. The Civil Protection Brigade is on track for full operational capability by 31 December 2006. Its first full-scale field training exercise, from 5 to 8 September, successfully tested its capabilities. The Brigade was inaugurated on 6 June 2005 and has operating capability in search and rescue, explosive ordnance disposal, firefighting and hazardous material protection.

Kosovo Protection Corps: challenges ahead

93. Despite positive recruitment policies, active engagement among Kosovo Serb communities and no internal evidence of discrimination, KPC still has difficulty in attracting and retaining recruits from the Kosovo Serb community.

94. Difficulties are apparent as KPC starts to face the coming challenge of transformation following a final status settlement. Donor support will be needed for resettlement programmes and other engagement to ensure that KPC is able to respond to that challenge.

95. Other donor support is also needed to enable KPC to become more professional.

[1] Figures for convictions quoted in previous technical assessments have aggregated minor offences and more serious charges, but it is now deemed more useful to present the figures in this way.

Annex II

A. Composition and strength of the police component of the United Nations Interim Administration Mission in Kosovo (as at 31 October 2006)

Argentina	11	Malaysia	2
Austria	22	Nepal	19
Bangladesh	3	Netherlands	1
Brazil	2	Nigeria	24
Bulgaria	45	Norway	19
China	18	Pakistan	155
Croatia	9	Philippines	45
Czech Republic	13	Poland	123
Denmark	21	Portugal	7
Egypt	17	Romania	170
Finland	4	Russian Federation	33
France	53	Slovenia	8
Germany	182	Spain	13
Ghana	15	Sweden	35
Greece	10	Switzerland	6
Hungary	6	Timor-Leste	10
India	78	Turkey	125
Italy	26	United Kingdom of Great Britain and Northern Ireland	60
Jordan	58		
Kenya	16	United States of America	208
Kyrgyzstan	5	Ukraine	183
Lithuania	8	Zambia	9
		Zimbabwe	18
Total			**1 895**

B. Composition of the Kosovo Police Service(as at 31 October 2006)

Category	*Percentage*	*Number*
Kosovo Albanians	83.94	6 031
Kosovo Serbs	10.30	740
Other ethnic minority members	5.76	414
Total	**100**	**7 185**
Men	86.40	6 208
Women	13.60	977

Annex III
Composition and strength of the military liaison component of the United Nations Interim Administration Mission in Kosovo (as at 31 October 2006)

Country	*Number of liaison officers*
Argentina	1
Bangladesh	1
Bolivia	1
Bulgaria	1
Chile	1
Czech Republic	1
Denmark	1
Finland	2
Hungary	1
Ireland	4
Italy	1
Jordan	2
Kenya	1
Malawi	1
Malaysia	1
Nepal	1
New Zealand	1
Norway	1
Pakistan	1
Poland	1
Portugal	2
Romania	2
Russian Federation	2
Spain	2
Ukraine	2
United Kingdom of Great Britain and Northern Ireland	1
Zambia	1
Total	**37**

2. Report of the Secretary-General on the United Nations Interim Administration Mission in Kosovo, 9 March 2007 (S/2007/134)

I. Introduction

1. The present report is submitted pursuant to Security Council resolution 1244 (1999) of 10 June 1999, by which the Council decided to establish the United Nations Interim Administration Mission in Kosovo (UNMIK) and requested the Secretary-General to report at regular intervals on the implementation of the mandate. It covers the activities of UNMIK and developments in Kosovo (Serbia), from 1 November 2006 to 19 February 2007.

II. Political assessment

2. My Special Envoy for the Future Status Process for Kosovo, Martti Ahtisaari, and his team continued consultations with Belgrade and Prishtinë/Priština as well as international actors on elements of a comprehensive settlement proposal for Kosovo's future status. My Special Envoy submitted a draft comprehensive proposal for the Kosovo status settlement ("Settlement Proposal") to the parties on 2 February. He invited the parties to engage in a consultative process on the Settlement Proposal starting from the first week of February.

Political situation

3. The future status of Kosovo has remained the principal political issue in Kosovo over the reporting period. The announcement by my Special Envoy on 10 November that his presentation of the Settlement Proposal to the parties would be delayed until after 21 January to allow for the holding of parliamentary elections in Serbia was received with deep disappointment by Kosovo Albanians. The reaction among the population was generally restrained, with the exception of a demonstration by the Kosovo Albanian self-determination movement Vetevendosje on 28 November, Albanian Flag Day, in which both the Government and UNMIK headquarters in Prishtinë/Priština were attacked by approximately 4,000 demonstrators throwing projectiles.

4. The Settlement Proposal was generally well received on 2 February by Kosovo Albanian leaders and the public, though a number of concerns were voiced on its elements such as the proposed disbandment of the Kosovo Protection Corps (KPC) and decentralization. Radical Kosovo Albanian elements and Kosovo Serbs both rejected the Settlement Proposal, though for opposite reasons. Vetevendosje again held a protest against the plan, the Kosovo negotiating team, UNMIK and the future envisaged International Civilian Office on 10 February, the intent of which was clearly violent. Tragically, two protesters died from rubber-bullet wounds to the head. The Minister of Internal Affairs of the Kosovo Provisional Institutions of Self-Government and the UNMIK Police Commissioner resigned shortly afterwards, while the leader of the Vetevendosje movement's remains in pre-trial detention. An inquiry into the deaths and an investigation into Vetevendosje are ongoing. While there is little mainstream support for the actions of this movement, the continued lack of clarity on Kosovo's status, which hampers social, economic and political progress, creates a fragile environment which was exploited by radical elements.

5. The Kosovo negotiating team, which comprises the President, the President of the Assembly, the Prime Minister of Kosovo and the leaders of the two main governing parties and two main opposition parties, maintained unity and intensified activity in explaining their proposals and role in the future status process. They reached out to all of Kosovo's communities and held a number of town hall meetings at which the effects of decentralization measures envisaged in the Settlement Proposal for Kosovo's municipalities and communities were debated. These efforts are welcome, but need to be increased as the future status process moves forward. While the negotiating team remained unified, pressures on members mounted from some radical elements who increasingly criticized the team for taking part in the future status process at all, especially after the delay in connection with the Serbian parliamentary elections.

6. Political developments within a number of Kosovo's political parties were also a source of pressure on the unity of the negotiating team. This was particularly true of the Democratic League of Kosovo (LDK), which held a leadership contest during the reporting period. The President of Kosovo, Fatmir Sejdiu, emerged victorious from party elections held on 9 December 2006 and suspended his role as party leader in order to retain his post as President, as required by the Kosovo Constitutional Framework. The losing candidate, the former President of the Assembly, Nexhat Daci, who won a significant proportion of votes, started preparations to form his own party. The split within LDK has so far been most evident at the municipal level. The other main Government coalition partner, the Alliance for the Future of Kosovo (AAK), also faces a challenge as its party leader, Ramush Haradinaj, is due to be tried at the International Tribunal for the Former Yugoslavia in March on charges of war crimes. There have been isolated security incidents which may reflect tensions within and between political parties. An unidentified explosive device went off inside the LDK branch office in Gjilan/Gnjilane on 28 January. On 20 December 2006, UNMIK police and the Kosovo Force (KFOR) found and confiscated a large cache of weapons in Prishtinë/Priština region; three AAK members were arrested in connection with the case.

7. Kosovo Serbs have continued to take very little part in the political institutions in Kosovo. Against a background of active discouragement by Belgrade, Kosovo Serbs in the Assembly and the Government have not taken up their seats and the only Kosovo Serb Minister in the Government, the Minister for Communities and Returns, was forced to resign on 27 November at the recommendation of the Prime Minister after an audit uncovered evidence of financial irregularities and mismanagement. A Kosovo Serb is currently acting Minister. General engagement of the Kosovo Serb community in and with the Provisional Institutions at both central and local level remains very limited. The influence of the Government of Serbia, through the Serbian Coordination Centre for Kosovo, is particularly strong in the north of Kosovo, owing to its control of wages and employment in parallel structures. To a large extent, reaction by Kosovo Serbs to the status proposal depends on the reaction of Belgrade. The political leadership of the three Kosovo Serb municipalities in the north of Kosovo continued to boycott most contacts with Prishtinë/Priština. After cutting off political links, they are now fully dependant on Serbian state financial support, with minor exceptions for Kosovo Albanian staff and projects, funded by the Provisional Institutions.

Security

8. With the exception of the violent demonstration on 10 February led by Vetevendosje and the explosion in central Prishtinë/Priština on 19 February that damaged three

United Nations vehicles, the security situation remained generally calm. There was a relatively small number of potentially destabilizing incidents. General crime levels decreased during 2006 in comparison to 2005. In specific categories, crimes against persons dropped 11 per cent and weapons-related crimes by 10 per cent. Murders fell by 15 per cent. The only area of significant increase was in crimes against property, which rose by 5 per cent. Potentially ethnically motivated incidents also dropped significantly, by 70 per cent.

9. Vetevendosje and their linkages to other groupings such as the War Veterans' Association remain a cause for concern. Radical groups are likely to continue to exploit any public dissatisfaction ensuing from my Special Envoy's proposals and the future status process, including delays in the process. Other fringe elements may seek to use the charged atmosphere of the future status process to provoke inter-ethnic violence for their own ends. There are strong concerns about the possibility of sudden and confrontational action by radical political leaders north of the Ibar River and the reactions that this may provoke in the rest of Kosovo. Some Kosovo Serb leaders have made statements implying the possibility of unilateral initiatives in reaction to the decision on Kosovo's future status.

Standards and European integration

10. During the reporting period, the Government has continued to make progress on standards implementation. The basic reference document on standards implementation, the 2004 Kosovo Standards Implementation Plan, has been replaced by the European Partnership Action Plan, approved by the Government in August 2006. The 109 standards goals contained in the original Implementation Plan are all incorporated into the Action Plan, but the actions agreed in 2004 have been updated and revised to reflect current challenges and to respond to both the standards goals and the European partnership priorities. As a result, the Agency for European Integration is now the main coordination mechanism within the Provisional Institutions on standards, and the European Partnership Action Plan is the main guiding tool for Kosovo's European integration process. It is expected that the European integration process will remain a Kosovo Government priority for the foreseeable future, which will ensure that the principles underlying the standards programme will be preserved and promoted beyond the life of UNMIK.

Decentralization

11. Decentralization continues to be a contentious issue in the context of the status process. Although the Kosovo negotiating team has improved outreach to municipalities to explain their proposals for new municipalities, it has faced criticism from those living in affected areas and others who perceive decentralization as a means of establishing the territorial control of Belgrade over Kosovo Serb-majority areas. Decentralization is not only problematic politically. Practical difficulties have also become evident in the establishment of Pilot Municipal Units foreseen at present, including the recruitment and training of qualified staff and obtaining necessary funding. In a recent assessment of their performance, the Government decided that, owing to challenges faced by the Units in the exercise of additional competencies, their conversion to fully fledged municipalities should be postponed until July 2007.

12. In addition, the establishment of new municipalities should be synchronized with the holding of new municipal elections, which were postponed because of the status process. The Government is carefully monitoring the performance of Pilot Municipal Units in the

exercise of newly acquired competencies with a view to preparing them for additional transfer of competencies. The difficulties encountered by the Government and host municipalities in establishing the Units indicate that further decentralization, such as that proposed in the Settlement Proposal, will require considerable time and resources, as well as much international support, to be implemented.

Cultural and religious heritage

13. There were a small number of incidents, mostly theft-related, against Serbian Orthodox Churches during the reporting period. The drop in incidents corresponds with increased Kosovo Police Service (KPS) patrols at Serbian Orthodox cultural heritage sites. In January, UNMIK had to exert pressure on the Provisional Institutions to remove illegal constructions in the vicinity of the Serbian Orthodox Visoki Deçan/Decani monastery. Other issues of concern with regard to that monastery are the plans by the Provisional Institutions to construct an interregional road to Montenegro, which is to bisect the special zoning area established to protect this World Heritage Site. On 6 November 2006, my Special Representative, Joachim Rücker, promulgated the Law on Cultural Heritage, which allows for potential amendments to harmonize the law with future status arrangements.

14. The reconstruction of Serbian Orthodox churches damaged or destroyed during the violence of March 2004 has moved forward. Extensive interventions were carried out on seven sites under the direction of the Reconstruction Implementation Commission, chaired by the Council of Europe, from August to December 2006. The Commission's workplan for 2007 envisions further works on these and up to 13 additional sites. Following the memorandum of understanding signed by the United Nations Educational, Scientific and Cultural Organization (UNESCO) and UNMIK on 11 September 2006, which provided a framework for the implementation of projects arising from pledges made at the 2005 UNESCO donors conference, a further memorandum of understanding to allow for implementation of a project using the $1 million contribution from the United States Government was signed on 29 January 2007. UNESCO is expected to begin work soon on the seven sites selected for this project, which include both Ottoman and Orthodox monuments.

Dialogue

15. Two of the four working groups for dialogue on technical issues between Prishtinë/Priština and Belgrade remained dormant during the reporting period. However, the Missing Persons Working Group held two closed meetings, on 7 December 2006 and 7 February 2007, while the Sub-Working Group on Forensics held regular conference calls every four to six weeks. The Technical Sub-Working Group of the Returns Working Group held its first meeting on 12 December 2006 in Prishtinë/Priština. A deadlock over starkly different interpretations of the scope of the Protocol on Return signed earlier that year was overcome and the outcome of the discussions was positive. Cooperation with the Belgrade authorities on cultural matters covered arts exchange and the return of documentation and archaeology.

Returns

16. The primary factors affecting returns, which remain low, continue to be lack of economic opportunities, uncertainty about the future status of Kosovo, and, to a much lesser degree than in the past, security. The funding shortfall of €15.4 million also negatively

affects the return rate. Municipalities are increasingly demonstrating the capacity to directly implement components of returns projects, making them more sustainable and less expensive. After the change of leadership, the Ministry of Communities and Returns needs to continue restructuring, paying particular attention to implementing the recommendations of the audits performed in 2006. The funding shortfall affects 18 approved return projects at present, all of which have been either re-evaluated with stakeholders or are in the process of re-evaluation to bring down projected costs. Cooperation on returns between the Provisional Institutions and the Government of Serbia continued at the local level, particularly on matters of humanitarian concern.

17. In 2006, the overall number of persons involuntarily repatriated from host countries reached 3,598. Repatriation functions are in the process of being transferred to the Provisional Institutions. Another 90,000 Kosovans are subject to deportation and return to Kosovo, adding urgency to the Government/UNMIK plan to address reintegration needs.

Economy

18. A number of significant economic developments occurred during the reporting period. The first draft of the Kosovo Development Strategy and Plan was completed at the end of December 2006, though much work remains to be done on prioritizing its proposed policy measures and formulating concrete, cost-specific projects. Following its completion in the first half of 2007, the Kosovo Development Strategy and Plan is expected to become the strategic framework for public policy priorities and government and donor spending. Its ultimate objective is to improve the impact of public policies and the effectiveness of public spending.

19. On 19 December 2006, UNMIK on behalf of Kosovo signed the enlarged Central Europe Free Trade Area Agreement, which constitutes a single free trade agreement among its parties, namely, Albania, Bosnia and Herzegovina, Croatia, Moldova, Montenegro, Serbia, the former Yugoslav Republic of Macedonia and UNMIK on behalf of Kosovo. The Agreement will liberalize and simplify trade relations among the parties, giving them access to a large market of consumers.

20. Two significant projects in the energy and telecommunications sectors have moved forward. On 4 December, the Ministry of Energy and Mining announced that 10 companies had expressed interest in the Energy Sector Development Project, which includes the construction of a new electricity-generating plant in Kosovo. Four of these fulfilled the eligibility criteria, and will be invited to submit detailed proposals. The World Bank Lignite Power Technical Assistance grant for $8.5 million that will support the Project was signed on 13 December 2006. Secondly, the deadline for submitting bids to the tender for the second mobile telephone operator for Kosovo, which had been launched on 3 November 2006, was 17 January 2007. Five bids were presented, including from local companies acting in consortium with international partners. The evaluation of the bids is currently under way.

Future international arrangements and transition

21. Preparations and planning for the handover of UNMIK responsibilities at the end of its mandate following a political settlement intensified during the reporting period. These preparations, which have remained a top priority for UNMIK and its international and local

partners, are being carried out by means of five technical working groups in the areas of rule of law, governance, civil administration, legislation, economy and property. Preparatory work has also started on a post-UNMIK constitutional arrangement and elections although without prejudice to an eventual political settlement. There has been good progress at both the political and technical level in preparing for a transition. My Special Representative has continued to chair the local Steering Group on future international arrangements, which has included representatives from the Office of the Special Envoy of the Secretary-General for the future status process for Kosovo, the preparation teams of the future International Civilian Office and the future European Security and Defence Policy mission. Current planning is geared to preparing the ground for a rapid and robust build-up of the future international authorities which will ensure that no gaps arise in international political authority and capacity during the transition period. In addition, the Office of the Special Envoy has held a number of meetings in Vienna with representatives from UNMIK, the preparation team of the future International Civilian Office, and the future European Security and Defence Policy mission to brief them in detail on the Office's proposals and to discuss necessary implementation steps.

III. Observations

22. During the reporting period and over the course of the future status process as a whole, Kosovo's institutions have demonstrated a sustained commitment to standards implementation. While overall progress has been mixed, and there remains scope for improvement, I welcome this commitment and the fact that it has led to concrete steps forward in many areas of standards, including in areas of vital importance to the minority communities of Kosovo. I call upon Kosovo's leaders and institutions to reaffirm and continue to act upon this commitment.

23. At the same time, it is important to acknowledge that further progress on standards implementation, and the sustainability and consolidation of what has been achieved thus far, will require both a sustained momentum in the future status process and concrete prospects for a conclusion of the process.

24. After almost eight years of United Nations interim administration, Kosovo and its people need clarity on their future. The Security Council and key Member States are called upon to meet this challenge. Moving towards a timely conclusion of the Kosovo future status political process and a sustainable solution to the future status of Kosovo should be a priority for the international community as a whole.

25. Such a solution must entail a Kosovo that is stable and in which all communities can coexist in peace. The use of violence by extremist groups in Kosovo to achieve political objectives cannot be tolerated and should be strongly condemned. I note with concern the violent demonstrations on 10 February in Prishtinë/Priština that led to the tragic loss of life, and I call upon the organizers to exercise restraint and responsibility in peacefully furthering their political aims.

26. My Special Representative and his staff will continue to focus on creating an enabling environment for the future status process, both by working closely with the local leaders in managing the overall political context in Kosovo and by bringing forward preparations for a transition to future international arrangements following settlement of the future status of Kosovo. It is crucial that in doing so my Special Representative continues to receive the

backing and support of the Security Council, the Contact Group, the European Union and the wider international community.

27. UNMIK will need to remain adequately resourced until the completion of its mandate, and I ask that Member States ensure that all appropriate measures are put in place to ensure that UNMIK has the necessary resources and staff to fulfil the mandate entrusted to it by the Security Council.

28. My appreciation goes to my Special Representative, Joachim Rücker, and to the staff of UNMIK for their commitment to the Organization. Their dedication and steadfastness in carrying out their tasks deserve special mention at this critical and difficult stage for UNMIK. I would also like to extend my appreciation to KFOR, our partners within UNMIK—the European Union and the Organization for Security and Cooperation in Europe—and to the United Nations agencies, funds and programmes and other contributors for their commitment and support.

Annex I
Technical assessment of progress in implementation of the standards for Kosovo

Prepared by the Special Representative of the Secretary-General for Kosovo, 6 February 2007

1. The status settlement process dominated the reporting period. Nevertheless, progress continued to be achieved in the implementation of the standards and the transition from the Kosovo Standards Implementation Plan to the European Partnership Action Plan is well under way.

2. Implementation also continued of the remaining items in the programme of 13 priority points presented to the Kosovo Government by the Contact Group in June 2006.

The 13 priorities for standards implementation

3. **Priority 1.** The Laws on Religious Freedom, Languages, and Cultural Heritage were promulgated on 24 August, 20 October and 6 November 2006, respectively.

4. **Priority 2.** The reconstruction under the leadership of the Kosovo Protection Corps (KPC) of properties damaged in March 2004 in Svinjarë/Svinjare was declared complete by the UNMIK/Provisional Institutions of Self-Government Decision-Making Board on 15 December. An UNMIK/Provisional Institutions/KPC engineering commission declared all properties fit for habitation. However, the displaced Kosovo Serb homeowners have chosen not to return. Consequently, and despite increased Kosovo Police Service (KPS) patrols, some burglary of unoccupied houses has required minor extra repairs. The commission suggested that there should be no further repair unless people undertake to immediately return to live in their properties, since otherwise the unoccupied houses will remain vulnerable to the weather and other hazards and need repair all over again. By the same reasoning, the Kosovo Government is not proceeding with repair of the 24 remaining commercial claims.

5. **Priority 3.** Following the initial pilot project in the Prishtinë/Priština region, the Kosovo Property Agency has extended the rental scheme to all of the 5,247 residential properties currently under its administration. By 31 January, 1,402 property right holders had included their property into the scheme. Forty occupants are currently paying rent and an amount of €23,490 was collected. The first 12 evictions of occupiers who have declined to pay rent

were also carried out in January, and the Agency initiated an outreach campaign to identify tenants for these properties.

6. **Priority 4.** Six hundred and seventy-two decisions made by the Housing and Property Directorate/Housing and Property Claims Commission remained to be implemented, down from 1,150 in November. Implementation should be complete by the end of March. Cooperation between the Kosovo Property Agency and the police remains satisfactory.

7. **Priority 5.** On 1 January, the competency to provide humanitarian train and bus services for minority communities, including the €2,675,000 budget, was transferred from UNMIK to the Ministry of Transport and Communications. Initial monitoring shows that the minority community members continue to use and are generally satisfied with the humanitarian bus service.

8. **Priority 6.** The Government has allocated returns funding according to the agreement reached with UNMIK on 30 June 2006.

9. **Priority 7.** On 16 January, the Prime Minister, the Minister of Justice, the President of the Supreme Court and the Chief Prosecutor issued a joint statement calling for witnesses to the March riots to cooperate with the police, and publicized the various means available to the public for giving information to the police. Figures issued on 10 January by the Office of Judicial Administration of the Kosovo Judicial Council regarding March 2004 cases show that 326 criminal charges have by now been brought before local courts, excluding Minor Offences courts. These resulted in 200 indictments which in turn have brought 134 convictions. Twenty-nine cases remain under investigation. These figures represent very little change from the last report. International courts have indicted 31 defendants of whom 26 have been found guilty and 4 are on or awaiting trial; 13 new cases are in preparation. Work continues on a comprehensive database of March 2004 cases, within the specialized police unit created in 2006 to handle these cases. On 14 December, the police made a new arrest of a woman on charges of grievous assault and arson.

10. **Priority 8**. On 1 September, the Ministry of Public Services issued an administrative instruction defining rules and procedures of the central-level monitoring of the use of official languages. The Government also compiled the first CD-ROM containing all government decisions and regulations in the official languages, which was distributed to ministries and municipalities.

11. **Priority 9.** A special commission reviewed 31 applications for minority media fund grants; 11 media were selected and the grants were distributed on 11 July 2006.

12. **Priority 10.** All 17 new sub-municipal police stations agreed on 6 September 2006 by the Police Commissioner and the Minister of Internal Affairs have now been established, even the two in communities where the local population had initially indicated they were unwanted.

13. **Priority 11.** The Director of the Anti-Corruption Agency was appointed by the Assembly on 17 July.

14. **Priority 12.** The Independent Media Council was established on 28 August 2006 and now replaces the Temporary Media Commissioner. On 11 January, the Assembly of Kosovo appointed two candidates for the Media Appeals Board, thus completing the formal establishment of all bodies required for the functioning of the Independent Media Council.

15. **Priority 13.** The draft law to amend the Law on Public Procurement is with Assembly committees and awaits its second reading.

Functioning democratic institutions

16. Kosovo has 38 registered political parties. Three parties face possible suspension for failing to submit their twice-yearly financial reports. While the existing formula for distributing funds to political parties is equitable, the law on Political Party Financing, adopted by the Assembly, needs to be revised to regulate this distribution without being discriminatory to parties holding reserved seats.

17. The Government continues to hold in trust the salaries of the Kosovo Serbs who have left the payroll of the Provisional Institutions. A simplified procedure was introduced for their reinstatement after complaints about procedural delays at the municipal level. To date, 51 Kosovo Serbs have been reinstated and their salaries have been paid.

18. Civil service employs 68,460 with 40,191 in municipalities and 28,269 at the central level. Minority employees represent 11.2 per cent.

19. Despite an administrative instruction of the Ministry of Finance and the Economy on the implementation of fair-share financing issued on 10 August 2006, only 16 of the 27 reporting municipalities had prepared the Annual Plan for Minority Projects and Expenditure for the 2007 budget (as at 19 January). The Ministry of Finance and the Economy has threatened the non-compliant municipalities with sanctions. The third-quarter report on fair-share financing in 2006 shows that 20 of the 27 municipalities reached or exceeded their target, which was slightly better than the second quarter, in which 17 did. Zvečan/Zveçan has still not submitted any fair-share financing reports for 2006 despite receiving funds from the Kosovo consolidated budget.

20. The implementation of the Law on Languages commenced, albeit with a slight delay. In January, the Ministry of Local Government Administration issued an administrative instruction defining steps required to implement the Law, including the issuing of 10 subsidiary acts. An administrative instruction to determine the composition and competencies of the Language Commission is in preparation.

21. Municipal language service is provided by 28 municipalities, 23 municipalities have established language units and 5 have hired interpreters/translators. Zveçan/Zvečan and Gllogoc/Glogovac did not employ any interpreter/translator. Units or translators function well in 16 municipalities. All ministries and most municipalities now have simultaneous translation equipment, although in 10 municipalities it is either underutilized or not properly installed. Most municipalities are fully or partially language compliant in respect of road and street signs and municipal buildings.

Functioning democratic institutions: challenges ahead

22. The unwillingness of many Kosovo Serbs to cooperate with the Provisional Institutions remains a challenge and an obstacle to progress towards the integration of Kosovo Serb communities into mainstream society.

23. Compliance with the Law on Languages is important and necessary. While monitoring of language compliance has improved, enforcement needs to develop further. The Language Commission needs to be established.

24. The Agency for Gender Equality needs to continue implementing its long-term strategy to increase the number and improve the position of women in the Provisional Institutions, with a special emphasis on municipalities and implementation of its memorandum of understanding with the Ministry of Local Government Administration.

25. Efforts to avoid politicization of the civil service and local governance structures should be strengthened. In at least two municipalities the proper functioning of the Municipal Assembly and other municipal bodies is affected by political divisions (Malishevë/Mališevo and Gjilan/Gnjilane).

26. The Office of the Official Gazette still lacks a systematic approach to the publication of laws and secondary legislation, as well as a database and index to make accessible the extensive existing body of laws.

Rule of law

27. The Administrative Direction required to implement the vetting process for reappointment of judges and prosecutors was promulgated at the end of 2006. A memorandum of understanding among the European Union, UNMIK and the United States Office Pristina and the related project document on funding and implementation of the vetting process is now finalized for signature. Meanwhile, UNMIK has continued the discussion with the Kosovo Judicial Council on the allocation of the budgeted 421 judicial and prosecutorial posts between various courts in Kosovo.

28. Transition of relevant competencies to the Ministry of Justice continues with the transfer of penal management and missing persons and forensics. Minority representation in the Ministry has dropped slightly, to 14.9 per cent from 15.16 per cent, in the last reporting period since new recruits have been mostly Albanian. Vacancy announcements should be advertised in the Serbian language printed media.

29. The Ministry of Internal Affairs is continuing to build capacity in order to deal with migration, repatriation, oversight of KPS, emergency preparedness and management. Minority representation is 9.4 per cent, down from 10.97 per cent in the last reporting period since new recruits have been mostly the Albanians. Sixty-four remaining vacancies (out of 779 posts) are expected to be filled soon; 39.7 per cent of posts are occupied by women.

30. The civil court backlog increased from 2.46 per cent during the reporting period, to 47,105 cases. A strategy to reduce the backlog of property and other civil cases is in preparation and is expected to be finalized by the end of February. Possible remedies include reform of legislation, civil cases monitoring, reallocation of judges, improvement in delivery of court summons, solution to stayed property cases, and improvement in case management.

31. On 27 November, 12 persons were appointed to the Kosovo judiciary by the Special Representative of the Secretary-General. Five were from underrepresented communities. Non-Albanian representation is now 10.86 per cent for judges and 9.09 per cent for prosecutors. Women's representation is at 26.83 per cent for judges, and 20.45 per cent for prosecutors.

32. The establishment of the Kosovo Special Prosecutor's Office is on track. Three prosecutors were selected in January and are to be approved by the Kosovo Judicial Council and appointed by the Special Representative. If approved, the number of Kosovo Special Prosecutors will increase from one to four.

33. Inter-ethnic crime continues at a low level but cases continue to receive maximum exposure in the Serbian-language media. Following the shooting and subsequent death on 3 January of a KPS officer on the Prishtinë/Priština-Mitrovica highway near Babimovc/Babin Most, a predominantly Serb village, KPS officers supported by UNMIK police carried out searches of 17 houses, which brought heavily publicized allegations from villagers that excessive force had been used. Investigations by the KPS Professional Standards Unit, closely monitored by senior officials of UNMIK police, have so far revealed no malpractice by the officers involved.

34. The Local Public Safety Committees have been established in 13 of the 17 communities originally planned. Efforts continue in the four communities that have not to date accepted the establishment of those committees.

35. KPS and the Kosovo Correctional Service (KCS) continue to be multi-ethnic, with 16 per cent minority staff (10.3 per cent Serb) in KPS and 14.35 per cent (10.65 per cent Serb) in KCS. Female officers make up 13.54 per cent of KPS and 12.27 per cent of KCS.

36. The Directorate of Planning and Development transitioned from UNMIK to KPS on 31 December.

37. The Anti-Corruption Agency is now functioning but has suffered a budgetary cut reducing its staff to 8 instead of the 35 approved by the Assembly. A two-week anti-corruption campaign was carried out in December publicizing a confidential hotline for citizens to report corruption cases. The Agency received 105 alleged cases of corruption. During 2006, 24 people were arrested and 1 person was convicted on corruption charges. An additional case of embezzlement was concluded on 24 January resulting in one two-year prison sentence and one suspended sentence. Investigation continues into the misappropriation of €236.500,00 allocated to buy an armoured car, paid for but never delivered, for the Office of the President of the Assembly of Kosovo (under the previous Assembly President). Three suspects have been arrested, including two Assembly officials.

Rule of law: challenges ahead

38. Further efforts are needed to protect witnesses from intimidation. Legislation on witness protection is awaiting finalization. The final assessment by the United States and the European Union on the Kosovo witness protection programme should be released in the next reporting period, paving the way for donor funding and financial support for any future Kosovo witness protection programme.

39. More work is still needed to increase the number of underrepresented communities among judges and prosecutors.

40. The implementation of the Case Management Information System is well behind schedule and requires additional efforts. Judges, prosecutors and court staff need to be encouraged to use the system.

41. The Government needs to ensure the full functioning of the Anti-Corruption Agency. All ministries should appoint vigilance officers. The Agency needs to start with the collection and investigation of property and assets declarations by Assembly members, ministers and senior staff from the ministries, the judiciary and the police. Ministries need to submit the lists of senior official persons.

42. The problems that hinder transfer of competencies for civil status registry functions from the Ministry of Public Services to the Minister of Internal Affairs need to be resolved as soon as possible. The fact that the Departments of Registration Services and Civil Status continue to be under the operational control of two different ministries violates the regulatory and legal framework.

Freedom of movement

43. On 23 January, the humanitarian minority bus transported Kosovo Serbs from Rahovec/Orahovac to Zveçan/Zveçan and Graçanicë/Graçanica, with "KS" number plates and without United Nations emblems and escort for the first time in seven years.

44. The police continue to assess the security situation as stable but fragile. Regular surveys conducted by KPS consistently show that over 90 per cent of minorities travel outside their area of residence; and that their perception of freedom of movement remains good (92-98 per cent of those interviewed). In illustration, Serbs from Kosovo and Serbia travelled unescorted in private cars to Visoki Dečani monastery to celebrate Saint Stefan's Day on 24 November.

45. However, the mining of the railway line that runs from Fushë Kosovë/Kosovo Polje to Mitrovicë/Mitrovica, the stoning of a bus carrying Kosovo Serbs to Shtërpcë/Štrpce in December and a roadblock in November which detained a bus carrying Kosovo Serbs show that further progress is needed.

46. Escorts continue to be reduced. According to the latest police estimates, less than 1 per cent of minorities travelling in Kosovo now request escorts. Checkpoints are now rare in Kosovo.

47. Kosovo leaders generally continue to speak out against violence. Following an attack against a Serb resident in Klinë/Klina on 29 December, the President of the Municipal Assembly condemned the attack. While there was no public statement from the central government, the Prime Minister received a delegation of Kosovo Serb urban returnees from Klinë/Klina, accompanied by the Municipal Assembly President, and pledged to support their reintegration.

Freedom of movement: challenges ahead

48. The central government needs to take the lead in condemning violent crime wherever it occurs, building on their good record in recent years.

49. The Ministry of Transport and Communications needs to implement a consultative process to determine the selection of future humanitarian bus routes.

Sustainable returns and the rights of communities

50. On 27 November, the Minister of Communities and Returns, Slaviša Petković, resigned following many months of criticism from the international community. The Permanent Secretary, Branislav Grbić, was appointed Acting Minister and quickly established a more productive relationship with the international community, showing commitment to taking ownership of the returns process. He has initiated the long overdue restructuring of the Ministry, which will allow resumption of the postponed transfers of competencies from UNMIK to the ministry.

51. According to the Office of the United Nations High Commissioner for Refugees, 1,608 minorities (593 Serbs) returned voluntarily in 2006, the lowest minority returns figures

since 2001 and the lowest Kosovo Serb returns figures since proper monitoring was established in 2000. The low figures are partly due to the improper management of the budget of the Ministry of Communities and Returns in the previous years.

52. The current funding gap of €15,400,000 for 18 organized multisectoral returns projects remains the single most important obstacle to returns. An amount of €5,200,000 have been allocated in the 2007 budget for returns projects. The Ministry of Communities and Returns has indicated that it will focus on individual returns—a more cost-effective and economically viable approach to displacement.

53. During the reporting period, returns projects were completed in Siga/Sigë, Brestovik, and Ljevoša/Levosha (Pejë/Peć) and Babush i Serbëve/Srpski Babuš (Ferizaj/Uroševac) for 40 and 74 Kosovo Serb families, respectively. However, some of them postponed their return until spring. Another project for 27 families was completed in Klinafc/Klinavac thus making Klinë/Klina the first municipality in Kosovo to fully implement a returns project.

54. On two separate occasions, the municipalities of Kaçanik/Kačanik and Shtime/Štimlje have prevented internally displaced persons from participating in go-and-see-visits, alleging their involvement in war crimes.

55. The Belgrade authorities continue to cooperate with the municipal structures on some returns projects. The Llugë/Lugovo and Gjurakovc/Djurakovac (Istog/Istok) returns project is ongoing and the Prishtinë/Priština Planning, Urbanism and Construction Committee endorsed the allocation of land for the Novi Badovac II/Badoci i Ri II project.

56. Following the recruitment of nine staff of the Directorate of Border Management, Asylum and Migration of the Minister of Internal Affairs, the pace of the transfer of competencies in the field of repatriation should gather momentum.

Sustainable returns and the rights of communities: challenges ahead

57. The Ministry of Communities and Returns needs to continue restructuring with particular attention to implementing the recommendations of the audits performed in 2006, a necessary step to take full responsibility for its mandate, including the management of its budget.

58. With an estimated 90,000 Kosovans subject to deportation and return to Kosovo, the Government and UNMIK need to implement the joint plan to address their reintegration needs and implement the transfer of competences to the Provisional Institutions.

59. The central government needs to ensure that the municipalities comply with their obligations to promote the returns process, including the requirement to engage in dialogue with internally displaced persons.

Economy

60. Early indications suggest that spending on wages and salaries in 2006 was broadly in line with the 2006 budget mid-year review. However, total expenditures in 2006 were 10.1 per cent lower than budgeted, mostly because of underspending in capital projects. Some of these funds were carried forward to the 2007 budget, which was promulgated on 28 December, with authorized expenditure of €717,500,000.

61. Having boycotted the 2007 budget process since the summer of 2006, the northern municipalities of Zubin Potok, Zveçan/Zvecan and Leposavic/q are not eligible to receive the 2007 funds appropriated to them under UNMIK regulation 2006/61. The Ministry of Finance and the Economy is in contact with the municipalities and has offered to assist them in complying with the 2007 budget regulation, a mandatory requirement to access the budget grants.

62. The hiring freeze imposed by the Government in September 2006, in accordance with the recommendations of the International Monetary Fund (IMF), will continue in 2007. However, lack of progress on public service reform and headcount reduction will raise the budgeted wage bill by approximately 1.4 per cent in 2007. The Ministry deadline of 1 January 2007 for municipalities to downsize a defined percentage of their staff has not been fully complied with. In some municipalities (Viti/Vitina, Fushë Kosovë/Kosovo Polje, Istog/Istok, Lipjan/Lipljan and Ferizaj/Uroševac) the minority communities have been disproportionately affected and in Viti/Vitina 24 of 36 employees downsized were women.

63. The Statistical Office of Kosovo has been working to correct its full consumer-price series, which is currently being reviewed by IMF prior to publication. Once published they will constitute the basis for the Office to calculate and publish the long overdue 2005 Kosovo economic accounts. Lack of technical capacity remains the most important obstacle to the timely production of reliable statistics.

64. A survey of the 14 municipalities audited by the Office of the Auditor General has found inadequate implementation of audit recommendations.

65. The Tax Administration of Kosovo has prepared a strategic plan for 2007–2010 and a business plan for 2007. The Tax Administration has also established five thematic working groups in order to address issues raised by the European Union Fiscal Blueprints exercise and the IMF mission to Kosovo in October 2006.

66. The Board of the Kosovo Trust Agency met regularly, approving the launch of the twenty-first and twenty-second waves of privatization. By the end of December 2006, 393 new companies derived from the assets of 256 socially owned enterprises had been tendered for sale, 216 sales contracts were signed, and 85 contracts were still pending signature. The total privatization proceeds amounted to €267,784,767. The Board had approved a total of 76 liquidations with total proceeds amounting to €2,856,040; and 20 per cent of privatization proceeds are due to be paid out to the eligible former workers of the privatized enterprises. As at 31 December 2006, this amount stood at €53,556,953, of which €9,867,284 had already been paid to the Independent Union of Trade Unions of Kosovo, which disburses the funds to the workers.

67. By the end of January 2007, the senior management of all publicly owned enterprises had been transferred to Kosovans.

68. Customs revenue collection figures for 2006 are the highest to date at €459,500,000, a 12.5 per cent increase from 2005.

Economy: challenges ahead

69. Compliance with IMF recommendations remains a major medium- to long-term challenge in the face of upwards pressures on expenditure, including those potentially related to a status settlement. The potential implementation of a number of social benefits laws

would constitute a serious burden to the Kosovo budget and be in violation of the letter of intent signed with IMF in 2005.

70. Responsiveness to, and implementation of, auditors' recommendations needs to improve.

71. Cash collection remains a major problem for a number of public utilities, and an obstacle to their economic viability.

Property rights

72. The Law on Housing is still awaiting adoption by the Assembly. The draft Law on the Treatment of Illegal Constructions and the draft Law on the Transformation of Real Estate Possessors into Owners are under review by the Assembly. The Law on Real Rights, a priority for the Government, is under review by the Provisional Institutions and requires further consideration by legal experts prior to promulgation.

73. On 11 January, the draft Spatial Plan 2005-2015 for Kosovo passed the first reading in the Kosovo Assembly. The plan promotes sustainable social and economic development, respect for environment and diversity, and includes protection of special zones such as national parks and cultural heritage sites.

74. The Kosovo Property Agency has received 8,536 claims, mostly covering agricultural and commercial properties. The first decisions are expected in March.

75. A joint initiative of the United Nations Human Settlements Programme (UN-Habitat), the Organization for Security and Cooperation in Europe (OSCE) and the Provisional Institutions is setting the basis for a long overdue action plan on informal settlements in consultation with affected communities. A campaign has begun involving posters and leaflets to promote the right to adequate housing.

76. The reconstruction of the cadastre has started in 25 cadastral zones with the support of the World Bank.

Property rights: challenges ahead

77. Illegal construction remains a major problem. Municipal authorities appear unable or unwilling to implement the existing legal framework. Separate spatial plans for areas of cultural heritage and environmental value need to be drafted, approved and implemented.

78. Municipalities, in cooperation with ministries, must remedy previous irregular expropriations and ensure that ongoing public works comply with the law by providing effective safeguards and access to legal remedies.

Cultural heritage

79. The Law on Cultural Heritage was promulgated on 6 November. As required by the Law, the Ministry of Culture, Youth and Sports is currently working with the Assembly towards establishing the multi-ethnic Kosovo Council for Cultural Heritage.

80. Progress has been made on the inventory of cultural heritage. By the end of December 2006, a total of 2,847 objects have been entered in a central database. The soon-to-be-established Kosovo Council for Cultural Heritage will have the final say on the classification of cultural heritage objects.

81. Reconstruction and restoration of cultural heritage sites by the Reconstruction Implementation Commission continue. The Commission held a meeting in January to agree on a workplan for 2007 which will include works on around 20 sites. An amount of €3,448,988 was allocated from the Kosovo consolidated budget to cover the works.

82. KPS reports a decreasing trend in the number of incidents, with 10 reported incidents against Serbian Orthodox churches during the period, of which seven were theft-related and three were minor acts of vandalism.

83. Security meetings between KPS and the Ministry of Culture, Youth and Sports focal points continue every two weeks and cooperation between them remains strong. Additional protection measures now include increased local patrolling by KPS at cultural heritage and religious sites, especially Orthodox sites under reconstruction. On average, more than 2,000 patrols across Kosovo are conducted by KPS every week.

Cultural heritage: challenges ahead

84. Fourteen subsidiary laws necessary for the implementation of the Law on Cultural Heritage should be drafted and passed within the timeframe allotted in the Law.

85. The Provisional Institutions should devise ways to ensure adequate protection of the cultural heritage sites, such as increased security measures, condemnation of acts against them, and issuing of positive reinforcement messages raising awareness of the value of cultural heritage.

Kosovo Protection Corps

86. Non-Albanian membership of KPC has decreased slightly in the reporting period and now stands at 213 (7 per cent), of whom 49 are Serbs (1.5 per cent). The decrease is mainly due to absenteeism and subsequent dismissal. Kosovo Serb officers remain subject to pressure from their own communities not to participate in KPC. No internal allegations of discrimination have arisen. Twenty-four vacancies remain reserved for non-Albanians. On 24 January, the KPC Commander signed into effect an action plan for 2007 for the recruitment, retention and support of ethnic minorities.

87. Women are represented at all levels of KPC though in comparatively small numbers (97 or 3.2 per cent in October 2006), and continue to occupy relatively more senior ranks in comparison with men.

88. Disciplinary compliance continues to improve, although further improvement in the staffing and investigation of disciplinary cases by KPC is still required.

89. The demining capacity of KPC has increased with the recruitment of 24 new deminers: KPC is on track to assume sole responsibility for all mine and unexploded ordnance clearance late in 2007. In 2006, by 15 December when the teams ceased demining activities for the winter season, KPC had located and destroyed a total of 1,962 mines and items of unexploded ordnance and cleared 781,237 square metres of land.

90. The capacity of the Civil Protection Brigade is increasing, with full operational capability expected to be endorsed soon in search and rescue, explosive ordnance disposal, firefighting and hazardous material protection.

91. A Technical Agreement on Cooperation on Civil Emergency Response between KPC, the Office of the KPC Coordinator and the Department of Emergency Management of the Ministry of Internal Affairs was signed on 22 December. The Parliamentary Security Committee held a public hearing for KPC on emergency management on 23 January.

Kosovo Protection Corps: challenges ahead

92. Despite positive recruitment policies, active engagement among Kosovo Serb communities, and no internal evidence of discrimination, KPC still has difficulty in attracting and retaining recruits from the Kosovo Serb community.

93. It is expected that a future Kosovo status settlement will also address KPC and its future. This may bring significant transformation, posing many challenges for KPC and its leaders. This is particularly the case with rationalizing numbers, equipment and infrastructure, all of which will have a resource cost. KPC will require significant donor and other support to meet a challenge of this nature.

94. Donor support is still needed for KPC humanitarian projects. Much of the equipment KPC possesses is obsolescent. New heavy equipment (such as graders and heavy trucks) would improve capacity.

Annex II
Composition and strength of the police component of the United Nations Interim Administration Mission in Kosovo(as at 19 February 2007)

Country	*Number*	*Country*	*Number*
Argentina	10	Nepal	17
Austria	28	Netherlands	1
Bangladesh	29	Nigeria	26
Brazil	2	Norway	18
Bulgaria	53	Pakistan	151
China	18	Philippines	44
Croatia	9	Poland	122
Czech Republic	16	Portugal	7
Denmark	24	Romania	182
Egypt	16	Russian Federation	42
Finland	2	Slovenia	15
France	51	Spain	13
Germany	164	Sweden	34
Ghana	35	Switzerland	6
Greece	10	Timor-Leste	9
Hungary	14	Turkey	141
India	71	Uganda	4
Italy	28	Ukraine	189
Jordan	38	United Kingdom of Great Britain and Northern Ireland	65
Kenya	15	United States of America	221
Kyrgyzstan	6	Zambia	9
Lithuania	6	Zimbabwe	18
Malawi	5		
Total			**1 984**

Composition of the Kosovo Police Service (as at 19 February 2007)

Category	*Percentage*	*Number*
Kosovo Albanians	83.99	6 060
Kosovo Serbs	10.31	744
Other ethnic minority members	5.70	411
Total		**7 215**
Men	86.44	6 237
Women	13.56	978

Annex III
Composition and strength of the military liaison component of the United Nations Interim Administration Mission in Kosovo (as at 19 February 2007)

Country	*Number of liaison officers*
Argentina	1
Bangladesh	1
Bolivia (awaiting a replacement liaison officer)	—
Bulgaria	1
Chile	1
Czech Republic	1
Denmark	1
Finland	2
Hungary	1
Ireland	4
Jordan	2
Kenya	1
Malawi	1
Malaysia	1
Nepal	1
New Zealand	1
Norway	1
Pakistan	1
Poland	1
Portugal	2
Romania	3
Russian Federation	2
Spain	2
Ukraine	2
United Kingdom of Great Britain and Northern Ireland	1
Zambia	1
Total	**36**

3. Report of the Secretary-General on the United Nations Interim Administration Mission in Kosovo, 29 June 2007 (S/2007/395)

I. Introduction

1. The present report is submitted pursuant to Security Council resolution 1244 (1999) of 10 June 1999, by which the Council decided to establish the United Nations Interim Administration Mission in Kosovo (UNMIK) and requested the Secretary-General to report at regular intervals on the implementation of the mandate. It covers the activities of UNMIK and developments in Kosovo (Serbia) from 19 February to 1 June 2007.

II. Political assessment

2. On 2 February, my Special Envoy for the Future Status Process for Kosovo, Martti Ahtisaari, submitted a draft comprehensive proposal for the Kosovo status settlement to the political leaderships in Belgrade and Prishtinë/Priština. My Special Envoy and his team then held further, intensive consultations with Belgrade and Prishtinë/Priština from 21 February to 2 March. A meeting of the Serbian and Kosovo leaders was held on 10 March in Vienna to discuss the settlement proposal, at which the parties were unable to make any additional progress. Following this meeting, my Special Envoy presented me with his report on Kosovo's future status (S/2007/168), containing his recommendation of independence for Kosovo supervised initially by the international community, and his settlement proposal (S/2007/168/Add.1). On 26 March, I conveyed both his future status report and his settlement proposal to the Security Council, with my full support.

3. Following my Special Envoy's briefing to the Security Council on his future status report and settlement proposal on 3 April, the Council undertook a mission to Kosovo and Belgrade from 25 to 28 April. The objective of the mission was to gain first-hand information on progress made in Kosovo since the adoption of resolution 1244 (1999). The Council met with the leaders of Serbia and of Kosovo's Provisional Institutions of Self-Government, with representatives of Kosovo's ethnic minority communities and with my Special Representative, Joachim Rücker, and UNMIK staff. A comprehensive and balanced programme enabled the Security Council to further its understanding of the political, social and economic situation in Kosovo, as reflected in the report of the mission (S/2007/256).

Political situation

4. The future status of Kosovo continued to be the main political issue for Kosovo's political establishment and for representatives of all of its communities throughout the reporting period. Expectations remained high among Kosovo Albanians that Kosovo would become independent in the near future. The Kosovo unity team, which represents Kosovo Albanian political parties from both the Government and the opposition, continued its work in three priority areas. It participated in the negotiations held in Vienna with the Belgrade negotiating team; it continued its outreach activities to all of Kosovo's communities to explain the settlement proposal; and it undertook efforts aimed at garnering international support for Kosovo's independence.

5. On 5 April, the Assembly of Kosovo met in an extraordinary session and approved a declaration in support of my Special Envoy's future status report and settlement proposal.

No Kosovo Serb member of the Assembly was present at the session. The declaration welcomed the report's recommendation on status, stating that it represented "a fair and balanced solution in accordance with the will of the people of Kosovo". The Assembly also committed itself to full implementation of the settlement proposal, adding that, if endorsed by the Security Council, it would be considered "legally binding" for Kosovo. Assembly members also welcomed, and pledged cooperation with, the future international civilian and security presences envisaged in the settlement proposal. On 14 April, unity team members signed a "declaration" in which they agreed to remain united during the 120-day transition period envisaged in the settlement proposal.

6. Kosovo Serb political leaders continued their near-total political boycott of Kosovo's central institutions, and were encouraged to do so by the authorities in Belgrade. However, a number of Kosovo Serb political actors who seek a more engaged approach entered the political arena in Kosovo. New Kosovo Serb political parties were established, such as the Independent Liberal Party in Graçanicë/Gracanica, some of which advocate that, irrespective of the future status of Kosovo, the Kosovo Serb community should remain in Kosovo and should participate in the future institutions of Kosovo. While these parties are small and have limited influence, this development reflects a growing concern among some Kosovo Serbs that the continued boycott of Kosovo's institutions is counterproductive and does not effectively address their practical needs.

7. It is evident that most Kosovo Albanians look forward to the resolution of Kosovo's status with confidence and anticipation, and that most Kosovo Serbs view this process with apprehension. Although the actual number of serious inter-ethnic incidents during the reporting period has remained low, the political uncertainty surrounding the status determination process continued to have a negative effect on perceptions of security within the Kosovo Serb community. It is also increasingly apparent that issues of common concern, such as unemployment and the state of the economy, are viewed with increasing pessimism by members of all of Kosovo's communities.

Economy

8. The economy in Kosovo showed some signs of continuing improvement. The gross domestic product continued to grow, following an estimated 3 to 4 per cent growth in 2006, while inflation remained close to zero. Exports increased as much as 40 per cent while Government revenues grew by 13 per cent, a rate which exceeds estimates made by the International Monetary Fund from the beginning of 2007. However, lack of foreign direct investment and access to international loans continues to hamper the Provisional Institutions' ability to effectively combat unemployment. The privatization process continued to move forward. By the end of April 2007, 460 new companies derived from the assets of 282 socially owned enterprises had been tendered for sale as part of the process. Total privatization proceeds amounted to over €303 million.

9. In terms of economic governance, the reporting period saw a number of positive trends. Fiscal management continued to improve, customs collections increased and the banking sector evidenced progressive growth. UNMIK continued to transfer competencies in the economic sector to the Provisional Institutions. With the exception of the Civil Aviation Regulatory Office, all regulatory bodies are currently headed by local professionals. Activities aimed at ensuring the long-term development of the energy sector also continued,

including the development of new mines and generation facilities and preparations for the construction of a new thermal power plant.

Security

10. During the reporting period, the overall security situation was calm, with few significant incidents. Rallies organized by the Kosovo Albanian self-determination movement "Vetevendosje" on 3 and 31 March, in protest against the current status determination process, had low attendance and were held peacefully. This stood in sharp contrast to the 10 February demonstration organized by Vetevendosje, during which two protesters were fatally wounded by UNMIK police and which led to the arrest of the movement's leader. This change in the nature of the Vetevendosje demonstrations can be attributed to outreach efforts by UNMIK police and the Kosovo Police Service (KPS) with rally organizers, and the continued detention of Vetevendosje's leader, as well as steps forward in the future status process.

11. On 17 April, the international prosecutor in charge of investigating the violence surrounding the 10 February Vetevendosje demonstration issued an interim report stating that there was a substantial basis upon which to conclude that members of the Romanian formed police unit were linked to the incidents. He also concluded that there was insufficient evidence to support a reasonable suspicion as to which Romanian police officers were responsible for firing the shots, and that therefore a judicial investigation could not proceed. On 18 April, the UNMIK Police Commissioner announced that an internal police review had found deficiencies in some areas of operational planning and command and control and indicated that measures had been taken to ensure that the police response to public disorder would be properly managed in the future.

12. The publication of the interim report, as well as the announcement by UNMIK police that an internal review would be undertaken, did much to defuse tensions. The relative calm during the reporting period was also attributable to a perception by the population in Kosovo that, as long as there is a clear forward momentum in the status determination process, there is no need to explicitly support more radical political options promoted by groups such as Vetevendosje.

13. Notwithstanding the general calm that prevailed during the reporting period, there were two high-profile incidents. These included a grenade attack on the Visoki Dečani monastery in Deçan/Dečani municipality on 30 March, and the attempted assassination on 28 February and 12 April of the head of the Telecommunications Regulatory Agency of Kosovo. Though little damage was done to the monastery, the attack was significant as it occurred only a few days after a successful outreach meeting in the municipality, which was attended by my Special Representative, senior officials of the Provisional Institutions, representatives of the Serbian Orthodox Church and representatives of the Kosovo Liberation Army War Veterans' Association. A suspect was subsequently identified in connection with the attack, but remains at large despite continuing efforts by KPS to locate and apprehend this individual, including public appeals for cooperation in the search. Thanks to swift action by KPS, three suspects were immediately arrested in the case of the assassination attempt on the head of the Telecommunications Regulatory Agency on 12 April.

Rule of law

14. Local institutions continued to assume additional responsibilities in the justice field. The Ministry of Justice continued to lead efforts to finalize an agreement with the Ministry of Health on the transfer of responsibility for missing persons and forensics. An memorandum of understanding between UNMIK, the European Union and the United States of America on funding and implementation of the vetting process for judges and prosecutors is under consideration. Consultations between UNMIK and the Kosovo Judicial Council on the allocation of 421 judicial and prosecutorial posts between various courts in Kosovo continued. Recruitment for the Kosovo Special Prosecutor's Office, including of members from minority communities, progressed.

15. Despite these ongoing, progressive steps to strengthen the justice sector, major challenges remain. It is still necessary for international judges and prosecutors to handle the most sensitive cases. The judicial system suffers from inadequate resources. This has a negative impact on the motivation of judges, as well as the recruitment process. To address these concerns, a justice system reform programme continued to work with municipal courts to reduce the backlog of civil cases pending since June 2006.

16. The Ministry of Internal Affairs has also taken on new competencies. It now reviews civil registration and documentation and has nearly completed drafting a police law that establishes the rights and duties of this Ministry and the police and clarifies the institutional relationship between them in line with European standards. The law will be submitted to the Government for approval, following which it is expected to be sent to the Kosovo Assembly for deliberation and then adopted. Participants and stakeholders from other sections of the Government, non-governmental organizations and the international community provided substantial inputs to the law and concur that it meets international and European standards.

17. The Ministry of Internal Affairs made significant progress in establishing the Department of Borders, Boundaries, Asylum and Migration and strengthened its capacity to implement current readmission procedures. Progress was also made in clarifying the chain of command in cases of civil emergency, in converting the Kosovo Police Service School into the Kosovo Centre for Public Safety Education and Development, and in creating an independent professional standards board.

Standards and European integration

18. Work on standards implementation continued to progress within the framework of the European Partnership Action Plan. A technical assessment on progress in the implementation of the standards for Kosovo, prepared by my Special Representative, is contained in the annex to the present report. Standards implementation continues to strengthen Kosovo's institutions and helps to improve the delivery of public services to the people of Kosovo. It is particularly important that the principles underlying the standards have been incorporated into the Action Plan. Fulfilling the requirements of the Action Plan remains a priority for the Kosovo institutions.

Governance

19. The consolidation of Kosovo's government structures continued, especially at the central level through the strengthening of several independent agencies. However, obstacles remained, including in some instances a lack of sufficient capacity and the absence of

necessary secondary legislation, as well as insufficient adherence to procedures at the local level. At the central level, the Kosovo Assembly continued to show an increasing tendency to adhere to its rules of procedure and held a number of public hearings and consultations on numerous draft laws. The Central Election Commission continued to build up its capacity in all areas and is expected to take full responsibility for the conduct of the next elections, with the continued support of the Organization for Security and Cooperation in Europe (OSCE). The Transition Working Group on Elections, which includes representatives from both the Government and the opposition, prepared principles for draft legislation on elections. However, the Assembly's appointment of a new Ombudsperson has not progressed.

20. There was progress in the establishment and consolidation of a number of independent agencies in Kosovo. The consolidation of the Independent Media Commission continued; however, the implementation of the law governing the Commission and secondary-level legislation did not progress. The civil service Independent Oversight Board is now running effectively. There is, however, a need to provide for an effective mechanism to enforce its rulings and recommendations and to finalize its establishment as an independent body. The Anti-Corruption Agency became operational. The implementation of an anti-corruption strategy will now depend on the effectiveness of this Agency and its cooperation with the Provisional Institutions of Self-Government and the public.

21. The reporting period saw progress in municipal governance through a strengthening of both legislative and administrative structures. All municipalities, including the newly established pilot municipal units, now have rules and procedures that are incorporated into their statutes. Interdepartmental consultation is ensured through a board of directors. In addition, public consultation has become normal practice prior to the adoption of legislation and budget proposals by municipal assemblies. However, the general lack of meaningful consultation with minority communities is a cause for concern. In addition, the struggle between the Democratic League of Kosovo and the breakaway faction Democratic League of Dardania, led by the former President of the Kosovo Assembly, Nexhat Daci, in the key municipalities of Gjilan/Gnjilan, Viti/Vitina and Ferizaj/Uroševac has had negative consequences. Municipal assemblies in these municipalities have become dysfunctional and the appointment of senior civil servants has been delayed.

Decentralization

22. A transition working group has been established to consider the practical measures necessary to eventually implement the annex to the settlement proposal referring to decentralization. Transfer of responsibilities and capacity-building has continued in the three pilot municipal units of Hani i Elezit/Đeneral Jankovic, Junik and Mamushë/Mamuša. The Kosovo Government has requested the Ministry of Local Government Administration to recommend by 1 July whether pilot municipal units should be converted into fully functional municipalities.

Cultural and religious heritage

23. During much of the reporting period, work on the reconstruction of Serbian Orthodox cultural heritage sites damaged or destroyed during the March 2004 events slowed down significantly. This was mainly due to the paralysis of the Reconstruction Implementation Commission as a result of the non-participation of the representative from Serbia's Institute

for the Protection of Monuments. While a new representative was appointed to the Commission by the Serbian Minister of Culture in April, subsequent changes to the Government of Serbia led to a reversal of this appointment. The position needs to be filled before the Commission can recommence work. In an encouraging signal, the Assembly of Bishops of the Serbian Orthodox Church reiterated its readiness to cooperate with the Commission and the Council of Europe during its biannual meeting. The European Agency for Reconstruction began work in April on two Serbian Orthodox sites in Prizren under the Commission's mandate.

Returns

24. The number of Kosovo Serb returns remained low. Although conditions for returns have gradually improved, the factors that discourage large-scale return movements continue to exist, such as the lack of employment opportunities, unresolved property disputes and continuing perceptions of insecurity.

25. Despite these challenges, UNMIK and the Provisional Institutions have continued to focus their efforts on strengthening institutional and administrative structures to underpin the process of return. UNMIK continued to transfer competencies to the Ministry of Communities and Returns, which is led by the only Kosovo Serb minister in the Government. Transferred competencies include the coordination of municipal fair-share financing and of the work of municipal returns offices and municipal community offices. UNMIK maintains an advisory role and is building capacity with a focus on senior staff.

26. The Ministry continued to demonstrate a willingness to cooperate closely with UNMIK and the international community. It focused its efforts on supporting organized and individual returns of minorities and developing community development and stabilization projects. Four projects benefiting about 90 families were approved for funding by the Ministry and its partners for 2007, of which two (Berkove/Berkovo (Klinë/a) and Vushtrri/Vucitrn) have been launched; the remaining two will be launched in due course. In addition, two ongoing projects carried over from the 2006 Kosovo consolidated budget, in Lipjan/Lipljan and Abdullah Presheva/Presevo (Gjilan/Gnjilane), will benefit 45 internally displaced persons.

27. Individual returns have already begun this year. Returns to the Roma settlement in southern Mitrovicë/a began in early March and have now reached a total of 280 persons out of an expected 412. Though small in number, these returns are a highly symbolic breakthrough. They are expected to foster additional return movements, provided that international donor contributions and assistance to the Ministry continue.

Future international arrangements and transition

28. Joint work on transition to the future international presence envisaged in the settlement proposal continued, without prejudice to the outcome of the future status process. This work is carried out by UNMIK, in close collaboration with the planning teams for the envisaged international civilian representative and the European Security and Defence Policy rule of law mission, as well as the Kosovo Force (KFOR) and the Provisional Institutions of Self-Government.

III. Observations

29. I welcome and am encouraged by the continuing commitment to standards implementation shown by the Provisional Institutions of Kosovo throughout the reporting period. There has been concrete progress in many areas of standards, although results in some areas have been mixed and clearly much remains to be done. I call upon Kosovo's leaders and institutions to demonstrate an unambiguous continuing commitment to standards implementation, and to translate this commitment into concrete results.

30. In eight years of interim administration by the United Nations, Kosovo has made significant strides in the establishment and consolidation of democratic and accountable Provisional Institutions of Self-Government and in creating the foundations for a functioning economy. The Provisional Institutions have laid the basis for a peaceful and normal life for all of the people of Kosovo.

31. However, the process of full reconciliation and integration of Kosovo's communities will be a long-term one, and remains an uphill challenge. Further progress in consolidating peaceful coexistence in Kosovo will require firm determination on the part of Kosovo's leaders and a genuine commitment by members of all of its communities.

32. Regrettably, large segments of the Kosovo Serb population continue to feel that Kosovo's Provisional Institutions do not represent them. Kosovo Serbs continue to boycott these institutions at the central level, and instead rely for the most part on parallel structures supported by the authorities in Belgrade for the provision of basic services. At the same time, returns of Kosovo Serbs remain disappointingly low due to uncertain economic prospects and continuing security-related concerns.

33. While Kosovo's overall progress is encouraging, if its future status remains undefined there is a real risk that the progress achieved by the United Nations and the Provisional Institutions in Kosovo can begin to unravel. Sustaining and consolidating the progress made by Kosovo will require concrete prospects for the conclusion of the future status process and the active and constructive cooperation of all involved.

34. The determination of Kosovo's future status should therefore remain a priority for the Security Council and for the international community as a whole. My Special Envoy's settlement proposal and recommendation on Kosovo's future status contain the right elements for a sustainable solution to Kosovo's future status, including continued international supervision. I welcome the European Union's pledge to play the leading role in the future international presence in Kosovo, as envisaged in the settlement proposal.

35. I would like to express my appreciation and gratitude to my Special Representative, Joachim Rücker, and to his staff in UNMIK for their dedication and effort to move Kosovo forward. I would also like to extend my thanks to the United Nations partners—KFOR, the European Union and OSCE—and to the United Nations agencies, funds and programmes and other contributors for their support.

Annex I

Technical assessment of progress in implementation of the standards for Kosovo

Prepared by the Special Representative of the Secretary-General for Kosovo, 12 June 2007

1. The status settlement process continued to dominate the reporting period. Nevertheless, normal standards implementation work also continued, increasingly with its own momentum and with the Agency for European Integration in the lead.

2. Implementation also continued of the remaining items in the programme of 13 priority points presented to the Kosovo Government by the Contact Group in June 2006.

Functioning democratic institutions

3. There were no serious violations of the Kosovo Assembly rules of procedure during the reporting period. Monitoring of the Assembly has shown an increased number of plenary debates, public hearings, interpellations and consultations, with comments received on numerous draft laws. The Assembly has also strengthened the scrutiny of its budgetary expenditures.

4. In 2007 the Committee on Rights and Interests of Communities of the Kosovo Assembly has held 11 meetings and reviewed 10 amendments to draft laws, returning one draft law to the functional committee for review. However, the Committee did not forward any amendment for the Assembly's consideration. The problems faced by the Committee relate to internal political divisions, a low level of communication with the Assembly and a lack of concrete initiatives from Committee members.

5. The split in the Democratic League of Kosovo (LDK) and the establishment of the Democratic League of Dardania (LDD) have reduced the majority that the former enjoyed in many municipal assemblies. This has impaired the functioning of a number of assemblies, such as those of Kamenicë/a and Gjilan/Gnjilane, and has affected the tenure of members of the board of directors, including some chief executive officers (Lipjan/Lipljan). Six former LDK members formed their own LDD parliamentary group, but no difficulties have been noted in the functioning of the Assembly and the Government at the central level.

6. Representatives of the Serb List for Kosovo and Metohija (SLKM) continued their boycott of the Assembly and were joined in January by another elected Kosovo Serb representative, thus reducing the number of Kosovo Serbs participating in the Assembly to one. Eight other Kosovo Serb representatives participate in the work of the Assembly committees, but do not sit in the Assembly.

7. Against a background of budgetary constraints and pressure from the Government of Serbia, the participation of Kosovo Serbs in the civil service has not shown any significant improvement. In the central institutions, 11 per cent of civil servants come from minority communities, against a target of 16.6 per cent. Though incomplete, the statistics at the municipal level show that minority employment constitutes about 12 per cent of the total. (Because of the declared non-cooperation policy of the three Serb-run northern municipalities and the administration in northern Mitrovicë/a, these figures are incomplete for the municipalities.)

8. Two hundred Kosovo Serb civil servants, who had withdrawn from the Provisional Institutions' payroll following a directive from Serbian authorities to choose between the payrolls of the Serbian and Kosovo Governments, have requested reinstatement, and have received their accumulated salaries. The Kosovo Government continues to hold in trust the salaries of all remaining Kosovo Serbs who have left the Provisional Institutions' payroll (€4,910,810 remains in escrow while €237,584 has been paid out to those reinstated).

9. On 24 March, the Kosovo Government adopted a public administration reform strategy together with an action plan for its implementation. The total budget required for its implementation in 2007 amounts to some €6.5 million. Of this amount, €1.2 million has been allocated from the Kosovo budget, donors have provided €3 million, and the rest still needs to be found.

10. Women constitute 35.7 per cent of the civil service, but remain seriously underrepresented at the senior level. There are only 193 women, compared to 937 men, in senior posts at the central level, with only one minister and one permanent secretary who are women. There are only 56 women, compared to 731 men, at the municipal level, with only two chief executive officer posts occupied by women.

11. To address this discrepancy the Prime Minister declared 2007 the Year of Affirmative Action for Women in Kosovo. The Provisional Institutions issued an administrative instruction which promotes preferential treatment for the employment of women in the civil service. All municipalities have gender equality officers and so far 20 municipalities have committees for gender equality

12. The Independent Oversight Board and the Senior Public Appointments Committee are now functioning normally. The Office of the Prime Minister has established a commission to oversee the transformation of the Independent Oversight Board into an independent body which reports directly to the Assembly.

13. The Anti-Corruption Agency has been operational since 1 February. The public has since started to contact the Agency and several corruption cases have been brought to the attention of police and the judiciary. The implementation of the anti-corruption strategy will now depend on the effectiveness of this Agency and the collaboration it obtains from the Provisional Institutions and the public. Of the 732 senior officials at the central level, 712 have declared their properties and assets in accordance with the anti-corruption law. Ministries have yet to appoint vigilance officers to implement the anti-corruption action plan.

14. The implementation of the law on languages continued with the adoption of administrative instructions setting out the composition and competencies of the Language Commission and the administrative sanctions to be imposed in cases of violation. The Municipal Assembly of Mitrovicë/a has adopted Turkish for official use and similar decisions are expected in other municipalities including Prishtinë/Priština.

15. The Ministry of Public Services and the Ministry of Local Government Administration continue to monitor language compliance at the central and local levels respectively. The Kosovo Institute for Public Administration is conducting training sessions for approximately 60 interpreters and translators. Except in the Serb-run northern municipalities and the mono-ethnic Kosovo Albanian municipalities, signs outside municipal buildings

generally appear in all official languages. However, defacing of place names on road signs is quite common; officials usually take corrective action only at the behest of UNMIK.

16. Of the 117 licensed broadcasters, 42 broadcast in minority languages (34 in Serbian, four in Bosnian, two in Turkish, one in Gorani and one in Roma). Twelve radio stations, most of them broadcasting in the Serbian language, have a weekly programme in the Roma language.

17. Radio Television Kosovo broadcasts 16.4 per cent of its television programming and 12.5 per cent of its radio programming in minority community languages. Of the total television news programming, 20.7 per cent is in minority community languages.

18. Journalists and editors are increasingly adhering to the Press Council's code of conduct and its statute. As of 6 June, the Press Council had received a total of 38 complaints, 26 of which had been adjudicated.

Functioning democratic institutions: challenges ahead

19. The existing administrative instruction on the composition and competences of the Language Commission needs to be revised to ensure adequate minority participation.

20. Existing gender structures need adequate support and should be fully involved in decision-making processes and selection of personnel. The long-term strategy to increase the number and improve the position of women in the Provisional Institutions should be further implemented at both central and local levels.

21. There should be no further delay in the appointment of an Ombudsperson in accordance with the amended regulation on the ombudsperson institution in Kosovo. Amended rules of procedure need to be adopted before the summer recess and a new call for applications should be issued immediately.

22. The Minority Media Fund should continue its operation with a new round of grants. Radio Television Kosovo should transfer 5 per cent of the 2006 and 2007 broadcast fee to the Minority Media Fund.

23. The implementation of the Independent Media Commission Law needs to be expedited, including the allocation of adequate resources. However, the amounts set by the adopted license fee regulation for broadcasters could pose a heavy financial burden for stations, particularly those serving minority communities.

Rule of law

24. As of 2 April, the Police Task Force, established in April 2006 to investigate March 2004 cases (a Contact Group priority), had investigated 1,526 cases, of which 754 were under review, 177 remained open, 315 were closed, 120 were under active investigation and 160 were being investigated by the Kosovo Police Service (KPS).

25. International prosecutors have indicted 36 people for the most serious March riot-related offences, resulting in 26 convictions and one acquittal. Nine defendants in three cases are awaiting trial. Local prosecutors have brought over 300 criminal charges resulting in 142 convictions, with another 22 persons currently under investigation.

26. A memorandum of understanding between the European Union, UNMIK and the United States on the funding and implementation of the reappointment of judges and prosecutors is under review. The Kosovo Judicial Council approved on 20 March the new allocation of 326 judicial positions for the supreme, district, municipal and minor offences courts. A number of judicial staff have been transferred from low-volume to high-volume courts as part of this process. The Ministry of Justice plans to complete its new allocation of the prosecutorial positions by the end of June.

27. A strategy to identify and reduce current civil case backlogs (including those related to property cases) and to prevent future backlogs was developed in February by a group of international and local stakeholders.

28. Legislation on witness protection is still awaiting finalization. With United Kingdom and United States support, all district courts are now equipped with a witness protection system that will improve the ability of the Kosovo justice system to conduct investigations and prosecutions in a variety of sensitive cases with protected witnesses.

29. The Kosovo Special Prosecutor's Office is operational. Six special prosecutors are now in place, including one woman and one member of an ethnic minority group.

30. In March, an additional police substation was established for Roma returnees to the Roma settlement in Mitrovicë/a, raising the number of existing substations to 18. An additional nine substations are under consideration.

31. Minority representation within KPS remained constant at 16 per cent (10.3 per cent Kosovo Serbs) and in the Kosovo Corrections Service (KCS) at 14.4 per cent (10.3 per cent Kosovo Serbs). Female representation stands at 13.6 per cent for KPS and 17.4 for KCS.

32. A memorandum of understanding on the transfer of competencies covering the civil status registry from the Ministry of Public Service to the Ministry of Internal Affairs was signed on 4 April. Minority representation in the Ministry of Internal Affairs is 9.8 per cent (7.2 per cent Kosovo Serbs). There are still 53 vacancies out of 779 posts. Forty per cent of posts are occupied by women.

33. Minority representation of judges and prosecutors is at 8.9 per cent (4.2 per cent Kosovo Serbs) and 9.1 per cent (3 per cent Kosovo Serbs) respectively. Women's representation is at 26.8 per cent for judges and 20.5 per cent for prosecutors. Minority representation in the Ministry of Justice, including KCS, prosecutors and their support staff, is currently at 13.2 per cent (9 per cent Kosovo Serbs).

Rule of law: challenges ahead

34. Further work is needed to effectively protect witnesses from intimidation.

35. Efforts to increase the number of judges and prosecutors from underrepresented communities and to increase minority recruits within the Ministry of Internal Affairs need to continue.

36. The Kosovo Judicial Council needs to proceed with the restructuring and rationalization of the court system. A first step would be to reduce the number of judges assigned to the lowest volume courts. Similarly, the Ministry of Justice needs to restructure the 95 prosecutorial posts.

37. The Kosovo Judicial Council needs to institute stronger accountability mechanisms and to tighten its supervision over court administration. An effective coordination mechanism between the Council and the Ministry of Justice is needed.

Freedom of movement

38. No crime related to freedom of movement was reported during the reporting period. However, some Kosovo Serbs continue to express concerns over the security situation and some members of all communities continue to limit their movements to areas where they are in the majority.

39. On 6 May, some 400 Serbs from Prizren and other parts of Kosovo, currently displaced in Serbia, visited the village of Gornjasellë/Gornje Selo (Prizren) for the annual celebration of St. George. On 7 May, some 280 Serbian children from various parts of Kosovo, including Shtërpcë/Štrpce, Graçanicë/Gračanica and Partesh/Parteš, attended an annual children's folklore music festival in Zubin Potok.

40. Beneficiaries of the humanitarian transport programme, which was handed over to the Government on 1 January, continue to use it in great numbers.

Freedom of movement: challenges ahead

41. Even though KPS surveys suggest that individuals from minority communities have a positive perception of their freedom of movement, the Government needs to continue to condemn inter-ethnic crimes and identify new ways to address the security concerns of minority communities.

Sustainable returns and the rights of communities and their members

42. Restructuring of the Ministry of Communities and Returns (MCR) is ongoing and Minister Grbić continues to build constructive relationships with all stakeholders. As a result, the Ministry is taking an increasing leadership role in the returns process, including participation in municipal working groups and direct project implementation.

43. Five organized return projects, costing €3.2 million, for the return of 120 minority families have been launched in 2007 in Lipjan/Lipljan, Gjilan/Gnjilane, Vushtrri/Vučitrn, Klinë/a and Fushë Kosovë/Kosovo Polje. While additional projects continue to be developed at the municipal level, funding remains the most important obstacle to returns. The Ministry of Communities and Returns has approved 47 community development and stabilization projects worth €2.08 million to facilitate integration of all communities in Kosovo.

44. The first 69 families have returned to the Roma settlement in Mitrovicë/a and construction is under way to accommodate 24 more families.

45. The Government has assessed all outstanding compensation cases for commercial properties damaged or destroyed during March 2004 (a Contact Group priority) and the funds have been transferred to the beneficiaries.

46. Compliance with fair-share financing quotas and with the administrative instruction issued by the Ministry of Finance and Economy on the administration of fair-share financing by municipalities has improved. Of the 24 municipalities south of the Ibar River, only three failed to comply with the 2006 targets.

47. An administrative instruction defining the competencies of human rights units in the ministries was adopted by the Government on 28 February. This administrative instruction adds the monitoring of implementation of recommendations of the Ombudsperson to the units' responsibilities. The units comprise three to seven staff members covering gender, the rights of minorities, equal opportunities, anti-discrimination, children's rights, anti-trafficking and the rights of persons with disabilities.

48. The draft readmission policy and procedures for repatriation of refugees to Kosovo were finalized on 10 May and submitted to the Government for approval. The reintegration strategy for repatriated persons is to be finalized soon.

Sustainable returns and the rights of communities and their members: challenges ahead

49. Despite the existence of an anti-discrimination law, a comprehensive implementation plan and an administrative instruction to implement the law, little has been done. There is still no comprehensive mechanism for tracking discrimination cases, and ministries have not been tasked with specific duties for its implementation.

50. The Government needs to continue to build capacity to implement its repatriation responsibilities. A comprehensive action plan and monitoring mechanisms should be put in place.

51. The Prishtinë/Priština Municipal Assembly needs to allocate land for the Novi Badovac II/Badoci i Ri II project. The returns project has been coordinated with Belgrade and approved by the municipal working group and the relevant municipal committee.

Economy

52. The draft law to amend the law on public procurement (a Contact Group priority) was adopted by the Assembly on 8 February and promulgated on 13 June.

53. Fourteen of the 30 municipalities audited last year by the Office of the Auditor General have been revisited to determine whether they adopted the mandatory action plans to address the audit findings. Of the 14, three have already implemented their action plans, seven are in the process of doing so and four have not demonstrated any progress. The remaining 16 municipalities will be visited in the coming months.

54. The Board of the Kosovo Trust Agency has approved the launching of the twenty-seventh wave of privatization. By the end of May, 476 new companies derived from the assets of 287 socially owned enterprises had been tendered for sale. Two hundred and seventy-seven sales contracts had been signed, with an additional 127 pending signature. Total privatization proceeds amounted to €310,411,684. The Board had approved a total of 90 liquidations. The estimated value of liquidation sales contracts signed amounted to €2,036,837, and of contracts pending to €2,260,405. The 20 per cent of privatization proceeds to be paid out to the eligible former workers of privatized enterprises stood at €62,082,337, of which €11,784,115 had already been paid to the Independent Union of Trade Unions of Kosovo, which disburses the funds to the workers.

55. There were no reports of unauthorized annexing of socially owned enterprises' property by municipalities during the reporting period. Following the issuance of criteria under

which municipalities may seek to obtain plots of land under the auspices of the public good, several land swaps have been proposed and approved. Prizren is the only municipality to have surrendered land previously annexed without authorization; it returned the property of four socially owned enterprises and of two publicly owned enterprises.

56. The incorporation of the water enterprises is proceeding well; the incorporation of the waste and irrigation enterprises commenced in March.

57. On 12 June, the Economic and Fiscal Council endorsed the expenditure ceilings for the 2008 budget, amounting to €852 million. This represents an increase of 17 per cent compared to 2007. The medium-term expenditure framework was approved by the Government at the beginning of June.

58. The Tax Administration of Kosovo first quarter report shows that tax receipts are nearly 2 per cent ahead of budget projections, and 16 per cent higher compared to the same period in 2006.

59. Revenue collection figures for the Kosovo Energy Corporation for the first quarter of 2007 show overall progress compared to the same period in 2006. The billing of supplied energy increased from 47 to 62 per cent. Although revenue collection on bills decreased from 75 to 67 per cent, revenue collected against energy supplied increased from 35 to 42 per cent, so that the Corporation collected a greater amount of revenue in 2007.

Economy: challenges ahead

60. Audit recommendations need to be better implemented, including by the municipalities audited last year.

61. The Government should systematically consider the costs of legislation when drafting it. The Provisional Institutions need to make improvements in enacting subsidiary legislation and complying with the deadlines envisaged for the adoption of secondary acts.

62. Serious concerns remain about the quality, coverage and timeliness of economic statistics in Kosovo, despite substantial international technical assistance.

63. Revenue collection remains a challenge for the Kosovo Energy Corporation and other public utilities; further efforts are necessary to achieve progress.

Property rights

64. The law on expropriation, the law on arbitration and amendments to the law on cadastre have been approved and are pending promulgation. The law on real rights, a priority for the Government, is still under revision by the Assembly. The draft law on housing and the draft law on the treatment of illegal construction are awaiting adoption by the Assembly. The draft law on the organization of cadastral institutions has been discussed with the municipalities and will be presented to the Assembly.

65. On 6 June, the Housing and Property Claims Commission was officially replaced by the new Kosovo Property Claims Commission, which has adjudicated in the first instance all 29,160 cases it received. Of these, 368 claims still need to be implemented (a Contact Group priority). Implementation of the rental scheme for illegally occupied properties continues (a Contact Group priority). To date, 2,546 property right holders have included their

property in the scheme. Three hundred and ninety-two properties have been rented and €118,248 collected.

66. The Kosovo Property Agency has received 23,343 claims covering agricultural (90.5 per cent), commercial (3.2 per cent) and residential properties (6.3 per cent). Nine hundred and fifty-five cases were brought before the Kosovo Property Claims Commission at its first session, held on 4 and 5 June. First claims including 4,551 agricultural properties, 360 residential properties and 296 commercial properties have been published to enable persons with potential legal interests to become parties to the claim.

67. A strategy to reduce backlog of property cases in courts, drafted by the Organization for Security and Cooperation in Europe (OSCE) in consultation with all relevant stakeholders, was completed and circulated for comments in April.

Property rights: challenges ahead

68. Courts need clear guidance on the mandate of the Kosovo Property Agency over conflict-related property claims, and on the final binding force of all decisions of the Housing and Property Claims Commission, in order not to pass judgement on cases within the jurisdiction of the former or those already decided by the latter.

69. The Kosovo Property Agency needs to ensure that displaced persons belonging to the Kosovo Roma and other vulnerable groups are aware of the claims process and have effective access to it.

70. Concerns remain over the proper implementation of expropriations by Kosovo institutions, and the proper implementation of demolitions.

71. Spatial plans for special zones deemed of particular cultural and environmental value need to be prepared, drafted and implemented before further urbanization projects are launched.

72. The action plan on informal settlements needs to be drafted and implemented.

73. The strategy to reduce judicial property backlogs needs to be implemented.

Cultural heritage

74. The Reconstruction Implementation Commission held its only 2007 meeting thus far in January and agreed to make further interventions on six of the seven sites undergoing work in 2006, as well as another 10 to 12 sites. However, the absence of the Serbian Government representative since February has prevented further progress by the Commission. Discussions are under way between the Council of Europe, the Serbian Orthodox Church, the Ministry of Culture of Serbia and UNMIK to resolve the issue.

75. Over the reporting period, 34 incidents targeting heritage sites were reported. While the vast majority were vandalism (10 cases) or theft-related (20 cases), one serious incident occurred when the Deçan/Dečani monastery sustained slight damage from a rocket-propelled grenade attack on the site.

76. The Provisional Institutions, in coordination with the Serbian Orthodox Church and with support from UNMIK and the Council of Europe, have drawn up a project proposal to hire 24-hour guards and/or install surveillance equipment at 15 sites considered vulnerable.

The Ministry of Culture, Youth and Sports is preparing to allocate €20,000 to €50,000 for these additional security measures.

77. The Ministry of Culture, Youth and Sports established a group of experts to prepare drafts for the 14 sub-laws necessary to implement the cultural heritage law. At workshops held with Council of Europe experts in April and May, it was agreed to merge some provisions so that only seven sub-laws instead of 14 would be necessary. Texts for three sub-laws were finalized. A draft proposal on the composition and terms of reference of the Kosovo Cultural Heritage Council was prepared and presented to the Commission on Culture of the Kosovo Assembly for discussion.

Cultural heritage: challenges ahead

78. Full support for the work of the Reconstruction Implementation Committee is needed from all stakeholders.

79. Seven subsidiary laws necessary for the implementation of the law on cultural heritage should be drafted and passed within the time frame allotted in the law. A non-discriminatory policy for the allocation of funding for cultural heritage protection should be defined in subsidiary legislation. The Kosovo Cultural Heritage Council should be in place by the end of June 2007.

80. The Provisional Institutions should continue to work on ways to ensure adequate protection of cultural heritage sites, such as increased security measures, condemnation of violent acts perpetrated against them and positive reinforcement messages raising awareness of the value of cultural heritage.

81. Following the establishment of a new Government in Serbia, the Belgrade-Prishtinë/Priština cultural dialogue needs to be re-energized.

Dialogue

82. Three of the four working groups of the direct dialogue between Prishtinë/Priština and Belgrade on technical issues were inactive during the reporting period.

83. The Missing Persons Working Group held an ad hoc session in Prishtinë/Priština in early April under the auspices of its chair, the International Committee of the Red Cross (ICRC). The Prishtinë/Priština and Belgrade delegations subsequently met on 18 April in Niš, Serbia, to exchange information on a suspected mass grave site in Raška, Serbia. A conference on Kosovo missing persons issues, organized by the Sarajevo-based International Commission on Missing Persons, was held in Ohrid, in the former Yugoslav Republic of Macedonia, on 16 and 17 May. It was the first opportunity for groups of Serbian and Albanian family members of the missing from the 1998-1999 conflict to meet face to face.

84. A plenary session of the Missing Persons Working Group, its first in a year, had been scheduled for 31 May in Prishtinë/Priština but was postponed after the Prishtinë/Priština delegation threatened to boycott the session if a leader of the Serbian family association of missing persons, who had participated in the 5 May inauguration of a Serbian vigilante group that intends to "liberate" Kosovo, formed part of the delegation. An ICRC proposal to substitute the individual was refused, resulting in postponement of the meeting.

Kosovo Protection Corps

85. Minority community membership in the Kosovo Protection Corps (KPC) slightly decreased in the reporting period and now stands at 195 (6.7 per cent), of whom 42 are Serbs (1.4 per cent). The decrease is in part due to absenteeism and subsequent dismissal, resignations and a general suspension on recruitment and promotion since 12 February. In addition, 92 members have left KPC as part of the resettlement pilot programme (see para. 88 below). Efforts are focusing on ethnic minority outreach, retention and the implementation of humanitarian projects. Kosovo Serb members remain subject to pressure from their own communities not to participate in KPC. No internal allegations of discrimination have arisen.

86. Women are represented at all levels of KPC though in comparatively small numbers (89 or 3.1 per cent).

87. Disciplinary compliance continues to improve, although further improvement in the staffing and conduct of disciplinary investigations by KPC is still required.

88. The resettlement pilot programme for the redundancy of 80 KPC personnel was launched on 23 January. An additional 12 members have since joined the programme, thus exhausting its current funding capacity. The programme consists of a nine-month resettlement package provided by the International Organization for Migration (IOM), funded by the United Kingdom, and a severance payment of the participant's remaining salary for the year 2007, taken from the KPC budget.

89. The demining capacity of KPC has increased with the completion of training for 32 new deminers. KPC is on track to assume sole responsibility for all mine and unexploded ordnance clearance in late 2007. A United States-funded project for the donation of four mine detection dog teams began on 17 April.

90. The capacity of the civil protection brigade is increasing. In the coming year its full operational capability is expected to be endorsed in search and rescue, explosive ordnance, disposal and firefighting and hazardous material protection, upon receipt of further specialist training and equipment. Its new purpose-built headquarters was officially inaugurated on 12 March.

Kosovo Protection Corps: challenges ahead

91. Despite its positive personnel policies, active engagement among Kosovo Serb communities and apparent lack of internal discrimination, KPC still has difficulty in retaining Kosovo Serbs and gaining support from this minority community.

92. Donor support is needed to repair and replace equipment to increase KPC capacity to implement humanitarian projects and respond to civil emergencies.

Annex II
Composition and strength of the police component of the United Nations Interim Administration Mission in Kosovo (as at 1 June 2007)

Country	*Number*	*Country*	*Number*
Argentina	9	Nepal	17
Austria	22	Netherlands	1
Bangladesh	31	Nigeria	14
Brazil	2	Norway	15
Bulgaria	52	Pakistan	174
China	18	Philippines	44
Croatia	9	Poland	122
Czech Republic	18	Portugal	4
Denmark	24	Romania	182
Egypt	16	Russian Federation	38
Finland	2	Slovenia	15
France	47	Spain	13
Germany	151	Sweden	35
Ghana	35	Switzerland	6
Greece	10	Timor-Leste	8
Hungary	12	Turkey	148
India	68	Uganda	4
Italy	29	Ukraine	189
Jordan	68	United Kingdom of Great Britain and Northern Ireland	65
Kenya	15	United States of America	222
Kyrgyzstan	8	Zambia	7
Lithuania	6	Zimbabwe	18
Malawi	4		
Total			**1 997**

Composition of the Kosovo Police Service (as at 1 June 2007)

Category	*Percentage*	*Number*
Kosovo Albanians	83.99	6 060
Kosovo Serbs	10.31	744
Other ethnic minority members	5.70	411
Total		**7 215**
Men	86.44	6 237
Women	13.56	978

Annex III

Composition and strength of the military liaison component of the United Nations Interim Administration Mission in Kosovo (as at 1 June 2007)

Country	*Number of liaison officers*
Argentina	1
Bangladesh	1
Bolivia	1
Bulgaria	1
Chile	1
Czech Republic	1
Denmark	1
Finland	2
Hungary	1
Ireland	4
Jordan	2
Kenya	1
Malawi	1
Malaysia	1
Nepal	1
New Zealand	1
Norway	1
Pakistan	1
Poland	1
Portugal	2
Romania	3
Russian Federation	2
Spain	2
Ukraine	2
United Kingdom of Great Britain and Northern Ireland	1
Zambia	1
Total	**37**

E. Lebanon: Hariri Attack Investigation

1. Fifth Report of the International Independent Investigation Commission, 25 September 2006 (S/2006/760)

Letter dated 25 September 2006 from the Secretary-General addressed to the President of the Security Council

I have the honour to transmit herewith the fifth report of the International Independent Investigation Commission, which was prepared pursuant to Security Council resolutions 1595 (2005), 1636 (2005), 1644 (2005) and 1686 (2006).

The report details progress made by the Commission since its previous report dated 10 June 2006 (S/2006/375) in investigating the assassination of former Lebanese Prime Minister Rafik Hariri and 22 other victims, and in providing technical assistance to the Lebanese authorities in their investigation of certain other attacks perpetrated in Lebanon since 1 October 2004. The report highlights the Commission's steady advancement in its investigations, despite experiencing difficulties in accessing witnesses and information as a result of the conflict in Lebanon.

I wish to thank the staff of the Commission for their dedicated and systematic work in difficult circumstances, particularly in the light of the volatile security situation in Lebanon during the reporting period. I also wish to thank Mr. Brammertz for his continued leadership in advancing the investigation of the attack, and the Government of the Lebanese Republic for its continued support for, and cooperation with, the Commission.

I should be grateful if you would bring this matter to the attention of the members of the Security Council. Meanwhile, I am transmitting the report to the Government of Lebanon.

(*Signed*) Kofi A. **Annan**

Serge Brammertz, Commissioner
Beirut, 25 September 2006

Summary

In resolution 1644 (2005) of 15 December 2005, the Security Council requested the International Independent Investigation Commission to report to it on its progress, including on the cooperation received from the Syrian authorities, every three months.

The present report outlines the progress made by the Commission in its investigative activities between 15 June and 15 September 2006. This period was marked by the conflict and unstable security situation in Lebanon, and resulted in the temporary relocation of the Commission to a base in Cyprus on 21 July 2006, as required by the United Nations. All efforts were made to manage the impact of the relocation on the work of the Commission, and operations resumed immediately upon arrival in Cyprus. The gradual process of moving international personnel back to Beirut has started.

While the Commission faced delays and logistical difficulties in accessing witnesses and information as a result of the conflict in Lebanon, these problems were minimized. As a result, progress has been made in all investigative areas, and the Commission continues to investigate systematically and thoroughly all possible leads. The Commission continues to interact closely with the Lebanese authorities on all matters relevant to its mandate and appreciates their support.

The Commission has also continued to provide technical assistance to the Lebanese authorities in their investigation of other attacks perpetrated in Lebanon since 1 October 2004. The expanded mandate given to the Commission by the Security Council in resolution 1686 (2006) has enabled the Commission to take a more proactive role in these cases, resulting in tangible progress both in individual cases and in their potential linkage to each other.

The assistance the Commission receives from States continues to be critical to the progress of the investigation, especially as it develops its more complex investigative themes. The cooperation that the Commission has received from the Syrian Arab Republic has remained generally satisfactory, and the Commission continues to require its full support in providing information and facilitating interviews with individuals located on Syrian territory.

I. Introduction

1. This report is submitted pursuant to Security Council resolution 1644 (2005) of 15 December 2005, in which the Council requested the International Independent Investigation Commission to report every three months on the progress of its inquiry, and on cooperation matters, including cooperation received from the Syrian authorities. The report accounts for the progress the Commission has made in implementing its mandate, as laid out in Security Council resolutions 1595 (2005), 1636 (2005), 1644 (2005) and 1686 (2006) since its previous report dated 10 June 2006 (S/2006/375).

2. The Commission has continued its investigation into the killing of former Lebanese Prime Minister Rafik Hariri and 22 others (Hariri investigation) and has reinforced the level of technical assistance it provides to the Lebanese authorities in their investigation of

certain other attacks perpetrated in Lebanon since 1 October 2004. Although the work of the Commission has been affected by the unstable security situation in Lebanon during the reporting period, and the subsequent need to evacuate the Commission staff to a temporary base in Cyprus, progress has been made in all main areas of the investigations. The Commission continues to interact closely with the Lebanese authorities on all matters relevant to its mandate and appreciates their ongoing strong support, especially in the light of the difficult security situation in Lebanon during the reporting period.

3. In the Hariri investigation, 20 major investigation and analysis projects and themes, subdivided into numerous subprojects, are ongoing. They include investigations of the crime scene and convoy, interviews with key witnesses and sensitive sources, and the investigation and analysis of telecommunications, organizational structures and linkages. Each project is undertaken by a multidisciplinary team of individuals equipped with the appropriate skill sets.

4. While the Commission focused in its last report on the results of its forensic examination of the crime scene and of the blast that killed Hariri and 22 others, in this reporting period it also focused on the investigation of those who participated at different levels in the perpetration of this crime. That elicited further forensic tasks, such as DNA research and analysis; electronic, communications and digital devices examination and analysis; fingerprints research and comparative analysis, mobile telephone analysis, and forensic examination of documents.

5. In line with the revised mandate given by the Security Council in resolution 1686 (2006), the Commission has further expanded the technical assistance it provides to the Lebanese authorities in their investigation of certain other attacks perpetrated in Lebanon since 1 October 2004. Specifically, the Commission has focused on three main areas: forensic investigation and analysis, communications analysis and the conduct of interviews. A key component of these activities is to obtain evidence concerning horizontal multiple-case linkage, including any commonalities with the Hariri case. This increased assistance has allowed progress in the investigations of these other cases, with the Commission first concentrating on the cases involving attacks against specific individuals.

6. The assistance of States continues to be necessary to the success of the work of the Commission. During the reporting period, 27 requests for assistance were sent by the Commission to 11 States and entities, in addition to the requests sent to Lebanon. As a result, the Commission has enjoyed broad and detailed assistance from a number of States in a wide range of investigative and analytical areas. The cooperation of the Syrian Arab Republic with the Commission remains an important component of the ongoing work. Over the past three months it remained generally satisfactory, with regular working level meetings having been held with senior Syrian officials to manage the timeliness of the responses, the facilitation of witness interviews and the provision of information. The Commission has continued to receive the assurances of the Government of the Syrian Arab Republic that all Commission requests will be met in a timely and satisfactory manner.

7. During the reporting period, the Commission continued to develop its internal procedures, as directed by the Security Council in paragraph 6 of its resolution 1595 (2005), and has further standardized its work, notably in the light of the possible establishment of a tribunal of an international character.

8. In view of the extension of the mandate of the Commission until 15 June 2007 by the Security Council in resolution 1686 (2006), the Commission has gradually increased its capacity and resources to meet its significant investigative, legal and analytical obligations, together with developing and maintaining the appropriate security, language services, administration, recruitment and logistics support associated with its mandate. As part of its management tasks, new budget proposals have been prepared and submitted to enable planning continuity and the fulfilment of management objectives.

II. Progress in the investigations

9. During the reporting period, the investigative focus of the Commission in the case of the murder of Mr. Hariri and 22 others was on three main objectives: continuing crime scene and associated work; broadening its knowledge and evidence in relation to the linkage and perpetrator aspects of the case; and developing new projects.

10. As regards the other 14 cases, the Commission began conducting interviews following the expansion of the mandate by the Security Council in June, focusing in the first instance on six of these cases, namely those of targeted attacks. As ever, the imperative remains to achieve realistic results of an evidential standard in the best possible time frame.

11. As in its previous report, the Commission is providing a "snap-shot" of its ongoing work on the different layers of the case, with as much detail as possible, bearing in mind the underlying need to preserve confidentiality and investigative leads.

A. Hariri investigation

1. Crime scene and associated topics

Forensic exploitation of the crime scene

12. Following the Commission's final collection of forensic evidence at the crime scene, completed in June 2006, a number of results have been established that enable further confirmation of the current case theory, regarding the crime scene and its associated aspects, and provide new investigative leads. The Commission is also establishing a comprehensive forensic inventory and database of all exhibits in the possession of the Lebanese authorities and in the possession of the Commission.

13. A total of 56 exhibits of human remains were found in June 2006, with four other parts found that could not be analysed owing to their condition. The parts were scattered over a large area, with human remains found in all six of the subdivided areas of the crime scene. The DNA analysis conducted on these remains produced 27 mitochondrial DNA profiles and 14 nuclear DNA profiles. Three new independent DNA profiles were extracted from exhibits found at the crime scene, one drawn from blood stains found in the Byblos building and one on the roof of the St. George Hotel annex. The third one has particular significance in that the sample was taken from the key ignition mechanism in the vicinity of the so-called "building 367", adjacent to the Byblos building, which may be relevant to associated evidence close to the blast. The Commission is undertaking steps to ascertain whether these new DNA profiles can be attributed to known injured persons, or represent as yet unidentified persons most likely injured in the explosion.

14. The tooth found on the crime scene during the investigations carried out just after the explosion in 2005 belongs to the same male person whose 27 parts were previously

recovered. Odontological examinations showed it is an upper middle right incisor that belonged to a man, possibly in his early 20s, and unlikely to be older than 25, showing a distinguishing mark to the surface of the crown, which is a feature rarely seen among people from Lebanon. Another complete tooth was collected during the recent investigations of the crime scene in June 2006, in the same vicinity where the 27 parts belonging to this person had been found. Further forensic tests are being undertaken to establish, if possible, the regional origin of the person from the examination of the tooth. In addition, five pieces of human remains were also found in the same vicinity, all matching the DNA of the 27 other parts of the same male person, and a number of other bone fragments belonging to a skull were found in the same area. Although they were too burned for DNA profiles to be extracted, the Commission believes that they belong to the same male likely to be the individual who detonated the bomb, and not to another unidentified person.

15. A trajectory analysis of physical and biological exhibits is nearing completion. In order to achieve this goal, a 3D-reconstruction of the crime scene, above and also under the ground, is being finalized and will be linked to the database of the exhibits inventory. The objective of this exercise is to determine the relative location of the carrier of the bomb, i.e. the Mitsubishi van, the seat of the explosion and the location of the male identified as the person who most likely detonated the improvised explosive device (IED). Two other separate and independent series of experiments conducted to assist in the understanding of the properties and associated features of the explosion, the cratering, the explosion fireball, the trajectories of primary and secondary high velocity fragments and their collision with vehicles and buildings have all demonstrated very similar properties to those of the actual blast on 14 February 2005.

16. Documentation and technical information from the Mitsubishi Fuso Truck and Bus Corporation in Japan received recently by the Commission will enable identification of the vehicle parts and metal fragments allegedly originating from the Mitsubishi van collected from the scene of the crime. Similarly, vehicle parts found at this scene should be conclusively identified with the assistance of an external expert by matching the parts to technical drawings and to identical and fully intact components from an undamaged vehicle of the same production batch, model, make and year.

17. Such potentially key parts as the piece of metal, possibly the roof of a vehicle, retrieved approximately 50 m above the ground from the arm of the crane attached to a building at the crime scene (Byblos building), the ignition key device collected adjacent to the unsafe building (building 367), and the gearing mechanism of a vehicle found embedded in the ground inside the crater, some 40 cm below the surface, will be examined and subjected to the above-mentioned analysis for final identification and assessment of relevance for the case. Other parts, such as those taken from inside the crater, where a further 48 metallic and non-metallic parts or components from a vehicle or vehicles were found, and parts found among the rubble at the crime scene, where a large rear-view mirror and a rear light fragment, together with electrical wiring, number plates, electronic devices and other metallic unidentified fragments were recovered, will also be subjected to final identification and an assessment of their relevance for the case.

Characteristics of the explosion

18. Independent tests carried out in two separate environments conducted earlier in the year, as well as scaling explosion experiments, have corroborated the findings of the Commission

with regard to the characteristics and nature of the actual explosion of 14 February 2005, i.e. the Mitsubishi Canter van, carrying a very large bomb of a minimum of 1,200 kg of TNT equivalent most likely detonated by a man (to whom the 32 human parts belong) within or immediately in front of the van. The nature of the fireball, the pressure range, the properties of the carrier, the effects on the surrounding vicinity, including on the impacted vehicles, adjacent buildings and the road, the trajectory findings, the amount of explosives used and the nature and form of the crater have all been corroborated by these experiments. A new hypothesis relating to an aerial delivery means as a method of causing the explosion, advanced to the Commission recently, is being examined for its validity. The Commission is unable at this stage to conclude if it has any impact on its existing findings at the crime scene, which were corroborated by two separate and independent series of tests.

19. The Commission has developed its findings as to exactly how the explosive charge would have been placed in the van to achieve the intended effects, and how the explosives must have been wired to detonate in the manner they did. Experiments conducted with explosive charges packed and laid out in different configurations have led to an understanding of how and where the explosives would have been placed in the Mitsubishi van, and how the detonation of the device would have been effected.

20. In the previous report, the Commission discussed varying possibilities concerning the amount of explosives used in the attack. It suggested that the amount used to produce a crater of the size that was created on 14 February 2005 would be approximately 500 kg of TNT equivalent, if the IED was placed at 1.7 m under the ground; or 1,200 kg of TNT equivalent if placed just above the ground; or 1,800 kg of TNT equivalent if the IED was approximately 0.80 m above the ground. This data has been confirmed by a separate series of experiments relating to the effects of differing explosive amounts packed in differing configurations and detonated at varying heights above the ground. Once the trajectory analysis, 3D-reconstruction of the crime scene, video analysis and formal identification of all Mitsubishi van parts have been completed, the Commission will be able to establish the height above ground of the IED and, as a consequence, the quantity of explosives used in the IED. Subject to these final results, the Commission estimates that the quantity of explosives would be closer to 1,800 kg than to 1,200 kg.

Convoy route

21. The project of systematically interviewing or re-interviewing all members of Mr. Hariri's security staff, including the surviving members of his convoy, those managing his security and those in his immediate personal staff, has been largely completed. The Commission has established to its satisfaction the convoy's route; the exact timing of its progress; stop and start times; timing and knowledge of route selection; the use of one or more identical armoured Mercedes Benz S600 vehicles in the convoy both on the day of the attack and before; patterns of operational activity demonstrating when the route along the St. George Hotel was previously selected; and the use of electronic countermeasures.

22. Certain individuals interviewed by the Commission have emphasized that government security arrangements for Mr. Hariri had been reduced, in terms of his security detail and convoy facilities, in the period following his resignation as Prime Minister of Lebanon. The impact of that is being evaluated by the Commission, both in the political context and from an operational perspective.

23. The Commission is examining information and developing investigative hypotheses that Mr. Hariri was the subject of earlier operational activity by the alleged bombing team, including surveillance of him and his convoy and reconnaissance of various locations. The Commission also has information indicating that a number of opportunities may have arisen to deliver the attack on Mr. Hariri but were not acted upon by that team for reasons as yet to be fully understood by the Commission.

24. For example, the Commission has received information that earlier movements of Mr. Hariri during February 2005 may have been responded to by the alleged bombing team either as a rehearsal for the attack on 14 February or indeed as an attempt to kill him. This aspect of the investigation is an important component in understanding the capabilities, operational support mechanisms and intent of the alleged bombing team, as well as in providing indications of the timing of the decision to kill Mr. Hariri. Because of this alleged earlier activity, further investigative leads have become available beyond those offered by the attack of 14 February 2005 alone.

25. It is apparent that the operational methodologies and associated mechanisms relating to the security panoply of Mr. Hariri during the period since he had ceased to be Prime Minister created a number of vulnerabilities, which enabled the attack on him to be perpetrated more easily than it would otherwise have been. For instance, the time of day the convoy needed to depart from Parliament to return to Hariri's residence meant that only one obvious route option was available to return Hariri in a timely manner for his next appointment.

26. Similarly, a working hypothesis is that the alleged bombing team knew that electronic countermeasures may have been a factor in protecting the convoy and Hariri. They therefore may have chosen a method of attack that rendered the use of such countermeasures and their technical capability, deterrent effect and operational capacity on the day in question irrelevant to their plan.

27. It may also be a contributing factor to the successful execution of the crime that the position of Hariri's vehicle within the convoy was regular and largely predictable over a period of months leading up to the actual attack, and that Hariri chose to drive his vehicle himself. The Commission is aware that this was not an unusual practice by Hariri, and it may have enabled him to be more easily identified and pinpointed than he would have otherwise been. The Commission continues to investigate the relevance of this particular aspect of the crime.

28. Other relevant issues have been clarified to the satisfaction of the Commission. For example, a vehicle alleged to have been following the convoy as it left a local café and the vicinity of Parliament has been discounted from its current working hypotheses as most likely not relevant. Similarly, the supposed deliberate delay in the final leg of the convoy's route caused by a combination of vehicles and traffic lights is not deemed relevant, as the interviews of convoy personnel did not elicit such evidence. Additionally, the likely modus operandi of the alleged bombing team did not demand such a complex and precise action within their overall plan.

29. The Commission believes the plan was sufficiently professional in its compilation and flexible in its execution that the exact timing of the convoy's movement towards St. George Hotel was not critical, and that the success of the operation was not conditional upon precise movements of the vehicles. This is exemplified by the relatively unpredictable nature

of Hariri's actions once he left Parliament and crossed the road to visit the café, instead of departing in his convoy immediately.

30. This spontaneous pause lasted approximately 15 minutes and could not have been predicted by the alleged bombing team. The communications traffic between alleged members of that team went silent during that period, and resumed only after Mr. Hariri had left the café and departed on the route back to his residence. Thus, the plan of the alleged bombing team coped with such latitude in the time taken by Mr. Hariri to commence the return to his residence, and the team was still able to execute the plan.

Crime scene witnesses

31. A series of systematic interviews and re-interviews of over 25 crime scene witnesses has been largely completed. The Commission is now satisfied with a number of previously unclear issues; for example, the exact movements and positioning of the Mitsubishi van at the final stages of the operation, and establishing a commonality of understanding of the events at the time of the explosion, including whether two sounds were heard.

32. Blast-scaling explosion experiments have been conducted to collect data regarding the possibility of one or two explosions, above or under the ground. The objectives were to visualize the fireball, assess the effects on structures, estimate the behaviour of high velocity fragments, estimate the size and features of the crater, and register the shock pressures and record sound pressures with microphones at different distances, combining incident and reflected waves from any reflecting surface. Numerical simulations will enable the Commission to establish if the location and situation of each witness at the time of the explosion is consistent with their likelihood of hearing one or two sounds at the moment and immediately after the explosion. One final phase of interviewing is necessary to conclude this aspect of the investigation, in which the noise recordings of blast or sound wave experiments, conducted in part to identify the aural properties of the blast relative to the location of each witness at the scene, will be replayed to each witness. Subject to those findings, at this stage, the Commission's favoured hypothesis is that there was only one blast, and that the phenomenon of two sounds being heard by a number of witnesses can be scientifically explained.

Rafik Hariri timeline

33. The Commission has expanded its investigations into the last days of Mr. Hariri's life, and has extended the period of scrutiny backwards in time. Important information is emerging through the interviews to date of 15 individuals associated in some context with Hariri over the months prior to his murder. Such people include those with influence in Lebanon and in the broader region, those who worked and managed his personal and professional affairs, visitors to his residence in Beirut and other residences, staff in the residences, and those with whom he had business or political relations.

34. The Commission is reconstructing Mr. Hariri's life in the period leading up to his assassination from a number of different perspectives, including examining his political situation and his relationships domestically and internationally, his meetings with his associates and other prominent individuals, his movements inside and outside Lebanon, his private and personal discussions with friends, his expressed opinions, thoughts and moods as perceived by others, his business affairs, including the management of his media interests and

media portrayal of his interests and activities, relevant financial matters as they affected his political position, professional relationships and private arrangements, and his personal movements both within and outside his residence.

35. It is apparent that there are converging business, political, economic, and personal factors that provide the context of Hariri's life during this period. When these themes are integrated into a heightened threat environment and matched against alleged operational activities of the bombing team, they create a picture of Hariri's last weeks seen from a number of perspectives. Similarly, these themes are being developed by the Commission in order to understand if any or all of them led to conditions that prompted the decision to assassinate him. This area of the Commission's work will continue to develop and expand with further interviews and the collection of information planned throughout the next reporting period.

New and ongoing investigation leads

36. The Commission has identified a considerable number of new leads for investigation relating to the crime scene, its vicinity and the immediate perpetration of the crime, and has begun investigative and analytical work on each one of them. The topics include the investigation of the circumstances surrounding particular individuals and vehicles at the crime scene before, during and in the immediate aftermath of the explosion, other associated items after the explosion and the examination of allegations of tampering with the crime scene following the explosion.

37. These investigation leads arise from analysis of existing information and from the collection of new information, and vary in their relevance and their magnitude; however, they all require considerable development. The Commission anticipates that once completed, further information arising from the crime itself and the immediate environs will provide additional links towards those who perpetrated the crime.

38. The Commission also continues its investigations into other key aspects of the case, including the acquisition of the Mitsubishi van, the acquisition of the explosives and the preparation of the van as the carrier of the device, and the identity and manner of participation of the individual initiating the detonation of the IED, either from within or close to the front of the Mitsubishi van.

2. Individuals involved in the commission of the crime

Communications analysis and investigation

39. The Commission has devoted considerable resources to the analysis and investigation of the communications traffic aspects of the case. This topic has yielded important results, and enables the Commission to establish links that otherwise would not be evident. Much of the work is reactive in nature. However, some of the analytical work is also proactive and speculative, and builds upon known facts and develops investigation themes. It has elicited a number of leads and continues to provide the Commission with better understanding of the communications linkages relevant to the crimes.

40. The links that are being established through the communications work demonstrate a complex network of telecommunications traffic between a large number of relevant individuals, sometimes through intermediary telephone numbers or locations and sometimes directly.

A series of investigation leads has been developed as a result of these analyses, which the Commission regards as a priority. Much painstaking work is required to track down each individual connection or link and exempt it from the enquiries or continue with it as a working lead. Similarly, the Commission understands better the preparatory aspects of the attack through its communications analysis; this work remains ongoing in conjunction with timeline analyses, and is one of a number of areas where comparative analysis with the 14 other cases is being pursued. For example, knowledge of the activities of the six subscriber identity module (SIM) card holders who are alleged to have been part of the bombing team, both geographically and in communications terms, has become clearer and more detailed.

41. The Commission has also developed direct and indirect linkages between significant individuals in disparate groups that are relevant from an investigative perspective. Explanations for these linkages are in some cases not immediately apparent, and the Commission is working to understand their relevance to the crime itself, to those potentially linked to it and to other individuals.

42. The international dimension of the communications analysis continues to provide investigative leads, as the Commission develops its knowledge of the complexities of international call routing and receives responses to its requests from States where telephone call traffic has been traced. To date the Commission has engaged 17 States in this aspect of its work, and has received considerable assistance and responses from a number of them.

43. The relevant communications links emanating from within Lebanon or outside the country of those individuals whom the Commission wishes to interview and/or continues to investigate are being systematically reviewed, and the results are providing further investigative leads.

44. The Commission also continues to examine local, regional and international linkages between numbers associated with Ahmed Abu Adass and other individuals, a number of which are of specific interest. The Commission continues to analyse telephone traffic activity emanating from those numbers alleged to have been used by those allegedly involved in the attack on the day of 14 February 2005.

Ahmed Abu Adass and associated aspects

45. Following extensive investigative steps and analysis of electronic data, documents, artefacts and other items, the emerging profile of Ahmed Abu Adass and his activities is becoming clearer. His profile is distinct in that he seemingly had more academic and intellectual interests and less technical orientation than that associated with members of terrorist groups engaged in the operational aspects of terrorist activities, at least in Lebanon.

46. The Commission continues its examination in detail of every aspect of Ahmed Abu Adass's involvement in the crime, including the validity of the claim of responsibility he delivered in the videotaped message. It continues to work along two investigative tracks, one being that he was a willing participant in the crime, and the other that he was coerced into delivering the message. Either avenue remains a factual possibility at present, and further investigations are ongoing to ascertain the correct hypothesis.

47. The Commission is investigating the events surrounding the delivery of the tape and note to a location in downtown Beirut, and the five associated telephone calls to *Reuters*

and Al Jazeera following the attack. Two of the calls claimed responsibility for the attack and three were related to the tape and the note that were provided.

48. General forensic analysis, DNA and fingerprint research, media forensic analysis and document examinations of the tape in which Ahmed Abu Adass claims responsibility for the attack, on other associated items and on the physical modalities of delivering the message have been completed. thirty-two identifiable fingerprints, three palm prints and three mitochondrial DNA profiles have been collected from the exhibits. The Commission is making comparative analyses of these results with other records, and is evaluating them with a view to conducting further interviews of relevant persons in connection with this aspect of the case and undertaking further comparative forensic analyses.

49. The Commission also maintains its awareness of individuals who have operated in Lebanon and the region in the recent past in a criminal context, and continues to assess their activities for the relevance or otherwise of their possible involvement in the crimes. The Commission is also undertaking further work in relation to the hypothesis of compartmentalization of the crime, as well as on the circumstances regarding the placing of the videotape on which the claim of responsibility by Ahmed Abu Adass was recorded.

Knowledge of the crime

50. The Commission is pursuing leads concerning individuals who apparently had some degree of substantive information in varying degrees of detail about the attack prior to its execution. This investigative theme falls into two categories: those who knew something about the forthcoming attack in some context or another but said or did nothing about it, or were unable to do anything about it; and those who knew something or were informed of some aspect of the attack and somehow tried to deliver a warning to Hariri or a person close to him.

51. Each of the above-mentioned categories is of interest to the Commission. For example it is apparent that a number of individuals from various backgrounds believed that Hariri was likely to be subject to an attack, even more so than in the ordinary context of his status, past professional life, regional dynamics and existing circumstances. There is also information that leads the Commission to believe that certain individuals knew that an attempt on his life was imminent. In this regard, the Commission is undertaking a series of interviews with those whom it believes can assist it in these lines of inquiry.

52. There is evidence to believe that Hariri was aware of a heightened threat against him, and that he himself had discussed that situation at length with a number of individuals, and had factored the unusually elevated threat environment into his thinking, approach, activities and movements over the last few weeks of his life. The Commission has been collecting evidence on this topic. It is an important aspect of its work, as it assists in understanding the extreme nature of the crime.

The political, military, police and intelligence environment of Lebanon

53. The Commission continues to conduct a number of interviews and re-interviews of representatives or former representatives of the Syrian and Lebanese Government structures. This work will remain ongoing throughout the next reporting period, and remains of key importance in understanding the political structure and security environment that existed in Lebanon at the time of the attack. This work is augmented by additional interviews and the collection of information from persons of influence and other individuals of

relevance in Lebanon and the region, to obtain the required knowledge of different perspectives of the systems that were in place at the time and better understand the contextual environment in which the attacks took place.

3. Persons who commissioned the crime

Motives for the attack

54. The Commission continues to investigate both the possibility that a single group, with a singular intent and capacity, committed the crime, or that a well-defined or disparate collection of individuals or groups joined together with differing motives and intentions to commit the same crime.

55. The Commission has identified several different potential motivations, not necessarily mutually exclusive, that may have led to the decision to carry out the assassination of Hariri, and it remains seized of the possibility that there may be more theories to consider. Some of these motives may be similar to those of other attacks the Commission is investigating in Lebanon. Such motives are apparently of varying levels of international, regional and national relevance, and relate to political, economic, financial and business matters.

56. The Commission is, for example, establishing to an evidential standard information on the political environment that surrounded Mr. Hariri at the time of and prior to his assassination, such as the introduction of Security Council resolution 1559 (2004), the issues surrounding the then forthcoming national elections in Lebanon, relations with other States in the region, the Al Madina Bank affairs, business and media factors, and his personal relations with political actors and other relevant individuals at all levels. As stated before, the Commission appreciates the possibility that there may have been more than one motivating reason for perpetrating the crime. This area of the Commission's work is to be further developed in the next reporting period, and a number of investigative steps will be undertaken, including the conducting of a considerable number of interviews in Lebanon, the region and internationally, and the analysis of documents and other information currently in the possession of the Commission and of future anticipated data.

B. Technical assistance in the other cases

57. In line with its mandate as expanded on 15 June 2006 by the Security Council in its resolution 1686 (2006), the Commission has extended further its technical assistance to the Lebanese authorities in the 14 cases discussed in its last report. The Commission dedicated a multidisciplinary project team to this task comprising legal, investigative, analytical, forensic and communications expertise, which continues to work closely with the Prosecutor General of Lebanon.

58. In the previous report, the Commission stated that it had created analytical files for each of the 14 cases, based upon the existing information available during that period. During this last reporting phase, the Commission translated over 1,000 pages of documents relevant to the cases, and developed the case files for each case by adding to the existing information previously collected. This work remains ongoing, with over 3,000 further pages to be translated. The Commission will develop further its support mechanisms with the Prosecutor General of Lebanon and the relevant investigating magistrates during the next reporting period.

59. The Commission has also focused its technical assistance on three specific areas for each case. The first area is the support of forensic investigation and analysis for each case. The second is communications research, where horizontal analysis of each attack and the associated communications traffic is being undertaken. The third is the conduct of interviews, where the subjects chosen for interview can provide individual case depth of knowledge and potentially also horizontal multiple case commonalities, including the necessary development of potential factual and evidential themes relating to the Hariri case.

1. Forensic analysis

60. The Commission continues to review in detail the forensic evidence available concerning the cases, and recognizes the varied levels of detail in each individual case. It is preparing to implement a plan designed to maximize the forensic investigation possibilities, which will be discussed with the Prosecutor General of Lebanon and the investigative magistrates. Upon agreement, the Commission will begin with a collection phase designed to augment the forensic acquisition of data for each case. It is the intention to arrive at the best possible level of forensic information that can be acquired at this stage of each of the cases, given that all 14 of the attacks occurred between nine months and almost two years ago.

61. As this work progresses, the objectives will be to enhance each case where possible, and to seek forensic evidence linking the cases. Thus, the work with the forensic laboratory of the Lebanese Internal Security Forces performed earlier in the year to evaluate the scientific results will be finalized by the analysis of the crime scene management of each case. This will be undertaken through meetings and interviews with the first responders at each scene of the crime.

62. The Commission is currently studying all the pictures and images of the sites where the explosions occurred, comparing them with the results obtained from the explosions experiments conducted, to enable it to establish, if possible, the nature of the IED used and its probable location for each case. This forensic comparative analysis will be augmented by the comparative seismological analysis of the records of the signals recorded by the National Center of Geophysics in Lebanon. Also, the forensic evidence found in these cases is being compared with that of the Hariri case, for instance by using common fingerprints and DNA databases to establish horizontal forensic linkages.

2. Communications

63. The Commission has assembled millions of telephone call records and separated those of interest that span a selected time period surrounding each of the 14 attacks. The objective of this project is to lift from the vast amount of communications traffic occurring in Beirut during the period of the attacks those numbers that have commonality between the attacks and links to other potentially relevant numbers.

64. For example, from the perspective of mobile telephone communications traffic alone, one individual using multiple numbers has been preliminarily linked in a broad geographic context and within a specific common temporal period to a number of the attacks. Four other people have been linked to this person in some of those attacks. The Commission will continue such analytical work and assist the Prosecutor General of Lebanon by investigating the links, conducting appropriate interviews and developing further leads for follow-up.

3. Interviews

65. Following the expansion of the mandate on 15 June 2006, this aspect of the work began, and the Commission has conducted a number of interviews relevant to the six targeted attacks. These interviews have elicited information and evidence of considerable significance, and have provided many leads that require follow-up. In particular, a number of new interviews are being planned to maintain the momentum of this avenue of investigation over the coming reporting period, reinforcing results particularly in the significant area of linkage within the cases.

66. The immediate impact of the interviews undertaken is evident in that a commonality of themes for the investigation is apparent between two or more cases. Links are being developed that relate to the motive and perpetrator aspects of the attacks and, as mentioned in the previous report as a hypothesis, the data being collected provides preliminary information of a "layering" of the motives for these crimes. At one level, the reason for the attacks may be based on motives associated with each victim individually. At another level, the attacks may fit into a broader scheme of intent. This concept of culpability remains critical to the cases and the commission of the crimes, and is one which the Commission will continue to consider and concentrate on.

67. The Commission has strengthened its preliminary conclusion that the 14 cases were not commissioned and executed by 14 disparate and unconnected persons or groups with an equal number of separate motives, and is developing evidence that links the cases into differing groupings. As such, the Commission is anticipating that further links between the cases may become evident upon further collection of information and evidence.

4. Further assistance

68. As indicated in the previous report, all the cases are at varying stages of their development by the Lebanese authorities. The Commission's primary objective for the 14 cases in the coming reporting period is to expand the quality and the quantity of the information and the evidence for each case, where possible, by providing investigative capacity, coordinating capability, horizontal analysis and technical assistance to the Prosecutor General of Lebanon, and through his office to the respective investigative magistrates.

69. Another objective of the Commission is to work with the Prosecutor General of Lebanon in developing operational interconnectivity between the investigative magistrates in support of the conjoined direction on all cases. The Commission believes there is added value to coordinating the investigative activities of all the cases and scrutinizing them not only individually, but in a number of different ways as a single unified group of 14 cases, or as two or more smaller groups, linked to one another by one or more factors.

III. External cooperation

A. Interaction with the Lebanese authorities

70. The Commission has continued to interact closely with the Lebanese authorities on practical, investigative and legal issues that are relevant to its mandate. A total of 12 new written requests were sent to the Lebanese authorities during the reporting period. The Government of Lebanon, the Prosecutor General and his senior staff, the investigating judges assigned to the cases and the liaison officer appointed by the Internal Security Forces have remained clearly committed to the mandate of the Commission and have

supported its efforts throughout the reporting period, despite the tense security situation in Lebanon caused by the recent conflict. The Commission would like to thank them for their support and assistance.

71. The Commissioner met twice with the Prime Minister of Lebanon and held regular meetings with the Minister of Justice and the Prosecutor General during the reporting period. Technical working-level interaction also continued, even after the Commission's temporary relocation outside of Lebanon. As part of the Commission's provision of technical assistance to the Lebanese authorities, meetings were also held with the civilian and military judges and investigating judges in charge of the different cases to discuss the progress of each case, their possible links to one another and all other matters related to the provision of technical assistance.

72. The Commission has continued to share with the competent Lebanese authorities all relevant documentary, testimonial and physical information obtained in the course of its investigations, with the exception of information that could compromise the safety of a witness or the national security interests of a State. Even in such cases, the substance of the information is communicated to the Lebanese authorities in a manner that does not compromise the interest of the witness or the State.

73. The Commission also continues regularly to provide the Lebanese judicial authorities with information, interviews and documentation relevant to those detained, to enable them to take any steps they deem appropriate or necessary. In this connection, the Commission is finalizing the conduct of interviews and the review of extensive documentation in order to assess the credibility of witnesses in the Hariri case. The Commission will continue to regularly provide the Prosecutor General of Lebanon with any information in relation to this matter.

74. The Commission remains available to provide further technical assistance in relation to any other incident or case within the scope of its expanded mandate, should the Lebanese authorities so request.

B. International cooperation

75. The Security Council, in its resolutions 1636 (2005) and 1644 (2005), adopted under Chapter VII of the Charter of the United Nations, reiterated its call upon all States to cooperate with the Commission. Unlike situations involving mutual legal assistance, where each State can negotiate a framework for cooperation on criminal matters, States are required to cooperate with the Commission and to take any steps necessary under their own law to implement their obligations under the above-mentioned resolutions.

76. Acting on that basis, the Commission has continued to request the cooperation of States in technical, judicial and legal matters relevant to the fulfilment of its mandate. Specifically during the reporting period, the Commission submitted a total of 28 separate requests to different States and international organizations seeking to obtain information and documents, facilitate witness interviews, and provide technical assistance and expertise.

77. As it has done in previous reports, the Commission requests that States contact the Commission if they possess or have access to any information that may be relevant to the Hariri investigation or the Commission's other cases. The Commission welcomes any information from States that would advance the investigation, whether it is directly linked

to the assassination of Mr. Hariri, the other attacks being investigated, or the general political and security situation prevailing in Lebanon at the time of the attacks. At this stage of its investigation, the Commission would also find it very useful to receive assistance from States in such matters as interviews with diplomatic representatives and the provision of further technical intelligence and imagery products.

1. Cooperation with the Syrian Arab Republic

78. The Syrian Arab Republic is required to cooperate fully with the Commission, as specifically mandated by the Security Council in its resolutions 1636 (2005) and 1644 (2005), adopted under Chapter VII of the Charter of the United Nations. Pursuant to the common understanding reached between the Commission and the Syrian Arab Republic earlier in the year, the cooperation of the Syrian Arab Republic with the Commission has continued to be timely and efficient.

79. During the reporting period, the Commission submitted 11 formal requests for assistance to the Syrian Arab Republic, seeking information and documentation about certain individuals and groups as well as statements obtained from persons in the course of investigations conducted by Syrian authorities. Working meetings were held with Syrian officials, and extended discussions took place as a result of requests to meet with persons with knowledge of particular topics of relevance to the Commission's work.

80. Documentation was also provided by the Syrian Arab Republic relating to experiments conducted concerning the properties and impacts of various controlled explosions, and follow-up meetings have taken place with experts of the Commission and the Syrian Arab Republic to discuss those experiments. Further information has been received recently concerning this topic, and is currently being evaluated and researched by the Commission.

81. In addition, the Commission requested the Syrian Arab Republic to assist in the facilitation of witness interviews in the Syrian Arab Republic. During the reporting period, the Commission conducted a number of missions to the Syrian Arab Republic, during which 11 interviews were carried out, including of Syrian Government officials. The interviews were arranged by the Syrian authorities in accordance with the requests of the Commission, and the Commission is satisfied with the speed with which that was done, as well as with the logistical and security arrangements for those interviews. In terms of the qualitative cooperation of Syrian officials being interviewed, the Commission continues to closely monitor the depth and validity of responses provided, and finds it necessary to undertake corroborative interviews. This aspect of cooperation is driven by the individual responses of each person being interviewed on a topic-by-topic basis, and the Commission has found the level of cooperation to be variable.

82. The level of assistance provided by the Syrian Arab Republic during the reporting period remained generally satisfactory, with the Syrian Arab Republic responding to the requests of the Commission in a timely manner. The Commission will continue to insist on the Syrian Arab Republic's full cooperation, which remains crucial to the swift and successful completion of its work.

2. Cooperation with other States

83. The Commission continues to require the expeditious assistance and full support of States on technical, legal and judicial matters relevant to the investigation. During the

reporting period, there were a number of requests for assistance submitted to States and international organizations, and a number of follow-up letters. Since 15 June 2006, a total of 16 new formal requests for assistance have been sent to nine States, in addition to the requests for assistance addressed to the Syrian Arab Republic and the regular interactions with the Lebanese authorities.

84. As in previous reporting periods, most States responded in a positive and prompt manner to the requests of the Commission, and have supported its work, including by providing forensic technical assistance, technological support, tracking and analysis of telephone communications, and facilitating witness interviews. In the light of the importance of the cooperation of States for the furtherance of the investigations without delay, the Commission trusts that it will enjoy the full and prompt cooperation of all States during the next reporting period.

IV. Organizational support

A. Internal procedure

85. The Commission continues to adopt and streamline its internal procedures, in accordance with Security Council resolution 1595 (2005) and in view of the possible establishment of a tribunal of an international character. These internal procedures are based on relevant international standards, but also take into account Lebanese law and judicial procedures, and the practice of the Commission since its establishment.

86. The Commission is also consulting with States about further support that can be given to enable it to offer a range of protective measures to witnesses and sensitive sources.

87. Further to Security Council resolution 1686 (2006), in which the Council expresses its support for the Commission's intention to provide further technical assistance to the Lebanese authorities in relation to the other cases, the Commission has also been reviewing its procedures. The Commission investigators have conducted interviews pertaining to those investigations, without the presence of representatives of the Lebanese judiciary, using the Commission's own standards and procedures to conduct the interviews. The Commission notes that there are certain differences between the standards and procedures for conducting interviews under Lebanese law and those that arise under international law. On one hand, the Commission considers that it should respect all due international standards. On the other hand, it is aware of the responsibility to ensure that the testimonial, forensic or other evidence that it collects during the course of its work on all the cases shall be admissible before any Lebanese court in which any accused persons may ultimately be tried.

B. Temporary relocation in Cyprus

88. The reporting period was marked by the rapidly deteriorating security situation in Lebanon, which ultimately resulted in the temporary relocation of all international staff of the Commission to Cyprus. As the general security environment in Lebanon deteriorated significantly beginning on 12 July 2006, the Commission commenced business continuity planning for a possible emergency situation affecting the main operating base or for partial or full relocation of its international staff. Meetings were held with the Prosecutor General of Lebanon to discuss plans to preserve case materials, including evidence, documents, electronic files, exhibits, artefacts and legal materials in the Commission's possession, notably those collected at the crime scene. Following a change in the security phase level

for Lebanon from phase three to phase four, all international staff were required to leave Lebanon in accordance with United Nations security regulations. On 21 July 2006, the Commissioner informed the Prime Minister of Lebanon of the temporary relocation of all international staff, who departed that day to continue activities from Cyprus.

89. While the events in Lebanon and the relocation to Cyprus undoubtedly affected the operations and productivity of the Commission during the reporting period, that impact has been kept to a minimum, thanks notably to the generous assistance of the United Nations Development Programme and the United Nations Peacekeeping Force in Cyprus in ensuring that the Commission could make use of temporary office accommodations immediately upon its arrival. The Lebanese and Cypriot authorities, the United Nations Interim Force in Lebanon, the Economic and Social Commission for Western Asia, and the relevant departments at United Nations Headquarters, supported the Commission throughout the process of evacuation and relocation. The Commission also wishes to acknowledge the very helpful support provided by certain States in facilitating regular missions for Commission personnel back to Lebanon to carry out investigative activities, including interviews.

C. Systems management

90. During the reporting period, significant advances have been made in the area of information management, where a new investigations and analysis information system incorporating state-of-the-art analytical tools has been designed and implemented. This system will further increase the ability of the Commission to analyse and exploit its information and evidence holdings. In addition to this system, a number of other ancillary information systems have been enhanced, finalized and introduced. Further standard operating procedures and workflows have been developed to assist and guide staff in information acquisition practices and document management.

D. Administration

1. Recruitment

91. The rapid strengthening of the Commission's institutional capacity continued to be one of the key tasks of the Commission during the reporting period. The recruitment of competent personnel within appropriate timescales remained a significant challenge for the Commission and delays in the recruitment process impacted the Commission's ability to fulfil its mandate in a timely manner.

92. While vacancy rates decreased in the previous reporting period, they went up during the current reporting period, owing to an increase in the number of posts approved in June 2006 and the disruption to the recruitment process caused by the conflict in Lebanon.

93. An assessment of candidates put forward by States and international agencies is in progress. It is therefore anticipated that the vacancy rates will again continue to decline steadily as more candidatures are received, reviewed and recruited. The Commission is grateful for the positive responses received so far from States and international institutions, and would like to emphasize the need for their continued assistance in making qualified and skilled human resources available to the Commission on a regular basis to ensure continued stability and progress.

2. Budget

94. The Commission recently submitted a new budget for the year 2007. The budget proposal, submitted in August 2006, makes provision for 188 international staff, reflecting a small increase of 13 international staff. The increase comprises five investigations personnel for the technical assistance cases, one additional security officer and seven administrative posts.

E. Security

95. The security of the Commission staff, premises and assets continues to be a priority. The deterioration of the general security environment in Lebanon and the wider region during the reporting period has worsened the situation, while the focus of the investigation increases the probability of individuals or groups attempting to execute threats against the Commission or its personnel for the purpose of disrupting its mandate. The primary focus of security operations is therefore to enable the continuation of the mandate of the Commission by ensuring maximum security for all personnel, facilities and assets.

96. The Commission's security operations team, in coordination with the Lebanese Armed Forces and Internal Security Forces, coordinated a safe and secure relocation of the international staff of the Commission and essential investigation materials from Beirut to Cyprus, while maintaining security of the Commission's main operating base in Beirut. The Commission's security team continues to review and update the threat and risk assessments relating to the Commission to ensure that all critical aspects of security are consistent with security standards. As required, standard operating procedures and contingency plans are developed or adjusted on the basis of the current threat and risk analysis.

F. Supplemental memorandum of understanding

97. The negotiations with the Government of Lebanon regarding the terms of a supplemental memorandum of understanding to supplement and modify the original memorandum of 13 June 2005 were put on hold when the Commission temporarily relocated to Cyprus. They are expected to resume and conclude soon. The draft supplemental memorandum of understanding, which has been prepared in consultation with the Office of Legal Affairs of the United Nations Secretariat, addresses such issues as the legal status of the Commission's premises and the privileges and immunities of the Commission and its staff.

V. Conclusions

98. The Commission is grateful for the outstanding support and work undertaken for the benefit and security of Commission personnel and property by the Lebanese authorities, in particular the Armed Forces and the Internal Security Forces, especially considering the particularly difficult circumstances that marked the reporting period.

99. In the Hariri investigation, the Commission continues to finalize its primary crime scene work, including its forensic research and analysis, and it is satisfied that it has largely established the facts to an evidential standard. The crime scene and associated elements now are providing investigative leads of a secondary nature, as the Commission delves deeper into some of the issues that have arisen from its work on these topics.

100. The Commission will continue to develop its understanding of linkage to the perpetrators at all levels in the Hariri investigation. In the coming reporting period, the Commission's strategic objectives are to undertake approximately 50 key linkage-related interviews;

collect and analyse a large amount of already identified electronic data, technical intelligence and documentation; develop its communications, horizontal and vertical linkages between all the cases; continue with its forensic programme; and develop further sensitive sources.

101. The Commission's work in relation to the 14 other cases helps place the attacks into the prevailing context at the time, and is beginning to produce links notably in identifying potential conjoining motives. Establishing the depth, breadth and nature of those links to an evidential standard is an investigation priority over the next months.

102. As the investigation narrows its focus methodologically and refines its working hypotheses, progress will be accelerated from the development of further witnesses with inside knowledge of the crime and its associated elements. The Commission is putting in place witness protection mechanisms in order to allow more individuals with the appropriate knowledge to step forward and assist it in this sensitive area of its work.

103. The Commission emphasizes the importance of international support from States for its work. This is crucial in order for the Commission to maintain its progress and ensure the completeness of its work, and is exemplified by the 72 requests for assistance that have been sent to States and entities in the last six months. The Commission looks forward to receiving further support and interaction with States as it continues its progress in its investigations.

104. The above-mentioned strategic objectives are contingent on the Commission's operational support systems being able to function at the same operational tempo as its investigation activities. This is especially important in the recruitment of personnel, where the Commission will work with the broader United Nations system to ensure that employment timescales match the current operational demands.

105. Noting the progress made towards the establishment of a tribunal of an international character, and given its current mandate regarding the provision of assistance to the Prosecutor General of Lebanon, the Commission will ultimately hand over responsibilities to a prosecutor's office in either case. By applying the principles of objectivity and balance and by respecting international legal standards in its working methods, the Commission aims to provide the best possible platform for either office to continue the work.

2. Report of the Secretary-General on the Establishment of a Special Tribunal for Lebanon (S/2006/893), 15 November 2006

I. Introduction

1. In my report to the Security Council pursuant to paragraph 6 of its resolution 1644 (2005) (S/2006/176), I set out at the Council's request the nature and scope of the international assistance needed to try before a tribunal of an international character those responsible for the terrorist bombing that killed former Lebanese Prime Minister Rafiq Hariri and others. In so doing, I put forward the general principles of a tribunal of an international character, its personal and subject matter jurisdiction, composition, location and the question of financing, on the basis of consultations between the United Nations Secretariat and the Lebanese authorities.

2. By resolution 1664 (2006), the Security Council endorsed the report and requested me to negotiate an agreement with the Government of Lebanon aimed at establishing a tribunal of an international character based on the highest international standards of criminal justice, taking into account the recommendations of my report and the views that have been expressed by Council members. The Council also requested me to submit for its consideration a report on the implementation of the resolution, in particular on the draft agreement negotiated with the Government of Lebanon, including options for a funding mechanism appropriate to ensuring the continued and effective functioning of the tribunal.

3. Following initial consultations with the Lebanese authorities in Beirut on 26 and 27 January 2006 and with two senior Lebanese judges from 24 to 28 February at United Nations Headquarters in New York, negotiations on the legal framework for the establishment of the special tribunal for Lebanon on the basis of the Security Council's mandate proceeded at the expert level between members of the Office of Legal Affairs of the Secretariat and the Government of Lebanon, represented by the Lebanese judges. The two delegations met between 31 May and 1 June 2006 at Headquarters and between 3 and 7 July 2006 in The Hague. In this latest round of negotiations the two delegations benefited from the advice and wealth of knowledge and experience of two former Presidents of the International Tribunal for the Prosecution of Persons Responsible for Serious Violations of International Humanitarian Law Committed in the Territory of the Former Yugoslavia since 1991. On 6 September, the Legal Counsel travelled to Beirut and presented the initial draft agreement and statute to the Prime Minister and to the Minister of Justice of Lebanon for their consideration.

4. Requested by the Security Council in its resolution 1664 (2006) to take account of the views that have been expressed by Council members, the Secretariat has, in the course of negotiations, taken into account the views expressed by interested members of the Council on the progress of the negotiations and the principles of the legal framework for the establishment of the special tribunal. These consultations have in many ways shaped the legal choices made in the tribunal's founding instruments.

5. The present report analyses the main features of the statute of the special tribunal and the agreement between the United Nations and the Government of Lebanon. It examines the

legal nature and specificities of the tribunal, its temporal, personal and subject matter jurisdiction, its organizational structure and composition, the conduct of the trial process, the location of the seat, the funding mechanism and cooperation with third States.

II. The legal nature and specificities of the special tribunal

6. The legal basis for the establishment of the special tribunal is an agreement between the United Nations and the Government of Lebanon, to which the statute of the tribunal is attached (see annex I). As a treaty-based organ, the special tribunal is neither a subsidiary organ of the United Nations, nor is it a part of the Lebanese court system.

7. The Security Council mandated the Secretary-General to negotiate an agreement aimed at establishing a tribunal of an international character based on the highest international standards of criminal justice. Although the features of such an international character were not specified, the constitutive instruments of the special tribunal in both form and substance evidence its international character. The legal basis for the establishment of the special tribunal is an international agreement between the United Nations and a Member State; its composition is mixed with a substantial international component; its standards of justice, including principles of due process of law, are those applicable in all international or United Nations-based criminal jurisdictions; its rules of procedure and evidence are to be inspired, in part, by reference materials reflecting the highest standards of international criminal procedure; and its success may rely considerably on the cooperation of third States. While in all of these respects the special tribunal has international characteristics, its subject matter jurisdiction or the applicable law remain national in character, however.

8. The special tribunal for Lebanon is distinguished from other international criminal tribunals established or assisted by the United Nations in two respects: (a) in the conduct of the trial process, more elements of civil law are evident than of common law; and (b) the investigative process conducted by the International Independent Investigation Commission constitutes, in fact, the core nascent prosecutor's office.

9. With the exception of the Extraordinary Chambers in the Courts of Cambodia, the conduct of the trial process as reflected in the constituent instruments of all other United Nations-based or assisted tribunals has included more common law elements. The special tribunal for Lebanon is the first United Nations-assisted tribunal to combine substantial elements of both legal systems. The applicability of the Lebanese Code of Criminal Procedure as a guiding principle alongside other reference materials reflecting the highest standards of international criminal procedure (art. 28), the enhanced powers of the Tribunal to take measures to ensure expeditious hearing and prevent any action that may cause unreasonable delay (art. 21) and the introduction of trials in absentia (art. 22) are the most notable manifestations of civil law elements.

10. The establishment of the special tribunal for Lebanon will have been preceded by the Commission established by Security Council resolution 1595 (2005) to assist the Lebanese authorities in their investigation of all aspects of the terrorist attack that killed former Prime Minister Rafiq Hariri and others. In establishing the Commission first, the investigative process has, for all intents and purposes, begun. In so doing, it will have the effect of reducing the lifespan of the tribunal and increasing the efficiency and cost-effectiveness of its operation.

III. The jurisdiction of the special tribunal: temporal, personal and subject matter

A. Temporal jurisdiction

11. In its resolution 1664 (2006), the Security Council envisaged the prosecution of those responsible for the single terrorist bombing that killed former Prime Minister Rafiq Hariri and others on 14 February 2005. The Hariri assassination, however, was committed in a context of other attacks bearing the same or similar characteristics committed between 1 October 2004 and 12 December 2005. Extending the jurisdiction of the tribunal beyond the assassination of Rafiq Hariri to other attacks is not, strictly speaking, an extension of the temporal jurisdiction of the tribunal, but rather an extension of its jurisdiction to include, within a specified period, other attacks that the tribunal might find to be connected to the Hariri assassination and similar to it in nature and gravity. The list of such attacks is included in the third report of the Commission (S/2006/161, para. 55; attached to this report as annex II).

12. The reasons for the inclusion of these other attacks are threefold:

(a) As the investigation of the Commission has progressed, potential links have emerged between the assassination of Rafiq Hariri and other attacks;

(b) The expansion of the mandate of the Commission to provide technical assistance to the Lebanese authorities in respect of the 14 other attacks is an indication of interest on the part of the Security Council in judicial accountability beyond the Rafiq Hariri assassination;

(c) Singling out for prosecution one attack in a context of other similar attacks is bound to create a perception of selective justice.

1. Linkage among the attacks

13. Article 1 of the statute of the special tribunal for Lebanon (see annex I, attachment) provides as follows:

> "The Special Tribunal shall have jurisdiction over persons responsible for the attack of 14 February 2005 resulting in the death of former Lebanese Prime Minister Rafiq Hariri and in the death or injury of other persons. If the Tribunal finds that other attacks that occurred in Lebanon between 1 October 2004 and 12 December 2005, or any later date decided by the Parties and with the consent of the Security Council, are connected in accordance with principles of criminal justice and are of a nature and gravity similar to the attack of 14 February 2005, it shall also have jurisdiction over persons responsible for such attacks. This connection includes but is not limited to a combination of the following elements: criminal intent (motive), the purpose behind the attacks, the nature of the victims targeted, the pattern of the attacks (modus operandi) and the perpetrators."

14. In investigating the potential links between some or all of these attacks, the Commission has identified certain potential linkages, notably the *mode of operation*, or the general pattern of using explosive devices; the *nature of the crime or the criminal intent underlying the attacks*, namely, targeting politicians or influential journalists, as well as creating widespread fear and anxiety among elements of the population by targeting public locations, destabilizing the security situation and causing damage to infrastructure; and *the identity of perpetrators,* of at least some of the attacks.[1] In its fourth report, the Commission reached

the preliminary conclusion that the 14 cases were not commissioned and executed by 14 disparate and unconnected persons or groups with an equal number of separate motives. Analytically, the cases can be linked in a number of different ways and from varying perspectives, notably their similarities in the modus operandi, and their possible intent.[2]

2. The expanded mandate of the Commission

15. The mandate of the Commission was originally limited to the investigation of all aspects of the terrorist attack of 14 February 2005 that killed former Prime Minister Rafiq Hariri and others (resolution 1595 (2005)). On 13 December 2005, a day after the assassination of Gebran Tueni, the Government of Lebanon requested the establishment of a tribunal of an international character and the expansion of the mandate of the Commission, or the establishment of another international investigation commission, to investigate the assassination attempts and assassinations and explosions that took place in Lebanon starting with the attempt on the life of Minister Marwan Hamadeh on 1 October 2004. In response to that request, the Security Council, in its resolution 1644 (2005), expanded the mandate of the Commission to include the provision of technical assistance as appropriate to the Lebanese authorities with regard to their investigations on the terrorist attacks perpetrated in Lebanon since 1 October 2004.

16. While the resolution expands the Commission's mandate with respect to the other 14 attacks for the purpose of extending its technical assistance to the Lebanese authorities and not for the purpose of its own investigation, it is an indication nonetheless that the Security Council is interested in judicial accountability for those responsible for those attacks as well.

3. A perception of fairness, impartiality and objectivity of the special tribunal

17. In establishing the temporal jurisdiction of any United Nations-based tribunal, the Organization strives to strike a balance between a temporal jurisdiction comprehensive enough to include the most serious crimes committed by those most responsible throughout the relevant period and a jurisdiction reasonably limited so as not to overburden the prosecutor's office and the tribunal as a whole. It is a balance struck, in fact, between fairness, objectivity and impartiality of the trial process, and its efficiency and cost-effectiveness.

18. In the present circumstances, singling out for prosecution the assassination of Rafiq Hariri, while disregarding a score of other connected attacks could cast a serious doubt on the objectivity and impartiality of the tribunal and lead to the perception of selective justice.

B. Personal jurisdiction of the special tribunal

19. In its resolution 1664 (2006), the Security Council did not prescribe the personal jurisdiction of the tribunal, although it was mindful of the demand of the Lebanese people that all those responsible for the terrorist bombing that killed former Lebanese Prime Minister Rafiq Hariri and others be identified and brought to justice.

20. Article 1 of the statute accordingly provides that the tribunal shall have jurisdiction "over persons" responsible for the crimes falling within its subject matter jurisdiction, whose modes of criminal responsibility are further elaborated upon in article 3. Within the all-inclusive definition of the personal jurisdiction of the tribunal, the prosecutor will be free to pursue her or his prosecutional strategy and to determine the list of potential indictees according to the evidence before him or her.

C. Subject matter jurisdiction

21. Article 2 of the statute provides as follows:

> "The following shall be applicable to the prosecution and punishment of the crimes referred to in article 1, subject to the provisions of this Statute:
>
> "(a) The provisions of the Lebanese Criminal Code relating to the prosecution and punishment of acts of terrorism, crimes and offences against life and personal integrity, illicit associations and failure to report crimes and offences, including the rules regarding the material elements of a crime, criminal participation and conspiracy; and
>
> "(b) Articles 6 and 7 of the Lebanese law of 11 January 1958 on 'Increasing the penalties for sedition, civil war and interfaith struggle'."[3]

22. While the Lebanese criminal law is the applicable law, its applicability is limited to the crimes and offences provided for in article 2 of the statute. It is also subject to the provisions of the statute and therefore to the exclusion of penalties (e.g. death penalty and forced labour) otherwise applicable under Lebanese law.

23. In keeping with the Security Council mandate requesting the Secretary-General to establish a tribunal of an international character and in the circumstances of Lebanon where a pattern of terrorist attacks seems to have emerged, it was considered whether to qualify the crimes as crimes against humanity and to define them, for the purpose of this statute, as murder or other inhumane acts of similar gravity causing great suffering or serious injury to body or to mental health, when committed as part of a widespread or systematic attack directed against the civilian population.

24. Mindful of the differences in scope and number of victims between the series of terrorist attacks committed in Lebanon and the killings and executions perpetrated on a large and massive scale in other parts of the world subject to the jurisdiction of any of the existing international criminal jurisdictions, it was nevertheless considered that the 14 attacks committed in Lebanon could meet the prima facie definition of the crime, as developed in the jurisprudence of international criminal tribunals. The attacks that occurred in Lebanon since 1 October 2004 could reveal a "pattern" or "methodical plan" of attacks against a civilian population, albeit not in its entirety. They could be "collective" in nature, or "a multiple commission of acts"[4] and, as such, exclude a single, isolated or random conduct of an individual acting alone. For the crime of murder, as part of a systematic attack against a civilian population, to qualify as a "crime against humanity", its massive scale is not an indispensable element.

25. However, considering the views expressed by interested members of the Security Council, there was insufficient support for the inclusion of crimes against humanity within the subject matter jurisdiction of the tribunal. For this reason, therefore, the qualification of the crimes was limited to common crimes under the Lebanese Criminal Code.

D. Individual criminal responsibility

26. Under article 3, paragraph 1, of the statute, all those who committed, participated as accomplice, organized or directed others to commit the crime, or otherwise contributed to the commission of the crime, shall be individually responsible. This is a reflection of the

Lebanese Criminal Code and general criminal law principles, evidenced, inter alia, by article 2, paragraph 3, of the International Convention for the Suppression of Terrorist Bombings of 1997 (General Assembly resolution 52/164, annex). Article 3, paragraph 2, reflects the principle of command responsibility both under international law and national criminal and military codes as more fully articulated in article 28, subparagraph (b), of the Statute of the International Criminal Court. Under article 3, paragraph 3, obedience to superior order is no defence, but may be considered in mitigation of punishment.

IV. Organizational structure of the special tribunal

A. The organs of the special tribunal

27. The special tribunal for Lebanon will consist of the following organs: the chambers (a pre-trial judge, a trial chamber and an appeals chamber), the prosecutor, the registry and the defence office. The composition of the chambers is mixed, with a majority of international judges in the trial and the appeals chambers. An international prosecutor, assisted by a Lebanese deputy prosecutor, is responsible for the investigation and prosecution of persons who may have committed the crimes falling within the jurisdiction of the tribunal. The registrar is appointed by the Secretary-General and is a staff member of the United Nations. The establishment of the special tribunal with a majority of international judges, an international prosecutor and a registrar is consistent with the long-established United Nations position that in the establishment of any mixed tribunal a substantial international component is a guarantee for the independence, objectivity and impartiality of the trial process.

B. Pre-trial judge

28. Pre-trial proceedings exist in different forms in all international criminal tribunals. However, unlike the pre-trial judge of either of the ad hoc tribunals for the former Yugoslavia and Rwanda, or of the Special Court for Sierra Leone, who is designated by the presiding judge of a trial chamber from among the members of that chamber, the pre-trial judge of the special tribunal for Lebanon is a dedicated, single international judge serving as a pre-trial judge only and not as a member of any of the chambers.

29. The role of the pre-trial judge is primarily to review the indictment and, if a prima facie case is established, to confirm the indictment. At the pre-trial phase and throughout the investigation, the pre-trial judge may issue any orders or warrants of arrest, detention or transfer of persons as may be requested by the prosecutor for the purpose of the investigation. In the decade-long experience of United Nations-based tribunals, the role of the pre-trial judge has proved crucial to ensuring the efficiency and expediency of the trial process.

C. Defence office

30. The need for a defence office to protect the rights of suspects and accused has evolved in the practice of United Nations-based tribunals as part of the need to ensure "equality of arms", where the prosecutor's office is an organ of the tribunal and is financed in its entirety through the budget of the tribunal. The statute of the special tribunal institutionalizes the defence office. The head of the office is appointed by the Secretary-General, although, in carrying out its functions, the office is independent. The defence office of the special tribunal

is to protect the rights of the defence, draw up the list of defence counsel and provide support and assistance to defence counsel and persons entitled to such legal assistance.

V. Conduct of the trial process

A. Due process of law

31. With all the specificities of the special tribunal for Lebanon, its standards of justice and guarantees of due process of law are modelled on the highest international standards of criminal justice. In addition to listing the rights of the accused, including an elaborated provision on the presumption of innocence and the burden of proof, the statute provides for the rights of suspects during investigation, including the right not to be compelled to incriminate oneself, to be informed of the charges against him or her, to have legal assistance and to be questioned in the presence of counsel. The statute also protects the rights of victims whose personal interests are affected and, while not recognizing them as "*parties civiles*", it permits their views and concerns to be presented and considered at all stages of the proceedings.

B. Elements of civil law and common law systems combined

32. The proceedings before the special tribunal, while essentially adversarial, contain elements of both civil and common law systems. While distinctive features of civil law, namely, the institution of an investigating judge and the participation of victims as *"parties civiles"* are absent, the trial process before the special tribunal is inspired by the civil law system in the following two respects, the active role of the judges and the conduct of trials in absentia:

(a) The judges of the special tribunal will take a more active role in the conduct of the trial process and the examination of witnesses. Under article 20 of the statute, unless otherwise decided by the trial chamber, "examination of witnesses shall commence with questions posed by the presiding judge, followed by questions posed by other members of the Trial Chamber, the Prosecutor and the Defence". The trial chamber may also *proprio motu* "decide to call additional witnesses and/or order the production of additional evidence";

(b) The institution of trials in absentia is common in a number of civil law legal systems, including Lebanon's. In addition, in the present case, where the conduct of joint trials for some or all of the cases falling within the jurisdiction of the tribunal is likely, it would be crucial to ensure that the legal process is not unduly or indefinitely delayed because of the absence of some accused.

33. In introducing the institution of trials in absentia on the conditions that the accused has waived his or her right to be present, that he or she has not been handed over or absconded, or otherwise cannot be found, the statute of the special tribunal takes account of the relevant case law of the European Court of Human Rights, which determined the regularity of trials in absentia in full respect for the rights of the accused.[5] Accordingly, and as a supplement to the Lebanese Criminal Procedure, article 22 of the statute provides that, where hearings are conducted in the absence of the accused, the special tribunal shall ensure that the accused has designated a defence counsel to be present in the trial or that, if he or she has refused to do so, one will be assigned to him or her by the tribunal's defence office. In case of conviction, the accused shall have the right to be re-tried in his or her presence, if the accused has not designated a defence counsel of his or her choosing in the first trial. Otherwise, the conviction will stand.

C. Receivability and admissibility of evidence collected prior to the establishment of the special tribunal

34. It will be necessary to have a coordinated transition between the work of the Commission and the special tribunal. While the modalities of such transition would be determined taking into account the progress of work of the Commission, it is necessary at this stage to ensure that the work of the Commission is preserved and that evidence collected by it prior to the establishment of the tribunal is nevertheless receivable by the tribunal.

35. In this connection, the Commission noted in its fourth report (S/2006/375, para. 111), that:

> "While based on relevant international standards, the internal procedure takes into account Lebanese law and judicial procedures, as well as the practice of the Commission since its establishment. In defining the standards to be applied, the Commission considered the procedures of international criminal jurisdictions and the minimum guarantees afforded by international criminal law and international human rights law. The internal procedure will therefore help ensure that any information collected or obtained by the Commission is admissible in future legal proceedings, notably before a tribunal of an international character".

36. In the circumstances, it is necessary to provide for the receivability of evidence collected by the national authorities of Lebanon and by the Commission in accordance with its mandate, on the understanding that its admissibility and the weight to be given to such evidence shall be determined by the tribunal in accordance with international standards on the collection of evidence.

VI. Agreement between the United Nations and the Government of Lebanon

37. The agreement between the United Nations and the Government of Lebanon would govern the terms of United Nations cooperation in establishing the tribunal. It stipulates the composition of the tribunal, the procedure for the nomination and appointment of judges (both international and Lebanese), of the international prosecutor and the Lebanese deputy prosecutor and of the registrar and other members of the tribunal, as well as the privileges and immunities to which they are entitled.

38. As a non-United Nations organ, the special tribunal would not be entitled to the privileges and immunities of the Convention on the Privileges and Immunities of the United Nations of 1946. For the special tribunal, its premises, funds, archives and all members of the tribunal, to enjoy comparable privileges and immunities, the agreement between the United Nations and the Government of Lebanon, as well as the future headquarters agreement between the United Nations, the Government of Lebanon and the host State, will have to provide for the necessary privileges and immunities.

39. The agreement between the United Nations and the Government of Lebanon draws, for the most part, upon the agreements signed between the United Nations and the Governments of Cambodia and of Sierra Leone. The provisions relating to the location of the seat and the funding mechanism, however, are Lebanon-specific.

A. Location of the seat

40. For a variety of reasons, the parties share the view that it would be desirable to locate the seat of the tribunal outside Lebanon. In the choice of the seat, considerations of justice

and fairness, administrative efficiency, the rights of victims and proximity to witnesses, existence of suitable facilities—both for the tribunal and its detention facilities—security arrangements and affordable costs, would be fully taken into account.

41. The location of the seat outside Lebanon will require the conclusion of a headquarters agreement between the United Nations, the Government of Lebanon and the host State. It is envisaged that when an agreement, in principle, is reached on the location of the seat, the Secretariat will dispatch a United Nations planning mission to identify adequate premises and negotiate the terms of the headquarters agreement.

42. Like the "split seat" of the Office of the Prosecutor of the International Criminal Tribunal for the Prosecution of Persons Responsible for Genocide and Other Serious Violations of International Humanitarian Law Committed in the Territory of Rwanda and Rwandan Citizens Responsible for Genocide and Other Such Violations Committed in the Territory of Neighbouring States between 1 January and 31 December 1994, where the Prosecutor conducts some investigations through his office in Kigali, while the seat of the Tribunal is in Arusha, the choice of the seat of the special tribunal outside Lebanon will not affect the operation of the prosecutor's office and the conduct of investigations in Lebanon, as necessary and subject to the conclusion of appropriate arrangements with the Government of Lebanon. The arrangements governing the presence of the Commission in Lebanon under the Memorandum of Understanding between the Government of the Republic of Lebanon and the United Nations regarding the Modalities of Cooperation for the International Independent Investigation Commission, signed on 13 June 2005 (see S/2005/393), depending on the circumstances prevailing at the time of the establishment of the tribunal, may be expanded to apply, mutatis mutandis, to the presence of an office of the prosecutor in Lebanon.

43. As is customarily the case with respect to tribunals of all kinds, the possibility that the special tribunal for Lebanon will meet away from its seat when it considers it necessary for the efficient exercise of its functions is provided for in article 8, paragraph 2, of the agreement.

B. Funding mechanism

44. In its resolution 1664 (2006), the Security Council requested the Secretary-General to submit options for a funding mechanism appropriate to ensure the continued and effective functioning of the tribunal. Without prejudice to the authority of the General Assembly in budgetary matters under Article 17 of the Charter of the United Nations, several options are, in principle, available in the determination of the funding mechanism of the special tribunal: assessed contributions in whole or in part; voluntary contributions; or assessed and voluntary contributions combined. As the Government of Lebanon has expressed its willingness to bear a substantial part of the expenses of the tribunal,[6] all options but one include a provision that 49 per cent of the expenses of the tribunal would be borne by the Government of Lebanon. An indication of possible options and a proposed corresponding article are described below.

1. Assessed contributions

45. The merits of assessed contributions—the funding mechanism of the two ad hoc tribunals, the International Tribunal for the Former Yugoslavia and the International Criminal Tribunal for Rwanda—were debated at the time of the establishment of the Special Court for Sierra Leone. In his report to the Security Council (S/2000/915), the Secretary-General expressed the view that only regular, predictable, assessed contributions could produce a

viable and sustainable mechanism affording secure and continuous funding. It was also his view (para. 70) that:

> "A financial mechanism based entirely on voluntary contributions will not provide the assured and continuous source of funding which would be required to appoint the judges, the Prosecutor and the Registrar, to contract the services of all administrative and support staff and to purchase the necessary equipment. The risks associated with the establishment of an operation of this kind with insufficient funds, or without long-term assurances of continuous availability of funds, are very high, in terms of both moral responsibility and loss of credibility of the Organization, and its exposure to legal liability."

46. Funding through assessed contributions could be either in whole or in part. If considered an expense of the Organization under Article 17 of the Charter of the United Nations, it should be financed from assessed contributions. Any voluntary contributions, including the contribution of the Government of Lebanon, would be supplemental and be used to implement specific non-core activities. It is recalled in this connection that if a decision to fund the special tribunal through assessed contributions is adopted, it would be for the General Assembly, as the authority entrusted under Article 17 of the Charter with the responsibility to consider and approve the budget, to decide on the source of funding, as well as on any budgetary and administrative arrangements to be put in place. It is also recalled that funding through assessed contributions would trigger the applicability to the special tribunal of the United Nations Financial and Staff Regulations and Rules.

47. If the mechanism of assessed contributions in whole is accepted, the relevant provision of the agreement would read:

> "The expenses of the Special Tribunal shall be considered expenses of the Organization in accordance with Article 17 of the Charter of the United Nations."

48. If the mechanism of assessed contributions in part is accepted, the relevant provision in the agreement would read:

> "The expenses of the Special Tribunal shall be borne in the following manner:
>
> "(a) Fifty-one per cent of the expenses of the Tribunal shall be considered expenses of the Organization in accordance with Article 17 of the Charter of the United Nations;
>
> "(b) Forty-nine per cent of the expenses of the Tribunal shall be borne by the Government of Lebanon."

2. Voluntary contributions

49. Voluntary contributions was the funding mechanism of the Special Court for Sierra Leone and the Extraordinary Chambers in the Courts of Cambodia, although in the former case a one-time subvention was granted by the General Assembly to replenish the dwindling reserves of the Special Court. If the option of voluntary contributions, as the sole funding mechanism of the tribunal, is adopted, then the corresponding article would read:

"The expenses of the Special Tribunal shall be borne in the following manner:

"(a) Fifty-one per cent of the expenses of the Tribunal shall be borne by voluntary contributions from States;

"(b) Forty-nine per cent of the expenses of the Tribunal shall be borne by the Government of Lebanon."

3. Combined funding mechanism

50. While the Secretary-General maintains his principled position in support of assessed contributions as the funding mechanism of international criminal jurisdictions, the uniqueness of the special tribunal for Lebanon may warrant a different approach to the establishment of the financial mechanism. The formula proposed is a combined formula of both voluntary and assessed contributions. It provides for a continuation of assessed contributions to fund investigations (as is currently the case with the Commission) and this may be considered more viable and sustainable than other options wholly reliant on voluntary contributions. If accepted, the corresponding article would read:

> "The expenses of the Special Tribunal for Lebanon shall be borne in the following manner:
>
> "(a) The expenses incurred for investigations shall continue to be considered expenses of the Organization in accordance with Article 17 of the Charter of the United Nations;
>
> "(b) Fifty-one per cent of the expenses of the Tribunal, excluding those related to investigations, shall be borne by voluntary contributions from States;
>
> "(c) Forty-nine per cent of the expenses of the Tribunal, excluding those related to investigations, shall be borne by the Government of Lebanon."

51. With regard to the options described in paragraphs 49 and 50 above, both of which involve voluntary contributions, the sufficiency of funds must be guaranteed before the Secretary-General can be expected to commence the process of establishment of the tribunal. In any of these options, therefore, the following text should be inserted as paragraph 2 of the corresponding article:

> "It is understood that the Secretary-General will commence the process of establishing the Tribunal when he has sufficient contributions in hand to finance the establishment of the Tribunal and twelve months of its operations, plus pledges equal to the anticipated expenses of the following twenty-four months of the Tribunal's operation. Should voluntary contributions be insufficient for the Tribunal to implement its mandate, the Secretary-General and the Security Council shall explore alternate means of financing the Tribunal."

C. Cooperation with the special tribunal

52. Article 15 of the agreement places an obligation on the Government of Lebanon to cooperate with the tribunal at all stages of the proceedings and to comply with its requests for assistance in the identification and location of persons, service of documents, arrest and detention of persons, and the transfer of indictees to the tribunal.

53. In maintaining the logic of Security Council resolutions 1595 (2005), 1636 (2005) and 1644 (2005), under which Member States are obliged to cooperate fully with the Commission in its investigation of the Hariri assassination, the Council may wish, at the appropriate stages and as necessary, to consider similar measures to enable the special tribunal more effectively to prosecute those responsible for the attack against Rafiq Hariri and for other attacks falling within the jurisdiction of the tribunal.

VII. Conclusion

54. On 10 November 2006, I transmitted to the Prime Minister of Lebanon the draft agreement between the United Nations and the Government of Lebanon on the establishment of a special tribunal for Lebanon, to which was annexed a draft statute for such a tribunal. By his letter to me of 13 November 2006, the Prime Minister informed me that the Lebanese Council of Ministers had agreed in its session of that date to the draft and looked forward to the completion of the remaining steps leading to the establishment of the tribunal. By a note verbale dated 14 November 2006, the Permanent Mission of Lebanon forwarded to me a copy of observations made by the President of the Lebanese Republic, including a challenge to the decision of the Council of Ministers. The negotiated instruments are now submitted to the Security Council for its consideration.

---

1 In the view of the Commission, the comparable modus operandi of each attack could point to a single group of perpetrators who aimed to conduct a series of sustainable repetitive attacks with a minimum of complications (S/2006/375, para. 69).

2 Ibid., para. 83. In its fifth report, the Commission confirmed its preliminary conclusion regarding the interconnectivity between the 14 cases and stated that, as it was developing evidence that linked the cases into differing groupings, it was anticipated that further links between the cases might become evident upon further collection of information and evidence (S/2006/760, para. 67).

3 Article 314 of the Criminal Code provides as follows:

> "The term 'acts of terrorism' includes all acts that are intended to cause a state of alarm and have been committed by means such as explosive devices, inflammable substances, toxic or corrosive products or infectious or microbial agents that are liable to pose a public threat."
>
> Articles 6 and 7, respectively, of the 1958 law provide:
>
> "All acts of terrorism shall be punishable by hard labour for life. Capital punishment shall be incurred if there were human fatalities or if a building has been wholly or partially destroyed when a person was inside, or if the act results in the destruction, even partial, of a public building, industrial installation, ship or other structure or damage to communications or transport links."
>
> "Conspiracy to commit one of the crimes mentioned in the preceding articles shall be punishable by hard labour for life."

4 Article 7, paragraph 2 (a), of the Rome Statute of the International Criminal Court defines an "attack directed against any civilian population" as "a course of conduct involving the multiple commission of acts... against any civilian population pursuant to or in furtherance of a State or organizational policy to commit such attack".

5 Case of *Krombach v. France*, European Court of Human Rights, Application No. 29731/96, Judgment, 13 February 2001; and Case of *Sejdovic v. Italy*, European Court of Human Rights, Application No. 56581/00, Judgment, 1 March 2006.

6 A firm commitment by the Government of Lebanon on defraying its share in the expenses of the tribunal would be required before the agreement could be signed by the Secretary-General.

Annex I
Agreement between the United Nations and the Lebanese Republic on the establishment of a Special Tribunal for Lebanon

Whereas the Security Council, in its resolution 1664 (2006) of 29 March 2006, which responded to the request of the Government of Lebanon to establish a tribunal of an international character to try all those who are found responsible for the terrorist crime which killed the former Lebanese Prime Minister Rafiq Hariri and others, recalled all its previous resolutions, in particular resolutions 1595 (2005) of 7 April 2005, 1636 (2005) of 31 October 2005 and 1644 (2005) of 15 December 2005,

Whereas the Security Council has requested the Secretary-General of the United Nations (hereinafter "the Secretary-General") "to negotiate an agreement with the Government of Lebanon aimed at establishing a tribunal of an international character based on the highest international standards of criminal justice", taking into account the recommendations of the Secretary-General's report of 21 March 2006 (S/2006/176) and the views that have been expressed by Council members,

Whereas the Secretary-General and the Government of the Lebanese Republic (hereinafter "the Government") have conducted negotiations for the establishment of a Special Tribunal for Lebanon (hereinafter "the Special Tribunal" or "the Tribunal"),

Now therefore the United Nations and the Lebanese Republic (hereinafter referred to jointly as the "Parties") have agreed as follows:

Article 1
Establishment of the Special Tribunal

1. There is hereby established a Special Tribunal for Lebanon to prosecute persons responsible for the attack of 14 February 2005 resulting in the death of former Lebanese Prime Minister Rafiq Hariri and in the death or injury of other persons. If the tribunal finds that other attacks that occurred in Lebanon between 1 October 2004 and 12 December 2005, or any later date decided by the Parties and with the consent of the Security Council, are connected in accordance with the principles of criminal justice and are of a nature and gravity similar to the attack of 14 February 2005, it shall also have jurisdiction over persons responsible for such attacks. This connection includes but is not limited to a combination of the following elements: criminal intent (motive), the purpose behind the attacks, the nature of the victims targeted, the pattern of the attacks (modus operandi) and the perpetrators.

2. The Special Tribunal shall function in accordance with the Statute of the Special Tribunal for Lebanon. The Statute is attached to this Agreement and forms an integral part thereof.

Article 2
Composition of the Special Tribunal and appointment of judges

1. The Special Tribunal shall consist of the following organs: the Chambers, the Prosecutor, the Registry and the Defence Office.

2. The Chambers shall be composed of a Pre-Trial Judge, a Trial Chamber and an Appeals Chamber, with a second Trial Chamber to be created if, after the passage of at least six months from the commencement of the functioning of the Special Tribunal, the Secretary-General or the President of the Special Tribunal so requests.

3. The Chambers shall be composed of no fewer than eleven independent judges and no more than fourteen such judges, who shall serve as follows:

(a) A single international judge shall serve as a Pre-Trial Judge;

(b) Three judges shall serve in the Trial Chamber, of whom one shall be a Lebanese judge and two shall be international judges;

(c) In the event of the creation of a second Trial Chamber, that Chamber shall be likewise composed in the manner contained in subparagraph (b) above;

(d) Five judges shall serve in the Appeals Chamber, of whom two shall be Lebanese judges and three shall be international judges; and

(e) Two alternate judges, of whom one shall be a Lebanese judge and one shall be an international judge.

4. The judges of the Tribunal shall be persons of high moral character, impartiality and integrity, with extensive judicial experience. They shall be independent in the performance of their functions and shall not accept or seek instructions from any Government or any other source.

5. (a) Lebanese judges shall be appointed by the Secretary-General to serve in the Trial Chamber or the Appeals Chamber or as an alternate judge from a list of twelve persons presented by the Government upon the proposal of the Lebanese Supreme Council of the Judiciary;

(b) International judges shall be appointed by the Secretary-General to serve as Pre-Trial Judge, a Trial Chamber Judge, an Appeals Chamber Judge or an alternate judge, upon nominations forwarded by States at the invitation of the Secretary-General, as well as by competent persons;

(c) The Government and the Secretary-General shall consult on the appointment of judges;

(d) The Secretary-General shall appoint judges, upon the recommendation of a selection panel he has established after indicating his intentions to the Security Council. The selection panel shall be composed of two judges, currently sitting on or retired from an international tribunal, and the representative of the Secretary-General.

6. At the request of the presiding judge of a Trial Chamber, the President of the Special Tribunal may, in the interest of justice, assign alternate judges to be present at each stage of the trial and to replace a judge if that judge is unable to continue sitting.

7. Judges shall be appointed for a three-year period and may be eligible for reappointment for a further period to be determined by the Secretary-General in consultation with the Government.

8. Lebanese judges appointed to serve in the Special Tribunal shall be given full credit for their period of service with the Tribunal on their return to the Lebanese national judiciaries from which they were released and shall be reintegrated at a level at least comparable to that of their former position.

Article 3
Appointment of a Prosecutor and a Deputy Prosecutor

1. The Secretary-General, after consultation with the Government, shall appoint a Prosecutor for a three-year term. The Prosecutor may be eligible for reappointment for a further period to be determined by the Secretary-General in consultation with the Government.

2. The Secretary-General shall appoint the Prosecutor, upon the recommendation of a selection panel he has established after indicating his intentions to the Security Council. The selection panel shall be composed of two judges, currently sitting on or retired from an international tribunal, and the representative of the Secretary-General.

3. The Government, in consultation with the Secretary-General and the Prosecutor, shall appoint a Lebanese Deputy Prosecutor to assist the Prosecutor in the conduct of the investigations and prosecutions.

4. The Prosecutor and the Deputy Prosecutor shall be of high moral character and possess the highest level of professional competence and extensive experience in the conduct of investigations and prosecutions of criminal cases. The Prosecutor and the Deputy Prosecutor shall be independent in the performance of their functions and shall not accept or seek instructions from any Government or any other source.

5. The Prosecutor shall be assisted by such Lebanese and international staff as may be required to perform the functions assigned to him or her effectively and efficiently.

Article 4
Appointment of a Registrar

1. The Secretary-General shall appoint a Registrar who shall be responsible for the servicing of the Chambers and the Office of the Prosecutor, and for the recruitment and administration of all support staff. He or she shall also administer the financial and staff resources of the Special Tribunal.

2. The Registrar shall be a staff member of the United Nations. He or she shall serve a three-year term and may be eligible for reappointment for a further period to be determined by the Secretary-General in consultation with the Government.

Article 5
Financing of the Special Tribunal

To be completed.

Article 6
Management Committee

The parties shall consult concerning the establishment of a Management Committee.

Article 7
Juridical capacity

The Special Tribunal shall possess the juridical capacity necessary:

(a) To contract;

(b) To acquire and dispose of movable and immovable property;

(c) To institute legal proceedings;

(d) To enter into agreements with States as may be necessary for the exercise of its functions and for the operation of the Tribunal.

Article 8
Seat of the Special Tribunal

1. The Special Tribunal shall have its seat outside Lebanon. The location of the seat shall be determined having due regard to considerations of justice and fairness as well as security

and administrative efficiency, including the rights of victims and access to witnesses, and subject to the conclusion of a headquarters agreement between the United Nations, the Government and the State that hosts the Tribunal.

2. The Special Tribunal may meet away from its seat when it considers it necessary for the efficient exercise of its functions.

3. An Office of the Special Tribunal for the conduct of investigations shall be established in Lebanon subject to the conclusion of appropriate arrangements with the Government.

Article 9
Inviolability of premises, archives and all other documents

1. The Office of the Special Tribunal in Lebanon shall be inviolable. The competent authorities shall take appropriate action that may be necessary to ensure that the Tribunal shall not be dispossessed of all or any part of the premises of the Tribunal without its express consent.

2. The property, funds and assets of the Office of the Special Tribunal in Lebanon, wherever located and by whomsoever held, shall be immune from search, seizure, requisition, confiscation, expropriation and any other form of interference, whether by executive, administrative, judicial or legislative action.

3. The archives of the Office of the Special Tribunal in Lebanon, and in general all documents and materials made available, belonging to or used by it, wherever located and by whomsoever held, shall be inviolable.

Article 10
Funds, assets and other property

The Office of the Special Tribunal, its funds, assets and other property in Lebanon, wherever located and by whomsoever held, shall enjoy immunity from every form of legal process, except insofar as in any particular case the Tribunal has expressly waived its immunity. It is understood, however, that no waiver of immunity shall extend to any measure of execution.

Article 11
Privileges and immunities of the judges, the Prosecutor, the Deputy Prosecutor, the Registrar and the Head of the Defence Office

1. The judges, the Prosecutor, the Deputy Prosecutor, the Registrar and the Head of the Defence Office, while in Lebanon, shall enjoy the privileges and immunities, exemptions and facilities accorded to diplomatic agents in accordance with the Vienna Convention on Diplomatic Relations of 1961.

2. Privileges and immunities are accorded to the judges, the Prosecutor, the Deputy Prosecutor, the Registrar and the Head of the Defence Office in the interest of the Special Tribunal and not for the personal benefit of the individuals themselves. The right and the duty to waive the immunity in any case where it can be waived without prejudice to the purposes for which it is accorded shall lie with the Secretary-General, in consultation with the President of the Tribunal.

Article 12
Privileges and immunities of international and Lebanese personnel

1. Lebanese and international personnel of the Office of the Special Tribunal, while in Lebanon, shall be accorded:

(a) Immunity from legal process in respect of words spoken or written and all acts performed by them in their official capacity. Such immunity shall continue to be accorded after termination of employment with the Office of the Special Tribunal;

(b) Exemption from taxation on salaries, allowances and emoluments paid to them.

2. International personnel shall, in addition thereto, be accorded:

(a) Immunity from immigration restriction;

(b) The right to import free of duties and taxes, except for payment for services, their furniture and effects at the time of first taking up their official duties in Lebanon.

3. The privileges and immunities are granted to the officials of the Office of the Special Tribunal in the interest of the Tribunal and not for their personal benefit. The right and the duty to waive the immunity in any case where it can be waived without prejudice to the purpose for which it is accorded shall lie with the Registrar of the Tribunal.

Article 13
Defence counsel

1. The Government shall ensure that the counsel of a suspect or an accused who has been admitted as such by the Special Tribunal shall not be subjected, while in Lebanon, to any measure that may affect the free and independent exercise of his or her functions.

2. In particular, the counsel shall be accorded:

(a) Immunity from personal arrest or detention and from seizure of personal baggage;

(b) Inviolability of all documents relating to the exercise of his or her functions as a counsel of a suspect or accused;

(c) Immunity from criminal or civil jurisdiction in respect of words spoken or written and acts performed in his or her capacity as counsel. Such immunity shall continue to be accorded after termination of his or her functions as a counsel of a suspect or accused;

(d) Immunity from any immigration restrictions during his or her stay as well as during his or her journey to the Tribunal and back.

Article 14
Security, safety and protection of persons referred to in this Agreement

The Government shall take effective and adequate measures to ensure the appropriate security, safety and protection of personnel of the Office of the Special Tribunal and other persons referred to in this Agreement, while in Lebanon. It shall take all appropriate steps, within its capabilities, to protect the equipment and premises of the Office of the Special Tribunal from attack or any action that prevents the Tribunal from discharging its mandate.

Article 15
Cooperation with the Special Tribunal

1. The Government shall cooperate with all organs of the Special Tribunal, in particular with the Prosecutor and defence counsel, at all stages of the proceedings. It shall facilitate access of the Prosecutor and defence counsel to sites, persons and relevant documents required for the investigation.

2. The Government shall comply without undue delay with any request for assistance by the Special Tribunal or an order issued by the Chambers, including, but not limited to:

(a) Identification and location of persons;

(b) Service of documents;

(c) Arrest or detention of persons;

(d) Transfer of an indictee to the Tribunal.

Article 16
Amnesty

The Government undertakes not to grant amnesty to any person for any crime falling within the jurisdiction of the Special Tribunal. An amnesty already granted in respect of any such persons and crimes shall not be a bar to prosecution.

Article 17
Practical arrangements

With a view to achieving efficiency and cost-effectiveness in the operation of the Special Tribunal:

(a) Appropriate arrangements shall be made to ensure that there is a coordinated transition from the activities of the International Independent Investigation Commission, established by the Security Council in its resolution 1595 (2005), to the activities of the Office of the Prosecutor;

(b) Judges of the Trial Chamber and the Appeals Chamber shall take office on a date to be determined by the Secretary-General in consultation with the President of the Special Tribunal. Pending such a determination, judges of both Chambers shall be convened on an ad hoc basis to deal with organizational matters and serving, when required, to perform their duties.

Article 18
Settlement of disputes

Any dispute between the Parties concerning the interpretation or application of this Agreement shall be settled by negotiation or by any other mutually agreed upon mode of settlement.

Article 19
Entry into force and commencement of the functioning of the Special Tribunal

1. This Agreement shall enter into force on the day after the Government has notified the United Nations in writing that the legal requirements for entry into force have been complied with.

2. The Special Tribunal shall commence functioning on a date to be determined by the Secretary-General in consultation with the Government, taking into account the progress of the work of the International Independent Investigation Commission.

Article 20
Amendment

This Agreement may be amended by written agreement between the Parties.

Article 21
Duration of the Agreement

1. This Agreement shall remain in force for a period of three years from the date of the commencement of the functioning of the Special Tribunal.

2. Three years after the commencement of the functioning of the Special Tribunal the Parties shall, in consultation with the Security Council, review the progress of the work of the Special Tribunal. If at the end of this period of three years the activities of the Tribunal have not been completed, the Agreement shall be extended to allow the Tribunal to complete its work, for a further period(s) to be determined by the Secretary-General in consultation with the Government and the Security Council.

3. The provisions relating to the inviolability of the funds, assets, archives and documents of the Office of the Special Tribunal in Lebanon, the privileges and immunities of those referred to in this Agreement, as well as provisions relating to defence counsel and the protection of victims and witnesses, shall survive termination of this Agreement.

In witness whereof, the following duly authorized representatives of the United Nations and of the Lebanese Republic have signed this Agreement.

Done at __________ on __________ 2006, in three originals in the Arabic, French and English languages, all texts being equally authentic.

For the United Nations: ______________

For the Lebanese Republic: ______________

Attachment

Statute of the Special Tribunal for Lebanon

Having been established by an Agreement between the United Nations and the Lebanese Republic (hereinafter "the Agreement") pursuant to Security Council resolution 1664 (2006) of 29 March 2006, which responded to the request of the Government of Lebanon to establish a tribunal of an international character to try all those who are found responsible for the terrorist crime which killed the former Lebanese Prime Minister Rafiq Hariri and others, the Special Tribunal for Lebanon (hereinafter "the Special Tribunal") shall function in accordance with the provisions of this Statute.

Section I
Jurisdiction and applicable law

Article 1
Jurisdiction of the Special Tribunal

The Special Tribunal shall have jurisdiction over persons responsible for the attack of 14 February 2005 resulting in the death of former Lebanese Prime Minister Rafiq Hariri and in the death or injury of other persons. If the Tribunal finds that other attacks that occurred in Lebanon between 1 October 2004 and 12 December 2005, or any later date decided by the Parties and with the consent of the Security Council, are connected in accordance with the principles of criminal justice and are of a nature and gravity similar to the attack of 14 February 2005, it shall also have jurisdiction over persons responsible for such attacks. This connection includes but is not limited to a combination of the following elements: criminal intent (motive), the purpose behind the attacks, the nature of the victims targeted, the pattern of the attacks (modus operandi) and the perpetrators.

Article 2
Applicable criminal law

The following shall be applicable to the prosecution and punishment of the crimes referred to in article 1, subject to the provisions of this Statute:

(a) The provisions of the Lebanese Criminal Code relating to the prosecution and punishment of acts of terrorism, crimes and offences against life and personal integrity, illicit associations and failure to report crimes and offences, including the rules regarding the material elements of a crime, criminal participation and conspiracy; and

(b) Articles 6 and 7 of the Lebanese law of 11 January 1958 on "Increasing the penalties for sedition, civil war and interfaith struggle".

Article 3
Individual criminal responsibility

1. A person shall be individually responsible for crimes within the jurisdiction of the Special Tribunal if that person:

(a) Committed, participated as accomplice, organized or directed others to commit the crime set forth in article 2 of this Statute; or

(b) Contributed in any other way to the commission of the crime set forth in article 2 of this Statute by a group of persons acting with a common purpose, where such contribution is intentional and is either made with the aim of furthering the general criminal activity or purpose of the group or in the knowledge of the intention of the group to commit the crime.

2. With respect to superior and subordinate relationships, a superior shall be criminally responsible for any of the crimes set forth in article 2 of this Statute committed by subordinates under his or her effective authority and control, as a result of his or her failure to exercise control properly over such subordinates, where:

(a) The superior either knew, or consciously disregarded information that clearly indicated that the subordinates were committing or about to commit such crimes;

(b) The crimes concerned activities that were within the effective responsibility and control of the superior; and

(c) The superior failed to take all necessary and reasonable measures within his or her power to prevent or repress their commission or to submit the matter to the competent authorities for investigation and prosecution.

3. The fact that the person acted pursuant to an order of a superior shall not relieve him or her of criminal responsibility, but may be considered in mitigation of punishment if the Special Tribunal determines that justice so requires.

Article 4
Concurrent jurisdiction

1. The Special Tribunal and the national courts of Lebanon shall have concurrent jurisdiction. Within its jurisdiction, the Tribunal shall have primacy over the national courts of Lebanon.

2. Upon the assumption of office of the Prosecutor, as determined by the Secretary-General, and no later than two months thereafter, the Special Tribunal shall request the national judicial authority seized with the case of the attack against Prime Minister Rafiq Hariri and others to defer to its competence. The Lebanese judicial authority shall refer to the Tribunal the results of the investigation and a copy of the court's records, if any. Persons detained in connection with the investigation shall be transferred to the custody of the Tribunal.

3. (a) At the request of the Special Tribunal, the national judicial authority seized with any of the other crimes committed between 1 October 2004 and 12 December 2005, or a later date decided pursuant to article 1, shall refer to the Tribunal the results of the investigation and a copy of the court's records, if any, for review by the Prosecutor;

(b) At the further request of the Tribunal, the national authority in question shall defer to the competence of the Tribunal. It shall refer to the Tribunal the results of the investigation and a copy of the court's records, if any, and persons detained in connection with any such case shall be transferred to the custody of the Tribunal;

(c) The national judicial authorities shall regularly inform the Tribunal of the progress of their investigation. At any stage of the proceedings, the Tribunal may formally request a national judicial authority to defer to its competence.

Article 5
Non bis in idem

1. No person shall be tried before a national court of Lebanon for acts for which he or she has already been tried by the Special Tribunal.

2. A person who has been tried by a national court may be subsequently tried by the Special Tribunal if the national court proceedings were not impartial or independent, were designed to shield the accused from criminal responsibility for crimes within the jurisdiction of the Tribunal or the case was not diligently prosecuted.

3. In considering the penalty to be imposed on a person convicted of a crime under this Statute, the Special Tribunal shall take into account the extent to which any penalty imposed by a national court on the same person for the same act has already been served.

Article 6
Amnesty

An amnesty granted to any person for any crime falling within the jurisdiction of the Special Tribunal shall not be a bar to prosecution.

Section II
Organization of the Special Tribunal

Article 7
Organs of the Special Tribunal

The Special Tribunal shall consist of the following organs:

(a) The Chambers, comprising a Pre-Trial Judge, a Trial Chamber and an Appeals Chamber;

(b) The Prosecutor;

(c) The Registry; and

(d) The Defence Office.

Article 8
Composition of the Chambers

1. The Chambers shall be composed as follows:

(a) One international Pre-Trial Judge;

(b) Three judges who shall serve in the Trial Chamber, of whom one shall be a Lebanese judge and two shall be international judges;

(c) Five judges who shall serve in the Appeals Chamber, of whom two shall be Lebanese judges and three shall be international judges;

(d) Two alternate judges, one of whom shall be a Lebanese judge and one shall be an international judge.

2. The judges of the Appeals Chamber and the judges of the Trial Chamber, respectively, shall elect a presiding judge who shall conduct the proceedings in the Chamber to which he

or she was elected. The presiding judge of the Appeals Chamber shall be the President of the Special Tribunal.

3. At the request of the presiding judge of the Trial Chamber, the President of the Special Tribunal may, in the interest of justice, assign the alternate judges to be present at each stage of the trial and to replace a judge if that judge is unable to continue sitting.

Article 9
Qualification and appointment of judges

1. The judges shall be persons of high moral character, impartiality and integrity, with extensive judicial experience. They shall be independent in the performance of their functions and shall not accept or seek instructions from any Government or any other source.

2. In the overall composition of the Chambers, due account shall be taken of the established competence of the judges in criminal law and procedure and international law.

3. The judges shall be appointed by the Secretary-General, as set forth in article 2 of the Agreement, for a three-year period and may be eligible for reappointment for a further period to be determined by the Secretary-General in consultation with the Government.

Article 10
Powers of the President of the Special Tribunal

1. The President of the Special Tribunal, in addition to his or her judicial functions, shall represent the Tribunal and be responsible for its effective functioning and the good administration of justice.

2. The President of the Special Tribunal shall submit an annual report on the operation and activities of the Tribunal to the Secretary-General and to the Government of Lebanon.

Article 11
The Prosecutor

1. The Prosecutor shall be responsible for the investigation and prosecution of persons responsible for the crimes falling within the jurisdiction of the Special Tribunal. In the interest of proper administration of justice, he or she may decide to charge jointly persons accused of the same or different crimes committed in the course of the same transaction.

2. The Prosecutor shall act independently as a separate organ of the Special Tribunal. He or she shall not seek or receive instructions from any Government or from any other source.

3. The Prosecutor shall be appointed, as set forth in article 3 of the Agreement, by the Secretary-General for a three-year term and may be eligible for reappointment for a further period to be determined by the Secretary-General in consultation with the Government. He or she shall be of high moral character and possess the highest level of professional competence, and have extensive experience in the conduct of investigations and prosecutions of criminal cases.

4. The Prosecutor shall be assisted by a Lebanese Deputy Prosecutor and by such other Lebanese and international staff as may be required to perform the functions assigned to him or her effectively and efficiently.

5. The Office of the Prosecutor shall have the power to question suspects, victims and witnesses, to collect evidence and to conduct on-site investigations. In carrying out these tasks, the Prosecutor shall, as appropriate, be assisted by the Lebanese authorities concerned.

Article 12
The Registry

1. Under the authority of the President of the Special Tribunal, the Registry shall be responsible for the administration and servicing of the Tribunal.

2. The Registry shall consist of a Registrar and such other staff as may be required.

3. The Registrar shall be appointed by the Secretary-General and shall be a staff member of the United Nations. He or she shall serve for a three-year term and may be eligible for reappointment for a further period to be determined by the Secretary-General in consultation with the Government.

4. The Registrar shall set up a Victims and Witnesses Unit within the Registry. This Unit shall provide, in consultation with the Office of the Prosecutor, measures to protect the safety, physical and psychological well-being, dignity and privacy of victims and witnesses, and such other appropriate assistance for witnesses who appear before the Special Tribunal and others who are at risk on account of testimony given by such witnesses.

Article 13
The Defence Office

1. The Secretary-General, in consultation with the President of the Special Tribunal, shall appoint an independent Head of the Defence Office, who shall be responsible for the appointment of the Office staff and the drawing up of a list of defence counsel.

2. The Defence Office, which may also include one or more public defenders, shall protect the rights of the defence, provide support and assistance to defence counsel and to the persons entitled to legal assistance, including, where appropriate, legal research, collection of evidence and advice, and appearing before the Pre-Trial Judge or a Chamber in respect of specific issues.

Article 14
Official and working languages

The official languages of the Special Tribunal shall be Arabic, French and English. In any given case proceedings, the Pre-Trial Judge or a Chamber may decide that one or two of the languages may be used as working languages as appropriate.

Section III
Rights of defendants and victims

Article 15
Rights of suspects during investigation

A suspect who is to be questioned by the Prosecutor shall not be compelled to incriminate himself or herself or to confess guilt. He or she shall have the following rights of which he or she shall be informed by the Prosecutor prior to questioning, in a language he or she speaks and understands:

(a) The right to be informed that there are grounds to believe that he or she has committed a crime within the jurisdiction of the Special Tribunal;

(b) The right to remain silent, without such silence being considered in the determination of guilt or innocence, and to be cautioned that any statement he or she makes shall be recorded and may be used in evidence;

(c) The right to have legal assistance of his or her own choosing, including the right to have legal assistance provided by the Defence Office where the interests of justice so require and where the suspect does not have sufficient means to pay for it;

(d) The right to have the free assistance of an interpreter if he or she cannot understand or speak the language used for questioning;

(e) The right to be questioned in the presence of counsel unless the person has voluntarily waived his or her right to counsel.

Article 16
Rights of the accused

1. All accused shall be equal before the Special Tribunal.

2. The accused shall be entitled to a fair and public hearing, subject to measures ordered by the Special Tribunal for the protection of victims and witnesses.

3. (a) The accused shall be presumed innocent until proved guilty according to the provisions of this Statute;

(b) The onus is on the Prosecutor to prove the guilt of the accused;

(c) In order to convict the accused, the relevant Chamber must be convinced of the guilt of the accused beyond reasonable doubt.

4. In the determination of any charge against the accused pursuant to this Statute, he or she shall be entitled to the following minimum guarantees, in full equality:

(a) To be informed promptly and in detail in a language which he or she understands of the nature and cause of the charge against him or her;

(b) To have adequate time and facilities for the preparation of his or her defence and to communicate without hindrance with counsel of his or her own choosing;

(c) To be tried without undue delay;

(d) Subject to the provisions of article 22, to be tried in his or her presence, and to defend himself or herself in person or through legal assistance of his or her own choosing; to be informed, if he or she does not have legal assistance, of this right; and to have legal assistance assigned to him or her, in any case where the interests of justice so require and without payment by him or her in any such case if he or she does not have sufficient means to pay for it;

(e) To examine, or have examined, the witnesses against him or her and to obtain the attendance and examination of witnesses on his or her behalf under the same conditions as witnesses against him or her;

(f) To examine all evidence to be used against him or her during the trial in accordance with the Rules of Procedure and Evidence of the Special Tribunal;

(g) To have the free assistance of an interpreter if he or she cannot understand or speak the language used in the Special Tribunal;

(h) Not to be compelled to testify against himself or herself or to confess guilt.

5. The accused may make statements in court at any stage of the proceedings, provided such statements are relevant to the case at issue. The Chambers shall decide on the probative value, if any, of such statements.

Article 17
Rights of victims

Where the personal interests of the victims are affected, the Special Tribunal shall permit their views and concerns to be presented and considered at stages of the proceedings determined to be appropriate by the Pre-Trial Judge or the Chamber and in a manner that is not prejudicial to or inconsistent with the rights of the accused and a fair and impartial trial. Such views and concerns may be presented by the legal representatives of the victims where the Pre-Trial Judge or the Chamber considers it appropriate.

Section IV
Conduct of proceedings

Article 18
Pre-Trial proceedings

1. The Pre-Trial Judge shall review the indictment. If satisfied that a prima facie case has been established by the Prosecutor, he or she shall confirm the indictment. If he or she is not so satisfied, the indictment shall be dismissed.

2. The Pre-Trial Judge may, at the request of the Prosecutor, issue such orders and warrants for the arrest or transfer of persons, and any other orders as may be required for the conduct of the investigation and for the preparation of a fair and expeditious trial.

Article 19
Evidence collected prior to the establishment of the Special Tribunal

Evidence collected with regard to cases subject to the consideration of the Special Tribunal, prior to the establishment of the Tribunal, by the national authorities of Lebanon or by the International Independent Investigation Commission in accordance with its mandate as set out in Security Council resolution 1595 (2005) and subsequent resolutions, shall be received by the Tribunal. Its admissibility shall be decided by the Chambers pursuant to international standards on collection of evidence. The weight to be given to any such evidence shall be determined by the Chambers.

Article 20
Commencement and conduct of trial proceedings

1. The Trial Chamber shall read the indictment to the accused, satisfy itself that the rights of the accused are respected, confirm that the accused understands the indictment and instruct the accused to enter a plea.

2. Unless otherwise decided by the Trial Chamber in the interests of justice, examination of witnesses shall commence with questions posed by the presiding judge, followed by questions posed by other members of the Trial Chamber, the Prosecutor and the Defence.

3. Upon request or proprio motu, the Trial Chamber may at any stage of the trial decide to call additional witnesses and/or order the production of additional evidence.

4. The hearings shall be public unless the Trial Chamber decides to hold the proceedings in camera in accordance with the Rules of Procedure and Evidence.

Article 21
Powers of the Chambers

1. The Special Tribunal shall confine the trial, appellate and review proceedings strictly to an expeditious hearing of the issues raised by the charges, or the grounds for appeal or review, respectively. It shall take strict measures to prevent any action that may cause unreasonable delay.

2. A Chamber may admit any relevant evidence that it deems to have probative value and exclude such evidence if its probative value is substantially outweighed by the need to ensure a fair trial.

3. A Chamber may receive the evidence of a witness orally or, where the interests of justice allow, in written form.

4. In cases not otherwise provided for in the Rules of Procedure and Evidence, a Chamber shall apply rules of evidence that will best favour a fair determination of the matter before it and are consonant with the spirit of the Statute and the general principles of law.

Article 22
Trials in absentia

1. The Special Tribunal shall conduct trial proceedings in the absence of the accused, if he or she:

(a) Has expressly and in writing waived his or her right to be present;

(b) Has not been handed over to the Tribunal by the State authorities concerned;

(c) Has absconded or otherwise cannot be found and all reasonable steps have been taken to secure his or her appearance before the Tribunal and to inform him or her of the charges confirmed by the Pre-Trial Judge.

2. When hearings are conducted in the absence of the accused, the Special Tribunal shall ensure that:

(a) The accused has been notified, or served with the indictment, or notice has otherwise been given of the indictment through publication in the media or communication to the State of residence or nationality;

(b) The accused has designated a defence counsel of his or her own choosing, to be remunerated either by the accused or, if the accused is proved to be indigent, by the Tribunal;

(c) Whenever the accused refuses or fails to appoint a defence counsel, such counsel has been assigned by the Defence Office of the Tribunal with a view to ensuring full representation of the interests and rights of the accused.

3. In case of conviction in absentia, the accused, if he or she had not designated a defence counsel of his or her choosing, shall have the right to be retried in his or her presence before the Special Tribunal, unless he or she accepts the judgement.

Article 23
Judgement

The judgement shall be rendered by a majority of the judges of the Trial Chamber or of the Appeals Chamber and shall be delivered in public. It shall be accompanied by a reasoned opinion in writing, to which any separate or dissenting opinions shall be appended.

Article 24
Penalties

1. The Trial Chamber shall impose upon a convicted person imprisonment for life or for a specified number of years. In determining the terms of imprisonment for the crimes provided for in this Statute, the Trial Chamber shall, as appropriate, have recourse to international practice regarding prison sentences and to the practice of the national courts of Lebanon.

2. In imposing sentence, the Trial Chamber should take into account such factors as the gravity of the offence and the individual circumstances of the convicted person.

Article 25
Compensation to victims

1. The Special Tribunal may identify victims who have suffered harm as a result of the commission of crimes by an accused convicted by the Tribunal.

2. The Registrar shall transmit to the competent authorities of the State concerned the judgement finding the accused guilty of a crime that has caused harm to a victim.

3. Based on the decision of the Special Tribunal and pursuant to the relevant national legislation, a victim or persons claiming through the victim, whether or not such victim had been identified as such by the Tribunal under paragraph 1 of this article, may bring an action in a national court or other competent body to obtain compensation.

4. For the purposes of a claim made under paragraph 3 of this article, the judgement of the Special Tribunal shall be final and binding as to the criminal responsibility of the convicted person.

Article 26
Appellate proceedings

1. The Appeals Chamber shall hear appeals from persons convicted by the Trial Chamber or from the Prosecutor on the following grounds:

(a) An error on a question of law invalidating the decision;

(b) An error of fact that has occasioned a miscarriage of justice.

2. The Appeals Chamber may affirm, reverse or revise the decisions taken by the Trial Chamber.

Article 27
Review proceedings

1. Where a new fact has been discovered that was not known at the time of the proceedings before the Trial Chamber or the Appeals Chamber and that could have been a decisive factor in reaching the decision, the convicted person or the Prosecutor may submit an application for review of the judgement.

2. An application for review shall be submitted to the Appeals Chamber. The Appeals Chamber may reject the application if it considers it to be unfounded. If it determines that the application is meritorious, it may, as appropriate:

(a) Reconvene the Trial Chamber;

(b) Retain jurisdiction over the matter.

Article 28
Rules of Procedure and Evidence

1. The judges of the Special Tribunal shall, as soon as practicable after taking office, adopt Rules of Procedure and Evidence for the conduct of the pre-trial, trial and appellate proceedings, the admission of evidence, the participation of victims, the protection of victims and witnesses and other appropriate matters and may amend them, as appropriate.

2. In so doing, the judges shall be guided, as appropriate, by the Lebanese Code of Criminal Procedure, as well as by other reference materials reflecting the highest standards of international criminal procedure, with a view to ensuring a fair and expeditious trial.

Article 29
Enforcement of sentences

1. Imprisonment shall be served in a State designated by the President of the Special Tribunal from a list of States that have indicated their willingness to accept persons convicted by the Tribunal.

2. Conditions of imprisonment shall be governed by the law of the State of enforcement subject to the supervision of the Special Tribunal. The State of enforcement shall be bound by the duration of the sentence, subject to article 30 of this Statute.

Article 30
Pardon or commutation of sentences

If, pursuant to the applicable law of the State in which the convicted person is imprisoned, he or she is eligible for pardon or commutation of sentence, the State concerned shall notify the Special Tribunal accordingly. There shall only be pardon or commutation of sentence if the President of the Tribunal, in consultation with the judges, so decides on the basis of the interests of justice and the general principles of law.

Annex II
Attacks perpetrated in Lebanon since 1 October 2004[a]

Following is an overview of the 14 cases in chronological order.

Number	*Date*	*Type of explosion*	*Area*	*Victims*
1	1 October 2004	Car bomb	Dar El-Mraisseh locality, California Street, Beirut	Marwane Hamadeh and driver wounded, bodyguard killed
2	19 March 2005	Bomb	New-Jdeidh, northern suburb of Beirut	11 persons wounded and serious material damage to buildings and cars
3	23 March 2005	Bomb	Altavista shopping centre, Kaslik, north of Beirut	3 persons killed, 7 persons wounded and serious material damage to buildings and cars
4	26 March 2005	Bomb	Sid-El-Bouchria, north-east of Beirut	6 persons wounded and serious material damage to buildings and cars
5	1 April 2005	Bomb	Plaza shopping centre, Broumana, east of Beirut	9 persons wounded and serious material damage to buildings and cars
6	6 May 2005	Bomb	"Voice of Charity" radio station, Jounieh, north of Beirut	11 persons wounded and serious material damage to buildings and cars
7	2 June 2005	Victim's car	Ashrafieh locality, Beirut	Samir Kassir killed
8	21 June 2005	Victim's car	Wata Msaytbeh, Boustany Street, Beirut	George Hawi killed
9	12 July 2005	Car bomb	Naccache area, Beirut	Elias El-Murr and 2 other persons wounded and 1 person killed
10	22 July 2005	Bomb	Monot Street, Ashrafieh locality, Beirut	13 persons wounded and serious material damage to buildings and cars
11	22 August 2005	Bomb	Zalka locality, near Promenade Hotel, north of Beirut	11 persons wounded and serious material damage to buildings and cars
12	16 September 2005	Bomb	Naoum Libki Street, Ashrafieh locality, Beirut	1 person killed and 10 persons wounded and serious material damage to buildings and cars
13	25 September 2005	Victim's car	Ghadir locality, suburb of Beirut	May Chidiac seriously wounded
14	12 December 2005	Car bomb	Mkalles, north of Beirut	Gebran Tueni and 2 other persons killed

[a] See S/2006/161, para. 55.

3. Sixth Report of the International Independent Investigation Commission, 12 December 2006 (S/2006/962)

Letter dated 12 December 2006 from the Secretary-General addressed to the President of the Security Council

I have the honour to transmit herewith the sixth report of the International Independent Investigation Commission, which was prepared pursuant to Security Council resolutions 1595 (2005), 1636 (2005), 1644 (2005) and 1686 (2006).

The report describes progress made by the Commission since its previous report of 25 September 2006 (S/2006/760) in investigating the assassination of former Lebanese Prime Minister Rafik Hariri and 22 other victims, and in providing technical assistance to the Lebanese authorities in their investigation of certain other attacks perpetrated in Lebanon since 1 October 2004.

During this period, the Commission returned from Cyprus, where it had been temporarily relocated from 22 July to 13 October 2006, to its main operating base in Lebanon and resumed full operations. The report provides information on the Commission's continued priority work in the forensic investigation of the Hariri case, focusing on the identification of the perpetrators as well as the advancement of its technical assistance on the 14 cases, including the establishment of linkages. Furthermore, the Commission, as mandated by the Security Council, started to provide technical assistance to the Lebanese authorities in their investigation of the tragic assassination on 21 November 2006 of Pierre Gemayel, the Minister of Industry of Lebanon.

I wish to thank the staff of the Commission for their extraordinary dedication in carrying forward their work in difficult circumstances, in particular in view of the volatile security situation in Lebanon during the reporting period. I also wish to thank Serge Brammertz for his continued leadership in advancing the investigation of the attack and the Government of Lebanon for its continued support for and cooperation with the Commission.

I should be grateful if you would bring this matter to the attention of the members of the Security Council. Meanwhile, I am transmitting the report to the Government of Lebanon.

(*Signed*) Kofi A. **Annan**

Serge Brammertz, Commissioner
Beirut, 12 December 2006

Summary

In its resolution 1644 (2005) of 15 December 2005, the Security Council requested the International Independent Investigation Commission to report to it on its progress, including on the cooperation received from the Syrian authorities, every three months.

The present report summarizes the progress made by the Commission in its investigative activities between 25 September and 10 December 2006. During this period, the Commission returned to Lebanon from Cyprus, where it had temporarily relocated from 22 July to 13 October 2006.

Since the Commission's return to Lebanon, it has operated in a volatile political environment, reflected in the assassination on 21 November 2006 of the Minister of Industry, Pierre Gemayel, and the national and international attention surrounding the establishment of a special tribunal for Lebanon.

The Commission's investigative direction in the Hariri case has remained focused on three areas: developing crime scene evidence from investigation and forensic analysis, investigating potential perpetrators and collecting evidence relating to the linkage and contextual aspects of the case. The Commission, in close cooperation with the Lebanese judiciary, has also continued to take a proactive role in the 14 other cases.

The assassination of Pierre Gemayel led to the request by the Security Council in a letter dated 22 November 2006 for the Commission to extend technical assistance in the Gemayel case to the Lebanese authorities. This constituted an expansion of the mandate contained in Council resolution 1644 (2005) and extended in its resolution 1686 (2006) in relation to the investigation of other terrorist attacks perpetrated in Lebanon since 1 October 2004. The Commission has responded by providing technical assistance, including forensic support, witness interviews and evidence collection and analysis, as requested.

The Commission's close interaction with the Lebanese authorities on all matters relevant to its mandate has been ongoing. The Commission continues to receive support from the Syrian Arab Republic in providing information and facilitating interviews with individuals located on Syrian territory. In addition, the Commission notes the assistance received from other Member States in response to its requests and highlights the need for such assistance to be provided in a timely manner as this is critical to the progress of the investigation.

I. Introduction

1. The present report is submitted pursuant to Security Council resolution 1644 (2005) of 15 December 2005, in which the Council requested the United Nations International Independent Investigation Commission to report every three months to the Council on the progress of its inquiry and on cooperation matters, including the cooperation received from the Syrian authorities. This report, the fourth submitted in 2006, provides an overview of

issues described in the previous reports and notes substantial progress in the work of the Commission, as well as new elements that have come to light since its last report of 25 September 2006 (S/2006/760).

2. During the reporting period, the Commission returned from Cyprus, where it had been temporarily relocated for a two-and-a-half-month period for security reasons, to continue its operations in Lebanon. As work continued in the temporary environment, the dislocation had minimal impact upon the momentum of the Commission's investigation.

3. The broader political climate in Lebanon has been volatile. Two major events have had an impact on the Commission's investigative activities and security requirements, namely the assassination of the Minister for Industry, Pierre Gemayel, in Beirut on 21 November and the national and international discourse surrounding the establishment of a special tribunal for Lebanon.

4. The Commission's investigative direction in the Hariri case has remained focused on three areas: developing crime scene evidence from investigation and forensic analysis, investigating potential perpetrators and collecting evidence relating to the linkage and contextual aspects of the case. Over the past three months, the Commission has continued with all the investigative projects identified in its previous reports, placing emphasis on the motives to assassinate Rafik Hariri, issues associated with Ahmed Abu Adass, linkage among the 14 other cases and on forensic analysis. In support of these objectives, the Commission has conducted 60 interviews during the reporting period.

5. With regard to the 14 cases in which the Commission is providing technical assistance to the Lebanese authorities in line with the revised mandate given by the Security Council in its resolution 1686 (2006), the Commission has focused on the six targeted attacks during this reporting period.

6. Following the request from the Security Council on 22 November 2006 (see S/2006/915), the Commission immediately committed managerial and operational staff from its existing resources to provide technical assistance to the Lebanese authorities concerning the assassination of Minister Pierre Gemayel.

7. The Commission continues to maintain its close working relationship with the Lebanese authorities on all matters relevant to its mandate. The assistance of other States is also necessary to the success of its work and, in general, the Commission has received assistance from a number of States in a wide range of investigative and analytical areas. However, it has also experienced delays and a lack of response from some States. The Commission continues to receive assistance from the Syrian Arab Republic in providing information and facilitating interviews with individuals located on Syrian territory. This cooperation remains an important component of the Commission's ongoing work.

8. The Commission is evaluating its work in the light of the creation of a special tribunal for Lebanon and is envisaging future planning activities to facilitate the transition to such a tribunal. The Commission is organizing its investigative outputs, evidence, data and files in such a manner as to ensure continuity and enable the tribunal to draw upon these resources and begin its work in as smooth a manner as possible, if and when it comes into being.

9. Renewed efforts during the reporting period to increase the capacity and resources of the Commission to enable it to meet the significant investigative, analytical, security, translation/interpretation and other challenges associated with its expanding mandate have so far yielded positive results. For example, the Commission has made considerable efforts to recruit new staff to fill international positions, resulting in a decrease in the vacancy rate from 29 per cent in August to 19 per cent in December.

10. The Commission has reached a critical stage in its investigations and, with this in mind, the Commission and the Prosecutor General of Lebanon believe that placing information concerning witnesses and suspects in the public domain would be contrary to the principles of fairness and justice and would defeat the purpose of, and be prejudicial to, any case presented before a tribunal. The Commission believes that this position is a standard investigative approach that also creates beneficial conditions under which witnesses, especially those considered sensitive owing to their placement and/or knowledge, can step forward to engage with the Commission in confidential circumstances.

II. Progress in the investigations

11. During this reporting period, the Commission's investigative direction in the case of the murder of Rafik Hariri and 22 others has continued to be focused on three main objectives: firstly, the development of crime scene evidence from investigation and forensic analysis; secondly, the investigation of potential perpetrators; and, thirdly, the collection of evidence relating to the linkage and contextual aspects of the case. In support of these objectives, and among other operational work it has undertaken, the Commission has conducted 46 interviews during the reporting period.

12. As regards the 14 cases in which technical assistance is being provided to the Lebanese authorities, the Commission has conducted 14 additional interviews relating to the six targeted attacks, focusing on two main objectives: to investigate each case individually and concurrently to establish links between each and any of the cases and the Hariri case. The remaining eight cases are gradually being integrated into the investigative activity, with the focus on modus operandi and perpetrator linkages between the cases.

13. During the reporting period, the Commission continued with the 20 projects that form the framework of its investigations. In particular, the Commission has focused upon and expanded its work on the motives for the Hariri assassination, the linkage between 6 of the 14 cases, the investigation relating to Ahmed Abu Adass and associated individuals, and forensic analysis to assist in identifying the perpetrators.

14. Such prioritization allows a logical development of the cases and enables management of the increasing workload. In this reporting period, for example, electronic data holdings doubled, thereby creating additional management and analytical tasks that accompany such a vast amount of newly acquired information.

15. Similarly, the workload for the 60 interviews undertaken for both the Hariri case and the other cases during this reporting period has been considerable. Each interview has taken on average one and a half days to complete, with sometimes over 50 pages of text per interview. The preparation time for the interviews is considerable and the time needed to analyse the content and integrate the information into the broader case after its collection is also significant. In this context, the Commission has continued to benefit from having

multidisciplinary teams working on all its investigative projects. This approach has ensured flexibility to respond to the priorities without delay or reduction in quality of output.

16. Following the request from the Security Council of 22 November 2006, the Commission also began the provision of technical assistance to the Lebanese authorities concerning the assassination of Pierre Gemayel on 21 November 2006. Work undertaken to date includes extensive forensic assistance and the conduct of 13 identification interviews.

A. Hariri investigation

1. Crime scene and associated topics

Forensic exploitation of the crime scene

17. Following the completion of the collection of forensic evidence at the crime scene in June 2006, the Commission has received the final report from the forensic experts who participated in that project. The detailed report provides many findings that are consistent with previous forensic work, confirms the main hypotheses of the modus operandi of the perpetrators and provides new information previously unknown to the Commission.

18. Among the findings from the report, it was confirmed that there was only one blast, that the Mitsubishi van was the carrier of the improvised explosive device (IED) and that the blast originated from inside the loading platform of the vehicle.

19. Investigations inside the crater showed that a rectangular depression of a further 40 centimetres in depth was present in a specific area. The rocky soil in that area was micronized and blackened, consistent with having been subjected to high pressure and high temperatures. This observation indicated that the van itself was finally situated slightly obliquely to the other parked vehicles. The report also provides new information relating to other aspects of the explosives and the van, which the Commission will continue to investigate over the next reporting period.

Findings to date regarding the explosives

20. In March 2005, many samples that originated from the crater wall indicated the presence of the explosive TNT. In November 2005, the swabs from the rear axle, wheel rim and crankshaft of the Mitsubishi Canter van showed significant amounts of the explosive RDX. In the last forensic analysis, in addition to RDX on the rear wheel flange, the explosives PETN, TNT and DNT were detected in lower concentrations, along with an indication of TNP (picric acid).

21. An estimate of the concentration ratios between the explosives has now been made, where the ratio between both RDX and PETN, and RDX and TNT/DNT have been calculated at approximately 10:1. The presence of such large amounts of RDX and the consideration of these ratios strongly supports the hypothesis that an RDX-based high explosive was used in the attack. RDX is a powerful high explosive that may be used either by itself or in combination with other materials, making it particularly useful in, for example, military applications.

22. According to the analysis conducted on behalf of the Commission to date, two hypotheses concerning the explosives have emerged: firstly, that the main charge was composed of RDX and TNT, with the detonating cord (PETN) linking together the explosive charges;

secondly, the explosive charge was composed of TNT and Semtex (RDX and PETN), an explosive that has been widely used previously in terrorist bombings within and outside the region.

Findings to date regarding the initiating system

23. The Commission's view concerning the initiating system is that triggering an explosion in order to deliver an impact upon a moving vehicle requires a high degree of precision in the timing. This precludes the possibility that a time-delay mechanism was used. Time-delay mechanisms incorporate mechanical, electrical or chemical timing devices that only function after a specified time period has elapsed. In this case, given the need for precision timing, the use of a remote-control mechanism or direct trigger (possibly a "suicide bomber") mechanism is more likely. However, the Commission considers that the use of a remote-control mechanism is highly improbable in this case for a number of reasons.

24. Firstly, all the electronic parts that were recovered at the crime scene have been subjected to expert analysis and the Commission has found that no parts originated from a remote-control activation mechanism of an IED.

25. Secondly, of the three electronic countermeasure devices in the convoy of Rafik Hariri, two were found to have most probably been operating at the time of the explosion. These devices were designed to disturb the signals from a remote-controlled mechanism intended to detonate an IED. The countermeasure device in the last Mercedes 500, the vehicle closest to the explosion, was completely destroyed. The device in the Mercedes 600 driven by Hariri was severely burned, but an expert examination revealed that it is likely that the device was operating properly when the explosion occurred. Finally, the device in the first Mercedes 500 was largely intact and was operating properly.

26. Thirdly, the 33 pieces of human remains of the unidentified male that were recovered at the crime scene are very small. The physical state and size of these human parts, and the fact that they were all found in the same area west of the crater, indicate that this male was very close to the IED. Also, a small number of the parts show the presence of plastic material that possibly comes from electric wires associated with the device.

27. In view of the above factors, the Commission considers that the most likely scenario for the activation of the IED is that a person directly triggered the IED from within or immediately in front of the Mitsubishi van.

Geographical origin of the bomber

28. The complete tooth and other biological parts belonging to the same male found on the crime scene during the investigations carried out in June 2006 and earlier are being analysed in order to establish, if possible, the geographical origin of the person. It is this individual who the Commission believes most probably detonated the IED.

29. The general methodology is to examine the ratio between isotopes in elements found in different parts of the person's body. The ratios are not constant, but vary depending on the geographical location of the individual and in other ways through physical, chemical and biological processes within the person's body. Different parts of the human body reflect different time windows relative to when body organs or tissues were formed, with which isotopic composition and in which geographical environment. Time windows for analysis

range from childhood for dense bones and tooth enamel to as recently as two weeks before the person's demise for the part of hair closest to the skin.

30. A number of samples have been analysed for their isotopic compositions in this project. These include hair, sternum and tooth samples of the unidentified man; samples of reference hair; samples of reference teeth of the approximate age of the man; and samples of soils, street dust and water.

31. The results of the expert report in this first phase of analysis show that the individual did not spend his youth in Lebanon, but was situated there in the last two to three months before his death. The report discusses the type of area in which the individual lived during the last 10 years or so of his life, although at this stage no specific region can as yet be derived from the analysis. The Commission has also received other information concerning geographical origin, which it is unable to disclose at this time. This forensic process will continue into the next reporting period.

32. A second phase of analysis will be undertaken during the next reporting period, with a wider analysis of hair, geochemical and other samples from relevant countries and other areas. As a result, the isotope analysis results may point towards the identification of a specific geographical origin of the man likely to have detonated the device.

Ethnic origin and description of the bomber

33. In a similar context, the Commission is undertaking forensic analysis to try to establish the ethnic origin of the man likely to have detonated the device. This is being done by analysing the alleles in the DNA profile of the 33 human parts and comparing them for similarities or variations in other allele frequency distributions from other States and regions. The findings of comparative frequencies enable a statistical probability analysis of the person's origin.

34. The upper right central incisor found at the crime scene in February 2005 and belonging to the unidentified male shows a distinguishing mark related to the lingual surface shape of the crown, which has the form of a spade. This feature is rarely seen among people from Lebanon. The tooth found on the crime scene during the investigations carried out in June 2006 is a lower right central incisor. Because of the time elapsed since the assassination, no DNA profile could be drawn from this tooth. Nevertheless, the odontological examination shows that this lower right incisor belongs to a male, and the X-rays indicate that this man had a similar age to the unidentified man. Considering that this tooth was found in the same vicinity as the 33 human parts, the Commission believes that this lower right incisor most likely belongs to the same individual.

35. In addition, the Commission is conducting an anthropological analysis of some of the 33 individual biological remains of the individual in order to develop a partial description of the man that will assist in future investigative steps.

36. The methodologies involved in identifying the geographical and ethnic origin of an individual are complex and time-consuming, as is the reconstruction of the bomber's physiognomy. Also, the specificity of the results may not be guaranteed. The Commission is mindful that results must therefore be interpreted carefully and the limitations clearly understood. The Commission will treat future results as forensic information to be used for lead purposes in the investigation.

Mitsubishi van identification

37. Documentation and technical information received by the Commission from Japan, together with its own sourcing of key manuals and documents, have enabled it to make a preliminary association of some of the vehicle parts found in the crater at the crime scene with those of a Mitsubishi van. An external expert will be brought in to confirm identification of those parts and will assist in other technical aspects of vehicle identification, using an exhibits inventory process to support the work.

Resolution of issues from crime scene investigations

38. The Commission has resolved certain aspects of its crime scene investigations to its satisfaction at present. These include the issue of the alleged missing closed-circuit television footage from the Phoenicia Hotel, which has been identified and is being analysed; establishing the reason for the last-minute arrival of a person in a rented van close to the scene of the crime some seconds before the explosion; investigating the reduction in government security for Hariri once he had ceased to be the Prime Minister; and issues concerning the position of Hariri in his vehicle and the position of his vehicle in the convoy.

Ongoing investigations

39. There are a number of leads that continue to be investigated, such as the allegations of tampering with the crime scene and obstruction of the investigation, and developing the information concerning alleged earlier operational activity against Hariri by the apparent bombing team and other individuals.

40. The Commission is also continuing to investigate the discovery at the crime scene in June 2006 of certain personal effects of a victim of the explosion and matters arising from a victim at the crime scene who had been discovered in a situation protected from the blast but who was killed by falling masonry. In addition, the Commission continues its work relating to seismological analysis, trajectory analysis and three-dimensional reconstruction of the crime scene, and the sounds of the blast phenomenon.

41. Similarly, with regard to the Mitsubishi van, investigations are ongoing concerning the acquisition of the van and its preparation with explosives. The Commission has received new information specifying details of the preparation of the van and establishment of the route of the van as it was brought to the St. George Hotel area prior to the attack. The Commission has developed working hypotheses based upon the recently acquired information.

42. Further interviews are required of crime scene witnesses and, upon receipt of the final forensic biological report, further DNA research and comparative analysis on profiles acquired from the June 2006 crime scene exploitation will lead to additional investigative work being undertaken.

2. Individuals involved in the commission of the crime

Communications

43. The Commission has conducted seven interviews in connection with the alleged bombing team and their use of six telephones to communicate on the day of the attack and in the days leading up to it. These interviews have provided new leads that are currently

being pursued and will lead to more interviews in the next reporting period. Analysis of the use of other associated subscriber identity module (SIM) cards is also ongoing.

44. The location of the telephones when used and the purposes for which some of the linking numbers were used have revealed the high degree of security-aware behaviour exhibited by the individuals under investigation. Some persons used multiple mobile cellular telephones during a short period of time or registered telephones using aliases. While such compartmentalization of telephone usage makes analysis more complex, it helps to provide an understanding of the modus operandi of the perpetrators.

45. During the reporting period, communications traffic analysis has continued in support of the other investigative projects. This work consists of preparation for interviews of key persons and preparing specific reports on communications between selected individuals. For the purpose of preparation of interviews, data relating to the different telephones used by the interviewee during a certain period of interest are gathered and organized into an exploitable electronic format. The analysis then focuses on the personal contacts and communications links of the interviewee, the use of intermediaries and the frequency, timing, type, duration and location of the calls, as well as international call activity.

Ahmed Abu Adass and associated individuals

46. The investigations into Ahmed Abu Adass have continued in this reporting period, focusing on a number of areas, including on the selection of Abu Adass for the role he played, as understood by the Commission at present. The Commission is working to establish how Abu Adass was identified, where and when this occurred, who involved him in the operation and what happened to him afterwards.

47. To further its investigation in this regard, the Commission has deconstructed the known time period from the time of Ahmed Abu Adass' alleged involvement with certain individuals in late 2004 through the period of his disappearance in January 2005 to the time of the video being recovered on 14 February 2005.

48. There are significant information gaps between known events on this timeline and the Commission is working to fill those gaps in order to establish the facts of Ahmed Abu Adass' involvement in the crime. The Commission has conducted interviews and forensic research, including DNA and fingerprint analysis, and computer forensic analysis. It has also examined numerous types of documentation, including notebooks, manuals, diaries, books and individual documents, and it has visited locations in Lebanon and elsewhere. This work will continue into the next reporting period.

49. The Commission has also undertaken investigations with regard to individuals associated with Ahmed Abu Adass in Lebanon and abroad. This aspect of the case has elicited some useful information and the Commission remains fully engaged in pursuing any new leads.

50. In this regard, the Commission has conducted 17 interviews to date in the Syrian Arab Republic and Lebanon and has held a number of meetings with relevant Syrian and Lebanese officials. It has collected substantial quantities of computer and electronic information and documentation and visited a number of locations in the Syrian Arab Republic.

51. In support of this work, the Commission has researched over 200 gigabytes of electronic data, examined hundreds of pages of documents, diaries and notebooks, analysed a number of mobile telephones and the records contained therein and examined large volumes of communications traffic.

52. Over 100 artefacts, some of potentially key relevance, have been sent to a forensic laboratory for fingerprint and DNA research, imagery analysis and for comparative analysis with previously acquired items. The Commission awaits the results of the current forensic analysis to determine the artefacts' relevance or otherwise to the Ahmed Abu Adass aspects of the case.

53. Researching and analysing the huge amounts of data collected to date on this single project absorbs considerable human resources and requires significant storage capacity and electronic-processing capability. To add to the complexity of this painstaking analytical work, some of the electronic data received by the Commission are written in code, some are encrypted and some had already been deleted. It has also been necessary to synthesize data where appropriate with communications traffic on mobile cellular telephones.

54. The process of analysis of communications traffic in preparation for interviews is rigorous and time-consuming. However, it represents an important corroborative tool to confirm or disprove information concerning the interviewee, as well as uncovering new information and providing investigative direction.

Other hypotheses

55. The Commission believes its role is to investigate all possible hypotheses that arise from the investigation and analysis of the Hariri assassination. To this end, it is investigating groups and individuals who are situated in Lebanon and beyond, including the group claiming responsibility for the attack in the Abu Adass video.

56. The Commission is examining allegations of the attack on Rafik Hariri being delivered via aerial means. Further collection work is being undertaken, including forensically and through the acquisition of technical data. This is done to clarify the likelihood of such a means being a viable attack option, prior to further investigative steps being taken. It is anticipated that the Commission will have established this understanding during the next reporting period.

3. Motives to assassinate Rafik Hariri

Rafik Hariri timeline

57. The Commission is expanding its investigations not only into the last days of Rafik Hariri's life, but also into the last 15 months of his life in considerable detail. The Commission has undertaken 17 more interviews during the reporting period, including with individuals in the international political arena. These interviews are lengthy, sensitive and drawn from individuals across the spectrum of persons with whom Hariri met and interacted.

58. The Commission has collected information concerning the increasing threat level and pressure exerted on Rafik Hariri over the last 15 months of his life. It has also established indications that he received assurances from his supporters, political allies and associates

that he would not be the focus of attack. It is alleged that even up to his last few days, he remained confident that he would not be the subject of an attack. This area of the Commission's work, which is highly sensitive and ongoing, focuses not just on establishing the contextual aspects of Hariri's life and working environment, but also on evidential leads in the investigation of criminal intent and capability.

Motives

59. The Commission continues to work on numerous alternative hypotheses in examining the motives to kill Rafik Hariri. Included among these are the following: that Hariri was the victim of an extremist group that assassinated him because of his links to other States in the region and in the West; Hariri's position regarding Security Council resolution 1559 (2004); that the extension of the term of the Lebanese President may have been a factor; that Hariri had to be killed before his possible success in the May 2005 elections; Hariri's involvement with the newspaper An-Nahar; or that Hariri was likely to expose publicly an alleged grand-scale financial misappropriation of funds from the Bank Al-Madina. Another hypothesis under consideration is that apparently obvious motives were used by the perpetrators as a convenient cover, with the real intent being to propel other individuals into the frontline of accusation.

60. The list outlined above is non-exhaustive and is indicative of the complexities in collecting evidence for each hypothesis, noting that combinations of the above are also feasible. At this stage in the Commission's investigations, a smaller number of motives to assassinate Rafik Hariri emerge as the most plausible. While the Commission will work on all hypotheses until they are no longer viable, during the next reporting period it will focus on collecting further evidence to clarify the more likely motives for his assassination.

B. Technical assistance in the other cases

1. The 14 other cases

61. During the reporting period, the Commission has extended further its technical assistance to the Lebanese authorities in the 14 cases and continues to work closely with the Prosecutor General of Lebanon and the investigative judges in support of each one. To date, the Commission has also translated over 2,500 pages of documents relevant to the cases and has received electronic data, which are under review.

62. In previous reporting periods, the Commission has provided technical assistance in forensic analysis, communications analysis and the conduct of interviews. In this reporting phase, the Commission has focused in particular upon interviewing witnesses associated in some respect with the victims of the six targeted attacks. It has conducted 14 interviews to date and has a number of interviews scheduled to be completed in the next reporting period.

63. The objective of the Commission in these interviews is to develop knowledge about each attack individually and also to develop linkages between the attacks. The Commission has collected evidence from its interviews to date of a considerable number of links between the six cases, and between these cases and the Rafik Hariri case, from a number of different perspectives. This evidence supports the analytical hypotheses discussed in the Commission's report of 10 June 2006 (S/2006/375).

(a) The nature of the attacks

64. The Commission believes that the six targeted attacks were deliberate attempts to assassinate the intended victims. Each attack was designed to kill the individual and the fact that three of the victims survived was by chance, not by design.

65. The eight other attacks were of an equally serious specific nature, although they differed in their execution. They were probably more indiscriminate in their nature in that a specific individual was not the target per se. However, the possibility that individuals would be killed as a result of the attacks was extremely high. In fact 4 people were killed and approximately 60 persons were wounded.

(b) The motives behind the attacks

66. In the six cases, there are factual links between a number of the victims, aligning them into a group with common objectives and interests. The Commission believes it is possible that the motive to kill at least some of the victims was associated with these common objectives and interests and that the attacks may fit into a broader scheme of intent.

67. In the eight attacks, a possible intent was to kill or wound individuals in order to spread fear among the population, to destabilize the security situation and to cause damage to infrastructure. The fact that no advance notice was given of any of the attacks supports this hypothesis.

(c) The nature of the victims targeted

68. In the six cases, Samir Kassir and May Chidiac were prominent media figures. Gebran Tueni was both a prominent media figure and a parliamentarian. Marwan Hamadeh and Elias El-Murr were then, and remain, government ministers; and George Hawi was the former Secretary-General of the Communist Party of Lebanon. Each victim was publicly known in his or her professional life, and each had a publicly known political orientation.

69. Some of the victims of the targeted attacks were directly or indirectly linked to the political coalition known as the March 14 Movement. Samir Kassir, Gebran Tueni and George Hawi were associated with it in one context or another. George Hawi and Samir Kassir supported the Democratic Left Movement, one of the political parties that fall under the umbrella of the March 14 Movement. Marwan Hamadeh was involved in the precursor to the March 14 Movement, a group known as the Bristol Group or Gathering, and remains closely associated with the March 14 Movement today.

70. Another link between Marwan Hamadeh, Rafik Hariri, Samir Kassir and Gebran Tueni was their association with An-Nahar newspaper. Some of the victims were also connected to each other or to Rafik Hariri through family ties, friendship or other personal associations.

71. In the eight attacks, the victims were not publicly known figures with political views that were broadly known to the Lebanese population. They could be best characterized as members of the general public.

(d) The pattern of the attacks, modus operandi and the perpetrators

72. As discussed in the Commission's report of 10 June 2006 (S/2006/375), the three specifically targeted persons who appeared to have had very limited personal protection

arrangements were Samir Kassir, George Hawi and May Chidiac. The modus operandi for these attacks appears similar in that all had IEDs placed underneath their cars.

73. In these cases, the operational capability and capacity to execute such attacks was high, yet the method chosen was simplified to maximize the chances of success with a minimum of complications. Each of the three attacks suggests that prior surveillance was carried out by the perpetrators to establish the level of personal security arrangements for the intended victims, including routines and protective measures, and to identify the relevant vehicle and seat for the placement of the device.

74. In the cases of the other three specifically targeted persons, namely Marwan Hamadeh, Elias El-Murr and Gebran Tueni, all three had some form of personal security arrangements. It is therefore possible that the reason for the different nature of the attacks on these persons, that is, a bomb being placed in a car parked along their respective routes, was to overcome their personal security arrangements. The modus operandi for these attacks appears similar, in that there was a high standard of operational capacity and capability. In particular, the attacks required good intelligence and more complex reconnaissance and surveillance coverage to maximize chances of success.

75. A claim of responsibility was made for both the Kassir and Tueni attacks by a previously unknown organization, the "Fighters for the Unity and Freedom of Bilad El-Cham". The Commission is conducting analysis of this group and has requested information from States to assist it in this matter.

76. In the eight other cases, the comparable modus operandi of each attack could point to a single group of perpetrators, who aimed to conduct a series of sustainable repetitive attacks with a minimum of complications. The operational capability to execute such attacks was high, yet the method chosen was as simple as possible to achieve the aim.

77. The explosive devices in each case were sufficiently small and light to be carried by a single person but large enough to ensure a significant impact. The devices were detonated either by using a timing device or by remote control. The choice of time and location of the eight attacks could be seen as a deliberate choice by the perpetrators, reflecting a carefully struck balance between the desired impact and the means of escape in each attack.

(e) Further assistance

Forensic analysis

78. The Commission continues to review in detail the forensic evidence available concerning the cases and to evaluate the crime scene management of each case. The comparative seismological analysis of the records of the signals recorded by the National Centre for Geophysics of Lebanon is ongoing, with the Commission expecting results from experts in the next reporting period.

Communications

79. The Commission continues to conduct communications analysis in support of witness interviews and in order to generate new investigative leads. One individual using multiple numbers has been preliminarily linked to a number of attacks and the Commission has conducted a number of interviews related to this issue. The objectives are to ascertain the

geographical location and timings of certain persons at the crime scenes where either the victims or associated individuals were present.

2. Pierre Gemayel case

Background

80. On 22 November 2006, the President of the Security Council sent a letter to the Secretary-General inviting the Commission to extend its technical assistance to the Lebanese authorities in this investigation (S/2006/915). The Commission received the letter on 23 November and that same day formal contact was made with the Prosecutor General of Lebanon to begin assisting in the case.

81. The Commission has met with the Prosecutor General and the Military Prosecutor in a series of working meetings to discuss the facts of the case in detail and a number of areas in which the Commission can provide technical assistance. The assistance is broadly grouped into two areas: helping with specific investigative aspects of the case and providing forensic expertise. The Lebanese authorities and the Commission have since continued their excellent relationship in all the working areas, as outlined below.

The assassination

82. On Tuesday, 21 November 2006, Pierre Gemayel, the Minister for Industry, left the Ministry at approximately 3 p.m. He was driving himself, with two armed bodyguards, in a vehicle that had been rented only a few days before. At approximately 3.30 p.m., while driving, he pulled over to the side of the road to wait for a person he was to meet with and at the same time he was making a telephone call.

83. A dark-coloured vehicle, probably a Honda CR-V, pulled up alongside Gemayel's vehicle and an individual from the front passenger's side began to shoot through Gemayel's car door window into the front driver's side. Gemayel's vehicle moved away and up a slight incline, and was blocked by another vehicle. At some point during these events, the assailants left their vehicle, moved to Gemayel's car, opened the front car doors and from a very close range continued to shoot into the vehicle. The attackers, who shot over 49 rounds using four different types of ammunition, then fled the scene.

Preliminary assessment

84. It is probable that Gemayel was the subject of surveillance as part of a planned assassination operation against him, although it is not yet clear for how long this plan had been conceived. The exact timing and precise choice of location of the attack can be characterized as opportunistic, given that Gemayel unexpectedly halted his vehicle while travelling.

85. It is likely that the plan was to assassinate Pierre Gemayel, not just to mount an attack against him, given that the assassins left their vehicle in order to keep firing at him until they completed their mission. In addition, the fact that the assassins had not made any attempt to disguise themselves or hide their faces may indicate that they had not intended to leave their vehicles to be seen at that precise time.

Technical assistance

86. The Commission is providing investigative support to the Gemayel case by helping to identify the perpetrators and the vehicles that were used in the attack. It is also working to reconstruct the modus operandi of the assassins before, during and after the attack.

87. The Commission's assistance includes an analysis of events in the vicinity of the crime scene and in locations prior to the actual attack, the actions and methodology of the perpetrators themselves, and events immediately after the attack occurred. It also consists of forensic work, including providing portrait artists to help reconstruct the appearance of the perpetrators, and carrying out investigation and analysis of the attacked vehicle for DNA, fingerprints and ballistic and transfer traces. The Commission is also assisting with interviewing eyewitnesses and other individuals, and it is investigating and analysing communications possibly related to the assassination.

88. The Commission has commenced a reconstruction of the crime scene so as to establish from a forensic perspective the modus operandi of the perpetrators. This reconstruction will include trajectory and ballistic analysis to establish which weapons were used, when, in what order and from which locations at the crime scene. The Commission is preparing weapons photo-boards and has acquired recordings of the sounds of different weaponry to assist in the interview process.

89. During seven days of investigations carried out on the crime scene, the Commission recovered 175 exhibits and examined the vehicle of Gemayel. In total, including items collected by the Lebanese authorities, 240 exhibits have been sent to a laboratory for forensic research and analysis. These include a vehicle bumper, some glass, car door handles, some of the victim's clothing and other exhibits. DNA and fingerprint research will be conducted on relevant exhibits.

90. The Commission will continue to provide technical assistance to the Lebanese authorities on this case for the foreseeable future and will allocate additional resources as required. It anticipates conducting more interviews of crime scene witnesses and other individuals, developing the case through further evidence collection and analysis and continuing to provide ongoing forensic support.

91. The Commission has identified a specific requirement arising from the provision of technical support to the Pierre Gemayel case. It is evident that the Lebanese authorities would benefit from immediate forensic capacity-building initiatives and training. This would be particularly useful for the management of crime scenes, immediate forensic handling and processing of evidence, and the necessary forensic coordination.

92. Such capacity-building is not within the Commission's scope to provide, but it suggests that States may consider the urgent provision of such assistance to the Lebanese national authorities. This would ensure that any future crime scenes are appropriately managed and would help maximize investigative leads for the Lebanese authorities in the immediacy of an incident, should other attacks occur.

III. External cooperation

A. Interaction with the Lebanese authorities

93. Throughout the reporting period, and in particular since it returned to Lebanon, the Commission has maintained close interaction with the Lebanese authorities on all aspects of its work.

94. The Government of Lebanon has extended its generous support throughout the reporting period, in particular by implementing extraordinary security measures to protect the

Commission's personnel and property. The Commission is very grateful for this support, especially at a time when the security situation in Lebanon remains volatile.

95. The Commission has made numerous requests to the relevant Lebanese authorities for assistance with its investigative work during the reporting period, including by addressing 22 formal written requests to the Prosecutor General. Members of the Commission have also met regularly with the Minister of Justice and the Prosecutor General, as well as with senior members of his staff, the investigative judges assigned to the cases that the Commission is investigating and the senior representative appointed by the Internal Security Forces.

96. The Commission regularly shares with the appropriate Lebanese authorities the substance of all relevant information that it obtains in a manner that does not compromise the interest of the source of this information, be it an individual, an organization or a State. This includes an analytical report on the credibility of a witness, recently transmitted to the Prosecutor General and the investigative judge assigned to the Hariri case. This process is of particular importance where the information is relevant to individuals who are detained, as it may assist the Lebanese authorities in taking any steps they deem appropriate or necessary in relation to detention.

B. International cooperation

97. Security Council resolutions 1636 (2005) and 1644 (2005), adopted under Chapter VII of the Charter of the United Nations, impose an obligation on States to cooperate with the Commission. The Commission continues to rely heavily on cooperation from States and regularly directs requests for assistance to States on a range of matters relevant to its investigations, including requests for information and documents, logistical help in establishing witness interviews and technical assistance and expertise. The full cooperation of Member States with the Commission is important as the investigation proceeds, especially as regards the timeliness and the quality of the information made available to the Commission by the State authorities.

Cooperation with the Syrian Arab Republic

98. Consistent with the Syrian Arab Republic's obligations under Security Council resolutions 1636 (2005) and 1644 (2005), and the common understanding reached between the Commission and the Syrian Arab Republic earlier in the year, the cooperation of the Republic with the Commission remains timely and efficient.

99. During the reporting period, the Commission submitted 12 formal requests for assistance to the Syrian Arab Republic, seeking information, artefacts, electronic media and documentation about certain individuals and groups, as well as statements taken from persons in the course of investigations conducted by Syrian authorities.

100. The Commission undertook a number of investigative activities and interviews of individuals in the Syrian Arab Republic. This work included conducting six interviews, holding five meetings with relevant Syrian officials and collecting considerable computer and electronic information and documentation. The Syrian Arab Republic provided the Commission with information as requested, notably on specific individuals and groups. It also forwarded to the Commission statements obtained in the course of investigations conducted by Syrian authorities.

101. All the Commission's investigative activities were arranged by the Syrian Arab Republic in accordance with the requests the Commission referred to the authorities over the reporting period, and the Commission is satisfied with the timeliness with which this was done and with the logistical and security arrangements for these activities. The level of assistance provided by the Syrian Arab Republic during the reporting period remains generally satisfactory. The Commission will continue to request the country's full cooperation, which remains crucial to the swift and successful completion of its work.

Cooperation with other States

102. The Commission requires the full and expeditious support of States on technical, legal and judicial matters relevant to the investigation.

103. Although most States have responded positively to the Commission's requests and have actively assisted in its work, including by facilitating witness interviews and providing other support and information, some States have provided late or incomplete responses, or have not responded at all. At the end of the reporting period, responses to 22 requests sent to 10 separate Member States are overdue. The lack of responsiveness by certain States has serious consequences in terms of delay for the work of the Commission and its investigative progress. In view of the crucial nature of the information that it seeks to obtain from States and the limited time frame in which it aims to complete its investigative activities, the Commission trusts that it will enjoy full and prompt cooperation from all States during the next reporting period.

104. Since 15 September 2006, a total of 10 new formal requests for assistance have been sent to five different States, in addition to the requests for assistance addressed to the Syrian Arab Republic and the Lebanese authorities.

IV. Organizational support

A. Internal procedure

105. The Commission has reviewed the internal procedure that it adopted pursuant to Security Council resolution 1595 (2005) in the light of the draft statute of the special tribunal for Lebanon. It remains aware of the responsibility to ensure that testimonial, forensic or any other evidence that it collects shall be admissible before this jurisdiction and, to this end, to respect all relevant international standards.

B. Administration

1. Recruitment

106. As stated in its last report (S/2006/760), the rapid improvement of the Commission's institutional capacity continued to be one of the key tasks in the reporting period. While timely recruitment of competent personnel is still a significant challenge and delays in the process have had an impact on the Commission's ability to fulfil its mandate, considerable headway has been made in the selection and recruitment of staff during the reporting period.

107. The vacancy rate had increased in the previous reporting period as a result of the disruption of the recruitment process caused by the conflict in Lebanon and the fact that additional posts had been approved in June 2006. However, there has been an overall steady

decline in the vacancy rate between August and December: the vacancy rate decreased overall for all international staff, from 29 per cent in August to 19 per cent in December. Most key positions are currently under recruitment. The investigations division currently has 29 international staff and 3 new staff members are under advanced recruitment. Twenty-eight additional candidates for investigations are being reviewed from the significant number of names received from Member States and international agencies and interviews are under way.

108. The Commission is grateful for the positive responses received so far from Member States and international institutions with regard to making qualified candidates available.

2. Budget

109. In August 2006, the Commission submitted a proposed new budget for the next 12-month period, from January to December 2007. The proposed budget makes provision for 188 international staff, reflecting an increase of 13. The increase comprises five investigations staff for the 14 cases, one additional security officer and seven administrative posts. The additional staff are necessary: (a) to meet the increased demands generated by the additional workload resulting from the technical assistance cases, where extraordinary amounts of data are expected and have already been acquired; (b) to address the increased workload generated by the anticipated growth in staffing levels as recruitment accelerates; and (c) to compensate for the loss of support from other Lebanon-based agencies (the United Nations Interim Force in Lebanon and the Economic and Social Commission for Western Asia), which are unable in the present circumstances to provide the same level of support as in the past.

3. Security

110. With the generous assistance of the United Nations Peacekeeping Force in Cyprus, the United Nations Interim Force in Lebanon and the Cypriot and Lebanese authorities, in particular the Lebanese Armed Forces and Internal Security Forces, the Commission's security operations team coordinated a safe and secure return of the Commission's international staff and essential investigation materials from Cyprus to Beirut, partially by ship and partially by air, over a one-week period, from 9 to 16 October 2006.

111. The security of the Commission's staff, premises and assets continues to be a priority. The post-conflict security situation in Beirut remains fragile. The ongoing political incidents have created further tension and instability. The focus of the investigation, together with a forthcoming transition towards a special tribunal may create an environment that makes the Commission's staff more vulnerable and could threaten its work. The primary focus of the Commission's security operations is therefore to enable the continuation of its mandate by ensuring maximum security for all personnel, facilities and assets.

112. The Commission's security team continues to review and update the threat and risk assessments relating to the Commission in order to ensure that all critical aspects of security are consistent with relevant security standards. As required, standard operating procedures and contingency plans are developed or adjusted based on the current threat and risk analysis.

4. Supplemental memorandum of understanding

113. On 13 October 2006, the Commissioner transmitted an updated draft supplemental memorandum of understanding, aimed at supplementing and modifying the original

memorandum signed by the Government of Lebanon and the Commission on 13 June 2005. The draft supplemental agreement is currently being reviewed by the Government of Lebanon.

V. Conclusions

114. The Commission's strategic objective remains to collect evidence against those responsible for the assassination of Rafik Hariri and the other victims of attacks being investigated that will be admissible before a future tribunal. It continues to balance the need for speed in the investigations with the exigencies of applying appropriate legal standards. During the next reporting phase, the Commission will maintain its current investigative focus as discussed in this report and it plans to undertake approximately 50 interviews, collect further documentation and acquire other forms of evidence.

115. The investigation into the assassination of Rafik Hariri is approaching a sensitive and complicated phase, and the Commission's work can only be undertaken with confidentiality in order to create a secure environment for its witnesses and staff. The Commission and the Prosecutor General of Lebanon remain in full agreement regarding this position.

116. The Commission's work on the 14 cases continues to bring to light significant links between each case and to indicate links to the Rafik Hariri case. Further work will continue with those links being the focal point of its investigative direction. Similarly, the Commission will continue to provide support in the Gemayel case and will concentrate on assisting in the identification of the perpetrators of the crime and on examining whether links to the other cases exist.

117. The Commission will require further support in the coming months in three main areas. Firstly, the Commission will work to ensure that the United Nations management systems in areas such as recruitment, procurement, administration and financial matters are able to support the necessary pace and direction of the Commission's work. Secondly, the Commission notes the varied commitment to the requests for assistance it sends to numerous States. Delays or lack of responses to its requests severely hamper the progress of the Commission's investigations in certain directions. Thirdly, it is of critical importance that the Commission has access to those political actors with whom Rafik Hariri had direct contact in the last months of his life and to individuals involved in the relevant political dynamics in Lebanon, the broader region and internationally. The Commission looks forward to future cooperation with such individuals and, where appropriate, State representatives, in order to ensure the completeness of its investigations.

118. The Commission notes that the overall environment within which it conducts its work may be characterized as highly unpredictable. The security situation, the political environment, the previous conflict, the potential for ongoing violence and issues regarding the future special tribunal may contribute to the reticence of witnesses to engage with the Commission and makes it more difficult for the Commission to recruit and retain staff.

119. Finally, the Commission recognizes its additional obligations and role, given that a special tribunal is likely to be established in the forthcoming although undetermined period. The dynamic of the Commission will alter as necessary to accommodate the establishment of the tribunal and, to that end, the Commission will realign its objectives in part to hand over its fact-finding work to date to the prosecutor's office.

4. Seventh Report of the International Independent Investigation Commission, 15 March 2007 (S/2007/150)

Letter dated 15 March 2007 from the Secretary-General addressed to the President of the Security Council

I have the honour to transmit the seventh report of the International Independent Investigation Commission, which was prepared pursuant to Security Council resolutions 1595 (2005), 1636 (2005), 1644 (2005) and 1686 (2006).

The report describes progress made by the Commission since its previous report dated 12 December 2006 (S/2006/962) in investigating the February 2005 assassination of former Lebanese Prime Minister Rafik Hariri and 22 other victims, and in providing technical assistance to the Lebanese authorities in their investigation of a number of other attacks perpetrated in Lebanon since 1 October 2004.

The present report provides information on the Commission's progress in the investigation of the Hariri case, with particular emphasis on developing crime scene leads and collecting evidence relating to perpetrators as well as linkage and contextual aspects of the case. The Commission also continued to provide significant technical assistance on 15 other cases, pursuing possible linkages between these and the Hariri case. It has also worked in conjunction with the Lebanese authorities on the investigation of the 13 February 2007 bombings, in which three people were killed and at least 20 people were injured when two explosions occurred on two buses travelling through the village of Ain Alaq, near Beirut.

I wish to take this opportunity to express thanks to Commissioner Brammertz for his leadership and to the staff of the Commission for their dedication and commitment in often demanding circumstances.

I also wish to thank the Government of Lebanon for its enduring cooperation with, and support for, the Commission. In addition, I would like to welcome the request of the Lebanese Government transmitted in Prime Minister Siniora's letter of 21 February 2007 for a further extension of the mandate of the Commission for a period of up to one year, from 15 June 2007.

I should be grateful if you would bring this matter to the attention of the members of the Security Council. Meanwhile, I am transmitting the report to the Government of Lebanon.

(*Signed*) **Ban** Ki-moon

Serge Brammertz, Commissioner
Beirut, March 2007

Summary

The Security Council, in its resolution 1644 (2005) of 15 December 2005, requested the International Independent Investigation Commission to report to it on its progress, including on the cooperation received from the Syrian authorities, every three months.

The present report summarizes the progress made by the Commission in its investigative activities since the last report to the Council (S/2006/962). During the reporting period, the Commission remained focused on its primary objective in the investigation of the Hariri case and provided technical assistance to the Lebanese authorities in 16 other cases, including the assassination of Minister Pierre Gemayel and, most recently, the Ain Alaq bombings of February 2007.

In the Hariri case, the Commission has made progress in collecting new evidence and in expanding the forms of evidence collected. This has enabled the Commission to narrow its focus in a number of areas during the reporting period, particularly in relation to establishing the motive behind the execution of the crime.

The Commission continues to maintain a close working relationship with Lebanese authorities on all matters relevant to its mandate. The Commission also continues to receive responses to its requests to other Member States, including the Syrian Arab Republic. This cooperation remains an important component of the Commission's work.

Since the last report, the political and security environment in and around Lebanon has remained unstable. The Commission continues to monitor the political situation in the region and its potential impact on its investigations and requirements for its security.

In the light of the current and planned investigative activities, it is unlikely that the Commission will complete its work before its current mandate expires in June 2007. The Commission therefore welcomes the request for an extension of its mandate beyond that date.

I. Introduction

1. The present report is submitted pursuant to Security Council resolution 1644 (2005) of 15 December 2005, in which the Council requested the International Independent Investigation Commission to report every three months to the Council on the progress of its inquiry and on international cooperation, including the cooperation received from the Syrian authorities.

2. This report, the seventh report of the Commission, provides an update of issues covered in previous reports to the Council and notes progress in the work of the Commission since the last report, of 12 December 2006 (S/2006/962). As outlined in earlier reports, the Commission remains mindful of its obligation to protect the confidentiality of its investigations in order to ensure the integrity of the legal process and to protect those who have

cooperated with the Commission. This approach is taken in full agreement with the Lebanese judicial authorities. Hence the present report provides an overview of activities undertaken in the reporting period rather than a detailed account of ongoing investigations.

3. Since the last report, the security environment in and around Lebanon has remained unstable, as illustrated by the bombings of two buses in the village of Ain Alaq, near Beirut, which resulted in the death of three people and injuries to 20 others on 13 February 2007. Also, discussions about the creation of a special tribunal for Lebanon remain at the top of the political agenda in Lebanon and in the region. The Commission therefore continues to monitor these issues for potential impact on its investigation activities and requirements for its security.

4. As in the past, the Commission maintains a close working relationship with Lebanese authorities on all matters relevant to its mandate. During the reporting period, the Commission also received extensive and timely assistance from a number of other States in a wide range of substantive areas. The Commission also continues to receive responses from the Syrian Arab Republic, which provides information and facilitates interviews with individuals located on Syrian territory. This cooperation remains an important component of the Commission's work.

5. The Commission has remained focused on its primary objective: the investigation of the assassination of former Prime Minister Rafik Hariri and 22 others. It has made progress in collecting new evidence and in expanding the forms of evidence collected. This is done to enhance case knowledge and corroborate existing information. This approach has enabled the Commission to narrow its focus in a number of areas, in particular in relation to developing its understanding of the motive behind the execution of the crime.

6. Following requests from the Security Council, the Commission has been providing technical assistance to the Lebanese authorities for the 14 other cases, the case of the assassination of Minister Pierre Gemayel and, more recently, the Ain Alaq bombings. In doing so, the Commission has sought to identify areas of work where it can add value to the investigations, while expending appropriate resources to achieve the required results. The objective remains to assist in each individual case, while identifying possible linkages between them.

7. The forensic programme of the Commission continues to form a particularly important component of the investigative work in support of all cases. Further corroboration of findings through forensic work was achieved during the reporting period, and a number of new tasks were undertaken. With that in mind, the Commission introduced internal and external capacity-building measures to manage its complex and interlinked forensic projects.

8. The Commission intends to compare selected DNA profiles and fingerprints with relevant databases, access to which will be facilitated by an international law enforcement organization. The Commission is also developing its own database of relevant DNA samples, and will continue to work with Lebanese authorities and foreign experts to gain access to materials and conduct further analyses, as appropriate.

II. Progress in the investigations

9. During the reporting period, the Commission's investigation of the Hariri assassination concentrated on its main objectives and expanded the scope of information and evidence being collected. In support of those objectives, and in addition to other operational work it undertook, the Commission conducted 42 interviews linked to the Hariri case during the reporting period.

10. The provision of technical assistance to the Lebanese authorities has continued in the 16 other cases, including the Pierre Gemayel case and the Ain Alaq bombings. The Commission has conducted 27 interviews, carried out forensic investigations on the crime scenes, undertaken the collection and examination of crime scene exhibits, conducted portrait sketch activities with witnesses, and collected closed-circuit television footage in support of these other cases. The overarching objective remains to develop each case individually, while seeking evidence of possible linkages between the cases. Linkages may include the characteristics of the victims targeted, motive, purpose of the attacks, the modus operandi employed, and perpetrators of the attacks.

11. In the reporting period, the Commission developed and implemented a broader plan for collection of evidence in relation to all cases currently under investigation to enhance the evidential base for the cases in conjunction with conventional interview processes. This was done to corroborate and substantiate the witness statements. It is made possible through the acquisition of documentary information such as government and national agency records; and the management of forensic collection, research and analysis projects, including the development of inventories and databases, the coordination of external analysis by forensic experts of exhibits provided by the Lebanese authorities, the systematic exploitation of communications intercept material, further development of communications traffic analysis, further analysis of considerable electronic data holdings and the development of confidential witnesses and contacts.

12. By applying this methodology, the Commission believes it can establish a more detailed picture of events around the crime, elicit new leads and corroborate witness statements. This is especially important when investigating the linkage and knowledge aspects of the cases, where the establishment of the facts can sometimes be clouded by individual subjectivity.

13. The Commission devotes the majority of its time and resources to the Hariri case by developing crime scene leads and collecting evidence relating to the perpetrators, linkage and contextual aspects of the case. It is mindful of the balance that needs to be struck between the Hariri case, the provision of support in the 14 other cases, and the Gemayel and Ain Alaq cases. This is a changing equation over time, but the Commission strives to take advantage of methodologies that add the most value to all the cases while making the best use of available resources.

A. Hariri investigation

1. Crime scene and associated topics

Properties of the blast—seismological analysis

14. The analysis of seismological data registered on 14 February 2005 by the National Centre of Geophysics in Lebanon is ongoing and aims to establish the properties of the

blast that killed Hariri. The preliminary report, which was received from external experts, corroborates the Commission's earlier assessments that only one blast occurred and that the precise time of the blast was 12:55:05.

15. The phenomenon of more than one sound being heard by a number of witnesses is now satisfactorily scientifically and experimentally explained. In fact, three distinct phases of the blast can be observed on the seismograms, owing to the different propagation speeds of three different waves: the primary and secondary volume waves, the surface waves and the sound waves. At a sufficient distance from the explosion, these waves can be mistaken for the signature of more than one explosion. The sound recordings performed during the scaling explosion experiments confirm these theoretical explanations.

16. The final report on the characteristics of the explosion, which will be provided to the Commission in the next reporting period, will include an assessment of the power of the explosion, and a comparative analysis of other explosions that have occurred in Lebanon.

Properties of the blast—scaling explosion experiments

17. The analysis of scaling explosion experiments confirms previous conclusions that the physical phenomena observed at the crime scene are fully compatible with an above-ground explosion. For example, the fireball, deposit of carbon residues on the facades of the hotels, and damage sustained to the buildings and the surroundings, due to the blast effects, are not compatible with an underground explosion.

18. In addition, a full analysis of the autopsy and injuries records and associated photographs of the victims will be undertaken to examine the wound phenomena for the primary blast (for example: the presence of pulmonary lesions and lesions of the eardrums) and secondary blast (projections of debris) associated with an above-ground explosion. A preliminary assessment of the data corroborates that the explosion occurred above the ground. These findings are being confirmed by numerical simulations.

Aerial delivery theory

19. The validity of the hypothesis of an aerial delivery of the explosive device, put forward to the Commission in August 2006, is being examined. The Commission is conducting a scientific, technical and investigative analysis of the possibilities of the bomb being delivered in this way. Preliminary technical findings indicate that this theory is unlikely. The Commission intends to conduct a fact-finding mission, to include interviews and meetings with relevant experts, in order to develop its understanding of this possibility, and will draw some conclusions during the next reporting period.

Forensic examination of exhibits recovered on the crime scene

20. As previously reported to the Council, the Commission was able to make a preliminary association between certain vehicle parts found in the crater at the crime scene and those of a Mitsubishi van. This was done using documentation and technical information received by the Commission from Japan, as well as the Commission's own-sourced manuals and documents. The process of creating a complete inventory of these exhibits is ongoing, in conformity with international standards, and, once complete, the alleged parts of the vehicle will be submitted for formal identification in cooperation with external technical experts.

Visualization projects

21. Three digital visualization projects have been completed, and a new one is ongoing to enable evidence and case facts to be presented in a way that will facilitate the identification of further investigative steps to be taken. The first two projects are the visualization of the city and the crime scene at various points along the route taken by the Hariri convoy on 14 February 2005, using panoramic and three-dimensional (3D) satellite imagery. The third project is the visualization of a time line reconstruction of Hariri's last day, including the alleged communications traffic activity of the bomb team as the convoy proceeded along its route. A fourth project entails the creation of a model that will allow users to "walk through" the crime scene showing the exact locations where various exhibits were found.

22. Themes being placed into the model include the plotting of trajectories and final locations of physical and biological evidence; the reconstruction of events; animations of the Mitsubishi van and the convoy vehicles as they arrived at the crime scene; the damage caused by the explosion; witness information; video recordings from the closed-circuit television system of a nearby branch of the HSBC bank; and test explosions data.

Geographical origin of the alleged bomber

23. The project to attempt to determine the geographical origin of the bomber is being developed through two approaches. One method uses a team of experts that is conducting a statistical analysis on allele frequencies based on the nuclear DNA profile of the 33 human parts collected from the crime scene. These human parts belong to the man likely to have detonated the device, and are compared with the allele frequencies of profiles provided by several countries. This work should provide a probability-based assessment on the possible place of origin of the alleged bomber.

24. The second method focuses on the study of isotope data. In the Commission's previous report, the results of the first phase of analysis showed that the individual did not spend his youth in Lebanon, but was likely situated there in the two to three months before his death. The Commission can now also add that the man had significant exposure to lead pollution in an urban environment up to the age of about 12, and that such exposure was low during the last 10 years of his life, possibly indicating that he lived in a more rural environment during this period.

25. In order to advance this line of inquiry, the Commission has collected a total of 112 samples from 28 locations in the Syrian Arab Republic and Lebanon. Over the coming weeks, it will collect samples in three other countries in the region, and further countries are identified for another series of sampling missions.

26. As stated in the previous report, the Commission is mindful that results should be carefully interpreted and the limitations clearly understood. The Commission will treat future results as forensic information to be used primarily for lead purposes in the investigation.

Ongoing crime scene investigations

27. The preliminary results of examinations of the personal effects of a victim discovered at the crime scene in June 2006 have resolved outstanding questions, but further investigative work will be undertaken to finalize the matter in the near future.

28. The issue of a victim who was killed at the crime scene, found in a location where normally he should have been protected from the blast, continues to be investigated. Documentary information in relation to this matter is being translated and will be analysed before a decision is taken on the relevance of this individual to the investigation.

29. The issue of alleged tampering with the crime scene and obstruction of the investigation as a result of removal of artefacts remains under investigation. The Commission is conducting analyses and will undertake further investigative steps to clarify if there was deliberate intent in this matter.

30. A number of interviews were conducted in the reporting period to clarify issues relating to the crime scene prior to the blast, new leads arising from the analysis of witness statements and communications traffic, and the acquisition of artefacts as possible evidence. A minimum of 15 further crime scene witness interviews are planned in the next reporting period in support of these objectives.

31. Investigations are ongoing into the acquisition and storage of the Mitsubishi van, and its preparation with explosives. The Commission has received a body of new information relating to this topic, and over 500 pages of data are being prioritized for translation and analysis. The Commission is developing recent leads concerning the van, investigating the history of the vehicle from the most recent time it was known to be in Lebanon, and working backwards in time from that point.

32. The Commission continues to work on establishing the route of the Mitsubishi van as it was brought to the area prior to the attack, then towards the St. Georges Hotel area, and then on its final path on 14 February 2005.

33. The Commission has largely resolved the allegation that a red car was parked outside the St. Georges Hotel, apparently reserving a space for the Mitsubishi van before its arrival on the crime scene. It has been suggested that the vehicle had driven off to make way for the van to park in its place. It has been established by witness interviews and the examination of photographs of the scene immediately after the explosion that the position of the red car was some 15 metres before the place where the crater was created. The conclusion at this stage, subject to further information coming to light, is that there is no direct connection between that vehicle and the arrival of the Mitsubishi van.

2. Individuals involved in the commission of the crime

Communications

34. The Commission's analysis of communications traffic continues in order to support and validate different points arising from the investigations. Much work has been done to support the interviews conducted, in order that respective communications contact with other persons of interest to the case can be discussed with witnesses. Patterns of communications traffic, including frequencies and timings of calls, and linkages and clear associations to others, are all developed and elicit investigation leads.

35. In relation to the six mobile cellular telephone SIM cards allegedly used by the team that executed the operation on the day of 14 February 2005, the Commission has developed further information of interest relating to associated earlier operations, including possible surveillance and reconnaissance activity, possible practice-runs or earlier attempts to kill

Rafik Hariri, and other actions undertaken by the team. New areas of interest have emerged from this analysis and are currently being examined.

36. The Commission has also undertaken an investigative project examining the role of the persons using the six SIM cards and activities that can be inferred from their use. This exercise is supported by the Commission's existing communications traffic analysis projects in relation to the cards. The objective is fourfold: first, to reaffirm the validity of the hypothesis that the cards could indeed have been used by the bomb team to execute its task; second, to establish whether other modes of communication must have been used between the members of the team, and also perhaps with other individuals, in order for the attack to take place; third, to allow the Commission to establish a better understanding of how the crime was committed on 14 February; and finally, to understand further what other activity the bomb team undertook, and what locations it travelled to and why, in the days leading up to the attack.

37. Such extensive analysis enables the Commission to reach a better understanding of the bomb team, its role in the crime and its other activities. This in turn creates further investigative leads geographically and temporally, and pointing to the activities of individuals outside the immediate bombing team the Commission believes were using the six SIM cards.

38. This detailed examination of the activities of the six SIM cards has resulted in a number of significant elements for ongoing investigation. These include, but are not limited to: potential identification of the role of each participant in the preparation, planning, surveillance and actual attack; the bombing team's anticipation of Hariri's activities and movements; and possible earlier attempts on Hariri's life.

39. One working hypothesis is that the bomb team had to ensure that Hariri was indeed dead after the explosion in order for the video claim of responsibility to be delivered and to have resonance with its intended audience. It is possible that the team, and those commissioning the crime, could not afford to deliver a claim of responsibility to the global media if Hariri had survived the attack. Thus, the Commission is exploring the hypothesis that one member of the team, or an associate, was tasked with confirming the death of the principal target as soon as possible and may have contacted someone waiting for the news. Based on existing information, the time frame for this activity would have been within approximately 45 minutes of the explosion.

40. This in turn led to the series of events related to the taped claim of responsibility and the subsequent telephone calls made to media outlets. The Commission is examining the hypothesis that one or more members of the bomb team was responsible for delivering the tape and making the subsequent telephone calls to the media. Other variations on this hypothesis are being explored to establish the numbers of perpetrators who may have been involved on the day of the attack.

Ahmed Abu Adass

41. In the reporting period, the investigation developed its understanding of how Ahmed Abu Adass was identified and chosen to be the person to make the video claim of responsibility, who involved him in that activity and where and when that occurred. A working hypothesis is that he was identified because of his personality and other specific characteristics. It is possible that his association and relationship with one or more individuals whom

he met at his place of worship led him to depart his home on 16 January 2005, for reasons that are currently unknown.

42. The Commission is aware that Ahmed Abu Adass was acquainted with individuals associated with extremist groups, at least because they attended the same place of worship, which he frequented regularly and where he occasionally conducted prayers. The Commission also conducted extensive analysis of communications traffic records associated with Ahmed Abu Adass, including analysis of the telephone communication at his home and place of work and on lines belonging to his alleged associates.

43. A working hypothesis is that Ahmed Abu Adass was either coerced or duped into making the videotaped claim of responsibility. The claim he read out on tape was made on behalf of a group, and Ahmed Abu Adass himself did not state he would be the one who would carry out the attack. In relation to the tape's production, it is of note that relatives and persons who knew him before his disappearance have stated that his appearance on the videotape was physically different from that before 16 January 2005. To some, he appeared even thinner than previously; his beard had markedly grown, indicating that he may have made the tape towards the end of the approximately four-week period between his disappearance and 14 February 2005. His clothing was also different from his usual style in that he had headwear and clothing that his close friends and family had not seen him wearing before.

44. It is of interest to the investigation that a note was included with the video on 14 February 2005, which stated that the bomber was indeed Ahmed Abu Adass. From its forensic findings, the Commission believes this to be highly unlikely. One working hypothesis is that the video and the accompanying note could have been designed to deceive. Another working hypothesis is that while an extremist group may have been involved in part in committing the crime as outlined in the tape and note, this group was actually manipulated by others for another objective not related to its own organizational aspirations.

45. Thus, the Commission continues to investigate the various possibilities concerning the group that executed the crime. The Commission has received information in relation to individuals who operated in Lebanon and beyond who may have been involved in the production of the Ahmed Abu Adass tape, and also may have participated in the attack on Rafik Hariri in more than one context. In connection with this information, the Commission has undertaken a number of missions outside Lebanon, conducted 23 interviews to date, researched over 200 gigabytes of data from numerous computers, USB devices, CD-ROMs, mobile telephones and SIM cards, and analysed large volumes of communications traffic.

46. A working hypothesis is that a small number of individuals belonging to a larger group may have come together to undertake the filming of the claim of responsibility, acquire the Mitsubishi van and have it prepared with explosives. They may also have participated in the acquisition of an individual who was to detonate the bomb, and may have assisted in delivering him and the bomb to the scene of the crime.

47. The Commission has a number of investigative leads to follow up, further interviews to conduct, and further communications traffic analysis and forensic collection missions to perform. It also awaits the final forensic analysis of various artefacts that are possibly associated with this working hypothesis, including video cameras and related equipment,

cassette tapes, computer hardware and other items. These artefacts were submitted for DNA/fingerprint research and forensic digital analysis during the last reporting period. To date, 118 samples have been taken and will be analyzed for nuclear and mitochondrial DNA profiling, and 127 fingerprints have been collected.

Individuals with prior knowledge of the attack

48. The Commission believes that beyond those directly involved in the crime and those who decided it should take place, certain other individuals may have had prior knowledge of the attack. Some of those individuals possibly only had partial information; for example, knowing about the bomb, but not for whom it was intended, or knowing that Hariri was to be killed, but not knowing precisely when. The Commission is also exploring hypotheses that some knew both the target and the timing of the attack, and were informed for specific reasons.

49. The Commission is developing a hypothesis whereby the final phase of the operation to assassinate Hariri took shape by early February 2005, at which point all necessary components for the operation were assembled. These include the van, acquired and prepared with explosives and ready for use; the bomber, prepared, briefed and ready to be deployed; the minimum necessary information acquired, and surveillance and reconnaissance conducted, to be able to undertake the operation; the bomb team undiscovered and able to execute the operation; the videotaped message of Ahmed Abu Adass completed and ready to be delivered upon the success of the operation; and, most importantly, the intent still present in the minds of those who ordered the crime to go ahead with the operation.

50. A working hypothesis is that the bomb team was working within a "window" of opportunity to deliver the attack on Hariri, rather than one specific day, given the significance of the target and the time that would have been spent in overall preparation of the attack. That preparation time was most likely measured in weeks rather than days.

51. The activities of some potentially relevant individuals were noticeably altered during this period, as the bombing team began what became the final activities prior to the attack. The Commission is investigating such issues, and is finding that attitudes, behavioural patterns and comments made by certain persons in the period before the killing could have relevance.

3. Motive to assassinate Hariri

Rafik Hariri timeline

52. As indicated in earlier reports to the Council, the Commission had collected a significant amount of evidence and information related to Rafik Hariri during the last 15 months of his life. The picture assembled is complex and multilayered, and provides part of the backdrop for the motive behind the decision to assassinate him. This aspect of the Commission's investigation is ongoing, and is unlikely to be completed in the next reporting period given the significant amount of work required.

53. The following issues shaped Hariri's environment in this period: the adoption of Security Council resolution 1559 (2004) and the political implications of its implementation; the extension of the term of Lebanese President Emile Lahoud; the personal and political dynamics that existed between Hariri and other political parties and leaders in Lebanon, the

Syrian Arab Republic and other countries; the preparation and manoeuvring ahead of the parliamentary elections due to be held in May 2005, as well as other business matters in which he was involved. All of these factors came together and were handled by Hariri, sometimes proactively, and sometimes in reaction to events around him. The Commission believes it is likely that a combination of these factors may have created the environment in which the motive and intent to kill him arose.

54. Whereas the Commission had previously adopted a broad focus in the investigation of possible motive, the current reporting period saw these significantly narrowed down to the group of inquiries linked to Hariri's political activities. The Commission is developing a detailed picture of the factual reality that is substantially beyond its earlier understanding of events.

55. From this understanding of the dominating themes, it has become more evident that Hariri was perceived to be in a position of vulnerability from a security perspective. There are indications nevertheless that he received assurances that he would not be the focus of an attack, and that even up to his last few days, he remained confident, at least for external consumption, that he would not be the subject of an attack.

56. The Commission continues to develop the hypothesis that Hariri's threat environment was sufficiently serious for measures to have been taken in attempts to ameliorate the underlying situation, both in the Lebanese political establishment and in the international community.

57. In the last months of Hariri's life, he was very focused on the forthcoming 2005 elections. The nature of his intentions for the planned elections and his perceived likelihood of success, as well as his political and personal relationships with other parties and their leaders, are particularly significant aspects of the Commission's work in this area, particularly given the rivalries existing between certain political figures at the time.

58. Negotiations unfolded during that period between Hariri and other individuals, including potential candidates, and intense interest was focused upon the draft electoral law, including the drawing of electoral district boundaries in Lebanon and, in particular, in Beirut. Throughout that period, Hariri was also adjusting his political stance, and on the day of his murder had made public that position.

59. It is of some note that Hariri was killed on the day that Parliament was scheduled to debate the electoral law to be applied in the forthcoming elections. Another working hypothesis for the Commission is that those who decided upon the assassination saw it as beneficial to kill him before he formally began his election campaign, especially given the perception in the media at the time that he was likely to win.

60. The Commission has established that Hariri worked on differing political and professional levels, which was reflected in the nature and extent of information, views and positions he discussed with those with whom he interacted. That is evident from the information the Commission has collected from some of his friends, acquaintances, political interlocutors and apparent rivals.

61. It is therefore critical that the Commission continue to have access to those political and diplomatic interlocutors with whom Hariri dealt, and those individuals involved in the relevant political and diplomatic dynamics at all levels. The Commission looks forward to

continuing cooperation with such individuals, including, where appropriate, Government officials, in order to ensure the completeness of its investigations.

62. The Commission is developing a working hypothesis that in the period immediately prior to his death, Hariri and others in the national and international political arena were taking steps to defuse the tensions that had arisen between him and others on the political stage. These initiatives apparently included the development of diplomatic and political dialogue between Syrian and Lebanese individuals and Hariri. This dialogue had previously been managed through other Syrian and Lebanese channels, which had apparently fuelled misperceptions and aggravated the already tense political environment.

63. A working hypothesis is that the initial decision to kill Hariri was taken before the later attempts at rapprochement got under way and most likely before early January 2005. This leads to a possible situation in the last weeks before his murder in which two tracks, not necessarily linked, were running in parallel. On one track, Hariri was engaged in rapprochement initiatives and, on the other, preparations for his assassination were under way.

Other investigative areas of interest

64. In a wider context, the Commission continues to seek information that broadens and deepens its knowledge of the political and security environment in Lebanon at the time leading up to and beyond Hariri's assassination. To that end, the Commission has received significant documentary information from certain Lebanese agencies, and continues to seek more, based upon strictly focused requirements. It will continue to request documents of relevance, and anticipates expanding the concept to incorporate other agencies and other forms of data as necessary.

65. Similarly in this context, the Commission conducted three interviews with Syrian officials in relation to the location of parts of the archive brought back from Lebanon at the time of the Syrian withdrawal in 2005. Following those interviews, two document exploitation missions to those archives at two locations in the Syrian Arab Republic were undertaken, in order to acquire those historical documents created within a strict time period that were of relevance to the broader contextual knowledge objective. The missions were undertaken in conjunction with Syrian authorities, and have elicited useful results with the selection and provision of documentary information. It is anticipated that further requests for assistance will be forthcoming in this regard throughout the next reporting period.

66. The Commission continues to clarify issues surrounding individuals alleged to have engaged in financial transactions with Rafik Hariri, especially during the period immediately leading up to 14 February 2005. This area of the investigation is complex, and the Commission is ensuring that it is pursued only to the extent that it is linked to its investigative objectives.

B. Technical assistance in the other cases

1. The 14 other cases

67. The Commission's focus in the provision of technical assistance to the Lebanese authorities during the reporting period continued with work aimed at interlinking a number of investigative projects. That work will continue to develop in the same manner in the next

period. A seismological analysis of the 14 cases is also being conducted by external experts, and the Commission anticipates that it will receive the results before the end of the next reporting period.

Six targeted attacks

68. The Commission has conducted 17 interviews relating to the six targeted attacks in this reporting period, and in doing so it has almost concluded its interviews with the surviving victims of the six attacks, as well as with the victims' families and close associates. The primary purpose of these interviews has been to establish the victims' movements on their last days; determine possible motive for the attacks; understand the victims' security arrangements, if any; identify whether they were under surveillance; and determine any threats or assurances they received. Various leads have emerged from these interviews, and these will be followed up in the coming weeks and months.

69. The Commission has also completed a number of internal analytical reports relating to the Lebanese authorities' case files of the six attacks, and has submitted 12 related requests for assistance. It has also conducted communications traffic analysis in support of other interviews related to a number of the cases, and continues to examine potential communications linkages in the modus operandi of the attacks, and potential commonalities between cases. This work will continue for the next reporting period, and the Commission will also undertake an analysis of exhibits found at each crime scene, including the possible remains of the improvised explosive devices (IEDs), and other associated items, as deemed relevant. In conjunction with this analysis, an assessment of the modus operandi used by those placing the bombs will be undertaken to develop further the Commission's understanding of commonalities between each attack.

70. The Commission is in the process of prioritizing and translating a number of forensic and crime scene reports provided by the Lebanese authorities, which will be sent for further analysis to an external team of forensic experts. It will also examine all remaining relevant forensic documents and materials in the possession of the Lebanese authorities, develop an exhibits and documents inventory and conduct further forensic examinations on the information and exhibits.

71. The Commission also requested that the Lebanese authorities facilitate an examination of the victims' vehicles and other cars containing the IEDs that were used in the attacks. The Commission conducted a preliminary examination of the available vehicles. These cars have been examined by a visiting forensic expert team in order to develop leads regarding the modus operandi of these attacks and, potentially, to establish horizontal and vertical linkage to other attacks. A number of additional exhibits and residues were taken by the experts for further forensic examinations.

72. The Commission has also recently received a draft report from visiting forensic experts who examined the scene where Gebran Tueni was killed. In addition to 32 exhibits previously recovered by the Lebanese authorities, these experts collected and examined an additional 190 exhibits.

73. The experts confirmed that an amount of high explosives was used in the attack on Tueni, and that the IED in this case was contained in a Renault Rapid vehicle. The bomb was activated when Tueni's Range Rover drove by. The Commission believes that the IED

was most likely triggered by a remote control device. A time delay activation mechanism is unlikely to have been used because it was not known in advance precisely when Tueni would drive by the location of the IED. It is also very unlikely that the IED was triggered by a suicide bomber, as there were no human remains found at the site arising from any individuals other than the three victims who were killed in the attack.

74. The experts also found that the attack on Tueni occurred at a location that was conducive to a bomb attack. It took place on a narrow road, along a mountain ridge, which could be viewed clearly from the area surrounding and opposite the crime scene. This location chosen provided a clear unobstructed view of the vehicle-borne IED and, as such, allowed for an effective position to trigger the device remotely.

75. In the El-Murr case, the Commission arranged for an international law enforcement sketch artist to develop the image of two individuals seen acting suspiciously, one of whom was seen the night before the crime, and another who fled the scene at the time of the attack. At this stage, the Commission does not believe the sketches identify the man as being the same person.

Eight bomb attacks

76. The Commission continues to implement the plan for the provision of technical assistance to the Lebanese authorities in the eight bomb attacks where no specific individuals appear to have been targeted, by reviewing and analysing the files as received from the Prosecutor General and the investigating judges.

77. The Commission has sent seven requests for assistance to the Lebanese authorities, requesting, inter alia, additional witness and suspect statements, closed-circuit television footage relevant to the cases, intercepted communications if available and information relating to vehicles of interest.

78. The preliminary objective in this exercise is to conduct individual case analyses for each of the eight cases and make some suggestions as to further investigative steps that may be taken by the Lebanese authorities. Through that exercise, the next aim is to continue to develop horizontal analysis in relation to perpetrator identification, motive, intent and modus operandi.

79. In support of these objectives, and as in the six targeted attacks, the Commission will also undertake a preliminary analysis of exhibits found at each crime scene, and will study each location with relevant experts to conduct a first assessment of the modus operandi used by the perpetrators.

2. Pierre Gemayel case

80. The Commission continues to provide technical investigative support to the Lebanese authorities by conducting interviews, analysing witness statements, collecting closed-circuit television imagery, performing forensic work, conducting communications analysis and reconstructing the crime scene events. In support of this work, the Commission has submitted 10 requests for assistance to the Lebanese authorities.

81. Following the Commission's investigations conducted at the crime scene in November 2006, three days after the assassination, 240 exhibits, including DNA samples, fingerprints, mobile phones, and ballistic and transfer traces, were submitted to forensic examination and analysis.

82. Preliminary results show that there was no global positioning system in the victim's car, which may have given useful tracking information. The specific make and model of at least one vehicle used by the perpetrators has been established. Also, 22 DNA samples taken from a number of places on the vehicle used by Gemayel have been analysed. The DNA profiles of the two victims were found at many locations, and eight DNA samples taken from the doors gave the profile not only of Gemayel, but also of more than one unknown individual.

83. The Commission has conducted a detailed ballistics analysis on the 49 cartridge cases and 55 bullets or parts of bullets found at the crime scene. It can now be concluded that a minimum of five different weapons were used. In addition, the Commission has prepared weapons photo-boards and has acquired recordings of the sounds of different weapons used, in order to assist in the interview process. Statements collected from witnesses are compatible with the scientific findings and have allowed the Commission to refine its understanding of the weapons used in this crime.

84. Sketches of the alleged assassins of Pierre Gemayel provided by the Commission to the Lebanese authorities were recently released and publicized, and they will form part of a broader sketch database that will be developed during the next reporting period.

85. The Commission has developed further investigative leads, including those arising from additional closed-circuit television footage discovered in the proximity of the scene of the crime. The footage has been sent to a technical laboratory for enhancement of the images. This work is ongoing, as is a 3D-reconstruction and forensic examination of items relating to the crime scene and other items that may have association with the crime. The Commission will continue to provide technical assistance to the Lebanese authorities on this case for the foreseeable future.

3. Ain Alaq bombings

86. The Commission has taken a series of investigative and forensic steps to support the Lebanese authorities in their investigations into these bombings, in which three people were killed and a number of individuals were injured on 13 February 2007. A team of forensic experts was provided to conduct forensic examinations on the crime scene, including examining the Mitsubishi and Kia buses that were bombed, a process which took five days to complete, between 20 and 24 February 2007.

87. The team recovered 127 relevant exhibits, as well as 242 steel ball bearings associated with the explosions. The team provided a preliminary analysis of its findings, and will submit a full report during the next reporting period. The findings indicate that there had been one IED inside each bus, and that the explosive in each, possibly TNT, was approximately 1.5 kg in weight. There were approximately 750 grams to 1 kg of steel ball bearings of the same diameter. Ballistic examinations confirmed that the ball bearings were placed around the explosive.

88. The devices were placed in each bus in a similar position, towards the rear and under a seat on the left-hand side. At the time of explosion, the IED in the Mitsubishi bus was approximately 0.75 m above the ground, and in the Kia bus approximately 1.10 m above the ground. A small number of exhibits were collected that may have come from the initiation system of the IED, and it was assessed that the devices were likely detonated by a time

delay device or possibly by remote control. Several fragments of bags that could have been used to carry the bombs were recovered and submitted for forensic examination.

89. The final report on these crime scene investigations and the results of the forensic examinations conducted on exhibits (DNA, fingerprints and explosives) will be received during the next reporting period.

90. It remains unclear at this stage what the motive was in executing these attacks, in the place, on the date and at the time they occurred. In terms of modus operandi, the use of ball bearings may be indicative of the intent to injure as many people as possible with the relatively small amount of explosive used. It is unclear at present whether the bombs were placed by one or two persons, and whether more individuals were involved in the attacks. The Commission is working upon a number of hypotheses in this regard in support of the Lebanese authorities.

III. External cooperation

A. Interaction with the Lebanese authorities

91. During the reporting period, the Commission has continued to work closely with the Lebanese authorities in the Hariri investigation and the 16 other cases. This close interaction has taken the form of regular meetings between the Commission and the Prosecutor General and senior members of his office, as well as communication with the investigative judges assigned to the various cases and with the senior representative appointed by the Internal Security Forces.

92. The Commission has also exchanged a significant amount of information, including documents, reports and other materials, with Lebanese authorities. Specifically, the Commission continues to share with the appropriate institutions the substance of relevant information that it obtains in the course of its investigations in a manner that does not compromise the interest of the source of this information. This continues to include information that may be relevant to individuals who are detained by the Lebanese authorities.

93. During the reporting period, the Commission also continued to rely on the cooperation and assistance of the Lebanese authorities, especially as its caseload had increased and its investigations into the Hariri assassination, the 14 cases, the Gemayel murder and the Ain Alaq attacks had advanced and necessitated a broader range of investigative actions.

94. Thus, during the reporting period, the Commission addressed 57 formal requests for assistance to the Prosecutor General seeking, inter alia, his help in obtaining documents and other information and in facilitating interviews and other missions on Lebanese territory. The Lebanese authorities responded fully and expeditiously to these requests.

B. Cooperation with the Syrian Arab Republic

95. Pursuant to the Syrian Arab Republic's obligations under Security Council resolutions 1636 (2005) and 1644 (2005), and the common understanding reached between the Commission and the Syrian Arab Republic in 2006, the cooperation of the Republic with the Commission remains generally satisfactory.

96. During the reporting period, the Commission submitted four formal requests for assistance to the Syrian Arab Republic seeking information regarding individuals, groups and

issues of interest to the Commission and requesting the facilitation of interviews and other missions on Syrian territory.

97. Following the transmission of its requests for assistance, the Commission has, since December, undertaken a number of investigative activities in the Syrian Arab Republic, including conducting interviews, where, once again, responses by individuals can be characterized as variable in quality on occasion; the holding of meetings with relevant Syrian officials; the collection of samples from locations in the Syrian Arab Republic to support the geographic origin forensic project; and the collection of documents from two archive storage sites. The last three missions in particular were arranged and facilitated in a professional and timely manner by the Syrian authorities.

98. The Syrian Arab Republic has continued to provide the Commission with assistance in response to its requests within the appropriate timescales, and the Commission is grateful for the logistical and security arrangements provided by Syrian authorities for its activities in Syria. The Commission will continue to request the full cooperation of the Syrian Arab Republic, which remains crucial to the swift and successful completion of the mandate of the Commission.

C. Cooperation with other States

99. The Commission continues to rely on the willingness of States to provide information and expertise and facilitate its work on their territories when required. During the reporting period, a total of 40 new formal requests for assistance were sent to 23 States, in addition to the requests for assistance addressed to the Syrian and Lebanese authorities.

100. The Commission has greatly benefited from the responses of States to its requests where full and prompt cooperation has been forthcoming. The Commission is very grateful for this cooperation.

101. As the Commission noted in its last report to the Council, a lack of responsiveness by certain States to the Commission's requests could have serious consequences for the Commission's work, in areas such as arranging interviews, providing information on the whereabouts of certain individuals, and technical assistance.

102. In its last report, the Commission noted that responses to requests from 10 Member States were overdue. In view of the importance of the assistance requested and the time frame in which it aims to complete its investigative activities, the Commission concentrated on following up on all outstanding requests for assistance. The Commission held a series of meetings with relevant ambassadors to discuss past requests. As a result of those meetings, almost all outstanding matters were resolved to the Commission's satisfaction, with responses received, and, where appropriate, mechanisms introduced to facilitate the resolution of pending issues.

IV. Organizational support

A. Recruitment

103. During the past three months, the Commission undertook a series of management measures to streamline its internal processes in operational support activities and maintain its recruitment initiative to fill its outstanding positions. In this period, the Commission recruited 35 international and 5 national staff with the assistance of the Department of

Peacekeeping Operations. As of March, a further 30 candidates are under active recruitment. These efforts will be maintained until the Commission has reached a satisfactory level of staffing.

104. The investigation division has 41 staff and consultants in March 2007, compared to 29 in December 2006. Additional analysts, investigators, legal officers, forensic experts and a database administrator are currently being recruited.

105. The Commission has been working closely with the Department of Peacekeeping Operations to afford the Commission the operational flexibility it needs to carry out its mandate, particularly regarding staffing issues. The Commission has formally approached several Member States to assist it in the identification of much-needed database information management specialists. Positive responses from Member States to this request would be invaluable to the Commission's work in this important area.

106. All additional posts requested for 2007 were approved in the budget, bringing the total number of international posts in the Commission to 188. The additional posts will assist the Commission to execute its mandate more expeditiously by allowing more concurrent investigative activity to take place and improving the efficiency of the operational support aspects of its work. Out of the 188 budgeted posts, 104 have so far been filled. Of the 51 posts approved for national staff, 41 have been filled with the remaining 10 under active recruitment.

107. Problems remain regarding the recruitment and retention of international language staff such as Arabic language interpreters, translators and transcribers. The Commission is experiencing serious difficulties in finding suitable candidates for recruitment. So far, only 3 of 27 such posts have been filled. This creates significant bottlenecks resulting in delays in investigative activities. The Commission is undertaking varied recruitment initiatives in order to acquire resources in this critical area.

B. Security

108. Since the Commission's last report, the security situation in Lebanon and in the region has remained uncertain and unpredictable. The bombing of the two buses in Ain Alaq, together with numerous discoveries of explosives and IEDs around Beirut and beyond, contribute to this unstable security environment. The Commission continues to enjoy excellent coordination and cooperation with the Lebanese security forces, who have spared no effort in meeting the safety and security needs of the Commission in carrying out its mandate. The Commission is very grateful for this support.

109. Security concerns and restrictions impact the work of the Commission and its investigative activities, and, as a result, a number of steps to mitigate anticipated risks have been taken to maintain a safe and secure environment within which all Commission personnel can function effectively.

110. Emerging security trends are continually being analysed and integrated into the operational context of the Commission's work. Crisis management measures, evacuation procedures and business continuity planning are maintained based on the variables in the security environment surrounding the Commission's work.

V. Conclusions

111. The Commission's primary strategic objective remains the continued investigation into the killing of Rafik Hariri and 22 others, as well as the provision of technical assistance to the Lebanese authorities in the other cases. In pursuit of the goals in the Hariri case, the Commission aims to further establish the facts and to continue to seek links between the other cases and the Hariri case. In so doing, the Commission seeks to conduct its work in the most expeditious investigative timescale, while respecting a framework of appropriate legal standards.

112. During the next reporting period, the Commission will maintain the investigative focus discussed in this report. A total of around 250 individuals have been identified for interview, and the Commission will seek to interview approximately 50 of them in the next three months. The Commission also plans to acquire further documentary information, additional electronic material and communications data for analysis.

113. The Commission is grateful for the full support of the Prosecutor General of Lebanon in conducting its work, in particular as it relates to sensitive and complicated investigative steps that have been undertaken and that are being planned. Both the Commission and the Prosecutor General will continue to create a secure and confidential working environment for witnesses and for the Commission's staff.

114. The Commission recognizes the complexities of the Hariri case as it develops. During the reporting period, the Commission narrowed down possible motives to those linked with Hariri's political activities. The Commission's understanding of the facts has advanced substantially, producing valuable links within and between the main components of the case. In the next reporting period, and potentially beyond that, the Commission believes that it will be able to develop further a unifying factual theory built upon newly identified linking evidence. The aim remains to link together the most responsible perpetrators with others who knew about the crime, those who participated in the execution of it, and those who assisted in the preparation of the necessary components for its execution.

115. The Commission's work on the other cases remains focused upon the provision of technical assistance to the Lebanese authorities by identifying and applying investigative support that adds value to each case without putting excessive strain on the Commission's resources. The Commission also continues to identify horizontal links between each case, and with the Hariri case, where possible. The Commission believes that in the next reporting phase, the depth of knowledge of each case will be further enhanced to allow such potential linkages to emerge.

116. The Commission notes that requests for assistance it has addressed to Lebanon, the Syrian Arab Republic and other States have received mostly positive and timely responses. Assistance from all these States remains essential to allow the Commission to carry out its investigative work effectively.

117. The Commission also notes that the volatile political and security environment in Lebanon and the ability to recruit and retain qualified staff have an impact on the Commission's ability to fulfil its mandate in a timely fashion. The Commission will continue to concentrate its efforts on managing these factors as it works towards its objectives.

118. Finally, the Commission continues its work in anticipation of the creation of a special tribunal for Lebanon. In the light of the current and planned investigative activities outlined in this report, it is unlikely that the Commission will complete its work before its current mandate expires in June 2007. The Commission therefore welcomes the request for an extension of its mandate beyond that date.

5. Eighth Report of the International Independent Investigation Commission, 12 July 2007 (S/2007/424)

Letter dated 12 July 2007 from the Secretary-General addressed to the President of the Security Council

I have the honour to transmit the eighth report of the International Independent Investigation Commission, which was prepared pursuant to Security Council resolutions 1595 (2005), 1636 (2005), 1644 (2005), 1686 (2006) and 1748 (2007).

The report describes progress made by the Commission since its previous report dated 15 March 2007 (S/2007/150) in investigating the February 2005 assassination of former Lebanese Prime Minister Rafik Hariri and 22 other victims, and in providing technical assistance to the Lebanese authorities in their investigation of a number of other attacks perpetrated in Lebanon since 1 October 2004.

The present report provides information on the Commission's priority work in the investigation of the Hariri case, and into 17 other cases, including the assassination of former Member of Parliament Walid Eido in June 2007. The Commission also undertook a comprehensive review of its past and current investigations, which has yielded positive results, including the refinement of the workplan to maximize the utilization of its limited resources. Furthermore, the report highlights, pursuant to Security Council resolution 1757 (2007), steps taken by the Commission to ensure a coordinated transition of its activities to the Special Tribunal for Lebanon.

I wish to express my thanks to Commissioner Brammertz for his tireless leadership, and to the staff of the Commission for their dedication and commitment, particularly in the light of the deterioration in the political and security environment in Lebanon.

I should be grateful if you would bring this matter to the attention of the members of the Security Council. Meanwhile, I am transmitting the report to the Government of Lebanon.

(*Signed*) **Ban** Ki-moon

Serge Brammertz, Commissioner
Beirut, July 2007

Summary

The Security Council requested the International Independent Investigation Commission to report to the Council on progress in its inquiry, including cooperation received from the Syrian authorities.

The present report outlines progress made in the different aspects of the investigations into the assassination of Rafik Hariri and the 17 other cases for which the Commission has been mandated to provide technical assistance to the Lebanese authorities, including the June 2007 assassination of Member of Parliament Walid Eido.

Since its last report to the Council on 15 March 2007 (S/2007/150), in addition to actively pursuing these investigations, the Commission completed a comprehensive review of all its information, analysis and findings on all past and current investigations. This significant undertaking, which involved all the investigative staff of the Commission, has produced several positive results outlined in this report. Among others, this effort has allowed the Commission to refine its workplans for the next reporting period, making the best possible use of its limited resources.

During the reporting period, the Commission continued to receive generally positive responses to its requests for assistance to Lebanon, the Syrian Arab Republic and other States. Cooperation from all States remains crucial to the Commission's work, and the Commission calls upon all States to be forthcoming in their responses to its requests for assistance.

The Commission notes with concern the deterioration in the political and security environment in Lebanon since its last report to the Council. Although the Commission, in close cooperation with the Lebanese authorities, has put in place mitigating measures to protect its staff and premises, the deterioration in the political and security environment is likely to have a negative effect on the Commission's activities in the coming months.

In the light of the establishment of a Special Tribunal for Lebanon by the Security Council in resolution 1757 (2007), the Commission has taken several steps to facilitate the handover from the Commission to the Special Tribunal for Lebanon at a time when the latter shall begin functioning.

I. Introduction

1. The present report is submitted pursuant to Security Council resolutions 1595 (2005), 1636 (2005), 1644 (2005), 1686 (2006) and 1748 (2007), in which the Council requested the International Independent Investigation Commission to report every four months to the Council on the progress of its inquiry, and on international cooperation, including the cooperation received from the Syrian authorities.

2. This report, the eighth report issued by the Commission, provides an update on issues covered in previous reports to the Council and notes progress in the work of the Commission since its last report of 15 March 2007 (S/2007/150).

3. As outlined in earlier reports, the Commission remains particularly mindful of its obligation to protect the confidentiality of its investigations both in order to ensure the integrity of the legal process and to protect those who have provided information and assistance to the Commission. This approach is taken in full agreement with the Lebanese judicial authorities.

4. Since the last report to the Council, the security situation in Lebanon has deteriorated significantly, as illustrated by the prolonged combat between the Lebanese army and militants in the north of the country, the assassination of Member of Parliament Walid Eido and seven others in central Beirut on 13 June 2007, and the attack on a convoy of the United Nations Interim Force in Lebanon (UNIFIL) in the south of Lebanon on 24 June 2007 in which six peacekeepers were killed. The reporting period also saw several other major bomb attacks throughout the country. This degradation in the security environment comes hand-in-hand with increased political tension in Lebanon and in the region. The Commission, in close cooperation with the Lebanese security forces and with other United Nations bodies, continues to pay close attention to these developments and to try to mitigate the effect these may have on its investigations and on the security of its staff.

5. The Commission continues to maintain close and collegial interaction with the Lebanese authorities on all matters related to its work. Responses from other States, including the Syrian Arab Republic, remain generally satisfactory. The Commission's interaction with all States, including Lebanon and the Syrian Arab Republic, remains an important factor in the Commission's ability to carry out its mandate.

6. The Commission notes the adoption of Security Council resolution 1757 (2007) on 30 May 2007, calling for the establishment of a Special Tribunal for Lebanon. The Commission looks forward to cooperating closely with the Special Tribunal for Lebanon during a transition phase in which the Commission's work will be transferred to the Office of the Prosecutor of the Tribunal. The Commission has taken several important steps to ensure a smooth handover at the appropriate time in the near future.

7. In this regard, the reporting period was marked by a significant exercise of consolidation of all of the Commission's information, findings and recommendations of all of the investigations it is conducting. This complex exercise has produced comprehensive confidential consolidated reports totalling more than 2,400 pages, including a 2,000-page report on its investigation into the assassination of former Prime Minister Rafik Hariri and 22 others in Beirut on 14 February 2005, which the Commission is ready to hand over to the Prosecutor of the Special Tribunal for Lebanon at the appropriate time.

8. During the reporting period, the Commission also made progress in the different areas of the Hariri investigation. Following requests of the Security Council, the Commission also continued to provide technical assistance to the Lebanese authorities in their investigations of 17 other cases, including the assassination of Walid Eido, and to investigate any possible links between these cases and the Hariri case. In total, 84 interviews were conducted during the reporting period by the Commission, covering all current investigations.

II. Consolidation of findings and progress in the investigations

9. Since its last report to the Security Council, one of the main tasks undertaken by the Commission was a comprehensive internal consolidation of information held by the Commission in order to take stock of progress made in all areas of the investigations and to prioritize the next investigative steps. In parallel, the Commission pursued its investigations into the Hariri case and continued to provide assistance to the Lebanese authorities in the 17 other cases, including the assassination of Walid Eido.

A. Consolidation of findings, analysis and recommendations

10. The consolidation of findings, analysis and recommendations was launched in March 2007, and consists of a thorough review of the large amounts of information held by the Commission related to all of its investigations. It was completed in June 2007, and resulted in a number of detailed analytical reports, totalling over 2,400 pages, covering different aspects of the investigation.

11. To achieve the common objective of consolidation, the format and methodology adopted for each investigative project varied according to the topic at hand. Each report presents a critical review of all factual findings held by the Commission, including those emanating from investigations undertaken by the Lebanese authorities. Where appropriate, the reports lay out and evaluate the Commission's past and current investigative hypotheses. The reports also present a detailed assessment of results achieved to date, as well as gaps in the knowledge and understanding of the Commission, and make prioritized recommendations regarding the next steps to be undertaken in each investigation project.

12. This time-consuming undertaking has yielded several positive results. First, it has enabled the Commission to critically and comprehensively assess all the information and analysis it has collected since the start of the investigations, as well as progress made to date. Second, by providing the Commission with an up-to-date bird's eye view of the different strands of the investigations, the exercise has allowed the Commission to effectively prioritize the use of its limited resources in the months to come. The consolidation exercise has also helped identify important aspects and individuals of common interest across several areas of the investigations.

13. Finally, against the backdrop of Security Council resolution 1757 (2007) establishing the Special Tribunal for Lebanon, the consolidated reports, which will be updated to include new findings and analysis, will provide a useful starting point in the transition from the Commission to the Tribunal.

14. In parallel to the consolidation effort, the Commission carried out a thorough inventory of its data holdings during the reporting period. This inventory reveals that, since its creation in 2005, the Commission has accumulated more than 9,200 individual documents amounting to more than 120,000 pages of information related to the investigations. This includes about 1,200 statements, 1,800 investigator notes and over 6,200 other documents, including numerous internal analytical reports and documents received in response to requests for assistance sent to Lebanon, the Syrian Arab Republic and other States.

15. As indicated in previous reports, in order to increase efficiency and facilitate the investigations, the Commission has created and implemented an industry-standard information

management system that ensures that the Commission's considerable information holdings are stored in a systematic, secure and user-friendly manner. In addition, the system provides users with powerful search functions and analytical tools. This system has been developed on the basis of best practices used in existing ad hoc international tribunals, and it is foreseen that it will be a particularly useful tool to the Special Tribunal for Lebanon. This is a considerable undertaking and one which, given current resources, the Commission expects will have to be carried over beyond the Commission's current mandate.

B. Hariri investigation

16. During the reporting period, the Commission continued to devote most of its resources to the Hariri investigation. The consolidation of the Commission's sizeable holdings and analysis in this case amounts to a broad review of the work conducted to date in the numerous different areas of the investigation, including the large amounts of forensic and communication analysis used to support the investigations. This effort resulted in a 2,000-page consolidated report covering all areas of the Hariri investigation.

17. The Commission also continued to actively pursue investigative steps during the reporting period. Since the Commission's last report to the Council, 32 interviews were conducted by the Commission in relation to the Hariri investigation, including several particularly significant and extensive interviews in Lebanon, the Syrian Arab Republic and other countries.

1. Crime scene and associated topics

18. The Commission has methodically consolidated its considerable information and findings on the forensic aspects of its investigations in the Hariri case. These findings include a series of detailed analytical reports produced by the Commission and the Lebanese authorities, in conjunction with several international experts, on the explosive and other forensic aspects of the crime scene investigation. These analytical reports were compiled on the basis of 58 different forensic examinations undertaken by the Commission and by external experts on the Hariri case, the majority of which has been finalized. In total, more than 10,000 pages of information have been produced on the crime scene aspects of the investigation.

19. The results and analysis of all the different examinations and reports concerning the forensic aspects of the Hariri investigation were summarized and critically assessed in one consolidated report. The report also highlights some remaining questions, which continue to be investigated.

Improvised explosive device

20. Regarding the issue of the improvised explosive device used in the attack, the Commission has consolidated its findings on the type and quantity of explosives used, the type of initiating system used and the container used to carry the improvised explosive device. Since the establishment of the Commission, several hypotheses were tested on these points using the analysis of exhibits found at the crime scene, real explosion experiments as well as results derived from bloodstain research, document analysis, metallographic and paint analyses, fingerprint and DNA research, wound analysis, analysis of the damage sustained by nearby buildings, 14 scaling explosion experiments and numerical simulations conducted at the Commission's behest. The Commission also reviewed results from

seismological analyses conducted to test hypotheses on the number of blasts, time of the blast and sound signature of the blast.

21. As concerns the type of explosive used in the attack, the Commission brought together the results obtained from samples taken at the crime scene and chemical analyses. These confirm that the explosive used was composed of a mix of RDX, PETN and TNT. The Commission's consolidation of its analysis of the crater formed by the explosion, compared with the results derived from the explosion experiments and other aspects of the investigations, confirm the Commission's previous conclusions that a single blast was caused by an above-ground charge consisting of approximately 1,800 kg of explosive detonated at 12:55:05. Ongoing efforts to determine the precise origin of the explosives and to ascertain possible forensic links with other cases will be pursued as priorities in the next reporting period.

22. The Commission's holdings on the type of initiating device covered several possible hypotheses by examining the electronic parts recovered from the crime scene and investigating the status of the electronic countermeasures used in the Hariri convoy. These analyses, and the presence of a number of body parts belonging to an unidentified male at the crime scene, confirm the Commission's previous conclusions that the improvised explosive device was most likely triggered by a suicide bomber. The theory of an aerial attack has largely been excluded by the Commission.

23. The Commission has also consolidated all of its information and findings concerning the container of the improvised explosive device. The Commission has reviewed its examinations of the exhibits collected at the crime scene and the results obtained from analyses of characteristics of the fireball caused by the explosion, thermal effects of the blast on surrounding objects, analysis of the characteristics of the crater caused by the explosion in conjunction with results obtained from explosion experiments and the trajectory analysis of vehicle fragments. The consolidation of findings has reinforced the Commission's previous conclusion that the improvised explosive device was most likely detonated from within a Mitsubishi Canter van.

Investigations on the Mitsubishi van

24. During the last reporting period, progress was made in the line of inquiry around the Mitsubishi Canter van most likely used to carry the explosives. The origin and recent history of the van have been established to the satisfaction of the Commission. According to investigations led by the Commission and by the Lebanese authorities, the van left a Mitsubishi factory in Japan in February 2002 and was reported stolen in Kanagawa, Japan, in October 2004. The van was then shipped to the United Arab Emirates and transported to a showroom close to Tripoli in northern Lebanon in December 2004, where it was sold. The Commission has recently acquired information regarding the sale of the van to individuals who could be involved in the final preparation of the van for the attack on Rafik Hariri. This line of inquiry is being pursued as a priority.

Identity of the alleged suicide bomber

25. Regarding the identity of the suicide bomber, the Commission has brought together and reviewed the results from a large number of ongoing and completed orthodontic, isotope and allele frequency analyses and investigative examinations. Based on preliminary results, the Commission's findings remain that the suicide bomber was a male, probably between

20 and 25 years old; that he had short dark hair; that he originally came from a region more arid than Lebanon; and that he did not spend his youth in Lebanon but lived there in the two to three months before his death, which corresponds to findings in other areas of the Commission's investigations. The Commission's experts also reached the preliminary conclusion that this individual lived in an urban environment for the first 10 years of his life and in a rural environment during the last 10 years of his life.

26. Experiments are ongoing to determine the geographic origin of the unidentified male thought to be the suicide bomber. As reported in the Commission's last report, the Commission collected a total of 112 soil and water samples from 28 locations in the Syrian Arab Republic and Lebanon for comparison purposes. Numerous additional samples were also collected from 26 locations in other countries during the reporting period. On the basis of preliminary results, the Commission has been able to identify a limited number of countries which could be the country of origin of the suicide bomber.

27. The Commission is able to confirm previous conclusions that Ahmed Abu Adass, the individual who appeared in the video claim of responsibility, is not the suicide bomber.

Other forensic issues

28. As part of the consolidation effort, the Commission is in the process of creating a DNA and fingerprint database to be able to store and make use of the 256 nuclear DNA profiles and 66 mitochondrial DNA profiles, 159 fingerprints and two palm prints recovered from the crime scene and on seized items of particular relevance to the investigations. These are currently being compared with existing databases held by several national and international law enforcement agencies.

29. During the reporting period, the Commission initiated an inventory of all the physical and biological exhibits that it has accumulated in the course of its investigations. This process started with the creation of a specific database, standard operating procedures and the establishment of a dedicated laboratory. About 2,200 exhibits, representing about half of the forensic exhibits currently held by the Commission, have so far been entered into this database. At current capacity, the time-consuming process of entering these exhibits into the database should be completed by the end of the next reporting period.

30. In addition, the Commission has brought together the results of all of its biological examinations, including the detailed results derived from the identification of all the victims in the attack of 14 February 2005. In total, more than 300 biological examinations were conducted in the Hariri investigation, and the results of each of these, including DNA profiles and orthodontic and photographic records, were brought together into one consolidated report.

31. The Commission has also designed a database to store and easily search the sketches of individuals described by eyewitnesses in the course of the investigations. A total of 24 sketches have so far been finalized by sketch artists and entered into this database, which represents a particularly useful tool for interviews and to compare physical descriptions of individuals across different areas of the investigation and across cases.

32. Three digital visualization projects have been completed by external experts to assist investigators to get a clear picture of the city and the crime scene, of the route taken by the convoy and of the movements of Rafik Hariri during his last day, including the alleged communications traffic activity of the bomb team as the convoy proceeded along its route.

A fourth project, which will allow users to "walk through" the crime scene, is also ongoing. These visual aids could be of particular use to present certain facts in a possible future court setting.

Other crime scene investigations

33. Through the consolidation of findings related to the crime scene, a number of other issues were resolved to the satisfaction of the Commission. These include, among others, the circumstances behind the choice of the convoy's route from Parliament to the Hariri residence, the status of the electronic jamming devices used by Rafik Hariri's security, the list of persons who knew about the convoy's movement and the composition of Rafik Hariri's convoy on the day of the assassination.

34. In addition, the Commission has reached a satisfactory understanding of the context surrounding specific vehicles present at or near the crime scene. The presence of suspicious road works in the vicinity of the crime scene prior to the attack and allegations of interference with the crime scene after the attack have also been clarified to the satisfaction of the Commission.

35. A number of other areas related to the crime scene remain under active investigation, including a review and finalization of the identification and interview of all the people present at the crime scene at the time of the crime and immediately afterwards.

36. It is worthy of note that the crime scene was released and the road where the attack took place was reopened to vehicle traffic during the reporting period.

2. Individuals involved in the commission of the crime

Ahmed Abu Adass

37. The Commission has completed an extensive review of information and findings related to Ahmed Abu Adass, the individual who appeared in the video claim of responsibility for the attack on Rafik Hariri. This information was drawn from over 70 interviews and a detailed review of all relevant documents. A number of items, including all items seized from the Abu Adass family home, have also been reviewed by the Commission in order to assess their relevance to the investigation. Information retrieved from items seized from other associated individuals and groups has also been reviewed and incorporated into this consolidation exercise, including 10 computers and hard drives, memory sticks and numerous CDs, floppy discs, mobile phones and subscriber identity module (SIM) cards.

38. This consolidation has allowed the Commission to reach a more comprehensive understanding of the background and profile of Ahmed Abu Adass, including his personality, family and associates, employment history, and political and religious views. It has also helped to provide a thorough overview of the Commission's current understanding of his disappearance from his home and the activities of his relatives and friends in the months leading up to and after his disappearance. All of the Commission's information related to the making, acquisition and handling of the videotape has also been reviewed.

39. As indicated earlier, the Commission is able to conclude that Ahmed Abu Adass is not the suicide bomber who carried out the attack on Rafik Hariri. The Commission continues to investigate two possible hypotheses: (a) that Ahmed Abu Adass was forced or duped into recording the video claim of responsibility for the assassination of Rafik Hariri, and then

presumably killed; and (b) that Ahmed Abu Adass willingly recorded the video together with individuals belonging to a wider extremist group who may have come together to undertake the filming of the claim of responsibility, acquire the Mitsubishi van and have it prepared with explosives. They may also have participated in the identification of a suicide bomber and may have assisted in delivering him and the bomb to the scene of the crime. In this regard, the Commission has established that some associates of Ahmad Abu Adass had links to networks involved in extremist activities in Lebanon and elsewhere in recent years.

40. In addition, the consolidation effort has helped to identify gaps in the Commission's information and to verify some of its working hypotheses regarding Ahmed Abu Adass. These mainly relate to what happened to him in the period between his disappearance from his home on 16 January 2005 and the assassination of Rafik Hariri and beyond. The Commission is also refining its understanding of the motivation behind the creation of the videotape, the persons involved in its production and delivery and Abu Adass's relationship and links to certain other particular individuals and groups. Key priorities and next steps have been identified to help clarify these matters and to obtain a clearer understanding of the identity and role played by certain persons of interest who may have had a motive, opportunity and capability to carry out the attack.

Communications analysis

41. The Commission has consolidated its sizeable holdings of call records, communications data and analyses related to specific time periods, institutions and individuals of relevance to the Hariri investigation. Since its inception, the Commission has acquired more than 5 billion records of telephone calls and text messages sent through cellular phones in Lebanon, as well as communications data from a number of other countries. The Commission has also acquired a very large number of detailed subscriber call records. Since 2005, the Commission has issued more than 300 requests for assistance to support its communications analysis related to the Hariri investigation.

42. The Commission's communications analysis provides valuable input to the investigations in establishing links between individuals, analysing the behaviour and activity of a number of persons of interest to the investigations and analysing call patterns for specific numbers, times and locations. It is also a very valuable resource in preparing for witness interviews. Given the proven investigative value and potential of communications analysis, the Commission has recently sought outside expertise to help exploit its communications data holdings and analysis. The Commission has also recently acquired new hardware and software, which will allow it to conduct more comprehensive data searches.

43. On the basis of the consolidation exercise, the Commission has confirmed and advanced its earlier conclusions that individuals using six mobile cellular telephone SIM cards acted in a coordinated manner to conduct surveillance on Rafik Hariri in the weeks prior to his assassination. A detailed analysis of the use of these cards on the day of the assassination indicates that these individuals played a critical role in the planning and execution of the attack itself, as demonstrated by their movements and call patterns. The Commission has established the origins of the SIM cards and is finalizing its understanding of the circumstances around the sale of the cards and a number of handsets to the individuals who made use of them in the surveillance of Rafik Hariri. A number of interviews were held during the reporting period to advance this line of inquiry.

44. The Commission also conducted extensive analysis of communications traffic records associated with Ahmed Abu Adass, including analysis of the telephone communication at his home and place of work and on lines belonging to his alleged associates. This revealed interesting information regarding the circumstances around his disappearance from his home and confirms the Commission's conclusions that some of the people with whom he associated had links to networks involved in extremist activities in Lebanon and elsewhere in recent years. In total, 18 communications analysis reports were produced on the topic of Ahmed Abu Adass.

45. Steps have also been taken to learn more about the individuals who placed the calls to the media about the Ahmed Abu Adass video claim of responsibility. The Commission continues to try to identity the callers and to ascertain if any links exist between the callers and individuals or groups of interest to the investigations.

46. The Commission has also been focusing on establishing horizontal and vertical links between individuals linked to the crime scene and those who may have been involved in the preparation of the attack or may have had prior knowledge of the attack through the analysis of telephone communications. Several telephone numbers have been identified and scrutinized as a result of this line of inquiry.

3. Motives and persons of interest

47. A significant share of the Commission's resources has been devoted to the analysis of the factors that are likely to have shaped the motive to assassinate Rafik Hariri. The consolidation of the Commission's understanding under this heading amounts to a substantial analysis of Rafik Hariri's political and other activities. This also includes a systematic review of the political and security environment in and around Lebanon in the years prior to the attack as it may relate to the motive to carry out the crime.

48. The Commission has reached a satisfactory understanding of the events surrounding the Bank Al-Madina scandal as they relate to the investigations. The Commission is able to conclude that the Al-Madina affair was not a principal motive for the assassination. However, the Commission's holdings on the Al-Madina case have allowed it to reach a much clearer understanding of the financial relationships existing between several individuals through Bank Al-Madina in the period under scrutiny.

49. As indicated in its previous report to the Council, the Commission has significantly narrowed down its investigation into possible motives to those linked to Rafik Hariri's political activities and to the political and personal relationships between Rafik Hariri and political leaders and officials in Lebanon, the Syrian Arab Republic and other countries during that period. The Commission has consolidated its information and findings in a number of areas related to the political environment in Lebanon, with a focus on the 2004–2005 period. It is worthy of note that, although mainly used in the Hariri case, this has also been useful in the investigations of the other attacks targeted at specific individuals.

50. The Commission has consolidated its understanding of the context around the adoption of Security Council resolution 1559 (2004). The Commission has also consolidated its findings on certain relevant aspects of the possible roles played by Rafik Hariri and other prominent Lebanese and international political leaders in the adoption of the resolution and

of the perception of those roles by some external parties. While some events surrounding the adoption of resolution 1559 (2004) need to be further investigated, the Commission's working hypothesis is that it is likely that these events played an important role in shaping the environment in which the motives to assassinate Rafik Hariri emerged.

51. The Commission has also focused on the sequence of events that led to the vote to modify the Lebanese Constitution to extend the mandate of President Emile Lahoud and its relevance to the investigation. The Commission has reached a satisfactory understanding of the overall role and position of various political actors during that period and of the impact they could have had on the motive to carry out the attack.

52. The Commission has further focused on reviewing its holdings regarding the new electoral law being discussed during the period under examination and its impact on the different political formations contending the 2005 parliamentary elections, including that of Rafik Hariri. The Commission has also focused on the perception of possible outcomes held by different parties in Lebanon and elsewhere, the basis for such perceptions and their relevance to the investigation.

53. Although it has focused on this group of inquiries into the motives behind the assassination of Rafik Hariri, the Commission also continues to explore alternative hypotheses. These include the possibility that Hariri was targeted, for example, by extremist groups because he was widely considered in Lebanon and the Arab world as a leading figure in his community. It cannot be excluded that the motives to assassinate Hariri could have arisen from a combination of political and sectarian factors. A number of aspects related to this hypothesis are still being investigated.

54. The Commission has brought together and summarized its findings regarding the organization of certain security and intelligence institutions of relevance to the investigation and present in Lebanon in the period prior to the assassination of Rafik Hariri, particularly during 2004 and early 2005. To advance this line of inquiry, the Commission has increased its understanding of the de facto and de jure structures of various organizations of interest to the investigation.

55. Following a detailed review of all its information and findings, the Commission has broadened its understanding of the environment in which the motives to assassinate Rafik Hariri emerged. On the basis of this understanding, and supported by a number of findings in other areas of its investigations, the Commission has identified a number of persons of particular interest who may have been involved in some aspects of the preparation and commission of the crime or could have had prior knowledge that such a plan was under way. The Commission has consolidated its information and findings and recommended next steps concerning the possible involvement of these individuals in the assassination of Rafik Hariri. This line of inquiry will be pursued as a priority in the next reporting period.

4. Other investigative issues

56. The Commission continues to evaluate reports about several specific threats, warnings and assurances conveyed to Rafik Hariri through different intermediaries in the last months of his life. The Commission's preliminary conclusion remains that tension had escalated in the months prior to the assassination to such an extent that certain issues concerning Rafik Hariri's personal safety had been discussed at a high level both in Lebanon and in other countries. The Commission is also continuing to look into reports that certain individuals

were attempting to broker a rapprochement to diffuse these tensions by developing alternative channels of communication. This remains an open line of investigation, which the Commission will pursue in the next reporting period.

57. The Commission has reached a satisfactory understanding of the activities of Rafik Hariri in the days leading up to the attack. In addition, the Commission has established a comprehensive list of the important meetings conducted by Rafik Hariri over a period of several months prior to his assassination. In addition, the Commission has looked into events related to his resignation as Prime Minister in October 2004. The Commission is continuing to complete and confirm details concerning some of these important meetings and events.

5. Witness protection

58. The requirement to ensure the security of witnesses in a manner that will preserve the integrity of evidence remains a priority for the Commission, particularly in view of the transition to the Special Tribunal for Lebanon. Although the Commission is confident that it can provide a timely and appropriate operational response to such a situation if the need arises, the Commission is also aware that a review, formalization and extension of these arrangements will need to be conducted in the near future.

C. Technical assistance in other cases

59. The Commission has consolidated its information, findings and recommendations on each of the other cases and has reviewed the Lebanese authorities' case files. In total, over 400 pages of consolidated reports were produced on these other cases, and the final and preliminary findings from 25 forensic examinations undertaken by the Commission and by external experts on these cases have been reviewed. The consolidation of findings in the 17 cases was carried out with a particular focus on identifying possible links between the cases and with the Hariri case, in line with both the mandate of the Commission and with the Agreement on the establishment of the Special Tribunal for Lebanon, referred to in Security Council resolution 1757 (2007).

60. During the reporting period, as mandated by the Security Council, the Commission continued to provide technical assistance to the Lebanese authorities in their investigations of these 17 other cases, including the assassination of Member of Parliament Walid Eido and seven others on 13 June 2007 in central Beirut. In total, 25 interviews were conducted on the nine bomb attacks and 27 interviews were conducted on the targeted attacks during the reporting period.

1. Nine bomb attacks

61. The Commission has consolidated information received from the Lebanese authorities and its own investigative work on the nine bomb attacks in which no specific individuals appear to have been targeted, including the 13 February 2007 Ain Alaq bombing. Based on this consolidation, the Commission has identified next steps to be taken in these investigations.

62. Regarding the Ain Alaq bombings, the Commission, working in conjunction with the Lebanese authorities, has established that in each case of the two buses that were targeted, a male boarded the bus, placed an improvised explosive device under one of the seats and then got off the bus before the explosion took place.

63. Some progress was made in the reporting period, through interviews conducted by the Commission and the Lebanese authorities, to establish the identities of the perpetrators. The Lebanese authorities have arrested a number of individuals in connection with the Ain Alaq bombings. One of these individuals has confessed to having placed a bomb in one of the buses. According to statements taken from these individuals, the perpetrators may be linked to extremist groups currently active in Lebanon.

64. A preliminary forensic report indicates that there was only one explosion in each bus, and that in each case the improvised explosive device was placed on the left hand side of the bus, between the fourth and seventh rows. The report also confirms that the improvised explosive device in the Mitsubishi bus contained about 1.5 kg of explosives combined with between 0.5 and 1 kg of steel ball bearings and that the explosive substances used in the two buses were of a high velocity similar to TNT. These findings are compatible with information given by a number of witnesses and suspects in their statements.

65. Over 120 exhibits, as well as DNA samples, have been collected from the Ain Alaq crime scene, and forensic analysis on these exhibits and samples is ongoing. The Commission has also collected potentially relevant closed-circuit television footage, which will be reviewed in the next reporting period.

66. At this stage, no forensic links between the Ain Alaq bombings and any of the other cases under investigation have been firmly established. Evidence and statements collected by the Commission and the Lebanese authorities indicate that the choice of the date, on the eve of the second anniversary of the assassination of Rafik Hariri, may however be connected with the motives for the attack. The Commission is continuing to investigate this information and other leads relevant to potential links between the Ain Alaq case and other cases within the mandate of the Commission.

67. The Commission has conducted a similar review of information and findings received from the Lebanese authorities in relation to the other eight non-targeted bomb attacks, on which it has been asked to provide assistance to the Lebanese authorities. The objective of this review is twofold: to make a constructive assessment of the investigation conducted by the Lebanese authorities into each case and to identify possible linkages with other cases or areas of interest to the Commission, particularly related to the Hariri case. In total, the Commission has produced three detailed analytical reports comparing these attacks. It should be noted, however, that, owing to resource limitations within the Commission and to other investigative priorities, progress in the investigation of these cases has been limited.

2. Eight targeted attacks

68. The Commission has brought together all of its information, findings and recommendations regarding the attacks targeted at Marwan Hamedeh, Samir Kassir, George Hawi, Elias El-Murr, May Chidiac, Gebran Tueni, Pierre Gemayel and Walid Eido. The Commission has also continued to pursue its investigations into these cases during the reporting period.

Victim profiles and possible motives

69. As part of the consolidation, the Commission has refined its profile of each of the principal victims and has continued to develop a detailed case narrative for each case.

70. Given the profile of the victims, the Commission has given particular attention to the public and political activities of each of the victims in the period preceding the attacks because the Commission's working hypothesis is that it is likely that these played an important role in shaping the environment in which motives to carry out the attacks emerged. This was conducted in tandem with similar steps taken in the Hariri investigation, as detailed above.

71. The Commission has also consolidated its holdings and understanding of the public stance taken by the victims regarding several of the major events that shaped the Lebanese political landscape in recent years, including, among others, the adoption of Security Council resolution 1559 (2004), the extension of the term of President Emile Lahoud, the assassination of Rafik Hariri and the withdrawal of Syrian troops from Lebanon. This analysis has revealed both interesting commonalities as well as some potentially relevant differences in the positions taken by the individuals targeted.

72. In addition, the Commission has consolidated its information and analyses regarding the relationships between each of the victims and several individuals and institutions of particular interest to the investigations. In this line of investigation, the Commission's working hypothesis is that some of these relationships are connected with areas of particular interest in the Hariri investigation.

Modus operandi

73. All of the attacks, except for the assassination of Pierre Gemayel, involved an improvised explosive device placed either in the victim's own vehicle or in a vehicle parked along the route that the victim took on the day of the attack.

74. The modus operandi in each of the attacks involving an improvised explosive device is only different to the extent that a different level of sophistication was necessary to maximize the chance of success. In the attacks targeting May Chidiac, Samir Kassir and George Hawi, an explosive device was placed under each victim's vehicle while it was parked unguarded.

75. In the Marwan Hamadeh, Elias El-Murr and Gebran Tueni cases, where the targeted person had some security arrangement in place, a different modus operandi, involving a roadside vehicle containing a remotely triggered improvised explosive device, was chosen in order to overcome those security arrangements.

76. The Commission's consolidation and comparison of its findings in each of the cases suggest further similarities related to the explosives and to the vehicles used in several of the attacks. The Commission is also using its DNA, fingerprints and sketch databases in the context of these investigations. The Commission will pursue this line of investigation in the coming months.

Threats and claims of responsibility

77. The Commission has also collected a significant amount of information about threats that some of the victims received and has identified common individuals who allegedly threatened several of the victims in the cases under investigation. These individuals may also be linked to the Hariri investigation.

78. In addition, and as noted in previous reports, the Commission's findings suggest that there may be a link between the group claiming responsibility for the Hariri killing and the group that claimed responsibility for the attacks on Samir Kassir, Gebran Tueni and Pierre Gemayel. The Commission has conducted several interviews that relate to this line of inquiry and continues to explore issues relating to these groups.

Communications analysis

79. The analysis of relevant communications traffic has significantly advanced the investigation of the targeted attacks. The nature of the targeted attacks and the profile of the victims suggest that the perpetrators conducted surveillance in the days and weeks preceding the attacks. In addition, it is likely that telephone contact was maintained within each team of perpetrators in the period immediately prior and immediately subsequent to each attack.

80. The Commission has conducted detailed communications analysis to assess whether traces of this surveillance can be identified using call records of persons of interest and call patterns in specific geographical areas over specific time periods. Overall, the Commission notes progress in this analysis, which has helped to uncover interesting leads.

81. Communications analysis conducted so far has helped confirm the Commission's hypothesis that a number of individuals may be relevant to the Hariri case and one or more of the other cases. The Commission will be conducting a number of interviews to further assess the linkages identified so far.

Pierre Gemayel case

82. The Commission has supported the Lebanese authorities by conducting eight interviews relating to the Gemayel case since March 2007, bringing the total number of interviews conducted by the Commission as part of the Gemayel investigation to 19. The Commission is looking into a number of potential motives for the crime, and it is also continuing to investigate whether Pierre Gemayel was under surveillance during the days preceding his attack and who may have known about his intended movements at the time he was killed. Based on witness statements collected so far, the Commission's findings suggest that Mr. Gemayel may have been selected among a small group of potential targets because he had minimal security arrangements in place.

Walid Eido case

83. On 13 June 2007, at around 17.45, Walid Eido, his son, two bodyguards and four other individuals were killed when an improvised explosive device exploded near Mr. Eido's vehicle. Mr. Eido was a member of the parliamentary majority bloc and was considered to be close to Rafik Hariri. The attack took place in the area known as the Manara Corniche in central Beirut, which generally sees heavy vehicle traffic at the time the attack took place.

84. On 14 June 2007, following a request from the Lebanese Prime Minister to the Secretary-General of the United Nations, the Commission was mandated to provide technical assistance to the Lebanese authorities in their investigation into this attack.

85. A team from the Commission visited the crime scene on 15 June 2007, accompanied by six international forensic experts. Subsequently, the Commission and the Lebanese authorities conducted a detailed two-week-long forensic examination of the crime scene.

86. The investigation into this attack is still at an early stage, and the Commission awaits the results from the forensic experts. However, the Commission, working in close cooperation with the Lebanese authorities, has been able to determine a few elements of interest. Primary conclusions provide some information on the type of vehicle used to carry the improvised explosive device. Further analysis is under way to confirm this finding and to determine the type and quantity of explosives used in the attack.

87. The Commission has also started to establish possible motives for the attack, and has started to put together a profile of the targeted victim and to build a case narrative. The Commission will also continue to identify possible links with other attacks and with the Hariri case. This investigation will be pursued in the next reporting period.

III. External cooperation

A. Interaction with the Lebanese authorities

88. Since its last report to the Council, the Commission has continued to interact closely with the Lebanese authorities on all cases under investigation. Regular meetings and briefings have continued to take place between the Commission and the Prosecutor General and his staff, as well as with the investigative judges assigned to the different cases.

89. During the reporting period, the Commission renewed its efforts to ensure that the Lebanese authorities are regularly kept abreast of the Commission's activities and progress made in its investigations. The Commission continued to share significant amounts of information with the relevant Lebanese authorities, including interviews and analytical reports.

90. Since the last report to the Council, the Commission addressed 88 requests for assistance to the Prosecutor General seeking, inter alia, to obtain relevant documents and help in arranging interviews and other missions in Lebanon. This brings the total number of requests for assistance addressed to the Lebanese authorities since January 2006 to 218. The Lebanese authorities have continued to respond fully and expeditiously to these requests. The Commission gratefully acknowledges this positive cooperation.

91. The Commission also continues to enjoy a close and collegial working relationship with the Internal Security Forces and the Lebanese Army, which provide security to the Commission staff and facilities. The Commission is grateful to these institutions for their excellent support.

B. Cooperation with the Syrian Arab Republic

92. In line with the obligations of the Syrian Arab Republic under Security Council resolutions 1636 (2005) and 1644 (2005), and the common understanding reached between the Commission and the Syrian Arab Republic in 2006, the cooperation of the Syrian Arab Republic with the Commission remains generally satisfactory.

93. Since its last report to the Council, the Commission has submitted 11 formal requests for assistance to the Syrian Arab Republic, asking it to facilitate a number of interviews and

seeking to obtain information about individuals and events of interest to the Commission. This brings the total number of requests for assistance addressed to the Syrian authorities since January 2006 to 57. The Syrian authorities were also forthcoming in making arrangements for four missions to Syria during the reporting period.

94. During the reporting period, the Syrian Arab Republic continued to provide the Commission with assistance in response to its requests within the appropriate timescales. The Commission is also grateful for the logistical and security arrangements provided by Syrian authorities for the Commission's various activities in the Syrian Arab Republic.

95. The Commission will continue to request the full cooperation of the Syrian Arab Republic, which remains crucial to the successful completion of the mandate of the Commission.

C. Cooperation with other States

96. During the reporting period, a total of 18 requests for assistance were sent to 12 States, in addition to the requests for assistance sent to Lebanese and Syrian authorities. This brings the total number of requests for assistance addressed to other States since January 2006 to 106.

97. The Commission has greatly benefited from the responses of States to its requests where full and prompt cooperation has been forthcoming. The Commission is very grateful for this cooperation.

98. It remains of paramount importance that the Commission should be able to rely on the support of States to provide information, assistance, expertise and access when required. During the reporting period, the Commission received particularly helpful and timely assistance from a number of States.

99. The Commission also gratefully acknowledges the expertise and other forms of assistance it received from several States and international institutions during the reporting period. The Commission reiterates the need for continued assistance from these entities in making qualified and specialized human resources available on a regular basis to ensure progress in the investigations.

100. As the Commission noted in its last report to the Council, the Commission will be able to effectively carry out its mandate only if it can count on the cooperation of all States to provide the Commission with the information requested, access to certain individuals, including current and past Government officials, and other forms of technical assistance.

IV. Security

101. The security situation in Lebanon has markedly deteriorated since the Commission's last report. Lebanese armed forces have been engaged in sustained combat for several weeks with fighters associated with Fatah al-Islam in the refugee camp of Nahr al-Barid, near the city of Tripoli in the northern part of the country.

102. Violence during the reporting period was not confined to these areas. Several other significant incidents took place, including the assassination of Walid Eido and seven others on 13 June 2007. In addition to that attack, a significant number of incidents involving improvised explosive devices took place in Lebanon during the reporting period causing several casualties.

103. On 24 June 2007, six peacekeepers serving with UNIFIL were killed when their convoy was struck by an improvised explosive device near the southern town of Khiam.

104. Security analysis conducted by the Commission in conjunction with several other organizations indicates that the security outlook for Lebanon over the coming months appears to be bleak. This is owed in large part to the combined negative effects of the ongoing political stalemate between the majority and the opposition in Lebanon and the deterioration in the security situation in the region. The period in the run-up to the Lebanese presidential elections, scheduled for later this year, is widely expected to be one of growing tension, possibly marked by further security incidents. In addition, it is unclear what impact the creation of the Special Tribunal for Lebanon will have on the security situation in Lebanon and on the Commission in particular in the months to come.

105. The Commission is very mindful of this general threat environment and of specific threats it faces because of the nature of its mandate. During the reporting period, the Commission conducted regular assessments on all aspects of its security in close cooperation with the Lebanese security forces. Based on these assessments, the Commission, with the full support of the Lebanese authorities, has implemented additional mitigating measures.

106. While measures have been taken to reduce the risks facing the Commission and its staff, the degradation in the security environment in Lebanon has had several negative effects on the ability of the Commission to carry out its mandate. First, this may affect progress in the investigations in that it restricts the Commission's ability to conduct interviews and other investigative activities as freely as was previously the case. Second, the current insecurity and political instability may cause some witnesses to hesitate to cooperate with the Commission. Finally, security concerns may impact the Commission's ability to attract and retain qualified staff in the months to come.

V. Organizational support

A. Recruitment

107. During the past four months, the efforts of the Commission to improve its staffing have borne some positive results, particularly in the investigation, security and language sections, but recruitment remains an area of concern. Of the approved 188 international posts, 125 are filled, compared with 104 at the end of the last reporting period. Of the 51 approved national posts in the Commission, 44 have been filled. The investigation division currently consists of 50 international staff, including 30 investigators, analysts and technical experts.

108. In its last report to the Council, the Commission noted with concern the problem of recruitment of qualified language staff, which remains an essential component of the Commission's ability to carry out its mandate effectively. During the period under review, the Commission made progress in this area. A total of 17 language staff posts have been filled in the language section, up from three at the end of the last reporting period. The Commission also relies on a number of qualified freelance interpreters to fill the human resource gaps in this area. The Department for General Assembly and Conference Management of the Secretariat has been forthcoming in providing one staff interpreter and one staff translator for a period of three months. The Commission is grateful for this support.

B. Budget

109. In June 2007, the Commission submitted a budget proposal for 2008. Since it will be a maintenance budget, no major changes in staffing are envisaged except for a modest increase in security staff resulting from the need to maintain separate premises for office space and accommodation of staff.

VI. Conclusions

110. The substantial consolidation of the Commission's information, analysis and recommendations, which was started and completed during the reporting period, amounts to a significant step in the investigation into the assassination of Rafik Hariri. The 2,400 pages of reports produced as a result of the consolidation effort on the Hariri and the other cases offer both a comprehensive overview of the considerable progress made to date and a valuable tool to further identify and explore remaining investigative steps to be taken in order to complete the Commission's understanding of the facts surrounding these attacks.

111. This undertaking has been a significant step forward in several ways. The consolidation has helped highlight the large number of questions that have been resolved to the satisfaction of the Commission in each area of the investigations. The consolidation effort has equally allowed the Commission to identify a number of key questions that remain open and where further investigative steps will need to be taken. By providing an overview of the status of all the areas of the investigations, the consolidation effort has also allowed the Commission to identity a number of important commonalities between the cases under investigation. These commonalities will be explored in greater depth in the next reporting period. Finally, the consolidated reports emerging from this effort represent a valuable starting point in the transition from the Commission to the Special Tribunal for Lebanon.

112. The Commission notes that the consolidation effort undertaken has helped identify a number of persons of particular interest who may have been involved in some aspect of the preparation and execution of the attack on Rafik Hariri or the other cases under investigation or could have had prior knowledge that plans to carry out these attacks were under way. The Commission will pursue this line of inquiry as a priority in the coming months.

113. Based on the results of the consolidation effort, the Commission produced detailed workplans to identify the priority objectives in each area of the investigation. These workplans, which amount to 150 pages, include, among others, forensic examinations, documents to be reviewed, interviews to be conducted and plans for the collection of further evidence. The workplans are also very helpful to make the best use of the Commission's limited resources. The Commission foresees that the next reporting period will be particularly active in carrying out the priorities identified as a result of the consolidation effort. More than 200 interviews are planned in the Hariri investigation and about 100 interviews are being scheduled in the 17 other cases.

114. In all aspects of its work, the Commission continues to enjoy close and collegial cooperation with the Lebanese authorities, particularly with the Prosecutor General and his staff. Illustrating the sustained pace of the investigations, the number of requests for assistance addressed to the Lebanese authorities has considerably increased since the Commission's last report to the Council. Nevertheless, the Lebanese authorities have continued to respond fully to these requests.

115. The Commission also notes that the Syrian Arab Republic and other States have continued to provide mostly positive responses to its requests for assistance. Cooperation from all States remains of paramount importance in order for the Commission to implement its mandate in a timely manner. The Commission therefore calls on all States to continue to respond fully to the Commission's requests.

116. Since the Commission's last report to the Council, Lebanon has experienced a phase of increased political and security volatility, as illustrated by the prolonged fighting in the refugee camp of Nahr al-Barid, the assassination of Walid Eido and the attack on UNIFIL troops. As indicated above, the Commission is taking all possible measures to mitigate the risks to its staff and premises. The Commission is particularly grateful to the Lebanese security forces for their outstanding support in this respect.

117. Against the backdrop of Security Council resolution 1757 (2007), the Commission is working to ensure a smooth handover between the Commission and the Special Tribunal for Lebanon when the Tribunal begins to function. The Commission stands ready to cooperate with the Secretary-General of the United Nations and with the Special Tribunal for Lebanon on all issues pertaining to this transition.

6. Report of the Secretary-General submitted pursuant to Security Council Resolution 1757 (2007) of 30 May 2007 (S/2007/525), 4 September 2007

I. Introduction

1. The present report is submitted pursuant to paragraph 3 of resolution 1757 (2007) of 30 May 2007, by which the Security Council requested me to undertake, in coordination, when appropriate, with the Government of Lebanon, the steps and measures necessary to establish the Special Tribunal in a timely manner and to report to the Council on the implementation of the resolution within 90 days of its adoption and periodically thereafter.

2. By resolution 1757 (2007), the Security Council decided, acting under Chapter VII of the Charter of the United Nations, that the provisions of the document annexed thereto (the "Annex") on the establishment of the Special Tribunal, including the statute attached thereto (the "Statute"), would enter into force on 10 June 2007, unless the Government of Lebanon had notified the United Nations in writing that the legal requirements for entry into force had been complied with before that date.

3. On 10 June 2007, as no notification had been received prior to that date, the provisions of the Annex and the Statute entered into force. Thereafter, as mandated by the Security Council in its resolution 1757 (2007), I commenced to undertake the steps and measures necessary to establish the Special Tribunal in a timely manner. The most immediate actions taken since 10 June relate to: (a) the location of the seat of the Special Tribunal; (b) the appointment of the judges, the Prosecutor, the Deputy Prosecutor, the Registrar and the head of the Defence Office; (c) the staffing requirements and budget of the Tribunal; (d) the funding of the Tribunal, including both its establishment and operation; (e) the Management Committee; (f) security issues; and (g) communications and outreach.

4. The present report discusses in detail the steps already undertaken towards the establishment of the Special Tribunal and provides an outline of the next steps.

II. Location of the seat

5. Pursuant to article 8, paragraph 1, of the Annex, "[t]he Special Tribunal shall have its seat outside Lebanon". In the paragraph it is further stipulated that "[t]he location of the seat shall be determined having due regard to considerations of justice and fairness as well as security and administrative efficiency, including the rights of victims and access to witnesses, and subject to the conclusion of a headquarters agreement between the United Nations, the Government and the State that hosts the Tribunal".

6. After considering possible seats and noting that having the Special Tribunal located in the Netherlands would fully meet the criteria set forth above, on 23 July 2007, I wrote to the Prime Minister of the Netherlands inviting his Government to consider hosting the Special Tribunal. In my letter, I emphasized that the experience and knowledge gained by the Netherlands in hosting several international courts and tribunals was invaluable. I cited the unique and essential role of the Netherlands in the development of international justice and the rule of law. In a letter dated 14 August 2007, the Prime Minister of the Netherlands informed me that his Government was favourably disposed towards hosting the

Special Tribunal. From 27 to 30 August 2007, the Legal Counsel of the United Nations led a delegation to The Hague to initiate discussions with the authorities of the Netherlands regarding the modalities for the establishment of the Special Tribunal. The delegation visited possible sites for the Special Tribunal, identified issues for discussion and agreed upon further steps to achieve progress in a timely manner. In the coming weeks, subsequent meetings will be held to follow up the discussions.

III. Appointment of the judges, the Prosecutor, the Deputy Prosecutor, the Registrar and the head of the Defence Office

7. I will describe below the appointment processes for the judges, the Prosecutor, the Deputy Prosecutor, the Registrar and the head of the Defence Office.

A. Judges

8. In accordance with article 2, paragraph 5 (c), of the Annex, the Secretary-General and the Government of Lebanon will consult on the appointment of the judges. Paragraph 5 (a) stipulates that the Lebanese judges will be appointed by the Secretary-General from a list of 12 persons presented by the Government of Lebanon upon the proposal of the Lebanese Supreme Council of the Judiciary. In accordance with paragraph 5 (b), the international judges will be appointed by the Secretary-General upon nominations forwarded by States at the invitation of the Secretary-General, as well as by competent persons. Pursuant to paragraph 5 (d), the Secretary-General will appoint all of the judges upon the recommendation of a selection panel composed of two judges, currently sitting on or retired from an international tribunal, and the representative of the Secretary-General.

9. On 10 July 2007, the Government of Lebanon forwarded to me, in a sealed envelope, a list of the 12 judges proposed by the Lebanese Supreme Council of the Judiciary. The list will remain sealed until the selection process of all judges begins. With a view to appointing both Lebanese and international judges at the same time, the Legal Counsel sent a letter on 1 August 2007 to all Member States, on my behalf, inviting them to consider submitting candidates for appointment as judges of the Special Tribunal no later than 24 September 2007.

10. In the meantime, I have begun the process of establishing the selection panel, which will take up its task by October 2007. In keeping with article 2, paragraph 5 (d) of the annex, I will indicate my intention to the Security Council before appointing the members of the panel. The selection panel will interview the candidates during the third quarter of 2007, and I hope to appoint the judges by the end of 2007.

11. Pursuant to article 17 (b) of the annex, the judges will commence their judicial functions on a date to be determined by me, in consultation with the President of the Special Tribunal, who will be elected in accordance with article 8, paragraph 2, of the Statute. In order to draft the rules of procedure and evidence of the Special Tribunal, as envisaged in article 28 of the Statute, and to address other organizational matters as set out in article 17 (b) of the Annex, the judges may be convened on an ad hoc basis prior to the commencement of their judicial duties.

B. The Prosecutor and the Deputy Prosecutor

12. Pursuant to article 3 of the Annex, the Prosecutor will be appointed by the Secretary-General upon the recommendation of a selection panel (established in the same manner as

that for the international judges), in consultation with the Government of Lebanon. A Lebanese Deputy Prosecutor will be appointed by the Government of Lebanon, in consultation with the Secretary-General and the Prosecutor, to assist the Prosecutor in the conduct of investigations and prosecutions.

13. The recruitment of the Prosecutor will begin in due course. With regard to the Deputy Prosecutor, the Government of Lebanon has forwarded to me, in a sealed envelope, a list of suggested names in preparation for her or his appointment. The list will remain sealed until the selection process begins.

14. The provisions set out in article 17 (a) of the Annex call for appropriate arrangements to be made to ensure that there is a coordinated transition from the activities of the International Independent Investigation Commission (the "Investigation Commission") to the activities of the Office of the Prosecutor. The Secretariat has initiated discussions with the Investigation Commission aimed at achieving that end and will remain in close contact with the Commission to ensure effective coordination during the period of the establishment of the Special Tribunal.

C. The Registrar

15. Pursuant to article 4 of the annex, the Secretary-General will appoint the Registrar, who will be a staff member of the United Nations. I will start the process of identifying suitable candidates before the end of the year. He or she will take office at an appropriate time in order to develop the administrative and judicial infrastructure of the Special Tribunal so as to enable it to be operational on the date of the commencement of its functioning. The Registrar will also assist with the transition from the Investigation Commission to the Special Tribunal.

D. Head of the Defence Office

16. Pursuant to article 13, of the Statute, an independent head of the Defence Office, responsible for appointing the Office staff, drawing up a list of defence counsel and providing support and assistance to defence counsel and persons entitled to legal assistance, will be appointed by the Secretary-General in consultation with the President of the Special Tribunal.

17. I will initiate the process of identifying appropriate candidates for the position before the end of the year. The head of the Defence Office will be appointed at a later stage.

IV. Staffing requirements and estimated budget

18. A preliminary estimate of the staffing requirements and the budget of the Special Tribunal has been made for the three years to which reference is made in article 5, paragraph 2, of the Annex. In making the estimate, attention was paid to the experiences of other international tribunals, in particular that of the Special Court for Sierra Leone, which shares characteristics with the Special Tribunal.

19. While it is possible to determine the organizational and operational framework of the Special Tribunal, many issues which may have significant budgetary consequences, relating, inter alia, to the premises of the Tribunal, the number of accused persons, witnesses and trials, and the level of security required, have yet to be clarified. Therefore, the budget allocation herein presented constitutes an overall estimate rather than a precise evaluation

of the funding necessary to support the operation of the Special Tribunal throughout its mandate.

20. In addition, the staffing requirements and the budget were necessarily developed on the basis of a number of assumptions, many of which may vary depending on the course of events during the establishment and operation of the Special Tribunal. Those assumptions are as follows:

(a) The work of the Office of the Prosecutor will be directed by the Prosecutor, based on the efforts already being carried out by the Lebanese authorities assisted by the Investigation Commission. The Prosecutor will benefit greatly from the work of the Lebanese authorities and the Investigation Commission in that regard. However, the Prosecutor will need the necessary time to complete the investigation work, as well as to prepare and submit an indictment;

(b) The terms and conditions of service for both judges and staff will be guided by those of the judges and staff of the Special Court for Sierra Leone, with appropriate modifications;

(c) A phased-in approach to the establishment and operation of the Special Tribunal will be adopted in accordance with the chronology of the legal process;

(d) The President of the Tribunal will take up his or her full-time duties on the date on which the Special Tribunal commences functioning;

(e) There will be three working languages with regard to the trial proceedings: Arabic, English and French;

(f) An office of the Special Tribunal will be established in Lebanon.

21. At this stage, no assumption can be made concerning the cost involved in providing for a courtroom, detention facility or office accommodation for staff.

22. Consequently, mindful of the considerations addressed above, including the required estimates referred to in article 5, paragraph 2, of the Annex, and taking into account established trends, in particular at the Special Court for Sierra Leone, it is estimated that the Special Tribunal will require a staffing level of between 415 and 430 posts and a total budget of $35 million for the first 12 months of its operations, $45 million for the second 12 months and $40 million for the third 12 months.

23. It may be necessary to consider budgeting in the second and third years of the Special Tribunal for a second Trial Chamber. As provided for in article 2, paragraph 2, of the Annex "[t]he Chambers shall be composed of a Pre-Trial Judge, a Trial Chamber and an Appeals Chamber, with a second Trial Chamber to be created if, after the passage of at least six months from the commencement of the functioning of the Special Tribunal, the Secretary-General or the President of the Special Tribunal so requests". This would entail, if required, the appointment of four additional judges and an examination of how to accommodate an additional Trial Chamber within the existing physical infrastructure. Should a second Trial Chamber be created, it is estimated at the present time that the additional annual financial requirements would be $8 million.

24. A draft budget including staffing requirements across the organs of the Special Tribunal, will be prepared in due course.

V. Funding

25. As provided for in article 5, paragraph 1, of the annex, the expenses of the Special Tribunal will be borne in the following manner:

(a) Fifty-one per cent of the expenses will be borne by voluntary contributions from States;

(b) Forty-nine per cent of the expenses of the Tribunal will be borne by the Government of Lebanon.

26. Pursuant to article 5, paragraph 2, of the Annex, "[i]t is understood that the Secretary-General will commence the process of establishing the Tribunal when he has sufficient contributions in hand to finance the establishment of the Tribunal and 12 months of its operations plus pledges equal to the anticipated expenses of the following 24 months of the Tribunal's operation".

27. On 26 July 2007, the Secretariat created a trust fund to receive contributions for the establishment and activities of the Special Tribunal. A letter to Member States inviting them to contribute to the trust fund will soon be sent.

VI. Management Committee

28. In accordance with article 6 of the Annex, the United Nations and the Government of Lebanon "shall consult concerning the establishment of a Management Committee".

29. Accordingly, on 9 July 2007, the United Nations and the Government of Lebanon agreed to establish a Management Committee, which, inter alia, would (a) provide advice and policy direction on all non-judicial aspects of the operation of the Special Tribunal, including questions of efficiency; and (b) perform other functions as agreed by the members of the Committee. They also agreed that the United Nations would be entrusted with establishing the Management Committee, including drafting the terms of reference in consultation with the Government of Lebanon.

VII. Security

30. Ensuring the security of the Special Tribunal's officials is a matter of the highest priority in order to preserve the integrity and the independence of the Tribunal. Overall security arrangements will be made in consultation with the authorities of the Netherlands and of the Government of Lebanon.

VIII. Outreach and communications

31. The creation of the Special Tribunal has already attracted significant interest in both Lebanon and the international community. That interest will only increase as the establishment of the Special Tribunal moves forward. Therefore, a communications strategy, including an outreach programme for the region, must be developed and implemented.

32. Adopting an effective communications strategy to provide accurate information about the establishment, role and activities of the Special Tribunal is of the utmost importance.

It is also crucial to ensuring that the entire process is perceived as transparent, fair and accessible.

33. A key element for the success of the Special Tribunal is not only that justice be done but also that justice must be seen to be done. As the Special Tribunal's seat will be located outside Lebanon, the development of an effective and comprehensive outreach programme bringing the activities of the Special Tribunal closer to the population of Lebanon and the wider region is a priority.

IX. Next steps

34. In order to support the successful and timely implementation of Security Council resolution 1757 (2007), the establishment of the Special Tribunal will proceed in three phases: (a) a preparatory phase; (b) a start-up phase; and (c) the commencement of functioning.

A. Preparatory phase

35. During the preparatory phase, which is currently under way, the following actions will be undertaken:

(a) Identifying the premises for the seat of the Special Tribunal, in coordination with the authorities of the host State, that would provide for the detention of accused persons, the conduct of trial proceedings and offices;

(b) Negotiating a headquarters agreement with the host State;

(c) Making preliminary legal and administrative arrangements with respect to the presence in Lebanon of an Office of the Special Tribunal for the conduct of investigations;

(d) Appointing the judges, the Prosecutor, the Deputy Prosecutor and the Registrar;

(e) Identifying candidates for the head of the Defence Office;

(f) Finalizing the drafting of the terms and conditions of service of judges and of the staff;

(g) Developing a draft budget, including a staffing table, for the Special Tribunal;

(h) Initiating fund-raising for the establishment and operation of the Special Tribunal;

(i) Drafting the terms of reference of the Management Committee and determining its composition, in consultation with the authorities of the Government of Lebanon and interested Member States;

(j) Formulating and implementing communications and outreach policies for the period before the Special Tribunal becomes operational.

B. Start-up phase

36. The start-up phase will begin when the Registrar has been appointed. This phase of activity includes the following actions:

(a) Working on the preparation of the premises identified for the Special Tribunal;

(b) Beginning the process for the recruitment and appointment of staff;

(c) Establishing a core unit of Registry personnel to assist the Registrar in preparing for the Special Tribunal to become operational.

37. In addition, during the start-up phase, the Commissioner of the Investigation Commission, working together with the Registrar, should begin taking administrative measures to ensure a coordinated transition from the Investigation Commission to the Office of the Prosecutor.

C. Commencement of functioning

38. The responsibility falls upon me to determine when the Special Tribunal will commence functioning. This can occur when sufficient financial means have been received pursuant to article 5, paragraph 2, of the Annex. In addition, pursuant to article 19, paragraph 2, of the Annex, the Special Tribunal will commence functioning on a date to be determined by me, in consultation with the Government of Lebanon, taking into account the progress of the work of the Investigation Commission.

39. Once the Special Tribunal is ready to commence functioning, the judges, the Prosecutor and the Registrar will be sworn in and the first plenary meeting convened. The purpose of the meeting will be twofold: (a) to elect the President of the Special Tribunal; and (b) to adopt a schedule for the drafting of the rules of procedure and evidence and other necessary documents (such as the directives on the assignment of defence counsel, on the detention of persons awaiting trial or appeal and on the code of professional conduct for defence counsel). After his or her election, I will consult with the President regarding the appointment of the head of the Defence Office, pursuant to article 13 of the Statute.

40. As set out in article 17 of the annex, the judges will serve on an ad hoc basis during this initial period of operation of the Special Tribunal. I envisage that the judges of the Trial and Appeals Chambers will only commence their official judicial functions at a later stage. However, the pre-trial judge would start her or his duties earlier than the other judges in order to issue any warrants and orders required for the conduct of investigations and for the preparation of trials.

X. Final observations

41. It is my belief that the establishment of the Special Tribunal will contribute to ending impunity in Lebanon for the crimes under the Tribunal's jurisdiction. The United Nations remains committed to assisting the Government of Lebanon and the Lebanese people towards this end by creating a tribunal of an international character grounded in the highest standards of international justice. As the process to establish the Special Tribunal advances, I will keep the members of the Security Council apprised of this important work.

The manufacturer's authorised representative in the EU for product safety is Oxford University Press España S.A. of El Parque Empresarial San Fernando de Henares, Avenida de Castilla, 2 - 28830 Madrid (www.oup.es/en or product.safety@oup.com). OUP España S.A. also acts as importer into Spain of products made by the manufacturer.
Printed and bound by CPI Group (UK) Ltd, Croydon, CR0 4YY
14/09/2026
02216290-0018